Supporting Children with Communication Difficulties in Inclusive Settings

School-Based Language Intervention

Linda McCormick
University of Hawaii

Diane Frome Loeb
University of Kansas

Richard L. Schiefelbusch
University of Kansas

Allyn and Bacon
Boston   London   Toronto   Sydney   Tokyo   Singapore

To Susannah, Beau, and Taylor Gresham, Natelise Loeb,
and Jordan and Sarah McCormick.

Executive Editor: Stephen D. Dragin
Vice President, Education: Nancy Forsyth
Editorial Assistant: Christine Svitila
Marketing Manager: Kathy Hunter
Editorial Production Service: Barbara J. Barg
Manufacturing Buyer: Megan Cochran
Cover Administrator: Linda Knowles

Copyright © 1997 by Allyn & Bacon
A Viacom Company
Needham Heights, MA 02194

Library of Congress Cataloging-in-Publication Data
McCormick, Linda
    Supporting children with communication difficulties in inclusive
settings : school-based language intervention / Linda McCormick,
Diane Frome Loeb, Richard L. Schiefelbusch.
    p. cm.
    Includes bibliography references and index.
    ISBN 0-02-379272-8
1. Speech therapy for children. 2. Children—Language.
3. Communicative disorders in children. 4. Mainstreaming in
education. I. Loeb, Diane Frome. II. Schiefelbusch, Richard L.
III. Title.
LB3434.M396 1997
371.91'4—dc20   96-21866
                                                    CIP

Printed in the United States of America
10 9 8 7 6 5 4 3 2 1   01 00 99 98 97 96

Photo Credits:
Page 1: Brian Smith; 43 and 59: Will Faller; 71: Jim Pickerell; 109, 149, and 162: Will
Faller; 179 and 186: Stanford Loeb; 223: Will Faller; 243: Stanford Loeb; 257: Stephen
Marks; 287 and 307: Will Faller; 325: Stanfoed Loeb; 335: Will Faller; 369: Stephen Marks;
395 and 405: Will Faller; 433: Stephen Marks; 446: Stanford Loeb; 467: Robert Harbison;
498: Stephen Marks

CONTENTS

iii

PART III: SPECIAL POPULATIONS

CHAPTER 9   *Language Intervention with Infants and Toddlers*   **307**

Ken M. Bleile

CHAPTER 10   *Language Intervention in the Inclusive Preschool*   **335**

Linda McCormick

When we began writing this text, the intention was to produce a third revision of the text *Early Language Intervention*. At about the halfway mark, it became evident that a revision summarizing the history and the present state of our knowledge about language disorders and language intervention could not do justice to the progress that has been made in the field of language and communication disorders as well as to the substantial literature that has emerged over the past decade describing strategies for supporting students in inclusive environments. *Supporting Children with Communication Difficulties in Inclusive Settings* reflects our commitment to new ideas and new directions. It is not about the traditional service delivery model—in which teachers, working alone, try to meet the educational needs of one group of students; speech-language interventionists (*or* physical therapists, *or* occupational therapists), also working alone, try to meet the needs of other students; and parents try to do what they can at home. It is about a service delivery model where parents and professionals collaborate with one another, sharing both expertise and responsibility to maximize and support language and communicative competence in classrooms with wide ability and cultural, racial, ethnic, linguistic, and economic diversity. It is about a service delivery model where the needs, abilities, and ways of living of *all* children, including those who may be seen as culturally and developmentally different, are included a priori in the articulation and implementation of program and school goals and practices.

This book is an effort to translate our commitment to collaboration and meeting the needs of all children in general education classrooms and other inclusive settings into practical guidelines for teaching/intervention arrangements. Our experience has led us to believe that collaborative efforts result in improved outcomes. We have observed that the success of inclusion for children with communication difficulties has little to do with the severity of the children's disability or disabilities and everything to do with whether language interventionists and teachers are committed to providing an environment that recognizes, supports, and enhances every child's strengths.

There is no intent to suggest that every activity in the school day and all special assistance and support (e.g., remedial math, mobility training, computer activities) should be provided in the general education classroom. All children (those labeled as having a disability *and* those considered "typical") need special help (e.g., special tutoring or extra drill) at one time or another, and they may need to leave the general education classroom to receive that assistance. Most important is for all children to know that it is acceptable to need help sometimes and for that help to be there when they need it. Needing help should not mean that you don't "belong" with your peers. Nor does being culturally or developmentally "different" mean that you cannot share social and academic resources and opportunities with your peers. Children need to know that, as it is okay to need help, it is also okay to be different.

This text is intended to prepare language interventionists and special education teachers to work with colleagues and families on collaborative teams in public school settings. It provides a solid foundation in basic procedures for natural environment-based and classroom-based intervention for all children with language and communication difficulties, with hands-on activities to give students practice in applying the procedures.

Organization

The 14 chapters are organized into three major sections: an introductory section that presents essential background information, a general assessment and intervention section, and a third section that considers the assessment and intervention needs of special populations. Chapter 1 introduces important terms and concepts, followed by an overview of language acquisition. Chapter 2 presents the contributions of major researchers and theorists in language acquisition, with a focus on the practical implications of their offerings. Chapter 3 describes characteristics of students with language and communication difficulties. Chapter 4 presents practices for building effective partnerships with family members. Chapter 5 summarizes legislative regulations, with implications for language interventionists and special education teachers. It also highlights recent paradigm shifts that have significantly impacted what type of services are provided, how services are provided, and where services are provided for children with language and communication difficulties. Finally, this chapter highlights important concepts related to the development and functioning of collaborative teams.

In Section II, Chapter 6 discusses formal and informal language assessment. Chapter 7 presents a rationale for ecological assessment and planning and the steps in the ecological assessment and planning process, with specific guidelines for their implementation. Chapter 8 considers the focus of intervention, methods, and procedures for special instruction, the instructional environment, professional relationships and responsibilities, scheduling, and measurement and evaluation.

Chapter 9, which begins Section III, describes language assessment and intervention with infants and toddlers. Chapter 10 presents strategies to encourage language and communication in inclusive preschool settings. It includes a section that looks at the needs of young children from culturally and linguistically diverse populations. Chapter 11 overviews the language demands of beginning literacy instruction, optional literacy approaches, combined approaches, and programs for learners with special needs during early childhood. Chapter 12 provides focuses on the special needs of young children with severe disabilities. The field of augmentative and alternative communication (AAC) is overviewed in Chapter 13, with particular attention to assessment and planning for an AAC system. The final chapter, Chapter 14, considers second-language learning. Specifically, this chapter prepares students to facilitate the linguistic and academic achievement of bilingual/bicultural children with language difficulties.

Acknowledgments

We wish to thank the reviewers, Ruth Harris, California State University, Northridge; Diane Klein, California State University, Los Angeles; and Patricia Prelock, University of Vermont, who provided valuable assistance and feedback of the final product. We also express our appreciation to the editors for their patience. Finally, we recognize and appreciate the fact that no major project such as a textbook could possibly be completed without the support and encouragement of our colleagues and students. The children and the families with whom we worked are ultimately the ones who deserve the most credit because they are our teachers!

FOREWORD

The unique vitality of this book is that it combines and synthesizes two relevant frames of reference, one in educational practice and one in language intervention. In educational practice I refer, of course, to educational inclusion for learning and to environmental supports for language acquisition. The first emerges from at least forty years of research and practice in special education. This field emerged somewhat timorously in its early states. Children with disabilities were placed in secluded educational environments—if indeed, they were placed at all. Forced into environments that were minimal at best, these children acquired limited language skills, and what skills they did acquire did not serve them well in the social mainstream.

In speech and language intervention, the same type of segregating and formal instruction occurred and the result here, too, was to minimize the acquisition of socially functional learning. Children received formal, adult-directed word and phrase training that had limited functional value, when what they needed was social experiences with their peers.

The truth is that even when we knew that our approaches were of limited value for the children for whom we were supposedly instructional experts, we did not know how to make appropriate modifications. It seemed radical, indeed, to place them in "regular" classes and to let them have a full identification with their normal peers. Acquisition of the confidence and the expertise to plan and to undertake altered arrangements that would produce improved results required many years of innovation. School systems were not well disposed or equipped to undertake these changes, and language specialists were tentative in their efforts to push innovation.

This book, more than any other, combines relevant information about early language acquisition and stimulating social arrangements. It provides information about early language features that vary among children, together with the conditions that must be varied to accelerate desired features. This language information is relevant for both the inclusive classroom and other natural environments. It is a privilege for me to advocate the concept of inclusion to my colleagues in the language-support fields, as well as to those in the schools. This book provides both background and designs for inclusion.

Inclusion is a complex and many-sided concept. This text focuses on both the educational systems that make the inclusion strategy feasible and on the content and functions of language that render them appropriate and functional for the children.

A significant difference from other texts in the field is the unique blending of disciplines. Special educators and speech-language pathologists provide a joint reference toward the common goal of increasing children's language abilities in the surroundings most amenable to learning. It is most encouraging for both teachers and clinicians to see such an expert juncture of the language and the intervention traditions.

Finally, this text provides the most up-to-date data and procedures from both language acquisition and intervention fields. Readers from all relevant disciplines and levels of expertise can use this book to update their professional knowledge base. The student trainee, the educational specialists, and the language interventionists can all benefit from information provided here. The text serves the purpose of both undergraduates and graduate faculty and active research scientists in the education and the developmental language fields. It reflects the shift in the way that educators, both special and regular, and speech-language pathologists view services to enhanced language and communication skills. Working with children in inclusive settings requires a change in philosophy that, in turn, requires us to reevaluate and question our current practices and the assumptions upon which those practices are based. Such shifts in thinking set the stage for further learning and understanding. It is with these thoughts that we hope the readers become engaged with this text.

—Richard L. Schiefelbusch

CHAPTER 1

Introduction to
Language Acquisition

Linda McCormick

Of all the singular gifts bestowed on humans, the ability to acquire and use language at an early age is by far the most miraculous. Long before their first words are produced, children demonstrate well-developed patterns of intentional communication, repair misunderstood messages, use others to accomplish goals, and participate in turn-taking routines (Bates, 1976). By age 2, most have a vocabulary of 50 words, and many are producing short but intelligible sentences. By age 3, they have begun to master tenses, and most children start kindergarten with a vocabulary of 8,000 words or more.

That children learn to talk even before they are out of diapers is a misleading assumption. Even for normally developing children, language acquisition is enormously challenging. For children with biological and/or environmental risk conditions, language acquisition may be impossible without special intervention/instruction.

Many infants are talking even before they can walk.

The goal of this book is to provide an introduction to concepts and practices of language and communication intervention/instruction, with an emphasis on practical guidelines, strategies, and methods, that can be implemented in inclusive settings. This first chapter presents key terms and concepts in linguistics, a discussion of the bases of normal language acquisition, and an overview of early language learning processes.

IMPORTANT TERMS AND CONSTRUCTS

Two problems that complicate study in a new area are (1) learning new terms, and (2) learning new meanings for familiar terms. Of the two, learning new terms is often easier because all you have to do is learn the meaning of the new term and you have a new vocabulary item. Familiar terms with new meanings are more difficult because you have to form new associations. Many of the terms in this first section are of the latter type. They are familiar terms with more refined and specialized or different meanings. For example, you know the terms *language, speech,* and *communication,* but you may not be altogether clear about how the three concepts differ and how they relate to one another.

Language

Languages are abstract systems with rules governing the sequencing of their basic units (sounds, morphemes, words, sentences) as well as rules governing meaning and use. Lahey (1988) defines language as "a code whereby ideas about the world are represented through a conventional system of arbitrary signals for communication" (p. 2). The term *code* is basic to defining language. Language is a code in the sense that it is not a direct representation of the world but, rather, something with which to represent ideas or concepts about the world. These ideas or concepts about the world are inherent in people—*not* in words and not in what words represent.

Language is a marvelously versatile system that allows us to convey our thoughts and feelings to others.

When you know a language, you know both its basic units and the complex rules governing relationships among sounds, words, sentences, meaning, and use. The term *know* is used here in the sense of "being able to apply." The implicit knowledge of language, which allows native speakers of that language to judge sentences as being grammatical, ungrammatical, or ambiguous, and to generate sentences in the language, is called *linguistic competence* (Chomsky, 1965). The production of utterances that demonstrate or realize this knowledge is *linguistic performance.* Language has five components or elements: **phonology, morphology, semantics, syntax,** and **pragmatics.**

PHONOLOGY. The **phonology** of a language includes the sounds that are characteristic of that language, the rules governing their distribution and sequencing, and such variables as the stress and intonation patterns that accompany sounds. The task facing language learners is twofold: (1) how to recognize and produce the sounds of the language they are learning, and (2) how to combine the sounds into words and sentences with the proper intonation.

Phonemes are the smallest units of sound that signal a difference of meaning in a word. To demonstrate what a phoneme is, say the words *bat* and *pat* to yourself. Note that the only difference between the two words is the initial sound. The sounds /b/ and /p/ produce two different words—each with a different meaning. This difference in meanings is the reason that /b/ and /p/ are categorized as separate phonemes in English.

> Phonemes are the smallest units of sound that signal a difference in meaning in a word.

MORPHOLOGY. The **morphology** of a language includes the rules governing how words are formed. Morphemes are the smallest units of meaning in a language. A morpheme cannot be broken into smaller parts without violating the meaning or leaving meaningless remainders. Words consist of one or more morphemes. Examples of words that consist of a single morpheme are *cat, danger, toy,* and *big*. These are called *free morphemes:* they have meaning standing alone. Other morphemes, called *bound morphemes,* cannot function alone. They are always affixed to free morphemes as prefixes or suffixes. Examples include *-s, -er, re-,* and *un-*.

There are two types of bound morphemes: inflectional morphemes (sometimes called grammatical morphemes) and derivational morphemes. Inflectional morphemes modify words to indicate such things as tense, person, number, case, and gender. There are a limited number of inflectional morphemes in English, and they are all suffixes. They are used to form plurals ("two boy*s*"), possessives ("the boy*'s* wagon"), third-person present tense ("she comb*s* her hair"), past tense ("she comb*ed* her hair"), and the past participle ("she has comb*ed* her hair"). There is a complex set of rules that enable speakers to form a past tense or plural of a word that they have never heard before.

Derivational morphemes make a new word that is often, but not always, in a different grammatical class. An example is *-ness*. When added to the adjective *happy,* a noun is derived. Another example is *-ish*. When added to the noun *boy,* an adjective is derived. Derivational morphemes may be either prefixes or suffixes, and in many cases they are borrowed from other languages, particularly Latin or Greek.

> Morphemes are the basic meaningful units of language.

SEMANTICS. The **semantic** aspect of a language specifies rules that speakers use to create and understand the meaning associated with words and word combinations. At the most basic level, semantics involves the lexicon (vocabulary) of a language. It is the linguistic realization of what the speaker knows about the world—what people talk about. Semantics is concerned with relationships: (1) between words and meanings, (2) between words, (3) between word meanings and sentence meanings, and (4) between linguistic meaning and nonlinguistic reality.

With one exception, the relationship between a word and its meaning is arbitrary. The exception is onomatopoeic words. (An onomatopoeic word is formed by imitating the sound made by, or associated with, its referents.) That the piece of furniture you are sitting on is called a *chair* rather than a *cup* is an accident of linguistic history. Other languages, of course, have different words to represent the piece of furniture that English speakers call a chair. When thinking about words and their meanings, remember

1. the meaning of a word is a concept or an idea in the head of the speaker—the thing the word represents is the referent; and
2. words have an arbitrary relationship to the things they represent—they are elements of a code that have been arbitrarily assigned meanings.

The second type of relationship is the relationship between words. Words may have a synonymous, homonymous, or antonymous relationship with one another. Words that have the same meaning are synonymous (e.g., *sofa* and *couch*). Words that sound the same but have different meanings are homonymous with one another (e.g., *flower* and *flour*). Words that have opposite meanings are said to have an antonymous relationship (e.g., *tall* and *short*).

Semantic knowledge is necessary to interpret the meaning of words and sentences.

The third type of semantic relationship is between word meanings and sentence meanings. The meaning of a sentence is not the sum of the meanings of the words combined to form the sentence. If this were the case, then sentences that have the same words (i.e., "The boy loved the girl" and "The girl loved the boy") would also have the same meaning. Rather, the meaning of a sentence is determined by both the meaning of its words *and* its word order. Making a sentence is something like building with blocks. The number of blocks in a set is limited, but there are unlimited possibilities for combining the units to form different structures.

Finally, the fourth type of relationship is between linguistic meaning and nonlinguistic meaning (cognitive knowledge). Cognitive knowledge is the structure we give to our experiences as we organize them into categories for efficient storage and retrieval. When words become linked with cognitive knowledge, the cognitive knowledge becomes semantic knowledge. Thus, semantic knowledge is a subset of cognitive knowledge.

SYNTAX. The **syntax** of language contains rules for how to string words together to form phrases and sentences, what sentences are acceptable, and how to transform sentences into other sentences. Knowledge of the syntax of a language allows a speaker to generate an infinite number of new sentences and to recognize sentences that are not grammatically acceptable. For example, native speakers of English know immediately that one of these sentences is ungrammatical:

1. The waitress poured the coffee.
2. The poured coffee the waitress.

Now consider these sentences:

1. Visiting grandparents can be boring.
2. Jason gave his cousin a sock.

Both sentences are ambiguous. However, because you have linguistic competence in English, you are able to paraphrase them to eliminate the ambiguity. These examples illustrate the wealth of knowledge underlying the ability to form and understand sentences.

> Syntactic rules specify how words are to be combined to form sentences.

PRAGMATICS. The major concern in **pragmatics** is the effectiveness of language in achieving desired functions in social situations. Attitudes, personal history, the setting, the topic of conversation, and the details of the preceding discourse are among the social and contextual factors that determine how speakers cast their sentences (and how listeners interpret them).

Lahey (1988) describes three types of pragmatic knowledge and skills. First is knowing how to use language forms and structures to accomplish certain personal and/or social goals and functions. An example of this type of pragmatic competence is persuading a person to act in a particular manner. Language is used for an extraordinarily wide range of functions. A speaker's utterance can serve as a request for an object, or for information, attention, action, or acknowledgment; an utterance can also convey facts, attitudes, and beliefs, as well as promises and threats. These functions are called **speech acts.** A speech act is a speaker's goal or intent in using language. For example, "Do you think there is enough green paint?" might be interpreted as a request for information. However, when said to the teacher by a child preparing to paint, it might be interpreted as a request for action—an indirect directive to replenish the paint jar. Or, if the green paint jar was about to overflow, the utterance (by an older child or an adult) might be an attempt at sarcastic humor.

> Children must learn when to say what to whom.

Some speech acts are called **performatives** because the intent or goal is actually accomplished by the act of speaking. For example, when you say "I apologize for _____," you are actually apologizing; when someone says "I christen this ship _____," the ship is actually being christened; and the words "You are fired!" actually terminate someone's employment.

A second type of pragmatic competence is knowing how to use information from the social context to determine what to say in order to achieve personal and social goals. Speakers must decide the appropriate form of a message to use in different contexts to accomplish desired functions. They must infer what the listener already knows (and does not know) and adapt their messages accordingly. Judgments about the capacities and needs of listeners in different social contexts are called **presuppositions.**

Rules for engaging in social exchanges or conversational abilities constitute the third type of pragmatic competence. Among the most critical abilities is the ability to initiate, maintain, and terminate conversations. To initiate a conversation, the speaker must first solicit the potential conversational partner's attention. Then, to maintain a conversation, the speaker must know how to take turns, how to assert a position or opinion, and how to respond or react to what the listener has asserted. Finally, the speaker must know how to "sign off" the conversation in a way so that neither partner is left feeling abandoned. The rules for entering and initiating conversations, leaving or terminating conversations, taking turns, shifting topics, handling regressions, asking questions, and temporal spacing of pauses are called **conversational postulates.**

Speech

Speech is the oral modality for language, the expression of language with sounds. Other language modalities include manual signing and writing. Although humans are not the only species to produce sounds, humans are the only species with the unique structure of the human vocal tract necessary to produce the variety and complexity of sounds that are required for speech.

Production of speech sounds depends on respiration, phonation, resonance, and articulation.

Speech production depends on precise physiological and neuromuscular coordination of respiration, phonation, resonance, and articulation. Respiration is the act of breathing; phonation is the production of sound by the larynx and vocal fold; resonance is the vibratory response that controls the quality of the sound wave; and articulation is use of the lips, tongue, teeth, and hard and soft palates to form speech sounds. Exhaled air from the lungs is modified by the vocal folds in the larynx and/or the structure of the mouth to produce speech sounds.

Speech is willed, planned, and programmed by the central nervous system—the brain, the spinal cord, and the peripheral nervous system, which includes the cranial and spinal nerves. The different parts of the nervous system are bound together by neurons to form a complex information exchange network that transmits motor impulses to and from the muscles of the speech mechanism.

Communication

At the broadest level, **communication** is the exchange of ideas, information, thoughts, and feelings. Each person's role in the exchange is clearly defined (e.g., as either speaker or receiver) as the participants take turns sending and receiving messages. The communication process begins when a person has an idea or intention and wants to share it. The idea or intention is formulated into a message and then expressed to another person or persons. The other person or persons receives the message and reacts to or acknowledges it. Thus, the behavior of one participant is directed toward and affects the behavior and/or thoughts of a receiver (or receivers). Then the subsequent behavior and/or thoughts of the message sender are influenced by the response to the message. In any communication there is always a high probability that the message will be distorted because of the many possible message modalities and the many possible connotations and perceptions of the communication partners.

Communication does not necessarily require speech or language. Examples of nonlinguistic communication behaviors are gestures, posture, eye contact, facial expression, and head and body movement. Nonlinguistic communication modes may be used as the only method of communication or they may be used in conjunction with linguistically encoded messages. When they are used in conjunction with speech, there is a complex interrelationship between verbal and nonverbal behavior. Even the distance between participants provides information (Higginbotham & Yoder, 1982). Specifically, it sends a message about the level of interpersonal intimacy of the participants. In Western cultures, participants in a formal, public exchange typically maintain a distance of 12 feet or more. A distance of 4 to 12 feet is common for social-consultive exchanges, and a distance of 18 inches to 4 feet is usual for personal exchanges. Participants in intimate exchanges typically maintain a distance of direct contact to 18 inches.

Communication is possible without speech or language.

There are numerous perspectives on communicative competence. The sociolinguistic perspective, which is heavily influenced by the early work of Hymes, emphasizes the appropriateness of communication with respect to the conversational parameters discussed above. Communicative competence is defined as the language user's ". . . knowledge of sentences, not only as grammatical but also as appropriate" (Hymes, 1972, p. 277). According to Hymes, communicative competence is "knowing when to speak and when not to speak, what to talk about with whom, when, where, and in what manner" (p. 277). Psychologists tend to emphasize the intelligibility of the communicative signal (the degree to which the message is conveyed or received), rather than appropriateness, as the most important aspect of communicative competence (Wang, Rose, & Maxwell, 1973). Others, particularly professionals concerned with speech acts analyses of language, define communicative competence in terms of successful performance of speech acts (Searle, 1969). (Recall that a speech act is a speaker's goal or intent in using language.)

This section has reviewed basic terms and constructs in language development and intervention. Other terms are defined and explained as they occur throughout the text. The next section considers language development—specifically, the contributions of biological preparation, successful nurturance, sensorimotor experiences, and linguistic experiences to the language acquisition process.

THE BASES OF LANGUAGE ACQUISITION

The four sets of variables that seem to have the most profound influence on language learning are (1) biological preparation, (2) successful nurturance (particularly social experiences), (3) sensorimotor experiences, and (4) linguistic experiences. The relative weight given to each of these factors depends on your theoretical biases regarding language acquisition. (Chapter 2 describes language acquisition theories.)

Biological Preparation

In some respects, even newborns are competent learners.

That all cultures have language and all humans learn to talk (unless limited by sensory, neuromuscular, or cognitive impairment) are the strongest evidence for the contention that language is a biologically determined capability. Infants arrive in this world with certain neuromotor capabilities, a supply of attentional and perceptual abilities, and a strong desire to interact with others. If provided with an appropriate variety of experiences, they will become competent communicators. The persistence and attentiveness with which they go about this momentous task are testimony to what has been called the "motivational characteristic of infancy" (Hunt, 1965).

NEUROMOTOR POTENTIALITIES.   As noted above, speech is an enormously complex motor skill. It depends on coordination of the muscles of the vocal organs (tongue, lips, and vocal cords) and appropriate instructions from the brain. Impulses along the motor nerves set the vocal muscles into movement. This movement produces minute pressure changes in the surrounding air (sound waves).

There is a symmetry (called **lateralization**) between the left and right hemispheres of the brain for many motor and sensory processes. Whether one has left- or right-hand dominance, the left cerebral hemisphere controls the right side of the body and is specialized for language in all modalities (oral, visual, and written), temporal- or linear-order perception, arithmetic calculations, and logical reasoning.

The right hemisphere controls the left side of the body and specializes in processing music and other nonspeech sounds. It also carries out spatial activities such as visualizing designs.

At one time it was thought that lateralization takes place gradually throughout infancy and childhood and is not complete until adolescence. Lenneberg's (1967) contention (called the **critical-period hypothesis**) that there is a critical period for language learning was based on the belief that the brain's left hemisphere is no longer able to acquire language after lateralization for language has taken place. The critical-period hypothesis takes the position that humans are most proficient at language learning between age 2 and puberty: A person is no longer prepared to learn language fully after that time because lateralization is complete.

Quite a different picture of lateralization has emerged over the last two decades. There is now some evidence that brain lateralization is present at birth (Kinsbourne & Hiscock, 1983; Michel, 1981). Electrophysiological studies of infants tell us that the young brain is already organized in a lateralized fashion long before the development of specific abilities (e.g., Gardiner & Walter, 1976; Kinsbourne & Hiscock, 1983). If this is the case, then the difficulties that people experience in learning to use a second language like a native speaker would have to be related to variables other than lateralization.

SENSORY AND PERCEPTUAL CAPABILITIES. In addition to special anatomical and physiological structures and unique neurological asymmetry, infants have impressive sensory and perceptual capabilities. Even newborns are sensitive to the basic sound differences in language, which seems to be the minimal prerequisite for acquisition of spoken language (Miller & Eimas, 1983). In a short time they can discriminate between sounds differing in various dimensions (e.g., voicing, place of articulation) and distinguish loudness or intensity, pitch, and duration of sound (Hirschman & Katkin, 1974; Jusczyk, 1992). Four-month-old infants can discriminate between vowels and imitate vocally the main features of the vowels (Kuhl, 1990). Six-month-olds can discriminate vowels and recognize them as the same or different when they are spoken by different speakers (Grieser & Kuhl, 1989).

Infants also demonstrate some visual abilities and rather startling gustatory and olfactory abilities. By 2½ months they are spending approximately 35 percent of their waking hours visually scanning the environment (Rose, 1981). They prefer objects that move, objects with sharp contours, and objects with light-dark contrasts (Kagan, 1985). By three days after birth, infants can differentiate smells and tastes (Desor, Maller, & Andrews, 1975). Most prefer the sweetness of fruit (bananas and applesauce are first choices) over vegetables. (This comes as no surprise to parents, most of whom have been sprayed at least once with strained spinach or some other vegetable.)

Lateralization refers to the specialization of the two hemispheres of the cerebral cortex.

INTERACTION PROPENSITIES. Interaction is a reciprocal process that infants are well prepared to learn. They are responsive to all other humans from birth, but they are especially and differentially responsive to their caregivers. Infants seem to know that they can create change in their environment with certain behaviors. They seem to have clear expectations for caregiver behavior patterns.

During the latter half of the first year, normally developing infants discover that their vocalizations and gestures affect their caregivers' reponses in predictable ways. They use such behaviors as gaze, smiling, touch, and vocalization to motivate their caregivers to attend to them and to respond to their needs, and, in so doing, they actually prompt provision of the type of experiences that will assist the continuing growth of their language skills. There is a high level of mutual coordination and responsiveness between the partners, with the infant influencing the communication process and contributing to the interactions. Infants learn to be message senders as well as message receivers and to coordinate gaze, vocal, and gestural behavior into a fairly complex, patterned exchange that parallels the structure of a conversation.

Nurturance

Sameroff and Fiese (1988) describe the nurturing environment as one in which there is a "mutual dynamic regulation of the child's capacities to understand and [of] the experiences that are presented to be understood" (p. 10). For example, caregivers take advantage of social exchanges to help the infant learn (1) the rules of turn-taking, (2) the meaning of particular gestures, (3) imitation of sounds and gestures, and (4) mutuality. Development of shared meanings, shared intentions, shared codes of conduct, sensorimotor concepts, and symbolic representation will eventually emerge from these attainments.

Caregivers treat babies as if they are intentional communicators long before they actually are. At the same time, they never seem to lose sight of the infant's language and communication limitations. The term that Vygotsky (1978) and his interpreters (Rogoff & Wertsch, 1984; Rogoff, 1990) use in conceptualizing the dynamic regulation that goes on between the infant and caregivers in a nurturing environment is the **zone of proximal development.** The zone of proximal development is the distance between actual and potential development. It is essentially the difference between the developmental level of the child when independently engaged in problem solving and the child's competence when guided by caregivers or in collaboration with more capable peers. It suggests pacing in the presentation of new stimuli. Although this concept is most frequently applied to analyzing the effects of formal educational intervention, it also applies to language acquisition. A common metaphor for this is "scaffolding."

Human infants are social beings from birth.

The distance between actual and potential development is called the zone of proximal development.

Caregivers temporarily support the infant's emerging skills and abilities in much the same way that a temporary framework supports builders and materials when a building is being erected. They regulate presentation of both linguistic and nonlinguistic stimuli.

It is primarily in the context of nurturance that infants acquire the social knowledge essential for language (Dore, 1986; Rice, 1984; Snow, 1984). During routine interactions with caregivers, they discover that communication exchanges have a predictable structure, and they realize that others are responsive to their signals. Over time, they begin to use vocal and gestural signals to *intentionally* influence the attention and actions of others. Thus, in the course of exploiting their "power to direct," infants come to understand the **directive function** of language.

A nurturing environment is an environment in which the pace at which new stimuli are imposed upon the child is mediated by responsiveness. The dynamic regulation of stimuli is evident in caregiving rituals such as feeding and diapering, joint action routines such as peekaboo, and a variety of other daily exchanges. When language development and learning occur, they occur at the fluid boundary (the zone of proximal development described above) where the infant interacts with the nurturing environment.

Sensorimotor Experiences

The relationship between cognitive development and language development continues to be a matter of intense scrutiny and heated debate. Certain language achievements seem to closely follow mastery of selected cognitive skills in children who are developing at a normal rate (Corrigan, 1975) *and* children with disabilities (Mundy, Seibert, & Hogan, 1984). It is not clear, however, that language development is contingent upon mastery of any specific subset of cognitive abilities as was once argued (Lenneberg, 1967). The most likely explanation of the cognitive development–language development relationship is that they are parallel. Arguments by Gopnik and Meltzoff (1984, 1987) avoid the "which comes first?" issue by simply asserting that children learn specific words related to specific cognitive problems that interest them at any point in time. Thus, mastery of certain cognitive and language skills often seem to coincide.

It is clear that acquisition of sensorimotor abilities is precursive (if not prerequisite) to language and communication development. From birth to age 2, the infant's sensory and motor behaviors undergo significant integration, refinement, and reorganization, which permit development of increasingly more complex cognitive abilities. These abilities enable the young child to share a subset of basic meanings with caregivers and to grasp the relationship of words to meanings.

The acquisition of sensorimotor abilities is precursive to development of language skills.

"Knowing" in the sensorimotor sense of the term begins with reflexes that are present at birth, ultimately resulting in the ability to use mental images for problem solving. Infants are active, intrinsically motivated learners. It is not accurate to say that children's minds are totally programmed by learning experiences or that they are born with innate ideas that impose order on reality. Indeed, according to Piagetian theory (Piaget, 1952) children construct their understanding of the world by acting on the world, both physically and mentally. Like tireless little scientists, they explore, hypothesize, test, and evaluate. Acquisition of sensorimotor abilities affords children the critical skills necessary for achieving higher-level thought processes.

Piaget uses the term **schemata** (the singular is **schema**) to describe the models, or mental structures, that humans create to represent, organize, and interpret their experiences. Schemata are patterns of thought or action similar in many respects to what we think of as a concept or strategy. Their knowledge of the world, their schemata, changes as children organize and reorganize their existing knowledge and adapt to new experiences. Among the most important things they learn are that the world is a permanent place with predictable effects and that there are any number of means for controlling the events that occur around them.

According to Piaget (1952), the basic processes of cognitive development, or *ways of learning,* stay essentially the same from birth through adulthood. What differs across stages are the products—the knowing. Both the content and the structure of cognitive functioning become progressively more complex (qualitatively different) as the child moves through the four broad stages of cognitive development: sensorimotor, preoperational, concrete operational, and formal operational. Piaget believed that all cognitive structures are created through the operation of two inborn intellectual functions. He called these basic processes of cognitive development **organization** and **adaptation** (Piaget, 1952).

> Organization is the tendency to combine and integrate available schemata into coherent and complex systems.

Organization is the process by which existing schemata are combined into new and more complex intellectual structures. It is the tendency to reduce, systemize, and categorize the environment into cohesive, orderly, and ultimately more manageable proportions. Learning comes about through progressive, qualitative organization and reorganization of actions and perceptions. Consider, for example, looking and grasping, which are two of the infant's earliest means of operating on the environment. Initially, each functions independently; the infant can grasp an object or she can look at it, but she cannot manage both at the same time. With practice, the infant comes to organize these two actions into a pattern and is able to look at what she grasps and grasp what she is looking at. The result of this organization of initially unrelated schemata into a complex structure—visually directed reaching—enables the infant to reach out and discover the characteristics of many interesting objects in the environment.

The goal of organization is to further the adaptive function. The second key process, **adaptation,** is the process of adjusting to the demands of the environment. Adaptation has two complementary and mutually dependent aspects, **assimilation** and **accommodation.** Assimilation is the process by which new information and new experiences are incorporated into the organism's existing cognitive schemata. Not all stimuli will fit into existing structures, however, so the cognitive structures must be adapted. For example, the young child who sees a cow for the first time will try to assimilate it into one of his existing schemata for four-legged animals and thus may think of this creature as a "doggie." He notices, however, that this creature is very big and if indeed the sound it makes is a bark, it is a very peculiar bark. If the child recognizes that the creature is not a dog and makes an effort to understand it and adopt a label for it, he will have to modify his schema for four-legged animals to include a new category of experience—cows. This is accommodation, modifying existing cognitive structures in accordance with new information. Assimilation and accommodation never occur in isolation. They are two sides of the same coin, complementary aspects of all intellectual acts.

The end result of accommodation and assimilation is a state of **equilibrium** between the child's cognitive structures and the environment, a more complex and sophisticated repertoire. For example, 4-month-old Jessica has encountered a small teddy bear for the first time. She applies her limited "learning strategies" to this strange new "thing." She grasps it by one ear, mouths it, hits it, and shakes it vigorously before throwing the bear to the floor. The teddy bear has two properties that are presumably new to Jessica: softness (for cuddling) and furriness (for stroking). If she seems to be attending to these properties (if she begins to cuddle and rub the bear), then she is learning something from her experience with this new object. The new experience and the new information have been assimilated into Jessica's existing schemata for toys and her existing schemata have changed as a function of the new information (accommodation). What has been accomplished is equilibrium or equilibration: learning has occurred.

> Equilibration acts like a thermostat, accommodating or adjusting thought whenever we perceive something we do not fully understand.

Infants begin constructing some concepts at birth. Piaget called these early schemata **preconcepts** in the course of development. Through the innate activities of adaptation and organization, infants construct a progressively greater understanding of the world in which they live. Over time, their cognition or thinking becomes qualitatively different. Between the ages of 18 and 24 months, infants progress from sensorimotor intelligence, which is reflexive, self-centered, and disorganized, to concepts that are sophisticated, refined, well-organized, and adapted to the demands of the environment.

A substage is never skipped: the sequence is stable. However, some infants progress more rapidly than others. By the end of the sensorimotor stage (18 to 24 months), the young child has constructed the following broad concepts: (1) object permanence, (2) schemata for relating to objects, (3) spatial relationships, (4) means-end understanding, (5) causality, and (6) imitation.

Object permanence is understanding that objects continue to exist even when not immediately perceptible: that people, places, and things exist independent of one's own perceptions. Object permanence begins with the ability to visually fixate on an object (animate or inanimate) and then track its disappearances and appearances. In early infancy, before infants have the notion of object permanence, the disappearance of an object causes no more than a fleeting glance in the direction where it disappeared. Infants act as though the object does not exist unless they can see it. By the end of the first year, however, infants begin to show searching behaviors that are appropriate to the recovery of a desired object (*if* they observed the object's disappearance). More prolonged search will indicate that children have some mental representation of the object. Many consider mental representation to be the crowning achievement of the sensorimotor period, at least for language (e.g., Morehead & Morehead, 1974), possibly related to a spurt in vocabulary growth at the end of the second year. Representational thought continues to develop as children become increasingly able to deal with complex relationships that are not directly perceptible in the environment. Table 1.1 summarizes development of object permanence and the object concept (described in the following paragraphs).

Schemata for relating to objects refers to the infant's ability to perform specific actions or action sequences consistently and habitually on a variety of objects. The scheme itself is the mental organization of the overt actions. These object-specific action patterns are possible because of cognitive capacity.

Initially, schemata for relating to objects are more like reflexes than voluntary behavior. They are behavior sequences directed at the infant's own body. For example, the young infant who sucks everything that finds its way into her mouth would be said to have a sucking scheme. Initially she is indiscriminate, but in time she will develop the ability to discriminate "suckables" and apply this action scheme only in response to these particular objects. Similarly, we can talk about listening, grasping, looking, hitting, kicking, and other schemes that will eventually come to be refined actions applied only to particular objects or events.

Schemes for relating to objects represents a kind of action-based scientific method that the infant uses to learn about objects. At first, all objects elicit the same action schemes (sucking, grasping, shaking),

Object permanence is understanding that objects continue to exist when they are not detectable to the senses.

The infant's grasping actions and sucking responses are early behavioral schemata.

TABLE 1.1 Representative sensorimotor behaviors: Object permanence and schemes for relating to objects

Stage (Ages)	Object Permanence	Schemes for Relating to Objects
Stage 1: (0–1 month) Reflexive	Continuously practices reflexes No active search for objects that drop out of view Demonstrates some visual pursuit when lying on back	No discernable separation of self from objects
Stage 2: (1–4 months) Primary Circular Reactions	Gradually coordinates sensory schemes—vision and hearing, sucking and grasping, and vision and grasping Able to visually follow a slowly moving object through a 180-degree arc in a smooth tracking response Very little, if any, visual or manual search for a vanished object—"out of sight is out of mind" Lingers with a brief glance at the point where a slowly moving object disappears	Shows incidental object use in the process of practicing different behaviors such as grasping and looking Mouths some objects Holds and briefly inspects various objects
Stage 3: (4–8 months) Secondary Circular Reactions	Visually anticipates the future position of a moving object Continues manual search for an object if grasping movements are interrupted while in process Recognizes and obtains an object that is partially hidden Behaves as if an object no longer exists when it is completely covered or drops out of sight	Shows systematic object use in practicing different behaviors Bangs objects together Shakes a rattle, bell, and other objects Visually inspects an object while tactually exploring it Displays other differentiated actions with objects, including crumpling (of paper), sliding (of toys on surface), tearing, stretching, rubbing, mouthing
Stage 4: (8–12 months) Coordination of Secondary Reactions	Looks for an object after it has vanished behind a screen and reliably retrieves it Reacts with only mild surprise or puzzlement when object retrieved differs from the one hidden Continues searching for an object at point A (where it is usually found) even after watching it being hidden at location B	Demonstrates new actions on objects resulting from (related to) object properties Intentionally drops and throws objects Uses objects in a socially relevant manner Combines functional relationships, such as placing cup in saucer, to some extent

(continued)

TABLE 1.1   Representative sensorimotor behaviors: Object permanence and schemes for relating to objects (continued)

Stage (Ages)	Object Permanence	Schemes for Relating to Objects
Stage 5: (12–18 months) Tertiary Circular Reactions	When the hiding is visible, infant will search in the place where it was last seen (even with 3 screens) Not successful at retrieving objects if hiding is not visible because infant cannot yet "think" where an object might be	Varies action on objects to "experiment" with different effects (such as dropping objects to study their trajectory) Links more objects in functional relationships: Puts cup in saucer, pretends to drink from cup, slides brush or comb over his hair
Stage 6: (18–24 months) Invention of New Means through Mental combinations	Systematically searches for an object that has undergone as many as 3 invisible displacements— searches each hiding place (sometimes in reverse order)	Demonstrates understanding of the functions and social meanings of a large number of objects: Holds telephone to ear and vocalizes, tries to put shoes and socks on, names familiar objects

which are part of the infant's reflexive repertoire. Gradually, schemes become differentiated and are applied according to object properties.

Spatial relationships involve two related concepts: the infant's recognition of an object's position in space and the recognition of one object in relation to another. Development of the awareness of spatial relationships begins with visual tracking of moving objects. Soon after, the infant begins to act on objects as though they have a given location and to rotate them in relation to perceived spatial orientation. For example, if presented with a bottle with the nipple turned away, the infant will turn the nipple toward her and begin to suck it. Finally the infant gives evidence of mental representation of the spatial relationship between two objects (without testing the relationship with her own body). For example, the child unhesitatingly goes around a hedge to retrieve a ball, rather than first trying to go through it. Mental representation of space is also evident in the child's recognition that an object that is usually in a given location is missing from that location.

Means-end understanding is the ability to separate problem-solving processes from problem-solving goals. It begins with simple reflexive responses to external stimuli during the period of 1–4 months. An example is the infant's sucking in response to her lips being stimulated by mother's nipple. During the third sensorimotor substage, these behaviors become less reflexive. They are now behavior sequences that the infant has discovered through repeated experiences with positive consequences. An example would be an infant's hitting the top of the jack-in-the-box toy because she has discovered that this makes the clown pop out.

By the first half of the second year, infants are beginning to vary the components of a behavior sequence systematically to observe changes in the outcomes. By the sixth substage, infants are solving problems without overt trial and error. Piaget calls this the ability to invent new means through mental combinations. Means-end relationships are closely related to causality concepts.

Causality is the ability to anticipate what consequences will follow from a certain cause or, conversely, what cause is likely to produce a particular consequence. Infants learn about causality when they accidentally create pleasurable effects through such behaviors as hand waving and kicking. Once they learn that they can cause effects and thus control their environment effectively through systematic application of certain motor behaviors, they begin to use more complex control behaviors. As experiences with pleasurable effects increase, infants begin to anticipate results and events and they begin to search for activating or causal mechanisms to produce the anticipated pleasurable outcomes.

> Means-end understanding and causality are closely related concepts.

The 1-year-old is aware only of causal relations that have some personal consequence for her (e.g., crying causes mother to pay attention). It is not until 18 months that she becomes aware of causal relations involving other people and objects and she realizes that her behavior can be affected by, as well as affect, other people and things in the environment. Two-year-olds are able to classify many of their own behaviors and the behaviors of others in terms of the consequences they produce. Table 1.2 presents some parallels between development of means-end and causality concepts and emergence of communicative functions.

Imitation is performance of a response that matches, or approximates, the behavior of a model. Piaget recognized the adaptive significance of imitation. At the very least, imitation requires the ability to pay careful attention to, and precisely copy the topographical features of, a behavior produced by another, *immediately* after the model. Table 1.3 summarizes the development of imitation in the sensorimotor period. Imitation is a device that infants use to add new behaviors to their repertoire. In the early months, infants can imitate only actions that are already in their repertoire. It is not until Stage 4, when they are able to coordinate secondary schemes, that they can accommodate their behavior to imitate novel actions. Imitation becomes more efficient at 12 to 18 months, but the greatest accomplishment is in the latter part of their second year when infants engage in **delayed or deferred imitation.** Deferred imitation,

TABLE 1.2   Parallels between means-end and causality development and emergence of communicative functions

Sensorimotor Stage (Ages)	Means-End Behavior and Causality Development	Interaction-Communication Strategies
Stage 1: (0–1 month) Reflexive Reactions	Repeats/practices reflexes No understanding of causal relationships	Perlocutionary acts Quiets and responds to human voice
Stage 2: (1–4 months) Primary Circular Reactions	No differentiation of self and moving objects Immediately repeats behaviors that have accidentally produced interesting results (e.g., attempting to keep a mobile in motion)	Perlocutionary (unintentional) acts Smiles and coos in response to adult smiling and/or vocalization Shows anticipation when about to be picked up Emits distinguishable cries for anger, hunger, pain
Stage 3: (4–8 months) Secondary Circular Reactions	Uses such behavior as consistent vocalization, kicking, waving as if attempting to "cause" continuation of an interesting sight	Perlocutionary acts Shows enjoyment when played with Vocalizes states such as pleasure, satisfaction, anger Follows adult gaze (if adult breaks eye contact to look elsewhere) "Recognizes" caregiver Performs joint action "rituals" with caregiver (turn-taking routines)
Stage 4: (8–12 months) Coordination of Secondary Circular Reactions	Intentional, goal-directed behavior apparent in releasing or pushing aside one object to grasp another, pulling a support to obtain desired toy Appreciation of causality outside the self demonstrated by pushing the adult's hand to continue an interesting sensory effect, anticipating the occurrence of events from signs (e.g., crying when mother gets her coat out)	Perlocutionary acts Extends arms to be picked up Withdraws from approach of a stranger Reacts negatively when a toy is taken away Waves "bye-bye" Shows affection to parents and other adults Looks at caregiver's face when receiving an object as if to acknowledge receipt Plays peekaboo, hiding face for another to watch
Stage 5: (12–18 months) Tertiary Circular Reactions	Experiments with means and ends as if to see what will happen Demonstrates considerable interest in novelty for its own sake	Illocutionary acts Tries to turn doorknobs as a request to "go outside" Uses gestures such as pointing to direct adult attention

TABLE 1.2 Parallels between means-end and causality development and emergence of communicative functions (continued)

Sensorimotor Stage (Ages)	Means-End Behavior and Causality Development	Interaction-Communication Strategies
Stage 5: (12–18 months) Tertiary Circular Reactions	Uses an attached string or stick to obtain a desired toy without demonstration (even if toy is not in direct view) Hands a mechanical toy to an adult to be reactivated Shows object to others to instigate social interaction	Hands book to adult to request reading of a story Pulls adult to view certain situations or a new location Shows/displays/points out objects to others to elicit attention and social interaction
Stage 6: (18–24 months) Invention of New Means through Mental Combinations	Ability to use mental problem solving (mental foresight of effects) Immediately looks for causes of own actions Able to infer a cause, given only its effect, or foresee an effect, given a cause	Locutionary acts Asks for desired object (with conventional symbol) Uses words to make wants/desires known Names objects in the presence of others Says "What's that?" for adult attention

the imitation of models who are no longer present, is a clear indication of mental representation.

Vocal imitation and gestures have been found to be significantly correlated at about 9 months of age (Bates, Benigni, Bretherton, Camaioni, & Volterra, 1979). (An increase in one was typically associated with an increase in the other.) While imitation cannot account fully for language acquisition, it undoubtedly plays some role in the process. Vocal and gestural imitation have been positively correlated with language level (Snow, 1989).

Vocal and gestural imitation are positively correlated with language level.

THE ROLE OF PLAY. Play has a cognitive, social, and integrative function in development. It is both a learning strategy and a learning context. The function of play seems to be to exercise and develop manipulative and interactional strategies that can later be integrated into more sophisticated task-oriented sequences (Bruner, 1975). Almost from birth, infants and caregivers engage one another in familiar patterns of interaction. In analyzing children's early games and routines such as peekaboo, Ratner and Bruner (1978) found a highly structured pattern of mother-child exchanges, with rules that teach the infant about communication. Over time, as the infant continues to play games with the mother, the infant's behavior gradually changes from passive recipient

Table 1.3   Development of sensorimotor imitation

Stage (Ages)	Type of Imitation	Characteristics
Stage 1: (0–1 month)	Vocal contagion	Infant is incapable of "true" imitation, but acts that appear to be imitative do occur. One crying newborn is likely to stimulate the other infants to cry. Piaget describes this phenomenon as the triggering of existing response patterns through external stimulation.
Stage 2: (1–4 months)	Mutual imitation	The infant will often repeat a habitual response (gesture or vocal) if someone has immediately mimicked the production. Reproductions are limited and are only gross approximations of the model.
Stage 3: (4–8 months)	Systematic imitation	Since the child is now able to coordinate vision and prehension, she can imitate many more acts. She can now imitate movements, such as opening and closing the fist, but cannot imitate acts, such as opening and closing the eyes, that she cannot see herself performing. The child apparently needs a visual impression that matches that which she has seen the model create in order to duplicate the model. Also, the child will imitate only those sounds and movements that are already in her repertoire. Thus, imitation at this stage is less a learning strategy than a strategy to prolong or continue those events the child finds meaningful.
Stage 4: (8–12 months)	Imitation of new behaviors	The ability to imitate movements that she cannot see herself, and to produce and imitate some acts that are not already known, emerge simultaneously. Imitation undergoes a transition from being a means for continuing interesting events to being a means for learning new ones. However, only actions and vocalizations similar to those in the child's repertoire are imitated.
Stage 5: (12–18 months)	Expanded imitation of new behaviors	Reproductions of new models are immediate, deliberate, and usually quite accurate. Imitation is used in a trial-and-error fashion to discover the properties of objects. Novel vocalizations will be imitated repeatedly as if to perfect the reproduction.
Stage 6: (18–24 months)	Deferred (or representative) imitation	Imitation no longer requires that the model be immediately present. The child is now capable of mental representation and long-term memory for what was modeled. She is also capable of imitating complex new acts and objects as well as persons.

to initiator of actions. By 5 to 9 months of age, the infant has learned to be a partner in the exchange process that is inherent in social games. During the second 6 months of life, object play increases, with infant and mother participating in ritualized give-and-take of objects. The importance of these games is the shared meaningful communication at a completely nonverbal level.

Piaget (1952) discussed play in the sensorimotor period as setting the stage for practice and mastery of emerging cognitive skills. Because play centers on the children's interests, it permits them to reenact environmental experiences and to construct rich fantasy worlds for themselves. The earliest forms of pretend play begin around 11–13 months. Like language, pretend play is initially very dependent on the "here and now." Infants pretend to engage in familiar activities such as eating, sleeping, or drinking from a cup.

In later writing, Piaget (1962) emphasized the parallel courses of play and language development. Similar to language, play is a manifestation of the symbolic function. At about the time that children begin to combine symbols, they begin to play symbolically. In symbolic play, children learn to "know" objects in more than one way. It is evident when children begin to substitute one object for another. For example, a child demonstrates that he has established a relationship between an absent object (a car) and a symbolized object (a block) when he moves a small block along a groove in the dirt while making a motor sound. Development psychologists have hypothesized that early symbols emerge out of an underlying, generalized symbolic capacity called the **semiotic function** (e.g., Bates, Bretherton, & Snyder, 1988).

As children enter their third year, their play becomes much more complex. They begin to role-play. They use toys in imaginative ways and exhibit much make-believe play. Unlike 2-year-olds, they are likely to play in groups and they are learning to take turns and share toys. The play of 3-year-olds is accompanied by sounds and words as they explain their actions, make environmental noises, and take various roles in pretend play.

Symbolic play is pretend play in which one actor, object, or action represents another.

By about age 4, children are able to role-play a baby using higher pitch, phonetic substitutions, and shorter and simpler utterances (Sachs & Devin, 1976). They are also able to play "Mother and Dad." (Andersen, 1977). Mother is portrayed as more polite, using more indirect requests, and with a higher pitch and longer utterances than Dad.

Thus, we see infants progress, in two short years, from being totally reflexive and largely immobile to becoming planful thinkers who can move about on their own and communicate many of their intentions—a truly remarkable achievement. During the preconceptual period (2–4 years of age) children become increasingly proficient at constructing and using mental symbols to think about objects, situations, and events (called symbolic thought or mental representation) and using words to make reference to objects, persons, and events.

Linguistic Experiences

Linguistic input (called child-directed speech) plays an important role in language learning. Caregivers continuously adjust the phonologic, semantic, syntactic, and pragmatic characteristics of their speech when they address infants and young children.

Motherese is a term that was coined to describe the less complex linguistic style that mothers use when talking to infants, but it has come to refer to any child-oriented language by an adult. Even adults who are inexperienced with infants and children as young as 4 years modify their speech when addressing infants (Papousek, Papousek, & Haekel, 1987). Presumably, adults make modifications (without even being aware of it) in order to capture and hold the infant's attention (Snow, 1984). Fernald (1989) suggests that the exaggerated prosodic patterns may ensure the infant's attention and help the infant become aware of the general communicative intent of a message.

> Motherese is a term for the less complex language that caregivers use when talking to infants.

Language directed to very young children is less diverse. There are fewer *different* words and they are used less often. Caregivers tend to use more modifiers, and the frequency of questions increases as the child gets more competent. They are selective about the words they use with young children. When speaking to young children, caregivers seem to be guided by three assumptions: (1) that some words are easier for children to pronounce than others; (2) that some words are more useful for children than others; and (3) that some words and word endings should be omitted and others should be avoided (because they are difficult to understand).

Caregivers use repetitions when infants seem unable to understand a word or statement or to comply with a request (Messer, 1989). They also simplify their linguistic input semantically and syntactically. They use "here and now" language, talking about only those aspects of the world that are present in the immediate environment.

Caregivers provide running commentaries on what children are doing when objects and events, or pictures of objects and events, are the focus of the child's attention. They play what can be called a "naming game" in many interactions, particularly during picturebook reading activities. When the child looks at a picture, caregivers name the object or action that is depicted. Syntactic simplification is reflected in the brevity, concreteness, and reduced number of contractions and pronouns in child-directed speech.

Caregivers model words and sentences for their children to reproduce and they specifically direct the child to imitate ("Say _____"). Using imitation as a learning strategy varies among children, but there is some evidence that children who *do* imitate, imitate selectively (Bloom, Hood, & Lightbown, 1974). Young children reproduce words and phrases that they are in the process of learning. They may not imitate words and syntactic structures that are either very familiar or very unfamiliar. Also, children are more likely to imitate if the prior adult utterance is a repetition or expansion of the child's previous utterance. Children's imitation of adult utterances decreases with increasing language development. After age 2, when language becomes more complex, imitation is not as important a language-learning strategy.

Adults use both expansion and extension when responding to young children. **Expansion** is responding to a child's utterance with a more sophisticated version of the utterance: The response preserves the word order of the child's utterance. For example, if the child says "Daddy bye-bye," the adult might respond with "Daddy is going bye-bye." Expansions make up a substantial proportion of child-directed speech. When repeating and expanding the child's utterances, caregivers take care not to change or add to the intended meaning, thus confirming that the child has been understood. Very often, when adults imitate and expand children's utterances, children imitate the expansions.

> Expansion is responding to a child with a more sophisticated version of the child's utterance.

Extension is responding with a comment that adds information to the topic established by the child. For example, when the infant says "Daddy bye-bye," the adult responds "Yes, Daddy is going to work." Adult extensions and length of child utterances have been found to be significantly correlated (Wells, Barnes, Gutfreund, & Satterly, 1983).

> Extension is responding with an utterance that adds new information to the child's topic.

Adults begin asking questions of infants as young as 3 months of age. They also, of course, supply the answers (Snow, 1984: Stern, 1984). The questions caregivers ask their infants demonstrate that they have precise understanding of the infant's knowledge and his language abilities. They reformulate and "break down" the structure of a question if the child does not respond to the original form.

Adults also use many fill-ins in their speech directed to children. For example, the adult might say "This is a _____ ," and pause for the child to supply the final element. If the child does not respond or responds incorrectly, the adult will usually provide a prompt or cue ("This is a b _____ ") or a model ("You can say 'baby.' This is a 'baby.' "). What seems uppermost in the mind of the adult is maintaining the interaction at a level that allows the child to participate and keep the conversation going.

OVERVIEW OF EARLY LANGUAGE ACQUISITION

The routines established in play and daily caregiving activities provide settings for early language learning. By the latter half of their second year, through participation in these routines, infants have learned an enormous amount about the persons, objects, and events in their environment and communicative dialogues. While they have not *always* guessed correctly in their organization of internal representations of the world, and the "tags" they have attached to their concepts are not *always* correct, they are on their way to becoming competent language users.

Prior to beginning kindergarten, children demonstrate significant accomplishments in (1) phonological development, (2) types of words used, (3) types of sentences used, (4) the length of utterances, (5) number and variety of meanings expressed, (6) conversational/discourse abilities, and (7) the range of pragmatic functions.

Phonological Development

The English language consists of approximately 40 phonemes, categorized into vowels and consonants. Regardless of the linguistic community into which they are born, all infants seem to pass through the same states of vocal development (e.g., Ferguson, 1979; Prather, Hedrick, & Kern, 1975). From the moment of their first cry, infants begin learning precise control of their lips, tongue, and hard and soft palates, and how to coordinate their respiration, phonation, and resonance for speech.

During the babbling period there is a noticeable increase in the sounds made by the hearing child (in contrast to the infant who is hearing impaired). Around the third and fourth months, cooing and babbling monologues become more frequent, and sound use, more varied. Babbling sounds soon begin to resemble the consonants and vowels of adult speech in the child's culture. Between 6 to 10 months, infant babbling changes to experimentation with consonant-vowel syllable sequences (e.g., "da-da-da"). The repetitive syllable production that characterizes the infant's speech during this period is called **reduplicative babbling.** This sound pattern makes up about half of babies' noncrying sound from about 6 to 12 months of age (Mitchell & Kent, 1990).

"Ma-ma-ma" is an example of reduplicative babbling.

Infants begin to sound as if they are trying to produce words. At around 9 to 12 months, they begin to use imitation to expand and modify their repertoire of speech sounds. Initially they imitate only those sounds they have already produced spontaneously on their own. This stage is characterized by strings of sounds and syllables—called **conversational babbling,** or *jargon*—which are produced with adultlike stress and intonation patterns. Early words tend to use the same sound that the child preferred in babbling (the sounds that the baby has under voluntary control).

Pronunciations of first words vary. Some words may be perfect according to adult standards while others are difficult to understand.

Some of the sound sequences produced at this stage are not based on adult words. These are called **vocables** or **phonetically consistent forms** (PCFs), (Dore, Franklin, Miller, & Ramer, 1976). Infants may develop as many as a dozen vocables (and use them consistently) before producing their first words. An example of a PCF would be the use of "b" for "ball."

Children learning English must learn to correctly articulate 25 consonants and 21 vowels and diphthongs, and they must learn to produce these sounds individually and in swift-moving speech. There is enormous variability among children. The age of acquisition for some sounds may vary as much as 3 years (Werker & Pegg, 1992). By age 3, most children can produce all of the vowel sounds and nearly all consonant sounds (though not with total accuracy in all words). As the normative data previously presented indicate, even at 4 and 5, there will be some consonants that are in error. The acquisition process continues well into early elementary school as children continue to work on mastery of a complete repertoire of speech sounds and two sets of rules: the rules that govern the position of sounds in words, **distributional rules,** and the rules for sequencing these sounds, **sequential rules.**

Distributional rules govern the position of sounds in words.

Types of Words Used

First words, produced around the end of the first year, are typically a combination of lexical, vocal, and gestural forms. By 13 to 15 months, most infants have acquired 10 words. The majority of these words are names for favorite toys or foods, family members, or pets. Action words such as "up" and "bye-bye," modifiers such as "pretty," and grammatical function words such as "what" are also represented in this first vocabulary, but much less frequently. These single words are typically used for different functions: requesting, commenting, and inquiring (as well as naming). Early vocabulary growth is slow, with short periods of time when the child does not add any new words and may even stop producing some of the words in his initial vocabulary. This is usually due to changing interests and improved production capabilities.

Although there is wide individual variation, it is not uncommon for a child's receptive vocabulary to be as much as four times the size of the expressive vocabulary in the first half of their second year (Griffiths, 1986). Some meanings will be similar to adult meanings, but most will be very restricted compared to adult definitions.

Vocabulary growth accelerates as the child nears a 50-word vocabulary. Composition of the second set of 40 words, typically acquired by 18 to 20 months, is two-thirds nouns for many children. Action words account for less than 20 percent of the total (Benedict, 1979; Nelson, 1973). In Nelson's listing of the nominals used by the

Children's first words are
names for things that move or
can be acted upon.

18 children in her study, there was no noun that was used by all of the children. The fact that very few words were shared by even half the children is impressive evidence for the influence of environmental differences. Children learn names for different objects and events because they encounter different objects and events.

The one commonality among all children is that they learn names for things that move or that they can act upon. Such common nouns as stove, lamp, tub, and the like, labeling objects that are not acted upon by the young child in any significant way, are notable by their absence from early vocabulary lists. Instead, we find many words for food and drink, animal names, clothing, and toys. All of the latter are objects children directly experience or objects that move. Another variable is pronunciation: Children learn words that contain sounds they can produce (Leonard, Schwartz, Morris, & Chapman, 1981).

As discussed, children are capable of representational thought by age 2, in preparation for the more advanced cognitive period that Piaget calls preoperational thought. They know that object existence is absolute—that objects exist and continue to exist even when not immediately visible—and that different objects have different perceptual and functional properties. Similarly, they know (1) that "things" can cease to exist and then recur, (2) that people (including themselves) can relate to objects in certain prescribed ways (e.g., owning them, locating and relocating them), and (3) that objects also relate to themselves and each other in a relatively consistent manner. Their single-word utterances reflect this growing knowledge of the world. Most early single-word utterances can be classified as either substantive or relational (Bloom & Lahey, 1978). **Substantive words** refer to specific entities or classes of entities that have certain shared perceptual or functional features. Examples include *cup, bottle, mama, doggie,* and *ball.* When children begin combining words into two-word combinations, they classify substantive words on the basis of action. Words are classified as agents—the source of action—or objects—the recipient of action.

Relational words make reference across entities. Relational meanings transcend the individual objects involved. Use of relational words is evidence that the child is able to conceptualize and encode the dynamic state of the entity separately from the entity itself. They may refer to dynamic relations that an entity shares with itself or with other entities. In relation to itself, an entity can exist or not exist, disappear and reappear. An example is "all gone," which can apply to an empty bowl or a vacant dog house. Other entities may share static states such as possession and attribution, dynamic states (actions), or locations.

In the years from age 2 to age 6 there are marked changes in the *kinds* of words children use. As noted, a substantial proportion of a child's first 50 words are nouns and verbs, with labels for objects that move or can be acted upon and action verbs appearing most frequently. Modifiers (*hot, big*) and function words (*no, more*) begin to appear around 18 to 20 months. Expressions for temporal relations (*then, after, before*), causality (*if, because*), and quantity (*many, few, three*) appear much later.

At around age 2, children begin both to recognize that a pronoun can refer to an already established referent and to use some pronouns correctly. Their first pronouns signal notice, such as *this* and *that* (e.g., *That* a birdie). The pronoun *it* also appears early, usually in the subject position (e.g., *It* a swing). Some other pronouns that occur when children begin to combine words include *one, some,* and *other.* The second set of pronouns to appear after age 2½ includes person pronouns. Subjective case pronouns (*I, you, they, he/she, we*) are acquired first; objective case pronouns are acquired somewhat later. Other pronouns emerge much later, with order of acquisition varying across children.

The most notable change in types of words used after age 2 or 2½ is acquisition of **grammatical morphemes.** The acquisition of grammatical morphemes is gradual and lengthy, beginning at around 27 months or when the mean length of the child's utterances is about 2.0. (Generally referred to as MLU, the concept of mean length of utterance is explained in the next section.) Although they do not carry independent meaning, grammatical morphemes (also called morphological inflections) subtly affect the meaning of sentences. Brown's (1975) study of the mastery of grammatical morphemes found that the rate of development varies but the order of acquisition (as listed below) is fairly predictable.

1. *-ing* making the present progressive tense (children first use this *without* an auxiliary verb). Example: I runn*ing*.
2. *In* and *on* used in locative state utterances. Example: Cookie *in* there. Ball *on* bed.
3. *-s* marking the regular noun plural (and some irregular forms). Example: My doll*s*.
4. Some past tense irregular verbs such as *went* and *came*. Example: She *went*.
5. *-'s* marking the noun possessive. Example: Daddy*'s* shoe.
6. Uncontractible copula forms of *to be: am, is, are, was,* and *were.* (The contractible forms are acquired much later.) Example: He *was* good.
7. Use of *a* and *the* to distinguish between definite and indefinite referents. Example: That *a* doggie.
8. *-ed* marking the regular past tense. Example: She cook*ed*.
9. *-s* ending on third-person regular verbs. Example: He move*s*.

Grammatical morphemes modulate the meaning of a sentence.

10. Third-person irregular verb forms. Example: *is, has, does*
11. Uncontractible auxiliary forms of *be* verbs preceding another verb: *am, is, are, were,* and *was.*
12. Contractible copula verbs. Example: It's my book.
13. Contractible auxiliary verbs. Example: He's reading a book.

While there are not definitive data on the acquisition of grammatical morphemes in all languages, what data there are suggest that grammatical morphemes are acquired in similar ways and at about the same stage of development in different languages (Pizzuto & Caselli, 1991). This evidence lends strong support to the notion that the cognitive relationship between the semantic and syntactic complexity of the earliest morphemes is the key to developmental order. The forms that are semantically and syntactically easier tend to be learned and produced earlier.

Types of Sentences Used

In the early stages of language learning, as mean length of utterance (MLU) increases, the complexity of children's utterances also increases. This relationship between length and linguistic complexity seems to maintain until an MLU of approximately 4.0. MLU is obtained by counting the morphemes in 50 (or 100) utterances from a spontaneous speech sample and then dividing by 50 (or 100).

By age 2½, most children are producing simple declarative sentences.

When children attain an MLU of 2.5 (at around 2½ years of age), most have mastered the elements of simple declarative sentences (Wells, 1985). They soon begin to experiment with modifying the basic pattern: They elaborate in noun phrase development and they begin to produce negative, interrogative, and imperative sentences.

NEGATIVE SENTENCES.   There are three periods in learning to produce negative sentences (Bellugi, 1967). First, at about age 2, children form negative sentences by attaching *no* or *not* to a simple declarative sentence, and they attach the negative form in the initial position. Sentences like "Not more juice" (said while holding up an empty cup) and "No can do it" (said while trying to force a wooden puzzle piece into the puzzle frame) are prevalent. The negative function used most often is *nonexistence* (e.g., *no cookie*, indicating the cookie is not in his pocket), but *rejection* (e.g., *not meat*, said while pushing the spoon away), and *denial* (e.g., *not my teddy*, said when offered someone else's bear) also appear. While children may initially express all three negative functions in the same way—by tagging on no or not—the different meanings are generally quite clear.

In the second period, children place the negative word next to the main verb within the sentence (e.g., "I no sleep," or "Mommy no go car"). In the third period, when children are around 42 to 48 months, their negative sentences approximate the adult form. By this age they have an extensive repertoire of negative possibilities. They use *can, does, do, did, will,* and *be* with *not* in uncontracted form. (Initially they use them in present tense.)

QUESTIONS. Children do not learn to ask some types of questions until they have learned to answer questions of the same kind. For example, they typically do not ask *why* questions until they are able to answer *why* questions. Ervin-Tripp (1970) studied the sequence in which five children responded to different questions after the age of 21 months. First they respond to these *wh-* questions, in this order: (1) *where,* (2) *what,* (3) *whose,* and (4) *who. Why, how,* and *when* were responded to somewhat later.

Klima and Bellugi (1966) described three stages in the development of question-asking skills:

Stage 1: At about 24 to 28 months (MLU around 2.0), children begin to use a few *wh-* words (*what* and *where*). However, most questions are like statements with a rising intonation. Possibly the reason these particular *wh-* words appear early is that they relate to the immediate environment, permitting the child to (1) gain labels, and (2) locate lost objects. Another possible explanation for the early appearance of *what* and *where* could be that they are used frequently by caregivers. Finally, a third possible explanation would be that *what* and *where* are learned first because they are related to two of the earliest semantic categories—nomination and location.

Stage 2: At about 26 to 32 months (MLU around 2.5), children begin to use the *wh-* forms, *why, where,* and *what,* to introduce statements. Examples include "Why you go?" and "Where my coat?" They have both a subject and a predicate but auxiliaries are notably absent. At this stage, questions of the *yes-no* type are still statements with a rising intonation. Mistaking one form of *wh-* question for another is common and lasts until about 36 months. Younger children (between about 20 and 28 months) will typically treat most *wh-* questions as *where* questions, but responses of older 2-year-olds indicate that they are mistaking *why* questions for *what* questions.

Stage 3: At about 33 to 36 months (MLU around 3.0), children produce inverted yes/no-type questions. Shortly thereafter they use inverted *wh-* forms. A variation at this stage is use of the carrier phrase *do you know* to introduce many questions.

Thus, the order of use of *wh-* forms is *what, where, who, when, why, how.* By about age 4, most of the necessary auxiliary verbs and

Children learn to answer certain kinds of questions before they learn to ask them.

pronouns are in place and children are using the adult question form.

IMPERATIVE SENTENCES.   Imperative sentences request, demand, ask, or command the listener to perform an action. Most imperative sentences have no overt grammatical subject and the verb is uninflected (e.g., "Give me the paper"). Children between the ages of 19 to 26 months (MLU around 1.75) produce forms (often accompanied by gestures) that serve an imperative or directive function. However. imperative sentences do not appear until around 31 months. By 35 months (MLU of 3.0), children have begun to use modal auxiliaries (e.g., *can, could, will*) in embedded imperatives (e.g., "Could you give me a cookie"). Production of the latter imperatives suggests that the child is beginning to understand the importance of modifying directives according to the status of one's listener.

Length of Utterances

Early multiword utterances are most accurately termed successive single-word utterances.

The multiword utterances that are evident as early as 16 months are more properly termed *successive single-word utterances* than short sentences (Bloom, 1973; Dore, 1975). Children use two words together (separate one-word utterances) to comment on two aspects of an ongoing event. These utterances are evidence that children are beginning to perceive relations among persons and objects. but they do not yet have sufficient language skills to express these relationships. After successive single-word utterances, encoding of semantic relations is the next step in the transition to syntactic constructions and a major contributor to increased length of utterances. The meaning of semantic relations (sometimes called semantic–syntactic relations), which are two- and three-word utterances, depends on *relationships* among the words rather than the meanings of the words themselves. An example is the utterance "Brendyn shoe," which expresses a possessor-possession relationship. (Semantic relations are discussed at more length below.)

A second factor accounting for increased length of utterances is **concatenation.** Concatenation (chaining together two-term semantic relations) is evident shortly after children begin producing single two-term semantic relations. For example, the agent–action relation *baby eat* and the action–object relation *eat cookie* would be combined (and the redundant term omitted to yield *Baby eat cookie*).

A third factor accounting for increased sentence length is expansion. Once children are understanding and expressing semantic relations, they begin to expand simple terms in these relations (i.e., agent, action, object) by adding modifiers and auxiliaries. These expanded constructions give the listener more accurate and precise information. Although the 3-year-olds who produce these expanded constructions are expressing the same intentions they expressed earlier with 2 or 3 words, interpretation is easier (and likely to be correct more often) because it is not dependent upon contextual information. The child who said "more juice" at 18 months and "want more juice" at 24 months, now at 30 months may say "want more apple juice."

A fourth factor in increased length of utterances is the emergence of grammatical morphemes at around age 2 or 2½. Acquisition of grammatical morphemes was described in the section, Types of Words Used.

Number and Variety of Meanings Expressed

Children have a range and variety of personal experiences with objects, action, and events in their physical and social worlds. These experiences are the source *and* the content for concepts about objects, actions, and events (nonlinguistic knowledge). Because the vast majority of these experiences also involve language, children have myriad opportunities to experience co-occurrences of words and phrases and their particular referents. Once concepts and ideas about the world become linked to, and expressed (and understood), through, language, they are classified as linguistic knowledge—more specifically, semantic knowledge.

Children progress steadily and gradually toward adultlike meanings. Slobin (1971) put it this way, based on analysis of data from his cross-cultural study of language acquisition: "New forms first express old functions, and new functions are first expressed by old forms" (p. 184). In other words, *children first use new words and phrases to express well-established (familiar) meanings and they use familiar words to express newly constructed meanings.* They try out either a new form or a new meaning, but not both. An example illustrates this premise. Slobin quotes his 3-year-old daughter as saying "Anything is not to break—just glasses and plates" (1971, p. 186). She has arrived at a new and complex (for a 3-year-old) idea: That only glasses and plates are breakable. Because she lacked the words to express this idea properly, she did the best she could with the words in her repertoire (with amusing results).

> Children use new words and phrases to express familiar meanings.

When you think about meaning in language you probably think about word meaning. A second type of meaning that has been noted several times throughout this chapter is relational meaning. Relational meaning maps the relationships among objects, actions, and events. Relational meaning can be encoding with a single word, but it is often difficult for the listener to interpret the intended meaning when only a single word is used. Consider the word *more,* for example. If the child with an empty cup and an empty plate simply says "more" and does not point to or otherwise indicate a cup, or dish, or food item, the intent of the utterance might not be accurately decoded. If the word is combined with a gesture or a second word, then the intent is clear. When a child uses a single word like *more* to communicate a meaning that an adult would say with a sentence (e.g., "I'd like more juice"), the one-word utterance is said to be **holophrastic.**

Semantic relations are multi-word utterances that incorporate two types of meaning.

Recall from the earlier discussion that earliest relational meanings, called **semantic relations,** are combinations of two or more words to convey more and different meaning than any one of the words used alone could convey. Semantic relations incorporate two types of meaning: the meaning of the individual words *plus* the meaning implicit in the way the words are ordered. Encoding of semantic relations, which begins around 18 months, is evidence of two things: (1) that the child's awareness and understanding of different types of nonlinguistic relationships has expanded; and (2) that the child now has some understanding of how to express nonlinguistic knowledge through language. The problem is that the former exceeds the latter: The range and variety of ideas and relational concepts children have acquired by this age generally exceed their expressive abilities. Thus, they are frequently in the position of having to use the same word or words to express more than one meaning. Those who are trying to understand the child's intention are dependent to a great extent on contextual information (where the child is, what she and others are doing and saying) in order to interpret the utterance.

The key role of semantic relations in language development was first highlighted by Bloom's (1970, 1973) research in the early seventies. A famous example from her research is the utterance "Mommy sock," which appeared several times in transcripts of the speech of a child just beginning to produce two word utterances. This utterance tells us that the child understands that things have names ("Mommy" and "sock"), but this is not all that we can learn from this utterance about understanding of language. One child in Bloom's research said "Mommy sock" when her mother was helping her put her socks on, conveying understanding of the relationship between an agent (in this case *Mommy*) and an object (*sock*). On another occasion she said "Mommy sock" while holding up her mother's stocking. This time the utterance conveys understanding of the relationship between a possessor and a possession.

The "Mommy sock" example makes two points: (1) that utterances with the same surface structure can have different intended meanings; and (2) that we can learn much about children's nonlinguistic knowledge *and* their linguistic knowledge if we pay close attention to the context of utterances. The child in Bloom's research knows that mommies can affect (act upon) socks in ways that socks cannot affect mommies (agent–action relationships) and that mommies can own socks but that socks' cannot own mommies (possession). She also knows the proper word order (in English) to express these relationships.

At about the same time that Bloom posited the notion that meaning relations are the basis for children's first word combinations, two other prominent psycholinguists, Brown (1973) and Schlesinger (1971) made a similar discovery. Working independently, each compiled a list of the most prevalent semantic relations expressed by children at age 2 (MLU around 2.0). Amazingly, the three lists agreed upon most categories. A synthesis of the semantic relations lists is presented in Table 1.4.

Considering the many things that young children could talk about, it is significant that the meanings they express in their earliest word combinations are as easily defined as they are. Even more remarkable is the finding that these categories are universal: There are striking parallels among children learning language in such widely different cultures as Germany, Russia, Finland, and Samoa (Brown, 1973). Children all over the world apparently attend to and talk about basically the same things with their first word combinations.

> Children all over the world attend to and talk about the same things.

The meanings shown in Table 1.4 provide criteria against which to judge the language development of a child in the two-word combination state. Keep in mind, however, that it is not possible to determine whether the child is expressing a particular semantic relation and/or which one, without knowledge of the context of the utterance. Form alone does not provide sufficient information to determine intended meaning and assign the utterance to a particular category.

Conversational/Discourse Abilities

The basic ingredients of conversation—turn-taking and reciprocity—are present in the earliest interactions of infants and their caregivers. They are observable beginning around three months in caregiving routines such as feeding and diaper changing and games such as "peekaboo" (Adamson & Bakeman, 1991). In these exchanges, both the infant and the adult are active participants, and there are clearly rules for each turn and expectations for particular words and actions within the action sequences. However, child–adult exchanges continue to be heavily dependent upon adult scaffolding until well into the child's preschool years (Gleason, Hay, & Cain 1989). Adults provide exchange frames in which the child is to produce appropriate responses, and they select and phrase their questions carefully so that the child's response options are very clear (e.g., "the big one or the little one?"). While children as young as 2 years old are quite good at introducing new topics, they typically do not sustain a topic

> Two-year-olds typically do not extend a conversation beyond two turns.

TABLE 1.4   Stage 1—Semantic relations: Prevalent meanings expressed in early two-word combinations

Semantic Relation	Form	Possible Context	Example
Existence	relational word + object name (introducer + entity)	child calls attention to an object picture of an object by pointing	"this car" "it ball"
Negation (3 meanings: nonexistence, rejection, denial)	relational word + object name (negation + entity)	if indicating nonexistence, child may be searching for lost cookie; if rejection, child may be refusing an offer of a cookie; if denial, child may be responding to the question, "Is this your cookie?"	"no cookie"
Recurrence	relational word + object name (more + entity)	child indicates awareness of the reappearance of an object or the desire for an additional amount (a new instance) of something	"more juice" "more swing"
Attribution	adjective + noun (attribute + entity)	child calls attention to some characteristic of an object	"big ball" "pretty baby"
Possession	noun + noun, or pronoun + noun (possessor + possession)	child indicates (pointing to or holding up) someone's property	"mommy sock" "my coat"
Locative (2 types: action, entity)	verb + noun/pronoun, noun/pronoun + verb (action + locative), or noun + noun (entity + locative)	child indicates a movement occurring in a specific place, or child indicates an object as existing in a particular place	"sit beach" "sweater chair"
Agent–action	noun/pronoun + verb	child indicates the initiator of an action and the movement	"mommy go" "doggie run"
Action–object	verb + noun/pronoun	child indicates a movement or process with someone or something receiving it	"hit ball" "drink juice"
Agent–object	noun/pronoun + noun/pronoun	child indicates someone or something in direct interaction with another person or thing	"daddy ball" "mommy baby"

beyond one or two turns. Moreover, because they have not yet learned about linguistic contingency or contextual contingency, their responses may be unrelated to partner comments. Linguistic and contextual contingency develop slowly. Even at age 3½, only about 50 percent of children's utterances demonstrate contingency (Bloom, Rocissano, & Hood, 1976; Garvey, 1977).

Children as young as age 2 make distinctions in their speech on the basis of who they are addressing (Gordon & Ervin-Tripp, 1984). Awareness of social relationship variables such as power and familiarity is evident in their use of significantly more imperatives when addressing their mothers than when talking to their fathers. Additionally, they use polite request forms with visitors rather than the type of direct orders addressed to siblings. Other instrumental language strategies, such as gaining a listener's attention and providing explanations or justifications when making requests, are evident at about age 4.

Children learn discourse and conversational skills in the context of social relationships—first with caregivers and later, when they start school, with a broader social community. The following conversational and discourse skills are fairly well developed by school age:

- **Ability to sustain simple three-term *contingent queries*** where there is a comment, a request for clarification, and a clarifying response.
- **Ability to participate in conversations** by introducing a topic, sustaining it through several turns, and then closing or switching topics.
- **Speech adjustments** (e.g., elaboration) for listeners with different and/or less sophisticated language abilities.
- **Elimination of redundant information** in recognition of listener's knowledge about the topic with the understanding that information shared with a partner does not need to be repeated.
- **Ability to take the perspective of the listener** as evidenced by proper use of deictic terms (*here, there, this, that,* and personal pronouns).
- **Effective use of instrumental language** (to get a listener to cooperate with or carry out a goal) suggesting understanding of social relationship variables.

Range of Pragmatic Functions

By 12 months of age, most infants have learned to use their vocal and gestural abilities to intentionally engage their social environments. The infant's predisposition for social interaction (described earlier in the chapter) seems to be a powerful motivator for imitation of, interactions with, and eventually sharing their feelings, experiences, and thoughts with other human beings. Much of the infant's early language is directed toward maintaining contact with, and regulating the behavior of, others (Gleason, Hay, & Cain, 1989). These early social intentions have been described by a number of researchers (e.g., Bates, 1976; Halliday, 1975). Children gradually progress from reflexive, nonintentional communication to expression of intentions in a conventional manner. Development proceeds through three stages that Bates (1976) labeled the **perlocutionary stage,** the **illocutionary stage,** and the **locutionary stage.** Initially, in the perlocutionary stage, the infant's behaviors are undifferentiated and not intentionally communicative. Adults infer the meaning. Then, in the illocutionary stage, the child begins to use conventional gestures and vocalizations to intentionally affect the behavior of others. Finally, in the locutionary stage, the child uses words to convey intentions. Table 1.5 summarizes the development of language use skills from birth to age 3.

There have been a number of taxonomies listing the range of communicative intentions that develop prior to age 2 (e.g., Roth & Spekman, 1984). At the very least, early communicative intentions include the following:

- **Seeking attention.** Infants use gestures and speech (e.g., "look") to solicit and maintain attention.
- **Requesting.** Infants use gestures and vocalizations to get desired objects, to command the action of others, and to solicit information.
- **Protesting.** Infants use gestures and speech to command cessation of, and to resist, undesired actions and to reject offered objects or events.
- **Commenting.** Infants use gestures and speech to call attention to, describe, and label objects and events.
- **Greeting.** Infants use gestures (typically waving) and speech to participate in such rituals as greeting and taking leave.
- **Answering.** Infants respond to requests for information.

TABLE 1.5   Emergence of language use

Age Range	Characteristics
0–1 month	Regards faces momentarily Quiets in response to voice Eyes follow a moving person Cries in reaction to physiological distress
1–4 months	Smiles/coos in response to voice and smile Becomes "excited" when caregiver approaches Quiets upon seeing or hearing caregiver Shows anticipatory response upon seeing bottle Shows anticipation when about to be picked up Shows awareness of strange situations or strange person

TABLE 1.5   Emergence of language use (continued)

Age Range	Characteristics
4–8 months	Increases activity at the sight of a desired toy or caregiver Initiates mutual interactional dialogues with caregivers Cries and shows other indications of distress when caregiver leaves the room Smiles, head movements, and gestures in interactional dialogues with caregivers Turn-taking in play and other interactional dialogues Deliberate imitation of movements and vocalizations Vocalizes to accompany different attitudes (pleasure/displeasure, satisfaction/anger, eagerness) Responds differentially to interactional partners
8–12 months	Vocalizes deliberately to initiate interpersonal interactions Shouts to attract attention, listens, then shouts again Shakes head for "no" Gives affection to caregivers and other familiar adults Waves "bye-bye" Repeats a behavior if people laugh at it Expresses anger and distress if a toy is taken away Looks at caregiver's face when receiving an object (as if to acknowledge receipt)
12–18 months	Indicates wants by gesturing and vocalizing Hands mechanical toy to an adult to "request" reactivation Shows and offers objects to "request" social interactions Tries to turn the doorknob and looks at adult to "request" outside play Uses gestures, such as pointing, to direct adult attention Hands book to adult to "request" a story Pulls adult to certain locations to "request" attention to an object or event Gestures and vocalizes loudly to "request" desired objects and events
18–24 months	Gestures and vocalizes loudly to "request" proximity of caregiver or familiar adult Uses words to request desired objects and events Names objects spontaneously in the presence of others Vocalizes immediately following the utterances of another
2–3 years	Talks about objects and events that are not immediately present Initiates spontaneous vocal interactions Adds information to the prior utterances of communication partner Uses an increasing number of utterances that serve interpersonal functions (i.e., call attention to self or objects and events, regulating the behavior of others, obtaining desired objects and services, participating in social interaction rituals, commenting about objects and events)

Children gradually begin to use more pragmatic functions and a greater variety of forms for their functions.

As children grow older, they use more pragmatic functions and a greater variety of forms for all functions. They become more effective in using language (1) to attract and hold the attention of others, (2) to share and understand the emotions, goals, and intentions of others, (3) to mediate relationships, and (4) to acquire cultural values and expectations.

Throughout the infancy and early childhood period, caregivers and other adults treat children as effective communicators, and eventually they do become very skilled conversationalists. By kindergarten (and often before), they are ready for the rhymes, songs, and word games so important to engagement in social and instructional activities. Also, by school age they are ready for what Owens (1988), with tongue in cheek, calls "those special oaths and incantations passed along on the 'underground' from child to child" (p. 321).

SUMMARY

Although socialization alone does not fully account for language acquisition, there seems little question that children's early socialization experiences drive the language learning process. Children learn language by using it to communicate within a social context. Ultimately, our understanding of children's difficulties with language and communication and the impact these difficulties have on children's lives hinge on our understanding of the nature of language and communication and the early socialization process.

This chapter has reviewed the terms and concepts most essential for understanding the normal development research, which tells us how, why, and when children learn language. It has also discussed the variables that have the most profound influence on language learning and use. Finally, the chapter presents some discussion of children's major accomplishments in the areas of language and communication prior to beginning kindergarten.

REFERENCES

Adamson, L. B., Bakeman, R. (1991). The development of shared attention during infancy. In M. H. Bornstein & J. Bruner (Eds.), *Interaction in human development* (pp. 241–260). Hillsdale, NJ: Erlbraum.

Andersen, E. (1977). Learning to speak with style. Unpublished doctoral dissertation, Stanford University.

Bates, E. (1976). *Language and content.* New York: Academic Press.

Bates, E., Benigni, T., Bretherton, I., Camaioni, L., & Volterra, V. (1979). *The emergency of symbols: Cognition and communication in infancy.* New York: Academic Press.

Bates, E., Bretherton, I., & Snyder, L. (1988). *From first words to grammar: Individual differences and dissociable mechanisms.* New York: Cambridge University Press.

Bellugi, U. (1967). *The acquisition of negation.* Unpublished doctoral dissertation, Harvard University.

Benedict, H. (1979). Early lexical development: Comprehension and production. *Journal of Child Language, 6,* 183–200.

Bloom, L. (1970). *Language development: Form and function in emerging grammars.* Cambridge, MA: The MIT Press.

Bloom, L. (1973). *One word at a time: The use of single-word utterances before syntax.* The Hague: Mouton.

Bloom, L., Hood, L., & Lightbown, P. (1974). Imitation in language development: If, when and why. *Cognitive Psychology, 6,* 380–420.

Bloom, L., & Lahey, M. (1978). *Language development and language disorders.* New York: Wiley.

Bloom, L., Rocissano, L., & Hood, L. (1976). Adult-child discourse: Developmental interaction between information processing and linguistic interaction. *Cognitive Psychology, 8,* 521–552.

Brown, R. (1973). *A first language: The early stages.* Cambridge, MA: Harvard University Press.

Brown, R. (1975). *A first language: The early stages.* Cambridge, MA: Harvard University Press.

Bruner, J. S. (1975). The ontogenesis of speech arts. *Journal of Child Language, 2,* 1–9.

Chomsky, N. (1965). *Aspects of the theory of syntax.* Cambridge, MA: The MIT Press.

Desor, J., Maller, O., & Andrews, K. (1975). Ingestive responses of human newborns to salty, sour, and bitter stimuli. *Journal of Comparative and Physiological Psychology, 24,* 966–970.

Dore, J. (1975). Holophrases, speech arts, and language universals. *Journal of Child Language, 2,* 21–40.

Dore, J. (1986). The development of conversational competence. In R. Schiefelbusch (Ed.), *Language competence: Assessment and intervention* (pp. 3–59). San Diego: College Hill Press.

Dore, J., Franklin, M., Miller, R., & Ramer, A. (1976). Transitional phenomena in early language acquisition. *Journal of Child Language, 3,* 13–28.

Ervin-Tripp, S. (1970). Discourse agreement: How children answer questions. In J. Hayes (Ed.), *Cognition and the development of language.* New York: John Wiley & Sons.

Ferguson, C. (1979). Phonology as an individual access system: Some data from language acquisitions. In C. Fillmore, D. Kemper, & S. Y. Wang (Eds.), *Individual differences in language abilities and language behavior.* New York: Academic Press.

Fernald, A. (1989). Intonation and communicative intent in mothers' speech to infants: Is the melody the message? *Child Development, 60,* 1497–1510.

Gardiner, M., & Walter, D. (1976). Evidence of hemispheric specialization from infant EEG. In S. Harnad, R. Doty, L. Goldstein, J. Jaynes, & G. Krauthmer (Eds.), *Lateralization in the nervous system.* New York: Academic Press.

Garvey, C. (1977). *Play.* Cambridge, MA: Harvard University Press.

Gleason, J., Hay, D., & Cain, L. (1989). Social and affective determinants of language acquisition. In M. Rice & R. L. Schiefelbusch (Eds.), *The teachability of language* (pp. 171–186). Baltimore: Paul H. Brookes.

Gleitman, L. R., & Gleitman, H. (1992). A picture is worth a thousand words, but that's the problem: The role of syntax in vocabulary acquisition. *Current Directions in Psychological Science, 1,* 31–35.

Gopnik, A., & Meltzoff, A. (1984). Semantic and cognitive development in 15- to 21-month-old children. *Journal of Child Language, 11,* 495–513.

Gopnik, A., & Meltzoff, A. (1987). The development of categorization in the second year and its relation to other cognitive and linguistic developments. *Child Development, 57,* 1040–1053.

Gordon, D. P., & Ervin-Tripp, S. M. (1984). The structure of children's requests. In R. L. Schiefelbusch & J. Pickar (Eds.), *The acqui-*

sition of communicative competence. Baltimore: University Park Press.

Grieser, D., & Kuhl, P. (1989). The categorization of speech by infants: Support for speech-sound prototypes. *Developmental Psychology, 25,* 577–588.

Griffiths, P. (1986). Early vocabulary. In P. Fletcher & M. Garman (Eds.), *Language acquisition* (2nd ed.). New York: Cambridge University Press.

Halliday, M. A. K. (1975). Learning how to mean. In E. Lenneberg & E. Lenneberg (Eds.), *Foundations of language development* (vol. 1), (pp. 17–32). New York: Academic Press.

Higginbotham, D., & Yoder, D. (1982). Communication within natural conversational interaction: Implications for severely communicatively impaired persons. *Topics in Language Disorders, 2,* 1–19.

Hirschman, R., & Katkin, E. (1974). Psychophysiological functioning, arousal, attention, and learning during the first year of life. In H. Reese (Ed.), *Advances in child development and behavior.* New York: Academic Press.

Hunt, J. McV. (1965). Intrinsic motivation and its role in psychological development. In D. Levine (Ed.), *Nebraska symposium on motivation,* Lincoln: University of Nebraska Press.

Hymes, D. (1972). On communicative competence. In J. B. Pride & J. Holmes (Eds.), *Sociolinguistics.* Harmondsworth, England: Penguin.

Jusczyk, P. W. (1992). Developing phonological categories for the speech signal. In C. A. Ferguson, L. Menn, & C. Stoll-Gammon (Eds.). *Phonological development: Models, research, implications* (pp. 87–102). Parkton, MD: York Press.

Kagan, J. (1985, May). *Early novelty preferences and later intelligence.* Paper presented at the meeting of the Society for Research in Child Development, Toronto.

Kent, R. (1993). Speech intelligibility and communicative competence in children. In A. P. Kaiser & D. B. Gray (Eds.), *Enhancing*

children's communication (pp. 223–241). Baltimore: Paul H. Brookes.

Kinsbourne, M., & Hiscock, M. (1983). The normal and deviant development of functional lateralization of the brain. In M. M. Haith & J. J. Campos (Vol. Eds.; P. H. Mussen, General Ed.), *Handbook of child psychology: Vol 2. Infancy and developmental psychobiology* (4th ed.). New York: Wiley.

Klima, E. S., & Bellugi, U. (1966). Syntactic regularities in the speech of children. In J. Lyons & R. J. Wales (Eds.), *Psycholinguistic papers.* Edinburgh: Edinburgh University Press.

Kuhl, P. (1990). Auditory perception and the ontogeny and phylogeny of human speech. *Seminars in Speech and Language, 11,* 77–91.

Lahey, M. (1988). *Language disorders and language development.* New York: Macmillan.

Lenneberg, E. H. (1967). *Biological foundations of language.* New York: Wiley.

Leonard, L. B., Schwartz, R. G., Morris, B., & Chapman, K. (1981). Factors influencing early lexical acquisition: Lexical orientation and phonological composition. *Child Development, 5,* 882–887.

Messer, D. (1989). The episodic structure of maternal speech to young children. *Journal of Child Language, 7,* 29–40.

Michel, G. H. (1981). Right-handedness: A consequence of infant supine head-orientation preference. *Science, 212,* 685–687.

Mitchell, P. R., & Kent, R. D. (1990). Phonetic variation in multisyllable babbling. *Journal of Child Language, 17,* 247–265.

Miller, J. L., & Eimas, P. D. (1983). Studies on the categorization of speech by infants. *Cognition, 13,* 135–165.

Morehead, F., & Morehead, A. (1974). A Piagetian view of thought and language during the first two years. In R. L. Schiefelbusch & L. L. Loyd (Eds.), *Language perspectives— Acquisition, retardation and intervention.* Baltimore: University Park Press.

Mundy, R., Seibert, J., & Hogan, A. (1984). Relationship between sensorimotor and early communication abilities in developmentally delayed children. *Merrill-Palmer Quarterly, 30,* 33–48.

Nelson, K. (1973). Structure and strategy in learning to talk. *Monographs of the Society for Researching Child Development, 38,* 1–2.

Owens, R. E. (1988). *Language development: An introduction* (2nd ed.). Columbus, OH: Merrill.

Papousek, M., Papousek, H., & Haekel, M. (1989). Didactic adjustments in fathers' and mothers' speech to their three-month-old infants. *Journal of Psycholinguistic Research, 6,* 49–56.

Piaget, J. (1952). *The origins of intelligence in children* (Margaret Cook, Trans.). New York: International Universities Press.

Piaget, J. (1962). *The construction of reality in the child.* New York: W. W. Norton.

Pizzuto, E., & Caselli, M. C. (1991). *The acquisition of Italian morphology in a cross-linguistic perspective: Implications for models of language development.* Paper presented at the workshop on Cross-Linguistic and Cross-Populations Contributions to Theory in Language Acquisition, The Hebrew University, Jerusalem, Israel.

Prather, E., Hedrick, D., & Kern, C. (1975). Articulation development in children aged two to four years. *Journal of Speech and Hearing Disorders, 40,* 179–191.

Ramsay, D. S. (1984). Onset of duplicated syllable babbling and unimanual handeness in infancy: Evidence for developmental change in hemispheric specialization. *Developmental Psychology, 20,* 64–71.

Ratner, N. K., & Bruner, J. S. (1978). Games, social exchange and the acquisition of language. *Journal of Child Language, 5,* 391–401.

Rice, M. (1984). Cognitive aspects of communicative development, In R. L. Schiefelbusch & J. Pickar (Eds.), *Communicative competence: Acquisition and intervention* (pp. 141–190). Baltimore: University Park Press.

Rogoff, B. (1990). *Apprenticeship in thinking: Cognitive development in social context.* New York: Oxford University Press.

Rogoff, B., & Wertsch, J. V. (1984). *Children's learning in the "zone of proximal development."* San Francisco: Jossey-Bass.

Rose, S. (1981). Developmental changes in infants' retention of visual stimuli. *Child Development, 52,* 227–233.

Roth, R., & Spekman, N. (1984). Assessing the pragmatic abilities of children: Part 1. Organizational framework and assessment parameters. *Journal of Speech and Hearing Disorders, 49,* 2–11.

Sachs, J., & Devin, J. (1976). Young children's use of age-appropriate speech styles in social interaction and role-playing. *Journal of Child Language, 3,* 81–98.

Sameroff, A. J., & Fiese, B. H. (1988). The context of language development. In R. L. Schiefelbusch & L. L. Lloyd (Eds.), *Language perspectives* (pp. 3–20). Austin, TX: PRO-ED.

Schlesinger, I. (1971). Production of utterances and language acquisition. In D. Slobin (Ed.), *The ontogenesis of grammar.* New York: Academic Press.

Searle, J. (1969). *Speech acts.* London: Cambridge University Press.

Slobin, D. (1971). *Psycholinguistics.* Glenview, IL: Scott, Foresman.

Snow, C. E. (1984). Parent-child interaction and the development of communicative ability. In R. L. Schiefelbusch & J. Pickar (Eds.), *The acquisition of communicative competence* (pp. 69–108). Baltimore: University Park Press.

Snow, C. E. (1989). The use of imitation. In G. E. Speidel & K. E. Nelson (Eds.), *The many faces of imitation in language learning* (pp. 103–129). New York: Springer-Verlag.

Stern, D. (1984). *The interpersonal world of the infant: A view from psychoanalysis and developmental psychology.* New York: Basic Books.

Vygotsky, L. (1978). *Mind in society: The development of higher psychological processes.* Cambridge, MA: Harvard University Press.

Wang, M., Rose, S., & Maxwell, J. (1973). *The development of language and communication skills tasks.* Pittsburgh, PA: University of

Pittsburgh, Learning Research and Development Center.

Wells, G. (1985). *Language development in the preschool years*. New York: Cambridge University Press.

Wells, G., Barnes, S., Gutfreund, M., & Satterly, D. (1983). Characteristics of adult speech which predict children's language development. *Journal of Child Language, 10,* 65–84.

Werker, J. F., & Pegg, J. E. (1992). Infant speech perception and phonological acquisition. In Ferguson, C. A., Menn, L., & Stoel-Gammon, C. (Eds.), *Phonological development: Models, research, implication*. Parkton, MD: York Press.

Chapter 2

Language Theory and Practice

Diane Frome Loeb

For many years, researchers have described children's language abilities in multiple domains (i.e., pragmatics, syntax, semantics, morphology, and phonology). Such information has given rise to a greater understanding of the course of language development and the individual variation across children and languages. However, documenting the *course* of language development is but one step in understanding *how* language is learned. A complete theoretical account of language development that explains how children move from cooing and eye gaze interactions to complex syntax is necessary to guide optimal intervention.

Most individuals have some ideas about how language is learned or acquired. For example, some believe that children learn language in direct response to their caregivers' input. Others believe that

Our theoretical beliefs influence our approaches to intervention.

children may be born with certain capacities that mature over time, with input playing a minor role. One's own theoretical beliefs will influence many aspects of a language intervention program, such as: the definition of language impairment, the selection of children seen for language intervention, intervention techniques, creativity and flexibility, and quality control (Johnston, 1983; Brinton & Fujiki, 1989; Friel-Patti, 1994).

A **theory** is an orderly set of statements that explains and predicts behavior and is subject to scientific verification for continued existence (Berk, 1989). In contrast, a model is a working system based on theoretical assumptions. A theory of language development will need to be specific enough to lead to predictions and empirical tests, yet broad enough to encompass the variation seen in all the world's languages. It will detail the processes or mechanisms that drive language learning across the life span. Further, it should provide insight as to why some children are slow at learning language and why some children are precocious in their language skills. A theory of language development needs to inform us about the role of the input from caregivers as well as the role of the child in learning language, and it needs to specify the role of maturation. Last, it should consider those areas of development that are likely to influence learning—such as motivation and reinforcement—in a way that meaningfully ties teaching with learning (Kwiatkowski & Shriberg, 1993). Unfortunately, such a theory does not yet exist.

Current theories have been criticized as being too narrow, or too broad, or lacking in instructional function (Kamhi, 1993). Given these shortcomings, why should the language interventionist or other professional be informed about theory and utilize the theory of choice as the underlying foundation for intervention? Probably the best reason to base one's intervention on theory is that it sets a framework for proposing and testing hypotheses about a child's problem with language learning. It can be unique to the child's difficulties, yet broad enough to account for robustness of language learning in the general population. It allows for a systematic, rather than haphazard, way of approaching a problem. Alternatives to following theory are (1) "do what works" based on previous experience, and (2) an "eclectic" approach that borrows from many different theories. These alternatives are less desirable for one compelling reason—language learning is a robust phenomenon across nonimpaired populations and, as such, should have mechanisms and principles associated with it that are applicable across all children.

The purpose of this chapter is to show how current theories of language development inform both assessment and intervention. In order to understand some of the current thoughts and controversies, we need to revisit historical theoretical accounts. However, a majority of this chapter will be dedicated to theories that are currently impacting practices in early language intervention.

HISTORICAL TRENDS IN THEORY

The writings of Piaget (1954), Skinner (1957), and Chomsky (1957) gave rise to a rich history of events for language theory. Each theorist had his own perspective on how children learn language, especially in regard to the influence of the environment or the resources that the child brought to the task of learning. The extent that language and cognition were involved with one another and whether one system drove the other was topic for debate. A final difference was that the theories of Piaget and Skinner centered around ideas about learning in general; whereas Chomsky's theory was specific to language acquisition.

> Language interventionists need to explore reasons why a child is not learning language at the same rate as peers.

Piaget (1954) believed that a child's cognitive abilities guided the acquisition of language. Language was seen not as a separate ability, but as one of several cognitive achievements. Further, language was not considered innate; however, the cognitive ability to develop language was innate (i.e., given at birth). The interaction between cognition and environmental factors gave rise to language. The child was seen as an active learner in understanding the surrounding world. According to Piagetian theory, true language may occur only after the child can represent ideas symbolically. The child needs to attain sensorimotor development Stage 6 of object permanence (around 18 months of age) before symbolic representation may be achieved (see Table 1.1, p. 15). Thus, the child needs to be able to understand that objects exist when they are displaced or no longer present before she can produce true language. Symbolic play, or the ability to make one object represent another during play, should be demonstrated before words are used as symbols. Further, means-end behavior, which occurs around the second year of life, reflects a child's knowledge of ways to achieve goals. Because language is a tool that can be used to accomplish a goal, it is thought that means-end behavior is needed before a child can use language for different communicative intents and word combinations.

> Chomsky's theory deals specifically with language acquisition.

Skinner's (1957) operant learning theory, known as behaviorism, maintained that language learning occurred because of environmental influences. Verbal behavior was the gradual accumulation of vocal symbols and sequences of symbols learned through imitation, practice, and selective reinforcement. Skinner proposed that verbal behavior was similar to other types of learned behavior. Whereas other behaviors were subject to control by a variety of events, Skinner defined verbal behavior as "reinforced through the mediation of other persons" (p. 2). He argued that the distinctive characteristic of verbal behavior (as opposed to other behavior) is the nature of the consequences that come to control it. Skinner's operant theory emphasized the role of parents in modeling and reinforcing grammatical sentences. Language was learned through environmental contingencies and was not innate. The child's role was one of the passive participant.

Chomsky (1957) proposed a theory of grammar where the child is born with a language acquisition device that develops gradually over time. Referred to as the Standard Theory of Grammar, this theory provided elaborate explanations for how grammar was represented abstractly (as displayed by tree diagrams, phrase structure, and transformational rules). Chomsky's first version of his theory is well known for its claims that language is an infinite set of sentences that are rule-governed. That is, the number of sentences that we can produce is endless and we are able to generate sentences that we have never heard before. As speakers of a language, we have an innate knowledge of language, or a language competence, that allows us to recognize if sentences are ill-formed. This competence is revealed when we are able to determine if a sentence is grammatical or ungrammatical, regardless of whether it is a novel sentence. Chomsky characterized syntax as an autonomous system and rejected claims that language was a behavioral learning event or a by-product of cognitive achievement.

The language intervention programs used by language interventionists in the 1950s, 1960s, and 1970s reflected these latter theoretical orientations. Many programs emphasized the importance of the behavioral paradigm and relied on imitation, shaping, and drill-oriented procedures. Other programs focused on cognitive precursors and correlates. Still others focused on training sentence structures. Much of the early intervention was trainer-oriented (Fey, 1986) in that the clinician controlled what the child would learn, how he would learn it, and under which conditions mastery would be shown.

By the 1970s, interest in cognitive abilities and their relation with language dominated the field. Several researchers in the seventies supported the view that words are simply mapped onto sensorimotor concepts. This maxim of the cognitive view of language learning states simply that children talk when they have something to talk about, and they talk about what they understand. Language is an expression of developing conceptual knowledge. Cromer (1974) called this the **cognitive hypothesis;** Schlesinger (1977) referred to it as cognitive determinism. Further empirical data in the 1980s have to some extent supported the claim of a relationship between some cognitive and language skills. For instance, early symbolic play and

> Chomsky hypothesized that children are born with language competence.

first word usage have been found to be correlated. Likewise, higher means-end behavior and symbolic play are correlated with emerging word combinations. Finally, object permanence seems related to types of words used that refer to disappearance or absence of objects—"all gone," "find," and "more" (Gopnik & Meltzoff, 1987). One of the major problems with interpreting these studies is that a finding of a significant correlation indicates that the variables of interest are related in some fashion. It does not measure cause, or speculate that one is a precursor and one is not. One can only imply that these abilities are related or occur together in time. This is the homologous view of the language/cognition debate, where cognition and language are seen as parallel paths versus one path (or series of experiences) before the other (Brown, 1973; Bates, Benigni, Bretherton, Camaioni, & Volterra, 1977).

Bandura's theory of social learning was also proposed during this period of time. His theory emphasized the importance of social interaction to language learning (Bandura & Harris, 1966; Bandura, 1977). The child brought to the task of language learning the internal cognitive variables that interacted with the environment. The extent of learning was related to four interrelated variables: attention, retention, motor reproduction, and motivation. A process called **abstract modeling** was a key component to learning in this theory. In abstract modeling, the child observes various situations and the verbalizations that accompany the situations. Although imitation may be helpful, it is not required. The child extracts regularities from these situations and generates a rule-based system as a result of these observations. Intervention programs using Bandura's theoretical framework of modeling language targets have been successful in facilitating change in language abilities (Leonard, 1975).

Language intervention in the 1970s continued to utilize behavioral theory methods; however, theories that emphasized the child as an active learner of language also became increasingly popular. Researchers heightened our awareness of the important contributions of pragmatics and social interaction to the process of language learning, and these tenets were adopted to make language intervention more naturalistic and functionally oriented (Bates, 1976; Dore, 1979; Bruner, 1983). Language intervention programs frequently adopted Bloom and Lahey's (1978) psycholinguistic model of form, content, and use. Thus, emphasis was on semantic and pragmatic aspects of language, as well as syntax, phonology, and morphology.

During the 1980s, theory-building efforts escalated in multiple areas. Learnability issues, or models that explicitly describe how the child comes to learn language in a brief period of time, were proposed (Wexler & Culicover, 1980; Pinker, 1984, 1989). Linguistic theory was revitalized with the introduction of Chomsky's (1981) book

Bandura's social learning theory emphasizes the importance of social interaction to language learning.

Lectures on Government and Binding and Hyams's work in parameter theory (Hyams, 1986). Computer simulation of human language learning was detailed and implemented (Rumelhardt & McClelland, 1986; MacWhinney, 1987). Cognitive development through event learning influenced clinicians to use more scripted events in their interventions (Nelson, 1986). Theorists in the area of social interaction proposed new ideas that reshaped previous views (Nelson, 1987; Bates & MacWhinney, 1988). Behavioral theory continued to be used but in combination with more natural consequences, such as those seen in milieu teaching and enhanced milieu teaching (Warren & Kaiser, 1986; Kaiser, Yoder, & Keetz, 1992). Last, a past learning theory used in education and psychology that stresses the importance of social interaction, Vygotskian theory, has been applied by special educators and language interventionists. Thus far in the 1990s, cognitive science has offered a new version of how working memory and language are related (Gathercole & Baddeley, 1993).

Language intervention in the 1980s and 1990s has been dominated by social interaction approaches to language learning. Behavioral theory utilized within appropriate pragmatic contexts continues to be used within milieu teaching and enhanced milieu teaching (Hemmeter & Kaiser, 1994; Kaiser & Hester, 1994). In addition, there have been a few efforts toward incorporating linguistic theory with assessment and intervention (Connell, 1990; Loeb & Mikesic, 1992; Wilson, 1994; Rice, Wexler, & Cleave, 1995). The remainder of this chapter will focus on two theoretical orientations that continue to influence research and clinical practice: social interactionist theory and linguistic theory.

Current Trends in Theory

Social Interactionist Theoretical Approaches

According to the social interactionist theory, several factors are interrelated in the acquisition of language. These factors are social, linguistic, maturational, and cognitive in nature. All of these factors interact with and modify one another. This view further maintains that language is learned primarily through social interactions. Language is taught by parents and caregivers. It is taught through child-oriented talk such as motherese, recasts, and expansions. The child is an active participant in learning and to some extent guides the learning if caregivers are receptive to her cues.

A major criticism aimed at proponents of the social interactionist theory is that it is difficult to determine what features of interaction are necessary for language acquisition. There is evidence that some elements of motherese are related to language development (Cross, 1978). When children are between 18 and 24 months of age and their caregivers provide expansions of their children's utterances (i.e., repeat part or all of child utterance and add information to it), these children are more linguistically advanced and have greater sentence lengths compared to other children. However, it is unclear if this type of language facilitation is a necessary part of language learning. The lack of motherese in other languages raises the question of whether specially tailored interaction is required for language acquisition (Bernstein Ratner & Pye, 1984; Schieffelin, 1985). Another important criticism is that the theory lacks necessary and sufficient specificity in describing the internal process by which language is acquired.

> Social interactionist theory does not specify what particular features of interaction are necessary for language development.

Several theories and models of language learning hold the assumption that social interaction drives the process of language learning. Social interaction is not only important, but instrumental, to guiding the course of and causing the event of language learning. Four viewpoints that accept this assumption of the importance of social interaction will be discussed: the interactive model (Tannock & Girolametto, 1992); functional theory (Bates & MacWhinney, 1982), the rare event cognitive comparison theory (Nelson, 1987, 1989); and Vygotskian theory (Vygotsky, 1978).

Interactive Model

The interactive model is built on the premise that the child's active involvement in social interactions with peers and caregivers is crucial for language development. Not only does the child have to be an active participant in communication exchanges, but also these interactions need to be reciprocal in nature and frequently occurring. Interactions that occur as a result of the child's behavior or interests may be especially valuable to language learning. Importantly, in order to effectively facilitate language learning, caregivers need to have a style of interacting that is both a good match with their child's abilities and responsive to the child's interests. Thus, two key factors of this model are (1) child engagement (or involvement) in the activity, and (2) caregiver responsiveness to the child's interaction participation.

> Caregivers need to have a style of interacting that matches their child's abilities and is responsive to the child's interests.

There are three aspects of the interactive model that differ from other social interactionist models. First, the learning is wholly child-oriented. As such, no communication targets are selected for teaching. This means that the child is not required to produce certain target forms or functions. Second, there is no conscious use of operant procedures by the caregivers. For example, there is no shaping or differential reinforcement relied upon. Third, the caregiver is encouraged to use the techniques at all times of the day, not only at a specified period each day or in a specified setting.

APPLICATION TO LANGUAGE IMPAIRMENT. Tannock and Girolametto (1992) suggest that the ability of children with language impairment to assimilate and organize information may be a trouble source. As a result, social interactions with these children may require special adjustments. Tannock and Girolametto (1992) identified three intervention techniques based on the assumptions of the interactive model and evaluated parents' use of these techniques and the child's progress within a parent-child intervention program. These intervention techniques included child-oriented techniques, interaction-promoting techniques, and language-modeling techniques.

- Child-Oriented Techniques: The purpose of child-oriented techniques is to provide the child with opportunities for joint attention largely by responding to the child at his level and following his lead in play. The child guides the interaction. The caregiver needs to be sensitive and responsive to the child's cues and signals. Child-oriented techniques are believed to make the input to the child more salient. In order to be child-oriented, the caregiver needs to respond to what the child is interested in and participate in a way that puts him or her at the same level as the child (i.e., physical level, play level, and interest level).

> The goal of interaction-promoting techniques is to get the child actively involved in the interaction.

- Interaction-Promoting Techniques: The goal of interaction-promoting techniques is to get the child actively engaged in the interaction—not only as a responder, but also as an initiator. The inclusion of both responding and initiating leads to enhancing the child's ability to take turns within an interaction. The caregiver learns to take one turn at a time, uses waiting techniques to allow time for the child to respond, signals for turns, and decreases directiveness. By decreasing directives (i.e., telling someone what to do) the caregiver reduces the amount of responses, thus evening out the turn-taking events of initiating and responding.
- Language-Modeling Techniques: The purpose of language-modeling techniques is to help organize the linguistic input in such a way that facilitates the child's induction of form, content, and use. Caregivers are encouraged to talk about what the child is doing (description) and talk about what the caregiver is doing (self-talk) using short, simple sentences, expanding on the child's previous sentence, and repeating sentences in a meaningful context. The timing of the caregiver input is important, in that it should occur after the child's production or at the time of joint attention.

Tannock and Girolametto (1992) found that the parent-training language intervention program was effective in modifying the caregiver styles that led to more positive and responsive interactions with their children. Contrary to clinical and theoretical beliefs, there was little evidence that increasing parental responsiveness enhanced children's learning of *new* language skills. However, this type of program may be most effective in facilitating a child's *existing* language behaviors. On the other hand, in further studies, Girolemetto, Verbey, and Tannock (1994) learned that the previously described parent-implemented language intervention was successful in helping children acquire the beginning steps in joint engagement (i.e., joint attention and joint action).

Functional Theory

Functional theory seeks to explain the child's use of language (or functions) as well as the forms of a given language. The term "functionalism" was first used by Karmiloff-Smith (1979) and Bates and MacWhinney (1979). Bates and MacWhinney have expanded on the notion of functionalism as a theory of language learning drawing from the work of Givon (1979), Karmiloff-Smith (1979), and Slobin (1973). The strongest version of the functional theory says that grammatical forms are determined and maintained by communicative functions and processing constraints (Bates & MacWhinney, 1982, 1987, 1988). According to functional theory, the child does not start with an adult grammar that unfolds over time. Rather, the child's major task is to induce the relationship between form, content, and use. This results in putting together the form of a word with its meaning and use (i.e., form-function mappings). Form refers to surface word-order patterns and morphological markings; whereas function refers to underlying meanings or meaningful relations. Functionalists believe that grammatical surface forms arise from semantic and pragmatic functions. The child learns language through communicative interactions. In addition, a child's existing state of knowledge influences the course of development. It is not necessary that language be taught formally, because learning experiences occur in the natural contexts of interaction.

> According to functional theory, the child's major task in language learning is to induce the relationship among form, content, and use.

The competition model is a detailed model of the acquisition component of functional theory (MacWhinney, 1987). It employs a number of assumptions that are noteworthy. First, it adopts the idea of gradualism. Gradualism means that the child works through correct and incorrect hypotheses about language over time and does not begin with an adultlike grammar. Second, this model of language learning is lexically driven. That is, learning takes place at the level of the lexicon or word. It works from the bottom upward and is influenced by the "cues" in a child's given language. Cues are those events that provide evidence to the child about his native language. For example, word order is a strong and reliable cue in English, whereas in Italian it is less predictable. Cue extraction, or deriving the cues from one's native language, is an active undertaking for the child. Cues that are highly available (i.e., there when needed) and highly reliable (i.e., readily leading to a correct interpretation) will emerge from occasional exposure. If cues are not highly available or reliable, the child will work to increase his exposure to these cues.

As with functional theory, mapping occurs between the functional and the formal levels of language. However, this does not mean that there is a one-to-one relationship between form and function. Many functions can map with many forms. In the example "She is a great mom," "She" at the functional level is the agent or topic, at the formal level it is subject case marking and marked for verb agreement. Form and function mapping is accomplished through **cue validity**—how available and reliable a cue is in a language. For example, in English, the cue of preverbal positioning for the assignment of the noun phrase as the subject has high cue validity. It is almost always available and almost always reliable. Cue validity of verb agreement is low in English, because it is available only when there is competition between two nouns, and those nouns differ in number. Importantly, the major determinant of the order of acquisition and the strength of a cue is related to cue validity. Thus, the characteristics of a given language determine if certain structures are acquired early or late in that language.

The competition model is applicable to all languages, not just English. In fact, data from German-, Dutch-, and Hebrew-speaking children support the idea of cue validity as a viable explanation for some areas of language acquisition (Bates, MacWhinney, Caselli, Devescovi, Natale, & Venza, 1984; McDonald, 1986; Sokolov, 1988).

The competition model utilizes the neural network model used in the information processing accounts of learning. Thus, as lexical items are encountered in the input, the neuronal associations of these items are strengthened. There are constraints to learning, particularly when various semantic and pragmatic information is in competition. This competition is an occurrence of one event set against another. The "Principle of Competition" is that a given language will not allow a situation where two different forms express exactly the same meanings (e.g., "goed" versus "went"). This principle must be intact for a child to learn language. A competition is resolved by building up strengths of association in one lexical item versus another. As the activation of one item increases, its competitor decreases. Again, the strength of a cue is determined by the characteristics of the child's native language.

APPLICATION TO LANGUAGE IMPAIRMENT. MacWhinney (1989) suggests a number of problems that could occur in normal processing and learning that might result in impairment. These problems are related to "cue cost," that is, problems with processing information in the

> The characteristics of a given language determine when various structures are acquired in that language.

speech signal, with memory, with attention, with speed or accuracy of lexical access, with insufficient feedback, or with processing feedback. Mild problems in any of these areas would slow the rate of learning. Severe problems are hypothesized to result in major disruptions in language learning. According to functional theory, language is teachable if the teacher understands the principles of competition and the need to reinforce structures and functions. Competition will change depending on the input the child hears: The child who receives input for one competing form will decrease the activation for the other competing form. Another important aspect of the language-learning environment is that language learning should take place in meaningful contexts in order to enhance shared meaning and referential forms. Thus, frequent models should be presented in meaningful contexts. The child will learn language through positive instances. Recasts and expansions can be used to facilitate correct learning should the child produce an error. If a child makes more than one error that results in unclear sentence meaning, the language interventionist should request clarification (e.g., "What?") rather than provide recasts or expansions, to avoid teaching the child the wrong form-function mapping. Once the meaning is established, a recast or expansion can be provided. Finally, one can increase the child's attention to aspects of the sentence by increasing saliency. This increased saliency or heightening of certain aspects of the speech signal assists the understanding of form relationships.

Rare Event Cognitive Comparison Theory

Nelson (1987) proposes that children are active language learners who possess a powerful processing mechanism responsible for the development of language. The model of this theory claims that children have a rare event learning mechanism (hereafter RELM). This rare event mechanism is applicable to children at around Brown's Stage II or III of language development (MLU about 2:00 to 3:00). The mechanism gains strength as the child's language, cognitive skills, and age advance through the first four years of life. The learning mechanism is composed of the following components: selective attention, selective comparison, selective storage, retrieval, and hypothesis monitoring abilities. However, it is only on rare occasions that the child goes through the process of selectively attending and formulating new structural hypotheses about language. The rare event processing mechanism itself is driven by cognitive forces, rather than being a specific language learning device. Further, the child's interactions (self- and other-directed) and her ability to identify mismatches in the input will direct learning. The child needs to interact with proficient language users with whom there is an emotional, social, motivational, and communicative commitment.

The child develops "hot spots" or focal areas of attention that indicate where she is working at a particular point in development. They may arise because of some especially salient event or they may be a result of the child's current language system. Regardless, hot spots are areas undergoing intensive structural analysis. Selective attention, storage, retrieval, comparison, and hypothesis testing are dedicated to areas indicated as hot spots.

According to RELM, the young child concentrates on learning only a few structures at a time.

As an example, a child may learn modal auxiliaries (e.g., "will") by selectively attending to a small sampling of input during a conversational exchange. Imagine that the input sentence ("I will sing") is a mismatch with one already stored in the child's long-term memory (e.g., "I sing"). The child then compares the new input sentence to sentences that have been tagged in long-term memory. The child compares these sentences and comes up with a hypothesis about the structure that is being learned. The mismatches and the child's analysis combined make the "rare event." It is this latter type of abstraction (i.e., the process of noting a discrepancy, selectively retrieving and storing information, comparing and then hypothesizing new structures) that is crucial and driven by general cognitive abstraction processes. The child's hypothesis is then monitored with future input. The child keeps this newly learned language structure or rule if it is supported by the input. This type of cycle continues until the child has figured out her language system. Because hot spots differ from child to child, they nicely capture the range of individual differences observed in the process of language learning. In fact, different children receiving similar input can be working on different hot spots.

A recast is a repetition of a child's utterance that retains the child's meaning but uses a different linguistic structure.

The benefit that the child receives from interactions cannot be overstated. It is suggested that the child may benefit optimally from certain types of conversational exchange, particularly if the child is producing her highest level of complexity and the conversational partner is producing a simple recast at a slightly higher level of complexity. **Recasts** are types of utterances where the meaning of the child's utterance is maintained, but the new adult utterance has a different linguistic structure. For example:

> *Daughter: Mommy, sing "Edelweiss" to me.*
>
> *Mom: Will I sing "Edelweiss"? I will sing "Edelweiss."*

Research has found beneficial effects for the use of recasts in children with typical development. Specifically, Baker and Nelson (1984) found that, between 22 and 27 months, syntactic growth is greater in a group of children whose mothers used a high percentage of topic continuations and simple recasts (i.e., a change in only one sentence element, such as subject or verb).

APPLICATION TO LANGUAGE IMPAIRMENT.   Much of the application of the RELM has been to evaluate the effects of recasts on language change in children with typical development (Nelson, 1977; Baker & Nelson, 1984). RELM assumes that a child's eventual language ability will be a reflection of his interaction opportunities, differing levels of capability of the processing mechanism, and his motivation and emotional influence on the communicative exchange. Oftentimes, language assessment will involve collecting an audio- or videotape sample of caregiver–child or sibling–child interaction. According to the RELM, one cannot simply evaluate and tally the child and the partner utterances separately. Instead, the interaction between child and partner needs to be evaluated in context with an understanding of how one utterance is influencing another. Aligned with this view, Conti-Ramsden (1990) hypothesizes that differences seen in the interaction patterns between mothers and children with specific language impairment may be reduced by changing some of the discourse functions in which recasts are presented.

Another factor that may influence the course of language development is the child's past experiences or abilities in abstracting new language structures. Because the system strengthens and guides itself, the child who has been successful at language learning would continue to be successful; the child who has not been successful at this process will find future detriment. The importance of early intervention is implicated to help deter this course of development.

According to Nelson (1989), a child with a language impairment should benefit from recasts if his processing systems are similar to those of children developing language normally. Critically, the child's components of the rare event processing mechanism (i.e., selective attention, storage, retrieval, comparison, abstraction, and monitoring) need to be intact. An intervention assumption is that the frequency with which a child hears a language target would not be as important as the way in which it is presented. That is, it would be more beneficial for the child to hear particular structures in recasts versus a more structured, drill-type activity. However, once a child has hypothesized a new structure, frequent exposures to the structure may be helpful to confirm his hypothesis.

Regarding intervention targets, it may not be apparent what a child's current hot spot is. Thus, activities that follow the child's lead may be most effective. This leads to the question of "Can hot spots be created?" The experimental data from children with language impairment provide an affirmative answer to this question. Camarata and Nelson (1992) and Camarata, Nelson, and Camarata (1994) selected linguistic targets to use in recasts for four children with specific language impairment. They randomly assigned the children language

Children do not benefit from conversations unless they are active participants.

targets (areas of language to learn), taking into account their stage of language development. They found that the children learned the targeted structures with fewer presentations compared to a circumstance in which they were asked to imitate structures. However, they also found that the success of the recast intervention depended on the linguistic structure itself. That is, some structures were learned more readily than others. These studies provide evidence that the conversational-recast approach is an efficacious way to provide language intervention.

Finally, the child will not fully benefit from conversation if he is not an active participant. According to Nelson, when the child elicits information it may be an especially good indicator of the areas the child is working on. However, some children who are less willing to participate, or who are frequently off topic during conversation, may need specific assistance in becoming more involved with conversational partners prior to the onset of an intervention program designed to emphasize recasts of the child's utterance.

Vygotskian Theory

The concept of a zone of proximal development (introduced in Chapter 1) originated with Vygotsky.

Vygotskian Theory is based on the work of a Russian psychologist who sought to explain the process of learning within the context of social interaction. Vygotsky (1978) proposed that psychological functioning, including language, is learned through social interactions with a more capable member of society. The child is seen as an active participant in learning, assisted by an adult or more competent peer. There are two planes where development occurs: (1) the social plane (interpsychological category), and (2) the psychological plane (intrapsychological category). The social plane occurs between people and is termed "other-regulated." In contrast, the psychological plane occurs within oneself and is referred to as "self-regulated." The task of learning involves moving from "other-regulated" to "self-regulated" problem solving.

An important aspect of Vygotskian theory is the notion of the **zone of proximal development** (ZPD). The ZPD is the " . . . distance between the actual developmental level determined by independent problem solving and the level of potential development as determined through problem solving under adult guidance or in collaboration with a more capable peer." (Vygotsky, 1978, p. 86). There are four stages of the ZPD (Table 2.1). The child's developmental task is to move from "other-" to "self-regulated" behavior. In Stage 1, the child's performance is assisted by more capable others. van Kleeck and Richardson (1993) describe the process of learning in Stage I as involving "scaffolding" (Bruner, 1983), in which adults assist the child with cues in event scripts (i.e., familiar routines) (Nelson, 1986). The child's communication helps to determine the level of the cues given

TABLE 2.1   Four stages of the zone of proximal development

Stage 1   Capable other provides assistance to child using scaffolding within routines. During this stage, motivation to participate may be facilitated by the more capable other (i.e., entices the child to participate). For example, a parent provides models of vocabulary during routine such as dinnertime. The caregiver arranges environment and monitors the child's responses to the input.

Stage 2   Child assists self. Self-directed speech. For example, the child initiates own production of vocabulary words associated with dinnertime. Child internally monitors own language.

Stage 3   Child automatizes performance. No self- or other-regulation. For example, the child easily uses vocabulary associated with dinnertime without needing to monitor self or have assistance from others.

Stage 4   Child deautomatizes performance. This is when they may go back through earlier stages if needed. For example, the child attempts to use dinnertime vocabulary during pretend play and uses mother's phrasing or tone of voice to support his own context for the vocabulary. Deautomatization may also occur when outside stress factors or new conditions occur—for example, a child's milk is put in a different cup.

by the adult. In Stage II, performance is assisted by the child. Self-directed speech is an important occurrence at this stage, in which the child directs learning with speech directed toward oneself. Although assistance is not given at this stage, children have not fully learned the ability or task. Stage III is characterized by performance that has become automatic on the part of the child. At this stage, no "self" or "other" regulation is needed or occurs. If the child encounters assistance it is disruptive. At the final stage, Stage IV, performance becomes deautomatized and the child may once again go through earlier stages. The process is recursive, in that it can occur over and over again. The child may return to self-regulation, and perhaps other-regulation as needed. These stages of learning occur for adults as well as children in each new thing learned (Tharp & Gallimore, 1988). A good exercise to understanding these stages is to apply them to your own learning situations. Think back to the first time you had to prepare a lesson plan or transcribe a tape. At first, you needed the assistance of a more capable person; you progressed to being able to

Dynamic assessment determines where the child is functioning when supported by cues, models, and/or prompts.

do it by yourself without assistance; and finally, the procedure became automatic to you. However, when a new problem arose in planning or transcription that was not solvable through old, established methods, you may have had to seek the help of a more capable peer once again or do outside reading on your own.

APPLICATION TO LANGUAGE IMPAIRMENT. Within the last few years, Vygostkian theory has become increasingly prominent in its application to children with language impairment (Olswang & Bain; 1991; Olswang, Bain, & Johnson, 1992; van Kleeck & Richardson, 1993; Bain & Olswang, 1995). Prior to that, it was applied to individuals with mental retardation (Feuerstein, 1979) and in reading and learning disabilities (Braun, Rennie, & Gordon, 1987). Assumptions associated with this approach are that a child can learn from a more competent peer or adult, that learning takes place within a social context, and that a child moves gradually toward increasing ability depending on the zone of proximal development.

Integral to this theory's application to language impairment is the concept of "dynamic assessment." **Dynamic assessment** involves determining where a child is functioning with support from others such as cues, models, or prompts. A child's dynamic performance in a given task is compared to her static performance, which is her performance independent of assistance. The distance between these two, the static and the dynamic assessment, is the child's zone of proximal development for a given area (Olswang & Bain, 1991; Olswang, Bain, & Johnson, 1992).

Olswang and Bain argue that dynamic assessment may be used to determine whether a child may benefit from language intervention. They describe three possible child profiles where the ZPD differs. For the first child, there is no difference between the actual and potential performance—or no ZPD. For the second child, the difference is quite large, with the child responding greatly to assistance. The third child would be the one who makes some minimal gains with assistance. Olswang and Bain suggest that the third child would be the best candidate for language intervention. The first child may not be ready to learn and the second child may be in the process of accomplishing the task on her own. Data from two small groups of children, one learning single words (Olswang & Bain, 1991) and one learning two-term semantic relations (Olswang, Bain, & Johnson, 1992) support these predictions. In another study, Bain & Olswang (1995) found dynamic assessment to be a valuable tool for determining the readiness of children with specific expressive language impairment at the early word combination stage. They found that the children who were ready for immediate change responded to less cuing from adults (i.e., cues such as imitation, indirect models, and

sentence completion). In contrast, the children who were not as ready for change needed more supportive cuing.

Language interventionists could facilitate language within familiar events that involve social interaction appropriate to a child's ZPD until a given ability is learned. The early language interventionist must be aware when assistance is at too high or too low a level for a given skill and adjust assistance as needed. Otherwise, the child's progress may be hindered. Thus, one must be knowledgeable about the area targeted for intervention in order to track the child's developmental progress.

Finally, van Kleeck and Richardson (1993) suggest that, when a language interventionist uses the Vygotskian framework, errors that the child produces should be viewed differently than the traditional view of errors (i.e., something to be "corrected"). Errors are no longer seen as things that need fixing in the child's repertoire, but are part of the process of learning. These errors give clues as to where the child is functioning on the developmental path. As such, errors are responded to differently depending on the child's stage of ZPD.

Linguistic Theory

Since its inception in 1957, Chomsky's theory of language acquisition has undergone several major revisions. Earlier versions of linguistic theory were too powerful in that they could generate unrealistic patterns of language. The latest revision, presented in his book *Lectures in Government and Binding* (Chomsky, 1981), is referred to as the

Chomsky has proposed an innate universal grammar consisting of generic principles and specific parameters.

principles and parameters model. This model focuses more on how language is constrained so that it is learnable. It is constrained through the principles and learned through limited evidence from the environment.

Principles and Parameters Model

The principles and parameters model attempts to answer the question, "How does the mind represent language?" It proposes that all children at birth possess an innate **universal grammar** (UG). The UG is not only genetically determined, but also is separate from the conceptual system and pragmatic competence. That is, it is modular in nature. The UG consists of a set of principles that apply across languages as well as parameters that are "set" on the basis of language from the child's environment. The UG is the formal system of principles and well-formedness that constrain representation at each of four levels of representation: d-structure, s-structure, phonetic form (PF), and logical form (LF). D-structure, or deep structure, consists of two components: categorial and the lexicon. Categorial rules are sentence formulation rules that generate abstract syntactic structures. The lexicon assigns abstract syntactic and morphophonological details to each lexical item. The next level of representation is the s-structure, which is derived from the d-structure. The next two levels are phonetic form (PF) and logical form (LF). The PF is an abstract characterization of sound, including phonological rules. The LF is an abstract characterization of interpretation. Although meaning is generated at d- and s-structure levels, other rules are necessary to avoid ambiguity of interpretation.

Both principles and parameters influence language acquisition. Principles, in general, constrain or limit representation. Such constraints are needed because, without them, children (and adults) would utter incorrect sentences and could not learn language as quickly as they do on the basis of limited positive evidence. Although the principles are innate, they are believed to develop or mature over time. Principles are described within the subtheories of the principles and parameter model. These subtheories include bounding, government, case, binding, control, and θ (i.e., theta) theory. For an introduction to these subtheories, readers are referred to Leonard and Loeb (1988).

In contrast to principles, parameters are those components of grammar that can be changed or "set" to one of two values. The initial or "unmarked" setting is what every child is born with. However, if the child's native language is inconsistent with this setting of the parameter, the parameter can change to the "marked" setting. Typically, a parameter is reset once the child realizes certain "triggering" data. Triggering data is some specific input that the child is able to analyze from the language he hears in his native language that will cause a change in his grammar. Triggering data is parameter-specific.

That is, the type of linguistic input that will change a parameter setting will depend on the characteristics of the parameter itself.

A change in the setting of a parameter can result in changes throughout the entire grammar. After all the parameters of a language have been set, the child will be producing language comparable to competent adult speakers. Thus, the principles of UG are innate, yet some structural variation across languages is possible through parameter setting.

At this point, it is unclear how many or what parameters might exist. However, three parameters have been extensively written about and applied to language impairment. One parameter, the null subject parameter, accounts for the variations seen across languages with the optional use of subjects in sentences (Hyams, 1986, 1988, 1989). For example, some languages, such as Spanish, allow subjects to be omitted. In contrast, English does not allow optional subjects. English requires that the subject be present. English-speaking children have been noted to omit subjects in early language development. These subjectless sentences are observed in sentences such as "ride bike," "throw ball," and the like. Hyams has associated setting of the null subject parameter with the verb morphology of a language. For example, languages that have rich verb inflection systems are said to have "uniform" morphology. Languages, such as Chinese, that lack verb inflections are also "uniform" in morphology. Hyams proposed that English-speaking children start out with their null subject parameter set to the uniform morphology setting and need to reset it to a "nonuniform" setting to reflect the verb inflection system in English. English is a nonuniform morphology because we sometimes inflect verbs to change meaning and sometimes do not (i.e., "talk, talks, talking, can talk"). In order to trigger the null subject parameter to a nonuniform setting, the children will need to receive input data that help them to know that English sometimes inflects verbs and sometimes does not.

Wexler (1994a) has proposed two other parameters that are responsible for setting the word order of a language: the specifier-head parameter and the complement-head parameter. In English, specifiers or subjects occur before the head, whereas complements occur after the head of a phrase. For instance, in the phrase "Stan watched the football game," "watched" is the head of the verb phrase, it is preceded by "Stan," the specifier, and "football game" is the object or complement. Children learning English will need to set these parameters to specifier first and complement final in order to use and understand English word order. Lightfoot (1991) states that information associated with verbs may set or trigger the resetting of the complement-head parameter. Wilson and Fox (1994) suggest that sentences contrasting subjects of sentences, direct objects of sentences, and reversible sentences may reset these parameters.

Several criticisms have been aimed at the linguistic approach to language learning. Issues of debate rest largely on the extent to which the child is an active participant, how much of the grammar is innate, and the role of the environment. For instance, other theories do not accept the idea that a child is endowed with innate grammatical categories. Further, the emphasis on grammar and the lack of attention to areas related to the influence of pragmatic variables on language acquisition often have been criticized. Finally, the modular process of grammar is unacceptable for those who firmly believe in the guiding forces of cognitive processes to language learning.

APPLICATION TO LANGUAGE IMPAIRMENT.   The principles and parameters model is applicable to language impairment in many regards. One avenue that has been explored involves looking for differences in the underlying structural representations between children with normal language and those with language impairment. Preliminary results indicate that the morphological and syntactic problems exhibited by children with specific language impairment (SLI) may be related to relationships in the underlying grammar that differ when one compares children with typical language development (Hadley, 1993; Rice & Oetting, 1993; Rice, Wexler, & Cleave, 1995). Rice and others posit and provide data that support the idea that children with SLI are like their typical peers, with the exception that they extend the amount of time that they do not mark verbs for finiteness. In English, verbs appear in either finite or nonfinite contexts. Finite forms are marked for tense and agreement and appear in main clauses. Finiteness also can be marked by "be" and "do" forms. For example, a child who says "I walked to the store" is marking finiteness with the "ed" on the verb "walk." However, in the sentence "I wanted to go there," the verb "wanted" is marked for finiteness, but the verb "go" is a nonfinite context. Wexler (1994b) claims that English-speaking children with typical language development go through a period of time where they treat verbs as nonfinite and optionally mark finiteness. Rice and her colleagues have found this period of optionally marking finiteness to be extended in children with SLI. They refer to this phenomenon as the period of the extended optional infinitive. Importantly, this finding suggests that many morphological and syntactic problems are related to one underlying problem—not marking verbs for finiteness.

Application of the principles and parameters model to language impairment also results in a different way of thinking about the language learning problem. Connell (1990) suggests that the label of language disorder would not be a "delay" or a "simpler" language if a principles and parameters perspective were to be adopted by language interventionists. Instead, children with language impairment would be viewed as having the "wrong" or an "intermediate" grammar

Proponents of linguistic theory hypothesize that children with language impairment may have difficulty with levels of representation.

that is not the same as the adult language. This reconceptualization of the language learning problem would also have ramifications for intervention. The goal of language intervention would be to stimulate the child to choose the "right" or "input" language. In an inclusive service delivery, the "right" or "input" language could be presented through specific language models provided by the teacher or language interventionist to reset a given parameter. Specific types of language models might serve as "triggers" to switch a parameter. These language models with specific grammatical contrasts could be presented during play time, reading in large group, or during individualized language art instruction.

For many children with language impairment, there is a marked difficulty in learning morphology and syntax. Wilson and Fox (1994) suggest ". . . that treatment for problems with the grammar module should be directed specifically to this area and not addressed indirectly through pragmatics" (p. 1). Utilizing areas of intervention that focus on parameters is especially appealing because changes within one aspect of a parameter may alter other parts of a child's grammar. Thus, if a child with language impairment were experiencing difficulty due to some delay or impairment of the parameter process, then subsequent facilitation of a given parameter may result in widespread changes in the grammar. Under this framework, a child cannot be taught a missing structure that she is not ready to learn if the parameter has not been reset to the right setting. Instead, the clinician would direct the learner's attention to "trigger" information that would reset a parameter, thereby making possible a change in the grammar. To do so, precise input information would be needed in order for the child to reset the parameter. Also, the clinician would need to highlight and emphasize those aspects of the input that contain trigger material and de-emphasize those that do not. Following parameter setting, the language interventionist should provide information that gives the child many examples of the form and meaning to be learned.

It is not yet apparent whether children with language impairment have difficulties with parameter setting. Loeb and Leonard (1988) found that children with SLI did not display a "delay" in resetting the null subject parameter. The profiles of these children were not consistent with a child's grammar at an unmarked setting. However, Connell's (1990) training study with children with language impairment that was aimed at resetting the null subject parameter led to a number of the predicted positive changes in these children's language. His triggering data included making the subject of the sentence more salient. This was accomplished through left-dislocated topics. For example, in pointing to a picture that had two boys, one who was petting a deer, the clinician would point to the boy doing the petting and

> The role that theory plays in intervention design and implementation depends on the language interventionist's background.

say, "Him, he is petting the fawn." Connell suggests that the increased saliency of the subject resulted in the children's increased correct use of pronoun case marking, copula, auxiliary, third-person singular -s, and question inversion.

Another attempt to trigger changes in the null subject parameter contrasted verb inflections in the language models provided to children with language impairment (Loeb & Mikesic, 1992). The child who received the input that contrasted verbs with bare stems (walk) with verbs without bare stems (walking) made the most progress in pronoun subject case marking and verb morphology related to the null subject parameter.

Wilson (1994) and Wilson and Fox (1994) propose yet another intervention program aimed at resetting a parameter. Their approach provides contrasts as triggers for the child's complement-head parameter and the specifier-head parameter. For instance, the child needs to hear sentences contrasting objects to make the complement final position in English salient ("The girl ate the cookie" versus "The girl ate the cake"). Presentations of contrasting subjects focus the child's attention to the subject-verb order of English needed for the specifier-head parameter ("The boy chased the cat" versus "The girl chased the cat"). Finally, reversible sentences are suggested to be helpful for both parameters ("The girl kissed the boy" versus "The boy kissed the girl"). Importantly, they suggest that such an intervention program should occur before the child begins to combine words. Unlike current procedures that often wait until the child is much older, this approach gives focus on grammar early in development. Further examination of this parameter and other parameters in children with language impairment should shed some light on the nature of the child's problem as well as chart the course for intervention.

SUMMARY

All of the theories and models discussed in this chapter are continually undergoing change as new ideas and new data influence their direction. As the reader may have surmised, there are many areas of similarities as well as important differences among the theories presented (Table 2.2). While areas of difference are often the focus of heated debate, the common aim of researchers and theoreticians is an explanation of language development. The influence of these theories on how we understand the underlying difficulties and how we work with children exhibiting language problems cannot be overstated. Without such theories, we have to resort to treating symptoms without the knowledge of the underlying condition.

TABLE 2.2 Comparison and summary of theoretical assumptions

Question	Interactive Model	Functional Theory	Rare Event Cognitive Comparison Theory	Vygotskian Theory	Principles and Parameters Model
How is language learned?	Through social interactions with caregiver	Through child hypothesis testing via interactions with language environment	Through the interactions of cognitive abilities and social communication	Through social contexts with a more capable peer	Through innate universal principles and by setting parameters to be consistent with one's environment
What is the mechanism by which language is acquired?	Not specified, however, repeated exposures to joint attention episodes in daily routines are important	Cue validity: cue reliability and cue availability	A rare event that occurs once the child selectively attends, stores, compares, retrieves, and hypothesizes about input	The social plane and the psychological plane ZPD	Universal Grammar, which is an autonomous system of principles and parameters
Why do errors in typical development occur?	Child has difficulty organizing and assimilating information from context	Cue costs, Competition	Problems with attending, storage, comparing, retrieving, or hypothesis testing	It is part of the process of learning	Problems with the principles that constrain representation, setting a parameter, mapping from one level of representation to another, or an extended period of optional infinitive
What is the theory's application to language impairment?	Increased child engagement and caregiver responsiveness to improve child's ability to assimilate and organize contextual information	Meaningful context for intervention, frequent models using recasts and expansions: all designed to increase saliency of cues	Provides models in contingent, recasts; emphasizes need for early intervention, importance of evaluating language production within context	Dynamic assessment using ZPD tells of child's readiness for learning	Reset parameters: trigger data important to consider

Based in part on Houston (1972).

In a direct service delivery model, language interventionists apply the assumptions associated with their theory of language acquisition (i.e., behavioralism, linguistic theory, social interactive model, etc.) to the children with whom they work. When the language interventionist works with a parent, a child care provider, or a teacher as a consultant or team member, theory continues to be important. The team approach requires that those working together share a common theory (Coufal, 1993). The language interventionist and team members will need to discuss how they think language is learned and examine their assessment and intervention approaches for evidence of shared assumptions. When a shared theory is not achieved, it is likely that the intervention will vary depending on who provides the services. For instance, a teacher who strongly believes in behavioralism teamed with a language interventionist who is oriented toward social interactionalism will approach intervention differently. The teacher will emphasize the need for the child to respond, particularly through imitation; whereas the language interventionist will be satisfied with frequent models of the appropriate target without a required overt response from the child. Spontaneous use of the target by the child will suffice. Although it is not always possible for all team members to come to the same consensus of their theory of language learning, it is important that the team be able to discuss their differences and understand the impact of those differences on the course of assessment and intervention. Importantly, the exact role that theory will play when working with children with language impairment will vary depending on the interventionist's knowledge of the theory, the theory's breadth of application, and the extent to which we understand what has gone differently in the course of development in the child with language impairment.

References

Bain, B. A., & Olswang, L. B. (1995). Examining readiness for learning two-word utterances by children with specific expressive language impairment: Dynamic assessment validation. *American Journal of Speech-Language Pathology: A Journal of Clinical Practice, 4,* 81–91.

Baker, N., & Nelson, K. (1984). Recasting and related conversational techniques for triggering syntactic advances by young children. *First Language, 5,* 3–22.

Bandura, A. (1977). *Social learning theory.* Englewood Cliffs, NJ: Prentice Hall.

Bandura, A., & Harris, M. (1966). Modifications of syntactic style. *Journal of Exceptional Child Psychology, 4,* 341–352.

Bates, E. (1976). *Language and context: Studies in the acquisition of pragmatics.* New York: Academic Press.

Bates, E., Benigni, L., Bretherton, I., Camaioni, L., & Volterra, V. (1977). From gesture to first word: On cognitive and social prerequisites. In M. Lewis and L. Rosenblum (Eds.), *Interaction, conversation, and prerequisites*. New York: John Wiley and Sons.

Bates, E., & MacWhinney, B. (1979). A functionalist approach to the acquisition of grammar. In E. Ochs and B. Schieffelin (Eds.), *Developmental pragmatics*. New York: Academic Press.

Bates, E., & MacWhinney, B. (1982). A functionalist approach to grammar. In E. Wanner and L. Gleitman (Eds.), *Language acquisition: The state of the art*. New York: Cambridge University Press.

Bates, E., & MacWhinney, B. (1987). Competition, variation, and language learning. In B. MacWhinney (Ed.), *Mechanisms of language acquisition*. Hillsdale, NJ: Lawrence Erlbaum Associates.

Bates, E., & MacWhinney, B. (1988). What is functionalism? *Papers and Reports on Child Language Development, 27,* 137–152.

Bates, E., MacWhinney, B., Caselli, C., Devescovi, A., Natale, F., & Venza, V. (1984). A cross-linguistic study of the development of sentence interpretation strategies. *Child Development, 55,* 341–354.

Berk, L. (1989). *Child development*. Boston: Allyn & Bacon.

Bernstein Ratner, N., & Pye, C. (1984). Higher pitch in BT is not universal: Acoustic evidence from Quiche Mayan. *Journal of Child Language, 11,* 515–522.

Bloom, L., & Lahey, M. (1978). *Language development and language disorders*. New York: John Wiley and Sons.

Braun, C., Rennie, B., & Gordon, C. (1987). An examination of contexts for reading assessment. *Journal of Educational Research, 80,* 283–289.

Brinton, B., & Fujiki, M. (1989). *Conversational management with language-impaired children*. Rockville, MD: Aspen.

Brown, R. (1973). *A first language: The early stages*. Cambridge: Harvard University Press.

Bruner, J. (1983). *Child's talk*. New York: W. W. Norton.

Camarata, S., & Nelson, K. (1992). Treatment efficiency as a function of target selection in the remediation of child language disorders. *Clinical Linguistics & Phonetics, 6,* 167–178.

Camarata, S., Nelson, K., & Camarata, M. (1994). Comparison of conversational-recasting and imitative procedures for training grammatical structures in children with specific language impairment. *Journal of Speech and Hearing Research, 37,* 1414–1423.

Chomsky, N. (1957). *Syntactic structures*. The Hague: Mouton.

Chomsky, N. (1981). *Lectures on government and binding*. Providence, RI: Foris.

Connell, P. (1990). Linguistic foundations of clinical language teaching: Grammar. *Journal of Speech-Language Pathology and Audiology, 14,* 25–49.

Conti-Ramsden, G. (1990). Maternal recasts and other contingent replies to language-impaired children. *Journal of Speech and Hearing Disorders, 55,* 262–274.

Coufal, K. (1993). Collaborative consultation for speech-language pathologists. *Topics in Language Disorders, 14,* 1–14.

Cromer, R. (1974). The development of language and cognition: The cognitive hypothesis. In B. Foss (Ed.), *New perspectives in child development* (pp. 19–47). New York: Penguin.

Cross, G. (1978). Mothers' speech and its association with rate of linguistic development in young children. In N. Waterson & C. Snow (Eds.), *The development of communication*. New York: Wiley.

Dore, J. (1979). What's so conceptual about the acquisition of linguistic structures? *Journal of Child Language, 6,* 129–138.

Feuerstein, R. (1979). *The dynamic assessment of retarded performers*. Baltimore: University Park Press.

Fey, M. E. (1986). *Language intervention with young children*. Boston: College-Hill Press.

Friel-Patti, S. (1994). Commitment to theory. *American Journal of Speech-Language Pathology: A Journal of Clinical Practice, 3,* 30–34.

Gathercole, S. E., & Baddeley, A. D. (1993). *Working memory and language*. Hillsdale, NJ: Lawrence Erlbaum Associates.

Girolametto, L., Verbery, M., & Tannock, R. (1994). Improving joint engagement in parent-child interaction: An intervention study. *Journal of Early Intervention, 18,* 155–167.

Givon, T. (1979). *On understanding grammar.* New York: Academic Press.

Gopnik, A., & Meltzoff, A. (1987). Early semantic developments and their relationship to object permanence, means-ends understanding, and categorization. In K. Nelson & A. van Kleeck (Eds.), *Children's language* (Vol. 6) (pp. 191–212). Hillsdale, NJ: Lawrence Erlbaum Associates.

Hadley, P. (1993). A longitudinal investigation of the auxiliary system in children with specific language impairment. Unpublished doctoral dissertation, University of Kansas.

Hemmeter, M., & Kaiser, A. (1994). Enhanced milieu teaching: Effects of parent-implemented language intervention. *Journal of Early Intervention, 18,* 269–289.

Houston, S. (1972). *A survey of psycholinguistics.* The Hague: Mouton.

Hyams, N. (1986). *Language acquisition and the theory of parameters.* Norwell, MA: D. Reidel (Kluwer).

Hyams, N. (1987). The setting of the null subject parameter: A reanalysis. Paper presented at the Boston University Conference on language development.

Hyams, N. (1988). A principles-and-parameters approach to the study of child language. *Papers and Reports on Child Language Development, 27,* 153–161.

Hyams, N. (1989). The null subject parameter in language acquisition. In O. Jaeggli & K. Safir (Eds.), *The null subject parameter* (pp. 215–238). Norwell, MA: Kluwer Academic Publishers.

Johnston, J. (1983). What is language intervention? The role of theory. In J. Miller, D. Yoder, & R. Schiefelbusch (Eds.), *Contemporary issues in language intervention.* Rockville, MD: American Speech-Language-Hearing Association.

Kaiser, A., & Hester, P. (1994). Generalized effects of enhanced milieu teaching. *Journal of Speech and Hearing Research, 37,* 1320–1340.

Kaiser, A., Yoder, P., & Keetz, A. (1992). Evaluating milieu teaching. In S. Warren & J. Reichle (Eds.), *Causes and effects in communication and language intervention* (pp. 9–48). Baltimore: Paul H. Brookes Publishing.

Kamhi, A. (1993). Some problems with the marriage between theory and clinical practice. *Language, Speech, and Hearing Services in Schools, 24,* 57–60.

Karmiloff-Smith, A. (1979). *A functional approach to child language: A study of determiners and reference.* New York: Cambridge University Press.

Kwiatkowski, J., & Shriberg, L. (1993). Speech normalization in developmental phonological disorders: A retrospective study of capability-focus theory. *Language, Speech, and Hearing Services in Schools, 24,* 10–18.

Leonard, L. (1975). Modeling as a clinical procedure in language training. *Language, Speech, and Hearing Services in Schools, 6,* 72–85.

Leonard, L., & Loeb, D. (1988). Government-binding theory and some of its applications: A tutorial. *Journal of Speech and Hearing Research, 31,* 515–524.

Lightfoot, D. (1991). How to set parameters: Arguments from language change. Cambridge, MA: MIT Press.

Loeb, D., & Leonard, L. (1988). Specific language impairment and parameter theory. *Clinical Linguistics and Phonetics, 2,* 317–327.

Loeb, D., & Mikesic, E. (1992). Facilitating change in specifically language-impaired children's grammar. Poster presented at the American Speech, Language, and Hearing Convention, San Antonio.

MacWhinney, B. (1987). The competition model. In B. MacWhinney (Ed.), *Mechanisms of language acquisition.* Hillsdale, NJ: Lawrence Erlbaum Associates.

MacWhinney, B. (1989). Competition and teachability. In M. Rice & R. Schiefelbusch (Eds.), *The teachability of language.* Baltimore: Paul H. Brookes Publishing.

McDonald, J. (1986). The development of sentence comprehension strategies in English and Dutch. *Journal of Experimental Child Psychology, 41,* 317–335.

Nelson, K. (1977). Facilitating children's syntax acquisition. *Developmental Psychology, 13,* 101–107.

Nelson, K. (1986). *Event knowledge: Structure and function in development.* Hillsdale, NJ: Lawrence Erlbaum Associates.

Nelson, K. (1987). Some observations from the perspective of the rare event cognitive comparison theory of language acquisition. In K. Nelson & A. van Kleeck (Eds.), *Children's language* (Vol. 6) (pp. 289–332). Hillsdale, NJ: Lawrence Erlbaum Associates.

Nelson, K. (1989). Strategies for first language teaching. In M. Rice & R. Schiefelbusch (Eds.), *The teachability of language.* Baltimore: Paul H. Brookes Publishing.

Olswang, L., & Bain, B. (1991). When to recommend intervention. *Language, Speech, and Hearing Services in Schools, 22,* 255–263.

Olswang, L., Bain, B., & Johnson, G. (1992). Using dynamic assessment with children with language disorders. In S. Warren & J. Reichle (Eds.), *Causes and effects in communication and language intervention.* Baltimore: Paul H. Brookes Publishing.

Owens, R. E. (195). *Language Disorders* (2nd ed.). Boston: Allyn & Bacon.

Piaget, J. (1954). *The construction of reality in the child.* New York: Basic Books.

Pinker, S. (1984). *Language learnability and language development.* Cambridge, MA: Harvard University Press.

Pinker, S. (1989). *Learnability and cognition.* Cambridge, MA: MIT Press.

Rice, M., & Oetting, J. (1993). Morphological deficits of children with SLI: Evaluation of number marking and agreement. *Journal of Speech and Hearing Research, 36,* 1249–1257.

Rice, M., Wexler, K., & Cleave, P. (1995). Specific language impairment as a period of extended optional infinitive. *Journal of Speech and Hearing Research, 38,* 850–863.

Rumelhardt, D., & McClelland, J. (1986). On learning the past tense of English verbs. In J. McClelland, D. Rumelhart, & the PDP Research Group (Eds.), *Parallel distributed processing* (Vol. 2) (pp. 216–271). Cambridge, MA: MIT Press.

Schieffelin, B. (1985). The acquisition of Kaluli. In D. Slobin (Ed.), *The crosslinguistic study of language, Volume 1: The data.* Hillsdale, NJ: Lawrence Erlbaum Associates.

Schlesinger, I. (1977). Production of utterances and language acquisition. In D. Slobin (Ed.), *The ontogenesis of grammar.* New York: Academic Press.

Skinner, B. F. (1957). *Verbal behavior.* New York: Apppleton-Century-Crofts.

Slobin, D. I. (1973). Cognitive prerequisites for the development of grammar. In C. Ferguson & D. Slobin (Eds.), *Studies of child language development.* New York: Holt, Rinehart, and Winston.

Sokolov, J. (1988). Cue validity in Hebrew sentence construction. *Journal of Child Language, 15,* 129–155.

Tannock, R., & Girolametto, L. (1992). Reassessing parent-focused language intervention programs. In S. Warren & J. Reichle (Eds.), *Causes and effects in communication and language intervention* (pp. 49–80). Baltimore: Paul H. Brookes Publishing.

Tharp, R., & Gallimore, R. (1988). *Rousing minds to life: Teaching, learning, and schooling in social context.* New York: Cambridge University Press.

van Kleeck, A., & Richardson, A. (1993). What's in an error? Using children's wrong responses as language teaching opportunities. *National Student Speech-Language-Hearing Association, 20,* 9–21.

Vygotsky, L. (1978). Mind in society: The development of higher psychological processes. In M. Cole, J. Scribner, J. John-Steiner, & E. Souberman (Eds.), *Culture and thought: A psychological introduction.* Cambridge, MA: Harvard University Press.

Warren, S., & Kaiser, A. (1986). Incidental language teaching: A critical review. *Journal of Speech and Hearing Disorders, 51,* 291–299.

Wexler, K. (1994a). Triggers and parameter setting. Paper presented at the Linguistic, Cognitive Science, & Childhood Language Disorders Conference, City University of New York, April.

Wexler, K. (1994b). Optional infinitives. In D. Lightfoot & N. Hornstein (Eds.), *Verb movement*. New York: Cambridge University Press.

Wexler, K., & Culicover, P. (1980). *Formal principles of language acquisition*. Cambridge, MA: MIT Press.

Wilson, M. S. (1994). Early language intervention: Implications of the principles and parameters model. Presentation at the American Speech-Language-Hearing Association Annual Convention. New Orleans.

Wilson, M. S., & Fox, B. J. (1994). *Simple sentence structure*. Winooski, VT: Laureate Learning Systems.

CHAPTER 3

Characteristics of Students with Language and Communication Difficulties

Linda McCormick and Diane Frome Loeb

Every society has established standards to which the vast majority of people in that society conform. They look the way they are expected to look, behave the way they are expected to behave, learn the way they are expected to learn, and communicate the way they are expected to communicate. When, because of biological or environmental factors, *or both,* people deviate substantially from society's physical, social, and intellectual expectations, they are labeled in a way that is presumed to reflect the problem produced by the deviation from "normal" expectations (e.g., physically disabled, emotionally disturbed, learning disabled, sensory impaired). Efforts are then expended in trying to determine the cause of the problem, the assumption being that this will lead to intervention that will eliminate, or at least lessen, the deviation.

Attempts to determine etiology are generally not very productive because causality is multifaceted and extremely complex. Moreover, even when it *is* possible to establish causality with any certainty, there is not always a cause-and-effect relationship between the nature of the deviation and its effect on development and behavior. Thus, there is no guarantee that knowing the cause of a disability will result in useful information for intervention. Knowing the cause of a child's difficulties (in language and communication or any other area) simply does not translate to a prescription for appropriate instructional and support services. Generally, the most it can do is help us understand what the child is experiencing.

Knowing the cause of a disability is not a guarantee of effective intervention.

The reality is that the intervention needs of students who share the same disability category differ from each other as much as they differ from the needs of children in other categories: Children's individual differences override many, if not most, commonalities associated with a disability category.

This is not to say that there are no advantages to knowing the factors necessary for "normal" development. Information about these factors is extremely important in preventing delay, deviations, and dysfunction in development. Miller (1983) has listed the following factors as necessary for normal development of speech, language, and communication:

Neurological factors
Cognitive development
Information processing strategies (e.g., attention, discrimination, memory)
Motor output capabilities (neuromuscular control/coordination)
Social-emotional development and motivation

Structural and physiological factors
Sensory (auditory, visual, tactile, gustatory, olfactory) acuity
Oromuscular capabilities
Speech transmission mechanisms

Environmental factors
Social-cultural variables (socioeconomic level, language culture, dialect)
Experiences (caregiver-child interactions, linguistic input, responsiveness)
Physical context (availability of toys, pictures, manipulable objects)

Speech, language, and communication disorders are highly probable, if not a certainty, when there is delay, disruption, or dysfunction in any one of these factors. Because of the interrelatedness of these factors, the child's difficulties will be compounded when there is delay or dysfunction in more than one area. For example, there will be a direct relationship between delayed cognitive development (regardless of whether it is mild or severe) and acquisition of semantic knowledge and morphological, syntactic, and pragmatic rules. Similarly, the child with a visual impairment who experiences delayed social development (because she is not able to see and interpret social cues) and delayed physical development (because of restricted mobility) can be expected to have problems with the rate and course of early language development. Ultimately, how much of an effect any one or combination of these factors has on development of speech, language, and communication abilities will depend on (1) the degree of the deficit, (2) the type of deficit (e.g., structural and physiological factors may have more detrimental effects than environmental factors), (3) the age at which the problem occurs, (4) when the problem is identified, and (5) the quality of intervention efforts.

DESCRIPTIVE CLASSIFICATION OF LANGUAGE DIFFICULTIES

There are any number of possible descriptive classification systems for language and communication difficulties. They may be classified according to whether they are receptive language difficulties or expressive language difficulties, or according to the aspect (phonology, morphology, semantics, syntax, or pragmatics) of language that is affected. The latter option is not as straightforward as it sounds because children who have problems with one aspect of language generally experience some type of deficiency in one or more of the others. At the same time, there is usually one aspect where the child has greater problems.

Phonological Disorders

McReynolds (1990) notes that speech and hearing professionals have begun to use the label **phonological disorders** for problems that were previously termed *functional articulation disorders*. Phonological disorders are common in children with language difficulties. They are usually articulation problems that have no known or obvious organic, neurologic, or physical correlates. They may be due to speech-motor difficulties or to difficulties related to phonological organization. Leonard (1990) provides these examples to illustrate the two types of phonological disorders. The child whose phonological problems are associated with speech-motor difficulties might say "gup" for *cup* and "doo" for *two,* demonstrating an inability to coordinate the timing of voicing so that it begins after the release of the

Phonological disorders may be due to speech-motor difficulties or difficulties related to phonological organization.

consonant. The child whose phonological problems are associated with lack of phonological organization might say "tee" for *see* and "tack" for *sack,* while at the same time he demonstrates the capability of producing [s] (e.g., says "soo" for *shoe* and "sip" for *chip*). Phonological deficits are frequently observed in children who are experiencing reading and learning difficulties. Gerber (1993) posits the following phonological deficits as characteristic of many children with reading and learning disabilities: (1) delayed acquisition of a mature phonological system for speech production; (2) inferior perception and/or production of complex phonemic configurations; (3) inefficient use of phonological codes in short-term memory; and (4) impaired phonological sensitivity (which interferes with establishing phoneme-grapheme correspondences for reading and spelling).

Morphological Difficulties

Morphological difficulties include problems with verb tense, plurality, and possession.

Children with learning disabilities are prone to difficulties with morphological inflections (also called grammatical morphemes or grammatical markers). Recall from Chapter 1 that morphological inflections are inflections on nouns, verbs, and adjectives that signal different kinds of meanings; for example, adding the morpheme *-s* to dog indicates plurality. Specifically, these children seem to have problems with verb tense, plurality, and possession (Siegel & Ryan, 1984; Leonard, 1990) and they do not acquire the morphological rules at the same rate, and to the same degree of sophistication, as their peers (e.g., Vogel, 1977). They fail to learn the rules for words such as auxiliaries, modals, prepositions, and conjunctions (Wiig, 1990). Five-year-old Taylor is an example of a child with morphological difficulties: He omits *-ing* and confuses *a, an,* and *the,* and he is inconsistent in the use of suffixes indicating possession, gender, and number in nouns.

Semantic Difficulties

Semantic difficulties, especially problems with word finding (the ability to generate a specific word that is evoked by a situation, stimulus, sentence context, or conversation), commonly occur in children and adolescents identified as language disordered, learning disabled, dyslexic, and aphasic (Gerber, 1993; Leonard, 1990; Nippold, 1992). Students with semantic difficulties demonstrate restrictions in word meanings, difficulties with multiple word meanings, excessive use of nonspecific terms (e.g., *thing* and *stuff*) and indefinite reference (e.g., *that* and *there*), and difficulties with comprehension of certain conjunctions (e.g., *but, or, of, then, either, neither*) and relational terms (e.g., *in front of, more/less, before/after*). Tests of comprehension and their productive vocabularies indicate that word knowledge is restricted, literal, and concrete (Gerber, 1993; Wren, 1985).

Syntax Difficulties

Children with syntactic difficulties are experiencing problems acquiring the rules that govern word order and other aspects of grammar such as subject-verb agreement, evidenced by their problems processing sentences—even relatively simple ones. They typically produce shorter and less elaborated sentences than their peers, often failing to fully encode all possible relevant information. They also use fewer cohesive conjunctions than their peers without disabilities, and there is less variation in the types of conjunctions they use (Moran, 1988). They make many errors of omission, reversal, and substitution in sentence repetition tasks (Minskoff, 1976) and sentence completion tasks (Synder & Downey, 1991).

Syntactic difficulties include problems with word order and other aspects of grammar.

Pragmatic Difficulties

Included under the rubric of pragmatic skills are those skills that allow the child to use language as a social tool (i.e., communication functions, appropriate turn-taking, ability to adapt to the context). Children with pragmatic difficulties typically have problems related to listener needs (what and how much information they need to provide to their listeners). They may not understand the purpose of conversations or be reluctant to introduce topics (or introduce unusual or inappropriate topics). Many do not seem to know when to make eye contact, how close it is permissible to stand when talking to another person, when to request clarification of information (e.g., "Can you tell me again what you mean?"), or how to interpret direct and indirect requests. Not unexpectedly, considering the social deficits associated with autism, children with that diagnosis have a multitude of pragmatic difficulties (e.g., Mundy, Sigman, & Kasari, 1990). Deficits in the ability to interpret affective states, an important foundation for communication and language development, are especially pronounced.

Despite the fact that classification according to the aspects of behavior with which the child is having difficulty—what may be termed *educationally* or *instructionally relevant classification*—provides more information that is useful for planning and implementing intervention, it is not the prevalent method of classification. The most common means of grouping children with special needs is according to disability.

CLASSIFICATION ACCORDING TO DISABILITY

Disability grouping makes three totally unfounded assumptions: (1) that there are specific factors that have caused the disability; (2) that these factors can be identified; and (3) that all children with

Children must meet certain
eligibility criteria to receive
special education and related
services.

the same disability (or a significant number of characteristics in common) will benefit from the same intervention and/or instructional techniques.

The reason that the practice of grouping students by disability continues is that it is tied to our system for distributing state and federal funds. How many special education dollars a state or district receives depends on the number of children determined eligible for and provided with special services. The only way a student with special needs can receive individualized instructional activities and related services is if she meets the eligibility criteria for one of the disabilities categories specified in the Individuals with Disabilities Education Act (IDEA) (1992): visual impairment, hearing impairment, deafness and blindness, orthopedic impairment, other health impairments, mental retardation, specific learning disabilities, serious emotional disturbance, speech or language impairment, multiple disabilities, traumatic brain injury, and autism.

Most of the disability categories include students with communication disorders. These difficulties are the primary disability for students in the *speech or language impairment* category and a secondary disability for students in many of the other categories. Interestingly, identification of the etiology of a communication disorder is most likely when that disorder is secondary to another disability. Even then, however, when a presumed cause of the disorder *can* be specified, it is rarely possible to predict the precise nature and severity of the disorder. Children in the same disability group sometimes demonstrate very different language difficulties: In fact, their difficulties may be more similar to those of children in one or another of the other categories.

The remainder of this chapter considers *possible* causal factors, general characteristics, and language characteristics of students in the IDEA disability categories that have language components. As noted above, in the ideal world, children would be grouped for instruction according to descriptive, instructionally relevant variables. In the real world of the nineties, children are categorized according to the IDEA definitions. Therefore, it is critical for all school personnel to know these definitions and criteria for determining eligibility for special education and related services. The IDEA categories are grouped under these headings: (1) learning difficulties; (2) motor disabilities; (3) sensory impairments; (4) behavior disorders and autism; and (5) cognitive deficits.

Learning Difficulties

Among the labels used to refer to children with learning difficulties are (1) learning disabilities, (2) attention deficit disorder, and (3) specific language impairment. The common denominator across these subcategories is that, despite intelligence scores within the normal range, these children do not seem to learn in the same way or as efficiently as their peers. Because of their academic, social, and communication difficulties, they have many problems in school settings.

Learning Disabilities

Arguments about definition have been almost continuous since the inception of the field of learning disabilities (LD). The oldest and most well known definition was developed in 1967 by the National Advisory Committee on Handicapped Children. That definition became the basis of the federal definition, which was first printed in 1977 in the regulations for Public Law 94-142.

The federal definition is the same today:

> . . . *a disorder in one or more of the basic psychological processes involved in understanding or in using language, spoken or written, which disorder may manifest itself in an imperfect ability to listen, speak, read, write, spell, or to do mathematical calculations. The term includes such conditions as perceptual difficulties, brain injury, minimal brain dysfunction, dyslexia, and developmental aphasia. . . in the definition, but learning problems that are primarily the result of visual, hearing, or motor impairments; mental retardation; emotional disturbance; or environmental, cultural, or economic disadvantage are excluded. (Federal Register, 1992)*

Since 1977 there have been several other definitions of learning disabilities. In 1984 the Association for Children and Adults with Learning Disabilities (ACALD) adopted a definition that broadened the scope of the problem beyond academics. Another definition was adopted in 1988 by the National Joint Committee for Learning Disabilities (NJCLD). The definition put forth by this coalition of professional and parent organizations defines learning disabilities as:

Both the IDEA definition and the NJCLD definition define a learning disability by what it is *not*.

> . . . *a generic term that refers to a heterogenous group of disorders manifested by significant difficulties in the acquisition and use of listening, speaking, reading, writing, reasoning, or mathematical abilities. These disorders are intrinsic to the individual and presumed to be due to central nervous system dysfunction, and may appear across the life span. Problems of self-regulatory behaviors, social perception, and social interaction may exist with learning disabilities but do not themselves constitute a learning disability. Although learning disabilities may occur concomitantly with other handicapping conditions (for example, sensory impairment, mental retardation, serious emotional disturbance) or with extrinsic influences (such as cultural differences, insufficient or inappropriate instruction), they are not the result of those conditions or influences. (National Joint Committee on Learning Disabilities, 1994)*

This definition stresses the general nature of problems grouped under the term *learning disabilities*. It also refers to more specific abilities such as reading and writing, and it allows some overlap with other disabilities. Note that both definitions cited above have one thing in common: They define a learning disability by what it is *not*.

Most states and local districts require that the following criteria be met if a student is to be classified and served as learning disabled:

There must be a discrepancy between the student's potential and his actual achievement.

- *Discrepancy criterion:* This criterion states that there must be a discrepancy between the student's potential (as measured by a standardized intelligence test) and actual achievement (as measured by a standardized achievement test). Each state determines how large a discrepancy must be in order for the student to meet the inclusionary criterion. Many states have complicated discrepancy formulas to calculate this difference. The considerable debate over the use of discrepancy scores has focused on (1) the difficulty with reliable calculations, (2) problems related to the fact that test scores are likely to be negatively influenced by attention problems and lack of motivation, and (3) the enormous time and effort required (Gerber, 1993).

If another disability is causing the learning difficulties, then the child will receive special education services in that disability category.

- *Exclusionary criterion:* The exclusionary criterion states that the learning disability is not the result of other known factors such as mental retardation, sensory impairment, physical disabilities, emotional disturbance, or environmental disadvantage. If other disabilities are suspected, the student is evaluated in that area. If the student has another disability that does not *cause* the learning disability (e.g., a physical disability), then the student is eligible for learning disabilities services and may also be eligible for other services. If there is no other disability or factor present, the student must still meet the third criterion.

The child must be found to need individualized curriculum and procedures.

- *Need criterion:* The third criterion is a demonstrated need for special education services. There must be a demonstrated need for individualized curriculum and procedures.

While there is no such thing as a "typical" profile of a student with learning disabilities, there is extensive research documenting the characteristics associated with learning disabilities and the difficulties that these students experience, particularly in reading and written language. A summary of the research synthesized by Gearheart and Gearheart (1989), Gerber (1993), Mercer (1992), and Scott (1991) is presented in Table 3.1.

The etiology of the deficits summarized in Table 3.1 is not fully understood. The research concerned with neurological, genetic, and other medically based correlates of learning disabilities provides few answers concerning causal relationships and even less assistance for intervention. Both the IDEA and the NJCLD definitions presume an underlying neurological problem, but neurological evidence is inconclusive (Mercer, 1992).

TABLE 3.1   Summary of characteristics associated with learning disabilities

Characteristic	Description
Reading difficulties	Student makes many word recognition and comprehension errors; has difficulty keeping his place while reading.
Written language difficulties	Student has difficulties with handwriting, spelling, text structure, sentence structure, lexicon, and composition.
Deficits in the area of metacognition	Student uses inefficient or inappropriate learning strategies or is completely lacking in learning strategies.
Disorders of attention	Student is highly distractable, impulsive (responds very quickly without monitoring accuracy), and/or perseverative.
Poor spatial orientation	Student seems to become lost easily and has great difficulty orienting to new surroundings.
Difficulty with polar relationships	Student has particular difficulty with the concepts *big–little, light–heavy,* and *close–far.*
Confusion with directions	Student has difficulty with the concepts *right, left, north, south, east, west, up, down,* etc.
Poor motor coordination	Student is generally clumsy and poorly coordinated and has great difficulty achieving balance.
Poor fine motor ability	Student has difficulty manipulating small objects such as pencils, paint brushes, and scissors.
Insensitivity to social nuances	Student does not read facial expressions and body language or seem to know when actions are not socially appropriate.
Inability to follow directions	Student has difficulty following oral directions, particularly the first time they are given.
Inability to keep up with group discussions	Student cannot seem to follow the flow of thought and conversation in class discussions.
Inadequate time concepts	Student is frequently late and often does not seem to have a concept of time or responsibilities related to time.
Perceptual problems	Student cannot copy letters (without reversals) or discriminate shape differences; also has difficulty discriminating sound differences.
Memory problems	Student cannot remember simple sequences or find objects that are always in the same location.
Social immaturity	Student seems unable to predict the consequences of his behavior and tends to use less socially acceptable behaviors.
Auditory processing difficulties	Student has difficulties when there is competing noise in the background.

It is difficult, if not impossible, to separate problems with language from learning disabilities.

The two points that do seem clear are (1) children with these characteristics are ill-equipped to function without special assistance in school settings, and (2) problems with language and learning are connecting and overlapping (Wallach & Miller, 1988; Wallach & Butler, 1994). The American Speech-Language-Hearing Association's Committee on Prevention of Speech-Language and Hearing Problems (1984) estimated that 71 percent of all preschoolers with disabilities are diagnosed as having a speech or language disorder as their primary disability, but this percentage does not continue throughout the school years.

There are three possible explanations for this finding: (1) early intervention efforts are enormously effective; (2) language problems disappear with age; or (3) these children are reclassified into another disability category when they enter school. Many researchers favor the latter explanation: that the majority of learning disabilities are really language disabilities at school-age levels whose label has changed to fit the school context (e.g., Mallory & Kerns, 1988; Wallach & Miller, 1988). A study by Gibbs and Cooper (1989) seems to support this conclusion. In a study of 242 eight- to twelve-year-old children with learning disabilities, they found that 96.2 percent of these students exhibited a speech, language, or hearing problem. Slightly over 90 percent demonstrated language problems, 23 percent had articulation disorders, and 12 percent had voice disorders.

The label **language-learning disabled** is often used to refer to the substantial percentage of children in the learning disabilities category whose problems are exclusively in the areas of speech and language. Miniutti (1991) estimates that more than 75 percent of students with learning disabilities have difficulty learning and using symbols. Table 3.2, which provides an overview of the language difficulties of these students, reflects a synthesis of the research that has reported on the language difficulties experienced by children with learning disabilities (Bryan, 1991; Gerber, 1993; Moran, 1988; Nippold, 1992; Siegel & Ryan, 1984; Vogel, 1977; Wiig, 1990; and Wren, 1983).

Attention Disorders

Children with ADD may be classified and served in the Other Health Impairments category.

Attentional problems, including attention deficit disorder (ADD) and related disorders of behavior and learning (e.g., attention deficit-hyperactivity disorder [ADHD]) are thought to affect as much as 20 percent of the school-age population (Shaywitz & Shaywitz, 1992). Children classified as ADD demonstrate inattention and implusivity: A subset of these children also experience hyperactivity. Because ADHD is the formal diagnostic label from the psychiatric classification scheme (i.e., the Diagnostic and Statistical Manual of Mental Disorders [DSM-IV] 1994), this is the term used by family physicians, pediatricians, psychiatrists, and other mental health clinicians. Children with ADD are currently eligible for special education and related

TABLE 3.2 Language difficulties associated with learning disabilities

Language Dimension	Difficulties
Phonology	Delayed acquisition of sounds Inferior perception and/or production of complex sound configurations Inefficient use of phonological codes in short-term memory Impaired sensitivity to sounds
Morphology/Syntax	Production of shorter and less elaborated sentences than peers Failure to encode all relevant information in sentences Difficulty with negative and passive constructions, relative clauses, contractions, and adjectival forms Confusion of articles (*a, an, the*) Difficulty with verb tense, plurality, possession, and pronouns Delayed acquisition of morphological rules Difficulty learning the rules for using auxiliaries, modals, prepositions, conjunctions, and other grammatical markers
Semantics	Word-finding and definitional problems Restricted word meanings (too literal and concrete) Difficulty with multiple word meanings Excessive use of nonspecific terms (e.g., *thing, stuff*) and indefinite reference Difficulty comprehending certain conjunctions (e.g., *but, or, if, then, either*) Difficulty with relational terms (comparative, spatial, temporal)
Pragmatics	Difficulty with questions and requests for clarification Difficulty initiating and maintaining conversation

services under IDEA. They are classified and served in the Other Health Impairments category.

The diagnosis of ADD is separate from the diagnosis of learning disabilities, but there is considerable overlap in the two groups. Tarnowski and Nay (1989) estimate that 30 to 60 percent of children classified as ADD are learning disabled; the remaining children in the category are hyperactive but do not have learning difficulties. There is some evidence that early ADHD may predispose children toward reading problems (Ferguson & Horwood, 1992), but it is unclear whether it is the early problems with attention that create this risk or the problems with early language development.

Research considering the language difficulties associated with ADHD has produced contradictory findings. Some studies have found delay in developing language in children with ADHD (Hartsough & Lambert, 1985; Szatmari, Offord, & Boyle, 1989): The percentage of children with ADHD who are delayed in developing language is estimated to be in the range of 6 to 35 percent, compared to 2 to 5.5 percent for children without the ADHD label. Other studies have found no delays (Barkley, DuPaul, & McMurray, 1990).

Evidence supporting the observation that children with ADHD are likely to talk more than those without ADHD, especially during spontaneous conversation, is more conclusive (Barkley, Cunningham, & Karlsson, 1983; Zentall, 1985). However, in contrast to the data indicating an increased rate of spontaneous speech, there are other data that suggest that children with ADHD may be less verbal and more dysfluent in situations when they must organize and generate their speech (Hamlett, Pelligrini, & Conners, 1987; Zentall, 1985).

The substantial differences in the impulsivity, poor attention, and excessive activity among children with ADHD and across situations calls for a multidimensional approach to assessment. Parent, teacher, and even peer reports, plus observation in the classroom and other school settings, are essential.

Specific Language Impairment

When students demonstrate communication difficulties that do not seem to be the result of or directly associated with a hearing loss or an other disability, they are labeled as having a speech or language impairment. The IDEA definition for this disability group is

> . . . a communication disorder such as stuttering, impaired articulation, a language impairment, or a voice impairment that adversely affects a child's educational performance. (Federal Register, 1992)

The American Speech-Language-Hearing Association's (ASHA) (April 1980) definition of language disorders is more comprehensive with respect to communication. A major difference is that it does not mention the potential effect of the impairment. ASHA defines a language disorder as

> . . . the abnormal acquisition, comprehension or expression of spoken or written language. The disorder may involve all, one, or some of the phonologic, morphologic, semantic, syntactic, or pragmatic components of the linguistic system. Individuals with language disorders frequently have problems in sentence processing or in abstracting information meaningfully for storage and retrieval from short and long term memory. (ASHA, 1980, pp. 317–318)

SLI does not seem to affect or be affected by anatomical, physical, or intellectual problems.

The label **specific language impairment** (SLI) is used by many clinicians and researchers for children with language impairment that "cannot be attributed to deficits in hearing, oral structure and function, or general intelligence" (Leonard, 1987, p.1). It is important to note that while the term "specific language impairment" (SLI) is used as if it refers to a clearly defined group of children, in fact, there is no generally recognized or accepted definition for SLI (Aram, Morris, and Hall, 1993). Moreover, despite a great deal of research and thought committed to trying to understand why children with no other apparent problems have so much difficulty learning and using language, it is not clear what causes SLI. It does not seem to affect or be affected by anatomical, physical, or intellectual problems.

In contrast to the lack of definitive information regarding the cause or causes of SLI, there are some data concerning the educational and social impact of language impairment. There is a strong relationship between early speech-language impairments and reading disabilities (Tallal, Curtiss, & Kaplan, 1989). As noted in the section on learning disabilities, many children identified as having language difficulties in the preschool years (whether they are specifically labeled SLI or not), are later relabeled as language-learning disabled or learning disabled. Retrospective follow-up studies report that, when they enter school, 40 to 60 percent of these children will continue to experience difficulties with spoken language, and they will also have problems with reading and spelling (Aram, Ekelman, & Nation, 1984). Many students with language impairment also experience problems with social interaction (Bashir, 1989). Because relationships are based on communication, most students with language impairment have difficuly making friends, as they are not as likely to be selected as partners in social situations (Rice, 1993).

At the present time there is some agreement on exclusionary criteria—that the following factors should be excluded in defining SLI: peripheral hearing loss, neuromuscular disabilities, emotional disturbance, and mental deficiency. There is also some agreement concerning a discrepancy between actual language and expected language, but not how this discrepancy should be established.

As a group, children with SLI demonstrate a mild to moderate deficit in a range of language areas (Leonard, 1989). Most do not speak their first words until age 2 and do not combine words until age 3. Despite the fact that they constitute a heterogeneous group, it is possible to delineate these language difficulties. Table 3.3 provides a summary of information drawn from research by Craig and Washington (1993), Hadley and Rice (1991), Ingram (1972b), Lahey, Liebergott, Chesnick, Menyuk, and Adams (1992), Leonard (1989), Leonard, McGregor, and Allen (1992), Leonard, Schwartz, Allen, Swanson, and Loeb (1989), Loeb and Leonard (1991), Loeb and Pye (1993), Redmond (1993), Rescorla (1989), Rice and Bode (1993), Watkins, Rice, and Moltz, (1993), and Wetherby and Yonclas (1989).

As there is a lack of consensus as to a precise definition of SLI, there is also lack of consensus as to the underlying problem. It is possible, as some have suggested (e.g., Tallal & Piercy, 1973), that the mechanisms of language acquisition are impaired by an inability to process the incoming stream of speech. Leonard (1991) suggests that a language impairment represents the low end of the normal contin-

TABLE 3.3   Language difficulties associated with specific language impairment

Language Dimension	Difficulties
Phonology	Failure to capitalize on regularities across words Slow development of phonological processes Unusual errors across sound categories
Morphology/Syntax	Co-occurrence of more mature and less mature forms Fewer lexical categories per sentence than peers More grammatical errors than peers Slow development of grammatical morphemes Many pronoun errors
Semantics	Delayed acquisition of first words Slower rate of vocabulary acquisition Less diverse repertoire of verb types
Pragmatics	Intent not signalled through linguistic means Difficulty gaining access into conversations Less effective at negotiating disputes Less use of the naming function Difficulty tailoring the message to the listener Difficulty repairing communication breakdowns

uum of linguistic aptitude, not a different set of skills. This view pictures children with SLI as simply less skillful at the complex undertaking involved in language, rather than "disabled."

Motor Disabilities

Two of the IDEA disability groups demonstrate motor disabilities: orthopedic impairments and multiple disabilities.

Orthopedic Impairments

Many special educators and state and local educational agencies use the term *physical disabilities* for children with orthopedic impairments. The IDEA guidelines describe an orthopedic impairment as an impairment

> Physical disabilities may be a result of neurological damage or musculoskeletal impairments.

> . . . *that adversely affects a child's educational performance. The term includes impairments caused by congenital anomaly (e.g., clubfoot, absence of some member, etc.), impairments caused by disease (e.g., poliomyelitis, bone tuberculous), and impairments from other causes (e.g., cerebral palsy, amputations, and fractures or burns that cause contractures)* (Federal Register, *1992*)

There are two common classifications of physical disabilities: *neurological* and *musculoskeletal*. Neurological disabilities are disabilities that are caused by or related to the nervous system (e.g., spina bifida, cerebral palsy). Musculoskeletal disabilities are disabilities caused by or related to the muscles and skeleton (e.g., muscular atrophy). It is not difficult to understand why virtually all children with motor disabilities caused by damage to the brain or spinal cord experience problems with speech and language. Speech requires motor planning and precise and complex coordination of breathing, sound production, and articulation. Language requires complex and integrated brain function.

Imagine a continuum of motor involvement. The intellectual functioning of many of the children on this continuum will be within *or above* the normal range. Others, particularly many at the severe motor involvement end of the continuum, will demonstrate severe to profound retardation. Most children with minimal damage to the neuromotor system (at one end of the continuum) and many children with severe involvement (at the other end of the continuum) will learn to produce functional speech. Those who cannot use speech will be provided with augmentative and alternative communication systems (see Chapter 13).

The condition that accounts for the largest percentage of students with motor disabilities is **cerebral palsy.** Cerebral palsy is an umbrella term for any disorder of movement or posture that results from a nonprogressive abnormality (either damage or disease) to the immature brain. Some children with cerebral palsy have only very slight fine motor coordination problems; others are affected to the extent that they cannot move without assistance. Many children with cerebral palsy also have other disabilities such as retardation and sensory impairments. If they demonstrate severe and/or multiple disabilities, they are typically served in the category *multiple disabilities.*

> Cerebral palsy is the result of damage or disease to the immature brain.

A term that is often used in reference to the speech of children with cerebral palsy is **dysarthria.** Dysarthria is a group of related speech disorders that result from disturbed voluntary control over the speech mechanism. It includes impairment in the motor processes of respiration, phonation, articulation, and resonance (LaPointe, 1990). At the broadest level, dysarthria is a disturbance of motor function caused by damage to the nervous system. Because of an inability to coordinate resonation, articulation, and respiration mechanisms the child cannot speak with normal muscular speed, strength, precision, or timing. In some children with cerebral palsy, dysarthria is relatively mild; in others it is so severe that speech is virtually unintelligible. Dysarthria should not be confused with **apraxia,** which is a neurological disorder affecting the ability to *plan* speech movements. In apraxia, all speech mechanisms are functioning, but the child cannot get them to operate properly.

> Dysarthria is a disturbance of motor function caused by damage to the nervous system.

The type and extent of the speech, language, and communication difficulties problems of children with cerebral palsy depend on the degree of involvement of the neuromuscular system and the child's unique complex of associated disorders (i.e., sensory and perceptual impairments, retardation, seizures). There are some specific speech problems associated with the different types of cerebral palsy. Children with a general pattern of spasticity (high muscle tone with tight, stiff, and overactive muscles) typically demonstrate slow, labored speech. Children with what is called an athetoid pattern (fluctuating muscle tone with uncontrolled writhing movements) tend to have jerky speech. Children with an ataxic pattern (awkward and clumsy, poorly controlled movements) have a tremorous, quavering voice.

Multiple Disabilities

Because most states' services have a category and services for students with *severe and multiple disabilities,* many are surprised to find that the IDEA has separate definitions for multiple disabilities and severe disabilities. Students with multiple disabilities are those who have

> . . . *concomitant impairments (such as mental retardation–blindness, mental retardation–orthopedic impairment, etc.), the combination of which causes such severe educational problems that they cannot be accommodated in special education programs solely for one of the impairments. The term does not include deaf–blindness.* (Federal Register, *1992)*

In another part of the IDEA, children with severe disabilities are described as children

> . . . *who, because of the intensity of their physical, mental, or emotional problems, need highly specialized education, social, psychological, and medical services in order to maximize their full potential for useful and meaningful participation in society and for self-fulfillment.* (Federal Register, *1992)*

Two notable characteristics of students with severe and multiple disabilities are (1) they have severe impairments in intellectual functioning, and (2) they require intensive levels of support across environments to acquire functional and adaptive skills. Many have both sensory and motor impairments. (Chapters 12 and 13 deal extensively with assessment and intervention approaches for students with multiple and severe disabilities.)

Sensory Impairments

An impairment or limitation of any of the senses—auditory, visual, tactile, olfactory, or gustatory—deprives the child of critical information about the environment.

Hearing Impairment

Any loss or distortion of auditory input will have some effect on speech and language development but, as would be expected, children who are totally deaf have the greatest problems. The IDEA defines *deafness* as

> . . . *hearing impairment that is so severe that the child is impaired in processing linguistic information through hearing, with or without amplification, and that adversely affects a child's educational performance.* (Federal Register, *1992)*

The IDEA defines *hearing impairment* as

> . . . *an impairment in hearing, whether permanent or fluctuating, that adversely affects a child's educational performance but which is not included under the definition of deafness.* (Federal Register, *1992)*

There are three major types of hearing loss: **conductive, sensorineural,** and **mixed.** Each has a different prognosis and a somewhat different effect on language and communication. Conductive hearing losses are due to abnormalities or problems associated with the outer or middle ear. The problem is usually a malfunction or blockage that prevents clear transmission of sound waves to the inner ear. Examples are impounded wax, infections in the middle ear, excess fluid in the eustachian tube, or interruptions in the middle ear bones. The primary effect of a conductive problem is loss of hearing sensitivity because the level of sound reaching the inner ear is reduced. Conductive impairments are usually amenable to medical intervention (removal of the blockage) or amplification (a hearing aid).

Children may have conductive, sensorineural, or mixed hearing loss.

Sensorineural hearing loss is the result of damage or disease in some portion of the inner ear, auditory nerve, and/or the neural pathways. The signal may not reach the brain at all or may arrive in a highly distorted form. Usually sound impulses remain unclear and distorted even when amplification is provided. Medical and surgical procedures are of limited usefulness with this type of hearing loss.

Sensorineural hearing loss may be genetic in origin, or it may be caused by disease or injury before, during, or after birth. Genetic causes are thought to account for approximately 50 percent of all cases of severe loss (Northern & Downs, 1991). There are more than 50 genetic syndromes in which hearing loss may occur. Nongenetic causes of hearing loss include maternal rubella (commonly called German measles), meningitis, otitis media (middle ear infection), and congenital cytomegalovirus infection (CMV). (CMV is a viral infection in newborns that is transmitted through the placenta or picked up during the birth process.)

A mixed loss is a combination of conductive and sensorineural losses. The two exist simultaneously. There may be some benefits from amplification if the conductive loss is the greater; but, even then, the prognosis for sound discrimination is generally poor. In approximately half the population of students with hearing impairments, the cause or causes of the loss are not known.

Children who cannot hear speech do not learn to produce it without special training. Relatively few of the children with significant hearing loss develop *normal* oral language comprehension and production abilities. Ultimately, how much a particular child's hearing impairment affects his speech and development will depend on

- severity of the hearing loss,
- age of onset of the hearing loss,
- frequencies where hearing loss is greatest,
- age when loss was identified and intervention was initiated,
- amount and type of intervention, and
- the child's communication mode (whether manual, oral, or combined).

The effects of hearing loss are most deleterious when there is a severe loss that is present at birth or occurs shortly thereafter.

Speech and language problems invariably affect performance in other domains.

The interactive nature of cognitive, language, social, and motor development means that speech and language problems will invariably affect performance in other domains. Auditorily, children have to learn to make more out of less information if whatever hearing they have is to be useful. Thus, in addition to a language interventionist and a special education teacher specialized in education for the deaf, the support team for students with hearing impairment typically includes an audiologist. The fitting of amplification as early as possible is critical.

Teachers are a major source of referrals for audiometric evaluation. Table 3.4 provides a list of physical and behavioral signs suggesting the need for audiometric evaluation. The professional primarily responsible for this evaluation is the audiologist. However, screening is sometimes done by language interventionists and school or public health nurses because audiologists are not available in many school systems and all school systems do not have access to audiological services in the community.

Hearing is measured and reported in **decibels (dB),** which are a measure of the intensity of sound relative to a reference point. Zero decibels (0 dB) does not mean the absence of sound. Rather it is the point at which people with normal hearing can barely detect sound. Each succeeding number of decibels indicates some loss. The point at which an individual responds to sound 50 percent or more of the time is that person's hearing level, or *threshold of hearing.* Thus, the lower the threshold, the more acute or sensitive the child's hearing.

Once a child's hearing has been evaluated and described in decibels, it is possible to *estimate* the potential effect of the hearing loss

TABLE 3.4   Indicators for referral for audiometric assessment

Physical Indicators
1. Frequent complaints of earaches and colds
2. Discharge from the ears
3. Complaints of buzzing or ringing in the ears
4. Breathing through the mouth

Behavioral Indicators
1. Does not seem to understand simple directions
2. Fails to respond to questions
3. Requests many word and sentence repetitions
4. Frequently fails to respond when spoken to
5. Inattention and daydreaming
6. Articulation difficulties
7. Voice problems
8. Shows a preference for high- or low-pitched sounds
9. Disorientation and confusion when noise levels are high

Source: "Working with sensorily impaired children" by R. F. DuBose, in S. G. Garwood (Ed.), *Educating young handicapped children: A developmental approach* (2nd ed., pp. 235–276), 1983, Rockville, MD: Aspen Publications.

on the child's speech and language acquisition. Estimates of potential effect are presented in Table 3.5.

When mild to moderate hearing impairment is identified at an early age, early intervention targets vocal and phonological development. Ling's (1976) intervention approach for children with peripheral hearing impairment, which is one of the most widely used programs, is based on a view of language acquisition as an orderly and sequential process in which developmental advances occur on two developmental levels, simultaneously. On the phonetic level, children learn to produce and to differentiate sounds to the criteria of precise accuracy and automaticity, but without assigning meaning to the sounds. On the phonological level, children develop awareness of the meaningful use of speech sounds in their own speech and the speech of others.

There is considerable controversy over how and where students who are deaf or hearing impaired should be educated (Moores, Cerney, & Garcia, 1990). One side of this continuing debate argues that they should be educated to become as much like their peers with normal hearing as possible; that the goal should be to live and participate in "normal" society. They argue that children should not be taught a manual form of communication because they will prefer it and never develop auditory or oral skills. Rather, students with severe hearing impairment should learn to read lips, use their residual hearing, and use speech. The other side of the debate is in favor of teaching children to use manual communication, either alone or in combination

There is considerable debate over how and where to educate children who are deaf or hearing impaired.

TABLE 3.5   Relationship of degree of impairment to understanding of speech and language

Decibel (dB)	Effects
25–35 dB	Some difficulty hearing faint or distant speech and discriminating sound combinations.
36–54 dB	Understands conversational speech at 3–5 feet but may miss a significant percentage (as much as 50%) of class discussions. May demonstrate limited vocabulary and speech anomalies.
55–69 dB	Only hears/understands loud conversations and experiences difficulties with phone conversations and class discussions. Limited vocabulary and deficient in language usage and comprehension.
70–89 dB	May hear loud voices (about a foot from the ear) and may be able to identify environmental sounds and discriminate vowels (but not all consonants). Speech and language defective and likely to deteriorate (without therapy).
90 +	May hear some loud sounds but is more aware of vibrations. Relies on vision as the primary avenue for communication. Speech and language are of very poor quality and likely to deteriorate (without therapy).

with speech. They disagree with the argument that children with severe hearing impairment should strive for the goal of "normalcy." They contend that students should be given the communication skills they need (in any form possible), oral, manual, and written. They argue that the most appropriate goal should be integration into the world of work, and independence: Then they can socialize with other persons with hearing impairments, as well as hearing peers.

Arguments concerning inclusion of children who are deaf or severely hearing impaired in general education classes parallel the oral-manual communication debate. Although the trend is in the direction of inclusion, there seems little question that this controversy will continue. One side argues that, while the inclusive classroom may offer maximum opportunity for interactions with peers who are not disabled, it provides few opportunities for communication and social-ization with peers and adults who are deaf or hearing impaired. Some graduates from residential high schools for students who are deaf or hard of hearing take the position that their experiences were more positive "because of their teachers' ability to sign, ease of socialization with friends and participation in after-school activities" (Mertens, 1989). The other side contends that placing students who are deaf or hearing impaired in carefully chosen general education classes with appropriate support services (e.g., notetakers, interpreters, tutors) is academically and socially beneficial. This is borne out by research that reports increased achievement in both reading and mathematics for students in inclusive settings (Holt & Allen, 1989).

Visual Impairment

The IDEA defines children with visual handicaps as those who have

> . . . *a visual impairment which even with correction, adversely affects . . . educational performance. The term includes both partially seeing and blind children.* (Federal Register, *1992*)

Only about 1 percent of students receiving special education services have severe visual impairments. Students with visual impairments are similar to students in the other disability groups in that they are a heterogeneous population. They vary considerably with respect to type of visual disorder, degree of visual limitation, and extent to which the reduced visual capacity interferes with daily functioning. The one thing they have in common is the fact that their visual impairment creates a barrier to learning. How much of a barrier it is for a particular child depends on such variables as age of onset, degree of vision loss, etiology of the visual impairment, and the presence of other disabilities. Children blind from birth need special help to learn many concepts that are relevant to language acquisition because incidental learning is limited. Thus, the major contributors to the language delay observed in infants and very young children who are severely visually impaired are delayed cognitive development and difficulties with social interactions (Bigelow, 1987). Unless the child has another disability, the delayed cognitive development is most likely an effect of restricted mobility which limits experiences with objects and activities in the physical environment.

Restricted mobility limits the young child's experiences with objects and activities.

There are remarkable similarities in the language of children who are blind and the language of their sighted peers (Landau & Gleitman, 1985). Like their sighted peers, they use "sighted" words such as *look*. Moreover, by age 3 most have an appropriate MLU for their age. However, there are also some differences. In a longitudinal study of the language development of children with visual impairment, Orwin (1984) found limited naming or requesting; children relied heavily on routine phrases and people's names. Not unexpectedly, they did not refer to objects and events beyond their reach or touch and they rarely used function words (*there, more, no, gone*).

Because children with severe visual impairment lack the breadth of experiences of their peers without disabilities, they may learn the names for objects in their environment but not acquire words to describe object characteristics. Or they may provide detailed explanations of objects and events with little real understanding (Andersen, Dunlea, & Kekelis, 1984). Both circumstances have an impact on social interactions because communication is based on common experiences. Another commonly observed consequence of severe visual impairment is the development of unusual mannerisms. Because children cannot observe their partner's distance away when communicating, they often speak too loudly, and there is a tendency to smile too often and to use eyebrow movements that appear inappropriate to what is being said (Park, Shallcross, & Anderson, 1980).

A study by Kitzinger (1984) found a substantial number of echolalic utterances. The percentage of echolalic utterances in the spontaneous speech of a 3-year-old was 20.7 percent with her mother and 35.7 percent with another adult (with whom she was not well-acquainted).

As is the case where children with hearing impairment are concerned, teachers are a major source of referrals for children with mild to moderate visual impairment. Table 3.6 provides a list of physical and behavioral signs suggesting the need for visual assessment.

Most students with visual impairment attend general education classes with their sighted peers. In 1990–91, 42 percent of students with visual impairment were served primarily in inclusive general education classrooms. Another 23 percent were in inclusive general education classrooms for 60 to 79 percent of the school day (U.S. Department of Education, 1993).

Behavior Disorders and Autism

Our inclusion of language difficulties associated with behavior disorders and those associated with autism in the same section should not be misinterpreted. There is no intent to suggest a relationship between the cause (or causes) of the language impairments exhibited

---

Table 3.6   Indicators for referral for vision assessment

Physical Indicators
1. Crossed eyes
2. Watery or inflamed eyes
3. Recurring sties
4. Red, swollen, or encrusted eyelids
5. Dizziness, nausea, and frequent headaches

Behavioral Indicators
1. Frequent rubbing of the eyes
2. Tilting the head when looking at printed materials
3. Holding material close to the face
4. Squinting and/or frowning
5. Shutting or covering one eye when looking at printed material
6. Complaints about being unable to see distant objects

by children with behavior disorders and the cause of language impairments of children with autism. Nor is there an intent to suggest that the nature of their language difficulties is similar. The one commonality between the two groups is that the language difficulties of both are poorly understood.

Serious Emotional Disturbance

The area of serious emotional disturbance (SED), which is also called *behavior disorders* or *emotional disturbance,* tends to be a catch-all category for myriad child behaviors that are disturbing to adults, such as defiance, aggression, self-stimulation, depression, destructive behavior, social withdrawal, and noncompliance. The IDEA definition for serious emotional disturbance (SED) is virtually the same as the definition in the original legislation (PL 94-142). SED is defined as

> . . . *an inability to learn that cannot be explained by intellectual, sensory, or health factors; an inability to build or maintain satisfactory interpersonal relationships with peers and teachers; inappropriate types of behavior or feelings under normal circumstances; a general pervasive mood or unhappiness or depression; or a tendency to develop physical symptoms or fears associated with personal or school problems. The term includes children who are schizophrenic but not children who are socially maladjusted, unless they are seriously emotionally disturbed.* (Federal Register, *1992*)

Important terms in the IDEA definition for SED are not quantifiable.

This definition specifies three conditions that must be met: *chronicity* (the behavior must occur over a long period of time); *severity* (the behavior must occur "to a marked degree"); and *difficulty in school* (the behavior must adversely affect educational performance). The dissatisfaction with this definition expressed by many professionals is related to the fact that such terms and phrases as "normal," "over a long period of time," "to a marked degree," "adversely affect educational performance," and "satisfactory interpersonal relationships" are not quantifiable (Kauffman, 1993).

Over the past 10 years, a body of research has accumulated that points to a 50 to 60 percent co-occurrence of behavior disorders and communication disorders in children and adolescents (e.g., Baltaxe & Simmons, 1990; Ruhl, Hughes, & Camarata, 1992). Children referred to speech/language clinics have a higher rate of emotional/behavior problems than the noncommunication disordered population and, vice versa, children labeled as behavior disordered or emotionally disturbed have higher rates of communication disorders. Camarata, Hughes, and Ruhl (1988) found an incidence of 71 percent of communication problems in 38 children (8- to 12-year-olds) with mild to moderate behavior disorders. A study by Baltaxe, Russell, Simmons, and Bott (1987) showed that the histories of all 10 of their subjects with prepubertal onset of schizophrenia and three quarters of their subjects with prepubertal onset of schizotypal personality disorder also had a language delay, communication disorder, or learning and school problems prior to the appearance of their psychiatric disorder. Another study by Ruhl and colleagues (Ruhl et al., 1992) found the following linguistic deficits when they assessed the language skills (i.e., morphology, syntax, semantics) of 30 students (ages 9 to 16 years) labeled as having behavior disorders: (1) difficulty understanding and producing complex sentences; (2) delayed semantic functioning; and (3) delayed grammatical skills.

Autism

Autism is the result of abnormal brain development or brain trauma.

The term **autism** was first used by psychiatrist Leo Kanner in 1943 to describe a specific set of behaviors noted in some of his young patients. The primary characteristics of these children (all of whom had normal or above normal intelligence) were differences in speech (e.g., delayed acquisition, noncommunicative use of speech, delayed echolalia, pronominal reversals), poor relationships with people, an obsessive insistence on sameness, good rote memory, and poor imagination. Three decades later, in 1978, Rutter differentiated three broad groups of symptoms in children diagnosed as having autism: ". . . a profound and general failure to develop social relationships; language retardation with impaired comprehension, echolalia and pronominal reversal; and ritualistic or compulsive phenomena (i.e., an insistence on sameness)" (p. 4).

At one time autism was part of the Public Law 94-142 definition of severely emotionally disturbed. A subsequent revision of the definition removed autism from the emotional disturbance category and categorized it as a health impairment. More recently there has been some consensus that autism is a developmental disorder in the same genre as mental retardation: It is now a separate disability category in the IDEA. It is defined as

> . . . a developmental disability significantly affecting verbal and nonverbal communication and social interaction, generally evident before age 3, that adversely affects a child's educational performance. Other characteristics often associated with autism are engagement in repetitive activities and stereotyped movements, resistance to environmental change or change in daily routines, and unusual responses to sensory experiences. (Federal Register, 1992)

A term that is often used in association with autism is **pervasive developmental disorder (PDD).** This is a diagnostic category introduced in the 1987 revision of the manual of the American Psychiatric Association (DSM-1V). Psychiatrists and psychologists use this term for children who meet some but not all of the criteria for autism (or "autistic disorder" as it is called in DSM-1V).

After many decades of searching for causal factors, there is now consensus that autism is the result of some form of abnormality of brain development or brain trauma (Coleman & Gillberg, 1985). Approximately 65 percent of persons with autism have abnormal brain patterns (DeMyer, 1975) and most have unusually high levels of serotonin, a neurotransmitter and natural opiate (Schreibman, 1988). Autopsies of persons with autism show abnormalities in the cerebellum, the section of the brain that regulates incoming messages, and in the cerebral cortex (Courchesne, 1987).

While autism occurs in children at all levels of intellectual functioning (from gifted to profoundly mentally retarded), the majority of individuals with autism have mental retardation (Gillberg, 1991). Approximately 60 percent have IQs below 50, 20 percent have IQs between 50 and 70, and 20 percent have IQs in the normal range (Ritvo & Freeman, 1978).

The core features of autism, which distinguish it from other developmental abilities are (1) language and communication difficulties, (2) social impairment, and (3) challenging behavior. The language abilities of children with autism can be placed on a continuum of severity, from total absence of speech to language and communication that is generally adequate in terms of phonological and grammatical form but disordered from the perspective of semantic and pragmatic skills (e.g., poor eye contact, poor observance of the rules for referencing old and new information) (Baron-Cohen, 1988). Some students with autism never develop sufficient speech for oral communication to be a functional communication mode. Instead, they use an augmentative and alternative system (e.g., manual language, technology-assisted communication, communication boards) as described in Chapter 13.

Echolalia is another salient characteristic of children with autism. Echolalia may be immediate (an exact repetition produced within seconds) or delayed (an approximation produced some time after the original utterance. Analysis of many hours of videotape of echolalia by Prizant and Rydell (1984) indicated that, while not all echolalia is intended to be communicative, some echolalia may serve interactive communicative functions. For example, a child might use echolalia to gain an adult's attention (evidenced by the fact that the echolalia begins when the adult's attention is diverted and persists until the adult again focuses attention on the child) or to fill a conversational turn.

Communication is a reciprocal process based on mutual understanding, enjoyment, and benefit. Considering the requirements for effective communication—joint patterns of attending and affect between two individuals—it is not too surprising that children with autism have communication problems. They appear to lack intersubjectivity—the recognition that another person has a point of view—and they rarely show an interest in objects or activities that can be mutually shared (Kasari, Sigman, Yirmiya, & Mundy, 1993). Their lack of responsiveness to other people is pervasive. Most avoid eye

Children with autism seem unable to understand and interpret social cues.

contact or other forms of interaction with others, even when they are hurt or upset (Schreibman, Koegel, Charlop, & Egel, 1990). They voluntarily spend a disproportionate amount of time alone, developing a strong attachment to particular objects (Mundy, Sigman, & Kasari, 1990). Children with autism appear to be impaired in their ability to understand and interpret social cues accurately (Wing, 1988). The gestures and expressions that are an integral part of human communication seem to be confusing and lacking in meaning for children with autism. Most seem totally lacking in the ability to identify what others think and feel.

Children with autism demonstrate three types of challenging behavior: stereotypical behaviors, self-injurious behaviors, and aggression. **Stereotypical behaviors** are repetitive, rhythmic actions such as rocking, twirling objects, and waving fingers in front of the face. These behaviors may be the child's attempt to communicate boredom and agitation or a way in which to achieve some type of self-regulation (Helmstetter & Durand, 1991; LaVigna & Donnellon, 1986). **Self-injurious behaviors** exhibited by children with autism include head banging, biting, and scratching. Students who demonstrate severe forms of these behaviors may permanently injure themselves. **Aggressive behaviors** are similar to self-injurious behaviors except that they are directed toward others. It is important to note that students with autism are much less likely to engage in any of these challenging behaviors when they are involved in preferred and meaningful activities.

Table 3.7 provides an overview of the language difficulties associated with autism. These data draw from research by Baltaxe and Simmons (1990), Fay and Schuler (1980), Frith (1989), Kasari, Sigman, Yirmiya, and Mundy (1993), Loveland, Landry, Hughes, Hall, and McEvoy (1988), Mundy, Sigman, and Kasari (1990), Schreibman, Koegel, Charlop, and Egel (1990), Wetherby (1986), and Wetherby and Prizant (1989).

Stimulus overselectivity is responding to irrelevant stimuli or a limited subset of the relevant stimuli in an array.

Another contributor to the language difficulties of children with autism may be their observed **stimulus overselectivity** (the tendency to attend to irrelevant stimuli) (Kauffman, 1993; Rincover & Ducharme, 1987). When presented with an array of objects or object features, they tend to focus on only one aspect of that array (or a particular set of cues) to the exclusion of all others. Unfortunately, the stimuli they attend to are often irrelevant. Thus, they respond to irrelevant stimuli or a limited subset of the relevant stimuli in a complex array.

To acquire meaningful language, a child needs to hear the word representing a concept while simultaneously experiencing the labeled object, relation, or event. The tendency for stimulus overselectivity which is evident with both auditory and visual stimuli makes it difficult for the child to form the visual-auditory associations that are so necessary for language learning. Stimulus overselectivity may also affect social interactions. The child could easily miss nonverbal social

TABLE 3.7 Language difficulties associated with autism

Language Dimension	Difficulties
Phonology	Difficulty with expressive prosody (e.g., fluctuations in vocal intensity, monotonous pitch, tonal contrasts inconsistent with the meanings expressed)
Morphology/Syntax	Confusions of pronominal forms (e.g., gender confusion [*he* for *she* or *it*], case substitution [*him* for *he*], first- and second-person singular forms [*you* for *I* or *me*])
	Use of less complex sentences than peers
Semantics	Word-finding problems
	Inappropriate answers to questions
Pragmatics	Limited range of communicative functions
	Difficulty initiating and maintaining a conversation
	Few gestures
	Failure to make eye contact prior to or during communicative interactions
	Preference to follow rather than lead in a conversation
	Engaging of potential communication partners at a level that requires little actual sharing

cues because of preoccupation with what is being said, or the child may miss what is being said because he is attending to the speaker's facial expressions.

Views concerning what autism is and how it can and should be treated have changed more often and more drastically than perspectives in any other disability area. Recent research and intervention approaches may ultimately provide answers as to how to address the severe social and communication deficits that make inclusion of children with autism in general education classrooms especially challenging.

Cognitive Deficits

The fundamental role of social and cognitive functioning in the development of language and communication is most evident when these areas fail to develop at a normal rate. This section considers characteristics of children with mental retardation and characteristics associated with traumatic brain injury.

Mental Retardation

The IDEA definition for mental retardation is

> . . . *significant subaverage general intellectual functioning existing concurrently with deficits in adaptive behavior and manifested*

during the developmental period that adversely affects a child's edu-cation performance. (Federal Register, *1992*)

The cause of mental retardation is usually rooted in biological processes.

This definition does not define "subaverage general intellectual functioning." Intellectual functioning is determined from the results of an IQ test. The American Association on Mental Retardation (AAMA) recommends use of 70 as the cutoff for "subaverage," but each state is permitted to set its own levels (Grossman, 1983). There is a wide range of intellectual abilities among children categorized as mentally retarded. Children with mild retardation (IQ scores ranging from 56 to 70) constitute the largest segment of this population. Most of these youngsters achieve developmental milestones, but they attain them later (typically after special assistance). As adults, they hold jobs and live independently, or semi-independently, in the community. Children who are moderately retarded (IQ scores ranging from 41 to 55) generally learn to talk but they may experience difficulty with some aspects of communication. Children who are severely and profoundly retarded, particularly where they also demonstrate physical disabilities, require intensive intervention efforts to acquire basic functional communication skills (see Chapters 12 and 13). Many children with mental retardation have motor and sensory impairments, as well as health problems. Hearing impairment, which is especially prevalent in children with Down syndrome (Dahle & McCollister, 1986), multiplies their language difficulties.

When the cause of mental retardation is known, which is only about 50 percent of the time, it is usually rooted in biological processes (Coulter, 1992). The AAMD groups the biological causes of mental retardation into seven categories:

1. Infection and intoxification (e.g., rubella, syphilis, maternal use of drugs or alcohol)
2. Chromosomal abnormalities (e.g., Fragile-X syndrome, Down syndrome)
3. Gestation disorders (e.g., prematurity and low birth weight)
4. Unknown prenatal influences (e.g., hydrocephalus, microcephalus)
5. Traumas or physical agents occurring prior to birth, during delivery, or after birth (e.g., anoxia)
6. Metabolic or nutritional problems (e.g., phenylketonuria [PKU], Tay-Sachs disease)
7. Gross postnatal brain disease (e.g., neurofibromatosis)

The less severe the retardation, the less likely it is that a single cause can be specified. The majority of cases of mental retardation are the result of adverse psychosocial influences. Psychosocial causes can be categorized broadly into three subcategories: social, behavioral, and educational. Because the boundaries of these categories overlap, it is often difficult to isolate their effects. Mental retardation is frequently the result of complex interactions of multiple factors in all three subcategories. For example, teenage births are behavioral factors, but social factors (economic disadvantage) and educational factors (dropping out of school) complicate the picture.

While the label "mental retardation" does not describe a unique language pathology, it is safe to say that virtually all children with mental retardation experience some difficulties learning and using language (Grossman, 1983). Table 3.8 provides an overview of the language difficulties associated with mental retardation. These data represent a summary of information drawn from research by Abbeduto, Furman, and Davies (1989), Dahle and McCollister (1986), Fristoe and Lloyd (1979), McLeavey, Toomey, and Dempsey (1982), and Mervis (1990).

What is most helpful when working with children with mental retardation (as in working with other children with disabilities) is information concerning learning characteristics. Many of their learning problems are a consequence of learning strategy deficiencies or poor auditory processing.

Cognitive impairments place strong constraints on language development.

- **Learning strategy deficiencies:** They lack the learning strategies necessary to benefit from their experiences, frequently overlooking cues that could help them solve problems and they generally fail to take outcomes of previous trials into account.
- **Poor auditory processing:** They typically perform poorly on tasks requiring auditory memory and problem solving (Varnhagen, Das, & Varnhagen, 1987) and they fail to examine and evaluate their understanding of incoming messages (Ezell & Goldstein, 1991).

TABLE 3.8 Language difficulties associated with mental retardation

Language Dimension	Difficulties
Phonology	Delayed development of phonological rules Problems with speech production
Morphology/Syntax	Production of shorter, less complex sentences with fewer subject elaborations or relative clauses Delayed morpheme development Delayed development of syntax
Semantics	Use of more concrete word meanings Slower rate of vocabulary acquisition
Pragmatics	Difficulty with speech–act developmemt Difficulty with referential communication Difficulty initiating and maintaining a conversation Difficulty repairing communication breakdowns

The severity and pervasiveness of the language difficulties that a particular child with mental retardation experiences will be related to a host of factors, including sensory acuity, motivation, lack of social competence, and past instruction. In a review of research considering ways in which the cognitive, linguistic, social, and pragmatic impairments of persons with mental retardation may contribute to their problems with language, Abbeduto and Rosenberg (1992) concluded that the problem is more complex than simply a failure to master the linguistic system. It has to do with cognitive impairments that seem to place strong constraints on many aspect of linguistic communication.

Traumatic Brain Injury

The disability category *traumatic brain injury* (TBI) was added in the most recent amendments to the IDEA. TBI is defined as

> . . . *an acquired injury to the brain caused by an external physical force, resulting in total or partial functional disability or psychosocial impairment, or both, that adversely affects a child's education performance. The term applies to open or closed head injuries resulting in impairments in one or more areas, such as cognition; language; memory; attention; reasoning; abstract thinking; judgment; problem-solving; sensory, perceptual and motor abilities; psychosocial behavior; physical functions; information processing; and speech.* (Federal Register, *1992*)

More than one million children and adolescents incur traumatic brain injury (TBI) every year as a result of external physical force, such as a blow to the head received in an auto accident (Russell, 1993). Aphasia or acquired brain injury were the terms used in the past for children who developed language normally and then lost all or part of their linguistic abilities as a result of neurological damage.

Injury to the brain may be localized, confined to specific areas, or diffuse (spread over many brain regions). In general, the smaller the damaged area, the better the prognosis for recovery. The damage is a result of nerve cell death, which may come about directly (a result of the cells being removed or lack of oxygen) or indirectly (a result of degeneration of nerve cell connections). Outcome after brain trauma depends on a variety of factors, including preinjury characteristics (e.g., age, intellectual functioning, educational and vocational levels, personality); location and severity of the injury; and postinjury treatment, support systems, and emotional and behavioral reactions. Szekeres and Meserve (1994) note that, at the very least, there is likely to be evidence of

The smaller the area of the brain that is damaged, the better the child's prognosis.

- slowed processing and poor memory for new information and personal experiences;
- disorientation, confusion, and disorganization;

- problems with behavioral self-regulation and effective social interaction; and
- inconsistent performance (due to physical and mental fatigue).

The language difficulties associated with brain injury are summarized in Table 3.9. These data draw from research by Aram (1988), Blosser and DePompei (1992), Campbell and Dollaghan (1990), Ewing-Cobbs, Fletcher, and Levin (1985), Fennell and Mickle (1992), Jordan, Murdoch, and Buttsworth (1991), Long (1994), Mentis and Prutting (1991), and Russell (1993).

The definition of TBI as a disability category acknowledges delayed consequences of frontal lobe injury and the cumulative effect of the resulting learning problems. For children who have sustained traumatic brain injuries, the profound effects on later developing skills or skills in the process of development may be more serious than the loss of knowledge and skills acquired prior to the trauma (Lehr, 1990). Even what is considered to be relatively mild brain injury may have prolonged adverse effects on school performance. Traditional wisdom suggested that the younger the child when the injury occurred, the better the prognosis. However, the picture may be more complicated than this. Although spontaneous and complete recovery following brain injury often occurs, there is a substantial number of children who continue to exhibit persistent cognitive and language deficits (Blosser & DePompei, 1992; Ewing-Cobbs, Fletcher, & Levin, 1985) and, counter to conventional wisdom, some younger children experience more severe and persistent cognitive and language deficits following brain injury than either older adolescents or adults. The only summary statement that can be made is that

TABLE 3.9 Language difficulties associated with traumatic brain injury

Language Dimension	Difficulties
Phonology	Sound substitutions and omissions Slurred speech Difficulties with speech prosody (pitch, loudness, rate, and rhythm)
Morphology/Syntax	Deficits in syntactic comprehension Fragmented, irrelevant, and lengthy utterances Mutism immediately after the injury, followed by telegraphic production
Semantics	Small, restricted vocabulary Word-finding problems
Pragmatics	Difficulty with organization and expression of complex ideas Socially inappropriate and off-topic comments Less use of the naming function

children with TBI are certain to demonstrate a range and variety of social, cognitive, academic, and language problems.

Summary

This chapter has attempted to provide sufficient information to substantiate the heterogeneity of language abilities demonstrated by children within the same disability categories *and* the similarities in language abilities and difficulties across disability categories. In conclusion we reiterate our cautionary note about labeling: Because they provide little information about children's language intervention needs, labels should be avoided to the extent possible in favor of descriptions of learning and behavioral characteristics It may not be possible to avoid labeling altogether, but recognizing the pitfalls in the use of etiological categories can help us deal with the practice more intelligently.

All subsequent chapters in this text focus on intervention in inclusive settings. Thus, we will take this opportunity to briefly introduce what many consider to be one of the most important requirements of the IDEA—the **least restrictive environment (LRE) principle.** The LRE states that school systems must educate students with disabilities, to the maximum extent appropriate for the individual student, with students who do not have disabilities. This is called the "presumption of inclusion." It cannot be set aside unless there is evidence that the student cannot be educated appropriately with students who do not have disabilities (Turnbull, Turnbull, Shank, & Leal, 1995). Schools may not remove a student from general education unless the student cannot be educated successfully there even when supplementary aids and support services are provided. In the minds of many, the LRE translates to inclusion (e.g., Stainback and Stainback, 1990).

The premise underlying the LRE principle is best explained by Turnbull, Turnbull, Shank, and Leal (1995):

> *No matter what name you attach to the principle, its premise remains basically the same. When a state has a legitimate reason to intervene in a person's life (and educating its citizens certainly is such an interest), it must use the means that restrict the person's freedom to the least degree necessary to accomplish the state's purposes. (p. 106)*

There is no intent to suggest that placement in general education classrooms means that the student never leaves the class. Inclusion advocates note that there is a significant difference between being "based-in" and "confined to" general education classrooms. Brown, Schwarz, Udvari-Solner, Kampschroer, Johnson, Jorgansen, and Gruenewald (1991) note that "based-in" means "being a member of." While you may not spend all your time there, it is still your class and your classroom and "everyone knows it." "Confined to," on the other hand, means "spending 100 percent of each day" in the regular classroom and not leaving unless one's classmates without disabilities leave. How much time should be spent in the general education classroom depends on how much time it takes for the student to be considered a member of the class, rather than a visitor. If the student is young and engaged in meaningful activities, she should spend most, if not all, of the school day there.

This textbook takes the position that the vast majority of students with disabilities can and should be educated in, and be members of, general education classes. Inclusion will be successful only *if* students are provided with the supplementary services and supports they need (as specified in the IDEA); and *if* they have educators and support personnel whose attitudes and training have prepared them for collaboration and provision of appropriate curricula, instruction, methods, supplementary services, and related services.

REFERENCES

Abbeduto, L., Furman, L., & Davies, B. (1989). The development of speech act comprehension in mentally retarded individuals and nonretarded children. *Child Development, 59,* 1460–1472.

Abbeduto, L., & Rosenberg, S. (1992). Linguistic communication in persons with mental retardation. In S. F. Warren & J. Reichle (Eds.), *Causes and effects in communication and language intervention* (pp. 331–359). Baltimore: Brookes.

American Psychiatric Association. (1994). *Diagnostic and statistical manual of mental disorders* (4th ed.). Washington, DC: American Psychiatric Association.

American Psychiatric Association (1987). Diagnostic and statistical manual of mental disorders: Revision of 3rd edition. Washington, DC: American Psychiatric Association.

Anderson, E. S., Dunlea, A., & Kekelis, L. S. (1984). Blind children's language: Resolving some differences. *Journal of Child Language, 11,* 645–664.

Aram, D. M. (1988). Language sequelae of unilateral brain lesions in children. In Plum (Ed.), *Head injury rehabilitation: Children and adolescents* (pp. 171–197). New York: Raven Press.

Aram, D. M., Ekelman, B. L., & Nation, J. E. (1984). Preschoolers with language disorders: 10 years later. *Journal of Speech and Hearing Research, 27,* 232–244.

Aram, D., Morris, R., & Hall, N. (1993). Clinical and research congruence in identifying children with specific language impairment. *Journal of Speech and Hearing Research, 36,* 580–591.

ASHA Committee on Language Speech and Hearing Services in the schools. (1980, April). Definitions for communicative disorders and differences, *ASHA, 22,* 317–318.

ASHA Committee on Prevention of Speech-Language and Hearing Problems (1984). Prevention: A challenge for the profession. *ASHA, 26,* 35–37.

Barkley, R. A., Cunningham, C., & Karlsson, J. (1983). The speech of hyperactive children with their mothers: Comparison with normal children and stimulant drug effects. *Journal of Learning Disabilites, 16,* 105–110.

Barkley, R. A., DuPaul, G., & McMurray, M. (1990). A comprehensive evaluation of attention deficit-disorder with and without hyperactivity as defined by research criteria. *Journal of Consulting and Clinical Psychology, 29,* 546–559.

Baltaxe, C., Russell, A., Simmons, J. Q., & Bott, L. (1987, October). *Thought, language and communication disorders in prepubertal onset of schizophrenia and schizotypal personality disorders.* Paper presented at the Academy of Child and Adolescent Psychiatry, Washington, DC.

Baltaxe, C., & Simmons, J. Q. (1990). The differential diagnosis of communication disorders in child and adolescent psychopathology. *Topics in Language Disorders, 10*(4), 17–31.

Baron-Cohen, S. (1988). Social and pragmatic deficits in autism: Cognitive or affective. *Journal of Autism and Developmental Disorders, 18,* 379–402.

Bashir, A. S. (1989). Language intervention and the curriculum. *Seminars in Speech and Language, 10*(3), 181–190.

Bigelow, A. C. (1987). Early words of blind children. *Journal of Child Language, 14,* 47–55.

Blosser, J. L., & DePompei, R. (1992). A proactive model for treating communication disorders in children and adolescents with traumatic brain injury. *Clinics in Communication Disorders, 2*(2), 52–65.

Brown, L., Schwartz, P., Udvari-Solner, A., Kampschroer, E. F., Johnson, F., Jorgansen, J., & Gruenewald, L. (1991). How much time should students with severe intellectual disabilities spend in regular education classrooms and elsewhere? *Journal of the Association for Persons with Severe Handicaps, 16,* 39–47.

Bryan, T. (1991). Social problems and learning disabilities. In B. Y. L. Wong (Ed.), *Learning about learning disabilities* (pp. 195–229). San Diego: Academic Press.

Campbell, T. F., & Dollaghan, C. A. (1990). Expressive language recovery in severely brain-injured children and adolescents. *Journal of Speech and Hearing Disorders, 55,* 567–581.

Coleman, M., & Gillberg, C. (1985). *The biology of the autistic syndrome.* New York: Praeger.

Coulter, D. L. (1992). Reaction paper: An ecology of prevention for the future. *Mental Retardation, 30,* 363–369.

Courchesne, E. (1987). A neurophysiological view of autism. In E. Schopler & G. B. Mesi-

bov (Eds.), *Neurobiological issues in autism* (pp. 285–324). New York: Plenum.

Craig, H., & Washington, J. (1993). Access behaviors of children with specific language impairment. *Journal of Speech and Hearing Research, 36,* 322–337.

Dahle, A. J., & McCollister, F. P. (1986). Hearing and otologic disorders in children with Down's syndrome. *American Journal of Mental Deficiency, 90,* 636–642.

DeMyer, M. K. (1975). Research in infantile autism: A strategy and its results. *Biological Psychiatry, 10,* 433–540.

Ewing-Cobbs, L. Fletcher, J. M., & Levin, H. S. (1985). In M. Ylvisaker (Ed.). *Head injury rehabilitation: Children and adolescents* (pp. 71–89). Austin, TX: Pro-Ed.

Ezell, H. K., & Goldstein, H. (1991). Observational learning of comprehension monitoring skills in children who exhibit mental retardation. *Journal of Speech and Hearing Research, 34,* 141–154.

Fay, W., & Schuler, A. L. (1980). *Emerging language in autistic children.* Baltimore: University Park Press.

Federal Register. (1992). Washington, DC: U.S. Government Printing Office, September 29, 1992.

Fennell, D., & Mickle, P. (1992). Behavioral effects of head trauma in children and adolescents. In M. Tramontana & S. Hooper (Eds.), *Advances in Child Neuropsychology* (Vol. 1). New York: Springer-Verlag.

Ferguson, D. M., & Horwood, L. J. (1992). Attention deficit and reading achievement. *Journal of Child Psychology and Psychiatry, 33,* 375–385.

Fristoe, M., & Lloyd, L. (1979). Nonspeech communication. In N. R. Ellis (Eds.), *Handbook of mental deficiency, psychological theory and research* (2nd ed.). Hillsdale, NJ: Erlbaum.

Frith, U. (1989). A new look at language and communication in autism. *British Journal of Disorders of Communication, 24,* 123–150.

Gearheart, B. R., & Gearheart, C. J. (1989). *Learning disabilities: Educational strategies.* Columbus, OH: Merrill.

Gerber, A. (1993). *Languagae-related learning disabilities.* Baltimore: Brookes.

Gibbs, D. P., & Cooper, E. B. (1989). Prevalence of communication disorders in students with learning disabilities. *Journal of Learning Disabilities, 29,* 60–63.

Gillberg, C. (1991). Outcome in autism and autistic-like conditions. *Journal of the American Academy of Child and Adolescent Psychiatry, 30,* 375–382.

Grossman, H. J. (Ed.). (1983). *Classification in mental retardation.* Washington, DC: American Association on Mental Deficiency.

Hadley, P., & Rice, M. (1991). Conversational responsiveness of speech-and language-impaired preschoolers. *Journal of Speech and Hearing Research, 34,* 1308–1317.

Hamlett, K. W., Pellegrini, D. S., & Conners, C. K. (1987). An investigation of executive processes in the problem-solving of attention deficit disorder–hyperactive children. *Journal of Pediatric Psychology, 12,* 227–240.

Hartsough, C. S., & Lambert, N. M. (1985). Medical factors in hyperactive and normal children: Prenatal, developmental, and health history findings. *American Journal of Orthopsychiatry, 55,* 190–201.

Helmstetter, E., & Durand, V. M. (1991). Nonaversive intervention for severe behavior problems. In L. Meyer, C. Peck, & L. Brown (Eds.), *Critical issues in the lives of people with severe disabilities* (pp. 559–600). Baltimore: Brookes.

Holt, J. A., & Allen, T. E. (1989). The effects of schools and their curricula on the reading and mathematics achievement of hearing impaired students. *International Journal of Education Research, 13,* 547–562.

IDEA. 20 U.S.C. Secs. 1400–1485.

Ingram, D. (1972a). The development of phrase structure roles. *Language Learning, 22,* 65–77.

Ingram, D. (1972b). The acquisition of the English verbal auxiliary and copula in normal and linguistically deviant children. *Papers and Reports in Child Language Development, 4,* 79–91.

Jordan, F., Murdoch, B., & Buttsworth, D. (1991). Closed-head-injured children's performance on narrative tasks. *Journal of Speech and Hearing Research, 34,* 572–582.

Kanner, L. (1943). Autistic disturbances of affective contact. *Nervous Child, 2,* 217–250.

Kasari, C., Sigman, M., Yirmiya, N., & Mundy, P. (1993). Affective development and communication in young children with autism. In A. P. Kaiser & D. B. Gray (Eds.), *Enhancing children's communication* (pp. 201–222). Baltimore: Brookes.

Kauffman, J. M. (1993). *Characteristics of emotional or behaviorial disorders of children and youth* (5th ed.). New York: Macmillan.

Kitzinger, M. (1984). The role of repeated and echoed utterances in communication with a blind child. *British Journal of Disorders of Communication, 19,* 135–146.

Lahey, M., Liebergott, J., Chesnick, M., Menyuk, P., & Adams, J. (1992). Variability in children's use of grammatical morphemes. *Applied Psycholinguistics, 13,* 373–398.

Landau, B., & Gleitman, L. (1985). *Language and experience: Evidence from the blind child.* Cambridge, MA: Harvard University Press.

LaPointe, L. L. (1990). Neurogenic disorders of speech. In G. H. Shames & G. H. Wiig (Eds.), *Human communication disorders* (3rd ed.), (pp. 463–496). Columbus, OH: Merrill.

LaVigna, G. W., & Donnellon, A. M. (1986). *Alternatives to punishment: Solving behavior problems with non-aversive strategies.* New York: Irvington.

Lehr, E. (1990). *Psychological management of traumatic brain injury in children and adolescents.* Gaithersburg, MD: Aspen Publishers.

Leonard, L. (1987). Is specific language impairment a useful construct? In S. Rosenberg (Ed.), *Applied psycholinguistics* (pp. 1–39). New York: Cambridge University Press.

Leonard, L. (1989). Language learnability and specific language impairment. *Applied Psycholinguistics, 10,* 179–202.

Leonard, L. (1990). Language disorders in preschool children. In G. H. Shames & E. H. Wiig (Eds.), *Human communication disorders* (3rd ed.), (pp. 159–192). Columbus, OH: Merrill.

Leonard, L. (1991). Specific language impairment as a clinical category. *Language, Speech, and Hearing Services in the Schools, 22,* 66–68.

Leonard, L., McGregor, K. K., & Allen, G. D. (1992). Grammatical morphology and speech perception in children with specific language impairment. *Journal of Speech and Hearing Research, 35,* 1076–1085.

Leonard, L., Schwartz, R., Allen, G., Swanson, L., & Loeb, D. (1989). Unusual phonological behavior and the avoidance of homonymy in children. *Journal of Speech and Hearing Research, 32,* 583–590.

Ling, D. (1976). *Speech and the hearing-impaired child: Theory and practice.* Washington, D.C.: A. G. Bell.

Loeb, D., & Leonard, L. (1991). Subject case marking and verb morphology in normally developing and specifically language-impaired children. *Journal of Speech and Hearing Research, 34,* 340–346.

Loeb, D., & Pye, C. (1993). *Assessing the causative alternation.* Bethesda, MD: National Institutes of Health.

Long, S. H. (1994). Children with acquired language disorders. In V. A. Reed (Ed.), *An introduction to children with language disorders* (pp. 171–197). New York: Macmillan.

Loveland, K. A., Landry, S. H. Hughes, S. O., Hall, S. K., & McEvoy, R. E. (1988). Speech acts and the pragmatic deficits of autism. *Journal of Speech and Hearing Research, 31,* 593–604.

Mallory, B. L., & Kerns, G. M. (1988). Consequences of categorical labeling of preschool children. *Topics in Early Childhood Special Education, 8,* 39–50.

McLeavey, G., Toomey, J., & Dempsey, P. (1982). Nonretarded and mentally retarded children's control over syntactic structures. *American Journal of Mental Deficiency, 86,* 485–494.

McReynolds, L. V. (1990). Certiculation and phonological disorders. In G. H Shames & E. H. Wiig (Eds.), *Human communication disorders* (3rd ed.), (pp. 222–265), Columbus, OH: Merrill.

Mentis, M., & Prutting, C. (1991). Analysis of topic as illustrated in a head-injured and normal adult. *Journal of Speech and Hearing Research, 34,* 583–595.

Mercer, C. E. (1992). *Students with learning disabilities* (4th ed.). New York: Merrill/Macmillan.

Mertens, D. M. (1989). Social experiences of hearing-impaired high school youth. *American Annals of the Deaf, 134*(1), 15–19.

Mervis, C. B. (1990). Early conceptual development of children with Down Syndrome. In D. Circhetti & M. Beeghly (Eds.), *Children with Down Syndrome: A development perspective* (pp. 253–301). New York: Cambridge University Press.

Miller, J. F. (1983). Identifying children with language disorders and describing their language performance. In J. F. Miller, D. E. Yoder, & R. Schiefelbusch (Eds.), *Contemporary issues in language intervention* (pp. 61–74). Rockville, MD: American Speech-Language-Hearing Association.

Miniutti, A. (1991). Languagae deficiencies in inner-city children with learning and behavioral problems. *Language, Speech, and Hearing Disorders, 55,* 665–678.

Minskoff, E. H. (1976). Research on efficacy of remediating psycholinguistic disabilties: Critique and recommendations. In P. L. Newcomer & D. D. Hammill (Eds.), *Psycholinguistics in the schools* (pp. 80–98). Columbus, OH: Merrill.

Moores, D. F., Cerney, B., & Garcia, M. (1990). School placement and least restrictive environment. In D. F. Moores & K. P. Meadow-Orlans (Eds.), *Educational and developmental aspects of deafness* (pp. 89–103). Washington, D.C.: Gallaudet University Press.

Moran, M. R. (1988). Reading and writing disorders in the learning disabled student. In N. J. Lass, L. V. McReynolds, J. L. Northern, & D. E. Yoder (Eds.), *Handbook of speech-language pathology and audiology* (pp. 141–187). Philadelphia: Brian C. Decker Publishers.

Mundy, P., Sigman, M., & Kasari, C. (1990). A longitudinal study of joint attention and language development in autistic children. *Journal of Autism and Developmental Disorders, 20,* 115–128.

National Joint Committee on Learning Disabilities. (1994). Learning Disabilities: Issues on definition, a position paper of the National Joint Committee on Learning Disabilities. In *Collective perspectives on issues affecting learning disabilities: Position papers and statements.* Austin, TX: Pro-Ed.

Nippold, M. A. (1992). The nature of normal and disordered word finding in children and adolescents. *Topics in Language Disorders, 13,* 1–14.

Northern, J., & Downs, M. (1991). *Hearing in children* (4th ed.). Baltimore: Williams and Wilkins.

Orwin, L. (1984). Language for absent things: Learning from visually handicapped children. *Topics in Language Disorders, 4*(4), 24–37.

Owens, R. E. (1995). *Language disorders: A functional approach to assessment and intervention* (2nd ed.). Boston: Allyn and Bacon.

Park, K., Shallcross, R., & Anderson, R. (1980). Differences in coverbal behavior between blind and sighted persons during dyadic communication. *Journal of Visual impairment and Blindness, 74,* 142–146.

Prizant, B. M., & Rydell, P. J. (1984). Analysis of functions of delayed echolalia in autistic children. *Journal of Speech and Hearing Research, 27,* 183–192.

Redmond, S. (1993). *Arguing with SLI: The dispute characteristics of children with SLI.* Unpublished master's thesis, University of Kansas, Lawrence, KS.

Rescorla, L. (1989). The language development survey: A screening tool for delayed language in toddlers. *Journal of Speech and Hearing Disorders, 54,* 587–599.

Rice, M. (1993). "Don't talk to him; He's weird" A social consequences account of language and social interactions. In A. Kaiser & D. Gray (Eds.), *Enhancing children's communication: Research foundations for intervention.* Baltimore: Brookes Publishing.

Rice, M., & Bode, J. (1993). General all-purpose verbs. *First Language, 13,* 113–132.

Rincover, A., & Ducharme, J. M. (1987). Variables influencing stimulus overselectivity and "tunnel vision" in developmentally delayed children. *American Journal of Mental Deficiency, 91,* 37–42.

Ritvo, E. R., & Freeman, B. J. (1978). National Society for Autistic Children definition of the syndrome of autism. *Journal of Autism and Childhood Schizophrenia, 8,* 162–167.

Ruhl, K. L. Hughes, C. A., & Camarata, S. M. (1992). Analysis of the expressive and receptive language characteristics of emotionally handicapped students served in public school settings. *Journal of Childhood Communication Disorders, 14,* 165–176.

Russell, N. K. (1993). Educational considerations in traumatic brain injury: The role of the speech-language pathologist. *Language, Speech, and Hearing Services in Schools, 24,* 67–75.

Rutter, M. (1978). Diagnosis and definition of childhood autism. *Journal of Autism and Childhood Schizophrenia, 8,* 139–161.

Schreibman, L. (1988). *Autism.* Newbury Park, CA: Sage.

Schreibman, L, Koegel, R. L., Charlop, M. H., & Egel, A. L. (1990). Infantile autism. In A. S. Bellack, M. Hersen, & A E. Kazdin (Eds.), *International handbook of behavior modification and therapy* (2nd ed.) (pp. 763–789). New York: Plenum.

Scott, C. M. (1991). Problem writers: Nature, assessment, and intervention. In A. G. Kamhi & H. W. Catts (Eds.), *Reading disabilities: A developmental language perspective* (pp. 303–344). Boston: Allyn and Bacon.

Shaywitz, S. E., & Shaywitz, B. A. (1992). Introduction. In S. E. Shaywitz & B. A. Shaywitz (Eds.), *Attention deficit disorder comes of age* (pp. 1–12). Austin, TX: Pro-ED.

Siegal, L. S., & Ryan, E. B. (1984). Reading disability as a language disorder. *Remedial and Special Education (RASE), 5,* 28–33.

Snyder, L. S., & Downey, D. M. (1991). The language-reading relationship in normal and reading-disabled children. *Journal of Speech and Hearing Research, 34,* 129–140.

Stainback, W., & Stainback, S. (1990) *Support networks for inclusive schooling.* Baltimore: Paul H. Brookes

Szatmari, P., Offord, D. R., & Boyle, M. H. (1989). Ontario child health study: Prevalence of Attention deficit disorder with hyperactivity. *Journal of Child Psychology and Psychiatry, 30,* 219–230.

Szekeres, S. F., & Meserve, N. F. (1994). Collaborative intervention in schools after traumatic brain injury. *Topics in Language Disorders, 15,* 21–36.

Tallal, P., Curtiss, S., & Kaplan, R. (1989). *The San Diego longitudinal study: Evaluating the outcomes of preschool impairment in language development.* Final Report, National Institute of Neurological Communication Disorders.

Tallal, P., & Piercy, M. (1973). Defects of nonverbal auditory perception in children with developmental aphasia. *Nature, 241,* 468–469.

Tarnowski, K. J., & Nay, S. M. (1989). Locus of control in children with learning disabilities and hyperactivity: A subgroup analysis. *Journal of Learning Disabilities, 22,* 381–399.

Turnbull, A. P., Turnbull, H. R., Shank, M., & Leal, D. (1995). *Exceptional lives.* Columbus, OH: Merrill.

U.S. Department of Education. (1993). *Fifteenth annual report to Congress on the implementation of the Individuals with Disabilities Education Act.* Washington, DC: Author.

Varnhagen, C. K., Das, J. P., & Varnhagen, S. (1987). Auditory and visual memory span: Cognitive processing by TMR individuals with Down syndrome or other etiologies. *American Journal of Mental Deficiency, 91,* 398–405.

Violette, J., & Swisher, L. (1992). Echolalic responses by a child with autism to four experimental conditions of sociolinguistic input. *Journal of Speech and Hearing Research, 35,* 139–147.

Vogel, S. A. (1977). Morphological ability in normal and dyslexic children. *Journal of Learning Disabilities, 10,* 35–43.

Wallach, G. P., & Butler, K. G. (1994). *Language learning disabilities in school-age children and adolescents.* New York: Merrill/Macmillan.

Wallach, G. P., & Miller, L. (1988). *Language learning disabilities in school-age children.* Baltimore, MD: Williams & Wilkins.

Watkins, R., Rice, M., & Moltz, C. (1993). Verb use by language-impaired and normally developing children. *First Language, 13,* 133–144.

Wetherby, A. M. (1986). Ontogeny of communicative functions in autism. *Journal of Autism and Developmental Disorders, 16,* 295–316.

Wetherby, A. M., & Prizant, B. M. (1989). The expression of communicative intent: Assessment issues. *Seminars in Speech and Language, 10,* 77–94.

Wetherby, A. M., & Yonclas, D. G. (1989). Communicative profiles of preschool children with handicaps: Implications for early identification. *Journal of Speech and Hearing Disorders, 54,* 148–158.

Wiig, E. H. (1990). Language disabilities in school-age children and youth. In G. H. Shames & E. H. Wiig (Eds.), *Human Communication Disorders* (3rd ed.), (pp. 193–220). Columbus, OH: Merrill.

Wing, L. (1988). The continuum of autistic characteristics. In E. Schoper & G. Mesibov (Eds.), *Diagnosis and assessment.* New York: Plenum.

Wren, C. (1985). Collecting language samples from children with syntax problems. *Language, Speech, and Hearing Services in Schools, 16,* 83–102.

Zentall, S. S. (1985). A context for hyperactivity. In K. D. Gadow & I. Bialer (Eds.), *Advances in learning and behavioral disabilities* (Vol. 4). Greenwich, CT: HAI Press.

CHAPTER 4
Working with Families

Nancy Robinson

The practices that professionals use to work with families of children with disabilities have received considerably increased attention in recent years. However, the practices used to work with *families* have not received the same degree of attention that is applied to direct intervention practices with individual children. While service providers in special education, speech and language pathology, early childhood education, and regular education all have interactions with families, the focus on family members in the intervention process with young children is often inconsistent. This chapter will focus on family members as the *primary* communication and language intervention partners with young children. Clearly, when one considers that family members are typically the first and most constant language partners with young children through the developmental years, parent involvement in language intervention is a valid goal. However, this does not imply that parents must always meet professional expectations for involvement, such as implementing prescribed language intervention programs with children at home. Effective methods that are used to involve parents are responsive to individual family preferences, strengths, values, and needs.

Systematic attention to building partnerships with family members in the process of serving children with communication and language disorders is critical as a result of changing policy and practice in education, special education, and related services for children and youth. There are three major premises that support the rationale for family members and providers to work closely together around communication and language intervention with children. These premises are based on research in early language development, recent education legislation and policy, and diverse family demographics in the United States. Together, they support a significant shift in the way that professionals think and act toward parents and family members of children with disabilities. First, support for parents to provide positive communication interactions with young children with communication disorders contributes to positive outcomes for language assessment and intervention for children. Second, recent educational legislation related to young children with disabilities requires that families have a central role in decision making about programs for their children. Third, changing demographics of families in the United States and jurisdictions require expanded professional roles to work with families in increasingly diverse social and cultural contexts. Each of the above premises is discussed.

FAMILY ROLES IN COMMUNICATION AND LANGUAGE DEVELOPMENT.　For young children, communicative interactions occur most often within the context of the family. Research conducted over the past two decades (Snow, 1979; Snow & Ratner, 1984; Snow, 1984) has established the importance of caregivers' communication on the social, emotional, and language development of young children. Reported findings of studies in the area of parent-child interaction have yielded implications and guidelines for professional intervention with the parent-child dyad including the following:

- Parents' positive interactions with their children convey positive affect and security and contribute to an environment that invites further communication.
- Parents' interactions with their young children provide "scaffolding" and encouragement for children to develop more sophisticated communication and language forms.
- Parents' interactions with their children are related to the child's social interactions with siblings and peers in other settings, such as preschool and daycare.

Parent involvement in early language intervention is critical.

- Responsive interactions between parents and their infants are related to later communication and language development skills of those children.

Studies of the effects of the roles of parents and caregivers in support of language development of young children will be discussed later in this chapter.

CHANGES IN SPECIAL EDUCATION AND RELATED SERVICES POLICY. The role of family members as key decision makers in services for their children is strengthened by recent shifts in policy and legislation. Professionals involved in the identification, assessment, program planning, and remediation of communication disorders are currently challenged to consider the broader context of family and community environments, with family members at the center of services and supports provided to their children with disabilities. The professional roles and skills that are emphasized in clinical training programs with children are not adequate to accommodate family involvement and support in all phases of services for children with special needs in communication and language development. Attributable largely to the influence of early intervention legislation (Part H of the Individuals with Disabilities Education Act), a new focus on family roles in the intervention process with children with special needs has emerged. A central focus on family roles is particularly appropriate when applied to children with communication and/or language disorders.

FAMILY DIVERSITY. The rationale provided by studies of parent-child interaction for professionals to work closely with caregivers is clear. However, it must be tempered with the knowledge that current intervention models are based on families of North America, and that recommended strategies for positive parent-child interaction are culturally bound to a U.S. mainland, White American model. For example, parents of Asian, Pacific Island, Hispanic, and African American descent have reportedly more nonverbal styles of interaction with their children than White American families. The effects of diverse languages and cultural styles of interaction with children are not known; there is not one particular cultural style of parent-child interaction that is known to promote increased language development over another cultural style.

Most models for early language intervention do not consider the effects of culturally diverse backgrounds on language learning.

This chapter is focused on professional and family partnerships in communication and language intervention with young children and is divided into three major sections. The first section will examine the bases of family involvement in communication and language intervention from policy, research, and cultural perspectives. Initially, it is important to understand changing policies and legislation related to family participation and professional approaches to involve families in specialized services for children with disabilities.

The second section of the chapter will present strategies whereby the practitioner and student may enhance family involvement and family-professional partnerships in communication and language assessment. A summary of recommended practices to involve family members in assessment and intervention processes is presented.

The third and final section of the chapter addresses family-centered practices in intervention with children with communication disorders and family members. Three case studies are presented with direct application of recommended practices to maintain a central focus on the family as the most important context for language intervention activities.

In their recent textbook, Paul and Simmeonson (1993) stated six general principles to guide professionals in their work with families. In adopting these guidelines, professionals in speech, language, and communication intervention with children are encouraged to develop

1. an appreciation for the developmental course of the life of a family with a child with a disability;
2. a central interest in the experiences of the families;
3. respect for ethnicity as an organizing framework for understanding families;
4. a focus on the ethical implications of all aspects of professional decisions that affect families;
5. a particular emphasis on the social and cultural complexity of providing care for and with families who have children with disabilities; and
6. a commitment to both sharing the vision of diversity and sensitivity to the spiritual and social lives of families.

Throughout the remainder of this chapter, these guidelines will provide the parameters and quality indicators for family and professional partnerships in speech, language, and communication assessment and intervention services with children.

PREMISES OF FAMILY INVOLVEMENT IN COMMUNICATION AND LANGUAGE INTERVENTION

Roles of Family Members in Language Development: Motherese Reexamined

Interventionists should respect and appreciate the developmental stage of the family.

The importance of the family context as the most frequent communication environment for children emerges from the fact that family members or other primary caregivers (in the case of foster or adoptive care) are the first and foremost language partners with young children. Caregivers respond to even tiny infants with spoken language and nonverbal communication, providing stimulation and opportunities for infants to discriminate between subtle speech sounds, intonation, pitch, volume, and eventually the meaning of words. Infants learn that words are associated with daily events, people, actions, foods, and position in space through a process of interaction with caregivers and the environment. While language development is still not precisely understood, normally developing infants move into verbal language and toddlerhood through a process that demonstrates children's innate capacities and the supportive role of caregivers who respond to every burp, cry, vocal, and verbal utterance that they make with physical care and verbal language (Snow, 1979). The unique style of adult language used with young children has been called **motherese,** primarily because mothers and infants are most often studied in parent-child interaction. Motherese could easily be *fatherese,* or *siblingese.*

> Motherese might also be called fatherese, or siblingese.

The specific modifications that are commonly found when adults talk to young children include *raised pitch, slowed rate of speech, shortened phrase length, repetition, parallel talking,* and *simplified vocabulary* (Snow & Ratner, 1984). Grieser and Kuhl (1988) reported findings of universal characteristics of motherese across Chinese, English, and German, including shortened phrase length and heightened intonation. These findings indicate that caregivers and family members are keenly aware of the less developed communication and language skills of young children. Their accommodations are made in a natural and consistent manner.

The effects of motherese (used broadly to include other family members) have been reported to have variable effects on the verbal language development of young children. Several studies in the early 1980s reported positive effects of motherese on the language development of normally developing children, including increased vocabulary and phrase length (Kemler-Nelson, 1989; Weber-Olsen, 1984). In studies of this type, it is difficult to determine if gains in verbal language production were due to parents' heightened verbal stimulation of their children or maturational factors in children. More recently, Kennedy, Sheridan, Radlinshi, and Beeghly (1991) studied relationships between language comprehension, expression, and symbolic play schemes in children developing normally and in children with language delays. The findings reported greater variability in play and language behavior in children with language delays. Hampson and Nelson (1990) also reported findings that individual differences in children were more significant than the effects of motherese on the language development of children between the ages of 13 and 20 months.

Beyond motherese, which focused on the effects of caregivers' spoken language addressed to children upon the child's language development, the social context and more general characteristics of parents' responsiveness to their young children have been widely studied under the rubric of *parent-child interaction* (Swanson, Leonard, & Gandour, 1992; Comfort & Farran, 1994; Snow, 1979; Santarcangelo & Dyer, 1988; Barnard, 1978). There have been many studies over the past several years to examine similarities and differences of parents' communication styles (again, primarily mothers are studied) and the effects of different styles on the communication and language development of young children with disabilities. One hypothesis that is posed in studies of parent-child interaction is that children with disabilities communicate less with their family members and, therefore, require more sensitive and responsive partners. Conclusions to date show that parents of children with and without disabilities communicate generally the same way with their children, although parents of young children with developmental delays showed an increased *rate* of communication in some studies (Field, 1983). Increased rate in adult communication may be a result of the tendency for caregivers to provide more stimulation to a child who is less responsive. Findings regarding the impact of adult communication on the child's development of communication and language skills vary depending on the child's age, developmental level, and disability.

An additional variable of parents' interactions with young children with language delays includes differences between mothers and fathers. Girolametto and Tannock (1994) reported differences in interaction styles of mothers and fathers with their preschool children with developmental delays. Fathers were more *directive* in their interactions, changing topics and taking more turns in conversation, when compared to mothers' interactions with their children.

Adult responsiveness seems to impact child language development.

The degree of adult responsiveness to young children is reported to have an impact on child development outcomes. Responsivity is defined in one study as the adult's ability to recognize the child's behavioral cues and to provide contingent, appropriate, and consistent responses to those cues (Wilcox, Kouri, & Caswell, 1990). The context of communication between caregivers and children is established long before words are ever used, largely because the older family members (including parents, siblings, and relatives) attribute meaning to the infant's incidental behaviors. Sensitive responses from communicative partners (most often, family members) support children to expand the types of meanings they can convey through nonverbal means and to move into verbal means of communication and symbolic language. Consistent responsiveness of caregivers is thought to contribute to the child's understanding and use of consistent communicative signals (Snow, 1984).

While it has been hypothesized that mothers of children with disabilities are less responsive to their children than mothers of children who are nondisabled, Wilcox, Kouri, and Caswell (1990) found no significant differences in the responsiveness of adults to preverbal communication between children with disabilities and normally developing children. They also reported that caregivers of both types of children often "missed" communication from the children. They suggested that the most sensitive caregivers consistently responded in meaningful ways to children and that the presence of a disability did not cause consistent differences in caregivers' responsivity. The implications of this study are that caregivers of young children with disabilities need support to become aware of "missed opportunities" and to increase sensitivity to the child's communicative attempts.

The differences in adult responsiveness to children with specific language impairment (SLI) and children developing language normally (LN) were studied by Johnston, Miller, Curtiss, and Tallal (1993). Findings indicated that the children with SLI were more vulnerable to the style of adult language and verbal interaction with children. Children with SLI used single-word responses more often in their responses to questions than LN children of the same language age. The authors interpreted these findings to show that adult conversational style significantly affects the type of responses used by SLI children, limiting their opportunities to learn language variety and complexity.

Several recent studies have examined the effectiveness of teaching adults to increase their responsiveness to young children with developmental delays (Johnston, Miller, Curtiss, & Tallal, 1993; Warren, Yoder, Gazdag, Kim, & Jones, 1993; Yoder, Warren, & Gazdag, 1994). Positive effects to increase communication skills of the children in each study are related to both the techniques used by parents in addition to the individual characteristics and developmental stages of the children in each study.

For example, Warren and others (1993) found positive effects when using **milieu approaches** to increase prelinguistic communication skills of four young children with developmental delays. Milieu approaches to language intervention were adapted for children at the prelinguistic stage, and adults were instructed to use strategies found in typical parent-child interaction that include **contingent imitation, responsivity, following the child's lead, linguistic mapping,** and **social routines.** Three key milieu methods were used that included (1) eliciting child communication behaviors through the use of the above techniques; (2) providing language models through naming objects and actions that the child attended to; and (3) embedding teaching within developmentally appropriate routines. Results found in single-subject measures with each child showed increases in prelinguistic skills of requesting and increased commenting in one subject.

Further studies by Yoder and others (1994) generalized effects of adults use of milieu techniques to increase the *intentional* communication skills of young children. Intentional communication skills measured included the child's repeated looking, gesturing, and vocalizing toward parents and toys to signal requesting and/or commenting. A further finding reported in both studies was the effect of increased communication of young children to further prompt parents and other caregivers to respond. The effect of child behavior to further engage adults and to increase interaction is referred to as a *transactional* effect. The implications for intervention with young children with language delays, family members, and other adult caregivers are important not only to support communication development of the child, but also to increase the ability of the child to influence adult behavior and environmental responses.

In addition to studies with children at the prelinguistic stage, adult responses to children are studied in the preschool population. Kaiser and Hester (1994) employed **enhanced milieu teaching (EMT)** to include environmental arrangement of toys, responsiveness of adults, and incidental language teaching techniques with six children with communication delays. They reported increased communicative utterances and vocabulary.

Children with language
disorders are less capable of
maintaining conversations.

The above findings from studies of the effects of adult language and communicative responses with young children on the way that children learn to communicate nonverbally and verbally have implications for the models of language intervention that professionals develop with families. To date, there is increasing support that adult interactions with young children have a significant effect on prelinguistic and emerging language skills of young children with developmental delays, including nonverbal communication, vocabulary, and early semantic relations. Adults were found to communicate with children in similar ways regardless of the children's ability to use verbal language and preverbal communication. However, children with language disorders were found to be less capable "to keep conversations going" with caregivers. The limited verbal language and communication of children with language disorders may lead to "missed opportunities," as adults were found either to (1) speak for the child, or (2) limit the variety of responses to the child. Family members of children with communication and/or language disorders need support to understand the individual communication patterns of their children and to increase opportunities for their children to participate in communication interactions throughout the day, using gestures, sounds, words, or a combination of all communicative behaviors. The need for increased opportunities to communicate about daily experiences supports the milieu approaches to language and communication intervention. The primary focus of these interventions is to assist children with limited communication and language skills to learn about communication in natural contexts and to participate more fully in a variety of communicative behaviors, in addition to increasing spoken language.

POLICY PERSPECTIVES OF FAMILY INVOLVEMENT IN COMMUNICATION AND LANGUAGE INTERVENTION

Roles of Family Members in Communication and Language Intervention: Policy Perspectives

Parents have always played a critical role in services provided for children with disabilities. Professional perceptions and understanding of parents' roles have evolved in an ever-widening circle of awareness, with families at the center of that circle. The roles that parents have played in historical developments related to services for their children have always been the major force in the development of social policy and legislation for individuals with disabilities. Turnbull and Turnbull (1990) identified eight stages of development over the past several decades in which professional concepts of parents changed. Professional perceptions of parents have moved from casting parents in the role of being somehow to "blame" for disability in a child to understanding that parents are family members with multiple roles and responsibilities. The historical professional views of parents are outlined in Table 4.1.

> Professionals now have more respect for and better understanding of the multiple and complex roles and responsibilities of family members when there is a child with disabilities.

While current policies and practices with families are more supportive in involving families in flexible ways than in the past, stereotyped attitudes about parents are perpetuated and remain with many providers and health and educational service systems available today. Social change is uneven, particularly in established institutional practices. Models of service delivery were created in the 1960s and 1970s, following significant increases in federal and state funds for services to persons with disabilities. Following World War II, the return of veterans with a range of severe physical, emotional, and intellectual disabilities provided a rapid increase in social consciousness regarding persons with disabilities. Legislation flourished and, consequently, changes in social policy and program development were made to accommodate the vast numbers of veterans in need of services. Beginning in the late 1960s, children and elderly persons with disabilities also benefitted from increased services and attention to medical, educational, and social needs (Paul, Porter, & Falk, 1993).

The proliferation of political advocacy, research, treatment programs, educational services, and other activities intended to improve the welfare of persons with disabilities was perhaps more significant during this period than at any other time in history. However, the models developed at that time were largely based on medical intervention,

TABLE 4.1   Historical roles assigned to parents of children with disabilities

Parents as the Problem Source	Prior to the 1930s, the *eugenics movement* was established through documented cases of familial patterns of mental retardation and delinquency over several generations. While the conclusions that parents caused "defective traits" in their children were faulty, laws were made that prevented people with mental retardation from marrying and having children.
Parents as Organization Members	From the 1930s until the 1950s, parent organizations were the primary advocates. Today's organizations have their roots in parent organizations of this period in history, including the Association of Retarded Citizens, United Cerebral Palsy, the National Society for Autistic Children, the National Association for Down Syndrome, and the Association for Children with Learning Disabilities.
Parents as Service Developers	In the 1950s and 1960s, parent organizations took on the development of direct services, because their children were unserved. The focus of early programs was primarily on educational services for children with disabilities who were excluded from public school and recreation, residential, and vocational programs for family members with disabilities.
Parents as Recipients of Decisions	During the 1950s through the 1970s, increased educational services were opened up to children with disabilities. With more professional training available to serve these children, parents began to take a more passive role in the education process. As more children entered specialized services, professionals were expected to make decisions and parents were expected to agree and appreciate the services provided.
Parents as Learners and Teachers	From the late 1960s until the 1980s, intervention programs with children were considered to be most effective when parents also helped in teaching. The success of Head Start to involve parents in "Parent Training" and follow-through with young children was generalized to mean that *all* intervention programs required parent training and parent-as-teacher components.
Parents as Political Advocates	From the late 1960s until the present, parents are recognized as effective legislative advocates for their children with disabilities. Parent advocacy led to increased state services prior to 1975. While parent advocacy was effective in the legal system in landmark court decisions regarding *appropriate education;* the role of advocate also takes a toll on parents and families.
Parents as Educational Decision Makers	In 1975, the passage of the Education of the Handicapped Act (P.L. 94-142) established the role of parents as decision makers regarding educational programs for their children with disabilities. The role and responsibility to act as decision maker meant that parents were required to participate in educational planning through the IEP. While the intent of the law was to provide for *active decision making,* this expectation is not realistic for every parent.
Parents as Family Members	From the 1980s until the present, awareness of the family as a *system* of interrelated relationships and responsibilities has influenced professional expectations of parents. The needs of every member of the family must be considered for meaningful partnerships to develop.

Adapted from Turnbull and Turnbull (1990).

with physicians as the head and primary decision makers on the team. The imbalance in such a model continues today, due to the slowness of institutional change.

Recent changes in approaches to parent involvement for children with disabilities have occurred under the notion of **family-centered care,** a concept that shifts the focus of decision making from professionals to family members. The concept of family-centered care, its principles, and application have been widely discussed and demonstrated in early intervention services provided under recent federal legislation. For a more thorough discussion of family-centered care, the reader is referred to Shelton, Jeppson, and Johnson (1987).

One of the major proponents of a shift in the way service providers think about and interact with families is the Association for the Care of Childrens' Health (ACCH). In a 1987 publication, the ACCH outlined and defined guidelines of family-centered care for all professionals involved with families of young children with disabilities. Shelton, Jeppson, and Johnson (1987) summarized the elements of family-centered care as follows:

> Family-centered care recognizes that effective intervention depends on positive relationships with families.

1. Recognition that the family is the constant in the child's life while the service systems and personnel within those systems fluctuate.
2. Facilitation of parent/professional collaboration at all levels of health care including (1) care of an individual child; (2) program development, implementation, and evaluation; and (3) policy formation.
3. Sharing of unbiased and complete information with parents about their child's care on an ongoing basis in an appropriate and supportive manner.
4. Implementation of appropriate policies and programs that are comprehensive and supplying of emotional and financial support to meet the needs of families.
5. Recognition of family strengths and individuality and respect for different methods of coping.
6. Understanding and incorporating the developmental needs of infants, children, and adolescents and their families into health care delivery systems.
7. Encouragement and facilitation of parent-to-parent support.
8. Assurance that the design of health care delivery systems is flexible, accessible, and responsive to family needs. (p. 71)

The importance of family-centered care as a philosophy and approach to developing effective partnerships with families has far-reaching effects on professionals' interactions with family members.

The most critical elements of family-centered care are the understanding (1) that children are part of families, and (2) that effective interventions are built on positive relationships with individual families. Shelton, Jeppson, and Johnson (1987) cited Turnbull and Summers (1985), who compared family-centered care to the "Copernican Revolution." Copernicus reversed our conceptualization of the universe by placing the Sun, rather than the Earth, at the center of the universe. The parents, professionals, and policy makers who conceptualized family-centered care reversed our conceptualization of professional services. Rather than professionals at the center of the service system, making decisions about children and parents, *families* were placed at the center, with supports and services revolving around them.

Almost 10 years after the passage of P.L. 99-457 (now Part H of IDEA), professionals in health, human services, and education are making changes in policy and practices that move families to the center of decisions and services for their children. One of the major difficulties for full implementation of family-centered care is the need for professionals to become flexible and willing to forgo prior agendas.

The challenge for professionals has been to relinquish control over decision making to families.

The practice of family-centered care is based on knowledge of *family systems* theory, most clearly described by Turnbull and Turnbull (1990), "which views the family as a unique social system with unique characteristics and needs." When families are viewed as interacting systems, one can appreciate the impact of roles and responsibilities of parents, siblings, and other family members on all parts of the system. For example, if the language interventionist recommends that a mother spend time each day to review vocabulary words with her child, this may mean additional time that is not available in the daily schedule. In order to follow through, the mother will have to give up something else, such as reading the paper or taking a walk with her neighbor. While this may seem a small change to make, it may mean less opportunity for the mother to relieve her own daily stress and, consequently, affect her interactions with other family members. In subtle but significant ways, the practice of family-centered care requires that professionals work with families to provide services for children through the context of individual family needs and preferences.

Family-centered approaches provide opportunities to establish positive relationships with families and to create interventions for their children that fit into natural settings where families and children live. Crais (1991) recommends that professionals accept the following basic tenets in working with families of children with speech, language, or communication disorders:

1. Families are constant.
2. Families are equal partners in assessment and intervention.
3. The primary professional role is to support primary caregivers in the family to make decisions and to state individual preferences regarding services for children.

4. Families are individual systems, and professionals need to respond to this.
5. Families are community members first, so services should be conducted in "normalized" fashion.

The practice of family-centered care is not always easy. One of the first challenges is to develop consensus with family members regarding presenting concerns or preferences about the child's special needs. In order to build partnerships with families, professional understanding and acceptance of the family members' current perception of the problem is necessary.

For example, the assessment and diagnosis of speech and language disorders by the language interventionist is guided by the parents' perception of the problem. Rather than administering a standard protocol of assessment tools, the language interventionist first meets with parents or primary caregivers to define the communication behaviors of the child and to summarize presenting problems. Assessment then follows, based on the family definition of the problems. Following assessment by the language interventionists and related team members, the issue of diagnosis is very sensitive. The language interventionists may be required to use an official label such as "phonological disorder," owing to legal and agency policies. However, the diagnostic label poses a risk that the family's definition of the problem will be lost. Careful attention and communication with the family around this issue is critical, so as to develop terminology about the child's condition that includes family as well as professional terms.

The challenge to move from "client" or "child-centered" approaches to "family-centered" working with families requires that professionals relinquish control over decision making about services for the child. Crais (1991) recommends several steps that SLPs can take to change attitudes about decision making and assist families to gain skills in this area. These are:

1. comparison of personal beliefs and practices with those of family-centered care principles,
2. program evaluation and change, and
3. parent evaluation and consumer education.

Several tools are available for examination of personal beliefs and program evaluation. These include checklists developed by Shelton, Jeppson, and Johnson (1987) and others (Mahoney, O'Sullivan, & Dennebaum, 1990; Johnson, Jeppson, & Redburn, 1992). Evaluation of personal views and program practices is useful for individuals in preservice programs, practicing professionals, and program administrators. An example of such a tool for individual or group discussion is included in Figure 4.1. Parent evaluation and consumer education about family-centered practices will be discussed throughout the remainder of the chapter. The challenge for the remainder of the

Families and family life have changed dramatically in the past three decades.

FIGURE 4.1 Building family and professional teams: How are we doing?

		Never	Some-times	Always		Change Needed?	
1.	Do we ensure that parents have ready, direct access to all members of the team?	1	2	3	4 5	yes	no
2.	Do we provide parents with frequent opportunities to review the appropriate-ness and effectiveness of the IFSP/IEP?	1	2	3	4 5	yes	no
3.	Do we encourage parents to request a meeting of the team whenever they feel it is necessary? Are such requests honored?	1	2	3	4 5	yes	no
4.	Do we offer parents the option of being present at all team meetings concerning their children or family?	1	2	3	4 5	yes	no
5.	Does the team provide a supportive, comfortable atmosphere in which parents are free to ask questions and discuss their concerns?	1	2	3	4 5	yes	no
6.	Do team members provide parents with information that is understandable, meaningful, and responsive to their needs?	1	2	3	4 5	yes	no
7.	Do we issue a standing invitation for parents to share information with other members of the team and with other parents? Is the information parents provide acknowledged and used?	1	2	3	4 5	yes	no
8.	Are team reports written in clear, understandable language (free of technical "jargon") that is meaningful to parents?	1	2	3	4 5	yes	no
9.	Does the administration provide support to include family members as active participants on the team (e.g., variable scheduling, babysitting, access to records)?	1	2	3	4 5	yes	no
10.	Is there administrative support for staff to learn new skills to support each other in building effective teams (e.g., continuing ed.)?	1	2	3	4 5	yes	no

Ratokalu & Tada, 1993. Adapted from Johnson, B. H., Jeppson, E. S., & Redburn, L. (1992). *Caring for Children and Families: Guidelines for Hospitals*. Bethesda, MD: Association for the Care of Children's Health.

1990s and beyond will be in training professionals in clinical intervention and education settings to move from client to family-centered care, and from professional to family-driven systems of care. In practice, service providers are challenged to examine their personal and professional values regarding including key family members in decision making in all aspects of services for children with disabilities.

FAMILY DIVERSITY: LIFE-SPAN, SOCIAL-ECONOMIC, AND CULTURAL PERSPECTIVES

Related to the changing roles of parents in services for children with disabilities, expectations of parents in language assessment and intervention are also changing. As discussed in the preceding section, a greater understanding exists about the multiple roles that parents play as caregivers, partners to a spouse, family members, and community members. In addition to a more sensitive approach to individual differences among families—including cultural, social, geographical, and family structure—there is better understanding of the role of the caregiving environment in early child development outcomes. Early intervention and education for young children with disabilities have been shown to have positive effects on developmental skills in both short-term and long-term studies. Given the importance of the caregiving environment, the importance of parent involvement is compelling. However, if we are also to integrate sensitivity to differences among families, flexibility in professionals' expectations of family involved is required. Rather than seeking high levels of parent involvement as the outcome for working with families, other measures of success are needed. For example, families who report that services for their child were helpful and positive for the entire family are the critical measures of success.

> Family functioning is highly related to the life-cycle stage of the child with disabilities.

In order to enter into partnerships and to build positive relationships with families, certain considerations must be made of the changing social, economic, and cultural patterns of families in the United States and its territories and jurisdictions.

CHILDREN AND FAMILIES AT RISK.   In a recent review of the status of children and families nationally, the National Commission on Children (1991) reported on significant changes in family life. Table 4.2 shows risk factors that affect families nationwide. However, these trends are not new and not all are considered to have a negative impact on children. The increasing numbers of divorced parents as well as the resulting increases in the numbers of children who live with a single parent at some time in their developmental years have shown both positive and negative impacts on children. Some of the impacts include less time for parents to spend with children, yet children in

TABLE 4.2   Risk factors affecting families and children in America.

Changing Patterns of Families

- At any given time, $\frac{1}{4}$ of American children live with one parent.
- Most often, single parents are mothers.
- Less than $\frac{1}{2}$ of children of single parents have regular contact with fathers.
- Costs of housing, transportation, education, and health care have risen steadily since the 1970s.
- One-fifth of children live in poverty; children are the poorest Americans.
- Projections by the year 2000 show $\frac{1}{5}$ of women age 20 as mothers and more than 80% of these mothers as single parents.
- There are more mothers of young children working outside of the home than those who stay at home.
- One-third of single parents work more than 40 hours per week.
- Higher rates of immigration and mobility increase distances between members of extended families.
- There are increasing acts of random violence and predatory acts in urban areas of the United States.
- The Centers for Disease Control estimate that AIDS will infect up to 10,000 children by 1991.
- Nearly 10,000 children are homeless each night and families with children are the most rapidly growing group of homeless people.
- The number of children living apart from their families in foster homes, group homes, and residential treatment centers is increasing.

A Vision of America's Future, The Children's Defense Fund (1989); *Speaking of Kids: A National Survey of Children and Parents,* National Commission on Children (1991).

divorced families are found to be more independent and self-reliant than children in two-parent families.

The reported increases of violence and drugs in school settings have also heightened the anxiety for some families that their son or daughter will not survive adolescence. Increases in the numbers of children living in poverty as a result of being homeless, having divorced parents, and the trend for single mothers to live in poverty contribute to a complex set of environmental risks. Increased risk factors also add to the needs of these families for external supports through informal means such as churches, family, and friends, and through formal services in the community. For the professional who may intervene in situations of high risk for children, it is ever more important to determine the foremost concerns and needs for parents. For example, it may not be possible to involve families with multiple risk factors in traditional center-based services.

Life-Cycle Stages.   Another critical factor that influences families and the resources available to them is the **life-cycle stage.** Given points in the life cycle affect family participation in the system of care or services for the child with disabilities. Turnbull and Turnbull (1990) have described four life-cycle stages that influence family development and functioning including (1) early childhood, (2) elementary school, (3) adolescence, and (4) adult living. Changes within the family during each of these stages influence the level of family involvement in the services provided to children with disabilities.

For example, families of very young children often have competing tasks to accomplish, including the establishment of the *marital subsystem* within the family as well as the *parent-child subsystem*. The major concerns for families during the early childhood stage involve negotiating roles as couples, as individuals, and as parents. The birth of a child with a communication disorder during this time adds additional stress to the family system that is just becoming established. Parents are typically the ones to first report concerns if a child is not developing speech as expected. Parents are also the ones who then take on additional roles and responsibilities to seek appropriate services for the child. Professionals can more effectively build relationships with young families if they are sensitive to possible impacts of the early childhood life cycle for individual families.

Subsequent life-cycle stages, including elementary school, adolescence, and adult living, have unique challenges for families and the individuals within families. Elementary school years are characterized by less intensive parent-child interaction and involvement, as the child enters school and develops relationships with peers and teachers. Adolescence continues the development of individual values and socialization, with peer networks and sexual development as central in this process. Adult living is initiated as children are "launched" from the family home to independent lives in school or careers. Professional sensitivity to the life-cycle stages of individual families will enhance positive relationships with parents and family members around intervention with individual children.

CULTURAL DIVERSITY. The increasing cultural diversity in the United States in the past decade, with immigration of persons of Asian, Hispanic, African, Polynesian, Micronesian, and other non-White ethnicities, has important implications for professionals who work with families of young children. Current trends for increasing diversity in the United States are projected to continue with ethnic minorities increasing to one-third of the population by the year 2000. Adler (1990) has outlined the challenges for educators in general and for SLPs specifically. He stated that SLPs have greater challenges to meet the needs of diverse populations and to understand non-native English speakers than ever before. Adler further emphasized the need to address bilingualism and biculturalism directly. Not to do so, he cautions, is to send the message that indigenous cultures are of little value and that English-speaking educational institutions are inflexible and predominate for all persons.

The child's disorder may be in both languages, only in English, or only in the child's native language.

In identifying and addressing issues related to services and supports for families of diverse cultural groups with children with disabilities, there are several major questions posed in recent literature. These questions center on the determination of eligibility for specialized services for children with disabilities. The central questions are, "Does the child have (1) a disorder in both languages, (2) a disorder only in English, or (3) a disorder in the native language only?" Clearly, there are needs for professional involvement and services for children in all three of the above groups. Differing levels of professional involvement are needed in each, and professional roles cut across special education, ESL education, and regular education. Traditional discipline and service roles in school settings are challenged to accommodate the needs of the changing population of children of diverse cultural backgrounds and linguistic abilities. As a result, the consultant role for teachers and SLPs is becoming increasingly important. Professional and family relationships are the key to redefining the roles of educators and related service professionals who are mandated to serve children of diverse cultures who also have disabilities.

The challenges to professionals in education, early childhood, special education, speech pathology and audiology, and others include understanding and respecting diverse cultural styles, values, and preferences regarding child-rearing practices and, specifically, culturally acceptable communication styles with children. The challenges for professionals are to understand families' attitudes toward children with communication disorders, attitudes that may have a cultural base. Specific guidelines regarding cross-cultural attitudes and practices with respect to children with disabilities, specifically communication disorders, are limited.

In one relevant study, Bebour and Arthur (1992) surveyed college students of North American, Hispanic, Chinese, and Japanese birth regarding their attitudes toward communication disorders. Consistent significant differences were found between North Americans and the other three groups regarding attitudes toward persons with communication disorders. Persons of Hispanic, Chinese, and Japanese birth responded that emotional pathology and "lack of effort" were personality characteristics among persons with communication disorders, indicating the view that individuals with communication disorders were inherently responsible for their own disabilities. Attitudes among college students of North American birth toward persons with disabilities were found to be more variable and not focused on pathology of the individual.

Increasingly, attention in special education and related services, including speech and language pathology, is directed to the needs for professionals to increase knowledge and understanding of diverse cultures and educational practices. Several authors (Anderson, 1991; Hanson, Lynch, & Wayman, 1990; Terrell & Hale, 1992; Damico &

Damico, 1993) have stressed the importance of professional training and education to increase sensitivity to diverse cultures and traditions among newly immigrated groups for the purpose of improving multicultural services for children with disabilities. Anderson, in particular, has emphasized the impact of culture on family roles and responsibilities and the language development of young children. Anderson has advised professionals to recognize the limitations of personal belief systems and to learn about specific cultures that are most diverse from one's own. Hanson, Lynch, and Wayman (1990) provided guidelines to increase cultural competence in supporting families of children with disabilities:

Families' attitudes toward communication disorders are likely to be culturally based.

1. Describe the ethnic group with which the family identifies; for example, know the family's country of origin, its language, and the size of its ethnic community in the local area.
2. Identify the social organization of the ethnic community, including those organizations with leadership roles and related resources.
3. Describe the current belief system including values, ceremonies, symbols.
4. Learn about the history of the ethnic group and current events directly affecting family life.
5. Determine how members of the community gain access to and use social services.
6. Identify the attitudes of the ethnic community toward seeking help.

These steps can be specifically applied in the assessment and intervention planning process. As many authors have discussed, assessment instruments are often biased in favor of native English speakers. In order to minimize testing biases and to obtain valid information regarding the child's communication and language development status, building a relationship with families prior to assessment can be helpful in gaining knowledge of possible cultural expectations that parents may have of the child and perceptions of the child's abilities in the native language. Further, the need for an interpreter can be addressed through prior contact with the family, either through a home visit or meeting with parents and/or key representatives of the family in the school or clinic setting. Through prior contact and discussion with family members, the professional will gain understanding of the family concerns and values regarding the child's use of English and the degree to which the native language and/or English are used at home. Specific areas of information that parents can address include the following:

1. The issue of deficit or difference, as the child may not be considered to have deficit in native language.

2. Information regarding resources in home to follow through on language development in English. (Are there any other English speakers in the home?)
3. Family resources and expectations of the child. (Who are primary caregivers in daily routines?)
4. Paralinguistic (how child communicates nonverbally) information in communication.

Following assessment, the determination of appropriate intervention services requires team consensus with key family members, as well as with professionals in education, special education, and speech/language pathology.

Damico and Damico (1993) focus on the role of language to socialize children in a given culture. They suggest that differences in social practices across cultures also result in language development differences. In mainstream culture, children with cultural and linguistic differences may take passive roles as a result of differences in spoken language codes due to "stigma"—reducing social learning opportunities. Through involvement and discussion with family members, either through interpreter services or through direct conversation with parents, professionals can increase awareness of the conversational/communication expectations in other cultures for young children. For example, a practice that is commonly used in U.S. mainland intervention to encourage verbal language with young children is to provide choices, such as "Do you want an apple or a cookie?" The child is then provided with a model of both words and is more likely to respond with the name or phrase to indicate the desired item than a simple "yes" or "no" response. However, such choices may not be realistic or accepted in other cultural groups either because of beliefs that children under a certain age are not expected to make decisions or simply because economic circumstances do not allow for providing choices in daily items offered to the child. Regular contact and relationship building with family members can assist professionals both to understand parent-child interaction patterns in the home setting and to design appropriate interventions with family input.

Differences in social practices across cultures contribute to language development differences.

STRATEGIES TO IMPLEMENT PARTNERSHIPS WITH FAMILIES IN COMMUNICATION AND LANGUAGE ASSESSMENT

The goal of working with families is not merely to seek their involvement in a peripheral way, but to focus all interactions toward one primary goal. This goal is to impact the quality of life positively for children and families. Based upon current understanding of the central role of families and caregivers in the context of the child's daily life, professionals are challenged to enhance the system of support

Intervention should positively impact the quality of life for the family.

around individual children. Dunst, Deal, and Trivette (1988) have called this **empowerment,** a process that supports family members in gaining control over life circumstances and in providing nurturing and care for family members. Bailey and Simmeonson (1988) have stated that the primary goals for the early intervention professional are to support families to care for their children, to enhance child development outcomes, and to facilitate positive interactions between caregivers and children in the family context. In working with families, professional activities support families to understand the child and to integrate the child into the family. Those professionals who are involved in speech, language, and communication intervention can aim for increased positive communication between the child and other family members. In the following discussion, several strategies will be outlined that support practices to assist families to integrate the child with a disability within the family, to increase positive communication between the child and family members, and to enhance developmental outcomes for the child in a positive manner.

Based on the preceding discussion of changes in policy and practices pertaining to the way professionals seek to involve families in speech, language, and communication programs for their children, there are multiple variables to keep in mind. Family preferences and resources for involvement in formal intervention services are related to the degree of stress on the family system. As reviewed earlier, cultural, economic, marital status, and life-cycle variables influence how family members choose to interact with professionals. The increasing diversity among families with young children and school-age children creates increasing challenges for professionals to provide supportive services.

The remainder of the chapter will address strategies to support partnerships with family members for the benefit of their children with communication disorders. Approaches that are based on recommended practices in speech and language pathology, special education, early childhood education, and early intervention will be discussed as they relate to each step of the assessment and intervention process. Following discussion of the recommended components of building partnerships with families, three case studies will demonstrate family and professional partnerships in language and communication intervention.

Supporting Families in Identification and Assessment

Assessment of speech, language, and communication disorders offers the initial point of contact for partnerships with families. The identification of concerns regarding the child's development is most appropriately in the domain of the family. In most cases, referrals for assessment are based on parental concerns, even when a professional makes the referral. Through maintaining a focus on the definitions and statements of the problem made by parents or other caregivers in the family, the "ownership" of the problem remains with family members.

Practices that place families in control of the assessment process, rather than as recipients of professional decisions about assessment, are more effective in consistently building trust and communication between parent and professional. For example, special education practices require signed parental consent prior to assessment of childrens' speech, language, and communication development. It is also often the practice to have parents complete written information regarding their concerns prior to the formal assessment. These are positive steps to seek information from parents that can be used to plan more meaningful assessments with children referred for speech, language, and communication assessments. However, often parents provide the requested paperwork but do not hear the results and/or the application of the information provided to the school personnel. A more supportive practice for families would include a meeting with parents, the child's teacher, and specialists who will be involved in more formal assessment. The purpose of an initial contact with family members when there is a concern reported regarding speech, language, or communication development is to begin relationship building that will be addressed throughout the process.

Initial contacts need not be extensive. However, even a brief, focused interview with family members can communicate professional respect and reliance on information provided by family members. The roles that family members can play in initial meetings and contacts are important to convey information to professionals in the following areas:

1. Family definitions of the child's apparent speech, language, or communication problem.
2. Family perceptions of the child's language development in a native language other than English.
3. Family relationships at home; who are primary caregivers who spend most time with child?
4. The level of care that is required for the child at home.
5. Family reports of child's health history and efforts to date for addressing reported communication problems.
6. Family preferences for information and future contacts/involvement around the child's assessment results and program planning.

Information from parents to address these areas can be gathered informally through discussion and talking with the professionals involved. Professionals can then review parents' responses and ask further questions to determine areas of emphasis in speech and language assessment.

Parents should know how the information they provide is used.

Supporting Families in Report Writing

Following assessment, the summary of information is often completed in the form of a written report. The format of assessment reports varies from handwritten notes to formal typed reports. Often in educational settings, time constraints require brief reports to accompany the Individualized Educational Program (IEP). Although parents' legal rights to information indicate that copies of all reports are available to them, actual practices vary widely regarding the written reports that are routinely provided to parents. With the knowledge that parents are entitled to all information regarding their children, the preparation and presentation of assessment reports becomes critical. The need for information that is understandable, useful, accurate, and helpful to the parent in understanding communication and or language problems of the child requires that reports are carefully done. Attention to the content and format of reports is essential if the information presented is to be accessible to families of diverse backgrounds. Discussion of the content and format of reports follows.

CONTENT OF REPORTS.   Traditionally, assessment reports have followed a medical model, with the presentation of background and diagnostic observations of clinicians. While legislation and policy require reporting of assessment findings by a multidisciplinary team, there is flexibility within the requirements to design the content of assessment reports to include family members. The key to including families in the determination of content of assessment reports appears to be maintaining a central focus with family members as the "owners" of assessment information. As emphasized in the preceding section, beginning with the parent report and family perceptions of concerns regarding communication, speech, or language development in children provides the basis for partnership in assessment and intervention. The assessment report is the next step in that process. Assessment reports typically contain data and results of formal assessment tools, as required by schools, hospitals, and insurance companies, as well as state and federal agencies. In addition to the required information, Overbeck (1992) recommends that the content of assessment reports reflect a structure and process based on priorities and concerns of family members, as follows:

All information about children's intervention needs should be "family friendly."

- Statement of family goals/preferences for assessment
- Assessment observations
- Care principles
- Summary and recommendations

Each of the above components of an assessment report is found in varying sequence and format in most professional reports. A sample report format is presented in Figure 4.2.

FIGURE 4.2 Sample report format

COMMUNICATION/LANGUAGE DEVELOPMENT
TEAM ASSESSMENT REPORT

NAME: DATE OF ASSESSMENT:
B.D.:
C.A.:
TEAM MEMBERS:

Background

Assessment Observations

    Family Preferences:

    Developmental Processes:

    Individual Differences:

    Communicative Contexts:

    Team Model:

    Intervention Principles/Strategies:

Summary and Recommendations

The importance of these components is not derived from what they are called or the order of presentation, but from the content and representation of family concerns and preferences. The following suggestions are more detailed descriptions based on the recommended model developed and adapted from Overbeck (1992). Figure 4.3 provides an example of excerpts from one team report and the inclusion of the individual family concerns throughout.

STATEMENT OF FAMILY CONCERNS/PREFERENCES FOR ASSESSMENT. A suggested process to identify family concerns and preferences for assessment with children was outlined and discussed in a preceding section. Following initial conversations with family members regarding referral concerns, a summary statement is made to include family/parent descriptions of the child's communication problems as well as the major questions that the family wishes to have addressed in the assessment process. An example of one such summary statement is shown in Figure 4.3.

ASSESSMENT OBSERVATIONS. A subsequent section of the report contains summary information regarding child-specific performance using formal and informal assessment methods. In addition to the assessment data, observations of individual strengths are recommended. The focus on communication, speech, or language behaviors that the child uses to communicate with family members, peers, or others can assist families and professionals to work together in the identification of both the child's current abilities and future intervention steps.

CARE PRINCIPLES. Care principles refer to the basic information and approaches that are needed for all professionals to interact with a particular child and family. This information is not typically contained in assessment reports, and, if present, may appear in final recommendations. Critical in highlighting care principles separately within the report is the need to provide continuity of support across providers. An individual child and family may interact with nearly a dozen professionals, including the special education teacher, speech pathologist, occupational therapist, physical therapist, therapy assistant, social worker, physician, nurse, psychologist, and others. If basic care principles are stated by family members and written into reports, each of the individuals who interacts with the family will have critical information such as special health concerns, medication interactions, family stressors, cultural practices, and the like.

SUMMARY AND RECOMMENDATIONS. Summary and recommendations typically include assessment results and further referral and intervention recommendations. As a supplement to this section of traditional

All assessment information about a child belongs to the child's family.

The focus of observations is how the child uses speech and language to communicate.

FIGURE 4.3 Sample report content

One Team's Story

Portions of the team assessment report, completed with Naomi's mother, Ann, and her team members are highlighted. This first step was to develop an *Assessment Plan.* Ann met with her team to identify her family's preferences and concerns.

Ann's first concern was her request for clarification about her own expectations and those of the team. She stated her need to continue learning about Naomi's medical care and condition, to be knowledgeable of community resources, and to share her feelings of joy and challenge in caring for Naomi. She reminded the team to be practical and realistic in making recommendations. She stated her preference that issues be perceived as concerns raised in the course of her experiences in providing care for Naomi, rather than problems.

Ann and her team members further discussed *Care Principles,* or the way that she wants all professionals to interact with her family, and especially Naomi.

Caring for a child with special health needs, like Naomi, requires a lot of time, care, love, nurturing, and especially respect for her individuality. Respecting Naomi as an individual, no matter what her special needs are, opens up opportunities in creating a more natural working relationship in meeting her needs. For example, Naomi does not verbalize any words; therefore, Ann encourages her to develop ways of communicating her needs through gestures, noises, and/or movements to indicate what she wants. This form of respect allows Naomi to develop a sense of autonomy with her world.

Provision of care for a child with special health needs ultimately falls on the child's family. Naomi's family requires support, understanding, empathy, and, most importantly, respect for their abilities and capabilities as a family unit. Ann stresses her request that professionals address, listen, and hear her family's needs rather than make assumptions based on medical and other professionals' diagnosis. She also requested respect for her family's need for confidentiality, timetables, and their rights as individuals as well as a family in building a relationship.

To complete the report, the team provided *Summary and Recommendations* for other persons who may work together with Naomi and her family in the future.

Ann is very resourceful in seeking and obtaining needed services to help Naomi live a full and happy life and to enhance her family in functioning as a unit. Recommendations are addressed to those professionals who come into contact with Naomi and her family. First, include and encourage Ann's active input in the planning. Second, utilize and incorporate the family's daily schedule, other family members, transportation resources, etc., in all interventions. Finally, Ann stated, "Just because we are parents with a child with special health needs doesn't mean we have a problem. We are dealing with Noami's situation the best way we can and we don't see it as a problem."

assessment reports, specific intervention strategies are recommended. The integration of the preceding information, regarding family concerns/preferences, child strengths, and care principles forms the basis of intervention strategies. For example, Josh's family preferred that he attend a regular preschool. Although he communicated nonverbally, Josh demonstrated social responsiveness and gestures toward other children. As a primary care principle, his parents stated the need to provide Josh time to respond to new people and activities. Resulting strategies recommended by Josh's parents and team members included showing Josh new items such as foods, toys, and games before asking him to choose one item. The consistency between family preferences, assessment of the child's strengths, care principles, and specific intervention strategies provides continuity for families and children in the development of Individualized Educational Programs (IEPs), required in special education legislation for children ages 3 to 21 years and Individualized Family Support Plans (IFSPs), required by legislation for children with disabilities from ages 0 to 3.

STRATEGIES TO IMPLEMENT PARTNERSHIPS WITH FAMILIES IN COMMUNICATION AND LANGUAGE INTERVENTION

Supporting Families in Planning Intervention

One of the requirements of Part H of IDEA is "to enhance the capacities of families to meet the special needs of their infants and toddlers" (p. 238). If key family members are consulted in the assessment process, the development of goals together is a natural step in the process. Developing goals with families involves reviewing of assessment information, identifying child strengths and areas of need, prioritizing areas for further development, and deciding on the methods to achieve developmental gains.

Most professionals are familiar with the requirement to develop goals with families, particularly with legislated mandates for parental input to goals and objectives developed for individual program plans, through the IFSP or IEP process. The intent of the legislation—to develop goals, objectives, and intervention processes that match actual family concerns and preferences for young children with disabilities—is clear. However, development of collaborative goals is much less straightforward. In an attempt to accurately reflect family needs and preferences, the tendency in some early intervention programs in IFSP development has been to list family need statements as goals. However, this does not fully represent a collaborative discussion between family members and professionals expressing family expectations, preferences, and needs related to the child and professional assessment of the child's developmental strengths and needs.

The purpose of the IFSP process is to develop goals and objectives for infants and toddlers with disabilities and their families.

Bailey (1988) has suggested that goal statements in early intervention represent the *outcome* of a *process*.

> *Specifying family goals is a mechanism for clarifying the relationship between families and professionals and the expectations of that relationship. (p. 233)*

Inevitably, professionals question their role in becoming involved in issues with families that move beyond their specific role of providing therapy, education, and developmental support to the child. However, the context of intervention, particularly intervention around communication and language development, is clearly a family context. The inclusion of family needs and preferences in the identification, assessment, and intervention planning process will lead to more collaborative relationships and more collaborative goal statements with family members. Bailey further advises professionals to examine personal values carefully in the process of listening and responding to family preferences and choices, either explicit or implicitly stated. Similar to the assessment process, Bailey recommends several steps in the development of goals that include family concerns and preferences. These steps include: (1) develop a relationship with the parent or key family members; (2) identify strengths, needs of child; (3) identify family concerns, views of problem; (4) complete the professional assessment; and (5) determine the intervention target. Professionals are further advised to ask, "Are goals focused on the child, other family members, dyads within the family, or the whole family system?"

Supporting Families in Intervention

The planning to involve family members in the speech, language, and communication interventions includes consideration of family life. Naturalistic, or milieu, interventions are particularly suited to inclusion of family members. Several authors have recently presented intervention models in the context of natural, daily routines of children, families, and classrooms (Noonan & McCormick, 1993; Mac-Donald & Carroll, 1992; Norris & Hoffman, 1990a; Warren & Kaiser, 1986). Two of these approaches are described.

The **ecological communication model (ECO),** described by MacDonald and Carroll, has specific application to children with communication disorders and families in naturalistic settings. The context of play interactions is recommended for assessment and intervention processes with young children and family members. Assessment parameters in the ECO model focus on both communicative partners—the parent and the child—and include the activity level, joint focus of attention, balance of turns, imitation, initiated communication, and topic selections in the context of play. The reliability of the ECO assessment approach has been demonstrated to

The ECO assessment focuses on both partners in the communication process.

consistently rate the quality of child behavior during social play, turn-taking, nonverbal communication, language, and conversation. In the ECO approach to intervention, parents are supported to learn that communication "develops even from the (child's) simplest actions and sounds" and to respond to any child behavior that might be construed as communication. The effects of the ECO approach have been shown to increase levels of child imitation, vocalization, and turn-taking. Parents have demonstrated qualitative changes in communication behavior directed toward the child, with actions and words more closely matched to the child's play.

The validity of the ECO approach to focus communication and language intervention on the parent-child dyad, rather than on the individual child, is supported by the **continuity hypothesis** (Bates, Benigni, Bretherton, Camaioni, & Volterra 1979; Bates, Bretherton, & Snyder, 1988; Bates, Bretherton, Snyder, Shore, & Volterra, 1980; Bates, Camaioni, & Volterra, 1975; Bates, Thal, Whitesall, Fenson, & Oakes, 1989). The continuity hypothesis defines a continuous relationship from nonverbal communication in pre-language development to verbal language. The intervention approach used in the ECO model has demonstrated a positive effect to increase the "communicative match" between parent and child, thus facilitating the development of language in an interactive context.

Norris and Hoffman (1990b) have taken a similar approach to the ECO model, based on their findings that children in early stages of language development communicated with higher frequency and higher quality when interactions were child-initiated. Norris and Hoffman included children with complex medical histories between the ages of 2:6 and 2:10 years of age in their study. They found that children engaged in higher numbers of nonverbal gestures, vocalizations, and repeated actions with toys when adults provided "scaffolding" in order to structure and respond to the child's communication. Norris and Hoffman have outlined a three-step process, as follows:

1. Adults organize the play environment with developmentally appropriate toys and activities.
2. Adults provide communicative opportunities for the child through interpretation of child behavior, response, and expansion of child-initiated behavior. Suggested strategies include procedures referred to as: cloze, gestures and pantomime, relational terms, binary choices, turn-taking cues, and phonemic cues.
3. Adults provide natural consequences to extend communication in the forms of acknowledgment, nonverbal response, verbatim repetition, rewording, recounting physical actions/events, modeled dialogue, semantic contingency, personal reactions, questions/comments, predictions/projections.

While short-term effects of the naturalistic interventions described are promising, long-term effects of the above approaches are not reported. The benefits of naturalistic approaches for families are the informal implementation strategies and "goodness of fit" with daily routines in the home setting. Limitations are found in the extension of naturalistic interventions to older children. Further demonstration of these approaches will be provided in the case studies at the end of the chapter.

Summary of Family Support Practices in Communication Assessment and Intervention

In the preceding section, we discussed demonstrated strategies to support family members to play a central role in the assessment and intervention with children with communication disorders. The process to develop partnerships with family members was outlined and described. The underlying assumption of the support strategies described is that families have choices to determine the level and type of parent involvement that fits with other family variables. Variables present in today's families were discussed in the first section of this chapter. They include special needs of the child, parent-child interaction, parent and child rights, family economic welfare, marital status of parents, extended family involvement, diverse cultural backgrounds, and others.

> Intervention strategies are unlikely to be implemented unless they accommodate to the family's routines and lifestyles.

In order for professionals to be effective in working with families of diverse backgrounds at all levels of assessment, intervention planning, intervention activities, and evaluation, a range of skills and resources are needed. Key questions for professionals to ask themselves include the following:

1. What is the level of daily physical care involved for family members to assist the individual with a disability?
2. Who is at home during the day?
3. Who is the primary caregiver?
4. What cultural values and preferences are expressed regarding communication patterns in the family at home and in community settings?
5. What is the parent's estimation of child skills and problems?
6. Who are communicative partners for the child at home?
7. What is the English reading ability and language used by primary caregiver?
8. What are family goals and expectations for the child?
9. How will the family keep track of progress and observe daily gains?
10. What are services provided and what is frequency of parent contact?
11. What is the parent's preference for involvement in language intervention with the child?

Case Study Applications of Family-Centered Practices in Communication and Language Intervention

Three case studies are discussed to demonstrate support practices to involve families in communication and language assessment and intervention with young children.

Case Study No. 1: Infant

Tami, 8 months of age, is the youngest child born to Tony and Lea, who also have two young boys, ages 4 and 6. Tony originally immigrated from Cambodia to a major urban U.S. city over 20 years ago, and Lea recently immigrated. Tami requires considerable care from her family members. She was born full term but was readmitted to the hospital shortly after birth for heart surgery. Following surgery, Tami was discharged to her family with additional medical needs, including tube feeding. Since her discharge several months ago, Tami's parents and other caregivers in the home have found her to be often "fussy" and difficult to soothe. Recently, Tami's father reported that he is becoming very concerned about the amount of work that he must miss for this "special" child and the "fussy" state that she often exhibits.

FAMILY SUPPORT IN ASSESSMENT. The immediate need to support Tami's family members in the assessment process is to ensure that communication with the family is understood, by both the professionals and family members. Tami's father understands and speaks some English and his wife speaks in her native language from Cambodia. Discussion with the family is needed to determine their preferences for the use of an interpreter. If one is requested, that individual should be present in the initial meetings with parents to assist professionals to understand the primary concerns of family members. At times, limited English usage can become a barrier to fully supporting family members. In Tami's situation, her fragile health status requires that all professionals who interact with the child become aware of the high level of care required of her family members. Interpreter services are available through community organizations and cultural groups, and ready access to such services is essential in most urban areas.

> Understanding the demands that children's health care needs place on families is requisite to development of a support plan.

During the actual assessment, the professional team will need to determine the type of assessment that will address the concerns voiced by the family regarding Tami's developmental status and self-regulatory skills. Through a combination of observation with caregivers and play interactions, the team can establish Tami's responsiveness and receptive understanding of caregiving routines. Strengths observed will be shared with the family, and further description of Tami's communication and participation with family members will be requested. If an interpreter was requested by the family members, the interpreter will also be present to explain the team's assessment activities/questions and interpretation of observations with the parents.

FAMILY SUPPORT IN INTERVENTION.   Following assessment, review of the information gathered regarding Tami's particular strengths and needs may also require an interpreter for family members to fully understand the information shared. The multiple medical concerns and intensity of care for Tami need to be considered in planning intervention targets with her family. The family routine is focused on her physical care, nutritional intake, and calming Tami when she becomes distressed. Intervention planning and implementation will require that professionals and family members work together to find calming techniques to assist Tami to gain self-regulatory strategies. While developmental skills in feeding, communication, play, and social responsiveness to her family members are important, the priorities for intervention are determined by family concerns and preferences. Based on her parents' reported concerns, her high level of fussiness and sensitivity to the environment around her are the initial priority areas for further intervention.

Case Study No. 2: Preschooler

Naomi is now 3 years of age. She was the firstborn child of Ann and Mike, both in their late 20s. Naomi was born with multiple medical problems, including a heart defect, respiratory distress, cranial anomalies, and dislocation of her hip joints. Upon hospital discharge at 4 months of age, she had both tracheostomy and gastrostomy tubes in place to address respiratory and feeding needs. Since Naomi's birth, Ann has stayed home to provide round-the-clock care for Naomi, while Mike has become the sole breadwinner. Naomi has made slow but steady developmental gains and now can sit up independently. She enjoys playing with manipulative rattles, cause/effect toys, and face-to-face games. Naomi's communication with her family and other caregivers has always been nonverbal. Currently, Ann is concerned that Naomi is 3 years of age and facing transition to the school system. Ann has voiced her dream for Naomi to attend school and to communicate with other children. However, she worries that Naomi's many medical needs and nonverbal communication style require specialized care and intervention.

FAMILY SUPPORT IN ASSESSMENT.   To support Ann through this transition period and to include her expectations, needs, and preferences in the development of the IEP and subsequent services for Naomi, careful coordination with all sending and receiving team members is needed. Due to Naomi's individual communication needs, the SLP may be the most appropriate individual to assist Ann in the process. In order to determine the most effective ways to support Ann, it is important to discuss the degree of support that she will need at each step of the process.

Based on Ann's primary role in Naomi's care, it is expected that she will play a major role in the assessment process. All assessment processes need to begin with information provided by Ann and Mike, particularly Ann. Considering the extensive records that Ann maintains, it may be unnecessary for school personnel to repeat particular assessments, thus reducing the time and intrusion on Ann and Mike. Communication assessment may simply begin with Ann's descriptions of all forms that Naomi uses to communicate and the possible functions that she attributes to Naomi's communicative behaviors. Considering the extensive medical and health care needs that are provided to Naomi on a daily basis, professionals may find that an ecological assessment approach is most useful to determine the extent of Naomi's participation in daily care and social routines at home. An example of an ecological assessment of Naomi's care routines and participation in daily routines is shown in Table 4.3. The information gained from an ecological assessment such as the example shown provides more detailed assessment of Naomi's functional skills in daily routines and assists in the identification of the next steps in intervention.

FAMILY SUPPORT IN INTERVENTION. Following the completion of the ecological assessment profile with Ann, her priorities and goals for Naomi can be placed in the context of daily routines. This is especially critical for Ann, as Naomi requires continuous care related to her schedule of multiple medications, respiratory care, and tube-feeding routines. Upon examining Ann's schedule with her, the team may even feel that Ann is doing all she can to care for Naomi and to support her development within daily routines. Closer listening to Ann may reveal that her desire for Naomi to attend school, with proper supports, is a priority goal that is equal to skill development with Naomi. Underlying intervention with Naomi is the ongoing need to monitor her health and tolerance for new activities.

Support translates very simply to helping the family get whatever it is they want for their child.

Case Study No. 3: Kindergartner
Jon is 6 years of age and has been diagnosed with specific language impairment since he was 4 years of age, based on initial parent reports of difficulties in understanding his speech, dysfluency, and limited expressive vocabulary. Jon's parents, Alan and Kathy, just moved the family from an urban city on the East Coast to a rural area on the West Coast. He is the oldest of three children, with a younger brother age 3 years and a baby sister who is just 6 months of age. Jon's parents have accessed many resources and have found that the computer is an excellent tool to enable Jon to identify pictures and stories. Jon's parents have two major concerns: (1) they want him to have continuous speech-language services, and (2) they are concerned about the need for Jon to get along with other children his age in a regular classroom.

Table 4.3   Naomi's daily care routine

Context	Ann's Actions	Naomi's Actions	Possible Communication Goals
Bath time	Prepares bathing supplies, pours warm water in tub, holds Naomi with one arm and washes her with the other free hand	Smiles when seeing Ann pour the water in tub, reaches toward wash cloth, splashes her hands in the water	Increase Naomi's intentional communication with "bath time" objects
Aerosol treatment	Prepares aerosol materials, places mask on Naomi, and makes her comfortable during the 10-minute treatment	Allows Ann to place band around her head with aerosol mask, relaxes on pillow and Ann's leg during treatment	Increase Naomi's responsive actions to Ann's requests to "relax," "head back," etc., during aerosol treatment
Suctioning	Turns on suction machine in response to Naomi's coughing, assists Naomi to lift head up and back, inserts suction tube in Naomi's tracheostomy, and completes suctioning as needed	Coughs to alert Ann of need for suctioning, cooperates with Ann to lie back, allows suctioning to be completed and repeated, as needed	Increase verbal responses to Naomi's cues for suctioning and physical intervention
Dressing	Prepares clothing for Naomi, pulls on leggings with Naomi lying down, pulls Naomi to sit up and pulls on top	Cooperates in supine (lying on her back), reaches toward Ann to sit up, attempts to bring her trunk to sitting, sits up with help, puts arms up for dressing	Increase Naomi's initiated gestures to select clothing items she wants to put on first
Feeding	Prepares formula mixture, positions Naomi in reclining position on pillows, pours formula into feeding tube, and controls flow of formula into tube for 10–15 minutes until completely gone	Remains in reclining position, smiles at Ann, reaches toward Ann, and reaches toward feeding tube occasionally	Increase Naomi's demonstrated understanding of feeding implements and process through selecting items named by Ann
Going for walk	Places suction machine on back of wheelchair, packs extra supplies in large cloth bag, places Naomi in chair, straps her in, goes out for walk	Watches Ann prepare chair and supplies, lifts arms and trunk in attempt to sit up, looks and reaches toward chair, smiles when Ann puts her in chair, holds side handles of chair as they go outside	Increase Naomi's use of intentional gestures to indicate desires to go outside, be picked up, etc.

FAMILY SUPPORT IN ASSESSMENT.   Jon's parents clearly state their concerns for their son—to participate and to communicate with other children in a regular kindergarten classroom. The frequent moves made in the past several years have equipped his parents with complete records and experiences with multiple professionals, particularly SLPs. Their role as primary informants regarding Jon's communication, speech, and language abilities is evident. As Jon also requires occupational and physical therapy services, a team conference with his parents may be the most effective means to gather previous records and parent reports as the initial phase of the assessment. Further information regarding Jon's specific vocabulary and linguistic development can be gathered more carefully following his parents' review with the SLP and other team members. Supports needed by this family may be logistical in nature, as there are two younger children as well as adjustments to a new home. A home-based team assessment may be most effective for Jon's family. In the home setting, records maintained by Jon's parents can be easily reviewed. In addition, the team will have the opportunity to observe Jon's communication with his family members and other skills, including computer skills.

FAMILY SUPPORT IN INTERVENTION.   The concern expressed by Jon's parents to maintain continuity of SLP services, in particular, was defined as an equal priority to beginning in school. There is some immediacy in the needs for services for this particular child and family, as they are unsure of the length of stay in their new home before a new job assignment for the father will require a further move. In cases such as Jon's, an interim IEP is an option used in some states in order for immediate school placement and related services to begin. Completion of individual discipline assessment—the SLP assessment for example—may be ongoing for up to 30 days in some states prior to completion of the goals and objectives of the IEP. Advocacy and coordination roles may be necessary for the SLP to assist the team and Jon's family to provide timely services and educational placement. Further advocacy for Jon to access computer technology in the school setting, as an aide for language development and social interaction with other children, may be required.

Whether they provide medical, social, educational, or therapeutic services to children with disabilities, family-centered care is a challenge for all professionals.

SUMMARY

This chapter presented perspectives and strategies to build partnerships with families in the assessment and intervention with children with communication disorders. The central role of families to provide care and influence throughout the developmental years was emphasized. The point of view that family members are the primary contact point to begin and carry out speech and language assessment and intervention is supported with recent legislation and policy recommendations. The practice of family-centered care is a complex set of attitudes and skills on the part of professionals. The challenges to professionals in the area of communication, speech, and language intervention include the need to balance clinical excellence with support roles for individual families. In an era of cost containment for health, human services, and education, the challenge to provide clinical services to children and to support families will increase. However, policies and support roles for professionals and family members to work together in collaboration are established and demonstrated nationally. It is this author's hope that professional development for the reader will lead toward greater self-understanding and responsiveness to families with diverse cultures, strengths, and needs.

The effectiveness of involving parents in language intervention with young children has been demonstrated repeatedly. Recent publications support the role of parental involvement in language intervention in studies of the influence of parental stimulation and interaction with their young children on the academic and language abilities in early school years. There are many technologies and materials available to assist parents regarding effective interaction styles to support the language and learning development of the young child. However, with an increased emphasis on the importance of consistent caregiving and parental input in communication and language development, there is the temptation to require that all parents participate in similar ways to enrich the language and learning environments of their children. With a growing body of knowledge regarding strategies to provide family-centered care and culturally diverse approaches to child rearing and stimulation practices, professionals are required by best practice standards to empower families and to enable them to determine the most appropriate methods of intervention with their young children with disabilities. The challenge for all professionals who work with families and children in the development of communication and language behavior is to determine unique preferences, needs, daily routines, and communication patterns within individual families and, at the same time, to take advantage of the many parent education materials available to adapt and to implement with families of diverse needs and backgrounds in order to build on the communication strengths of both parent and child. More complex challenges and opportunities blur the traditional lines between roles of "parent" and "professional" to create partnerships with families and parents in the identification, assessment, and intervention process with young children.

REFERENCES

Adler, S. (1990). Multicultural clients: Implications for the SLP. *Language, Speech, and Hearing Services in the Schools, 21,* 135–139.

Anderson, N. B. (1991). Understanding cultural diversity. *American Journal of Speech and Language Pathology. 1,* 9–10.

Bailey, D. B., & Simeonsson, R. J. (1988). *Family assessment in early intervention.* Columbus, OH: Merrill Publishing Company.

Barnard, K. (1978). *Nursing child assessment satellite training.* Seattle: University of Washington Press.

Bates, E., Benigni, L., Bretherton, I., Camaioni, L., & Volterra, V. (1979). *The emergence of symbols: Cognition and communication in infancy.* New York: Academic Press.

Bates, E., Bretherton, I., & Snyder, L. (1988). *From first words to grammar: Individual differences and dissociable mechanisms.* New York: Cambridge University Press.

Bates, E., Bretherton, I., & Snyder, L., Shore, C., & Volterra, V. (1980). Vocal and gestural symbols at 13 months. *Merrill-Palmer Quarterly, 26,* 408–423.

Bates, E., Camaioni, L., & Volterra, V. (1975). The acquisition of performatives prior to speech. *Merrill-Palmer Quarterly, 21,* 205–226.

Bates, E., Thal, D., Whitesall, K., Fenson, L., & Oakes, L. (1989). Integrating language and gesture in infancy. *Developmental Psychology, 25,* 197–206.

Bebour, L., & Arthur, B. (1992). Cross-cultural attitudes toward speech disorders. *Journal of Speech and Hearing Research, 34,* 45–52.

Brazelton, T. B., & Als, H. (1979). Four early states in the development of mother-infant interaction. *The Psychoanalytic Study of the Child, 34,* 349–369.

Brazelton, T. B., Koslowski, B., & Main, M. (1974). The origins of reciprocity: The early mother-infant interaction. In M. Lewis & L. A. Rosenblum, (Eds.) *The effect of an infant on its caregiver* (pp. 49–76). New York: John Wiley & Sons.

Brown, W., Thurman, S. K., & Pearl, L. F. (Eds.). (1993). *Family-centered early intervention with infants & toddlers: Innovative cross-disciplinary approaches.* Baltimore, MD: Paul H. Brookes Publishing Company.

Bruner, J. (1983). *Child's talk: Learning to use language.* New York: Norton.

Clark, F. N., & Siefer, R. (1983). Facilitating mother-infant communication. *Infant Mental Health Journal, 4.*

Comfort, M., & Farran, D.C. (1994). Parent-child interaction assessment in family-centered intervention. *Infants and Young Children. 6,* 33–45.

Crais, E. (1991). Moving from "parent involvement to family-centered services." *American Journal of Speech-Language Pathology. 1,* 5–8.

Dale, P. S., Bates, E., Reznick, S., & Morisset, C. (1989). The validity of a parent report instrument of child language at twenty months. *Journal of Child Language, 16,* 239–250.

Damico, J. S., & Damico, S. K. (1993). Language and social skills from a diversity perspective: Considerations for the speech-language pathologist. *Language, Speech, and Hearing Services in the Schools, 24,* 236–243.

Dunst, C. J., Trivette, C., & Deal, A. (1988). *Enabling and empowering families: Principles and guidelines for practice.* Cambridge, MA: Brookline Books.

Field, T. (1983). High risk infants "have less fun" during early interactions. *Topics in Early Childhood Special Education, 3,* 77–87.

Girolametto, L., & Tannock, R. (1994). Correlates of directiveness in the interactions of fathers and mothers of children with developmental delays. *Journal of Speech and Hearing Research, 37,* 1178–1191.

Goldberg, S. (1977). Social competence in infancy: A model of parent-infant interaction. *Merrill-Palmer Quarterly, 23,* 163–177.

Gorenflo, C. W., & Gorenflo, D. W. (1991). The effects of information and augmentative communication technique on attitudes toward nonspeaking individuals. *Journal of Speech and Hearing Research, 34,* 19–26.

Gradel, K., Thompson, M. S., & Sheehan, R. (1981). Parental and professional agreement in early childhood assessment. *Topics in Early Childhood Special Education, 1,* 31–39.

Grieser, D. L., & Kuhl, P. K. (1988). Maternal speech to infants in a tonal language: Support for universal prosodic features in motherese. *Developmental Psychology, 24,* 14–20.

Hampson, J., & Nelson, K. (1990). Early relations between mother talk and language development: Masked and unmasked. In *Papers and reports on child language development, 29.* California: Stanford University, 787–785.

Hanson, M. (1983). Social Development. In M. Hanson, (Ed.). *Atypical Infant.* Baltimore, MD: University Park Press.

Hanson, M. J., & Krentz, M. S. (1986). *Supporting parent-child interactions: A guide for early intervention program personnel.* Integrated Special Infant Services Program, Department of Special Education. San Francisco State University.

Hanson, M. J., Lynch, E. W., & Wayman, K. (1990). Honoring the cultural diversity of the family when gathering data. *Topics in Early Childhood Special Education, 10,* 112–131.

Hart, B., & Risely, T. (1995). *Meaningful differences in the everyday experience of young American children.* Baltimore, MD: Paul H. Brookes Publishing Company.

Hayes, D. P., & Ahrens, M. G. (1988). Vocabulary simplifications for children: A special case of motherese? *Journal of Child Language, 15,* 395–410.

Ireton, H., & Thwing, E. (1974). *Manual for the Minnesota Child Development Inventory.* Minneapolis, MN: Behavior Sciences Systems.

Johnson, B., Jeppson, E. & Redburn, L. (1992). *Caring for children and families: Guidelines for hospitals.* Bethesda, MD: Association for the Care of Children's Health.

Johnston, J. R., Miller, J. F., Curtiss, S., & Tallal, P. (1993). Conversations with children who are language impaired: Asking questions. *Journal of Speech and Hearing Research, 36,* 973–978.

Kaiser, A. P., & Hester, P. P. (1994). Generalized effects of enhanced mileu teaching. *Journal of Speech and Hearing Research, 37,* 1320–1340.

Kaye, K., & Charney, R. (1981). Conversational asymmetry between mothers and children. *Journal of Child Language, 8,* 35–49.

Kemler-Nelson, D. G. (1989). How the prosodic cues in motherese might assist language learning. *Journal of Child Language, 16,* 55–68.

Kennedy, M. D., Sheridan, M. K., Radlinshi, S. H., & Beeghly, M. (1991). Play-language relationships in young children with developmental delays: Implications for assessment. *Journal of Speech and Hearing Research, 34,* 112–122.

Light, J., Dattilo, J., English, J., Gutierrez, L., & Hartz, J. (1992). Instructing facilitators to support the communication of people who use augmentative communication systems. *Journal of Speech and Hearing Research, 35,* 865–875.

MacDonald, J. D., & Carroll, J. Y. (1992). A social partnership model for assessing early communication development: An intervention model for preconversational children. *Language, Speech, and Hearing Services in the Schools, 23,* 113–124.

Mahoney, G., O'Sullivan, P., & Dennebaum, J. (1990). Maternal perceptions of early intervention services: A scale for assessing family-focused intervention. *Topics in Early Childhood Special Education, 10,* 1–15.

Mahoney, G., & Powell, A. (1985). *The transactional intervention program, preliminary teacher's guide.* Unpublished manuscript, School of Education, University of Michigan.

McCollum, J. A., & Yates, T. J. (1994). Dyad as focus, triad as means: A family-centered approach to supporting parent-child interactions. *Infants and Young Children, 6,* 54–63.

McDonald, L., & Pien, D. (1982). Mother conversational behavior as a function of interactional intent. *Journal of Child Language, 9,* 337–358.

National Commission on Children (1991). *Speaking of kids: A national survey of children and parents.*

Noonan, M. J., & McCormick, L. P. (1993). *Early intervention in natural environments: Methods and procedures.* Pacific Grove, CA: Brooks/Cole Publishing Company.

Norris, J. A., & Hoffman, P. (1990a). Language intervention within naturalistic environments. *Language, Speech, and Hearing Services in the Schools, 21,* 72–84.

Norris, J. A., & Hoffman, P. (1990b). Comparison of adult-initiated vs. child-initiated interaction styles with handicapped prelanguage children. *Language, Speech, and Hearing Services in the Schools, 21,* 28–36.

Overbeck, D. (1992). Transdisciplinary conjoint assessment with young children with special needs. Lanakila Infant Development Program. Honolulu, Hawaii.

Paul, J. L., Porter, P. B., & Falk, G. D. (1993). Families of children with disabling conditions. In J. Paul & R. Simmeonson (Eds.), *Children with special needs: Family, culture, and society.* (2nd ed.) (pp. 3–24). New York: Harcourt, Brace, Jovanovich College Publishers.

Paul, J., & Simmeonson, R. (1993). *Children with special needs: Family, culture, and society.* (2nd ed.). New York: Harcourt, Brace, Jovanovich College Publishers.

Ratner, N., & Bruner, J. S. (1977). Games, social exchange and the acquisition of language. *Journal of Child Language, 5,* 391–401.

Richard, N. (1986). Interaction between mothers and infants with Down syndrome: Infant characteristics. *Topics in Early Childhood Special Education, 6,* 54–71.

Santarcangelo, S., & Dyer, K. (1988). Effects on gaze and responsiveness in developmentally delayed children. *Journal of Experimental Child Psychiatry. 46,* 406–418.

Schubel, R. J., & Erickson, J. G. (1992). Model programs for increasing parent involvement through telephone technology. *Language,*

Speech, and Hearing Services in the Schools, 23, 125–129.

Shelton, T., Jeppson, E., & Johnson, B. (1987). *Family-centered care for children with special health care needs.* Washington, D.C.: Association for the Care of Children's Health.

Snow, C. (1979). The role of social interaction and the development of communicative ability. In A. Collins (Ed.), *Children's Language and Communication.* Hillsdale, NJ: Erlbaum.

Snow, C. (1984). Parent-child interaction and the development of communicative ability. In R. Schiefelbusch & J. Pickar (Eds.), *Their acquisition of communicative competence* (pp. 69–107). Baltimore, MD: University Park Press.

Snow, C., & Ratner, N. (1984). Talking to children: Therapy is also social interaction. Paper presented at the annual meeting of the American Speech and Hearing Association. November 1984, San Francisco.

Swanson, L., Leonard, L., & Gandour, J. (1992). Vowel duration in mothers' speech to young children. *Journal of Speech and Hearing Research, 35,* 617–625.

Terrell, B., & Hale, J. E. (1992). Serving a multicultural population: Different learning styles. *American Journal of Speech-Language Pathology. 1,* 5–8.

Turnbull, A. P., & Summers, J. A. (1985, April). *From parent to family support: Evaluation to revolution.* Paper presented at the Down Syndrome State-of-the-Art Conference. Boston, MA.

Turnbull, A., & Turnbull, R. (1990). *Families, professionals, and exceptionality: A special partnership.* (2nd ed.). Columbus, OH: Merrill Publishing Company.

Warren, S., & Kaiser, A. (1986). Incidental language teaching: A critical review. *Journal of Speech and Hearing Disorders, 51,* 291–299.

Warren, S. F., Yoder, P. J., Gazdag, G., Kim, K., & Jones, H. (1993). Facilitating communication skills in young children with developmental delay. *Journal of Speech and Hearing Research, 36,* 83–97.

Weber-Olsen, M. (1984). Motherese: The language of parent to child. Texas Tech, *Journal of Education, 11,* 123–141.

Wilcox, M. J., Kouri, T. A., & Caswell, S. (1990). Partner sensitivity to communication behavior of young children with developmental disabilities. *Journal of Speech and Hearing Disorders, 55,* 679–693.

Yoder, P. J., Warren, S. F., & Gazdag, G. E. (1994). Facilitating prelinguistic communication skills in young children with developmental delay II: Systematic replication and extention. *Journal of Speech and Hearing Research, 37,* 841–851.

CHAPTER 5

Policies and Practices

Linda McCormick

This chapter provides an introduction to key regulations of the Individuals with Disabilities Education Act (IDEA): assessment requirements, the Individual Family Service Plan (IFSP), the Individual Education Plan (IEP), the least restrictive environment mandate, and related services. This is followed by a discussion of recent paradigm shifts in the area of language intervention.

The new service delivery arrangements, which rely on collaboration, reflect radically different intervention priorities than past service delivery approaches. With respect to collaboration, diversity is both an advantage and a barrier. The key benefit of these arrangements is the wide range of skills that the different professionals contribute to the intervention process. However, the diversity of perspectives that the different professionals represent can also be an obstacle as it can be a barrier to collaboration and productive communication on behalf of children with disabilities. To be effective, consultation partners and team members must acknowledge differences in training, experiences, vocabulary, and underlying theoretical values; they then must work together to attain an integrated intervention. The last section of this chapter addresses this issue: how professionals can implement collaborative teaming and consultation arrangements in inclusive school settings.

IDEA REGULATIONS

In 1990, congress made two major statutory changes affecting special education law: (1) the Education for All Handicapped Children Act was given a new name—the Individuals with Disabilities Education Act (IDEA)—and amended to include provisions for transitional services and assistive technology as well as two new disability categories (autism and traumatic brain injury), and (2) the Americans with Disabilities Act (ADA) was passed. The ADA is basically a civil rights law that prohibits discrimination on the basis of disability and provides constitutional equal protection and due process. In a comparison of IDEA and ADA, Turnbull, Turnbull, Shank, and Leal (1995) note three major differences between the two laws. IDEA benefits persons with disabilities between the ages of birth and 21; ADA benefits *all* people with disabilities. IDEA benefits persons who are in school (or served by early intervention programs); ADA benefits persons with disabilities in employment and in a wide range of public and private services (in addition to educational settings). IDEA provides funds to state and local service agencies to help with the costs associated with serving persons with disabilities and it mandates provision of certain kinds of special services; ADA does not provide monies to support compliance (e.g., to defray the cost of building ramps and making restrooms more accessible facilities).

ADA is civil rights legislation.

IDEA regulations have an important and direct impact on assessment, planning, and special instruction. This section provides a brief description of these regulations.

Assessment Regulations

Recall from Chapter 4 that, under the IDEA, a child must meet the eligibility criteria for a disability group before special education or related services can be provided. The IDEA is very specific about the persons who can administer the assessment instruments used for eligibility determination and how they are to be administered. Evaluation must be by a multidisciplinary team. No single instrument may be used as the sole criterion for placement or planning. Assessment instruments must be

- administered in the child's native language,
- valid for the purposes for which they are being used, and
- administered by qualified personnel.

In addition to administering appropriate instruments and compiling a written report describing the tests and their results and findings, the multidisciplinary team members review and document anectodal records, work products, and data from classroom observations. After eligibility has been determined, decision making shifts to the IEP committee to determine the nature of the student's instructional needs and how and where they can best be met.

> The IEP committee determines the nature of the student's instructional needs and how and where they can be met.

The majority of children with moderate to severe disabilities are identified before they are 3 years of age. Others are identified when they demonstrate academic, social, or behavioral problems in preschool, kindergarten, or the primary grades. When a referral is made, the parents must consent to their child's evaluation. While the law does not require that parents be included in the assessment process, most school districts make every effort to solicit their participation. They provide information about their child's strengths and needs that is indispensable in helping to expand, clarify, and verify (or refute) test results.

> The law does not require involvement of parents in the assessment process but it is considered "best practice."

The Individual Family Service Plan (IFSP)

Part H of IDEA, which pertains to services for infants and toddlers with disabilities and their families, requires development of an IFSP for each eligible infant or toddler and his or her family. The IFSP is intended to be a dynamic *process* (gathering, sharing, and exchanging information) which, in addition to specifying services needed by the child and family, provides a context for establishing professional–family relationships. In most settings, the IFSP is continuously expanded and modified in response to the family's efforts to make informed choices about what early intervention services they want and need for their child and themselves. The IFSP process continues throughout the intervention.

Although the form used for the IFSP is relatively unimportant, there are very specific guidelines as to the information that needs to be assembled *in the course of the IFSP process*. Table 5.1 lists the types of information to include on the IFSP.

Note the requirement that the IFSP must include the name of a service coordinator or coordinators to coordinate and facilitate planning and intervention. This is one of a number of requirements for Part H that differ from mandates for children age 3 and above (Part B). Service coordination is intended to promote family independence and self-sufficiency by helping the family mobilize their resources to better meet their own and their child's needs.

Table 5.1   Required IFSP information

The IFSP should include
- a statement of the child's present functioning in cognitive, communication, social/emotional, physical, and adaptive development;
- the family's concerns, priorities, and resources related to their child's development;
- expected intervention outcomes, including criteria, procedures, and timelines;
- specific intervention services needed to meet the unique needs of the child and family;
- the natural environments where services will be provided;
- projected dates for initiation of services and expected duration of services;
- the name of a service coordinator(s) who will coordinate with other agencies and facilitate planning and intervention processes; and
- procedures to ensure successful transition from infant services to preschool services.

The service coordinator helps the family mobilize its resources on behalf of their own and their child's needs.

Some programs begin the IFSP process with blank sheets of paper rather than using a preprinted form (which can be intimidating to parents). Others use a simple form such as the IFSP form shown in Figure 5.1, which was developed by staff of the Zero-to-Three Hawaii Project. Note that Hawaii chooses to call the IFSP the Individual Family *Support* Plan. Also note that this IFSP was written by the child's parents. Similar to many other programs in the nation, the Zero-to-Three Hawaii Project encourages parents to write their own IFSP.

The Individual Education Plan (IEP)

The purpose of the IEP is to ensure that each eligible child receives appropriate and individualized education and special services. It is an agreement between the parents and the school stating what the child needs and what the school system will do to address the child's needs. The major components of the IEP are (1) the evaluation information indicating whether the student has a disabilitiy and that the student needs special education services and related services; (2) appropriate annual goals and short-term objectives, with criteria, procedures, and schedules that will be used to determine whether the short-term objectives are met; and (3) a statement of the appropriate special education placement and related services that the student needs, the amount of time the student will be in the general classroom with supplementary aids and services, and the specific related services the student will receive. Table 5.2 lists the information that the IEP must include.

FIGURE 5.1a

Zero-to-Three Hawaii Project
Hawai'i Department of Health

INDIVIDUAL FAMILY SUPPORT PLAN

Child's Name Nathan Takemoto   DOB 7-18-92
Prepared with Family By SELINA FLORES   Date 7-18-94

___ Interim
✓ Initial
___ Review

1. INFORMATION ABOUT THE CHILD

A. My Child Nathan has the following strengths, qualities & needs:

He is able to communicate through gestures. He knows what he wants and when he wants to do it. He is independent. He has good attention span and listening skills.

As Nathan's parent's we would like more information on what Nathan is doing, compared to other children his age, so we can determine if he has any needs.

B. Screening/Evaluation Tool: ______________ Date: ______________
Explanation/Notes:

C. Family strengths and resources related to enhancing the development of the child (optional):

As parents we understand Nathan's gestures and needs. We try to look at what he is doing through his eyes. We keep communication open with his sitter and she provides a nurturing environment. He has many relatives who cater to his every whim and are willing to do anything for him.

FIGURE 5.1b

INDIVIDUAL FAMILY SUPPORT PLAN

Zero-to-Three Hawaii Project
Hawai'i Department of Health

Child's Name _Nathan Takemoto_

Prepared with Family By _Selina Flores_   Date _7-18-94_

I/WE WANT:	WAYS TO GET IT & WHO CAN HELP:	TIME IT MAY TAKE:	WHAT HAPPENED:
1. Want Nathan to be able to communicate (talk) with us, to tell us what he wants, what's bothering him, or what he doesn't want.	1A. Mike/Patty can call Kapiolani Medical Center. 973-8235 and speak with Julie Robinson, who will schedule Nathan's appt. 1B. Mike/Patty will share information regarding Nathan's behavior with strangers, to promote a positive meeting.	by end of week - Friday 7/22/94 Prior to evaluation date	
2. Want to have Nathan's hearing tested to rule out any problems.	2A. Mike/Patty can call Kapiolani Medical center (973-8255), tell the receptionist they would like to schedule an audiology appt. for their son Nathan. 2B. Mike/Patty will call Selina (942-8245) with appointment dates & times for the authorization for services form (to ensure free services).	by end of week Friday, 7/22/94 As soon as the appts. are made.	
3. Want Nathan to interact with other kids (play, talk, defend himself).	3A. With Mike & Patty's permission Selina will write up their descriptions of Nathan's behavior and their concerns for 0-3 child psychologist M. Kопин, Ph.D. for a telephone consult. 3B. M. Kопин will contact family directly to schedule phone consult.	by end of day Wed. 7/20/94 one week, ending 7/25/94	

Child Enrolled in _Zero-to-Three Hawaii Proj_ (Program)

Parent Signature: _Patty Takemoto_   Date: _7/18/94_
Co-Care Coordinator: _Selina Flores_   Date: _7-18-94_

154

Table 5.2   Required IEP information

The IEP should include
- a statement of the child's present performance levels;
- annual and short-term instructional objectives;
- a statement of specific special education and related services to be provided;
- a statement of the extent to which the child will participate in regular education programs;
- projected dates for initiation of services and the anticipated duration of services;
- appropriate objective criteria, evaluation procedures, and schedules for measuring the student's progress toward the objectives; and
- a statement of the needed transition services for students (beginning no later than age 16).

The IEP is developed by a committee (usually called an "IEP team," a "placement team," or an IEP committee). This committee must include *at least* the following persons: the child's teacher, a representative of the school district (an administrator or designee), one or both of the child's parents or a guardian (or a court-appointed surrogate parent), a member of the multidisciplinary assessment team (or someone able to interpret the assessment results), and, where appropriate, the child. The child's and the parents' needs determine additional members. Very often, other professionals such as a language interventionist, medical personnel, a school psychologist, and physical and occupational therapists participate. Also, the parents may invite advocates and other family members.

IDEA requires that schools (1) *invite* parents to participate in developing the IEP, and (2) schedule IEP meetings at times and places convenient to parents who want to attend. The IDEA requires parental consent for the determination of necessary services, as well as placement in any type of special program, but the school can implement the IEP goals and objectives without parents' consent if they chose not to participate or give approval. Due process procedures are available to parents if they disagree about the content of the IEP.

The Least Restrictive Environment (LRE) Mandate

The LRE mandate of IDEA states that

> . . . *removal of children with disabilities from the regular education environment occurs only when the nature or severity of the disability is such that education in regular classes with the use of supplementary aids and services cannot be achieved satisfactorily. (Section 612 [5], Part B)*

Children with disabilities are to be educated with their nondisabled peers "to the maximum extent appropriate," and a continuum of placements must be made available to meet their needs. Placement in the general education class that the child would attend if she did not have a disability, called **full inclusion** or just **inclusion,** is the first and preferred option.

Interpretation of the LRE mandate has engendered debate and litigation for over two decades (Taylor, 1988; Rainforth, York, & Macdonald, 1992; Rothstein, 1995). The key is support. In the precedent-setting legal case defining LRE (*Daniel R. R.* v. *State Board of Education* [874 F.2d 1036m 5th Cir. 1989]), it was decided that the test for determining compliance with the LRE requirement of IDEA centers on the issue of whether education in the regular classroom can be satisfactorily achieved with the use of supplemental aids and services. Children cannot be removed from the classroom unless *every possible effort* has been made to accommodate them in the general classroom environment.

Despite the IDEA's stated preference for providing services and supports in general education environments, some school systems persist with the assumption that certain students cannot be educated in general education classes and that certain services cannot be provided in general education settings (Rainforth et al., 1992). Fortunately, the number of systems that hold to these assumptions is rapidly decreasing. Each year there is a marked increase in the number of students placed in general education classrooms with whatever supports are necessary for successful participation in those settings (USDOE, 1993).

Former Assistant Secretary of Education Madeleine C. Will formally introduced the inclusion movement in a series of speeches and articles in the late eighties. Sometimes referred to as the **regular education initiative (REI)** (Will, 1986), the basic premise of this philosophy is that general education should have primary responsibility for the education of *all* students, with support from special education. As outlined by Sailor (1991), the basic premises of the full inclusion philosophy are:

> Despite the IDEA's stated preference for inclusion, some schools continue to maintain that certain services cannot be provided in general education classrooms.

1. Students with disabilities should attend the community public school they would attend if they did not have a disability.
2. The population of the school should be representative of the school district at large, with a natural proportion of students with disabilities.
3. No student should be excluded from school based on the type or extent of disability.
4. Each student's placement should be age- and grade-appropriate.
5. General education practice should include cooperative learning and peer instructional methods.

6. Instructional supports and related services should be provided in the general education classroom and other integrated school environments.

Inclusion is somewhat different than mainstreaming or integration (Stainback & Stainback, 1990). Integration and mainstreaming attempted to help children fit into the mainstream of their schools. Inclusion is *not* about changing students so that they fit into the mainstream: Inclusion is about restructuring classrooms and schools so that they are able to support and nurture individual differences in a way that meets the educational and social needs of *all* students. It is also about supporting and nurturing professionals to work together in ways that they have not had much opportunity to do in the past.

The inclusion movement focuses on restructuring classrooms and other school environments to accommodate all students.

Related Services

As noted above, the IDEA states that the IEP must include a statement of the related services that the child will need in order to benefit from special education. Related services include speech pathology and audiology, psychological services, physical and occupational therapy, recreation, rehabilitation counseling services, social work services, medical services (for diagnosis and evaluation), school health services, transportation, transition services, and assistive technology services and devices.

In many states and districts, related services professionals and other special education personnel (e.g., teachers) are now called (and generally function as) *support personnel* (Rainforth, York, & Macdonald, 1992). Meeting the needs of students with disabilities in regular classrooms and other naturalistic environments is requiring new service delivery models and new roles for special educators and professionals in the disciplines that provide related services (e.g., speech-language pathology, occupational and physical therapy, psychology, etc.).

PARADIGM SHIFTS

A paradigm is an overall philosophy or a conceptual framework. Because they determine what we value and thus, view as relevant, the paradigms of service fields influence decisions having to do with (1) what *types* of services are provided; (2) *how* services are provided; and (3) *where* services are provided.

The inclusion movement is the paradigm shift in special education that has had the most far-reaching impact in the last decade. Paralleling that shift are several paradigm shifts in the area of language intervention. There have been major shifts from (Westby & Erickson, 1992)

The inclusion movement is paralleled by important paradigm shifts in language intervention.

1. standardized testing to naturalistic assessment;
2. exclusive concern for children's needs to concern for the child's social systems;
3. viewing children as much alike to awareness and concern for cultural and linguistic diversity;
4. focus on spoken language to focus on literacy; and
5. working with individual students and small groups in a therapy setting to working in natural environments (e.g., classroom, homes, community settings).

Not surprisingly, these trends have contributed to widespread changes in what *type* of services are provided for children with language and communication difficulties (whether as a primary or a secondary disability) and *how* and *where* services are provided.

NATURALISTIC ASSESSMENT.   Westby and Erickson (1992) describe the shift in assessment as a shift from "discrete point, decontextualized, standardized testing to integrative, descriptive, naturalistic assessment" (p. v). This shift reflects new conceptualizations about the nature of language and language learning. It reflects consensus that, although standardized language tests permit comparison of the performance of students with one another on some language-related skills, they do not provide information about children's use of language in natural environments or *why* language is not developing at the expected rate. Moreover, as we will discuss in Chapter 7, standardized tests rarely provide enough information or the type of information needed to develop and implement an appropriate, effective, and practical intervention plan.

> Standardized tests tell us little about the reasons for a child's language difficulties *or* how to develop an effective and practical intervention.

SOCIAL SYSTEMS INTERVENTION.   Social systems intervention reflects the premise that language and communication problems reside not within the child but, rather, in the child's interactions with family members and peers (Belsky, 1981; Bronfenbrenner, 1986). Social systems assessment identifies (1) the social communicative difficulties that the child is likely to encounter in daily interactions in natural environments (school, home, and community settings), (2) roles and functions in her particular social systems, and (3) the specific environmental supports *and* disincentives for language and communication efforts in those systems. Social systems intervention then has a dual focus: mobilizing and strengthening competency-enhancing supports and resources in the social systems and teaching the child a variety of positive social and communication strategies.

CULTURAL AND LINGUISTIC DIVERSITY.   It is estimated that, by the year 2000, one in every three persons will belong to a linguistically or ethnically diverse group; the population in our schools will undoubtedly mirror the makeup of the general population (Lynch & Hanson,

1992). The paradigm shift from a focus on student similarities to focus on student diversity is an acknowledgement of (1) the rapidly changing population demographics, and (2) the essential role that language plays in the socialization of children to their culture.

Certainly some minority children are quite competent in English when they enter school; others have had only minimal exposure to English. They may speak Spanish, the second most common language in the United States, one of the Asian languages, a native American dialect (e.g., Hawaiian pidgin), or some less common language, such as Arabic or Tongan. Concurrently, teachers and language interventionists are working to become culturally competent and knowledgeable about the discourse patterns and priorities of other cultures and to accommodate the cultural and linguistic diversity that is now the rule rather than the exception in most schools.

FOCUS ON LITERACY. A growing recognition of the interdependency of literacy and overall language abilities has precipitated the shift from exclusive attention to spoken language to a focus on "whole language." The "whole" in whole language emphasizes the integrity of language and the language process. It also recognizes the importance of language in the acquisition of literacy; that each area aids in the development of other areas (Goodman, 1986).

> Oral and written language abilities are interdependent.

Ultimately, adherence to whole language principles affects the way we view language, language learning, and curriculum (including instruction, materials, and evaluation). Oral and written language are no longer viewed as separate skill and instructional domains, with literacy "assigned" to teachers and language "assigned" to language interventionists. Recognition that oral and written language abilities are interdependent, that language abilities are a frequent and powerful contributor to academic success *and failure,* and finally, that literacy is, in fact, a fundamental dimension of normal language development in our culture *and* vice versa has led to collaboration toward the shared goal of facilitating language and literacy (Westby & Erickson, 1992).

INTERVENTION IN NATURAL ENVIRONMENTS. Historically, service delivery for students with language disorders adhered to a clinical model of one-to-one or small-group therapy provided in a separate setting. This service delivery approach, which is discussed at more length below, came to be called the isolated therapy model (or the pull-out model). It is no longer the preferred model for school services. The shift from one-to-one instruction provided in a separate setting to language and communication instruction provided in the context of daily activities in the classroom, the home, and other natural environments was prompted by research in both special education and language-communication development (e.g., Rainforth & York, 1987; Kamhi, 1993; Snow, 1991). The shift to **integrated intervention** (or **integrated therapy**) reflects recognition that language cannot be separated from other aspects of a child's daily life. To be effective, intervention must be provided when and where the child needs to understand and use language.

THE COLLABORATIVE ETHIC

When schools first began to include children with disabilities in daily activities in classrooms and other natural environments (in the early eighties), it soon became apparent that there was a need to discover ways to facilitate and support collaboration among professionals in general and special education, early intervention, and related services disciplines (e.g., speech-language pathology, psychology, occupational therapy, physical therapy). What evolved in response to this concern has been called "the collaborative ethic" (Phillips & McCullough, 1990). The collaborative ethic translates into collaborative team functioning and collaborative consultation. In practice, it has proved effective with children with speech, language, and communication disorders, including stuttering (Cooper, 1991), language disorders (Butterill, Niizawa, Biemer, Takahashi, & Hearn, 1989), reading and learning disabilities (Norris, 1989), and literacy learning (Dudley-Marling, 1987).

Teaming Models

When researchers first began to look for teaming models that would make it possible to combine resources to meet the multifaceted needs of children with disabilities, there was widespread discussion about and comparison of three approaches: the multidisciplinary, interdisciplinary, and transdisciplinary models (e.g., Hart, 1977; Lyon & Lyon, 1980; McCormick & Goldman, 1979; Sternat, Messina, Nietupski, Lyon, & Brown, 1977). The multidisciplinary model is the most limited with respect to collaboration. There is little, if any, information sharing, joint planning, or team accountability. With the multidisciplinary model, professionals from different disciplines implement separate assessment procedures and provide very separate discipline-specific services. The interdisciplinary and transdisciplinary models evolved in response to dissatisfaction with the lack of communication and the fragmented services associated with the multidisciplinary model. In an interdisciplinary team model, team members come together to develop joint intervention goals and discuss possible intervention strategies. In a transdisciplinary team model, team members collaborate in planning *and* share skills in implementing intervention. Additionally, in a transdisciplinary model, professionals *and* parents become consultants and trainers for one another (Hart, 1977; Lyon & Lyon, 1980; McCormick & Goldman, 1979; Sternat, Messina, Nietupski, Lyon, & Brown, 1977).

The transdisciplinary team model solved many of the problems inherent in traditional service delivery configurations. There was still one thing missing. Initial conceptualizations of this team model did not provide clear guidelines concerning *where* and precisely *how* assessment and intervention/instruction should be provided (Rainforth et al., 1992). There continued to be significant overlap and redundancy across assessment activities. Moreover, because special instruction (including language intervention) often continued to be provided in separate settings, there were problems related to lack of generalization of newly trained skills. Arena assessment and integrated intervention emerged as responses to these concerns.

Arena assessment (also called *joint assessment*) got its name from the way the professionals who are doing the assessment and the parents (and other family members) arrrange themselves for the assessment sessions. They usually sit on the floor in a circle or semi-circle around the child. One person, designated as an assessment facilitator, interacts with the child while the other members of the assessment team record observations and score their respective assessment protocol.

Arena assessment has a number of advantages over traditional individual assessment (Wolery & Dyk, 1984). One advantage is avoiding the redundancy that comes about because the same test items often appear in the assessment protocol of different disciplines. The effect of this redundancy is that the different professionals tend to present many of the same tasks to the child and they ask parents almost identical questions. With arena assessment all of the professionals on the team can observe and score the overlapping items at the same time.

A second major advantage of arena assessment is that, rather than seeing the child only from the perspective of their own discipline, team members get a more holistic view. Finally, a third advantage of arena assessment is the opportunity for collaboration among professionals and with parents and other family members and the opportunity to achieve consensus because everyone present observes the same constellation of behavior. Professionals and parents can talk to one another about what they are seeing, and parents can add information concerning the child's performance in other contexts and whether behavior observed in the assessment situation reflects his best efforts.

The most recent variation of arena assessment, for young children, is called **transdisciplinary play-based assessment** (TPBA). Linder's (1993) TPBA uses play (a normal activity for young children) in a natural environment (e.g., preschool classroom, home) as the assessment context. It provides guidelines for planning and implementing observations in four domains: social/adaptive, cognitive, communication/language, and sensorimotor. The guidelines are easy to use because they are stated in the form of questions to encourage

Arena assessment is a response to the concern that there was considerable overlap and redundancy among assessment activities.

observations of the qualitative aspects of "how" the child performs—
not just "if" the child performs—the task.

Integrated intervention is special instruction, facilitation, and
support provided in the general education classroom or some other
natural environment. (We prefer the term "integrated intervention" to
"integrated therapy," but much of the literature in this area uses the
latter term.) In the past, most language interventionists (and other
therapists) provided services in separate clinic or therapy rooms. The
rationale underlying the isolated therapy model was that children
acquire skills most efficiently when taught in a highly structured, distraction-free environment where there is access to specialized equipment. Cirrin and Penner (1995) provide a concise discussion of how
this service delivery approach emerged and some insights as to why it
persisted over so many decades. One explanation has to do with the
fact that services to children with language disorders evolved out of a
"speech clinic" model. In speech clinics, individual children or small
groups are provided intervention in separate therapy rooms. A second explanation for this service delivery approach was that, from the
perspective of maximizing opportunities to practice production of
specific linguistic targets, being able to control the communication
context had many advantages. Auditory and visual distractions can be
contolled (if not eliminated) and the child's attention and productive
capacities are relatively easy to manage. Third, in the past it was perfectly reasonable and sound to focus intervention on effecting change
in discrete linguistic units such as vocabulary or length or type of sentence because most descriptions of language emphasized phonology
and syntax. At that time there was less attention to the functions and

**Integrated intervention is much
more than simply relocating
therapy from contrived to natural environments.**

uses that language serves for the child in social contexts or the relationship between language and learning in school contexts.

Some of the factors that contributed to the shift away from the isolated therapy approach are:

- **Concerns about the lack of generalization of newly acquired language skills from the clinic room to natural settings:** Many children, particularly those with severe disabilities, have difficulty applying skills that are learned in one-to-one therapy settings at appropriate and necessary times in natural environments.

- **Holistic views of language learning and use that emphasize the role that language plays in social interactions and literacy:** There was growing recognition that the systematic, highly specialized, adult-directed instruction provided in traditional isolated therapy is incompatible with theories of language learning that stressed adult–child interactions and active engagement with the environment.

- **Apprehension about the potential negative effects of removing children from their classrooms (i.e., missing the general education curriculum):** There was growing consensus that removing a child from the classroom to receive therapy not only deprives the child of whatever instruction is in process, but also marks that child as different (in the eyes of his peers).

- **Lack of data supporting the notion that "more is better"— that providing more intensive therapy would result in proportionately greater gains:** There was growing disenchantment with the tendency to confound successful intervention with numbers of hours of therapy.

- **Concerns about fragmentation of services:** In addition to fragmentation, there is the potential for inadvertently sabotaging one another when the language interventionist (or other therapist) and the teacher do not know what the other is working on with a particular child.

- **Policy shifts at state and natural levels that emphasized the LRE mandate:** IDEA specifies that related services are to be provided as needed to make it possible for the child to benefit from instruction in the least restrictive environment.

In practice, integrated intervention is substantially more complicated than simply relocating services from separate settings to natural environments, and the benefits are much broader than increased generalization. It has required professionals to redefine both their responsibilities *and* their goals. However, the many advantages associated with integrated intervention make the effort well worthwhile. Some of these advantages are presented in Table 5.3.

As the relative superiority of integrated delivery of related services in natural environments has become accepted (e.g., Biklen & Zollars, 1986; Simon, 1985) the strongest evidence of its broad support base

TABLE 5.3   Advantages of integrated intervention

* The student gains and maintains access to "regular" educational opportunities and learning outcomes.
* Opportunities for team collaboration are maximized and fragmentation (gaps, overlaps, and/or contradictions) in services are avoided.
* The input and methods of all team members are synthesized as they address a shared vision for the student's participation in social, educational, and vocational settings.
* Skills taught through integrated intervention are likely to generalize because they were learned and practiced in the integrated, natural environments where they need to be used.

has been its endorsement by the professional organizations of the disciplines that work in school settings. The professional organizations of special education, occupational therapy, physical therapy, and speech-language pathology have all set forth guidelines promoting the tenets of integrated intervention in educational environments (American Occupational Therapy Association, 1989; American Physical Therapy Association, 1990; American Speech-Language-Hearing Association, 1989, 1991, 1993; Association for Persons with Severe Handicaps, 1986).

Collaborative Teams

A team is "a group of persons who have a shared goal and required actions to perform in order to achieve that goal" (McCormick, 1990, p. 262). When team members share responsibilities and accountability and pool their skills and resources they are a **collaborative team** (sometimes **cooperative team**) (Rainforth et al., 1992). The collaborative team model is basically an evolved version of the interdisciplinary and transdisciplinary team models. As set forth by Thousand and Villa (1992), a collaborative team is a group of people who

* agree to coordinate their work to achieve *common, agreed-upon goals;*
* hold *a belief system* that all members of the team have unique and needed expertise;
* demonstrate their belief in *parity* by alternately engaging in the dual roles of teacher and learner, expert and recipient, consultant and consultee;
* use a *distributed functions* theory of leadership wherein the task and relationship functions of the leader are distributed among all members of the group; and
* use a *collaborative teaming process* that involves face-to-face interaction; positive interdependence; the performance, monitoring and processing of interpersonal skills; and individual accountability.

Thousand and Villa discuss a sixth aspect which, in their opinion, is most important: The team must be an effective cooperative learning group. When the team functions as a cooperative learning group, the other five aspects tend to occur automatically. Drawing from Johnson and Johnson's (1987) definition of the requirements to be an effective cooperative learning group, the first is that members must interact face-to-face *on a frequent basis*. Second, they must have a mutual, "we are all in this together" feeling of positive interdependence. Third, they must be committed to developing small-group interpersonal skills (e.g., trust building, communication, leadership, creative problem solving, decision making, conflict management). Fourth, they must agree to setting aside time *regularly* to assess and discuss the team's functioning and set goals for improving relationships and accomplishing tasks more effectively. Finally, members must agree on methods for holding one another accountable for agreed-upon responsibilities.

FORMING A COLLABORATIVE TEAM. The size and the composition of collaborative teams vary. There may be as few as two or as many as six professionals from different fields and the parents. Ideally there is agreement that all services (including assessment) will be provided in the classroom and other natural environments.

> Forming a collaborative team takes considerable time as well as commitment.

Following are the steps to form a *collaborative team* (D. W. Johnson & F. P. Johnson, 1975, 1987). (When people are already working together, these steps can be used to restructure the team to function as a collaborative team.)

1. Spend the time necessary to get well acquainted. Share expectations about team activities and goals and talk about individual needs and desires that the group might help meet. One activity that helps to get people started talking about this is to ask people to complete sentences such as "When I first enter a new group I feel _____ " or "What I hope this team will be able to accomplish is _____ ."

2. Decide on operating ground rules. Formulate procedures concerning (1) how decisions are going to be made, and (2) how goals and objectives will be addressed. Talk about possible barriers to maximum effectiveness and consider ways of avoiding and/or working through these barriers.

3. Visualize ideal outcomes. Visualize desired outcomes and discuss strengths and resources of the team as a whole and those of the various team members as they contribute to these outcomes. Then develop team goals and objectives. These are examples of one team's goals:

- Implement collaborative assessment and generate a collaborative assessment report.
- Use a consensual decision-making process to develop a prioritized list of skills and environments for each student with disabilities.

- Develop IEP goals that integrate instruction strategies from the teachers, the language interventionist, and the therapists into a coordinated approach.
- Develop IEP goals that specify priority skills, priority environments, and activities.
- Provide all intervention in the classroom, the cafeteria, and on the playground in the context of activities in those settings.
- Discuss individual agendas, specifically the relationship of team goals and activities to each team member's individual skills and interests.

4. List and analyze potential supports and barriers. Discuss specific forces that will support and those that might hinder accomplishing team goals. Consider all types of positive and negative forces—for example, political, theoretical, attitudinal, logistical—that could conceivably affect the team's accomplishments.

5. Develop a plan. This is the point at which to discuss instructional *procedures*. Brainstorm different action plans, select a first choice, and work out procedures for implementing the plan. Among the instruction design issues that need to be considered are how often and where instruction will occur, how children will be prepared for instruction, what type of prompts will be used to elicit desired performance, what adaptations will be used to enhance performance, and how performance will be evaluated. Rainforth, York, and MacDonald (1992) urge collaborative teams to become informed as to the specific instructional philosophies and current best practices for school environments.

6. Plan monitoring procedures. Determine how progress toward goals will be monitored and develop specific criteria for goal attainment. This step is particularly important. Talk about ways for members to exchange feedback with one another as a means of continually improving individual effectiveness and team effectiveness. The collaborative team becomes an interdependent support system for obtaining the feedback essential to continued improvement of individual skills and group skills. Ultimately, the functioning of the students with disabilities for whom the team is responsible is the most valid indicator of the team's effectiveness.

ROLES AND RESPONSIBILITIES. Rainforth and others (1992) distinguish between core team members and support team members. **Core team members** are those team members who are directly involved in the design and implementation of the student's educational program. These are the child's key decision makers who need to be in frequent contact with one another. At the very least, the core team includes the student, family members, teachers (special and general educators), and one or more related services professional (e.g., language interventionist, phyiscal and/or occupational therapist, vision or hearing specialist, nurse) and possibly a paraprofessional or class-

The persons responsible for implementation of the student's program are the core team members.

room aide who helps to support the student in the classroom. Composition of the team depends on the child's needs.

Support team members are individuals who are not as closely involved with day-to-day programming. They may only participate in planning and decision making once or twice a year. Physical and occupational therapists are support team members for many children with mild disabilities. Other professionals who are often support team members include psychologists, social workers, nurses, dietitians, and orientation and mobility specialists.

Some roles and responsibilities are shared by all team members—core team members and support team members alike. Rainforth and others (1992) call these **generic team member roles.** They include (1) helping to set priorities and plan interventions; (2) participating in problem solving across all aspects of programming; (3) sharing discipline-specific information and competencies that will enhance the student's participation and progress; (4) supporting the contributions and efforts of fellow team members; and (5) continuing education about general practices to support and facilitate quality of life for all persons with disabilities in all aspects of family, school, and community life.

Other roles and responsibilities are specific to the different disciplines involved with children with disabilities. Tables 5.4, 5.5, and 5.6 present roles and responsibilities of the language interventionist, the special educator, and the general education teacher. Because each person's training, experiences, and interests are different, there are many differences among professionals in a discipline. However, all

> In collaborative consultation, the helper is a partner rather than an expert.

TABLE 5.4 Major roles and responsibilities of the language interventionist

1. Provide information about normal speech and language development.
2. Provide information about delays and disorders of speech, language, or communication.
3. Collect information about speech, language, and communication strengths and intervention needs to maximize participation in the classroom and other school settings.
4. Interpret assessment information to others and help to (1) develop intervention goals and objectives, (2) plan activities, and (3) select appropriate methods and materials.
5. Provide direct instruction for specific speech, language, and communication skills to individuals and small groups.
6. Demonstrate for, teach, and assist others (i.e., teachers, parents) to implement language and communication intervention procedures.
7. Participate in decision making related to provision of augmentative and alternative communication devices.
8. Evaluate and monitor student progress and program effectiveness.
9. Work collaboratively with others to promote student participation in age-appropriate activities and natural environments.

TABLE 5.5 Major roles and responsibilities of the special education teacher

1. Provide information about exceptional learners (students with disabilities and gifted students).
2. Provide information about special education laws and accompanying rules and regulations.
3. Develop and provide information to others about adapting curriculum, instructional materials, and equipment.
4. Implement assessment of abilities and disabilities or delays in cognitive, social, academic, and vocational skills and assist assessment of language and communication.
5. Provide direct instruction for a broad range of functional and academic skills (including language and communication) to individuals and small groups.
6. Demonstrate for, teach, and assist others (i.e., teachers, parents) to provide individualized instruction.
7. Manage, and assist others to manage, serious behavior problems.
8. Plan and implement environmental modifications to promote learning and generalization.
9. Evaluate and monitor student progress and program effectiveness.
10. Work collaboratively with others to promote participation of students with disabilities in normal activities and natural environments.

TABLE 5.6 Major roles and responsibilities of the general education teacher

1. Provide information about the curriculum philosophy, scope, and sequence.
2. Provide information about the classroom schedule and expectations for participation in routine activities.
3. Provide suggestions for adapting curriculum, instructional materials, and equipment.
4. Assist the language interventionist and the special educator to learn the skills for managing group activities.
5. Arrange peer interactions to teach social and communication skills.
6. Assist individual instruction.
7. Schedule planning time with support professionals and parents.
8. Implement environmental modifications to promote learning and generalization.
9. Co-teach with the special educator and the language interventionist.
10. Work collaboratively with others to promote participation of students with disabilities in normal activities and natural environments.

professionals in speech-language pathology/communication disorders and special education who work in the schools should have the skills necessary for the roles and responsibilities shown in Tables 5.4, 5.5, and 5.6.

Collaborative teams are effective to the extent that members are focused and committed to positive child outcomes more than to the specific concepts and methods and skills of their discipline. To be effective as a team, members must cooperate with one another, share information, and plan together to minimize the effects of the child's limitations on her functioning in natural environments.

CHARACTERISTICS OF EFFECTIVE COLLABORATIVE TEAMS.   Recognition of the importance of working together is clearly a prerequisite for collaborative teaming, but collaboration is more than an attitude. Groups who aspire to becoming collaborative teams should begin by studying and discussing characteristics of effective teams as well as guidelines for teaming skills and procedures (as presented in this section). Sources for this information include the group process literature (e.g., D. W. Johnson & F. P. Johnson, 1987; Napier & Gershenfeld, 1993; Parker, 1990), and theory and research in cooperative learning (D. W. Johnson, & R. T. Johnson, 1989). These sources suggest the following as key characteristics of effective collaborative teams:

1. Commitment to a shared vision. Effective teams agree on the reasons for their existence and the parameters of their activities. There is discussion and acceptance of ground rules (including how barriers and conflicts will be handled) and logistics of meeting times and locations. These ground rules and conflict resolution strategies are periodically reviewed and revised (if needed).

2. Clear goals. Effective teams formulate and agree upon a set of measurable and observable goals. All team members recognize that they must work together if the goals are to be accomplished. They use the goals to guide the team's activities.

3. Open communication and active listening. The members of effective teams trust one another. They communicate openly and honestly about where they stand and how they feel. Ideas and feelings are shared in an atmosphere of nonjudgmental acceptance so that team members feel that their contributions are valued. Equally important, they listen to one another (Parker, 1990). It is not sufficient to listen to hear; team members must learn to listen to understand. Active listening procedures can minimize misunderstandings and distortions about ideas and feelings. Active listening is a series of techniques developed by Gordon (1980) to ensure that messages are accurately received. Table 5.7 shows examples of the most common active listening strategies: clarification and "I" messages.

4. Shared leadership and consensual decision making. In effective teams, team members share leadership responsibilities as well as decision making. Who the leader is on different occasions

TABLE 5.7   Active listening strategies for collaborative teams

---

1. *Use Clarification*

When a team member makes a declarative statement, this is a way to request feedback to ensure that you understood what was said in the way the message was meant. Use one or another of the following phrases to request clarification (in a nonconfrontational way). Begin the request for clarification by saying

"Do you mean _____ ?"

"Am I hearing you say that _____ ?"

2. *Use an "I" Message*

"I" messages are a way for team members to communicate the issue that needs to be addressed and resolved in a nonthreatening way. The message includes your feeling about an action within the team, the consequence of the action, and a decision to resolve it.

Affect (feeling, wondering)	*"I feel frustrated."* or *"I feel uncomfortable."*
Behavior (action)	*"When we start the meeting late."* or *"When people come late."*
Consequence(s)	*"Because we aren't able to finish what we need to get done."*
Decision(s)	*"We need to talk about meeting times and time constraints."*

---

depends on the particular concern that the team is addressing. One important benefit of distributing and rotating leadership and decision-making powers among team members is that it encourages feelings of positive interdependence. While it may be unrealistic for all members on the team to agree on all decisions, consensual decision making is most desirable. The greater the agreement on a decision, the greater the commitment to its implementation. Table 5.8 shows the steps in consensual decision making.

   5. Constructive conflict resolution. Effective teams practice constructive conflict resolution to manage disagreements. When members disagree, the discussion takes place in a positive and cooperative atmosphere with a focus on generating creative and productive solutions. All ideas and feelings are listened to enthusiastically and uncritically. They are respected and valued. Members paraphrase one another's ideas and feelings as accurately as they can and without making value judgments about them. They try to view the messages of other members from their perspective, and negotiate the meaning of their colleagues' messages. The issue is not to establish who is "right" or "wrong" or who has the best answer but, rather, to get as much information as possible and explore different perspectives to come up with the best team decision possible.

6. Shared accountability. On effective teams, accountability is shared. Shared accountability is an important principle of collaborative teams. Working as a team clearly reduces the autonomy and freedom that teachers and support personnel have traditionally enjoyed when they have operated independently (Skrtic, 1991), but shared accountability relieves them of the onus of being (or at least feeling) solely responsible for programming decisions. Effective teams also keep records of and monitor the effectiveness of all team decisions and activities.

Collaborative Consultation

Tharp and Wetzell (1969) describe consultation as a triadic relationship involving interactions among a consultant, a consultee or mediator of change, and the person in whom change is sought. There are two major types of consultation models: collaborative models and expert models. Collaborative consultation differs from expert consultation in

TABLE 5.8 Steps in consensual decision making

Steps for Joint Decision Making and Problem Solving

1. *Clearly define the problem.* Separate relevant from irrelevant details, clarify vague or ambiguous terms, and assemble all the available information. Then write a consensus definition/description of the problem on the chalkboard or chart paper.
2. *Analyze the issue.* Clarify the problem and relationships among events that are associated with the problem situation as clearly as possible. Gather supporting evidence on the nature of the problem. Then use all available information to restate the problem in terms of a condition that exists and that, to some extent, needs to be modified. Then isolate specific causal factors. Finally, when all available data have been gathered, the problem has been stated as a condition to be changed, and various causal factors have been isolated, make a determination as to whether the team has the ability to solve the problem. If not, work to state the problem more realistically, bring others into the process (e.g., other professionals, other family members), or determine who *does* have the resources to solve the problem.
3. *Generate possible alternatives.* Brainstorm and list ideas for solutions. (Avoid any tendency to think about the "best" solution at this point.) Integrate and synthesize the ideas into a smaller number. Discuss and weigh the possible alternatives. Consider the consequences of each alternative. Then rank the solutions with "most preferred" as 1. There should then be decision by consensus that the group will support and try the first-ranked alternative.
4. *Select specific implementation strategies.* Discuss the solution and decide how it can be implemented. Write this on the chalkboard or chart paper: *What will we do? How will we do it? Who will do what? When will we do it?* Plan the sequence of steps for implementation of the solution and assign roles and responsibilities. Decide how much will be completed by the next meeting. Decide (and note) what part of the progress each team member will report on.
5. *Begin implementation of the agreed upon steps.*
6. *Reassess the situation and make modifications (if needed).* Use objective information to determine whether the strategy is producing the desired outcomes. If the intervention is not producing the desired outcomes, either modify it or reenter the problem-solving loop and select the next highest ranked solution to try.

that the consultant is not viewed (and does not view herself) as having more expertise than the consultee.

Collaborative consultation is more than just the *process* of planning and problem solving; it is also the essential relationship between persons from different backgrounds that makes the process possible. Drawing from early work by Caplan (1964), Tharp and Wetzell (1969), and Tharp (1975), the collaborative consultation model stresses reciprocity and mutuality. In educational applications the mediator is typically the general educator: The consultant may be the language interventionist, special educator, physical therapist, occupational therapist, or another support professional (e.g., a remedial reading teacher). The triadic model relies on parity between the partners: The consultant has the knowledge or skills to mobilize the mediator's influence and the mediator has the data to influence and inform the consultant (Idol, Paolucci-Whitcomb, & Nevin, 1987). Both the consultant and the mediator "own" the problem and both are accountable for the success or failure of whatever instructional practices they decide to implement.

Collaborative consultation is more than two professionals working together to provide special instruction or intervention in the general education classroom. It involves joint planning, shared responsibility, shared resources, shared accountability, and a willingness to invest the time and energy necessary to become familiar with one another's viewpoints, values, and vocabulary. Both participants must truly believe that "two heads are better than one" and that sharing will increase the probability for optimal outcomes (Thousand & Villa, 1992). Table 5.9, which reflects a synthesis of work by Idol and others (1987), Thousand and Villa (1992), and West and Cannon (1988), provides some guidelines for a successful collaborative consultation relationship.

Collaborative consultation may be direct or indirect. Which approach is used will depend on the classroom, students' needs, and teacher preferences. There are several possible *direct contact collaborative consultation* arrangements. The special educator and/or the language interventionist may work with the general education teacher to provide classroom-based individual or small-group special instruction, using modified classroom materials or special materials, with content drawn from the curriculum and/or the results of ecological assessment as described in Chapters 7 and 8. A second possible arrangement is co-teaching where the language interventionist and/or the special education teacher share responsibility for instruction (for the entire class) with the general education teacher.

There are also two possible *indirect contact collaborative consultation* arrangements. One is a collaborative support arrangement in which the language interventionist and/or the special educator provide minimal classroom-based services, *occasionally* teaching or

> Effective collaborative consultation operationalizes the tenet that "two heads are better than one."

> In co-teaching, the language interventionist or the special education teacher share responsibility for all classroom instruction with the general education teacher.

TABLE 5.9   Guidelines for a successful collaborative consultation relationship

- Behave in ways showing that you respect and trust one another's opinions, skills, and abilities.
- Share ownership of the problem as well as the proposed solutions.
- Learn from one another by regularly exchanging roles (shifting from consultant to consultee and vice versa).
- Use active listening and responding techniques (paraphrasing, perception checks, questions, acknowledging feelings) to facilitate communication.
- Give credit for each other's ideas and provide immediate positive feedback for one another when mutually agreed upon goals are achieved.
- Avoid professional jargon.
- Be available for one another.
- Review evaluation data often so that timely changes can be made when indicated.

demonstrating language activities and providing materials to the teacher. In this arrangement, the primary role of the language interventionist and the special educator is as support team members. They provide technical assistance, consultation, and in-service training. The second possibility is actually an expert support arrangement in which the language interventionist and/or the special educator provide *only* technical assistance and/or in-service training for the general education teacher. Staffing arrangements for both direct and indirect contact are discussed at more length in Chapters 7 and 8.

Based on five years' experience with collaborative consultation in 11 schools in California, Montgomery (1992) points out that no two applications of the collaborative consultation models will look and operate exactly the same because of differences in students' needs and differences in teaching styles. Montgomery argues that development of collaborative goals and objectives with the teacher must be a priority. She contends that all goals and objectives should be "shared by at least one other adult on the campus, such as the teacher, teacher's aide, bus driver, cafeteria worker, or resource teacher" (p. 363), so that there are opportunities for reinforcement throughout the day in different settings. The greatest challenge, according to Montgomery (and many others), is finding adequate time for planning and preparation. Over time, however, scheduling for planning and preparation becomes less a problem because consultation partners gradually become more informed and more efficient: The language interventionists come to know the curriculum in several subject areas and teachers become more adept at imbedding language instruction into the curriculum activities.

Scheduling time for planning and preparation becomes less a problem as both special and general education personnel become more informed about one another's activities.

Another example of collaborative consultation in practice is provided by Roller, Rodriguez, Warner, and Lindahl (1992). They describe an elementary school in Denver where there are teacher and language interventionist teams for classes at all grade levels. All classes include children who are developing language at an expected rate and students with severe language disabilities. The teacher-language interventionist teams share space, materials, resources, and responsibilities. As Roller and others put it:

> *Depending on the teams, responsibilities are divided in various ways. As speech-language pathologists and regular educators in the same room, we are responsible for teaching the appropriate grade-level curriculum to the entire group of students. We modify and adapt the curriculum as needed to ensure that Individual Education Plan (IEP) goals are met for the learners with disabilities and that school and district level goals are met for the typical students. We also share responsibility for parent conferences, evening programs, and decisions concerning report cards for all the students. (p. 23)*

The previous reports of successful collaboration highlight the importance of sharing information and joint training. The special educator and the language interventionist must schedule time with the teacher to plan how to learn about the curriculum with special attention to the vocabulary, the language skill expectations, the complexity of instructions, and the materials. (In addition to the teacher, another source of this information is teachers' manuals.) Additionally, they should arrange to analyze examples of the student's written language, assignments, and classroom tests and to observe in the classroom. Classroom observations should focus on (1) how well the student attends to tasks and instruction; (2) how the student's communicative attempts are responded to; (3) whether the student asks for help; (4) whether the student seems to understand directions; (5) the student's participation in discussions; and (6) whether the student communicates appropriately with the teacher and with peers.

Creating time and opportunity for collaboration requires the most creativity. West (1990) offers some suggestions for freeing up teacher time. One idea is to schedule special experiences (e.g., films, plays, guest speakers) that bring students together in a large group. Because fewer staff are needed to oversee large-group experiences, some teachers can use this time for collaborative planning. Or make arrangements for students to work on group projects in a setting in which they require minimal supervision. Another idea is for the principal or other support staff to teach a period a day on a regular basis. Having aides, student teachers, and/or volunteers guide and supervise transitions, lunch, and recess routines frees up teachers at those times. Finally, the faculty may vote to extend their instructional day for 20 minutes 2 days per week to provide time for planning meetings.

Many teams are very creative in figuring out ways to free up planning and preparation time.

SUMMARY

Development and maintenance of effective partnerships and successful team functioning are extremely difficult and time consumimg, and they require constant vigilance; but they are worth the effort for all involved (students, parents, *and* professionals). As discussed in Chapter 10, collaborative consultation and teaming in early intervention programs may be most challenging because professionals from different agencies (as well as from different disciplines) are involved. The challenges are both logistical and conceptual. Foremost among the logistical challenges are (1) resource management (specifically allocation of financial and time resources), and (2) division of responsibilities (for example, who will be responsible for developing the Individual Family Service Plan [IFSP]?). Conceptual challenges include difficulties establishing a parity relationship when professionals come from different agencies, and lack of familiarity with the vocabulary and procedures of one another's fields.

The basic reason for collaboration is pooling of staff expertise so that the needs of *all* students can be met. One method for continuing professional growth and support suggested by Johnson and colleagues (1987) is networking with other collaborative teams. Developing a schoolwide team support network in which teams can share ideas, lessons, and successes is a way to ensure continued support for and improvement of collaborative methods. Collaborative teaming empowers teaching staff, support personnel, parents, and students alike. They are enfranchised through their participation in decision-making processes. Regardless of the arrangement, special instruction and intervention can be embedded in the general education curriculum, and students with language and communication difficulties (whether the difficulties are primary or secondary) *can* remain in the general education classroom if a collaborative team model is implemented.

REFERENCES

Alsamit, D., & Alcorn, D. (1988). A preservice mainstream curriculum infusion model: Student teachers' perceptions of program effectiveness. *Teacher Education and Special Education, 11,* 52–58.

American Occupational Therapy Association. (1989). *Guidelines for occupational therapy services in the public schools* (2nd ed.). Rockville, MD: Author.

American Physical Therapy Association. (1990). *Physical therapy practice in education environments.* Alexandria, VA: Author.

American Speech-Language-Hearing Association (1993). Guidelines for caseload size and speech-language service delivery in the schools. *Asha, 35* (Suppl. 10) 33–39.

American Speech-Language-Hearing Association. (1989). Competencies for speech-language pathologists providing services in augmentation communication. *Asha, 31,* 107–110.

American Speech-Language-Hearing Association, Committee on Language Learning Disorders. (1991). A model for collaborative service delivery for students with language-learning disorders in the public schools. *American Speech-Language-Hearing Association, 3*(33).

Association for Persons with Severe Handicaps. (1986). *Position statement on the provision of related services.* Seattle, WA: Author.

Barker, J. A., & Christensen, R. J. (1989). *The business of paradigms: Discovering the future.* Burnsville, MN: Charthouse Learning Corporation.

Belsky, J. (1981). Early human experience: A family perspective. *Developmental Psychology, 17,* 3–23.

Beukelman, D. R., & Mirenda, P. (1992). *Augmentative and alternative communication: Management of severe communication disorders in children and adults.* Baltimore: Paul H. Brookes.

Biklen, D., & Zollars, N. (1986). The focus of advocacy in the LD field. *Journal of Learning Disabilities, 19,* 579–586.

Bronfenbrenner, U. (1986). Ecology of the family as a context for human development: Research perspectives. *Developmental Psychology, 22,* 723–742.

Butterill, J., Niizawa, J., Biemer, C., Takahashi, C., & Hearn, S. (1989). Serving the language-learning disabled adolescent: A strategies-based model. *Language, Speech, and Hearing Services in the Schools, 20,* 185–204.

Campbell, P. H., McInerney, W., & Cooper, M. A. (1984). Therapeutic programming for students with severe handicaps. *American Journal of Occupational Therapy, 38*(9), 594–602.

Caplan, G. (1964). *Principles of preventative psychiatry.* New York: Basic Books.

Cirrin, F. M., & Penner, S. G. (1995). Classroom-based and consultative service delivery models for language intervention. In M. E. Fey, J. Windsor, & Warren, S. F. (Eds.), *Language intervention: Preschool through the elementary years* (pp. 333–362). Baltimore: Paul H. Brookes.

Cole, K. N., Harris, S. R., Eland, S. F., & Mills, P. E. (1989). Comparison of two service delivery models: In-class and out-of-class therapy approaches. *Pediatric Physical Therapy, 1,* 49–54.

Cooper, C. S. (1991). Using collaborative/consultative service delivery models for fluency

intervention and carryover. *Language, Speech, and Hearing Services in Schools, 22,* 152–153.

Coufal, K. L. (1993). Collaborative consultation for speech-language pathologists. *Topics in Language Disorders, 14,* 1–14.

Coufal, K. L., & Butler, K. G. (1991). Collaborative consultation: Perspectives from special education and speech-language pathology. In *Critical issues in special education: Implications for personnel preparation.* Denton, TX: University of North Texas.

Dudley-Marling, C. (1987). The role of language interventionists in literacy learning. *Journal of Early Intervention, 11,* 81–90.

File, N., & Kontos, S. (1992). Indirect service delivery through consultation: Review and implications for early intervention. *Journal of Early Intervention, 16,* 221–233.

Ferguson, M. L. (1992). Clinical forum: Implementing collaborative consultation. *Language, Speech, and Hearing Services in Schools, 23,* 361–362.

Giangreco, M. (1990). Making related service decisions for students with severe handicaps in public schools: Roles, criteria, and authority. *Journal of the Association of Persons with Severe Handicaps, 15*(1), 22–31.

Goodman, K. (1986). *What's whole in whole language?* Portsmouth, NH: Heinemann.

Gordon, T. (1980). *Leadership effectiveness training (LET).* New York: Wyden Books.

Hart, V. (1977). The use of many disciplines with the severely and profoundly handicapped. In E. Sontag, J. Smith, & N. Certo (Eds.), *Educational programming for the severely and profoundly handicapped* (pp. 391–396). Reston, VA: Council for Exceptional Children.

Hutchison, D. J. (1978). The transdisciplinary approach. In J. B. Curry & K. K. Peppe (Eds.), *Mental retardation: Nursing approaches to care.* St. Louis: C. V. Mosby Co.

Idol, L., Paolucci-Whitcomb, P., & Nevin, A. (1987). *Collaborative consultation.* Austin, TX: Pro-Ed.

Johnson, D. W., & Johnson, F. P. (1975). *Joining together: Group theory and skills.* Englewood Cliffs, NJ: Prentice Hall.

Johnson, D. W., & Johnson, F. P. (1987). *Joining together: Group theory and skills* (3rd ed.). Englewood Cliffs, NJ: Prentice Hall.

Johnson, D. W., & Johnson, R. T. (1989). *Cooperation and competition: Theory and research*. Edina, MN: Interaction Book Company.

Johnson, D. W., Johnson, R. T., Holubec, E., & Roy, P. (1984). *Circles of learning*. Arlington, VA: Association of Supervision and Curriculum Development.

Kamhi, A. (1993). Some problems with the marriage between theory and clinical practice. *Language, Speech, and Hearing Services in Schools, 24,* 57–60.

Kuhn, T. S. (1970). *The structure of scientific revolutions*. Chicago: University of Chicago Press.

Linder, T. W. (1993). *Transdiciplinary play-based assessment: A functional approach to working with young children, Revised Edition*. Baltimore: Paul H. Brookes.

Locke, P. A., & Mirenda, P. (1992). Roles and responsibilities of special education teacher serving on teams delivering AAC services. *Augmentative and Alternative Communication, 8,* 200–214.

Lynch, E. W., & Hanson, M. J. (1992). *Developing cross-cultural competence*. Baltimore: Paul H. Brookes Publishing.

Lyon, S., & Lyon, G. (1980). Team functioning and staff development: A role release approach to providing integrated educational services for severely handicapped students. *Journal of the Association for the Severely Handicapped, 9*(2), 125–135.

Marvin, C. (1987). Consultation services: Changing roles for Language interventionists. *Journal of Childhood Communication Disorders, 11,* 1–15.

McCormick, L. (1990). Extracurricular roles and relationships. In L. McCormick & R. L. Schiefelbusch (Eds.), *Early language intervention* (pp. 261–302). Columbus, OH: Merrill.

McCormick, L., & Goldman, R. (1979). The transdisciplinary model: Implications for service delivery and personnel preparation. *AAESPH Review, 4*(2), 152–161.

Montgomery, J. K. (1992). Perspectives from the field: Language, speech, and hearing services in schools. *Language, Speech, and Hearing Services in Schools, 23,* 363–364.

Napier, R. W., & Gershenfeld, M. K. (1993). *Groups: Theory and experience* (5th ed.). Boston: Houghton Mifflin.

Norris, J. A. (1989). Providing language remediation in the classroom: An integrated language-to-reading intervention model. *Language Speech and Hearing Services in Schools, 20,* 205–218.

Parker, G. M. (1990). *Team players and teamwork*. San Francisco: Jossey-Bass Publishers.

Phillips, V., & McCullough, L. (1990). Consultation-based programming: Instituting the collaborative ethic in schools. *Exceptional Children, 56*(4), 291–304.

Rainforth, B., MacDonald, C., York, J., & Dunn, W. (1992). Collaborative assessment. In B. Rainforth, J. York, & C. MacDonald (Eds.), *Collaborative teams for students with severe disabilities* (pp. 105–156). Baltimore: Paul H. Brookes.

Rainforth, B., & York, J. (1987). Related services in community-based instruction. *Journal of Association for Persons with Severe Handicaps, 12*(3), 190–198.

Rainforth, B., York, J., & MacDonald, C. (1992). *Collaborative teams for students with severe disabilities*. Baltimore: Paul H. Brookes.

Roller, E., Rodriguez, T., Warner, J., & Lindahl, P. (1992). Integration of self-contained children with severe speech-language needs into the regular education classrooms. *Language, Speech, and Hearing Services in Schools, 23,* 365–366.

Rothstein, L. F. (1995). *Special education law*. New York: Longman.

Sailor, W. (1991). Special education in the restructured school. *Remedial and Special Education, 12*(6), 8–22.

Sileo, T. W., Rude, H. A., & Luckner, J. L. (1988). Collaborative consultation: A model for transition planning for handicapped youth. *Education and Training in Mental Retardation, 23,* 333–339.

Simon, C. (1985). *Communication skills and classroom success: Therapy methodologies for language-learning disabled students*. San Diego: College-Hill Press.

Skrtic, T. (1991). *Beyond special education: A critical analysis of professional culture and school organization*. Denver, CO: Love.

Snow, C. (1991). Diverse conversational contexts for the acquisition of various language skills. In J. Miller (Ed.), *Research on child language disorders: A decade of progress* (pp. 105–124). Austin, TX: Pro-Ed.

Stainback, W., & Stainback, S. (1990). *Support networks for inclusive schooling.* Baltimore: Paul H. Brookes.

Sternat, J., Messina, R., Nietupski, J., Lyon, S., & Brown, L. (1977). Occupational and physical therapy services for severely handicapped students: Towards a naturalized public school service delivery model. In E. Sontag, J. Smith, & N. Certo (Eds.), *Educational programming for the severely and profoundly handicapped* (pp. 263–287). Reston, VA: Council for Exceptional Children.

Stowers, S., Altheide, M. R., & Shea, V. (1987). Motor assessment for aided and unaided communication. *Physical and Occupational Therapy in Pediatrics, 7*(2), 61–78.

Taylor, S. (1988). Caught in the continuum: A critical analysis of the principle of least restrictive environment. *Journal of Association for Persons with Severe Handicaps, 13,* 41–53.

Tharp, R. G. (1975). The triadic model of consultation. In C. Parter (Ed.), *Psychological consultation in the schools: Helping teachers meet special needs* (pp. 133–151). Reston, VA: Council for Exceptional Children.

Tharp, R. G., & Wetzel, R. J. (1969). *Behavior modification in the natural environment.* New York: Academic Press.

Thousand, J. S., & Villa, R. A. (1992). Collaborative teams: A powerful tool in school restructuring. In R. A. Villa, J. A. Thousand, W. Stainback, & S. Stainback (Eds.), *Restructuring for caring and effective education* (pp. 73–108). Baltimore: Paul H. Brookes.

Tomes, L., & Sanger, D. D. (1986). Attitudes of interdisciplinary team members toward speech-language services in public schools. *Language, Speech, and Hearing Services in Schools, 17,* 230–240.

Turnbull, A. P., Turnbull, H. R., Shank, M., & Leal, D. (1995). *Exceptional lives: Special education in today's schools.* Columbus, OH: Merrill.

U.S. Department of Education. (1993). Fifteenth annual report to Congress on the implementation of the Individuals with Disabilities Education Act. Washington, DC: Author.

Vandercook, T., & York, J. (1990). A team approach to program development and support. In W. Stainback & S. Stainback (Eds.), *Support networks for inclusion schooling; Interdependent integrated education* (pp. 95–122). Baltimore: Paul H. Brookes.

Villa, R. A., & Thousand, J. S. (1993). Redefining the role of the special educator and other support personnel. In J. W. Putnam (Ed.), *Cooperative learning and strategies for inclusion* (pp. 57–92). Baltimore: Paul H. Brookes.

Weiss, A. (1993). Planning language intervention for young children. In D. K. Bernstein & E. Tiegerman (Eds.), *Language and communication disorders in children* (3rd ed.) (pp. 229–272). Columbus, OH: Merrill.

West, J. F. (1990). Educational collaboration in the restructuring of schools. *Journal of Educational and Psychological Consultation, 1*(1), 42–56.

West, J. F., & Cannon, G. S. (1988). Essential collaborative consultation competencies for regular and special educators. *Journal of Learning Disabilities, 21*(1), 56–63.

West, J. F., & Idol, L. (1990). Collaborative consultation in the education of mildly handicapped and at-risk students. *Remedial and Special Education, 11*(1), 22–31.

Westby, C., & Erickson, G. (1992). Prologue. *Topics in Language Disorders, 12*(3), v–viii.

Will, M. (1986). Educating children with learning problems: A shared responbility. *Exceptional Children, 52,* 411–415.

Wolery, M., & Dyk, L. (1984). Arena assessment: Description and preliminary social validation data. *Journal of the Association for the Severely Handicapped, 9*(3), 231–235.

York, J., Rainforth, B., & Dunn, W. (1990). Training needs of physical and occupational therapists who provide services to children and youth with severe disaiblities. In S. Kaiser & W. McWorter (Eds.), *Preparing personnel to work with persons with severe disabilities* (pp. 153–180). Baltimore: Paul H. Brookes.

CHAPTER 6

Diagnostic and Descriptive Assessment

Diane Frome Loeb

Assessment is a process, not a single procedure. It is ". . . a multi-level process, beginning with screening procedures and continuing through diagnosis, planning of intervention, and program monitoring and evaluation" (Richard & Schiefelbusch, 1991). Assessment involves multiple observations of the child over a period of time in as many social and physical contexts as possible. The processes of assessment parallel the five purposes for assessment, which this chapter will examine: (1) screening and identification; (2) diagnosis; (3) eligibility determination; (4) intervention planning; and (5) evaluating intervention progress. Diagnosis of a language impairment entails the use of both formal and informal methods. Because of the limitations of standardized and formal assessment tools, specific informal procedures used in the areas of form (morphology, syntax,

The processes of assessment parallel its purposes.

and phonology), content (semantics), and use (pragmatics) may be relied upon. These areas will be discussed at length in the following sections, with an emphasis on traditional methods of assessment.

SCREENING AND IDENTIFICATION

The goal of screening is to identify children who may have language and/or communication delays and disorders that place them at risk for social and/or academic problems. Screening tools may be comprehensive (covering motor, cognition, speech, language, and other areas of development) or may be specific to speech and language. Screening may be provided individually or through mass screening. Individual or selective screening occurs when a child is referred by a parent or teacher because of concern in his communication development. In mass screening, a large number of children are screened at one time. Preschool and kindergarten programs may have large-scale screening programs in place to identify children who may need special assistance. Klee, Carson, Hall, and Muskina (1994) found that mass screening by mail to parents was an efficient and cost-effective measure for screening 2-year-olds. They sent the Language Development Survey (LDS) (Rescorla, 1989) to parents who had contacted them requesting a speech-language evaluation. The parents completed the survey, which asks them to report their child's vocabulary and early word combinations. Parents mailed the completed LDS back to the clinic. Those children who did not meet the LDS criteria were seen for further speech-language assessment.

Screening involves a quick look to see if the child's language skills are adequate or whether there is a discrepancy from normal expectations that warrants further assessment. The screening procedure may last anywhere from 3 to 15 minutes. The results of a screening do not satisfy the objective of determining whether a child has a language problem: Children who do not pass a screening are referred for a complete speech and language evaluation.

Some children who need services may be missed (under-referral), and sometimes children who do not need services are referred for evaluation (over-referral). A screening tool's rate of over- and under-referral is related to its specificity and sensitivity. Tests that are sensitive appropriately identify children needing additional assessment, whereas a test that is specific will not refer children who do not require further assessment. The less sensitive a screening test is, the greater the number of under-referrals, and losses in specificity result in an increased number of over-referrals. The levels of specificity and sensitivity are measures of the screening tool's **validity.** Validity tells us the extent that a test measures what it says it measures. Unfortunately, a survey of preschool speech and language screening tests by

Screening is to identify children who may *have language and/or communication disorders.*

If tests are sensitive, they appropriately identify children needing further assessment.

Sturner, Layton, Evans, Heller, Funk, and Machon (1994) indicates that only a few screening tools contained the information necessary to make computation of validity possible. This finding highlights the importance of taking great care when selecting screening tools and interpreting screening results.

Screening tools typically use observations, parent report, or some combination of the two. Parental report is a valid method most commonly used with very young children and children with very limited language abilities (Rescorla, 1989; Dale, 1991; Glascoe, 1991). Parents may be asked to (1) complete a checklist of words the child understands and/or produces; (2) indicate the types of word combinations the child uses; and/or (3) report verbal and nonverbal communication attempts.

A summary of screening tools is provided in Table 6.1. Children who have an established risk for communication problems generally forgo the screening process. The category "established risk" includes children who have a diagnosed medical condition that is known to have a negative impact on development (e.g., Down syndrome, hearing impairment, cerebral palsy) (Tjossem, 1976). Children who have established risks should receive comprehensive evaluation of their abilities in multiple domains.

DIAGNOSIS

The first step in a speech-language evaluation is to determine the concerns of caregivers, teachers, and other significant adults. Next, procedures are implemented to collect as much descriptive information as possible about the child's language and communication abilities. Diagnostic information may come from a case history provided by caregivers, reports from other professionals, and direct observation of the child. Following collection of information about a child's communication skills, a diagnosis is made that describes the nature of the problem, severity of the problem, and possible causes and maintaining factors. The diagnosis has direct implications for the type and intensity of intervention. In order to provide a diagnosis, the language interventionist must perform a range of informal and formal procedures to determine the child's current level of functioning. The procedures used to accomplish this end are presented in the following section.

> The goal of diagnosis is to identify cause(s) and describe the nature and severity of the problem.

Formal and Informal Language Assessment

Assessment activities extend over a continuum of "formal" to "informal" procedures. Formal procedures typically are more structured and norm-referenced. Informal procedures tend to be more naturalistic;

TABLE 6.1 Summary of screening tools

Name of Test	Authors	Age Range	Areas Assessed	Method*
Birth to Three Developmental Survey	Bangs & Dobson (1986)	0–36 months	Language	DO
Early Language Milestone Scale-2	Coplan (1993)	0–36 months	Auditory expressive, auditory receptive, visual	DO, PR
Early Screening Profiles	Harrison, Kaufman, Kaufman, Bruininks, Rynders, Ilmer, Sparrow, & Cicchetti (1990)	2–6; 11 years	Cognitive, language, motor, self-help/social	DO, PR
Denver-II	Frakenburg et al. (1992)	0–6 years	Personal-social, fine motor–adaptive, language, gross motor	DO, PR
Mother-Infant Communication Screening	Raack (1989)	Infancy	Mother-infant interaction including language and synchrony, play and neutral state, distress, feeding, and rest	DO
Language Development Survey	Rescorla (1989)	2 years	Expressive language	PR
The Screening Kit of Language Development	Bliss & Allen (1982)	2–5 years	Receptive and expressive language	DO
Fluharty Preschool Speech-Language Screening Test	Fluharty (1978)	2–6 years	Receptive and expressive language	DO
Bankson Language Screening Test (BLT-2)	Bankson (1990)	3–6; 11 years	Receptive and expressive language	DO
Compton Speech and Language Screening Evaluation	Compton (1978)	3–6 years	Language, articulation	DO
Northwest Syntax Screening Test	Lee (1969, 1971)	3–7 years	Receptive and expressive language	DO
Patterned Elicitation Syntax Screening Test	Young & Perachio (1981, 1983)	3–7; 6 years	Expressive syntax	DO

Table 6.1　Summary of screening tools (continued)

Name of Test	Authors	Age Range	Areas Assessed	Method*
Pragmatic Screening Test	Prinz & Wenir (1987)	3; 5–8; 5 years	Expressive pragmatics	DO
Screening Children for Related Early Education Needs	Hresko, Reid, Hammill, Ginsburg, & Baroody (1988)	3–7 years	Multiple academic areas	DO
Test of Early Language Development-2	Hresko, Reid, Hammill (1991)	2–7; 11 years	Receptive and expressive language	DO
Language Identification Screening Test for Kindergarten	Illerbrun, McLeod, Greenough, & Haines (1984)	Kindergarten	Receptive and expressive language	DO

*Method is parent report (PR) or direct observation (DO).

however, the naturalness of an informal procedure will depend on the specific measure. Procedures in the middle combine structure and observation in a way that maximizes potential for data collecting.

FORMAL PROCEDURES.　Formal procedures are commercially available tests that are standardized and/or norm-referenced (Table 6.2 provides examples of norm-referenced, standardized tests). A standardized test is one that must be administered in a prescribed manner. A norm-referenced test compares one child's behavior with other children's behavior. Typically, such tests include mean and standard deviation scores that tell the extent to which a child deviates from same-age peers. The mean is the average performance of the normative group. The standard deviation gives the range of the variance or diverse range of scores in a population. Scores that fall within one standard deviation of the mean are generally considered within normal limits and account for 68 percent of the population. Often, two standard deviations below the mean is considered an indication of language impairment. This area of the normal bell curve accounts for 5 percent of the population. Percentiles are also used as a way to describe development. Percentiles indicate how a child performs relative to same-age peers. For example, if a child scores at the 10th percentile, 90 percent of the children performed better than she did.

Tests are only as good as the psychometric criteria on which they are based. Psychometric criteria reflect the **reliability** and validity of the test instruments. Reliability refers to the consistency of a test. The more stable a test is the more one can trust the results. Validity, as we have said, is how well a test measures what it says it measures.

> Formal procedures are generally norm-referenced and they tend to be more structured.

TABLE 6.2   Examples of formal tools for speech-language assessment

Name of Test	Authors	Areas Assessed	Expressive	Receptive	Ages
Assessing Semantic Skills through Everyday Language	Barrett, Zachman, & Huisingh (1988)	Semantics	✔	✔	3–9; 11 years
Comprehensive Receptive and Expressive Vocabulary Test	Wallace & Hammill (1994)	Semantics	✔	✔	4–17 years
Expressive One-Word Picture Vocabulary Test	Gardner (1982)	Semantics	✔		2–12 years
Full-Range Picture Vocabulary Test	Ammons & Ammons (1948)	Semantics			2–adult
Receptive One-Word Picture Vocabulary Test	Gardner (1985)	Semantics		✔	2; 10–11; 11 years
Peabody Picture Vocabulary Test–Revised	Dunn & Dunn (1981)	Semantics		✔	2–40 years
Test of Relational Concepts	Edmonston & Thane	Semantics		✔	3–8 years
Test of Word Finding	German (1986)	Semantics	✔	✔	6–12; 11 years
Miller-Yoder Test of Language Comprehension*	Miller & Yoder (1984)	Syntax, morphology		✔	3–8 years
Structured Photographic Expressive Language–Preschool	Werner & Kresheck (1993)	Syntax, morphology	✔		3–5; 11 years
Structured Photographic Expressive Language Test–II	Werner & Kresheck (1983)	Syntax, morphology	✔		4–9; 5 years
Test for Examining Expressive Morphology	Shipley & Stone, (1987)	Morphology	✔		3–8 years
Assessment of Phonological Processes–R	Hodson (1986)	Phonology	✔		Preschool
Arizona Articulation Proficiency Scale	Fudala (1978)	Articulation	✔		3–adult
Bankson-Bernthal Phonological Process Survey Test	Bankson & Bernthal (1990)	Phonology	✔		
Fisher-Logemann Test of Articulation Competence	Fisher & Logemann (1971)	Articulation	✔		

TABLE 6.2 Examples of formal tools for speech-language assessment (continued)

Name of Test	Authors	Areas Assessed	Expressive	Receptive	Ages
Goldman-Fristoe Test of Articulation	Goldman & Fristoe (1986)	Articulation	✔		2–16+ years
Khan-Lewis Phonological Analysis	Kahn & Lewis (1986)	Phonology	✔		2–5; 11 years
Phonological Process Analysis	Weiner (1979)	Phonology	✔		
Photo Articulation Test–Revised	Pendergast, Dickey, Selmar, & Soder (1992)	Articulation	✔		3; 6–8 years
Templin-Darley Test of Articulation	Templin & Darley (1969)	Articulation	✔		3–8 years
Communication & Symbolic Behavior Scales	Wetherby & Prizant (1993)	Pragmatics	✔		8–24 months
Test of Pragmatic Skills	Shulman (1985)	Pragmatics	✔		3–8; 11 years
Basic Language Concepts Test	Engelman, Ross, Bingham (1986)	Language	✔	✔	4–6; 5 years
Boehm Test of Basic Concepts	Boehm (1986)	Language		✔	3–5 years
Communication Abilities Diagnostic Test	Johnston & Johnston (1990)	Language			3–8 years
Clark-Madison Test of Oral Language	Clark & Madison (1986)	Language	✔		4–8 years
Criterion-Referenced Inventory of Language*	Wiig (1990)	Language	✔		
MacArthur Inventory of Language Development	Fenson, Dale, Reznick, Thal, Bates, Hartung, Pethick, & Reilly (1993)	Language	✔		8–30 months
Preschool Language Assessment Instrument	Blank, Rose, & Berline (1978)	Language	✔	✔	3–8 years
Preschool Language Scale–3	Zimmerman, Steiner, & Pond (1991)	Language	✔	✔	18 months– 17 years
Receptive-Expressive Emergent Language Test–2	Bzoch & League (1991)	Language	✔	✔	0–3 years

(continued)

TABLE 6.2   Examples of formal tools for speech-language assessment (continued)

Name of Test	Authors	Areas Assessed	Expressive	Receptive	Ages
Reynell Developmental Language Scales (U.S. Edition)	Reynell & Gruber (1990)	Language	✔	✔	1–6; 11 years
Sequenced Inventory of Communication	Hedrick, Prather, & Tobin (1984)	Language	✔	✔	4–48 months
Test of Problem Solving	Zachman, Barrett, Huisingh, & Jorgensen (1995)	Problem Solving	✔	✔	6–11 years
Test for Auditory Comprehension of Language–Revised	Carrow-Woolfolk (1985)	Language		✔	3–9; 11 years
Test of Language Development–Primary: 2	Newcomer & Hammill (1988)	Language	✔	✔	4–8; 11 years
Utah Test of Language Development–3	Mecham (1989)	Language	✔	✔	3–9; 11 years

*Indicates a criterion-referenced assessment tool.

McCauley and Swisher (1984a) evaluated preschool speech and language tests for their psychometric properties. They found that fewer than 20 percent of the 30 tests evaluated met half of the psychometric criteria (Table 6.3). This finding indicates that the validity and reliability of many speech and language tools were questionable.

TABLE 6.3   Properties of norm-referenced tests

Psychometric Criteria

1. Information about the standardization sample that includes geographic, socioeconomic, and normalcy should be present in the test manual.*
2. Adequate sample size should be present for the subgroups of the standardization (100 or more per subgroup).
3. Systematic item analysis should be reported.
4. Measures of central tendency and variability of the test results should be present.
5. There should be evidence of concurrent validity.*
6. There should be evidence of predictive validity.*
7. There should be an estimate of test–re-test reliability (0.90 or better significant at the 0.05 level).*
8. There should be evidence of inter-examiner reliability (0.90 or better at the 0.05 level).*
9. Test administration, scoring, and interpretation should be described in detail and be consistent with the standardization procedures.
10. There should be information about test administrator or scorer qualifications.

*Indicates which criteria were not achieved frequently.

More recently, Plante and Vance (1994) reported that validity and reliability of preschool language tests continue to be a major problem. They found that only 38 percent of the 21 tests evaluated met half of the psychometric criteria set forth by McCauley and Swisher. Plante and Vance further studied four of the tests that met half of the psychometric criteria by administering them to a group of children with normal language development and a group identified as language impaired. The tests were not able to differentiate normally developing children from children with language impairment.

The implications of these findings are that language interventionists need to evaluate the tests they administer carefully in terms of validity and reliability. Plante and Vance's findings emphasize the importance of comparing the test's population characteristics with those of the child being assessed. When tests do not include children with various language abilities in their normative sample, the variation is decreased, which makes it more likely that children with language impairment will appear very different from the normed population. Plante and Vance (1994) further suggest that language interventionists need to evaluate the test manual for evidence of discriminant analysis. Such an analysis will report the accuracy of a test in identifying language-impaired children and give an empirically derived cutoff score at each age level.

Look in the test manual for validity and reliability data.

Formal tests may not consider the child's ability to use language in natural and functional contexts.

What should the language interventionist do if he discovers that a widely used test has poor reliability and validity? There are three possible responses: First, and most extreme, would be not to use the test information, or the test, in the future. The second would be to use the test information with qualifications, cautioning the interpretation of the data based on the area of concern (i.e., the child is not part of the population on which the test was normed). Similarly, the language interventionist might use the information obtained descriptively as strengths and weaknesses. The last response would be to become an assertive consumer advocate for better test construction, involving contacting publishers of tests and sharing concerns.

Another disadvantage of formal tests is that they often lack ecological validity. That is, they fail to take into account the child's ability to use language in functional or everyday contexts. Many formats place the child as the "responder" in question-answer situations that are unlike any found in real-life situations. Thus, the artificial nature of the testing environment fails to tap into the child's use of language as she would interact in everyday situations. Further, with the exception of few specially designed tests (cf. Shulman, 1985; Wetherby & Prizant, 1993), it is difficult to assess a child's pragmatic skills using formal procedures.

A final weakness of standardized tests is their restricted usefulness outside the purpose of identifying a problem. Formal procedures have limited application to intervention planning and monitoring intervention progress. Because most tests are designed to assess fairly broad areas of skills, it is not appropriate to derive specific intervention targets from the tests (McCauley & Swisher, 1984b). This same reason has been used in arguing that formal tests should not be relied upon solely for evaluating the progress made during intervention. McCauley and Swisher (1984b) warn against using norm-referenced tests to assess progress because they may over- or underestimate change observed as a result of intervention. With respect to overestimation, children who show improvement on a norm-referenced test show a "gain score." For example, a pre-intervention score of 70 compared with a post-intervention score of 80 would yield a gain score of 10. The significance of a gain score is difficult to interpret, because the gain score can be a result of chance or a test's imperfect reliability. Thus, a child who makes no discernable progress in therapy, yet shows a gain score, may not have made the progress indicated by the gain score (McCauley & Swisher, 1984b). Underestimation occurs when a child does not show gains on a norm-referenced test, yet has clearly made gains in intervention. In this instance, the norm-referenced test is too broad to measure the specific changes observed.

Despite these many setbacks, formal procedures are relied upon to diagnose children with language impairment and to establish eligibility criteria for intervention. Speech-language pathologists (language interventionists) and others concerned with the limitations of formal procedures can use **clinical judgment** and informal procedures to guide decision making. Clinical judgment is a belief statement(s) about a client's abilities. The belief statement is derived from the professional's clinical experience, intuition, and knowledge of language development and language impairment. The best approach for making diagnoses and eligibility determinations is to use a combination of formal procedures, informal procedures, and clinical judgment.

INFORMAL PROCEDURES. Informal procedures include developmental scales, parent interviews, criterion-referenced tests (commercially available or self-constructed probes), and language sampling (see Table 6.2). These procedures allow a level of flexibility and in-depth testing not afforded by standardized tests. Developmental scales are checklists of speech-language behaviors or milestones that occur in children with normally developing speech and language. These might be administered by observing the child or through a caregiver's report. A developmental scale provides information about the child's overall development. In contrast, criterion-referenced tests probe specifically into one area of language learning.

Criterion-referenced tests typically evaluate a very specific area, such as pronouns, speech acts, or meaning relations in sentences (such as patient or agent). Criterion-referenced tests evaluate a child's performance on certain items. A number correct score is derived. Criteria are set at an arbitrary level, for instance, 80 percent success in order for the child to succeed. Criterion-referenced tests are thought to be more appropriate measures of change that occurs during intervention because of their specific focus. Unfortunately, with the exception of a few—for example, the Criterion Referenced Inventory of Language (Wiig, 1990) and the Miller-Yoder Test of Language Comprehension (Miller & Yoder, 1984)—there are a limited number of criterion-referenced tests available. Thus, language interventionists rely on constructing their own probes to evaluate specific areas of language ability. An example of an informal probe would involve assessing production of the final "s" and "z" in nonmorphophonemic contexts such as "bu*s*" or "fu*zz*" (i.e., words that do not have morphology expressed phonemically such as "bat*s*" or "goe*s*"). This type of probe might be used to determine if a child who is not producing some grammatical morphemes, such as plural-*s* or possessive -*s*, has a problem learning morphemes exclusively, or if the child also has a phonological component to the problem and has difficulty producing these sounds at the end of words that are not marked with grammatical morphemes (e.g., "house" or "rose"). This

Informal procedures allow more flexibility.

Criterion-referenced measures describe the skills that a child actually can display.

is an important thing to know because the child who cannot produce "s" or "z" in either morphological or nonmorphological contexts presents a different problem than the child who can produce final "s" and "z" in phonological, but not morphological context. The information derived from this probe would greatly influence whether grammatical or phonological goals were targeted for intervention.

Language Sampling

Spontaneous language samples provide a rich opportunity to observe a child's integrated communication abilities.

A very rich source of information about a child's expressive language can be derived from **language sampling,** which is the collection of the child's language during play, telling stories, or through everyday conversational exchanges. The advantage of this procedure is that it provides a detailed picture of the child's communication in a fairly naturalistic context. A drawback is that transcription and analyses of samples are time consuming. However, the gains in information derived from language sampling and the increase in computerized programs to assist with language analysis (Miller, Freiberg, Rolland, & Reeves, 1992) make this procedure a worthwhile investment.

The most important consideration when eliciting a language sample from a child is that it be representative. That is, the language the child produces represents a true picture of how the child interacts with others. Thus, akin to our concerns of validity and reliability for formal assessment procedures, we must also be concerned about the validity and reliability of language sampling by obtaining a representative sample. Miller (1981) suggests several factors to be taken into consideration to ensure a representative sample. These include:

1. The nature of the interaction
2. The setting where the interaction takes place
3. The materials used to elicit the language sample
4. The methods of recording the sample
5. The size of the language sample

The nature of the interaction concerns not only who interacts with the child, but also how the stage is set so that the child feels comfortable to talk. Speech-language pathologists, teachers, peers, and parents are excellent candidates for interactional partners. If the interactant is unfamiliar to the child, or if the child is placed in a new situation, he may be reticent to interact for the first few minutes of play. Rather than ask a series of closed questions that will elicit a minimal response, such as "What's that?" or yes/no questions, "Do you like dolls?" it is recommended that the child be given time to warm up to the environment with a short period of silent play. The danger with asking too many questions is that it could result in many one-word responses from the child, which in turn will negatively influence the representativeness of the sample. An alternative to a short silent period would be to have the individual who is interacting with the child produce "self-talk" or "parallel play." The technique of "self-talk" involves the interactor's playing with some of the materials and talking about what she is doing. "Parallel play" means to play alongside the child, either doing similar things as the child or a variation of the same theme. During parallel play, the interactant can talk about what the child is doing by using "description." Complying with the child's play agenda is referred to as "following the child's lead." The ability to follow the child's lead relies on the language interventionist's willingness to let the child control the pace and topic of play. Even with artful use of all the techniques available, the person collecting the language sample will not be successful if she is not enjoying herself or is not truly interested in the child and play. These types of procedures are illustrated in the following example:

> [Erik and the language interventionist are playing with a set of toys.]
> ERIK: [Moves a truck up a street ramp].
> LI: [*Follows his lead* by doing the same thing with a motorcycle.]
> LI: "You're going up the hill. (*Description of child's play*).
> I'm coming too. (*Self-talk*).
> I hope I can make it. (*Self-talk*).
> Uhoh. I stopped! (*Self-talk*).
> I need gas. (*Self-talk*)
> Someone, help me!"
> ERIK: [Pretends to give the language interventionist's car gas.]
> LI: [Gives the child's car some gas. (*parallel play*)]

Language samples can be obtained in many places, including the home, classroom, or clinic setting. There may be certain limitations on communication in some settings. The language interventionist should be aware of what these are and take them into account when determining representativeness. For example, there may be times in a child care setting, such as group reading, when it is inappropriate to take a language sample because the teacher is the main speaker and interaction is not encouraged.

Materials that are used to elicit a language sample should be interesting to the child. The child's developmental level and interests, as well as physical and sensory abilities, should be taken into consideration when selecting toys. The use of familiar books and games may elicit more routinized language. Puzzles may elicit locatives "on" and "in." Introduction of unfamiliar toys or toys with Band-Aids or other unusual characteristics (broken leg, pink hair, etc.) are novel and lead to child-initiated topics. Another common procedure is to use a play theme, such as a farm with many people and animals or a schoolhouse with children and teachers.

Language sampling can gather quantitative data to support a diagnosis of language disorder or it can be a source of qualitative data for planning intervention.

During the sampling, the language interventionist will audiotape or transcribe on-line what the child says (i.e., write down what is said as it is being said). In many cases it is not feasible to transcribe every word produced by the child on-line. Instead, the language interventionist can write down utterances on a time basis that would involve 5 minutes of transcribing and 5 minutes of rest, until a set-upon time or number of utterances had been attained. Regardless of whether on-line recording or audio-recording is used, it is very beneficial to make notes of the ongoing context (i.e., nonverbal occurrences or explanations) or to repeat what the child says when he is not understood.

The size of the language sample will vary depending on the child's willingness and ability to interact. Time sampling or a specified number of utterances can be used as guidelines for how many utterances to analyze or transcribe from a language sample. Miller (1981) recommends a 30-minute sample if the time sample format is used. The alternative is to set a number of utterances to be collected. The sample should have at minimum 50 child utterances in order to be representative. The larger the sample, the more representative the sample. However, because of time constraints, 50 to 100 utterances samples are common.

> **The language sample should have at least 50 child utterances.**

Once a language sample has been collected and transcribed, analyses deemed relevant to the child's needs can be initiated. All areas of language (syntax, phonology, morphology, semantics, pragmatics, and interactions thereof) can be performed on any language sample if careful attention is given to recording the verbal and nonverbal contexts of interaction.

Informal procedures will be relied upon more when the purpose of the assessment is to plan intervention or to monitor the progress of an intervention program. Procedures such as specific probes or language sampling provide a more detailed look at the child's skills. It is for this reason that they are appropriate for determining intervention goals. Additionally, informal procedures may be more effective at measuring gains observed during intervention because they can be tailored to evoke the child's speech and language targets.

Specific Informal Assessment Procedures

Assessment must determine not only *whether* a problem exists, but also *the nature* and *extent of the problem.* Typically, both receptive and expressive language functioning are assessed in multiple domains of language (i.e., form, content, and use). Following are a number of potential analyses for several areas of language with an emphasis on analyses that can be performed on language sample data.

> **Phonology, morphology, and syntax are assessed receptively and expressively.**

FORM. Form is divided into phonology, morphology, and syntax. When evaluating form, one will ask the following questions:

1. Does the child understand sentences of varying complexity?
2. Does the child have difficulty formulating grammatical sentences? If so, in what respect are they ungrammatical? Do they lack appropriate noun phrase marking or elaboration? Are negation and question formation skills at the appropriate developmental level?
3. Is age-appropriate morphology present? Is noun–verb agreement appropriate for the child's age?
4. Does the child produce grammatical sentences, yet produce short utterances that lack grammatical complexity? If so, what is the level of complexity used? What levels of complexity are absent?
5. Does the child produce sentences that are difficult to understand (i.e., unintelligible)? Is the unintelligibility due to a problem producing speech sounds or production of phonological processes?
6. Does the child have difficulty producing some sounds you would expect her to be able to make or is she producing phonological processes that you would predict to be absent at this point in her development?

Although there are several formal or standardized procedures available for assessing syntax, morphology, and phonology (see Table 6.2), the previous questions can also be explored using informal procedures. One commonly used index of syntax derived from a language sample is mean length of utterance. As discussed in an earlier chapter, mean length of utterance (MLU) is the average length of a child's utterance. It is a gross measure of complexity and is computed by counting the number of morphemes per utterance, adding the morphemes, and dividing by the number of utterances. An example is given below for a child who is 3½ years old. The child (C) is playing with a McDonald's toyhouse with an adult examiner (E). The morphemes per utterance are in parentheses. Chapman (1981) provides guidelines for counting morphemes to compute MLU based on Brown (1973). These guidelines are provided in Table 6.4.

MLU is a gross measure of complexity.

E: I almost sat on it.
    1. C: Yeah. (1)
    2. C: These go here. (3)
    3. C: That my fry. (3)
E: That's right.
E: That's your French fry.
    4. C: Open these me. (3)
E: Open that for you?
    5. C: Yeah. (1)
    6. C: Me not do. (3)
E: There you go.
    7. C: That up? (2)
E: Yep, that goes anywhere you want.
    8. C: Me go. (2)

E: You can go in there.
    9. C: Put this on. (3)
E: I'll put the lid on.
    10. C: Where this go? (3)
E: Where does that go?
E: It goes up here.

Total morphemes = 24
Dividing 24 by 10 utterances = an MLU of 2.4 morphemes

TABLE 6.4   Guidelines for MLU computation

Do Count:
1. Each meaningful morpheme.
   Example: Dog = 1, Dog/s = 2

Count as Only One Morpheme:
2. Words that are repeated for emphasis.
   "No!" "No!" "No!" = 1 morpheme per utterance in 3 utterances
3. Compound words (2 or more free morphemes), proper names, and ritualized or routinized forms.
   "Bye bye" "choo choo" "oopsadaisy" "snowman" "Big bird"
4. Irregular past tense verbs.
   "fell" "saw" "ran" etc.
5. The first instance of a disfluency.
   Example: "My, my *my baby is cry/ing*." Count only one of the "my"s.
6. Words such as "yeah" "nuuh" "no" "yes" "ok" "hi."
7. Semi-auxiliaries or catenatives such as "gonna" "wanna" "gotta."
8. Diminutive forms (-y) "daddy" "mommy" "puppy" "rainy."

Don't Count:
1. Fillers such as "oh" or "um." These forms serve to hold the conversational floor, but should not be counted as adding meaningful content or complexity to the child's message.
2. Counting, alphabet recitals, singing, nursery rhymes. Utterances that appear to be memorized strings of information should be excluded.
3. Conjunctions at the beginning of sentences that appear repeatedly throughout the language sample. Some children begin many sentences with "and" or "but."
4. Imitations of the adult utterances that exceed 20% of the entire sample and/or if their inclusion leads to an unrepresentative sample.
5. Frequent self-repetitions. Miller & Chapman recommend two analyses be conducted, one with and one without the self-repetitions. Self-repetitions should be excluded when their inclusion leads to an overall increase or decrease of MLU.

Based on Miller & Chapman (1979).

If this MLU value had been derived from 50 utterances and from a representative sample, it could be compared to normative guidelines to determine if this child was within normal limits for her age (Miller, 1981) (see Table 6.5). An MLU of 2.4 would be in Brown's Stage II of

TABLE 6.5   Mean length of utterance normative data

Early Stage I MLU					
	1.01	1.10	1.20	1.30	1.40	1.50
Predicted Age (+ 1 SD)	19.1 (16.4–21.8)	19.8 (17.1–22.5)	20.6 (17.9–23.3)	21.4 (18.7–24.1)	22.2 (19.5–24.9)	23 (18.5–27.5)

Late Stage I MLU					
	1.60	1.70	1.80	1.90	2.00	
Predicted Age (+ 1 SD)	23.8 (19.3–28.3)	24.6 (20.1–29.1)	25.3 (20.8–29.8)	26.1 (21.6–30.6)	26.9 (21.5–32.3)	

Stage II MLU					
	2.10	2.20	2.30	2.40	2.50	
Predicted Age (+ 1 SD)	27.7 (22.3–33.1)	28.5 (23.1–33.9)	29.3 (23.9–34.7)	30.1 (24.7–35.5)	30.8 (23.9–37.7)	

Stage III MLU					
	2.60	2.70	2.80	2.90	3.00	
Predicted Age (+ 1 SD)	31.6 (24.7–38.5)	32.4 (25.5–39.3)	33.2 (26.3–40.1)	34 (27.1–40.9)	34.8 (28–41.6)	

Early Stage IV					
	3.10	3.20	3.30	3.40	3.50	
Predicted Age (+ 1 SD)	35.6 (28.8–42.4)	36.3 (29.5–43.1)	37.1 (30.3–43.9)	37.9 (31.1–44.7)	38.7 (30.8–46.6)	

Late Stage IV–Early Stage V					
	3.60	3.70	3.80	3.90	4.00	
Predicted Age (+ 1 SD)	39.5 (31.6–47.4)	40.3 (32.4–48.2)	41.1 (33.2–49)	41.8 (33.9–49.7)	42.6 (36.7–48.5)	

Late Stage V MLU					
	4.10	4.20	4.30	4.40	4.50	
Predicted Age (+ 1 SD)	43.4 (37.5–49.3)	44.2 (38.8–50.1)	45 (39.1–50.9)	45.8 (39.9–51.7)	46.6 (40.3–52.9)	

Note: Age is in months.

Based on Miller (1981).

language development, with a predicted chronological age of 30.1 months (+ 1 standard deviation of 24.7–35.5 months). The child from whom we elicited the language sample was 42 months of age. Thus, the MLU was below age-level expectations by at least one standard deviation. It is critical to remember that MLU is a gross measure of syntax. It cannot be used by itself to indicate the presence or absence of an expressive syntax impairment. Klee (1992) found that mean syntactic length (MSL), a measure similar to MLU that excludes one-word utterances, was a good diagnostic indicator to differentiate between children with typical language and those with specific language impairment.

Additional informal analyses such as assigning structural stage (Miller, 1981), developmental sentence scoring (Lee, 1974; Hughes, Fey, & Long, 1992), or language assessment, remediation, and screening procedure (LARSP) (Crystal, 1979) are available to evaluate the use of sentence constituents and their relationships more precisely. These procedures allow a much closer examination of expressive syntax, and most of them can be computed by hand or via computer analysis programs (Long & Fey, 1993; Miller & Chapman, 1993).

Grammatical analysis evaluates production of Brown's 14 grammatical morphemes.

With respect to morphology, a grammatical morpheme analysis also can be performed on a child's language sample. This analysis evaluates the child's production of Brown's 14 grammatical morphemes in terms of percent correct usage in obligatory contexts. An obligatory context is the presence of a morpheme where it is required in adult language use. For example, a child who says "That mine" has omitted the copula "is" in an obligatory context. The copula can be contracted, so it is an omission of a contractible copula. A contractible copula or morpheme does not have to be contracted to be contract*ible*. For instance, in the sentence "She is happy," the "is" is contractible, because you could say "She's happy." Uncontractible copulas (and auxiliaries) are those that cannot be contracted, such as "There he is," which cannot be stated as "There he's." The following example shows the computation of the percent correct use of the contractible auxiliary in obligatory contexts.

1. C: Here's my hat.
2. C: I'm going home now.
3. C: My mom says it's cold outside.
4. C: But she *is fixing dinner.
5. C: She is making macaroni and cheese.
6. C: That's my favorite in the whole world.
7. C: I'm gonna eat my broccoli too.
8. C: It gives me muscles.
9. C: There's father.
10. C: He's driving the Volvo.

The occasions that the child produced the contractible auxiliary are underlined. The times that the child should have used an auxiliary, but omitted it, are indicated by an asterisk before the missing morpheme. Thus, utterance #4 was produced as "But she fixing dinner." Percent use in obligatory contexts is computed by counting the number of times the morpheme is used correctly divided by the number of times that it was obligated (present + omitted + used incorrectly). The ratio in the example presented would be 4/5 or 80 percent correct use in obligatory contexts. These data are then compared with developmental data, which tells us that the contractible auxiliary would be predicted to be mastered (90 percent correct use) at Post Stage V language stage.

Phonological disorders often occur in the child who is displaying a language impairment. These children may be described as being hard to understand or as not saying their sounds right. Crucial steps during assessment include understanding which sounds the child can produce, the contexts of correct and incorrect sound production, and the child's use or overuse of phonological processes. At this point, it is important to consider whether a child displays an articulation disorder or a phonological disorder, or a combination of the two. Articulation disorders can be of a *functional* (i.e., of unknown origin) or *organic etiology*. A distorted "s" sound, often referred to as a lisp, or a "w" for "r" substitution, such as saying "wing" for "ring," are common examples of functional articulation disorders. An organic articulation disorder is one for which there is a structural reason for the child's difficulty in making the sound(s), such as a cleft palate or weakness and inarticulate movements due to damage of the central nervous system.

> It is important to determine whether the child has an articulation disorder or a phonological disorder or both.

The key to why these are articulation disorders and are not associated with phonological disorders is that *a phonological disorder reveals a pattern of responses or a rule-based phenomenon*. These patterns of responses have been called phonological processes. One example of a phonological process that is common among children with and without language impairment is final consonant deletion. The child leaves off the end of a closed syllable (e.g., consonant-vowel-consonant) and says /d / ("daw") for "dog" and /kae/ ("cah") for "cat." In this case, a child will leave off many final consonants regardless of his ability to produce the sound itself. Thus, in the example given, it is not that the child cannot produce a "g" or a "t," but that the child has not learned to put a final consonant on CVC structures. However, it is important to note that often, even in the case of speech problems of an organic origin, phonological processes do occur. Thus, articulation and phonological problems may coexist in cases of functional or organic etiology.

Finally, a small number of children have been referred to as having developmental verbal apraxia. These children have difficulties with the sequencing of motor movements needed for speech production. Their speech is characterized as very difficult to understand and effortful. Evaluation of the child's oral motor structures and functions as well as prosody is warranted. A thorough understanding of the sounds and contexts that a child is able and not able to produce assists in determining the nature of the problem. This can be accomplished by generating a phonetic inventory for the child. A phonetic inventory consists of all the phones the child makes according to manner and placement. Syllable and word shape abilities of children also provide valuable information on their developing phonological systems.

Phonological abilities can be assessed using a variety of formal or informal procedures. Some tests assess articulation abilities on a sound-by-sound basis, others assess phonological processes, others provide evaluation of both. Further, analysis of spontaneous speech sound use from a language sample is often helpful in children with limited language skills. (Refer to Table 6.2 for a summary of these available procedures.)

CONTENT. Content includes understanding and production of vocabulary, semantic relations of meanings found in one-, two-, and three-word utterances, and case relations in sentences. Content also refers to the propositions or ideas within utterances. The language interventionist may ask the following questions with respect to age-appropriateness:

> Assessment of language content considers vocabulary, semantic relations, and case relations in sentences.

1. Does this child understand and produce a number of words and a variety of word types?
2. Does the child understand and express words to convey different meanings?
3. Is the child able to understand and express a variety of ideas at the sentence level?
4. Does the child have difficulty retrieving words to express his ideas?

Although there are numerous tests available to assess vocabulary understanding and production, fewer formal instruments are available to assess word type and relational meaning in utterances. In the past, the variety of words a child used was evaluated using the language sample with a measure called the **type-token ratio (TTR)** (Templin, 1957). The TTR is used to determine the diversity of words spoken. A TTR is computed by dividing the number of different words (types) used by the total number of words used (tokens) in a 50-utterance sample. A TTR of 0.50 is within normal limits. The usefulness of the TTR to determine language-impaired from nonimpaired populations has been challenged (Klee, 1992; Watkins, Kelly, Harbers, & Hollis,

1994). Instead of using the TTR, some clinical researchers have begun to look more closely at the types of words that children produce in their samples. Klee (1992) found that a child's **total number of words (TNW)** and **total number of different words (TNDW)** are two measures that differentiated children with specific language impairment from those without language impairment. Additional detailed information about a child's semantic diversity can be gained by examining the TTRs of individual parts of speech. For instance, Watkins, Rice, and Moltz, (1993) have examined verb type-token ratios in children. The same can be done with nouns, adjectives, or adverbs to provide clinically relevant information. Watkins and others (1994) suggest evaluating the child's total TNDW as well as TNDW for specific form classes such as nouns, verbs, adjectives, pronouns, and copula/auxiliary/modal verbs.

> The type-token ratio is a measure of the number of different words a child uses.

The evaluation of the relational meaning of the words involves a semantic relations analysis. This type of analysis can be performed when children are producing one-, two-, and three-word combinations. The analysis details the meaning expressed by words. For example, a child who says "daddy go," "mommy kiss," and "doggy jump" is expressing the meaning relation of "agent + action." During the language sampling, the language interventionist needs to be careful to note the contexts in which the child produces utterances in order to derive the child's intended meaning. The utterances are then coded according to their meaning. Categories for one-, two-, and three-word semantic relations are presented in Table 6.6.

> Semantic relations analysis is evaluation of the relational meaning of the child's words.

Many children who display language impairments in their first five years of life are later identified as having word finding problems. That is, children may know a word, but be unable to retrieve the word when they want to use it. There are only a few standardized tests available for assessing these difficulties (refer to Table 6.2). Evaluating a language sample for excessive use of nondescript terms (i.e., using "this" instead of the referent label) and a low NDW may be indications of problems in this area. In addition, McGregor and Appel (1994) provide three nonstandard probes to assess word finding problems. These include repeated confrontation naming (i.e., asking the child to label a picture three times in a row), story retelling and drawings, and cued naming (i.e., giving the child semantic, syntactic, or phonological cues to assist in retrieving the word).

USE. How children use language to communicate their needs and their ability to regulate conversation may be determined by asking the following basic questions:

> Assessment of language use considers the child's ability to communicate her needs and ability to regulate conversation.

1. Does the child understand and express a variety of intentions?
2. Does the child express a variety of intentions in appropriate ways? Is the child responding and initiating with a variety of

TABLE 6.6   Semantic relation analysis

Semantic Relation	Level		
	One word	**Two word**	**Three word**
Nomination "that" "that ball"			
Recurrence "more pie"			
Rejection "no juice"			
Disappearance "no bear"			
Denial "no boy"			
Notice "hi mommy"			
Agent + Action "daddy go"	*********		
Action (+ Object) "ride bike"			
Agent + Object "doggy ball"	*********		
Action + Location "sit blankie"	*********		
Locative State "me bed"			
Possession "sissy duck"			
Attribution "big frog"			
Instrument + Action "hammer nail"	*********		
Experience + Experiencer "baby sad"	*********		
Classificatory "toby boy"	*********		
Comitative "walk mommy"	*********		
Conjunction "daddy mommy"	*********		
Total			

Based on Bloom & Lahey (1978) and Brown (1973).

interactional partners? Does the child follow the topic of conversation and contribute appropriately?

3. Does the child participate in conversation in ways that lead to continued successful interactions? Can the child monitor interactions and repair conversations when they break down?

4. Is the child able to formulate and produce an appropriate narrative that is cohesive, free of communication breakdowns, with sufficiently complex syntax?

Several methods exist for evaluating language use in young children. Because of the need for functional contexts, assessment usually involves informal procedures such as language samples or setting up situations to elicit specific speech acts. However, a few formal assessment tools for very young children have emerged that assess functional language use (cf. Wetherby and Prizant, 1993). Brinton and Fujiki (1994) detail an assessment approach that places conversation as the context of choice for assessment. Their approach focuses on three essential components of conversation: turn exchange, topic manipulation, and conversational repairs. Brinton and Fujiki provide a list of observations concerning the child who may be experiencing difficulty conveying their message to others (Table 6.7).

TABLE 6.7 Observations in order to screen conversation skills

Observation	Not Observed	Sometimes Present	Frequently Observed
The child hesitates to interact with peers and adults.			
The child interrupts other speakers.			
The child does not introduce referents when a new topic begins.			
The child does not contribute to topics introduced by others.			
The child continues to persist with one topic, when the topic has been changed.			
The child focuses on tangential elements of the topic, not the "big picture" of the topic.			
The child is late in responding to questions.			
You have to work hard to interact with the child.			
The child does not respond appropriately to requests for clarification such as "Huh?" "What?" or "Which one?"			
The child does not ask for help if she does not follow the conversation.			
Certain aspects of the child's communication distract from the interaction process.			

Adapted from Brinton and Fujiki (1994).

There are several types of pragmatic analyses that can be used with language samples.

Speech Act and Conversational Participation. Informal procedures for evaluating language use include determining the types of communication intents children are expressing. Contextual notes on what is occurring during a language sample is crucial for a pragmatic analysis. Several types of pragmatic analyses can be performed on language samples that vary depending on the age of the child and the area of language use of interest. Speech acts for children at the one-word level can be identified using Dore's (1978) conversational acts (see Table 6.8).

Fey (1986) provides another useful system for evaluating the communication intents of children at various levels of language development. Fey's system involves analyzing children's utterances in terms of assertiveness and responsiveness (Table 6.9). The child's utterances are analyzed at fairly specific levels, allowing the language interventionist to evaluate production of speech acts. This analysis leads to a determination of the child's overall social-conversational participation. Social-conversational participation can fall along a continuum of assertiveness and responsiveness that result in four possible styles: passive, inactive, active, or nonverbal communicator (Figure 6.1). Intervention goals may be established based on these social-conversational profiles. For example, children who are inactive communicators may need to increase assertive acts. Alternatively, the intervention plan for a child who is a passive communicator may be to increase responding.

TABLE 6.8 Dore's speech acts

Speech Act	Example
Label	Child: Points to teacher and says "teacher."
Repeat	Adult: "That's a nice puppy." Child: "Puppy." All or part of the adult sentence is repeated.
Answer	Adult: Where's your bear?" Child: "Room."
Request Action	Child: Tries to button coat but can't do it. Child says or gestures for "Help."
Request	Child: Hears car door and says "Daddy?"
Calling	Child: Yells to other "Sister!"
Greeting	Child: "Hi" and "bye" at appropriate times.
Protesting	Child: Cries when parent washes hair (word may be produced).
Practicing	Child: "Book" is said when a book is not present.

Based on Chapman (1981).

TABLE 6.9   Fey's codes for conversational assertiveness and responsiveness

Utterance Level

Assertive Conversational Acts

Requests

Request for Information: Questions used to elicit new information. "Where baby?" "What that?"

Request for Action: Statements that ask the other interactant to perform an action. "You do it." "Put it there."

Request for Clarification: Questions used to clarify a previous utterance. "Huh?" "What did you say?" "The red one?"

Request for Attention: Statements used to gain the attention of or acknowledgment of the other interactant. These statements do not add new information to the interaction. "Look at this!" "Mom!" "Guess!"

Assertives

Comments: Statements that describe observable events. "I'm at school." "You look pretty."

Statements: Expressions of rules, explanations, and feelings not directly observable. "It's supposed to be a circle." "Those are dangerous."

Disagreements: Comments or statements that are in conflict with a previous assertion or that indicate noncompliance to requests. "I don't think so." "Nope." "Forget it."

Performatives

Jokes, teasing, protesting, and warnings. "Watch out!" "Mine!" "Nana nana boo boo."

Responsive Conversational Acts

Response to Requests for Information: Statements that give new information in response to interactants' requests. "That's a cow," in response to "What's that?"

Response to Requests for Action: Statements that occur along with an action in response to interactants' requests. "I did it," while drawing a star as requested by "You do it."

Response to Request for Clarification: Statements that attempt to clarify a previous utterance through repetition or some form of revision. "I said no more," in response to "What did you say?"

Response to Assertives and Performatives: Statements that provide acknowledgment or agreements with no new information added to previous sentence. "Yep," "Mhm" in response to an assertive or performative. When these statements occur along with an assertive, they are coded in an assertive category.

Imitations: Statements that repeat part or all of the prior sentence, with no new information added.

Others: Statements or questions that do not fit into one of the previous categories.

Discourse Level

Topic Initiation: Utterances that present new information unrelated to prior utterance.

Topic Maintenance: Utterances with no new unsolicited information, but that continue to be related to previous utterances.

Topic Extension: Utterances that continue previous utterances and add new information.

Topic Extension–Tangential: Extensions of one aspect of the topic, but in an adequate fashion.

Based on Fey (1986).

FIGURE 6.1   Fey's social-conversational system

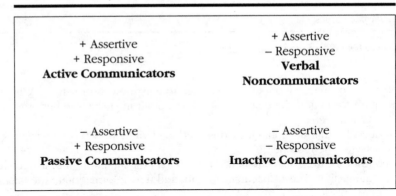

Based on Fey (1986)

Another procedure for coding children's responsiveness and assertiveness is the social interactive coding system (SICS) (Rice, Sell, & Hadley, 1990). SICS is an on-line procedure that codes a child's initiations and responses according to (1) the play activity (e.g., art table, block area, etc.); (2) the interactional partner (e.g., teacher or child); (3) whether the interaction is an initiation or a response and whether it was verbal or nonverbal; (4) the play level (e.g., solitary, adjacent, or social interactive); and (5) the language (e.g., English, other). The language interventionist follows a child for 5 minutes and codes her interactions (see Table 6.10 for the definitions used to code

TABLE 6.10   SICS definitions: Verbal interaction status and play level

Verbal Interactive Status
Initiations (I): A verbal attempt by the child to begin an interaction with another.
Repeat (Rep): Repetition of child's utterance if an initial initiation attempt is not successful.
Response: The verbal, nonverbal, or ignoring by the child in response to an individual.

Verbal	(R-V-1) one-word verbal response
	(R-V) multiword verbal response
Nonverbal	(R-NV) nonverbal response including head nods, smiles, gestures, pointing, etc.
Ignore	(ignore) child ignores interaction partner

Play Level
Play level is coded for the child's interactions with other children. There are three categories:

Solitary	(sol) the child is playing by herself one minute or longer.
Adjacent	(adj) the child is playing by himself but there is a child close by in the same area.
Social Interactive	(SI) the child is playing with another child.

behaviors). After a 5-minute rest, the language interventionist begins again, until a specified amount of sampling is completed. This procedure has been used in classroom settings and has the advantage of being less time-consuming than those that rely on contextually laden language samples or videotape analyses. As with all of these analyses, practice is required at identifying behaviors to ensure reliable and valid results.

A hypothetical transcript and an analysis form are presented in Table 6.11. In this hypothetical case the child tends to initiate to the adult and peer Y in the classroom. These initiations are verbal. Child A also responds to both interactants. Responses are at the verbal one-word level when interacting with a normally developing peer (child Y). However, note that verbal responses are longer than one word when the interactant is the adult (B). Because the sampling took place during one activity, art, it is unclear if initiations or responses would vary under slightly different conditions, such as snack or dramatic

TABLE 6.11 Hypothetical case application of SICS

Child A is the target child, B is the classroom teacher, and Y and Z are two other children. The activity is dramatic play.

1.1	A:	My dress pretty.	1.10	B: Maybe you can find something else to wear.
1.2	B:	Yes. You look very nice.		
1.3	A:	(tugs on dress)	1.11	A: Here my dress {hands dress to Y}.
1.4	B:	Do you want that off?	1.12	B: Oh, you're sharing.
1.5	A:	(nods head yes)	1.13	Y: Now it's my turn.
1.6	B:	(assists child) There you go.	2.1	A: What that? {points to feather boa}
1.7	Y:	Can I play with that now?	2.2	Y: You put it on your neck.
1.8	A:	(shakes head no)	2.3	Y: Like a scarf.
1.9	Z:	You're supposed to share.	2.4	A: Pretty.

SICS Coding Sheet: Form-LAP

Child's name: A   Date: Time: Observer:

Play Activity	Addressee	Verbal Interactive Status	Play Level	Language Used
Dramatic Play	B	(1.1) I (1.3) R-NV (1.5) R-NV X		English
	Y	(1.8) R-NV (1.11) R-V X	SI SI	English
	Y	(2.1) I (2.4) R-V-1 X	SI SI	English

play. Importantly, SICS illustrates the child's abilities under different interaction conditions. In the hypothetical case given here, the SICS supports a tentative hypothesis that this child could benefit from being encouraged to expand verbal responses to peers with the help of the adult in the classroom. The use of one SICS analysis may not be sufficient to assess the child's interactional skills. The child's interactions during other activities and with a range of interactants should be further confirmed with continued analysis.

Another procedure that takes a different approach to coding pragmatic behaviors has been proposed by Prutting and Kirchner (1987). Their procedure involves videotaping an interaction for 15 minutes and rating the interaction on several variables including speech acts, topic maintenance and change, turn-taking, repairs, cohesion, fluency, physical proximity, and eye gaze. The language interventionist judges whether the observed individual performs inappropriately in any of the variables rated. An inappropriate behavior is one that is distracting to the overall interaction. For example, if a child is interacting with a peer and makes no eye contact whatsoever during the interaction, it is likely that the interaction will suffer as a result. In this instance, the variable of "eye gaze" would be marked as inappropriate. The beauty of this coding system is that it rates several verbal, nonverbal, and paralinguistic behaviors. Prutting and Kirchner (1987) field-tested their procedure with children 5 years and older who had either Down syndrome, autism, or specific language impairment. Their results suggest interesting pragmatic profiles that may help to distinguish the groups of children. This procedure would seem particularly helpful in determining which areas of language use (i.e., physical proximity, turn-taking, or prosody) might benefit from intervention.

Situations must be specifically planned to sample infrequently occurring pragmatic behaviors.

Thus far, the pragmatic analyses presented have required the observer to code naturally occurring contexts. However, for infrequently occurring acts, it is advantageous to set up situations to assess the child's abilities. Margulies, Creaghead, and Rolph (1980) provide several helpful guidelines for eliciting speech acts with their pragmatic checklist (Table 6.12).

Narratives. The narrative requires the language interventionist to evaluate the child's formulation of sentences, selection of words, and connection of ideas to convey a story. The narrative analysis provides valuable information about how children bring these areas of language together as early as 3 years of age. Two types of analysis include (1) retelling a story (Paul & Smith, 1993), and (2) telling a personal story (McCabe & Rollins, 1994).

Paul and Smith (1993) used a story retelling task designed by Renfrew (1977)—"The Bus Story Language Test"—to determine differences between "late bloomers," children with normal language

TABLE 6.12 Pragmatic behavior checklist

Pragmatic Behavior	Elicitation Condition	Mode
Greeting	Check as the child enters the room.	
Request for Object	Have crackers in jar within child's view, but out of reach.	
Summoning, Request for Action	Give the child the jar with the cracker. The lid should be on too tight. Tell the child to open the jar and turn away from the child.	
Request for Information	Put peanut butter and jelly on the table and tell the child to get the knife.	
Commenting on Objects	Get the knife, come back to the table, and present a novel object (i.e., giant sunglasses).	
Making Choices	Ask the child if she wants peanut butter or jelly on her cracker.	
Denial	Hand the child the opposite of what she asked for.	
Request for Clarification	Mumble at some point during conversation with the child.	
Response to Request for Clarification	The examiner should request clarification, ask "What?" or "Huh?" at an appropriate time during the conversation.	
Commenting on Action	Drop the knife while spreading peanut butter on the cracker.	
Protesting	Eat the child's cracker (instead of your own).	
Closing	Check as the child leaves the room.	
Maintaining Topic	Check all of the remaining areas on the checklist during conversation with the child	
Changing Topic		
Initiating a Conversation		
Volunteering to Communicate		
Attending to Speaker		
Taking Turns		
Acknowledging		

Mode is Verbal (V), Nonverbal (N), or Not Observed (O).
Materials needed: Crackers, jar with lid, peanut butter, jelly, knife, and novel objects.

Based on Margulies, Creaghead, and Rolph (1980).

skills, and children with specific expressive language impairment at 4 years of age. The bus story is accompanied with pictures that the language interventionist uses as he tells the story to the child. The child is then asked to retell the story. The child's narrative is analyzed using an information score, MLU per T-unit, cohesion adequacy, and lexical diversity (Paul & Smith, 1993). The information score is a measure of relevant information provided by the child. There are normative data provided to evaluate the information score in Renfrew (1977). Analyses such as MLU per T-unit determine the average length of the child's clauses. Cohesion adequacy refers to how well the child links events within the narrative in a manner that logically keeps things together (Liles, 1985). Finally, lexical diversity is the number of word roots spoken by the child. Readers should refer to Paul and Smith (1993) for a report of normative data from a small sampling of children.

The conversational map is a way to elicit narrative from the child.

Another method of analyzing narrative skills is to ask the child tell a personal experience. Peterson and McCabe (1983) use a protocol called the "conversational map" to elicit such narratives. This protocol involves using a story prompt, collecting a minimum of three narratives from each child, using neutral subprompts during the storytelling, minimizing the child's self-consciousness, and giving the child enough time to tell the story. The story prompt is the event or thing that the examiner will ask the child to talk about. McCabe and Rollins (1994) point out that young children are likely to tell stories about being scared or hurt. However, they caution against using narratives that are about experiences with death because these narratives may have more confusion and be structured differently compared to other narratives. Story prompts might include a trip to the dentist, a ride at an amusement park, a fight with a friend or sibling, or something similar. Prompts about trips and birthday parties are discouraged because they might elicit a generic-type story, rather than a specific narrative.

Three narratives are elicited from the child; however, usually only one will be analyzed. The multiple story prompts are used because not all children will be interested in telling a story about the same thing. Thus, eliciting three narratives provides some assurance that the child will be interested in talking about one of the topics. While the child is telling the story, the language interventionist is encouraged to use neutral subprompts. These subprompts keep the child going with his story without too much interruption or interpretation on the part of the language interventionist. They include responses such as acknowledgments ("Oh"), open-ended statements ("Tell me more.") and questions ("Then what"?), and imitating in part or whole the child's last utterance (CHILD: "She was the prettiest princess of all," LANGUAGE INTERVENTIONIST: "She was the prettiest.").

Upon eliciting the narratives, the language interventionist selects the longest narrative for analysis, because narrative length has been found to be related to its complexity (McCabe & Peterson, 1990). Only narratives where the child was present should be used. The narrative macrostructure can be analyzed by using the definitions from McCabe and Rollins (1994) (Table 6.13). A small set of normative data is available by which to analyze the child's narrative structure (see Table 6.14 based on Peterson & McCabe, 1983; and McCabe & Rollins, 1994). It should be kept in mind that these data were derived from a small group of Caucasian, middle-class children and are not readily applied to children from different cultural backgrounds. For example, McCabe & Rollins (1994) indicate that children who are African American often use a "topic-associating narrative" (Michaels, 1981). This type of narrative combines things that happened at a variety of times into one narrative event. In contrast, McCabe and Rollins describe a narrative by a child of Japanese culture who produced very short narratives that may not contain the same level of details compared to Caucasian, North American, English-speaking children.

Teachers may have a particular expectation for narrative production that is not consistent with the narrative production of a child of diverse cultural background. For example, in discourse-based

TABLE 6.13 Hierarchy of narrative structure

Structure Type	Components
One-event narratives	A story that does not contain two past tense events.
Two-event narratives	A story that has no more than two past tense events.
Miscellaneous narratives	A story that has two or more past tense events, but does not match the real-world logical or casual sequence of events.
Leap-Frog narrative	A story the has two or more past tense events, but the order of events does not match the logical event sequence.
Chronological narrative	A story that has two or more past tense events, matches real-world sequence, and has an order that matches a logical sequence of events but no high point (i.e., concentrated evaluation comments).
End-at-High-Point narrative	A story that has two or more past tense events, matches real-world sequence, has an order that matches a logical sequence of events, and has a high point but no resolution following a high point.
Classic narrative	A story that has two or more past tense events, matches real-world sequence, has an order that matches a logical sequence of events, and has a high point and a resolution.

Based on McCabe and Rollins (1994).

TABLE 6.14   Percent occurrence of structural types for narratives

Narrative Structural Type	Age in Years						
	3; 6	4	5	6	7	8	9
Two Event	63.3	15	10	10	2	0	6
Miscellaneous	—	18	10	10	8	0	6
Leap-Frog	10	29	4	6	0	0	0
Chronology	20	23	25	15	25	21	13
End-at-High-Point	3	2	29	23	17	17	17
Classic	3	12	21	35	48	62	58

classroom events, such as sharing time, Micheals and Cazden (1986) found that white teachers with a middle-class background more highly rated oral narratives that had a single topic; high cohesion; clear organization with beginning, midpoint, and finish that has no time shifts; and clear vocabulary, including time and space concepts.

The decision of what should be the assessment focus depends on initial observations of the child and parents' and teachers' reports.

SUMMARY.   The preceding section has provided a wide sampling of the types of analyses that can be performed with young children to better understand their language abilities. The reader will need to read more about and practice each procedure before using it. The decision of which procedures to use and what areas to focus on depend on the observation of the child and reports from the caregiver and significant others in the child's environment. In many cases, young children need to be seen for multiple assessment visits before a diagnosis or plan for intervention can be determined. Young children also may participate in a period of "diagnostic therapy," where the children are enrolled in an intervention setting while data are collected on their speech and language abilities over a period of time.

Classroom Assessment Procedures

The language interventionist may share assessment functions.

The speech-language pathologist (language interventionist) traditionally has taken full responsibility for speech and language assessment. However, within school-based programs, current emphasis on meeting the least restrictive environment (LRE) mandate of IDEA (Individuals with Disabilities Education Act) has resulted in service delivery shifts that have modified the language interventionist's role in assessment and intervention. The parents, special education teacher, the regular education teacher, the language interventionist, the psychologist, and physical therapist work closely together. The language interventionist still has primary legal and ethical responsibility but is likely to share many assessment functions. The language interventionist needs not only to understand the speech and language development and disorders issues associated with a given child, but also to view the whole child. This requires an understanding of motor development, cognitive development (in particular, learning style), self-help skills, and play abilities. Some teams use a transdisciplinary assessment in order to learn about the child's skills from a wholistic perspective (Linder, 1993). (See Chapter 5 for a complete description of collaboration and teaming.)

In best practice circumstances, the teachers, parents, language interventionist, and other professionals will determine the best intervention context given the needs of the participants, the nature of the disorder, and the desired outcome of intervention (Coufal, 1993). Movements toward working with the child within their educational and child care settings indicate increased collaboration between the language interventionist and the caregiver, the regular educator, the special educator, and/or other professionals. This collaboration should be initiated early in the identification stage, following the principles of the collaborative/consultative model (Coufal, 1993). Recall that the purposes of assessment are multifaceted. Classroom assessment can be used to document a child's strengths and weaknesses within a classroom environment, determine eligibility (i.e., relevant educational outcomes), as well as assist in planning intervention. It should be noted that classroom assessment can take place not only in school settings, but also in child care settings. Cirrin (1994) poses three questions to ask when conducting classroom assessment. The same questions can be modified to include assessment of younger children in center-based preschools or home child care. The questions to ask are:

1. What is the child's ability to use language in the classroom/ child care with respect to spoken and listening tasks?
2. What are the characteristics of the teacher's/child care provider's language in the classroom/child care?
3. What concepts, vocabulary, sentence structures, scripts, and pragmatic skills does the child need to be successful in the classroom/child care?

Cirrin (1994) provides an excellent array of checklists for collecting data on the three questions he poses. To answer the first question, observation by the regular education teacher or child care provider is necessary. Information about the child's form and content, listening skills, ability to share and receive information, use of language in the classroom, and knowledge of scripts used in the classroom is necessary. After the teacher has completed the observation checklists, the language interventionist will need to observe the child within the instructional setting while reviewing the teacher-completed forms.

In order to answer the second question, a good collaborative/consultation relationship needs to be established. The assessment of teacher talk is voluntary on the part of the teacher, just as family assessment with the infant-toddler population is voluntary. This voluntariness is a key factor to the collaborative/consultation model (Coufal, 1993). If the teacher agrees to participate, the language interventionist will collect data regarding the length and rate of teacher instruction, the complexity of classroom language, and the effectiveness of questions, directions, and explanations. These data will be collected through direct observation or video- or audiotape recording.

The final question addresses the complexity of the sentence structures and vocabulary of the curriculum materials that the student encounters. The teacher will need to guide the language interventionist with respect to which materials are the most appropriate to examine at any given point. This type of assessment will need to be conducted many times throughout the school year if the student is to successfully link communication with educational outcome.

In addition to classroom demands, it is important to remember that the child's social use of language plays a role in the classroom. For example, many classrooms have group times or group collaboration efforts where certain communication behaviors are expected of the students. Gallagher (1991) suggests that priority should be given to assessing those areas of socialization that have been noticed as problematic by parents, teachers, and peers. Social tasks that may prove difficult for young children include (1) entering into peer groups; (2) responding to ambiguous messages of peers; (3) responding to their own failures; (4) responding to their own successes; (4) responding to group norms and expectations; and (5) responding to teacher expectations (Dodge, 1985). Children with language impairment may also have difficulty initiating with peers, despite being able to initiate conversation with adults (Hadley & Rice, 1991). Thus, the level of support that children need from adults relative to their participation with peer interactions should be evaluated.

> Priority should be given to assessing areas of socialization that have been identified by parents and teachers as problematic.

Children's abilities in all of the previously mentioned areas can be assessed systematically through observation of the classroom and by interviewing the child, teacher, parent, and peers. The answers to these questions should begin to provide a picture of how the child interacts within the classroom setting. Asking these questions should be helpful in determining not only how intervention might be implemented in the classroom environment, but also potential goals for the child's participation within that environment.

ELIGIBILITY CRITERIA

Public policy at the federal, state, and local level is instrumental in detailing the rights of children with special needs. At the federal level, several important pieces of legislation provide guidance for appropriate services within the school setting (Chapter 5 details this legislation). State policies implement federal policy by specifying methods of identifying children for services and providing guidelines for eligibility of services. Certification and/or licensure requirements are also established on a state-by-state basis. Local school policies may further interpret state guidelines.

Some children may be diagnosed with a language and/or communication impairment; however, they may or may not qualify for special services in the schools. To a great extent, eligibility determination is agreed upon by the state education department and local school district systems. Often such criteria are based on severity ratings and discrepancy scores. Severity ratings are rank orderings of the severity of a child's communication needs and its probable impact on educational needs. In some school districts, children need to have a moderate or severe disorder in order to qualify for services.

Discrepancy scores involve comparing the child with other children of the same age, or they may include a comparison of skills within a particular child. Comparing the child with other children is referred to as inter-referencing (Fey, 1986; Olswang & Bain, 1991). This is done when children are compared to other children in the population samples of standardized tests. Inter-referencing typically makes use of chronological age (CA) comparisons. When children score below their peers on particular measures of speech and language, they will qualify for services if that score is at the level prescribed by the state.

In contrast, intra-referencing allows evaluation of differences within the child's language system and/or cognitive abilities. For example, a child may have receptive language skills that are within normal limits, but display expressive language skills that fall below receptive abilities. Further, a child may have particular difficulty with language form and not with pragmatics or vice versa.

Another type of intra-referencing is known as **cognitive referencing** or MA (mental age) referencing. In cognitive referencing, the child's language abilities are compared with his nonverbal mental age. For instance, child A might have a mental age that is within normal limits but a language age below normal limits. According to the cognitive hypothesis, when mental age is greater than language age, a gap exists between what the child might be able to attain with respect to language and the child's current level of functioning. Child B might show no such gap, with the nonverbal cognitive functioning at the

Legislation is discussed at length in Chapter 5.

Comparing the child with other children is called inter-referencing.

The assumption underlying cognitive referencing is that children with a substantial gap between mental age and language age will make the most progress.

same level as language functioning, yet both are below the child's chronological age. Children who exhibit the largest gap are often given priority for intervention.

Casby (1992) reports that as many as 60 percent of the special education programs in state departments use cognitive referencing to establish speech-language eligibility criteria. The assumption is that the children with these gaps will make the most progress. This prediction is made because of the belief that cognition drives language development and, thus, those children whose language development is below their cognitive development will benefit the most from intervention. However, there are numerous studies to challenge this view, claiming that language might drive improvement in cognition (see Rice, 1983, for a review). In an effort to determine if cognitive referencing was a reliable procedure, Cole, Mills, & Kelley (1994) administered three commonly used nonverbal tests and three commonly used language tests to children who were identified as having language-cognition gaps. The results indicated poor agreement among the measures with respect to which children would receive services based on cognitive referencing criteria. Cole and others suggest that the poor agreement might be due to the level of reliability and validity of the assessment tools. As a result, some children might be denied services because of the poor psychometric characteristics of the tests that were selected for assessment. At issue is not the inclusion of children with gaps in abilities, but rather, the exclusion of children who do not display a gap. As an option, Cole and colleagues suggest that the child's "unmet communication needs" be used to qualify him for intervention. In addition, Olswang and Bain (1991) suggest that a child should be considered for intervention if the child improves in deficient areas when given some support during assessment.

> The problem with cognitive referencing is that it may result in denial of needed services for some children.

INTERVENTION PLANNING

The information gained from assessment should provide a picture of the child's strengths and weaknesses, as well as emerging areas of ability. The language interventionist needs to take this information and analyze it in respect to her knowledge of the process of normal language acquisition, hypothesize why the child has not progressed in the normal fashion, and develop intervention to assist the child in learning language in the most effective and efficient manner possible. In some cases, intervention planning is in part determined by the method of service delivery. (Chapter 7 discusses intervention planning in inclusive settings in detail.) However, the philosophy of intervention that is held by the language interventionist will also impact intervention planning.

> Intervention planning is discussed in Chapter 7.

Three philosophies to planning intervention are developmental logic, remedial logic, and theoretical logic. The language interventionist who uses developmental logic determines the next area of development a child should master and proceeds to intervene in this area (Guess, Sailor, & Baer, 1978). In contrast, remedial logic (Guess, Sailor, & Baer, 1974; 1978) focuses on the child's functional communication needs in the present environment. Remedial logic is supported by individuals working within the behavioral paradigm, particularly those working with children who display severe physical and mental disabilities. Another type of logic, theoretical logic, uses theory to predict which area(s) should be focused on during intervention. For instance, language interventionists adhering to the principles and parameters theory will focus on areas of grammar associated with specific parameters. In contrast, language interventionists who give more credence to the social interactionalist models will build upon what the child is producing by using recasts. Olswang and Bain (1991) utilize Vygotskian theory by using dynamic assessment to provide information as to what the child is ready to learn next. Dynamic assessment is akin to the notion of "stimulability," in which one determines if the child can imitate or produce a previously modeled target. Those areas that the child shows potential for producing are targeted before those areas that are not stimulable. Children who show a readiness to learn certain areas of language have been regarded as having more positive prognosis or better outcome than children not showing such an emergence. Regardless of which type of logic is used to plan intervention—developmental, remedial, or theoretical—an in-depth understanding of the child's abilities is necessary prior to intervention planning.

Evaluation is also discussed in Chapter 8.

EVALUATING INTERVENTION PROGRESS

Assessment for the purposes of evaluating an intervention program is called treatment efficacy evaluation. Many aspects of intervention may be evaluated, including the child's progress, the family's satisfaction with the program, and the long-term benefit to society, as examples of variables indicating the efficacy of intervention (Donahue-Kilburg, 1992). Most intervention programs assess the effectiveness of intervention by measuring the child's progress. The child's performance on particular language goals is measured at the beginning, during, and at the completion of intervention. Fey and Cleave (1990) specify four conditions that should be met in order to ascertain intervention effectiveness:

1. Some specific area of learning must be targeted.
2. Some behavior or behaviors that are valid representations of the targeted areas of learning must be selected.

3. Measurements must be taken in such a way that improvement can be detected reliably and objectively.
4. Steps must be taken to ensure that improvements observed are the direct or indirect result of the intervention program rather than the sole consequence of extraneous variables, such as maturation. . . . (p. 166)

There are a number of ways to ensure that the four conditions are met. One method for assessing change in intervention is a multiple baseline design (Kazdin, 1980, 1982), which involves taking repeated baselines across behaviors, settings, or individuals. This section will focus on the multiple baseline design across behaviors identifying two or more behaviors that a child has not yet achieved. There is a baseline phase where no treatment is given as well as a treatment phase where intervention is provided. However, not all behaviors are targeted for intervention at the same time. Following is an example of a multiple baseline design across behaviors for a child who is receiving intervention in the area of pragmatics:

Goal 1: To respond appropriately using verbal responses to same-age peers five times during dramatic play time with no prompting or redirecting from an adult.

Goal 2: To initiate appropriately using nonverbal means to same-age peers five times during art with no prompting or redirecting from an adult.

Using the terminology provided by Fey (1986), one of the goals will be designated the target goal, the other will be the control goal. The control goal should be chosen as a specific area that would not be expected to be influenced through intervention on the target goal, yet is still developmentally possible to attain for this particular child. The language interventionist collects data on both language goals during the baseline phase. The baseline phase must consist of at least three consecutive baselines and be stable or declining (McReynolds & Kearns, 1983). Once it has been determined that the baseline is stable or declining, then intervention begins on the target goal. After a specified amount of time, or at a specified level of gain, baseline probes are taken again for both goals. If there has been no change in the control goal, and there has been a change in the current treatment goal, then this is evidence that gains were a result of intervention. Thus, we want no change in the control goal to indicate experimental control. If we do not see change in the control goal, but there is change in the target goal, we can be reasonably sure that the intervention was responsible for that change. Progress is assessed by visually inspecting the graph for the amount of change over time. The rate of change or how quickly the child progresses over time can be evaluated by observing the steepness of the slope or the vertical line. A variation of this design given in Fey (1986) is the addition of a "generalization" goal. A generalization goal is a target that may be learned along with a "targeted" goal, without direct intervention. An example of a multiple baseline design across behaviors follows:

1. **Target goal:** Correct subject case marking on the pronouns "he" and "she" 90 percent of the time in five contexts during spontaneous conversation.
2. **Generalization goal:** Correct auxiliary "is" usage 90 percent of the time during spontaneous conversation.
3. **Control goal:** Correct use of articles 90 percent of the time during spontaneous conversation.

An efficient intervention program will produce gains in target and generalization goals, with no change in the control goal. One drawback to this design is that there is little empirical information on what areas of language would serve as good "control" and "generalization" goals for "target" goals. Lack of time is often cited as a reason why the multiple baseline is not used to evaluate efficacy. However, without a control for gains made from maturation or other sources it cannot be determined if the child's intervention plan has been successful.

Another method of evaluating intervention is through **social validity** measures. Social validity is the relevance of the child's advances in relation to her social system as determined by individuals other than the language interventionist (Goldstein, 1990; Wolf, 1978). Teachers, parents, and peers are all potential sources for social validity assessment of a child's intervention program. This might be accomplished through a set of questions concerning the child's speech and language skills and the importance of these skills in the child's eventual language functioning. This set of questions could be administered before and after intervention to assess the parents' (and others') opinions about the value of their child's success in the intervention program. Olswang and Bain (1994) suggest that both types of data—qualitative data that address social validity issues and quantitative data that are more objective in nature—should be used to evaluate treatment outcome.

> Social validity is the meaningfulness or importance of the behavior change as judged by significant others in the children's environment.

Dismissal from Intervention

Olswang (1993) suggests that there are both short- and long-term objectives for intervention. The short-term objective is change in the present. In this type of objective, discussed previously in this chapter, a target language goal is followed over time and the observed change or lack of change is recorded. It is the result of the current intervention at the current time. Long-term objectives are those that address the future status of the child. These objectives seek to answer the question, "Will current intervention influence the course of the child's future language skills by preventing or reducing the need for further intervention?" For some children with language impairment, dismissal from intervention with age-appropriate speech and language abilities is the long-term objective. For other children, the long-term objective may be a specified level of communication functioning. This type of long-term objective may change over time as the child learns more information and encounters new communication needs.

Dismissal from intervention is one of the most difficult team decisions derived from assessment, particularly if there has been little progress observed. Fey (1988) proposes some helpful guidelines for determining when a child might be dismissed from intervention. He suggests that dismissal criteria should be determined *prior* to the initiation of therapy. The decision to dismiss a child from intervention can be viewed as a hypothesis about the current functioning of the child that can be altered depending on the child's state. Three scenarios where dismissal is appropriate are

1. when the child is no longer making gains (or has "plateaued") despite efforts to modify intervention;
2. when the child has achieved all goals set forth and is no longer at risk for academic or social consequences as a result of a speech and language impairment; and
3. when the child's progress is general, and not specific to intervention.

Fey places arbitrary time guidelines on this decision-making process. He suggests that the intervention program should be reevaluated when at least one subgoal (i.e., a step below a goal) is not reached in one month's time. Reevaluation includes possibly changing the goals, the type of intervention approach, or the interventionist. If changing the intervention approach, goals, and/or interventionist still does not result in positive change for the child within 6 months, then the team may consider discontinuing the intervention. This decision should be made with extreme caution and should not result in penalizing the child because the team has not successfully implemented appropriate communication goals. Should dismissal occur, the language interventionist should consider reenrolling the child in intervention 6 months following dismissal. Importantly, it is recommended that the child be tracked following dismissal at 3-month intervals. Tracking the child's progress on specific criteria without intervention allows for an objective view of the child's development.

The best recommendation is to carefully monitor intervention and make decisions accordingly.

Treatment efficacy and dismissal of a child from language intervention are topics that continue to be studied. Until we know more about the influence of maturation and environmental factors, it will be difficult to determine how much intervention has contributed to a child's progress in language learning. For the time being, the best practice a language interventionist can adhere to is careful monitoring to determine if intervention is responsible for positive change and a prior determination of the ultimate outcome for each child.

SUMMARY

Assessment entails a myriad of events that allow professionals a better understanding of the child's speech and language abilities. The information derived reflects the performance of that child on a given day and is subject to error from the test instrument, the child, and the examiner. Keeping these cautions in mind, professionals who undertake assessment with young children should have a healthy respect for the complex task of describing a dynamic, interactional system such as speech and language primarily with tools that capture only parts of the child's capabilities. A key component in an accurate assessment is an accurate reflection of the child's current abilities in the context of the classroom and home with key providers and peers. Finally, it should be remembered that assessment is a continual process that repeats itself for each child—not only during specified periods of the year. As the child participates in intervention, the language interventionist needs to constantly assess changes in the child's communication, his environment, and his caregivers, modifying intervention accordingly.

REFERENCES

Bloom, L., & Lahey, M. (1978). *Language development and language disorders*. New York: John Wiley & Sons.

Brinton, B., & Fujiki, M. (1994). Ways to teach conversation. In J. Duchan, L. Hewitt, & R. Sonnenmeier (Eds.), *Pragmatics: From theory to practice*. Englewood Cliffs, NJ: Prentice Hall.

Brown, R. (1973). *A first language*. Cambridge, Massachusets: Harvard University Press.

Casby, M. (1992). The cognitive hypothesis and its influence on speech-language services in schools. *Language, Speech, and Hearing Services in Schools, 23,* 198–202.

Chapman, R. S. (1981). Computing mean length of utterance in morphemes. In J. F. Miller (Ed.), *Assessing language production in children*. Baltimore: University Park Press.

Chapman, R. S. (1981). Exploring children's communicative intents. In J. F. Miller (Ed.), *Assessing language production in children*. Baltimore: University Park Press.

Cirrin, F. M. (1994). Assessing language in the classroom and the curriculum. In J. B. Tomblin, H. L. Morris, & D. C. Spriestersbach (Eds.), *Diagnosis in speech-language pathology* (pp. 135–164). San Diego: Singular Publishing Group.

Cole, K. N., Mills, P. E., & Kelley, D. (1994). Agreement of assessment profiles used in cognitive referencing. *Language, Speech, and Hearing Services in Schools, 25,* 25–31.

Coufal, K. L. (1993). Collaborative consultation for speech-language pathologists. *Topics in Language Disorders, 14:1,* 1–14.

Crystal, D. (1979). *Working with LARSP*. London: Edward Arnold.

Dale, P. S. (1991). The validity of a parent report measure of vocabulary and syntax at 24 months. *Journal of Speech and Hearing Research, 34,* 565–571.

Dodge, K. (1985). Facets of social interaction and the assessment of social competence in children. In B. Schneider, K. Rubin, & J. Ledingham (Eds.), *Children's peer relations: Issues in assessment and intervention*. New York: Springer-Verlag.

Donahue-Kilburg, G. (1992). *Family-centered early intervention for communication disorders*. Gaithersburg, MD: Aspen.

Dore, J. (1978). Requestive systems in nursery school conversations: Analysis of talk in its social context. In R. Campbell & P. Smith (Eds.), *Recent advances in the psychology of language: Language development and mother-child interaction*. New York: Plenum Press.

Fey, M. E. (1986). *Language intervention with young children*. Boston: College-Hill Press.

Fey, M. E. (1988). Dismissal criteria for the language-impaired child. In D. Yoder & R. Kent (Eds.), *Decision making in speech-language pathology* (pp. 50–54). Philadelphia: B. C. Decker Inc.

Fey, M. E., & Cleave, P. L. (1990). Early language intervention. *Seminars in Speech and Language, 11,* 165–181.

Gallagher, T. (1991). Language and social skills: Implications for clinical assessment and intervention with school-age children. In T. Gallagher (Ed.), *Pragmatics of language,* San Diego: Singular Publishing Group.

Glascoe, F. P. (1991). Can clinical judgment detect children with speech-language problems? *Pediatrics, 87,* 317–322.

Goldstein, H. (1990). Assessing clinical significance. In L. Olswang, C. Thompson, S. Warren, & N. Minghetti (Eds.), *Treatment efficacy research in communication disorders* (pp. 91–98). Rockville, MD: American Speech-Language-Hearing Foundation.

Guess, D., Sailor, W., & Baer, D. (1974). To teach language to retarded children. In R. Schiefelbusch & L. Lloyd (Eds.), *Language perspectives: Acquisition, retardation, and intervention*. Baltimore: University Park Press.

Guess, D., Sailor, W., & Baer, D. (1978). Children with limited languages. In R. Schiefelbusch & L. Lloyd (Eds.), *Language intervention strategies*. Baltimore: University Park Press.

Hadley, P., & Rice, M. (1991). Conversational responsiveness of speech- and language-impaired preschoolers. *Journal of Speech and Hearing Research, 34,* 1308–1317.

Hughes, D. L., Fey, M. E., & Long, S. H. (1992). Developmental sentence scoring: Still useful after all these years. *Topics in Language Disorders, 12,* 1–12.

Kazdin, A. E. (1980). *Research design in clinical psychology*. New York: Harper & Row.

Kazdin, A. E. (1982). *Single case research designs: Methods for clinical and applied settings*. New York: Oxford Press.

Klee, T. (1992). Developmental and diagnostic characteristics of quantitative measures of children's language production. *Topics in Language Disorders, 12,* 28–41.

Klee, T., Carson, D., Hall, L., & Muskina, G. (1994). Screening language development in 24-month-old children. Poster presented at the 15th Symposium on Research in Child Language Disorders. University of Wisconsin-Madison, June.

Lee, L. (1974). *Developmental sentence analysis*. Evanston, IL: Northwestern University Press.

Leonard, L. B. (1974). A preliminary view of generalization in language training. *Journal of Speech and Hearing Disorders, 39,* 429–434.

Liles, B. Z. (1985). Cohesion in the narratives of normal and language-disordered children. *Journal of Speech and Hearing Research, 28,* 123–133.

Linder, T. W. (1993). *Transdisciplinary play-based assessment*. Baltimore: Brookes Publishing.

Loeb, D., & Leonard, L. B. (1988). Specific language impairment and parameter theory. *Clinical Linguistics and Phonetics, 2,* 317–327.

Long, S., & Fey, M. (1993). *Computerized Profiling*. Ithaca, NY: Steven Long.

Margulies, C., Creaghead, N., & Rolph, T. (1980). Pragmatic checklist. Presented at the OSHA Convention, March.

McCabe, A., & Peterson, P. (1990). What makes a narrative memorable? *Applied Psycholinguistics, 8,* 73–82.

McCabe, A., & Rollins, P. (1994). Assessment of preschool narrative skills. *American Journal of Speech-Language Pathology: A Journal of Clinical Practice, 3,* 45–56.

McCauley, R., & Swisher, L. (1984a). Psychometric review of language and articulation tests for preschool children. *Journal of Speech and Hearing Disorders, 49,* 34–42.

McCauley, R., & Swisher, L. (1984b). Use and misuse of norm-referenced tests in clinical assessment: A hypothetical case. *Journal of Speech and Hearing Disorders, 49,* 338–348.

McGregor, K., & Appel, A. (1994). Nonstandard approaches to assessment of word-finding problems in preschoolers. Miniseminar presented at the American Speech-Language-Hearing Association, New Orleans.

McReynolds, L., & Kearns, K. (1983). *Single-subject experimental design in communicative disorders.* Baltimore: University Park Press.

Michaels, S. (1981). "Sharing time": Children's narrative styles and differential access to literacy. *Language in Society, 10,* 423–442.

Michaels, S., & Cazden, C. (1985). Teacher/child collaboration as oral preparation for literacy. In B. Schieffelin & P. Gilmore (Eds.), *The acquisition of literacy: Ethnographic perspectives.* Norwood, NJ: Ablex Publishing.

Miller, J. F. (1981). *Assessing language production in children.* Baltimore: University Park Press.

Miller, J. F., & Chapman, R. S. (1979). The relation between age and mean length of utterance in morphemes. *Journal of Speech and Hearing Research, 24,* 154–161.

Miller, J. F., & Chapman, R. S. (1993). *Systematic Analysis of Language Transcripts (SALT).* Madison, WI: Waisman Center.

Miller, J. F., Freiberg, C., Rolland, M., & Reeves, M. (1992). Implementing computerized language sample analysis in the public school. *Topics in Language Disorders, 12,* 69–82.

Miller, J. F., & Yoder, D. E. (1984). *Miller-Yoder Language Comprehension Test* Clinical Edition. Baltimore: University Park Press.

Olswang, L. (1993). Developmental speech and language disorders. *American Speech, Language, and Hearing Association, 35,* 42–44.

Olswang, L., & Bain, B. (1991). When to recommend intervention. *Language, Speech, and Hearing Services in the Schools, 22,* 255–263.

Olswang, L., & Bain, B. (1994). Data collection: Monitoring children's treatment progress. *American Journal of Speech-Language Pathology, 3,* 55–66.

Paul, R., & Smith, R. L. (1993). Narrative skills in 4-year-olds with normal, impaired, and late-developing language. *Journal of Speech and Hearing Research, 36,* 592–598.

Peterson, C., & McCabe, A. (1983). *Developmental psycholinguistics: Three ways of looking at a child's narrative.* New York: Plenum.

Plante, E., & Vance, R. (1994). Selection of preschool language tests: A data-based approach. *Language, Speech, and Hearing Services in the Schools, 25,* 15–24.

Prutting, C., & Kirchner, D. (1987). A clinical appraisal of the pragmatic aspects of language. *Journal of Speech and Hearing Disorders, 52,* 105–119.

Renfrew, C. (1977). *The bus story language test: A test of continuous speech.* Oxford: Author.

Rescorla, L. (1989). The Language Development Survey: A screening tool for delayed language in toddlers. *Journal of Speech and Hearing Disorders, 54,* 587–599.

Rice, M. (1983). Contemporary accounts of the cognition/language relationships: Implications for speech-language clinicians. *Journal of Speech and Hearing Disorders, 48,* 347–359.

Rice, M., & Sell, M., & Hadley, P. (1990). The social interactive coding system (SICS): An on-line, clinically relevant descriptive tool. *Language, Speech, and Hearing Services in the Schools, 21,* 2–14.

Richard, N., & Schiefelbusch, R. (1991). Assessment. In L. McCormick & R. Schiefelbusch (Eds.), *Early language intervention.* Columbus, OH: Merrill.

Rosen, A., & Proctor, E. (1981). Distinctions between treatment outcomes and their implications for treatment evaluation. *Journal of Consulting and Clinical Psychology, 49,* 418–425.

Scarborough, H., & Dobrich, W. (1990). Development of children with early language delay. *Journal of Speech and Hearing Research, 33,* 70–83.

Shulman, B. (1985). *Test of Pragmatic Skills (Revised Edition).* Tucson: Communication Skill Builders.

Sturner, R. A., Layton, T. L., Evans, A. W., Heller, J. H., Funk, S. G., & Machon, M. W. (1994). Preschool speech and language screening: A review of currently available tests. *American Journal of Speech-Language Pathology: A Journal of Clinical Practice, 3,* 25–36.

Templin, M. (1957). Certain language skills in children: Their development and interrelationships. Child Welfare Monolg. No. 26. University of Minnesota Press, Minneapolis.

Tjossem, T. (1976). Early intervention: Issues and approaches. In T. Tjossem (Ed.), *Intervention strategies for high-risk and handicapped children.* Baltimore: University Park Press.

Watkins, R., Kelly, D., Harbers, H., & Hollis, W. (1994). Using form-class indices to measure children's lexical diversity. Poster presented at the Symposium on Research in Child Language Disorders. University of Wisconsin-Madison, June.

Watkins, R., Rice, M., & Moltz, C. (1993). Verb use by language-impaired and normally developing children. *First Language, 13,* 133–144.

Wetherby, A., & Prizant, B. (1993). *Communication and Symbolic Behavioral Scales.* Chicago: Riverside Publishing.

Wiig, E. H. (1990). *Wiig Criterion Referenced Inventory of Language.* San Antonio, TX: The Psychological Corporation (Harcourt Brace Jovanovich).

Wolf, M. M. (1978). Social validity: The case for subjective measurement or how applied behavior analysis is finding its heart. *Journal of Applied Behavior Analysis, 11,* 203–214.

CHAPTER 7

Ecological Assessment and Planning

Linda McCormick

Assessment, planning, intervention, and evaluation are overlapping activities. The purpose of the type of assessment described in this chapter is to collect information about the child's intervention needs. Planning focuses on formulating hypotheses as to reasons for identified deficiencies, and devising and describing intervention strategies. Then the planned interventions are implemented and evaluated.

As discussed in previous chapters, the close relationship between language, cognition, social skills, and motor abilities means that development in any one area cannot be understood apart from development in other areas. Separating language and communication skills from skills in other areas has an advantage for professionals; it allows us to examine language and communication skills more closely. We must keep reminding ourselves, however, that such a

A child's difficulties in language invariably affect and are affected by cognitive, social, and motor development.

separation is artificial. A child's difficulties are rarely confined to a single developmental domain: A disability in one developmental domain invariably affects and is affected by other areas. Even children with the label *specific language disability* (SLI) experience problems in other areas: for example, academics and/or social/adaptive behavior (Fey, Catts, & Larrivee, 1995).

Because a disability in one developmental domain affects and is affected by other domains, intervention in any one area cannot be implemented apart from intervention in the others. The different intervention areas—language and communication skills, motor skills, cognitive or academic skills, social/adaptive behaviors, and self-care—are not *parallel* processes. They are more like thick braids, which are interwoven almost to the point of fusion.

There are several problems with assigning intervention areas to professional disciplines; for example, saying that speech and language "belongs" to speech-language pathology, motor skills "belong" to physical therapy, cognitive, social, and academic skills "belong" to regular or special education, and self-care skills "belong" to occupational therapy. One problem is that such assignment ignores developmental interrelationships. Another problem is that it leaves the false impression that different disciplines have totally separate and distinct knowledge bases and practices. Finally, it is not reasonable to hold a single professional (or discipline) *solely* responsible for all assessment, planning, and instruction in a particular skills area. Effectively meeting the needs of children with disabilities is virtually impossible unless special education and general education resources are collaborative and integrated.

This chapter focuses on assessment and planning for all children with language and communication difficulties, regardless of the intensity of the difficulties or whether they are a primary disability (children labeled as speech or language impaired) or secondary to another disability (e.g., motor impairment, behavior disorders, autism, cognitive deficits, sensory impairments, or learning disabilities). After discussion of the rationale for an ecological approach, we will present the steps in an ecological assessment and planning process. Then, in Chapter 8 we will describe important dimensions of the instruction/intervention process: (1) the focus of intervention; (2) methods and procedures; (3) the instructional environment; (4) relationships and responsibilities; (5) scheduling; and (6) measurement and evaluation.

RATIONALE FOR ECOLOGICAL ASSESSMENT

Recall from Chapter 6 that assessment in school settings typically occurs at several different junctures. Initial assessment determines whether the child has a disability, whether special education is required, and what types of special or related services are needed. This type of assessment is usually implemented with 3-year-old children with disabilities, who are just entering the public school system, and with school-age children with mild to moderate disabilities who have been referred (usually by a concerned teacher) because they do not appear to be benefiting from instruction. Because eligibility is not an issue for children with severe and/or multiple disabilities, the focus of initial assessment for these children is on specifying what types of special or related services are needed.

For students with severe and multiple disabilities, the focus of initial assessment is on determining what types of special and related services are needed.

The type of information that is typically available at this juncture is described in Chapter 6. The data generated by the initial assessment process generally include developmental information (i.e., test scores, normative information), some information furnished by the family about behavior at home, and some information from past service delivery settings (e.g., early intervention program). If the child is determined to be eligible for special education and related services, the next questions (in this order) are:

What would be an appropriate educational program for this child?
What special services does this child need?
What is the least restrictive environment for this child?

Each child's IEP must be reevaluated every year, at which time there may be new decisions about placement, special services, and goals and objectives. After the initial assessment, however, the student may not have another *full* evaluation for three years (unless a comprehensive evaluation is requested by the parents or teachers). The exception is preschoolers who may be reevaluated more often.

Most important to realize is that the initial IEP development process rarely produces a useful instructional plan (e.g., Goodman & Bond, 1993). This is because, as Bateman (1992) puts it, the IEP is written at the wrong time and for the wrong purpose. Very often, goals and objectives on a child's first IEP cannot guide instruction/ intervention because (1) they are generated from assessment data collected for the purpose of establishing eligibility for services and the type of services needed, *not* the child's specific instruction and support needs in the inclusive classroom, (2) they are developed by persons who are unfamiliar with the child's daily functioning in natural environments, and (3) they are *not* generated by the persons who will be responsible for the child's learning and development.

The IDEA stipulation that an IEP must be finalized and signed *prior* to actual placement means that, in most school districts, the IEP committee may not include the child's teacher(s) or the related services personnel who, as the classroom support team, will be responsible for design and implementation of the child's day-to-day program. Moreover, when the initial IEP is developed, the child is not yet in his placement, and it is not clear what his strengths and needs are relative to the expectations of that setting.

Increasingly, teachers and support personnel are recognizing the importance of assessing child performance and learning outcomes in the context of the classroom and other school, community, and home environments. Results from standardized assessment instruments administered prior to placement provide little information about child learning characteristics and no information whatsoever about expectations of (1) the curriculum, (2) adults in the child's environments, (3) the surroundings in which learning occurs, or (4) social situations. The new assessment approaches such as curriculum-based assessment (CBA) and ecological assessment are prescriptive rather than descriptive. They provide instructionally relevant information and helpful teaching strategies.

The rationale for assessing the learning environment in addition to assessing the learner is based on the belief that child performance in school is a function of an interaction between the student and the contexts where learning takes place. This chapter will provide directions for an ecological assessment-planning process that is implemented after the child is in the classroom. Before outlining the basic procedures for this process, however, we will discuss (1) how it relates to and uses developmental information, and (2) the underlying philosophical and programmatic premises.

Developmental Information

The notion that teaching skills from the normal development sequence would effectively remediate language delays and prevent deviations that would lead to further delays and disorders was a major assumption underlying most past intervention efforts. Thus, the major source of information for formulation of goals and objectives was descriptive studies of stages of development of the various language dimensions—specifically, phonology, syntax, morphology, and semantics. Intervention then attempted to facilitate acquisition of knowledge and skills in the order in which they occur (or are thought to occur) in normal development.

Developmental information can be enormously useful in helping to explain learning barriers and design intervention procedures. However, relying *exclusively* on the developmental *stage* model as the source for intervention goals and objectives has several limitations (Goodman & Bond, 1993; Keogh & Sheeman, 1981; Leonard, 1987). It assumes (1) that the development of children with disabilities is essentially the same as that of children without disabilities, and (2) that children with disabilities are simply functioning at an earlier stage of development. There is a lack of data to support either of these assumptions. Leonard (1987) notes that, at least with some children, there may be more involved than simply developmental delay: Some children may have long-standing limitations in their abilities that prevent them from attaining normal development milestones.

Guess and Noonan (1982) note that the skills normally developing children are observed to demonstrate may not be necessarily sequential *or* indispensable. Moreover, they argue that reliance on data concerning developmental milestones as the sole source for goals and objectives may even have negative consequences. *If* interventionists are wrong—if, in fact, normal milestones are *not* appropriate intervention targets for children with disabilities—professionals may be wasting a great deal of valuable intervention time (the child's *and* their own). Yet another unfortunate consequence of preoccupation with teaching skills from normal development sequences may be restricted social experiences: So much of the instructional day may be taken up with intervention focused on teaching the skills observed in younger, normally developing children that the child misses out on opportunities for social and communicative interactions with peers. Limiting opportunities for interactions with, and learning from, peers (whether by design or inadvertently) ignores the child's communication needs and the fact that, even when the child's language *skills* are at a younger developmental age, the child's communication *needs* are likely to be similar to those of same-age peers.

> When much of the school day is taken up with teaching developmental skills, the child may miss valuable opportunities to imitate and interact with peers.

Developmental information must be used selectively. Information about the child's developmental skills contributes to understanding the child's language and communication limitations, adapting activities and materials, and developing intervention procedures, but it should not be the major source for intervention goals and objectives.

The Ecological Model

The central thesis for the **ecological model,** which originated in biology, is that an organism cannot be studied properly in isolation from its environment. Simply stated, *behavior cannot be understood without considering its context.* The basic assumptions of the ecological model are:

> The central tenet of the ecological model is that behavior cannot be understood without considering its context.

- Every individual is an inseparable part of a small social system.
- A disability is a discrepancy between the individual's abilities and the expectations or demands of the environment.
- Altering any part of the system—the individual, the environment, *or* environmental expectations—can benefit the entire system.

Rhodes (1967) was one of the first to apply the ecological perspective to developing intervention programs. Speaking specifically of students labeled "emotionally disturbed," he pointed out that viewing disturbance as something residing in the student leads to preoccupation with trying to "fix" the child's flaws. Rather, disturbance should be viewed as residing in the tension between the child and the demands of the environment. The label "emotionally disturbed" is not a disability: It reflects the fact that there is a discrepancy between the child's skills and abilities and the demands or expectations of the child's environment.

In the seventies, the writings of Bronfenbrenner focussed the attention of many psychologists on the ecological model. Bronfenbrenner described the laboratory approach to psychology that was prevalent at that time as "a science concerned with the strange behavior of children in strange situations with strange adults for the briefest possible periods of time" (1977, p. 513). He argued that the results of assessment had limited usefulness for planning intervention because they were not referenced against the social, behavioral, and educational expectations of activities and persons in the child's natural environments.

Ecological assessment differs from traditional assessment in that it considers the child's behavior in relation to environmental demands and expectations (rather than in relation to the performance of a test's standardized population). Table 7.1 highlights the differences between ecological assessment and traditional assessment. Ecological assessment examines the environments in which

> Ecological assessment considers the child's behavior in relation to environmental demands and expectations.

TABLE 7.1   Differences between ecological assessment and traditional assessment

	Ecological Assessment	**Traditional Assessment**
Reference	Compares child's performance to the demands and expectations of activities and tasks in the child's environments	Compares child's test performance with that of a sample of similar children who were administered the same test items
Focus	Child's ability to meet setting and task expectations and participate in activities and routines in natural settings	Language forms and structures described in the normal development research as representative of children at the child's age or stage of development
Procedures	Observes the child's behavior in daily activities and interviews with persons who know the child well	Elicits the child's responses to a set of standardized tasks thought to represent major skills/abilities in the area
Assessment Context	Natural settings: Assessment team includes parents and peers	Contrived settings: Independent assessments by discipline representatives
Best Use of Results	To generate individualized goals and objectives and plan special instruction	To determine child's status relative to same-age peers; for diagnosis and determination of eligibility for special education services

the child is expected to function in order to determine what adaptations need to be made and what needs to be taught to ensure the child's success in these environments. Where language and communication are concerned, the focus of assessment is on the adequacy of the child's language and communication skills in those natural contexts where she needs to know and use language in order to participate with peers.

The following philosophical and programmatic premises are basic to the ecological assessment, planning, and intervention processes as presented in this chapter and the next. They are expanded upon in the remainder of this section.

- There is no need for minimal criteria or prerequisites to justify communication intervention if language and communication difficulties prevent a child from fully participating in and benefiting from classroom instruction and social interactions.
- The focus of special education and related services should be providing whatever supports children need in order to be fully included in general education classes and other school settings.
- Teamwork is the key to developing an instructionally relevant description of children's strengths and their intervention and support needs.
- Professionals must acknowledge the influence that their own socialization has on their values, beliefs, and practices before they can work effectively with children, families, and colleagues.
- Children who lack language may behave in socially maladaptive ways because they lack other means of influencing people and events in their environment.

MINIMAL CRITERIA. Many states (31 of the 50, according to Casby [1992]) do not consider a child eligible for speech-language services unless there is a significant discrepancy between the child's language abilities and his cognitive functioning (as measured by a nonverbal intelligence test). The notion that communication intervention should not be provided unless there is a significant discrepancy between a child's language abilities and his cognitive functioning (as measured by a nonverbal intelligence test) is called **cognitive referencing.** The assumption underlying this discrepancy criterion is that children cannot demonstrate language and communication skills beyond the ceiling imposed by cognitive development.

Calculator (1994) and others call cognitive referencing a "misconception," citing evidence that children whose language abilities are already commensurate with cognitive ability derive as much benefit from language and communication training as those who demonstrate the required discrepancy. Actually, cognitive referencing is disturbing from two perspectives. Not only does it exclude children who may benefit from language and communication training, but also there is a

> Cognitive referencing assumes that children cannot demonstrate language and communication skills beyond the ceiling imposed by cognitive development.

potential for "over-labeling": labeling and providing intervention for children who are functioning within the normal range. Leonard (1987) reminds us that approximately 28 percent of the normal population has verbal IQ scores at least 15 points below nonverbal IQ scores. Thus, for some children a discrepancy between language abilities and cognitive functioning is a natural and predictable variation in language development (Cole, Dale, & Mills, 1990).

Possibly the relevant distinction is between speech-language services (direct *or* consultative) and communication instruction. Calculator (1994) argues that the fact that the initial assessment team did not consider a child an appropriate candidate for speech-language services "should not preclude that child from receiving communication instruction" (p. 119). Ideally there should not be minimal criteria or prerequisites to justify provision of whatever communication intervention and supports a child needs in order to participate in and benefit from classroom instruction and interactions with peers (Calculator, 1994; Cole, Dale, & Mills, 1990). The fact that language and communication difficulties prevent a child from full participation in daily cognitive/academic activities and social interactions should be reason enough to provide intervention.

> **There should not be minimal criteria to justify provision of communication assistance and support.**

Fortunately, recent trends are moving beyond decision making based on quantitative data to viewing individual children within the context of meaningful and functional interactions. Quantitative data may enhance communication among professionals, but they have little meaning to families or, ultimately, to the child's future. The position taken in this chapter and the next is that virtually all children with disabilities can benefit from instruction/intervention to facilitate and support language and communication skills.

INCLUSION.   The term *inclusion* has generally replaced the term *integration* in the educational arena. Stainback, Stainback, and Jackson (1992) prefer the term inclusion because it

> ". . . more accurately and clearly communicates what is needed—all children need to be *included* in the educational and social life of their neighborhood schools and classrooms, not merely placed in the mainstream." (p. 3)

The term inclusion reflects the shift from helping only those children identified as having a disability to addressing the needs of every member of the school (school personnel *and* children, alike) to be successful, secure, and welcome in the educational mainstream (Stainback et al., 1992). Unlike integration or mainstreaming, which imply a need to reinstate previously excluded children into the mainstream, inclusion begins with the assumption that the mainstream is where *all* children belong. The focus of inclusion is on the mainstream to accommodate children's needs, *not* vice versa.

> **The focus of inclusion is altering the mainstream to accommodate all children's needs.**

Inclusive classrooms are general education classrooms that include one or more children with disabilities and where there is unconditional acceptance of *all* children. In inclusive classrooms, teachers are provided with whatever supports and resources are needed to ensure that all children have beneficial and successful educational experiences. The emphasis is on what children *can* do, rather than what they can *not* do.

Inclusion is *not* episodic visits to the general education classroom for art, music, and/or circle time or joining the general education class for special activities (e.g., field trips): Inclusion is *"belonging."* It is *not* sacrificing or compromising support services: It is *every* child (whether eligible for special services or not) having whatever resources and support she needs *and* a challenging educational program that is geared to her abilities, needs, and interests. It is *not* promoting the needs of children with disabilities over those of children without disabilities: It is everyone (children and adults alike) welcoming and valuing abilities as well as disabilities and learning to respect and depend on one another.

> Inclusion is every child's having whatever resources and support are necessary to learn.

TEAMWORK. One of the most gratifying aspects of inclusive education is the opportunity it affords for teamwork. In traditional schools, because general education teachers and special education teachers each have separate classrooms, and because language interventionists, occupational therapists, and physical therapists typically have separate rooms, there are few opportunities to work together and learn from one another. The way that traditional schools are organized makes the type of ongoing collegial exchanges that lead to supportive and mutually empowering peer relationships all but impossible. Actually, other than very informal exchanges (i.e., saying "hi" in the teachers' lounge) and "expert exchanges" (when the special education teacher or the language interventionist gives advice to the general education teacher, or the language interventionist or therapists give advice to the special education teacher), there are few opportunities for interactions of any kind in traditional schools.

Inclusive schools are very different. As discussed in Chapter 5, there are frequent opportunities for collegial exchanges in the course of team teaching or other cooperative arrangements (e.g., collaborative consultation). Teaching staff, language interventionists, and physical and occupational therapists do not have an adviser–advisee or helper–helpee relationship with one another (or with families). Rather, they relate to one another as equal partners and equal team members. Team interactions provide almost continuous opportunities for sharing and mutual empowerment.

> In inclusive schools there are frequent opportunities for collegial exchanges.

Joint goal setting, ongoing problem solving and negotiation, and mutual support activities help team members (including family members) establish a common purpose or focus for instruction/intervention and support activities. Language interventionists, physical and occupational therapists, and other support personnel (i.e., psychologists, nurses, counselors, etc.) contribute to the continuing professional development and sense of efficacy of teachers by sharing the knowledge and skills of their respective disciplines. Teachers empower language interventionists, therapists, and other support personnel by sharing *their* expertise about curriculum development, classroom management, child learning characteristics, social abilities, and classroom behavioral requirements.

CULTURAL COMPETENCE.   One consequence of the rapidly changing demographics of the United States is the growing number of children from culturally and linguistically diverse backgrounds in preschools, early intervention programs, and schools—in *every* state. Faced with the reality of working with increasing numbers of children and families whose languages, beliefs, and practices differ in important ways from their own, professionals in these settings are working to develop culturally sensitive ways to carry out their responsibilities and create and nurture collaborative relationships with families and other professionals.

The term *culture* refers to the many different factors that shape our sense of group identity—race, ethnicity, religion, geographical location, income status, gender, and occupation. Everyone thinks of himself as belonging to a family. We also belong to a cultural group. The ways we think, feel, perceive, and behave reflect our cultural group membership.

> Our thinking, feelings, perceptions, and behavior are all shaped by our culture.

Cultural competence is "respect for differences, eagerness to learn, and a willingness to accept that there are many ways of viewing the world" (Lynch & Hanson, 1992, p. 356). Cultural competence depends on a complex and subtle interaction between feelings and understanding of cultural and linguistic differences and similarities. It requires every professional and every paraprofessional to recognize and acknowledge the influence of his or her culture on concepts, perceptions, and language and appreciate the relativity of every judgment. This requires examination and some level of understanding of socialization and its effects on views about family roles and relationships, childrearing practices, what is proper and appropriate social behavior, life expectations and aspirations, time and space, health, food, dress and personal appearance, and religion.

In general, cultural competence has been achieved when people are able to

- acknowledge and step outside their own cultural framework;
- understand how each family's cultural background influences family relationships, daily functioning, and family values, beliefs, and practices toward their child's disability;

- see strength in behaviors that reflect beliefs and assumptions that are different than their own; and
- understand that the very same functioning styles and behaviors that may appear at first glance to be problems are very often among the families' (and children's) greatest resources.

It is especially important to understand cultural assumptions underlying theory and practices that may bring us into conflict with families (Harry, 1992). An example of an area in which there is potential for dissonance between early intervention professionals and culturally different families is the meanings that are attached to a diagnosis of disability. The medical model, which is the dominant framework of many professionals in the United States who serve persons with disabilities, assumes that disabilities reflect intrinsic deficits that can be identified and treated through a scientific approach. However, the traditional beliefs among some Asian, Hispanic, and Native American groups suggest very different interpretations of a disability. For example, some Puerto Rican families view a disability as reflecting the health of the entire family, not just one family member (Canino & Canino, 1980). Some Mexican Americans, Native Americans, and Southeast Asian groups believe that the source of a disability lies in spiritual rather than physical phenomena (Adkins & Young, 1976; Chan, 1986; Locust, 1988). Thus, they believe that intervention should be spiritual rather than medical.

Meeting the instructional and support needs of children from linguistically and culturally diverse backgrounds requires professionals to go beyond the surface features of culture, such as food and holidays, to understanding the communication style of the cultural group (Kayser, 1995). A study by Kayser (1989) provides an example of this "closer look" at culture. Kayser observed the interactions of three Anglo and three Hispanic language interventionists during language screening sessions. The verbal and nonverbal behaviors of the two groups of professionals with the Hispanic children they were screening were strikingly different. The Anglo language interventionists kept a social distance of 48 to 60 inches from the children and they did not touch them. The Hispanic language interventionists sat much closer (a range of 18 to 48 inches); they used touch to control the children's behavior and to get their attention. Verbal communication was also very different. The Anglo interventionists used verbal reinforcements, questions, permission statements, statements of need, hints, explanations concerning a task, and "if-then" statements (e.g., "if you show me the car, then we can play with the toys") to coax the child to complete a task. The Hispanic clinicians were more directive: They used primarily performatives, such as *say, show me,* and *do this* (in Spanish). When clarification was necessary, the Anglo professionals tended to rephrase the utterance, whereas the Hispanic professionals repeated the utterance.

> Meeting the instructional and support needs of children with linguistically and culturally diverse backgrounds is enormously challenging.

COMMUNICATION-BASED INTERVENTION.   Communication-based intervention refers to intervention that teaches communication forms as a replacement for severe problem behaviors such as intense forms of aggression (punching, scratching, biting, and kicking others), self-injury (head-banging, self-biting, and self-slapping), property destruction, and tantrums (prolonged screaming and crying) (Carr, Levin, McConnachie, Carlson, Kemp, & Smith, 1994). Basic to communication-based intervention is the belief that there is a significant relationship between controlling the environment with communication and controlling the environment with problem behavior. This perspective argues that all behavior, regardless of its topography, is communicative (has message value), which is exactly what the pragmatic perspective of language would predict (Watzlawick, Beavin, & Jackson, 1967).

> **All behavior, regardless of its topography, has a message.**

Traditional behavior management focused on decreasing or eliminating problem behaviors. In recent years there has been a broad-based movement in the direction of understanding and using behavior analysis to change problem behaviors, with the goal of increasing the quality of life of the student. Referred to as communication-based intervention, nonaversive behavior management, positive behavior support, functional assessment, or functional communication training (Carr et al., 1994; Durand, 1990; Evans & Meyer, 1985; Reichle & Wacker, 1993; Voeltz & Evans, 1983), the defining characteristic of this approach is the emphasis on using positive procedures to promote development of adaptive behavioral repertoires. It is based on the assumptions that:

- problem behavior can serve specific, adaptive purposes or functions;
- successfully changing problem behavior depends on discovering the purpose or function of the behavior;
- the same problem behavior may serve many different purposes;
- achieving successful functioning depends on expanding limited response repertoires; and
- successful intervention involves changing social systems and lifestyles.

> **Functional analysis identifies the function or purpose of the problem behavior(s).**

The goal of functional analysis, the first step in the functional assessment process, is to define the behavioral function or purpose of the problem behavior or behaviors and the variables that influence their occurrence (the specific effects of the child's behavior on the environment). Basically, the outcome of function analysis is a set of predictions of when and where the problem behavior will be exhibited. Definition or description of these variables provides information about the effects of setting events (temporally distant phenomena that influence the behavior), immediate antecedents, and consequences of the problem behavior. Information provided by the functional analysis is used to develop an intervention plan. This plan describes (1) contextual variables (e.g., physical feature of the setting, social interaction patterns, the daily/weekly schedule), (2) physiological variables (e.g., sleep/eating cycles, allergies, medications), and (3) alternative response options. Once there is a thorough understanding of the purpose or function that the problem behavior serves, the focus shifts to identifying and teaching alternative communication responses that serve the same function as the problem behavior.

As noted above, the goal of functional analysis, the first step in the communication-based intervention process, is to identify accurately the purpose or function of the problem behavior—basically the messages that the behavior is conveying. One way to do this is a matrix observation format such as suggested by Donnellan, Mirenda, Mesaros, and Fassbender (1984). This observation tool, presented in Figure 7.1, lists communicative behaviors and communicative functions. Specific communicative behaviors are listed across the horizontal axis and possible functions are listed on the vertical axis. The communicative functions were derived from several taxonomies of pragmatic uses of language. They are divided into two categories: Interactive functions and non-interactive functions. The four types of interactive functions are (A) requests, (B) negations, (C) declarations about events, and (D) declarations about feelings. Non-interactive functions include (A) self-regulation (behaviors such as self-correction that are used to monitor one's own behavior), (B) rehearsal (behaviors used to practice an anticipated event), (C) habitual (behaviors which because of regular repetition have become set in a predictable sequence), and (D) relaxation/tension release (behaviors used for the purpose of self-entertainment or to calm oneself).

To get an idea of communicative function–behavior relationships, match possible functions and behaviors by moving across or down the page and noting the point(s) of intersection on the Donnellan and colleagues' matrix. This information is then used in formulating hypotheses about the functions of the different behaviors. Once communicative functions have been identified, decisions can be made about which behaviors need to be shaped into more appropriate communicative responses and where new communicative behaviors need to be taught.

Not all problem behaviors can be addressed through communication interventions (some may be related to physiological or environmental variables), but there are now impressive demonstrations that, in addition to building generalized communicative competence, functional communication training can decrease most problem behaviors of students with moderate to severe and pervasive disabilities (e.g., Carr & Durand, 1985; Prizant & Rydell, 1993).

Functional communication training is effective in decreasing most problem behaviors of students with moderate to severe and multiple disabilities.

FIGURE 7.1   An observation tool for analyzing the communicative functions of behavior

FUNCTIONS	AGGRESSION	BIZARRE VERBALIZATIONS	INAPP. ORAL/ANAL BEHAVIOR	PERSEVERATIVE RITUALS	SELF-INJURIOUS BEHAVIOR	SELF-STIMULATION	TANTRUM	FACIAL EXPRESSION	GAZE AVERSION	GAZING/STARING	GESTURING/POINTING	HUGGING/KISSING	MASTURBATION	OBJECT MANIPULATION	PROXIMITY POSITIONING	PUSHING/PULLING	REACHING/GRABBING	RUNNING	TOUCHING	DELAYED ECHOLALIA	IMMEDIATE ECHOLALIA	LAUGHING/GIGGLING	SCREAM/YELL	SWEARING	VERBAL/PHYSICAL THREATS	WHINING/CRYING	COMPLEX SIGN/APPROXIMATION	COMPLEX SPEECH/APPROXIMATION	ONE WORD SIGN/APPROXIMATION	ONE WORD SPEECH/APPROX.	PICTURE/WRITTEN WORD
I. INTERACTIVE																															
A. REQUESTS FOR																															
Attention																															
Social Interaction																															
Play Interactions																															
Affection																															
Permission to Engage in an Activity																															
Action by Receiver																															
Assistance																															
Information/Clarification																															
Objects																															
Food																															
B. NEGATIONS																															
Protest																															
Refusal																															
Cessation																															
C. DECLARATIONS/COMMENTS																															
About Events/Actions																															
About Objects/Persons																															
About Errors/Mistakes																															
Affirmation																															
Greeting																															
Humor																															
D. DECLARATIONS ABOUT FEELINGS																															
Anticipation																															
Boredom																															
Confusion																															
Fear																															
Frustration																															
Hurt Feelings																															
Pain																															
Pleasure																															
II. NON-INTERACTIVE																															
A. SELF-REGULATION																															
B. REHEARSAL																															
C. HABITUAL																															
D. RELAXATION/ TENSION RELEASE																															

Time: _____   Date: _____   Student: _____   Activity: _____

THE ECOLOGICAL ASSESSMENT–PLANNING PROCESS

The remainder of this chapter describes procedures for ecological assessment and planning. The scope of the discussion covers language and communication assessment and planning. Because language and communication skills permeate and are inextricably essential to success in all aspects of children's lives, completely removing this domain from the ongoing stream of daily functioning is counterproductive. Thus, assessment and planning for language and communication are highlighted in the context of ecological assessment and planning for overall functioning.

Ecological assessment or "the ecological inventory process" was conceptualized by Brown and colleagues (Brown, Branston, Hamre-Nietupski, Pumpian, Certo, & Gruenewald, 1979) in the late seventies as a method for generating functional goals and objectives for students with severe and multiple disabilities. Since that time it has been widely used with children with disabilities of all types and severity. Brown and colleagues originally conceived of the ecological inventory process as having five stages, of which Table 7.2 presents a brief description.

The ecological assessment process described in this chapter is a variation of the procedures developed by Brown and colleagues. A major difference is that the process is implemented *exclusively* in the school domain and, where appropriate, there is specific focus on language and communication skills. This process is applicable to all students. It is appropriate when planning for preschoolers who are entering inclusive classes; when planning for children who, though they have been identified as eligible for special education and related services, will remain in their general classrooms; when planning for children who are being moved (or have just been moved) from segregated to inclusive classes; or to revise or expand goals and objectives for children with disabilities who have been in inclusive classes for some time. The purpose of the ecological assessment–planning process is twofold:

> Ecological assessment is used to identify and develop opportunities to support participation in activities in inclusive environments and to develop specific language and communication skills.

- To generate information about the social, education, and functional activities and routines in natural environments (the classroom and other school environments) where the child with disabilities wants and needs to be an active and successful participant; and
- to determine what resources and support the child will need to participate in and receive maximum benefits from activities and routines in the classroom and other school environments.

The planning/support team should include the regular and special education teachers, the language interventionist, other therapists (e.g., OT, PT), parents, siblings, and the student. Table 7.3 shows the 10 steps of the individualized ecological assessment–planning

TABLE 7.2   Steps in the ecological assessment process as described by Brown and colleagues

Step	Procedure
1. *Identify curriculum domains.*	Identified four curriculum domains thought to represent the major life areas for most students: domestic, recreation/leisure, community, and vocational. (School was considered an environment in the community domain.) Because it is such a significant area in the lives of children, many now include school as a separate domain (York & Vandercook, 1991).
2. *Identify and survey current and future natural environments.*	Identified and described the environments in each domain in which student needs and wants to function. Also identified environments where the student would function in the future. For example, current environments in the community domain might include the grocery store, the beach, the park, the doctor's office, etc. Future environments: a fast-food restaurant.
3. *Divide the relevant environment into subenvironments.*	Identified locations in the environments with specific activities (that the student needs to participate in to be part of the environment) as subenvironments. For example, if it is decided that the student needs to be prepared to do grocery shopping, then subenvironments of the grocery store would be identified (e.g., the cart area, fruit/vegetable section, shelf displays, meat department, check-out).
4. *Inventory the subenvironments to identify the relevant activities that are performed there.*	Identified the activities and routines necessary for *basic* performance and participation in the subenvironments through observations and interviews at the subenvironment site. Extensive considerations given to how many times an activity is needed, the student's age and current skills, his interests, the priorities of the parents, and the physical characteristics of the setting that dictate the various behaviors.
5. *Examine the activities to isolate the skills required for their performance.*	Broke activities into teachable units or skills. Skills were then further task analyzed into precise performance sequences.

process as described in this chapter, with a summary of procedures and expected outcomes at each step. Ideally this process should not be undertaken until about 2 weeks after the child is in the classroom so that there is time for everyone to get to know one another.

STEP 1: Get To Know the Child

The purpose of the first step is for team members to begin to get to know the child and to get to know one another through a procedure

TABLE 7.3   Overview: The individualized ecological assessment–planning process

Step	Procedures	Outcome(s)
1. Get to know the child.	Schedule a team meeting. Use visioning to generate information about the child's strengths and challenges and what the family and peers want for the child.	A description of the child's strengths, capabilities, and preferences. A shared team vision for the child.
2. Get to know the environment.	Describe school subenvironments for a typical week for the child or a same-class peer. Prioritize subenvironments according to their potential to bring about the shared vision.	A schedule of a week's activities. A list with 3–5 first-priority subenvironments and 3–5 second-priority subenvironments.
3. State a goal for each subenvironment and list key activities/routines.	Develop a broad goal for each first-priority subenvironment. List activities and/or routines in each of the first-priority subenvironments.	Broad goals (3–5). Lists of activities and/or routines in priority subenvironments.
4. Determine component skills and concepts of the activities/ routines.	Record observations and conduct interviews to determine component skills and concepts of activities/routines. List the skills and concepts on the activity Discrepancy Analysis forms.	Lists of skills and concepts for all activities (in the first column of each of the activity Discrepancy Analysis forms).
5. Observe the child in each activity/ routine.	Record observations and describe what the child presently does in the activity—how and to what extent the child demonstrates the skills necessary for participation in the activity.	Descriptions of student's present participation (in the second column of each of the activity Discrepancy Analysis forms).
6. Perform a discrepancy analysis.	Discuss and compare the child's performance in each activity or routine with expected /desired performance.	Descriptions of the child's deficiencies in relation to expectations for all activities.
7. Determine factors contributing to performance deficiencies.	Categorize reasons why the skills that the activity requires are not performed. Strategy deficiency? Skill deficiency? Behavior problem? Instructional problem? Environmental arrangement?	Description of the different factors that prevent child's participation.
8. State instructional objectives.	State two or more instructional objectives for each activity. List these under the broad goals generated in Step 3.	At least two instructional objectives for each broad goal (from Step 3).
9. Determine resources and supports.	Determine needed modifications, adaptations, and supports. Decide the instructional foci for each objective (language? motor? academic? social? self-care?).	Description of needed modifications, adaptations, and support and instruction focus for each objective.
10. Plan an individualized program.	Plan modifications, adaptations, support, instructional procedures and materials (how? when? person responsible? monitoring?).	Plan for environmental manipulations and instruction for *first-priority subenvironments.*

The first step is visioning for the child.

called "visioning." The visioning framework, based on a planning system developed at McGill University is called *McGill Action Planning System,* or *MAPS* (Forest & O'Brien, 1989). MAPS is a systems approach designed to help team members plan for the inclusion of children with special needs into general age-appropriate classrooms. The process takes 2 or 3 hours. It can be completed in a single session or two sessions.

A meeting is scheduled. The meeting should involve all team members (family members, the child, all involved professionals and paraprofessionals), two to five classmates (if possible), and anyone else who expresses an interest in the child's future. (Inclusion of children in the planning process is a unique feature of MAPS.)

Team members sit in a semicircle with a facilitator positioned at the open side of the circle. The facilitator's role is to introduce the participants and the MAPS process, solicit input, encourage and support interactions, ensure equal participation, and record responses to the following questions.

The purpose of the first question is to give the team members a picture of what has happened in the child's life to this time. Parents are asked to summarize the key milestones that have affected their child's life and her school experiences.

What is _____'s history?

Family members and peers should be encouraged to talk about milestones in the child's life.

> **Example: These were Jennie's family's responses to the question "What is Jennie's history?"**
> She and her twin are the youngest of four children.
> Dad is in the military.
> The twins were premature.
> Janie was able to come home from the hospital 3 weeks before we were able to bring Jennie home.
> She has a history of seizures, ear infections, and asthma.
> Where we lived last year, Jennie was in a special education kindergarten class.
> She walked at about 20 months and said her first word at about age 3.

The next question is intended to encourage the family to think about what they want for the child and what they think the child would want. The goal is to project a vision that will give direction to planning. The parents are encouraged to talk about what they really want, not what they think is available for their child. Parents of very young children often find it difficult to think about adulthood. They may be more comfortable focusing on the nearer future (e.g., 5 years from the present).

What is your dream for _____'s future?

Example: These were Jennie's family's responses to the question "What is your dream for Jennie's future?"
She will participate in regular education classes all through school.
She will graduate from high school with her sister.
She will have friends like Janie.
She will some day be able to live independently in a place that she likes, with people she likes.
She will be able to carry on a conversation.
She will have an opportunity to do things that she likes and does well.

The next question is the most difficult to ask parents but it is extremely important. It makes explicit what is in the heart of the parents. The response tells the team what they must work to avoid.

What is your nightmare?

Example: These were Jennie's parents' responses to the question "What is your nightmare?"
She will not progress developmentally.
She will have to be in a special education class.
She will not have friends.
She will have to live in a group home.
She will not be able to go places with the family.
She will be placed in an institution.

The next question is intended to begin a general brainstorming session that continues until no one can think of anything else to say. Because they know the child best (and in different contexts) it is especially important for family members and peers to describe the child. They should be encouraged to share descriptive statements and anecdotes about the child's life and unique and positive characteristics. At the end, each team member may be asked to circle three words they feel best describe the child.

Who is _____?

Example: These were Jennie's family's and peers' responses to the question "Who is Jennie?"
She is a lovable, helpful, happy, and spunky little girl.
She is very motivated.
She is lively, curious, and full of energy.
She wants to learn—is inquisitive.
She is a twin, and her sister is her best friend.
She is excited about being in a "real" class like her sister.
Her favorite color is blue.

She is small and fragile looking.
She likes to be around people.
She has a good attention span.
She likes to go to birthday parties.
She likes to go to the beach.
She likes to be read to before bed.

The facilitator should ask team members to identify the child's strengths and unique gifts and abilities. The questions What can the child do? What does she like to do? and What does she do well? are asked to get everyone—especially the parents—to focus on positives

What are _____'s greatest strengths (or gifts)?

Example: This was the list that was generated in response to the question "What are Jennie's greatest strengths or gifts?"
People are drawn to her because she is so lovable and she is
    always happy.
She is almost able to dress herself.
Her motivation.
Her determination.
Her curiosity.
Her energy.
Her desire to learn.
Her sociability: She really likes people.
Her attention span.
She likes books.
She has Janie as a model for age-appropriate behaviors.
She's spunky and independent.

This question gives each team member an opportunity to identify the child's needs and challenges from his or her unique perspective.

What are _____'s greatest needs and challenges?

Example: This was the list that was generated in response to the question "What are Jennie's greatest needs and challenges?"
She needs to be able to communicate well enough that people
    who are not familiar with her will know what she wants.
She needs to be challenged to use language in more situations.
She needs more independence with dressing (especially shoes).
She needs more interactions with peers.
She needs words.
She needs consistent expectations.
She needs to initiate communication.
She needs to use the toilet without having to have a reminder.
She needs her own friends.

Ideally, the child' s school day will be the same as her peers. The issue is what supports need to be provided to achieve successful inclusion.

What would _____'s ideal school day be like? and What do we need to do to make it happen?

> **Example: These were the responses to the question "What would Jennie's ideal school day be like? and What do we need to do to make it happen?"**
>
> The schedule for Jennie's ideal school day would be the same as that of her first-grade classmates.
>
> The team needs to (1) adapt first-grade curriculum activities (especially the academic activities that call for beginning reading and writing), and (2) identify alternative activities that have the same format for some time slots.

STEP 2: Get To Know the Environment

The outcome of the visioning process is a shared vision for the student's participation in the school environment. The team is now ready to go step by step through the day and describe environments, activities, goals, and objectives. The goal is to get to know and decide first- and second-priority subenvironments. (Subenvironments are locations where important activities occur.) The team should identify settings in which significant activities occur (e.g., morning circle, playground, reading group, cafeteria, cooperative math groups).

The second step is to identify settings in which significant activities occur.

Language and communication skills are the means for establishing social relationships, participating in academic and literacy experiences, and functioning independently in classroom routines. All subenvironments can be expected to have extensive requirements for language and communication skills. School subenvironments will generally fall into one or another of three categories: (1) where the child's language and communication deficiencies preclude *any* type of participation at the present time; (2) where the child is partially participating at the present time; and (3) where the child is fully participating but full participation could be enhanced by more appropriate and effective use of language and communication.

A calendar-type grid such as those used for the sample schedules shown in Figures 7.2 and 7.3 helps to structure the discussion. Begin with the child's arrival on the school grounds each day and "talk through" the day until she leaves the school grounds in the afternoon. The format can be used in several ways. One strategy is to give each team member a blank grid to make notes on during the discussion, while the facilitator incorporates information onto a master form. Another strategy is to make the form into a transparency which the facilitator can work on as an overhead, transferring the information to another format at the end of the meeting. (The transparency form can be used again for planning for other children.) Or the grid can be drawn on the chalkboard and filled in during the discussion. The completed form should include all school subenvironments and time periods when the child is participating in activities in the subenvironment. This includes both extracurricular activities and informal interactions (e.g., waiting for the bus). If the child is not yet in the school, this form is completed for a peer in the same class who would be expected to have a similar schedule. This information can be verified or expanded if there is a question of accuracy. Figure 7.2 shows a weekly schedule for a second grader with severe disabilities. Figure 7.3 shows a weekly schedule for a sixth grader with severe disabilities.

After the weekly schedule is completed, the team prioritizes the subenvironments in terms of their significance to helping the child attain the team's shared vision. The team should agree on three to five first-priority subenvironments and three to five second-priority subenvironments.

How much time does this process require? The first time it will require considerably more time than traditional assessment and planning procedures. However, as the team accumulates activity/routine lists for all subenvironments in the school day and skill/concept lists for all activities and routines, it requires considerably less time for each child. These lists can be used with other children (in the current year or subsequent years).

FIGURE 7.2   Sample Schedule for second grader

Weekly Schedule for ___DAPHNE___ *from Arrival on Campus to Leaving Campus*

Time	Monday	Tuesday	Wednesday	Thursday	Friday
7:15–7:25	Arrival on the bus, toilet, wash hands ----------------------- (lanai area outside Rm. 3 and restroom outside Rm. 2 ---------				
7:25–8:45	Breakfast in cafeteria -------------------------				
7:45–7:50	Walk to Rm. 22 ------------------------- (walkway leading to 2nd grade wing)				
7:50–8:00	Arrival at class and morning business --------- (lanai, cubby holes, her desk)				
8:00–8:15	Announcements, notices, homework ----------- (teacher's desk, front of room, students at their desks)				
8:15–8:45	Writing (her desk)	Library (Library)	Writing -- (her desk) --		
8:45–9:20	Reading activities at her her desk --------------				
9:20–9:30	Clean up ------------------------- (her desk and cubby holes)				
9:30–9:45	Snack and toilet ------------------------- (lanai)				
9:45–10:00	Recess on 2nd grade playground ------------				
10:00–10:15	Wash hands and get a drink (sink or lanai)				
10:15–10:45	P.E. (playground)	MUSIC (floor)	HAWAIIANA (floor)	MATH (her desk)	MATH (her desk)
10:45–11:20	MATH (her desk)	MATH (her desk)	SOCIAL STUDIES (desk/floor)	HEALTH (desk/floor)	SCIENCE (desk/floor)
11:20–11:45	STORY AND DISCUSSION (floor) ------------				
11:45–12:00	Get ready for lunch–wash hands and toilet -- (lanai sink and restroom)				
12:00–12:30	Lunch in cafeteria -------------------------				
12:30–12:45	Recess on 2nd grade playground ------------				
12:45–1:00	Wash hands and get a drink ------------- (sink on lanai)				
1:00–1:45	SCIENCE (floor/desk)	SOCIAL STUDIES (floor/desk)	(1:00–1:15) Get ready for home	ART (desk)	HEALTH (floor/desk)
1:45–2:00	Get ready to go home --		Wait for the bus	Get ready to	go home --
2:00	Wait for the bus outside of Rm. 3			Wait for the	bus outside of Rm. 3

Second grade class, heterogeneous grouping, 19 students.
Developed by Dawn Hirata, 1995.

FIGURE 7.3 Sample schedule for a student in intermediate school

Intermediate School	7:30 Arrival/Free Time Monday	Tuesday	Thursday	Friday	Wednesday
Opening . . . . . . 5 min Homeroom . . . .10 min "Talk to Me" . . . .16 min	8:00–8:05 8:05–8:15 8:15–8:31	8:00–8:05 8:05–8:15 8:15–8:31	8:00–8:05 8:05–8:15 8:15–8:31	8:00–8:05 8:05–8:15 8:15–8:31	8:00–8:05 8:05–8:15 8:15–8:31
Module I . . . . . .53 min	Period 1 8:35–9:28 Story Hour	Period 1 8:35–9:28 Story Hour	Period 1 8:35–9:28 Story Hour	Period 2 8:35–9:28 Teen Health	Period 1 8:35–9:31 Story Hour
Module II . . . . .53 min	Period 2 9:32–10:25 Teen Health	Period 2 9:32–10:25 Teen Health	Period 3 9:32–10:25 P.E.	Period 3 9:32–10:25 P.E.	Recess Campus Walk 9:31–9:50
Recess . . . . . . .20 min	Campus Walk	Campus Walk	Campus Walk	Campus Walk	Period 2 9:54–10:50 Teen Health
Module III . . . .53 min	Period 3 10:49–11:42 P.E.	Period 3 10:49–11:42 P.E.	Period 3 10:49–11:42 CBI (community)	Period 4 10:49–11:42 CBI (community)	Period 5 10:54–11:51 Art
Module IV . . . .53 min	Period 4 11:46–12:39 CBI (Community)	Period 4 11:46–12:39 CBI (Community)	Period 4 11:46–12:39 Art	Period 5 11:46–12:39 Art	Lunch 11:51–12:21 Cafeteria Recess 12:21–12:30 Campus Walk
Lunch/Recess. . .40 min	Cafeteria/ Campus Walk	Cafeteria/ Campus Walk	Cafeteria/ Campus Walk	Cafeteria/ Campus Walk	Period 6 12:34–1:30 CBI (on campus)
Module V . . . .53 min	Period 5 1:23–2:16 Art	Period 6 1:23–2:16 CBI (on campus)	Period 6 1:23–2:16 CBI (on campus)	Period 6 1:23–2:16 CBI (on campus)	Optional Closing 1:30–1:35 Wait for father to pick up
Closing	2:16–2:20 Wait for father to pick up	2:16–2:20 Wait for father to pick up	2:16–2:20 Wait for father to pick up	2:16–2:20 Wait for father to pick up	Prep 1:35–2:15

Developed by Geri Souza, 1995.

STEP 3: State a Goal for Each Subenvironment and List Key Activities/Routines

State a broad goal for each priority subenvironment.

Example: Jennie will participate more effectively at arrival/free play time.

Then discuss and reach consensus on the key activities and routines in the priority subenvironments. This should yield three to five lists of activities and routines (depending on the number of priority subenvironments selected).

The third step is to state broad goals and key activities and routines.

Example: The activities at arrival/free play time (one of the priority subenvironments selected for Jennie) are:
1. Greetings and putting clothing and lunchboxes away
2. Selecting and participating in free play
3. Returning materials to shelves and preparing for reading group

STEP 4: Determine Component Skills and Concepts of the Activities and Routines

Record observations and conduct interviews of team members (including peers and regular education teachers) to determine component skills and concepts for each of the activities/routines in priority subenvironments. The goal is to generate a list of skill requirements (as performed by a child without disabilities). Team members should share responsibility for these observations and interviews. For example, the following behaviors might be expectations for the morning arrival routine in a second-grade class: (1) entering the room before the bell or when the bell rings at 7:45; (2) taking a seat at your desk; (3) responding to the teacher's "good morning"; and (4) responding to the teacher's questions about lunch count, the date, weather report, and the daily schedule.

The fourth step is to generate a list of required skills and concepts.

Figure 7.4 provides a form that (when enlarged) can be used for this step and subsequent ones. A Discrepancy Analysis form is completed for each activity. Component skills and concepts for the activity are listed in the first column of this form.

Observation and analysis of curriculum activities/lessons is especially challenging because academic lessons in each curriculum domain (i.e., language arts, science, math, social studies) have different (though related) goals, different materials, and different tasks each day. The observations should describe the typical lesson format and the teacher's objectives for the children over a reasonable period (six weeks or more). Every curriculum has many objectives, but only a few of these objectives are truly what might be called "benchmarks." These benchmark objectives are the ones that need to be considered in recording component behaviors in this step of the

FIGURE 7.4 Discrepancy analysis format

Discrepancy Analysis

Student: _____ Date: _____ Activity: _____

Team members present: _____

What does a typical peer do in this activity?	What does the student do in this activity?	Discrepancy: What does the student need to learn to do to participate in the activity?	What are possible reasons for the student's deficiencies?

process. Ultimately, in Steps 9 and 10, when decisions must be made about how the child with disabilities will participate in the lesson, the team will need to consider what types of adaptations are appropriate. (Specific adaptations are discussed in Chapter 8.)

STEP 5: Observe the Child in Each Activity or Routine

To this point in the process, information about the child's language and communication abilities has come from parent and professional reports and test results. The goal of this step is to record and describe how the child participates in key activities in the priority subenvironments. The focus is on how and to what extent the child performs the skills identified in Step 4. Does the child participate fully or is there only partial participation at the present time? Are there particular aspects of the various activities that the child seems to find especially interesting or motivating? Does the child exhibit any type of problem behavior during the activities and, if so, does this behavior appear to have communicative purposes? Other factors to note when observing the child perform the activity are (1) how well the child performs relative to expectations (e.g., How long does it take the child to perform the skill?); (2) whether the child seems aware of (and responds to) the natural cues and prompts for the skills; and (3) which peers might be potential supports for the child.

The fifth step is to observe the child in key activities and routines.

There are several possible data collection procedures that may be useful for this type of observation. However, the most appropriate procedure is a continuous recording method called anecdotal recording, or a variation of anecdotal recording, ABC analysis (see also Chapter 12). The observer positions himself in an unobtrusive location; the recording sheets are attached to a clipboard. Anecdotal recording then is simply recording careful and continuous descriptive notes about relevant aspects of the activity.

ABC is a somewhat more structured form of anecdotal recording. With ABC analysis, the blank sheet of paper is divided into three columns labeled A (for antecedent events), B (for behaviors), and C (for consequences). Events that precede relevant language/communication behaviors (antecedent events) are recorded in the first column; the behaviors themselves are noted in the second column; and whatever follows the behaviors is noted in the third column. The data collected in the ABC format make it fairly straightforward to identify the stimulus events for key language/communication responses, the form of the behavior, and its function or purpose. The child's utterances, comprehension (words, concepts, and structures the child seems to understand), and use of language should be recorded. Additionally, information about communication partners is useful, how consistent the language cues are in the activity (whether the child anticipates when language is indicated), and whether there are positive natural consequences that occur frequently enough to keep the child motivated. Also consider whether the child is likely to have opportunities to use the language and communication skills learned in this activity in other activities and other environments. (The more opportunities to practice the skills, the more likely they are to generalize.)

Ideally, the language interventionist, the OT and/or the PT, and the special and general education teachers should undertake these observations together until they have 3 to 5 days of performance data. If time constraints make this impossible or impractical, each may observe the child separately. Then team members can compare their lists and reach consensus regarding the child's present performance in the activities. The agreed upon list goes in the second column of the Discrepancy Analysis form.

STEP 6: Perform a Discrepancy Analysis

The sixth step is to compare what the child can do with required skills and concepts.

The Discrepancy Analysis compares the child's performance in each activity or routine with the component skills and concepts of the activity/routine. In analyzing the discrepancy between the child's performance in each activity or routine and the component skills and concepts for every activity or routine, development information from past assessments and observations should be considered. Description of the child's deficiencies in relation to the skill requirements and expectations of the activity are described in the third column of the Discrepancy Analysis form. The skill deficiencies should be analyzed, using task analysis, and effective cues and prompts should be indicated. Finally, description of the child's present language and communication performance in this third column should describe both the qualitative and the quantitative dimensions of the behavior and whether it is spontaneous or prompted. It should consider the child's language and communication in optimal as well as difficult conditions.

This step in the process is illustrated by the following example. Michael is a second grader with Down syndrome. The team are focusing their planning and instructional efforts for Michael on language and communication skills and social skills because the family has requested concentration in these areas. Michael's motor skills are considered adequate for participation in age-appropriate activities and routines. Data from observations in the morning arrival routine indicate that, when the bell rings, Michael moves with his peers into the classroom, finds his desk, and sits down. The teacher comments that he learned this without prompting by watching his peers during the first three days of school. He also joins the class's choral response to the teacher's "good morning class." Unfortunately, Michael's participation in the morning routine ends at this point. During the next 8 to 10 minutes, the teacher takes lunch count, points to the date on a calendar, asks questions about the day's weather report that is written on the chalkboard, and outlines the day's schedule of activities. Michael looks around the room, shuffles noisily through the contents of his desk, and turns his body to the side to look at (and occasionally touch) Brittney who sits across the aisle. Michael does *not*

- raise his hand in response to the question "Who is eating in the cafeteria today?" (he always buys his lunch in the cafeteria);
- attend to the teacher when she is talking about the weather or answer the question "What kind of weather are we having today?" with one of the weather words (i.e., *rain, warm, cold, hot, sunny, cloudy*);
- look at peers when they answer the weather question; or
- attend to the teacher's description of special activities for the day or write the words noting the activity on his daily schedule as the teacher instructs the class to do.

Perusal of the curriculum materials and observations during science and reading activities in Michael's classroom indicate that activities over the next month are related to the theme "our growing nature world." They incorporate vocabulary/concepts about time (e.g., *first, second, before, after, next, earlier, later*), causality (e.g., *if/then, why, when, therefore, because*), classification (grouping according to similarities and describing the basis for classification), and seriation (e.g., *first, second, third, big, bigger, biggest, small, smaller, smallest, long, longer, longest, short, shorter, shortest*). Available assessment information and observations in the classroom indicate that Michael has difficulty with comparatives. He also has difficulty understanding and using the vocabulary that expresses causality (*because, if/then, when, why*). The language interventionist and the special education teacher agree that, while Michael is able to classify objects by size, shape, or color, he is not able to explain the reasons for his groupings. Also, Michael has difficulty understanding the *wh-* questions that the teacher asks after reading a story to the class.

Required social/communication skills in Michael's subenvironments of "transition to lunch," " recess," and "waiting for the bus" are (1) initiate appropriately to ask to join a game, (2) assist others when asked (e.g., "Pass the napkins."), (3) cope with peer provocations (e.g., "Don't do that!" "No, I don't want to do that."), and (4) use persuasion and respond to the appeals of others (e.g., "Can I please use that next?"). When provided with prompts and other support, Michael can demonstrate these skills but he does not demonstrate them spontaneously. In looking at the discrepancy column of all of the activity forms, the team identified eight language/communication skills and social skills that appear more than three times across activities that are targeted for Michael.

STEP 7: Consider Factors Contributing to Performance Deficiencies

The seventh step is to explore reasons why the target child's behavior differs from that of his peers.

The purpose of this step is for the team to explore possible reasons for differences between the child's behavior and that of his peers in the same activities. Explanations might include

- *a strategy deficiency*—the child does not recognize the specific skill(s) that he is expected to perform at that particular juncture or does not attend to natural cues for performance of the skill;
- *a skill deficiency*—an inability to perform the required skill that is related to the child's disability (i.e., motor limitation, sensory deficit);
- *a behavior problem*—lack of motivation to perform the skill;
- *an instructional problem*—lack of instruction on the skill;
- *an environmental problem*—the way that the physical or temporal environment is arranged impedes the child's performance of the skill.

These possible explanations for the child's performance deficiencies are noted in the "possible reasons for deficiencies" column of the Discrepancy Analysis form. Recall the example of Michael above. In discussing factors that may contribute to his performance deficiencies in the arrival routine, the team raised these questions:

1. Is he able to *hear* the teacher's questions and directions? Is his hearing in the normal range? Is his desk location optimal?
2. Does he understand what the teacher is asking? In other contexts, is he able to answer questions about expected events and environmental conditions?
3. Does he know that the teacher expects each child to answer the questions?
4. Does he understand that the appropriate response mode is to raise his hand (for the lunch count)?

STEP 8: State Instructional Objectives

The eighth step is to develop objectives for each activity.

The team should generate at least two instructional objectives for each activity.

> **Example: Under the broad goal "Jennie will participate more effectively at arrival/free play time in the classroom each morning," the team stated these objectives:**

1. Every morning, when entering the classroom, Jennie will look at the teacher when the teacher greets her, return the greeting with a word and/or a gesture, and then (without a prompt) move to

her storage cubby and place her sweater/coat and lunch box there.

2. Every morning, when asked which activity center she would like to go to, Jennie will indicate her choice by vocalizing and pointing to a picture of the activity on the activity center communication board.

STEP 9: Determine Resources and Supports

When discussing resources, adaptations, and supports, remember two points: (1) there is no reason why all children in a classroom need to be doing the same thing at the same time, and (2) it is perfectly appropriate for individual children to participate differently in the same activities. Discuss the explanations for the child's lack of required/expected skills (from Step 7) and consider environmental manipulations and instructional strategies that address the identified strategy deficiencies, skill deficiencies, behavior problems, instructional problems, and problems related to environmental problems. List strategies to facilitate and support learning and performance of the targeted skills and skill, material, or equipment adaptations that may eliminate the need to teach specific skills or make learning easier. Identify classmates who might assist the child as special friends or serve as communication partners. When the team decides that a curriculum lesson is not appropriate for the child, consider precisely what adaptations will need to be provided. Options for adaptation are described in Chapter 8.

The ninth step is to decide what resources and supports will be needed.

STEP 10: Plan an Individualized Program

Discuss and plan environmental manipulations and instruction to support acquisition of the targeted skills. Instructional plans for each objective should show prompts, environmental modifications and supports, materials, and the persons responsible. Planning may be done on a form such as that provided in Figure 7.5. Instruction/intervention procedures are described in Chapter 8.

The tenth step is to plan an individualized program.

SUMMARY

Texts that focus on intervention for the child with language disorders (whether as a single disability or secondary to another disability) typically describe language assessment and intervention strategies as if they are activities that are (or can) be separated from the child's overall program. We agree with Jorgensen (1994) that "this practice, common to many related service disciplines, has resulted in fragmentation

FIGURE 7.5 Program planning form

Individualized Instructional Plan

Student: _____ Date: _____ Activity: _____

Objectives	Supports	Instruction	Adaptations
1.	Environmental: Personnel: Peers:	Methods: Prompts: Consequences:	Task modifications: Prosthetics: Environmental:
2.	Environmental: Personnel: Peers	Methods: Prompts: Consequences:	Task modifications: Prosthetics: Environmental:
3.	Environmental: Personnel: Peers:	Methods: Prompts: Consequences:	Task modifications: Prosthetics: Environmental:

of childs' programs" (p. 28). There must be a strong, direct linkage between assessment and intervention activities for children to receive maximum benefits from inclusion. Intervention should focus on two goals: (1) supporting the child's participation in all aspects of the inclusive classroom and other school settings; and (2) facilitating development of specific functional skills in inclusive contexts. This chapter has described an ecological approach to assessment and planning—one that looks at and plans for language and communication skills within the child's overall program.

REFERENCES

Adkins, P. G., & Young, R. G. (1976). Cultural perceptions in the treatment of handicapped school children of Mexican-American Parentage. *Journal of Research and Development in Education, 9*(4), 83–90.

American Speech-Language-Hearing Association Committee on Language Learning Disorders. (1989). Report on issues in determining eligibility for language intervention. *Asha, 31*(3), 113–118.

Bateman, B. D. (1992). *Better IEPs.* Creswell, OR: OtterInk.

Brown, L., Branston, M. B., Hamre-Nietupski, S., Pumpian, I., Certo, N., & Gruenewald, L. (1979). A strategy for developing chronological age-appropriate and functional curricular content for severely handicapped adolescents and young adults. *Journal of Special Education, 13,* 81–90.

Bronfenbrenner, U. (1977). Toward an experimental ecology of human development. *American Psychologist, 4,* 413–531.

Calculator, S. N. (1994). Designing and implementing communicative assessments in inclusive settings. In S. N. Calculator and C. M. Jorgensen (Eds.), *Including students with severe disabilities in schools* (pp. 114–181). San Diego: Singular Publishing Co.

Canino, I. A., & Canino, G. (1980). Impact of stress on the Puerto Rican family: Treatment considerations. *American Journal of Orthopsychiatry, 50*(3), 535–541.

Carr, E. G., & Durand, V. M. (1985). Reducing behavior problems through functional communication training. *Journal of Applied Behavior Analysis, 18,* 111–126.

Carr, E. G., Levin, L., McConnachie, G., Carlson, J. I., Kemp, D. C., & Smith, C. E. (1994). *Communication-based intervention for problem behavior.* Baltimore: Paul H. Brookes.

Casby, M. (1992). The cognitive hypothesis and its influence on speech-language services in the schools. *Language, Speech, and Hearing Services in Schools. 23,* 198–202.

Chan, S. (1986). Parents of exceptional Asian children. In M. K. Kitano & P. E. Chinn (Eds.), *Exceptional Asian children and youth* (pp. 36–53). Reston, VA: Council for Exceptional Children.

Cole, K., Dale, P., & Mills, P. (1990). Defining language delay in young children by cognitive referencing: Are we saying more than we know? *Applied Psycholinguistics, 11,* 291–302.

Donnellan, A., Mirenda, P., Mesaros, R., & Fassbender, L. (1984). Analyzing the communicative functions of aberrant behavior. *Journal of the Association for Persons with Severe Handicaps, 9,* 201–212.

Durand, V. M. (1990). *Severe behavior problems: A functional communication training approach.* New York: Guilford Press.

Evans, I. M., & Meyer, L. H. (1985). *An educative approach to behavior problems: A practical decision model for interventions with severely handicapped learners.* Baltimore: Paul H. Brookes.

Fey, M. E., Catts, & Larrivee, L. S. (1995). Preparing preschoolers for the academic and social challenges of school. In M. E. Fey, J. Windsor, and S. F. Warren (Eds.), *Language intervention: Preschool through the elementary years*. Baltimore: Paul H. Brookes.

Forest, M., & O'Brien, J. (1989). *Action for inclusion*. Toronto, Ontario: Center for Integrated Education, Frontier College.

Goodman, J. R., & Bond, L. (1993). The individualized education program: A retrospective critique. *Journal of Special Education, 26*, 408–422.

Guess, D., & Noonan, M. J. (1982). Curricula and instructional procedures for severely handicapped students. *Focus on Exceptional Children. 14*(5), 1–12.

Harry, B. (1992). Developing cultural self-awareness: The first step in values clarification for early interventionists. *Topics in Early Childhood Special Education, 12*(3), 333–350.

Jorgensen, C. M. (1994). Developing individualized inclusive education programs. In S. N. Calculator and C. M. Jorgensen (Eds.), *Including students with severe disabilities in schools* (pp. 27–74). San Diego: Singular Publishing Co.

Kayser, H. (1989, November). Communication strategies of Anglo and Hispanic clinicians with Hispanic preschoolers. Paper presented at the American Speech-Language-Hearing Association annual convention, St. Louis.

Kayser, H. (1995) Intervention with children from linguistically and culturally diverse backgrounds. In M. E. Fey, J. Windsor, & S. F. Warren (Eds.), *Language intervention: Preschool through the elementary years* (pp. 315–33). Baltimore: Paul H. Brookes.

Keogh, B. K., & Sheehan, R. (1981). The use of developmental test data for documenting handicapped children's progress: Problems and recommendations. *Journal of the Division for Early Childhood, 3*, 42–47.

Leonard, L. B. (1987). Is specific language impairment a useful construct? In S. Rosenberg (Ed.), *Advances in applied psycholinguistics* (Vol. 1, pp. 1–39). New York: Cambridge University Press.

Locust, C. (1988). Wounding the spirit: Discrimination and traditional American Indian belief systems. *Harvard Educational Review, 58*, 315–330.

Lynch, E. W., & Hanson, M. J. (1992). *Developing cross-cultural competence*. Baltimore: Paul H. Brookes.

Prizant, B. M., & Rydell, P. J. (1993). Assessment and intervention considerations for unconventional verbal behavior. In J. Reichle and D. P. Wacker (Eds.), *Communicative alternatives to challenging behavior* (pp. 263–298). Baltimore: Paul H. Brookes.

Reichle, J., Feeley, K., & Johnson, S. (1993). Communication intervention for persons with severe and profound disabilities. *Clinics in Communication Disorders, 3*, 7–30.

Reichle, J., & Wacker, D. P. (1993). *Communicative alternatives to challenging behavior*. Baltimore: Paul H. Brookes.

Rhodes, W. C., (1967). The disturbing child: A problem of ecological management. *Exceptional Children, 33*, 449–455.

Stainback, S., Stainback, W., & Jackson, H. J. (1992). Toward inclusive classrooms. In S. Stainback and W. Stainback (Eds.), *Curriculum considerations in inclusive classrooms* (pp. 2–17). Baltimore: Paul H. Brookes.

Voeltz, L. M., & Evans, I. M. (1983). Educational validity: Procedures to evaluate outcomes in programs for severely handicapped learners. *Journal of the Association for the Severely Handicapped, 8*, 3–15.

Watzlawick, P., Beavin, J. H., & Jackson, D. D. (1967). *Pragmatics of human communication*. New York: W. W. Norton & Co.

York, J., & Vandercook, T. (1991). Designing an integrated education for learners with severe disabilities through the IEP process. *Teaching Exceptional Children. 23*(2) 22–28.

CHAPTER 8

Language Intervention and Support

Linda McCormick

Language and communication instruction/intervention should be guided by what we know about how and why language is learned—that it is learned in the context of interactions in daily activities and routines, as a tool for communicating meanings and controlling the environment. Unfortunately, as Owens (1992) has noted, very often what we have instead are language intervention procedures that fail to consider "either the integrated nature of language or the context of language use" (p. 173). At the very least, broad outcomes for children who are experiencing difficulties with language and communication (whether a delay, a disorder, or minimal or severe difficulties) should be

- to increase the number of functions accomplished with language,
- to enhance and expand language and literacy competencies, and
- to increase the number of social and physical contexts in which language is used spontaneously and effectively.

These outcomes are sought through intervention that facilitates and supports effective teacher-student interactions, maximizes opportunities for developing and maintaining peer interactions and friendships, and ensures meaningful participation in classroom activities (both academic activities and routines). In short, it should facilitate and support the child's participation in all school environments (and, to the extent possible, home and community environments).

In inclusive schools, all students are provided appropriate educational opportunities and support to meet their individual needs (Stainback & Stainback, 1990). The resources, knowledge base, and personnel of special education (teachers, language interventionists, and therapists) combine with those of general education to facilitate and assist development and maintenance of challenging, supportive, and appropriate programs in all general education settings. In contrast, traditional schools tend to establish and maintain homogeneous environments. Children with disabilities are served in separate classes where they, alone, benefit from the special resources that personnel in special education can provide. Table 8.1 highlights the major differences between special education and speech-language intervention in traditional schools and special education and speech-language intervention in inclusive schools. This chapter is organized according to these differences, which range across at least six dimensions: (1) the focus of intervention; (2) methods and procedures for special instruction; (3) the instructional environment; (4) professional relationships and responsibilities; (5) scheduling; and (6) measurement and evaluation.

Intervention should facilitate and support the child's participation in all inclusive environments.

THE FOCUS OF INTERVENTION

The ecological assessment–planning process yields three to five specific goals, with at least two instructional objectives for each goal. The basic issues with respect to intervention are

1. How to modify and adapt existing environmental conditions; and
2. what methods and procedures will facilitate and support mastery of new language and communication skills and concepts.

This section will focus on modifications and adaptations of (1) teacher-child interactions, (2) peer interactions, and (3) the curriculum.

Teacher-Child Interactions

What children learn in the classroom (and how well they learn it) is largely dependent on teacher-child interactions. When the commu-

TABLE 8.1 Comparison of traditional and inclusive schools

| Dimensions | Traditional Schools | | Inclusive Schools |
	Special Education	Language Intervention	Special Education and Language Intervention
Focus of Intervention	Developmental skills Functional/adaptive skills	Linguistic concepts/rules Linguistic forms and structures	Teacher-child interactions Peer interactions Curriculum adaptations
Methods and Procedures	Contrived instructional contexts Adult controlled Individual instruction Massed trials	Contrived therapy contexts Adult controlled Individual instruction Massed trials	Milieu language teaching Scaffolding Routines and script training Interactive modeling Situated pragmatics Direct instruction
Instructional Environment	Special education classroom Resource room Homogeneous groupings	Therapy room Special education classroom Homogeneous groupings	Regular classroom Other school settings (playground, cafeteria, etc.) Home/community environments Heterogeneous groupings
Professional Relationships and Responsibilities	Autonomous decision making Little opportunity for collegial interactions Periodic unidiscipline in-service training	Autonomous decision making Little opportunity for collegial interaction Periodic unidiscipline in-service training	Interdependent/shared decision making Many opportunities for collegial interactions Continuous transdisciplinary training
Scheduling	Individual instruction Small-group instruction	Individual or small-group therapy weekly or biweekly	Block scheduling (half or full day blocks per class) Consultation weekly or biweekly
Measurement and Evaluation	Formative and summative evaluation Quantitative data	Formative and summative evaluation Quantitative data	Formative and summative evaluation Authentic assessment Qualitative *and* quantitative data

nicative competence that children bring to school matches their teacher's, then interactions are likely to be successful. There will be relatively few miscommunications, and the teacher will generally be effective in socializing the children into the school environment

The patterns of interaction that young children encounter in the classroom may be very different than what they have at home.

(Cazden, 1988). In many cases, however, the patterns of interaction that children encounter in their first classroom are completely new to them (Blank & White, 1986). Teachers have a type of role and absolute authority that many children have not experienced before, and they use communication patterns that differ from those of other adults in the child's environment (Garcia, 1992). Without a common linguistic environment, miscommunications and unsuccessful exchanges will far outnumber effective exchanges: Socialization efforts are likely to be tedious and demanding.

Communication in the majority of American classrooms has been characterized as "rigid" (Saville-Troike, 1982). There are rigid turn-taking rules (e.g., you must raise your hand and not speak until called upon), a prescribed space arrangement (everyone either in desks that are arranged in rows or sitting around tables), implicit control precepts (peer interactions are not supposed to occur except when the teacher permits them), and a great deal of question asking on the part of teachers. Even in classrooms where the focus is on child-guided learning, such as with whole language, although children have relatively more control, the teacher is "in charge."

Teachers ask questions for which they already know the answer.

Teachers use questions to elicit known (rather than new) information from children so that they can monitor and evaluate comprehension of materials. When they start school, children are not accustomed to having adults ask them questions for which they already know the answer. Similarly, many children have not had experience with the typical classroom discourse pattern. This turn-taking exchange pattern, known as the IRE exchange structure, repeats over and over again in most lessons. In this structure, the teacher **I**nitiates a question, the student **R**esponds, and the teacher **E**valuates the student response (Blank & White, 1986; Cazden, 1988). Learning the rules governing classroom interaction, even those that are stated explicitly (e.g., "Do not answer until you have been called on"), is particularly difficult for children with language/learning difficulties.

Most children with language difficulties will not be successful in the general education classroom unless they are specifically taught the IRE pattern and provided some practice with it. Instruction for the child should focus on

- how and when to respond during a teacher-directed lesson;
- how to penetrate the structure if they want to say something that is outside the format or content of the lesson;
- how to get the teacher's attention;
- when it is appropriate to speak to the teacher in front of the group and when they should speak in private;
- the appropriate way to answer the teacher;
- with whom they can interact; and
- when peer interaction is permitted (and when it is not).

In addition to helping children learn the specific language and communication skills they need to be successful in teacher-led lessons, teachers need to consider ways to modify their linguistic input to children. Au (1980) draws from research in the Kamehameha Early Education Program (KEEP) in Hawaii to provide an example of how teacher talk can be modified. Initial data from the KEEP suggested that the IRE interaction pattern (teacher initiates, student responds, teacher evaluates) was not effective with Hawaiian children. While they were quick to call out answers when a question was *not* directed to them or when it was directed to a group of students, individual children did not respond when a question was directed specifically to them. The research staff and teachers· concluded that the explanation for this response pattern is a discourse prototype, called "talk story." In the Hawaiian community, "talking story" is the traditional form of social interaction wherein conversants build upon each other's shared recollections to construct a story. The KEEP teachers changed their classroom communication expectations, allowing children to call out their answers and build on each other's responses until the group as a whole had a satisfactory answer. Rather than expecting one child to answer a question, they let the children know that it was perfectly acceptable for everyone in the small group to answer. The results of the KEEP experiment (permitting the children to engage in "talk story" responses) were evident within a year. The staff documented significant increases in the children's reading comprehension scores.

Another aspect of teacher-child interactions in the classroom, in addition to the IRE interaction pattern, is lesson presentation. Many teachers use the lesson presentation sequence recommended by Englert (1984) and Rosenshine (1983):

1. Review previous lessons with related information.
2. Tell students what they are expected to learn from the lesson.
3. Overview key points and planned activities to provide an anticipatory set.
4. Present salient information that is essential to acquisition of the targeted skills and concepts.
5. Maintain an appropriate pace of presentation and include active participation devices (e.g., games, self-assessment) to hold students' attention.
6. Provide examples and demonstrations before asking students to respond on their own.
7. Provide verbal and visual prompts and physical assistance to prevent incorrect responses.
8. Ask frequent and varied questions to maintain interest *and* test students' understanding.
9. Provide positive, clear, and immediate feedback for errors and provide an example or demonstration of the correct response.

There is not as yet a coherent theory addressing the contribution of auditory processing to language acquisition or to the difficulties experienced by children with language impairment (Rees, 1980). However, many children with poor language and poor listening skills are described as having auditory processing difficulties (Friel-Patti, 1994). These are children who, despite average or above-average cognitive abilities and normal peripheral hearing, seem to do reasonably well in one-to-one conversations but have great difficulty dealing with language when there is competing noise in the background. Note that each step in the lesson presentation sequence relies on the oral presentation of information. Thus, regardless of whether there are able to meet the academic task demands of the lesson, children with auditory processing difficulties are not likely to be successful if there is a noisy background.

The lesson presentation sequence is not an exception: Most of the information provided in the typical general education classroom (e.g., homework assignments, quizzes, field trips, special projects) is given orally, with minimal concern for whether there are distractions. Teachers and others who provide oral information in school settings need to be aware of the rate and loudness of their speech as well as potentially competing sounds. Topics and new vocabulary should be introduced with clear and simple explanations and then written out on the board or a large newsprint pad. Teachers and other speakers need to get into the habit of repeating important terms and providing alternative explanations or definitions for new vocabulary. Children should be encouraged to express directions for lessons and new concepts in their own words, both orally and in writing. And finally, students should be taught to monitor their own periods of inattention and develop strategies for staying focused on a task (Stark & Bernstein, 1984).

In summary, classroom observations by the language interventionist and/or the special education teacher should determine (1) how teacher communication expectations compare with the type of communicative competence that prevails in the child's cultural community, (2) specific reasons and possible remedies for teacher-child miscommunications, and (3) how the oral presentation of lessons can be supplemented and modified.

Peer Interactions

The second set of manipulable conditions that have a potential effect on language learning and use is peer interactions. Children learn language from (and during) reciprocal social interactions with more experienced language users. The "more experienced language users," once they enter school, are generally their peers. Peer interactions help children learn how to

> Children with auditory processing difficulties are not likely to be successful with academic tasks if there is background noise in the classroom.

> Children learn language from reciprocal social interactions with more experienced language users.

- express their needs and wants;
- exchange ideas, thoughts, and experiences;
- establish, maintain, and develop interpersonal relationships; and
- initiate and participate in conversations in a socially acceptable manner.

There is no area of a child's life where the impact of language impairment is greater than in the area of peer interactions. Children who are difficult or impossible to understand miss opportunities for interactions because they are not selected as social partners (Rice, Hadley, & Alexander, 1993). Data from a number of studies indicate that students who are very similar except for their speech or language abilities tend to be evaluated very differently by their peers (Hall, 1991; Rice, 1993; Vandell & George, 1991). Students with language impairments are perceived as less popular, less smart, less attractive and more insecure, more unpleasant, and more "weird" than their peers without language impairments. Missed opportunities for social interactions lead to further language and communication problems and diminished social competence. The effect is a low self-concept (Windsor, 1995). What occurs then is a self-fulfilling prophecy: Because students with low self-concept tend to be less motivated to achieve, their academic achievement is generally lower (Byrne, 1984).

At the preschool level, there seem to be at least three variables that predict the amount of peer interaction: (1) familiarity, (2) chronological age, and (3) functioning level. The role of familiarity is clear: The better children know one another, the more likely they are to initiate and maintain interactions (Doyle, Connolly, & Rivest, 1980). This finding makes one of the strongest arguments for full inclusions: Children who have limited time periods together (i.e., art, music, recess) are not likely to develop the type of relationships that foster language learning for children with language delays or disorders.

Findings related to chronological age are not so clear. Langlois, Gottfried, Barnes, and Hendricks (1978) found that older children had a suppressive effect on younger playmates. Lougee, Grueneich, and Hartup (1977) found just the opposite; that mixed-age groupings tended to increase interactions for the younger peers. Goldman (1981) found that mixed-age preschool groups engaged in more mature play than same-age peers. The findings with regard to functioning level are that preschoolers who were classified as language-delayed talked more in groups or classes composed predominantly of peers without language delays (Paul, Rogers-Warren, & Spradlin, 1978; Rogers-Warren, Ruggles, Peterson, & Cooper, 1981). As children develop, interactions become more sophisticated, with social communication skills playing an increasingly important role in sustaining child-child interactions.

Developing the type of relationships that foster language learning takes time.

The strategies described below were developed with preschool children: However, they can also be used with children in the primary grades. Approaches for increasing the peer interactions of young children with disabilities generally fall into four categories: (1) peer-mediated interventions; (2) adult-mediated interventions; (3) group interventions; and (4) direct instruction interventions.

In peer-mediated interventions children are taught to initiate interactions with their less competent peers.

PEER-MEDIATED INTERVENTIONS.   The basic strategy in peer-mediated interventions (also called confederate interventions) is to directly teach socially competent children to initiate interactions with their less-competent peers (Odom, Hoyson, Jamieson, & Strain, 1985; Odom, Stein, & Jenkins, 1983). Peers are taught to initiate (1) play organizers (i.e., "Let's play with the big blocks."), (2) shares (offering to give or exchange an object with a peer or suggesting mutual play with an object), (3) physical assistance (helping the peer in some way), and (4) affection (e.g., hugging, patting, holding hands).

According to Strain and Odom (1986), there are certain requirements for peer-initiated interventions to be optimally effective. They are

- selection and training of children without disabilities;
- careful selection of the specific peer initiation strategies (e.g., physical assistance, sharing materials);
- arrangement of the physical environment to promote interactions (e.g., providing toys that may be used cooperatively such as kitchen sets or cars); and
- conducting daily training sessions so that peers can implement the strategies.

Each session begins with the adult introducing the activity to the entire class and then reminding the children without disabilities of their roles. If the adult does not make the appropriate initiations, the peers without disabilities are prompted to do so. All children are praised for their participation in the activity. Ostrosky, Kaiser, and Odom (1993) stress the importance of also including systematic programming for maintenance and generalization of the new skills.

In adult-mediated interventions, parents and teachers teach and support social interactions.

ADULT-MEDIATED INTERVENTIONS.   Parents and teachers teach and support social interactions. The three types of adult-mediated interventions are (1) prompt-praise interventions; (2) environmental rearrangement interventions; and (3) milieu teaching interventions. With **prompt-praise interventions,** the teacher or another adult provides encouragement in the form of instructions or prompts and praise for social responses directed to peers (e.g., Apolloni & Cooke, 1978). For example, a child with disabilities might be prompted to imitate the sharing behavior of a peer and then be praised for the imitative behavior. Over time the prompts are gradually faded.

Environmental rearrangement interventions typically focus on arranging materials and equipment and activities to encourage social and communication interactions. For example, some ways to encourage sharing and cooperative play are (1) to select materials that children are familiar with and (2) to limit the amount of materials and toys. Because types of activities and activity structure seem to affect social interactions differentially, it is important to give careful attention to what activities are scheduled in order to achieve the curriculum objectives. In one study, young children without disabilities were more interactive during free play and least interactive during fine motor and circle activities; children with disabilities were more interactive during snacks (Kohl & Beckman, 1994). Burstein (1986) found children more interactive during outdoor play as compared to free-choice center times and story and music times; however, they were more interactive in free-choice center times than during story and music times. A study by Odom, Peterson, McConnell, and Ostrosky (1990) found similar results: Children with and without disabilities engaged in the most verbal social interactions during free-play and clean-up activities and had the least verbal social interactions during preacademic, story time, language lessons, and fine motor activities. Thus, the data *and logic* suggest that the less structure there is, the more likely children are to engage in social interactions. Less formal activities (e.g., free play and snacks) are likely to have higher levels of social interaction than more formal activities (e.g., circle time, story time, music, fine motor activities). However, if, during the low-structure activities such as free play, the teacher identifies a theme of play, sets some rules, and assigns roles, then children are likely to engage in more social interactions than if such structuring does not occur (DeKlyen & Odom, 1989).

> The less structure, the more likely children are to engage in social interactions.

Milieu teaching interventions are described at length later in this chapter and in Chapter 10. Milieu teaching begins when the child initiates an interaction in the context of naturally occurring routines and activities (Rogers-Warren & Warren, 1980). At that point the teacher or other adult uses modeling or a prompt strategy to elicit a social or communicative response, or the teacher may encourage a peer to model the social/communication behavior for the child with disabilities.

GROUP INTERVENTIONS. Group interventions for promoting peer interactions fall into two categories: (1) cooperative learning arrangements, and (2) affection activities. **Cooperative learning arrangements,** which draw from the work of Johnson and Johnson (1986, 1991), are a powerful instructional method for promotion of pro-social behavior and communication as well as academic achievement. The group dynamics become the vehicle as well as the context for social interactions and friendships. Group activities are structured in such a way as to teach children (1) to encourage one another, (2) to celebrate each

> Group interventions are cooperative learning arrangements and affection activities.

other's successes, and (3) to work toward common goals. The onus of responsibility for involving everyone in achieving the assigned task is on the group. Opportunities for practice of social and communication skills occur naturally in the course of working together to reach their common goal. The adult's role is to teach the necessary cooperative skills so that the cooperative learning groups will function effectively. Gallagher (1991) describes a cooperative learning activity in which the group was asked to work together to draw a picture of a sunny day. Each child was given a different colored crayon. To ensure that he would have an important role in producing the final outcome, the peer with a language impairment was given the yellow crayon.

Affection activities modify well-known games and songs (e.g., "Simon Says," "The Farmer in the Dell," "If You're Happy and You Know It") in such a way as to increase opportunities for social exchanges. Several researchers have been able to demonstrate positive effects of these activities on peer interactions (Brown, Ragland, & Fox, 1988; Twardosz, Nordquist, Simon, & Botkins, 1983). Implementation is straightforward. Children are taught a new song/game or they participate in a familiar song/game. The first time through they sing and move in the usual manner. Then they are told "we are going to play/sing this a little differently next time." The song/game is modified so that children exchange some form of physical affections (e.g., a pat on the back, "high five," or handshake). For example, instead of singing "the farmer takes a wife" or "the wife takes a child" in *"The Farmer in the Dell"* and then removing someone from the circle to stand in the middle, they would sing "the farmer *greets* a wife" and "the wife *greets* a child" and give high five to one another.

DIRECT INSTRUCTION INTERVENTIONS. Finally, the fourth category of approaches for increasing peer interactions is direct instruction of social-communication skills. In direct instruction interventions, training is more structured and systematic than in adult-mediated interventions. Sometimes training involves all children in the class; peers without disabilities are taught to respond readily to and encourage play with peers with disabilities. Children with disabilities are taught how to initiate interactions, appropriate turn-taking, and how to play. A typical direct instruction sequence would be to

- select three to four activities (3 to 13 minutes in length) as contexts for the training;
- perform a task analysis for each play activity and teach the component skills to the child with disabilities;
- coach the peers without disabilities (prior to each play session) to wait for their play partner with disabilities to initiate an interaction and then respond naturally;

- use unintrusive prompts and praise to encourage initiation and play behaviors if the child with disabilities does not approach the play context and initiate an interaction; and
- allow the children to play together for 2 to 6 minutes after the initiation sequence is complete.

Ostrosky, Kaiser, and Odom (1993) offer suggestions for facilitating peer interactions between children with and without disabilities, which serve as a summary of this discussion. These suggestions are presented in Table 8.2 as guidelines for facilitating social-communicative interactions.

TABLE 8.2 Guidelines for facilitating social-communicative interactions

- **Include peers without disabilities as facilitators,** not primary interventionists. They should not be expected to teach specific language/communication targets.
- **Teach social-communicative strategies to *all* children** (children with *and* without disabilities) during naturally occurring interactions.
- **Begin intervention activities with the children (with and without disabilities) who are most likely to be successful.** (Children with disabilities should be able to communicate consistently through either gestures, words, or signs.)
- **Focus preliminary individual instruction on developmentally appropriate initiation and response skills** for children *with* disabilities.
- **Teach the conversational strategies known to facilitate social-communicative interactions** (e.g., joint attention, establishing eye contact, commenting, responding, requesting information, turn-taking) to children without disabilities.
- **Use direct instruction and practice** (demonstrations, prompts, role playing, and feedback) **to teach specific peer interaction skills** for individual children with disabilities *if needed.*
- **Program for maintenance and generalization** by
  1. allowing adequate time for mastery of new skills;
  2. making skill training and opportunities for peer interaction a regular part of the classroom routine;
  3. systematically fading adult prompts and support; and
  4. concentrating on teaching those social-communicative skills that are likely to be most functional for the child.

Based on Ostrosky, Kaiser, & Odom (1993).

The Curriculum

Some educators define curriculum to include unplanned as well as planned experience—in fact, virtually everything that happens in the child's school day (e.g., Dittman, 1977). They view curriculum as a theoretical framework for experiences to promote the emotional, intellectual, and physical learning outcomes necessary for success in society. Others restrict the term to include what appears in the textbooks (or in the teacher's planbook) for a particular age or grade level (including goals and objectives, scope and sequence charts, teaching suggestions, environmental arrangements, materials and activities, and evaluation procedures, etc.) (e.g., Johnson-Martin, Attermeier, & Hacker, 1990). It may be easier to think about and describe curriculum in terms of what it is *not* than what it is. Curriculum is *not* teaching methods and procedures and it is *not* a set of activities: It is *what* is to be learned.

In the inclusive classroom (as in noninclusive classrooms) all children do not need to be doing the same thing at the same time. To the extent possible, however, they should be in the same curriculum. As Nelson (1994) puts it, in most cases, the value of keeping students in the regular curriculum "far outweighs potential disadvantages associated with any particular curriculum" (p. 105). There is one significant disqualifier for this statement. It assumes two things: (1) that the curriculum has a scope and sequence that is broad enough to accommodate students at a wide range of functioning levels, and (2) that the substance of what is taught and the instructional outcomes will not be affected by modifying the sequence of tasks and the way tasks are taught or by changing instructors.

Maintaining students with disabilities in the same curriculum as their peers without disabilities does *not* mean simply requiring them to practice certain skills more or repeat the lessons. Nor does it mean that language interventionists and special education teachers should abdicate total responsibility for language instruction and support to regular classroom teachers. It means using the regular curriculum as the context and the source for (1) determining the child's communication intervention needs and goals, (2) designing intervention activities, (3) selecting and modifying materials, and (4) monitoring student progress. It means thoroughly and deliberately analyzing the language and communication expectations of the curriculum, determining where the student is having (or is likely to have) difficulties, and selecting or designing and implementing appropriate adaptations. All of this is done by the general and special education teachers and the language interventionist as part of the ecological assessment process.

Functional life curricula (sometimes called a *functional curriculum approach* or *life skills instruction*) are curricula for students with moderate and severe disabilities. Development of functional

Curriculum is what *is to be learned.*

All children do not need to be doing the same thing at the same time, but they should be in the same curriculum.

curriculum approaches arose from the need to teach skills that would have direct and immediate utility in students' lives in their communities and, equally pressing, the need to prepare students for a successful transition from school to adult living (Brolin, 1991). The relationship between functional curricula and traditional academic curricula was among the most debated issues in special education in the early nineties (Clark, 1994). A major problem with implementing functional curricula was that they seemed to impede placement in inclusive classes. Students were forced to attend separate schools and segregated classes in order to receive functional instruction. Precluding students with moderate and severe disabilities from having full membership in the same school settings as their peers without disabilities profoundly limited their opportunities to learn the most important functional skills of all: (1) the social and communication skills necessary for independence in adult work and community environments, and (2) friendships and other relationships that are the basis of important social networks. (Falvey, Grenot-Scheyer, Coots, & Bishop, 1995). Thus, many came to view functional curricula as a barrier to successful independent adult living, which was precisely what functional curricula sought to promote (Clark, 1994).

> Implementation of functional curricula should not be a barrier to inclusion.

Without denying or deprecating the importance of life skills and facilitating functional outcomes for students with disabilities, current trends emphasize the importance of melding the opportunities of the general education program and environment with appropriate and individualized functional outcome goals. Using strategies such as ecological assessment and cooperative learning, support teams try to embed instruction of basic motor, personal care, communication, social interaction, and functional academic skills within the curriculum activities and daily routines of inclusive general education environments. One way to do this is to develop a matrix that lists objectives for the child along one axis and the daily schedule (both academic lessons/classes and routines (e.g., homeroom, lunch) on the other. The support team then decides which objectives can be taught logically and naturally during which activities and which objectives will require special scheduling because they cannot be taught naturally in the context of the day's activities. Chapter 12 provides an example of a matrix for a child with severe disabilities.

Examples of functional skills that cannot easily be taught in general education classes include dressing and grooming. Hamre-Nietupski, McDonald, and Nietupski (1992) suggest five possibilities for addressing this type of skills:

1. **If the skill can be performed with assistance in the context of classroom activities, a peer volunteer may be recruited and asked to provide partial assistance to the student.**
   Hamre-Nietupski and colleagues give the example of a student

who could easily remove her boots when she arrived at school in the winter but could not put on her shoes. The solution was to have her remove her boots upon arrival, take her shoes to the classroom, and ask a peer for assistance. (The peer had been shown how to give assistance in the difficult steps in putting on the shoes and to encourage independence on the easier steps.)

2. **Provide functional skill instruction during "down times" in the school schedule.** It is typically not too difficult to find some time between academic activities or routines for unobtrusive instruction. As little as 5 minutes several times a day may be adequate.

3. **Provide parallel instruction on functional skills while peers are involved with academic assignments.** For example, when peers without disabilities are working on place value in mathematics, that period can be used to teach functional mathematics skills.

4. **If there is no other alternative, brief removal from the classroom for specialized instruction may be considered.** For example, when peers without disabilities are receiving instruction on academic concepts and skills that are clearly beyond the level of the child with disabilities, it is appropriate to provide instruction on functional skills such as bathroom use and street crossing that should normally be done outside the classroom.

5. **Use ecological assessment** (as described in Chapter 7) **to select instructional goals and objectives.** When goals and objectives are drawn from observations in the general education classroom and other school environments, there is no difficulty teaching targeted skills in those settings, as these are the appropriate instructional contexts.

Responsibilities of the team's special education teacher, language interventionist, and therapists are to make whatever adaptations are called for, assist the general education teacher, coach peers, provide direct instruction when indicated, and facilitate positive interactions with peers.

CBA is a method to sample the child's performance on critical academic skills and concepts.

Curriculum-based assessment (CBA) is a method of analyzing and assessing the curriculum and then sampling the child's performance on critical academic skills and concepts. There are a number of CBA approaches, but they all generally share these salient features: test items are drawn from children's curricula; repeated testings occur across time; and the assessment information is used to formulate instructional decisions (Fuchs & Deno, 1991; Howell & Morehead, 1987; Tucker, 1987). CBA may be used as an alternative to the ecological assessment process. CBA is similar to the ecological assessment/intervention approach in that it is a general outcome measurement system, but it has a narrower focus. Whereas ecological assessment samples student performance in whatever activities are deemed important in the setting (academic or nonacademic), CBA is typically limited to sampling student performance on curriculum tasks and materials. It *generally* focuses specifically on performance in the areas of literacy and mathematics.

Both the curriculum-based language assessment approach and the ecological assessment/intervention approach emphasize adapting and individualizing instruction and the curriculum to reflect the interaction of the child's unique characteristics with curriculum expectations, teacher linguistic expectations, and peer interactions. In situations where there is clearly a need for a special instruction, it may still be possible to use pieces of the regular curriculum (Nelson, 1994). Children can be moved in and out of the regular curriculum as appropriate.

Whether the classroom team uses the CBA process and/or the ecological assessment process (or both, as we suggest in Chapter 7) to generate goals and objectives for children with language and communication difficulties, there is likely to be a need to adapt lessons, activities, and materials to make them accessible. Procedures for individualizing or adapting curriculum lessons and activities for students whose learning difficulties are primarily in the area of language and communication, and for those with more severe and/or pervasive language-learning disabilities, are on the same continuum. The range of possible adaptation for both groups is described in Table 8.3.

CURRICULUM ADAPTATIONS FOR CHILDREN WITH LANGUAGE-LEARNING DISORDERS. The fact that the difficulties that children with language disorders experience with oral language comprehension, auditory analysis, memory, and word finding and retrieval seem to translate to difficulties with reading, writing, and spelling skills is viewed as strong evidence for a relationship between oral language difficulties and literacy (Bashir,1989; Menyuk, 1983; Sawyer, 1991; Wiig, 1990). As children move through the grades, what was initially an oral language disorder may be manifested as serious difficulties with written language, specifically difficulties in processing and comprehending what they read (Westby & Costlow, 1991). Curriculum adaptations for children with language-learning disorders focus on providing extra support for (1) metalinguistic skills (Wallach & Miller, 1988), (2) conversational discourse skills (Brinton & Fujiki, 1989), and (3) language and learning strategies (e.g., Buttrill, Niizawa, Biemer, Takahashi, & Hearn, 1989).

> There is strong evidence for a relationship between oral language difficulties and problems with literacy skills.

Once they learn to read, reading can be a way to mediate and support language learning (Westby & Costlow, 1991). Because written language lends itself to repeated and careful examination of its properties, it can be examined and manipulated without the constraints of

TABLE 8.3   Guidelines for adapting lessons/activities

No Difference: The student with disabilities participates in the same lesson/activity with the same objective(s) and using the same materials as peers without disabilities. Since objectives for the student with disabilities are the same as for peers without disabilities, there is no need for adaptations.

Physical Assistance: The student with disabilities participates in the same lesson/activity with the same objective(s) and using the same materials, but the student with disabilities is provided with physical assistance to enable participation. For example, a buddy may help a peer with physical disabilities by placing shapes on the felt board for him, helping him dip the brush into the paint jar, or taking notes for him.

Adapted or Different Materials: The student with disabilities participates in the same lesson/activity with the same objective(s), but the student with disabilities uses adapted or different materials. For example, a student with physical disabilities might use adapted scissors and adapted writing implements (pen or pencil) and need to have the writing paper taped in place on her desk. A child with visual impairment might use a laptop computer for writing, rather than pen or pencil.

Different Stimuli: The student with disabilities participates in the same lesson/activity with the same objective(s), but the student with disabilities is provided with more or different instructional stimuli. For example, some children may benefit from having multisensory stimuli when new concepts or complex instructions are being presented. The steps in a task may need to be presented one at a time and then left visible on the board or an overhead.

Different Response Level: The student with disabilities participates in the same lesson/activity, but the objectives—the response requirements—are at a different level. For example, a child with severe language difficulties is not expected to respond verbally to all of the questions about the story: He is required to answer only one question "Was the story about a little boy or a little girl?" by pointing to a picture on his communication board.

Totally Different Objectives: The student with disabilities participates in the same lesson/activity with the same materials, but the objectives have a totally different focus because the student needs more functional goals with direct application to daily life. For example, when the focus of a science lesson for second graders is investigating how different kinds of liquids behave when poured (and recording their observations on a simple graph), the objectives for the student with disabilities may be (1) pouring without assistance, (2) making choices when presented with two options, and (3) following one-step directions.

memory and changing contexts that are characteristic of spoken language. Children with language-learning disabilities can examine and manipulate the various elements of language to learn how they function to communicate meaning. Specifically, Westby and Costlow (1991) suggest using scaffolding strategies to facilitate language learning in written contexts. (Scaffolding strategies are described in the next section.)

One aspect of adapting curriculum is modifying materials and/or developing different materials (see Table 8.3). Successful adaptation of materials for children with language-learning disorders must go beyond simplifying vocabulary and shortening sentences (or rewriting prose at a lower grade level). The information that is provided in daily lessons must be supplemented to make it more accessible. Some ways to supplement lessons are by

> Modifying materials and/or developing different materials is one aspect of adapting curriculum.

- providing advance organizers,
- highlighting important idea units,
- helping students identify different levels of importance of ideas, and
- teaching students to use task-appropriate cognitive strategies.

Pictures, charts, timelines, and outlines make information more accessible with a minimum of words. A series of pictures or a flowchart is a much more effective way to convey a process than a paragraph or two filled with transitional adverbs and complex compound sentences. Flowcharts are especially useful for children who are having difficulty learning how to compare and contrast ideas. Timelines can be used to demonstrate and teach sequencing, and outlines are a good format to highlight specific points *and* reduce extraneous information. With an outline, comprehensible chunks of words and phrases can convey essential information in a concise manner.

Usually the goal when adapting written material is to eliminate extraneous details by reducing the amount of text. Main ideas and the supporting facts are highlighted with bold typeface, underlining, and italics. (If, during the course of the lesson, students express an interest in details, they can be provided.) Once detail has been eliminated, the next consideration is the vocabulary and the grammar. New vocabulary should be clearly introduced and explained prior to reading; *after* reading, the new words can be reinforced with charts and discussion. Because synonyms are often confusing to students who are trying to grasp the essence of a new concept, they should be minimized. Finally, it is important to use simple verb tenses in explanations and descriptions and to simplify word order in sentences by eliminating clauses and relying on a simple sentence (subject-verb-object) format. Written instructions can be simplified by using the active voice and limiting the use of pronouns and relative clauses.

> One goal is to eliminate extraneous details.

How to teach new concepts is always a concern. Critical characteristics of new concepts (called *attributes*) should be identified through **concept analysis.** Critical or relevant attributes of a concept are those attributes that are present in *all* examples of the concept. These are the defining characteristics of the concept because they *must* be present for the concept to exist. Noncritical or irrelevant attributes may or may not be present in the concept. For example, concept analysis of the concept "square" yields these critical attributes: four sides, straight lines of equal length, four 90-degree angles, and enclosed space. Noncritical attributes include size, color, and orientation in space. Teaching the concept entails showing the student examples of instances of the concept and also examples of noninstances (in this case, examples of squares and examples of figures that are not squares) and then comparing the two. Understanding is assessed by asking questions that verify that the student has the meaning and recognizes critical components of the definition.

ADAPTATIONS FOR CHILDREN WITH SEVERE AND MULTIPLE DISABILITIES. Adaptations for children with severe and multiple disabilities are likely to involve modifications of the physical environment. The physical and/or occupational therapist should help others on the support team understand the child's mobility skills (how she travels within the classroom and other school and community environments), appropriate positioning (so the child can participate as efficiently as possible in classroom activities), and possible adaptations that can support and/or substitute for fine and gross motor control. (These adaptations are especially important when selecting and teaching an augmentative communication system.) The language interventionist and the special education teacher should help others on the support team understand the child's communication repertoire (symbols [e.g., words, signs, pictures] that the child understands and those she uses spontaneously), and communication modes (e.g., speech, gestures, manual signing, a communication device) that the student understands, uses, and/or needs.

> Physical and occupational therapists are major contributors to decision making about physical adaptations.

Goals and objectives for children with severe and/or multiple disabilities target specific skills and concepts that are within the child's communicative reach and are functional and relevant for the child's daily life and future goals. Adaptations for children with severe and multiple disabilities depend on the curriculum activities/lessons as well as the nature of the child's disabilities. Many children with severe and multiple disabilities are able to participate in some activities/lessons (e.g., creative movement, library book selection, homeroom, listening to a story or tape) with no adaptations (or only very minor adaptations). For others, participation depends on provision of modified or different materials (larger paper, adapted scissors), modified or different instructions (pictorial instructions, instructions on audiotape), modified or different outcome expectations (e.g., fewer and/or less sophisticated responses, gestural rather than verbal responses, partial rather than full participation), and/or full or partial support and assistance (by a peer partner or an adult).

For many children with severe and multiple disabilities, adaptations involve developing different objectives. These alternative objectives may come from what is sometimes called the implied curriculum (Dittman, 1977). Examples of implied curriculum skills and concepts that are important outcomes for children with severe and multiple disabilities include:

- sharing learning experiences and being part of a cooperative group with peers without disabilities;
- asking for (and giving) assistance;
- requesting materials;
- indicating activity and partner choices;
- following directions; and
- securing and organizing materials for an activity and returning them to their place when the activity has ended.

> Implied curriculum skills and concepts are important goals for children with severe and multiple disabilities.

Finally, as noted above in the discussion of functional life curricula, there may be a need to provide instruction focusing on specific skills and concepts that are functional and relevant for the child's daily life and future goals. A more detailed discussion of adaptations for children with severe disabilities is provided in Chapter 12.

INTERVENTION METHODS AND PROCEDURES

Traditional language training procedures relied on adult-directed procedures (the adult selected and controlled both the topic and the tasks of the instructional interactions), a rigid three-part presentation format ("request-response-correction"), contrived instructional materials (pictures and object replicas), and unnatural and repetitious feedback (e.g., "good talking" "say it right"). Over the past several decades, what has been learned about the nature of language and normal language acquisition has contributed to marked changes in procedures. In inclusive schools, language is taught in the context of daily routines and conversational interactions, using methods and procedures that are child-centered, interactive, and naturalistic.

Providing language instruction, facilitation, and support in the classroom and other school settings where children want and need to use language and communication has several major advantages:

- New skills and concepts are more likely to generalize because there are numerous opportunities to practice and use them in both social and academic interactions.

- Children receive more help because the teaching staff learns how to incorporate language instruction and practice into daily classroom activities and how to support carryover.
- Problems such as missed academic periods and increased isolation from peers that occur when students are regularly removed from their classrooms are avoided.

There is no one intervention method or set of instructional procedures that has been found to be superior for all children or all language goals (Yoder, Kaiser, & Alpert, 1991). Nor is it possible to designate specific instructional procedures to use with particular objectives. The instructional procedures planned and implemented with a particular child depend on the child's objectives, and his present functioning. Several procedures may be used to work on the same objective, and one procedure may be used to work on many objectives.

This section will describe six instructional/interventional procedures: milieu language teaching, scaffolding, routines and script training, interactive modeling, situated pragmatics, and direct instruction. Several of these procedures were originally developed to be implemented in separate therapy settings. However, all have now been demonstrated to be effective when used in the context of either small- or large-group activities in natural settings.

Several intervention procedures may be used to work on the same objective, and one procedure may be used to work on many objectives.

Milieu Language Teaching

Milieu language teaching is an umbrella term covering a number of naturalistic language teaching procedures (Kaiser, Hendrickson, & Alpert, 1991): (1) child-cued modeling (Alpert & Kaiser, 1992), (2) mand-model teaching (Warren, McQuarter, & Rogers-Warren, 1984), (3) time delay (Halle, Marshall, & Spradlin, 1979), and (4) incidental teaching (Hart & Risley, 1968).

Milieu language teaching is based on observations of caregivers interacting with their normally developing children (Hart & Risley, 1968), which found that parents tend to

- talk about objects, events, and/or relations that have attracted the child's attention;
- model, imitate, and expand desired and actual child communication efforts;
- repeat and clarify words, statements, and requests that the child does not seem to understand; and
- use techniques such as higher speech frequencies and stress to call the child's attention to important sentence elements.

Although grounded in a behavioral approach to language intervention, milieu language teaching does not use a rigid direct instruction format. The topic of each teaching interaction and the reinforcement are defined by the child. Typical intervention targets include increasing the frequency of communicative behaviors, production of longer and more complex utterances, and expression of familiar functions with more advanced forms. The basic elements of milieu language teaching are (1) arranging the environment to create reasons for communication, (2) identifying communication or language targets, and (3) applying the teaching procedures.

Milieu teaching procedures (modeling, mand-modeling, time delay, and incidental teaching) require the immediate presence of an adult to mediate between the child and the desired or needed object or activity. The major difference in the milieu teaching model and most other naturalistic intervention models is that it uses *explicit* prompts. The child is prompted to use more advanced ways to communicate whatever message he has just tried to communicate. Table 8.4 provides a summary of milieu language teaching procedures. Detailed instructions for implementing milieu language teaching are provided in Chapter 10.

> Milieu teaching differs from other naturalistic intervention models in that it uses *explicit* prompts.

Scaffolding

Scaffolding is supporting a child in such a way that he can understand and/or use language at a level that is more complex than could be grasped or produced independently. Scaffolding can be provided to assist a child to understand and use any element of language, including specific vocabulary words, figurative language, syntactic structures, or elements of discourse structure. As the child becomes more independent in the use of language, scaffolding is reduced and then gradually withdrawn. For example, when reading a story to young children or children with severe cognitive delay, scaffolding might take the form of explicit questioning about the elements of the story (e.g., Who was the story about? Where did it take place?). With older, more sophisticated students, scaffolding questions may focus on more complex aspects of the plot, such as the characters' motivations. The challenge is (1) knowing when there is a mismatch between the communicative demands of the task or situation and the child's abilities, and (2) determining the nature of the mismatch.

> Scaffolding enables the child to perform at a more complex level than would be possible if he performs independently.

Conceptually, scaffolding draws from the same caregiver–child research as the milieu teaching model. The major difference between the two is precisely when modeling and expansion strategies are applied and the degree of structure. The concept of scaffolding was introduced by Vygotsky (1962, 1978) in his conceptualization of the dynamic regulation that goes on between the infant and caregivers in a nurturing environment. It was later used by Bruner (1975, 1978) to describe parents' use of language and gestures to segment ongoing experiences into meaningful elements that are appropriate to their

TABLE 8.4   A summary of milieu language teaching procedures

Model Procedure	Mand-Model Procedure
Present model related to focus of child's interest	Present mand related to focus of child's interest
Correct child response receives immediate praise, verbal expansion, and (when material is being withheld) access to material	Correct child response receives immediate praise, verbal expansion, and (when material is being withheld) access to material
Incorrect child response is followed by a corrective model	Incorrect child response is followed by a second mand (when child's interest is high and he is likely to know the answer) or a model (when child's interest is waning and he is unlikely to know the answer)
Correct child receives immediate praise, verbal expansion and access to the material; incorrect response to corrective model is followed by corrective feedback and access to material	Correct response to mand or model is followed by immediate praise, verbal expansion, and access to material
	Steps of the Model Procedure follow incorrect child response to corrective mand or model

Time Delay Procedure	Incidental Teaching Procedure
Identify occasions when child is likely to need materials or assistance	Identify occasions when child is verbally or nonverbally requesting materials or assistance
Present time delay	Use occasion to teach more intelligible, complex, or elaborated language/communication skills by applying steps of the:
Correct child response receives immediate praise, verbal expansion, and materials or assistance	**1.** Model Procedure (use to train new or difficult forms or structures or to improve intelligibility), or the
Incorrect child response is followed by:	**2.** Mand-Model Procedure (use to train complex and conversational skills), or the
1. a second time delay (followed by use of the Mand-Model Procedure or Model Procedure if child responds incorrectly to the second time delay),	**3.** Time Delay Procedure (use to train the child to initiate communicative behavior about environmental stimuli)
2. the Mand-Model Procedure, or	
3. the Model Procedure	

From Alpert, C. L., and Kaiser, A. P. (1992). Training parents as milieu language teachers. *Journal of Early Intervention, 16*(1), 35. Used with permission.

child's level of understanding. In typical caregiver–child interactions, adults request only those behaviors (language and motor skills) from the child that they know the child can produce. As the difficulty of requests is gradually increased, just enough support is provided so that the child has an opportunity to be successful and, at the same time, sufficiently challenged in order to promote learning. Snow (1984) observed parents using scaffolding to assist their children's early literacy experiences. The parents read or tell a bit of a story in a storybook and then use the story (and the pictures) as a takeoff point for a series of questions appropriate to the child's functioning level.

Silliman and Wilkinson (1994) describe application of two scaffolding models in the classroom: directive scaffolding and supportive scaffolding. Both provide assistance to students who are having difficulty learning to communicate adequately on their own, but Silliman and Wilkinson favor the supportive model. They describe supportive scaffolds as providing a kind of "communication safety net." Providing supportive scaffolds within and across thematically meaningful learning activities can reduce the student's need to take risks in order to learn new skills.

As noted earlier in this chapter, in the section on adaptations, Westby and Costlow (1991) provide procedures for using scaffolding in the context of written language as a way to mediate language learning for children with language-learning disabilities. These procedures are basically an expansion of strategies suggested by Brown and Palincsar (Brown & Palincsar, 1987; Palincsar & Brown, 1984) to facilitate literacy. (Brown and Palincsar use the term *reciprocal teaching* for these interactive teaching procedures.) Evaluation data indicate that children learn to use the metacomprehension strategies independently (Brown & Palincsar, 1987; Palincsar & Brown, 1984) and they demonstrate significant improvement on criterion tests of reading comprehension, and classroom performance. They can be implemented by the language interventionist and/or the special education teacher in the general education classroom. The first step is to model these metacomprehension strategies:

- Summarize or review essential text information to confirm that it is understood and remembered.
- Generate the type of questions that might reasonably be asked on a test.
- Clarify anything that is ambiguous or involves inconsistent interpretations when there is not complete and accurate understanding.
- Predict information that might extend or follow the text information (in order to validate, disconfirm, or modify how the content fits with previous understanding).

Then have students read a portion of text and practice using the metacomprehension strategies to analyze it in the context of a small-group discussion. With each subsequent day of coaching and feedback, more and more responsibility for the group discussion is turned over to the students.

The scaffolding strategies that Westby and Costlow (1991) suggest to mediate language learning in the context of written language are summarized in Table 8.5 and described at more length below. Using these strategies, reading lessons proceed more as conversations than oral reading.

> Supportive scaffolds provide a "communication safety net."

TABLE 8.5   Strategies to scaffold language in written contexts

- Set the stage for what will be read
- Use a semantic map
- Provide extensions and/or invite the child to add elaborations
- Use "thinking-type" questions
- Emphasize and review old or previously stated information
- Restate or summarize important ideas and relationships
- Use flowcharts
- Teach metalinguistic knowledge
- Use repetition in the context of thematic units

1. Set the Stage

Provide a scaffold to help the student anticipate the concepts that will be presented in what will be read. For example, before reading the first sentence of a story, say "Listen to find out what this story is about." If a greater scaffold is indicated, provide a series of preparatory statements parsing the first sentence. Point to the appropriate clauses and say "This tells you who the story is about," "this tells you where main character lives," or "this tells you when the story took place." Westby and Costlow (1991) call these statements "preparatory set." If necessary, use scaffolds during every turn of the interaction to (1) focus students on the theme or topic of the passage, (2) highlight elements of discourse structure, (3) help students integrate the meaning and the structure of complex sentences, and (4) suggest an abstract interpretation of language when appropriate.

2. Use a Semantic Map

Semantic maps are a type of outline.

Semantic maps are a type of outline that help students brainstorm or generate ideas related to a central topic. They have four components: a key question or topic that establishes the purpose; strands that are answers to the key questions; strand supports, which provide details, facts, or other information to clarify or validate a strand; and ties or broken lines that show relationships among strands. The central topic or theme is placed in a circle in the center of the paper, and ideas that are associated with the theme are connected to the circle by lines. For example, when a story about Lindberg is read, the word *pilot* would be placed in the center circle. One cluster of associated words that might be generated and linked to the circle would be "things that pilots do." Other clusters might be "what pilots need to know about," "who can be a pilot," and "what pilots fly." The process of creating the map helps students learn to develop a topic, form associations, categorize, compare, and make inferences. They become very familiar with the information so they can invest attention to features of the language. Because it provides background information encountered in the text as well as new ideas, the map can be used as a scaffold for reading and a review or summary of what has been read.

3. Provide Extensions

Extensions are verbal comments that elaborate on the written language of the text. Providing extensions and/or inviting children to add elaborations is a way to clarify the text and ensure shared meaning. Extensions can also define unfamiliar vocabulary words or phrases. As children read a passage, the adult might point to and comment on an accompanying picture of the topic of the passage. Extensions should add clarification or function to elements of syntax, morphology, or discourse structure that may not be fully understood. Westby and Costlow (1991) give the example of using extensions to establish the temporal relationship between events. The adult might say "He *had* dreams. He's not sleeping or dreaming now, but last night, when he was sleeping, he *had* dreams." Thus, there is clarification of how a specific form ("had") expresses knowledge (that the event occurred in the past).

4. Use Questions

Questions should not test for comprehension or factual recall; they should extend the children's thinking by encouraging prediction, role assumption, generalization, formation of examples or exceptions, classification, justification, solutions, and inferencing (Westby & Costlow, 1991). "What do you think might happen if there was a big storm?" or "What are some other things the pilot should remember?" are examples of questions that extend the pilot theme previously mentioned. Another use of questions is to help children revise misinterpretations or repair miscommunications. Additionally, they can facilitate the integration of information across sentences.

Questions should extend the children's thinking.

5. Emphasize and Review Old Information

Reviewing old information that is relevant to new ideas serves as a scaffold to emphasize association of ideas within and across sentences. Reference to old information in the written text (when it is relevant to a new concept or recurs in a new context) helps children become aware of and understand complex aspects of discourse structure, such as story grammar. Further, it helps them interpret new information in thematically appropriate ways, draw conclusions, and/or verify beliefs.

6. Restate or Summarize

Restating important ideas and the relationships among ideas helps children categorize information and organize events in a logical manner. Pointing to relevant sentences or phrases when summarizing the ideas and having students summarize sentences and ideas is also useful. One approach is to use cloze procedures. For example, while pointing to the relevant information in the text you might encourage children to summarize important facts or events about pilots by saying, for example, "A pilot who flew only _____ wanted to learn to fly _____ so he went to _____ and _____ , but what he found when he got there was _____ ." This type of scaffold supports students to talk about a topic for an extended time, using syntactically complex sentences and cohesive ties that the children might not be capable of using independently. Over time the amount of support is gradually reduced.

7. Use Flowcharts

Flowcharts display key ideas in a hierarchical fashion.

Because they display key ideas in a hierarchical fashion, flowcharts can serve as a bridge between written and oral language. Similar to making a semantic map, making a flowchart helps children organize and talk about information. The main idea is entered at the top of the page with constituents, supporting ideas, and important details placed in subordinating positions. Elements that are equal in importance are parallel. Once completed, the flowchart is a visual scaffold that children can use to generate complex sentences to talk about and summarize the information. Creating and using a flowchart also helps students learn how to organize information, form categories, examine and use story structure, and order ideas hierarchically.

8. Teach Metalinguistic Knowledge in the Context of Written Language

Metalinguistic knowledge is an abstract appreciation for and understanding of language as an object. Before they can engage in flexible, nonliteral uses of words, children must have at least an implicit understanding that words are separable from their referents. They must be able to talk about and think about language: This means analyzing it, separating it from its context, and judging it. Development of metalinguistic abilities depends on the ability to separate or "pull back" from the immediate linguistic context in order to attend to how a message is communicated. Written language provides an ideal context in which to teach metalinguistic knowledge because of the opportunities to highlight patterns or regularities in language and help children develop concepts of syntactic categories. For example, while pointing to the word *big* in a sentence the adult might say "That's one *adjective* to describe the pilot. Another *adjective* for the pilot would be *tall*. What *adjective* would you use?"

9. Use Repetition

Repetition in a thematic context provides a scaffold for introducing new concepts.

Repeating the same story over an extended period of time in a thematic unit has many advantages. Using thematic units with the same story and the support of collaborative activities ensures that the language encountered in the story is discussed often enough and with enough contextual variability for generalization to occur. Repetition in a thematic context provides a scaffold for introducing new concepts or modifying the level at which old information is presented. Providing collaborative activities, such as writing or drawing, further reinforces the concepts. Children learn to organize information in large units, such as a logical story sequence. When they understand the context of the story, children may be asked to generalize events in the story to personal experiences or similar situations.

These strategies for scaffolding with written text can be used with individual children or with small groups. They make it possible to address many of the abstract, complex, and subtle aspects of spoken language that are difficult to address with procedures that are focused specifically on spoken language. Because the classroom curriculum provides many written language contexts, there are numerous opportunities throughout the day to work on language difficulties. Most children find these activities interesting and fun because they provide an opportunity for positive interactions with an adult.

Routines and Script Training

Routines are activities with a social or a maintenance purpose that are repeated frequently (usually on a daily basis) and always in almost the same way. They provide excellent opportunities to teach sequences of behavior, including language forms and functions. Social routines include games, rhymes, jokes, songs, storytelling, social amenities, and courtesies. Maintenance routines include classroom business activities (e.g., taking attendance, collecting lunch money), preparation activities (getting in line, preparing for a lesson, preparing for assembly, recess, lunch, or dismissal) and functional routines (cleaning up, distributing materials, toileting). Both social and maintenance routines may be viewed and taught as scripts.

Most classrooms (especially preschool and primary classrooms) have many routines that can be used as instructional contexts. Or routines can be developed. Once a routine is well established, children learn to anticipate what will happen next so they can be prompted to assume responsibility for the next language behavior in the routine.

Some routines are more suitable contexts for promoting language and communication skills than others. When selecting a routine to use as an instructional context, some considerations include the type of materials involved, time requirements, and the number and repetitiveness of the component actions and subroutines. The following questions can aid in the selection of routines to use for language facilitation and/or support (Halle, Alpert, & Anderson, 1984):

Some routines are better than others for promoting language and communication skills.

- Does the routine include a variety of attractive, interesting, and desirable objects and materials? *Interesting objects and materials are more likely to stimulate language and communication.*
- Can the routine be completed quickly? *The faster a routine can be completed and another begun, the greater the number of new communication opportunities.*
- Does the routine contain many actions? *Each action in a routine is an opportunity for language so the more actions, the more opportunities to prompt language.*

Once a routine is selected and established, and the children have learned the sequence of actions, then the routine can be interrupted or varied. The unexpected departure from the anticipated sequence or anticipated action is the prompt for a comment, protest, or request. Halle and colleagues (1984) suggest these strategies for interrupting routines:

Delay provision of an expected and desired material or event.
For example, consider the sequence of actions at snack time: one child distributes the napkins, another sets around the paper cups, the teacher pours juice or milk, and another child passes fruit or crackers. If, after the cups are set out, the teacher "forgets" to pour juice or milk, the children are likely to comment or protest the departure from routine (e.g., "No juice" or "I want juice" or "You forgot").

Provide an incomplete set of materials.
When a routine requires a prescribed set of materials, providing children with an incomplete set of materials (e.g., the toothpaste is missing from the tray with the other toothbrushing materials) generally elicits a protest or request for the missing object(s). The adult simply waits until the children notice and comment on the missing object.

Make "silly" mistakes.
Children are quick to comment on or protest absurdities and inappropriate actions, such as holding a book upside down. Intentionally violating expectations or calculated "silliness" also helps children develop a sense of humor (an additional advantage of this strategy).

The first two strategies are especially effective in stimulating peer prompting. For example, when a child is "inadvertently" missed while pouring juice, a peer might say something like: "Tell Miss Kim that you didn't get juice" or "Ask for some juice." The use of routines with preschoolers is also discussed in Chapter 10.

Scripts are generalized representations of familiar events or routines (Nelson & Gruendel, 1986) that show the established order of the elements. All people have scripts that they use when they describe routine events and when they want to predict what might happen in unfamiliar circumstances. Even very young children form scripted representations of routines and familiar events (e.g., a birthday party). Similar to older children and adults, they use their scripts, which are either temporally ordered (one event always follows another in time) or causally ordered (one event must occur before another can occur), to structure their verbal accounts of experience and to aid their recall. When events do not proceed as a child anticipates, adults generally help the child make comparisons and understand that there can be different versions of the same event (e.g., "I realize this isn't what you expected but, at some birthday parties, the gifts are opened *before* the cake and ice cream").

Although the line between them is often blurred, using naturally occurring routines and script training are somewhat different language teaching strategies. Whereas using routines involves identifying (and sometimes, teaching) naturally occurring routines to use as contexts for encouraging and teaching language and communication, script training typically involves actually writing and teaching something like a play script. Whereas the purpose of a natural routine may be toothbrushing, and the toothbrushing routine provides a context for encouraging language, the specific purpose of a script is to teach language and communication skills. The goal in script training is to create interactive, systematic repetitions of events where each "actor" plays her predictable role so that children can (1) practice social roles, (2) observe and model the language skills of others, and (3) learn to solve interpersonal conflicts. In the course of practicing the social roles in various events (e.g., going shopping, going to a restaurant, getting a haircut, a field trip to the zoo) they learn the expectations and the linguistic demands of the roles.

> The specific purpose of script training is to teach language and communication skills.

Bunce and Watkins (1995) found that script training (which they call *script play*) can serve three purposes in the preschool classroom: (1) enhancement of world knowledge and language; (2) stimulation of language exchanges; and (3) facilitation of social interactive skills. For enhancement of world knowledge and language to occur, there needs to be a preparatory discussion or demonstration in which children are given background, introduction, and priming for the dramatic play script. Roles are introduced, the use of props is demonstrated, and the basic goals of the play are discussed. As children practice their roles and exchange essential props, the familiar, repetitive structure of the play scripts enhances the likelihood of successful interactions.

Ross and Berg (1990) note that, when children are using scripts, they "use more semantically complex language (e.g., speak significantly more often of past and future events, speak of many different topics in one conversation) and are better able to answer questions than in other contexts" (p. 41). The reason may be that scripts seem to reduce the language processing demands placed on the child. The script provides an organizational framework for the content, and a support for recall, allowing the child to concentrate on linguistic demands. Scripts also provide a structure for children's conversations

> Scripts make it easier for children to process language.

during play. They use their scriptal knowledge to sustain these conversations (Nelson and Gruendel, 1981).

When a child seems to know what will happen next in a routine, whether that knowledge is verbalized or not, it is evidence that the child has some kind of generalized representation for the routine. For example, when a child knows what to do when the 8:20 bell rings and when he enters the cafeteria this indicates that he has a script for these routines (whether he can tell us about them or not). There are numerous classroom activities which, because they require a child to recall elements of a script, teach scripting. They begin with "show and tell" in the preschool years, through literacy activities (e.g., "what I did on my summer vacation") in the elementary grades, to expository discourse in middle school and high school.

There are a number of reasons why children with language disorders have difficulties forming scripts and then using them to describe routine events and to predict what may happen in unfamiliar circumstances. Reasons include problems with (1) the temporal-causal organization of knowledge, (2) limited expressive vocabulary, and (3) retrieving verbal labels (Donahue & Bryan, 1984; Naremore, Densmore, & Harman, 1995). Sometimes it is obvious that students do not have a causally or temporally ordered mental representation of a routine or event. At other times students give evidence of knowing what is expected (i.e., when the bell rings, in the cafeteria line) but they are not able to express that knowledge. For example, when asked to give directions to a new student on how to move through the cafeteria line, a student may not know the term for the "the bin where the silverware is stacked." Or the student may know the words but may not be able to retrieve them because of word-finding difficulties.

Script training is an effective strategy for teaching children the sequence, requirements, and roles for familiar events and routines when there is evidence that they have not developed generalized event representations on their own or lack the language ability to express their scripts. Goldstein, Wickstrom, Hoyson, Jamieson, and Odom (1988) taught "hamburger stand" and "barber shop" scripts to triads of preschoolers. In one of the experiments, each of the children with communication problems was taught to play each of three roles. Prompts were faded as the child began to act independently in her or his role. After the script was learned in structured training, the children were encouraged to enact the themes from the script during playtime. During play, teacher prompts reminding the children to stay in character were effective in getting the children to produce the theme-related communication behaviors. All of the children improved in their participation in the script during the training sessions, and most increased their use of socially directed, theme-related behaviors during free play. Most importantly, the script training increased the

overall frequency and quality of interaction among the children with disabilities and among children with and without disabilities.

Interactive Modeling

The basic premise underlying **interactive modeling,** which is also called *recasting* (Nelson & Gruendel 1986), *interactive language instruction* (Cole & Dale, 1986), or *focused stimulation* (Leonard, Schwartz, Chapman, Rowan, Prelock, Terrell, Weiss, & Merrick, 1982), is that increasing the frequency of exposure to targeted language features enhances their saliency (and thus, the probability that they will be learned). What interactive modeling does is give children with language difficulties more deliberate and focused practice, more time, more repetitions, and heightened focus on new words and concepts. With interactive modeling, students are presented with multiple exemplars of target forms or operations in contexts where the form is semantically and pragmatically appropriate. For example, target language forms or operations might be embedded in play activities (e.g., play activities such as "Simon says"), routines (e.g., making snacks), and/or curriculum activities. The child is neither requested nor required to respond.

Fey, Cleave, Long, and Hughes (1993) suggest using focused stimulation procedures with a *cyclical goal-attack strategy.* In this strategy, a number of different goals are worked on within a particular time period (e.g., month, semester, year) but each goal is presented individually within a session. For example, assume that a set of four goals is selected for the child. These goals would be presented in a cyclical fashion. Each week a new goal is targeted (regardless of the

Interactive modeling is discussed at more length in Chapter 10.

amount of observed progress exhibited on the last target). After each of the goals has been worked on sequentially over the time period, the targets are reevaluated and the cycle revised (goals added or taken away) or repeated. When the child begins to use a target syntactic structure productively, the goal is dropped from the cycle or combined with related goals. These are the steps in this procedure:

1. Identify specific grammatical targets for the student.
2. Determine activities that provide semantically and pragmatically appropriate conditions for the student to hear the targeted syntactic structure.
3. Model the target structure frequently during the identified activities.
4. Recast the student's attempts to produce the target structure through simple expansions or by changing the sentence modality (e.g., recast a declarative sentence as a yes-no question to highlight auxiliary form).
5. Use false assertions to encourage the child to produce sentences that use the target structure (e.g., "That's not your book" said to evoke "Yes, it is") and contingent queries to elicit semantic details omitted from an original message (e.g., "Which one did he take?").
6. Ask forced-alternative questions that provide a model of the correct use of the target structure (e.g., "You do want it or you don't want it?" to evoke "I don't want it") or ask questions about a story to give the student practice in producing the targeted features.

Interactive modeling is described at more length in Chapter 10.

Situated Pragmatics

Situated pragmatics is instruction that provides contextual support for language learning.

Duchan (1995) describes **situated pragmatics** as instruction that provides contextual support to help children with language and communication disorders understand and be more included in the social and cultural mainstream. Six possible support contexts are identified: the social context, the emotional context, the functional context, the physical context, the event context, and the discourse context. The basic goal in each of these contexts is to help the child make sense of what is going on and to provide an emotionally safe environment so that the child participates willingly and meaningfully.

Supports in the various contexts are tailored to fit the child's difficulties or to build on the student's strengths. According to Duchan, "specific methods in a situated approach depend on what is going on in the situation, who the interactants are, the child's needs in that context, and the supporter's goals for the child in that situation" (p. 165). Table 8.6 provides examples of possible supports in the six situated pragmatics contexts and some ideas for techniques to use in each of the contexts.

TABLE 8.6 Examples of support and possible techniques in the six situated pragmatics contexts

---

Examples of support for language learning in the **social context** *include:*
- helping the child identify and understand his or her role in the setting;
- helping the child understand his or her role in relation to the others in an interaction.

Possible technique(s)—enact scripts involving family roles, teacher–child roles, etc.

Examples of support for language learning in the **emotional context** *include:*
- helping the child and family members attune to the affect or emotional tone of one another;
- creating contexts in which the child can take a valued and important role, leading to positive self-esteem.

Possible technique(s)—use events in stories to develop understanding of emotions; provide emotional support when the child experiences frustration or difficulty.

Examples of support for language learning in the **functional context** *include:*
- helping the child associate intent with communicative acts, either nonverbal (e.g., pointing to request) or verbal (e.g., using a word, phrase, or sentence to make a request);
- helping the child detect the motivations behind the behavior and language of her communication partners.

Possible technique(s)—design events the child is excited about and ways the child can request the events and items within the event; use stories to interpret the motivations of others to the child.

Examples of support for language learning in the **physical context** *include:*
- offering interesting, manipulable objects and pictures as props for learning about the world;
- creating interesting and suggestive spaces (e.g., accessible theme areas) in the room.

Possible technique(s)—create alternative spaces in the classroom that the child can manipulate; provide communicative support at afterschool programs where children are able to socialize informally.

Examples of support for language learning in the **event context** *include:*
- allowing the child to watch and then act as an apprentice in an event until he is comfortable engaging directly in the event;
- helping the child expand familiar routines by inserting new elements into various slots in the routine.

Possible technique(s)—develop joint interaction routines between the child and different adults; create scripts with the child to help him understand and participate in complex or rule-based events.

Examples of support for language learning in the **discourse context** *include:*
- arranging space and allocating sufficient time for discourse;
- providing props that support initiations and enactments of discourse-based activities.

Possible technique(s)—create opportunities for the child to tell about an emotional event in the past; scaffold answers to questions about past events using a notebook that goes between home and school.

Based on Duchan (1995).

Duchan (1995) provides specific suggestions for applying the situated pragmatics approach to (1) developing vocabulary, (2) expressing targeted speech acts, and (3) understanding particular grammatical structures. When developing vocabulary, the focus is on teaching words as tools that can reference ideas in a domain of interest to the child. Overall, vocabulary learning is viewed as situated knowledge. Vocabulary goals should be words that are functional for the child. They should be taught as a related set in the context of an everyday event. Children who are considered to have a limited vocabulary should be supported to express, through words, their communicative intents or their favorite objects and ideas in order to better participate in the events and discourse of their daily lives. A situated pragmatics approach to teaching children to express particular intents, such as requests, would elicit and model expressions of the targeted intents in a variety of contexts. The aim is to support the child's efforts to use language to get what he wants. A situated pragmatics approach aimed at improving a child's language structure first looks for the pragmatic impact of the targeted structure. Then functional communicative contexts that highlight the importance of the structure are identified or developed.

Direct Instruction

Direct instruction is teacher-guided instruction toward the mastery of specific skills and concepts. It can be used for instruction of virtually any language and communication targets (e.g., Carr & Kologinsky, 1983; Rogers-Warren & Warren, 1980) and it can be implemented in natural environments. The behavioral methods most often associated with direct instruction are essentially the same procedures that are used in linguistic and naturalistic approaches: modeling, task analysis, shaping, prompting, and reinforcement. The primary difference is that direct instruction applies these procedures more systematically and in a more structured manner. To avoid the stigma associated with singling out a student for direct and intensive instruction it is best to use it in small groups in the context of ongoing classroom activities.

Direct instruction typically involves some drill and practice on specific forms and/or structures. The behavioral term for drill and practice is **massed trial instruction.** While linguistic and behavioral approaches may target different skills and concepts, both approaches have traditionally found it necessary to provide some drill and practice (particularly in the initial acquisition phase of instruction) (Cole & Dale, 1986). In linguistic approaches the targets for massed trial instruction usually include forms or structures exemplifying particular inflectional morphemes and specific syntactic rules. In a behavioral approach the targets for massed trial instruction might include

Direct instruction typically uses behavioral methods.

request forms (e.g., "more," "want _____") that can be used across a range of naturalistic contexts. Drill and practice procedures need not involve removing the learner from the natural environment to a distraction-free setting. As noted above, it is usually possible to provide practice trials in the context of ongoing activities. In fact, there are some activities and routines in which repetitions of a single response occur naturally (e.g., turn-taking in a social routine, saying "goodbye" to peers who are leaving a setting one at a time).

MODELING.   **Modeling** is "showing how" behavior. It should not be confused with imitation: Imitation is a *learning* strategy. Imitation is performance of a response that matches, or at least approximates, a model. Modeling is a *teaching* strategy in which there is a demonstration of a desired motor or verbal behavior. When modeling is used as a teaching strategy, the model or demonstration is usually preceded by a verbal direction (e.g., "do it like this," or "say _____"). An instance (or at the very least, a picture) of the concept being labeled should be present and should be the focus of the child's attention when modeling a word or manual sign. When modeling, placing stress on critical aspects of the stimuli increases the likelihood of imitation (Risley & Reynolds, 1970). For example, when teaching names of shapes, the format would be (1) display the circle shape, and (2) say "This is a circle. Say . . . *circle*" (with a pause between the words *say* and *circle* and the word *circle* emphasized.

Modeling is "showing how" behavior.

TASK ANALYSIS.   **Task analysis** is breaking down a skill into small steps to make it easier to teach. The target skill is first identified and stated as an instructional objective. Then these task analysis steps are implemented:

Task analysis is breaking down a skill into small steps so it is easier to teach and easier to learn.

1. Perform the skill (or watch someone else perform the skill) and record component steps in performing the skill.
2. Eliminate unnecessary or redundant steps.
3. Sequence the steps in the order in which they are performed or in terms of difficulty.
4. Prompt the student through the task and make any modifications in step size that is necessary (based on the student's performance).

Task analysis must be individualized for a particular student because the size of the steps depends on a child's ability level. There should be just enough steps to allow efficient instruction. One student might need a 10-step task analysis to acquire a particular skill while another might need to have the same behavior broken down into a 20-step process. Each step in a task analysis should be clearly stated in order to measure the student's performance of the behavior objectively.

Shaping is reinforcement of slight changes in behavior toward a complex target behavior.

SHAPING. **Shaping** is a procedure for teaching the steps in the task analysis. Shaping begins with reinforcement of the closest approximation of the first step and systematically builds on slight changes in that behavior (called reinforcement of successive approximations). Each step or approximation is reinforced until it is learned, and then the next behavior (the next closer approximation) is taught until eventually the complex target behavior is produced. Shaping can be used with prompts to further encourage the development of new skills when reinforcement of successive approximations alone does not have the desired results.

Prompting is assisting or supporting performance of a correct response.

PROMPTING. **Prompting** can be thought of as "priming" a desired response. Prompts are assists or supports that are provided to increase the likelihood that the learner will give a correct response. Prompts are introduced during the acquisition phase of instruction and faded as soon as the desired behavior is occurring at a predictable frequency. There are response prompts and stimulus prompts. Response prompts include verbal directions, modeling, and physical guidance. Stimulus prompts are cues that are used in conjunction with the task materials to ensure a correct response. Examples include movement cues (e.g., the teacher points to the correct picture), position cues (e.g., the correct picture is placed closest to the student's right hand), and redundancy or exaggeration cues (the stimulus is altered by exaggeration, repetition of adding a dimensional cue such as color, size, or shape). The two criteria for judging the effectiveness of instructional prompts are (1) whether they are able to elicit the desired response, and (2) whether they can be faded.

Prompt-dependency, waiting for a prompt rather than attempting a response, is a major concern when using prompts. To avoid a student becoming prompt-dependent, always

- develop and use a written plan for when and how prompts will be delivered and what correction procedures will be used;
- select prompts that minimize errors but do not interfere with the instructional sequence;
- have the student's attention before delivering the prompt;
- pair natural prompts with instructional prompts and fade the instructional prompts as soon as possible; and
- use prompts that focus the student's attention on the most relevant characteristics of the stimuli (Noonan & McCormick, 1993).

Fading is the gradual removal of an instructional prompt.

FADING. **Fading** is the gradual removal of an instructional prompt so that the desired behavior is performed independently or with only naturally occurring supports. Fading may be accomplished by shifting from partial prompts, or by reducing the amount of assistance.

The primary concern is maintaining correct responding as prompts are removed. The type of fading strategy used depends on the type of prompt: The sound intensity of auditory prompts can be faded; the size of spatial and movement prompts can be decreased; the color intensity of visual prompts can be faded. If, as prompts are being faded, the student begins to perform the behavior incorrectly, or stops performing the behavior at all, this means that the prompts were faded too fast. When fading procedures are properly executed, the student maintains the high level of responding that was evident with the prompts.

REINFORCEMENT.   **Reinforcement** is any event that immediately follows a response and has the effect of increasing the probability that the response will be repeated. Reinforcement and reinforcers are often misunderstood and misrepresented. Defining reinforcement as the act of providing a treat (e.g., candy, raisins, trinkets) or praise after an appropriate behavior is common but inaccurate. The only way to determine whether an object or event is reinforcing is by reference to its effects on the response that it follows. An event is not a reinforcement *unless* it increases (qualitatively and/or quantitatively) the behavior it follows. There are individuals for whom treats and praise are *not* reinforcers.

> Reinforcement is any event that immediately follows a response and has the effect of increasing the probability that the response will be repeated.

Similarly, it is inaccurate and misleading to state that use of reinforcement is limited to behaviorists and behavioral programs. Everyone provides reinforcement of one type or another. The major difference between behaviorists and others is the way the event is described and how systematically it is implemented.

Availability of a reinforcer in the learner's natural environment is an important consideration in selecting reinforcers for a particular child. Contrived and artificial reinforcement conditions should be avoided in favor of naturally occurring events. If contrived reinforcement must be used, it should be replaced or faded as quickly as possible toward natural consequences. In normal learning circumstances, a child's efforts to communicate are reinforced, not the form of the communication. Even primitive communication efforts are typically responded to with attention, if not the receipt of a requested object or event. The more meaningful and appropriate the child's communicative efforts, the greater the likelihood that the intent of the message will be correctly interpreted and responded to.

THE INSTRUCTIONAL ENVIRONMENT

Where instruction is provided is a major difference between traditional and inclusive schools. In traditional schools, special instruction is likely to be provided in a special education classroom, a resource room, or a therapy room. In inclusive schools, special instruction for language and communication and other skills occurs in heterogeneous groups in the regular classroom and other school settings (i.e., the playground, cafeteria, halls, gymnasium). When students with disabilities spend the school day alongside their peers who are not disabled, the message to peers, families, school personnel, and others in the community (and most importantly, to the students themselves) is clear. They belong: They have equal footing in society. When functional independent living and vocational skills are taught in nonschool environments (e.g., home, vocational, and other community settings), the contexts in which these skills naturally occur, they are encouraged and supported by appropriate special education and vocational rehabilitation staff. However, the actual instruction should be provided by the people who are responsible for those settings (e.g., parents, employers).

In a cooperative classroom, both children and adults look for and find ways to support and nurture each other's learning.

The defining characteristic of a cooperative classroom environment is children and adults who look for and find ways to support and nurture each other's learning so that everyone can succeed. To create a cooperative classroom environment (Sapon-Shevin, 1990):

- **Eliminate all symbols of competition.** Examples of competitive classroom symbols include star charts and other visual displays that show the "best" performance in any area. Create bulletin boards and other displays that feature the work of *all* children, not just the work of the "bests."
- **Use "we" language.** Using "we" rather than singling out individual students or small groups within the class (e.g., "the first reading group") encourages and supports group achievement and solidarity. When there is an issue with a particular child or a small group, the whole class should be engaged in problem solving. Inclusive ("we") language helps students see that they have an important role in supporting their peers to be contributing and productive class members.
- **Plan activities that build the classroom community.** Examples of activities that help to draw the class together and build a sense of community are plays, choral singing, and sharing situations. Students can be involved in writing the script for a play, producing scenery, painting posters, making popcorn for the production, etc. For singing, students can take turns teaching and leading songs, or small groups of students can take responsibility for directing the morning's music.
- **Encourage students to see each other as sources of information, instruction, and support.** Sapon-Shevin gives the example of one teacher who arranges her students' desks in clusters and sets this rule: If one person in the group has a problem of any sort, she must consult with her group before coming to the teacher for help.
- **Prompt students to notice each other's accomplishments.** Tattling and recriminations are evidence that students are being

attentive to the misdeeds of their classmates. This can be turned around by focusing attention on positive acts and achievements, making it clear that there is no competition; that everyone can succeed and everyone can be happy for others' accomplishments.

- **Select and read books that have cooperation and/or conflict resolution as a theme.** Reading books with cooperation themes provides opportunities for discussing personal and classroom application of cooperation and conflict resolution. Another idea is for the class to write their own book about cooperation in which they record the things they have accomplished as a class that would not have been possible without cooperation and collaboration.

PROFESSIONAL RELATIONSHIPS AND RESPONSIBILITIES

As noted earlier in this chapter, the organization of traditional schools had the effect of isolating special and regular education teachers from one another and isolating therapists from each other and from teachers. Regular education teachers were primarily concerned with *their* children and *their* rooms; special education teachers were concerned with *their* children and *their* rooms. Therapists worked independently to facilitate development of specific skills for specific children (children assigned to their caseloads). Because people were never in the same place at the same time, it was all but impossible to form any type of professional (or personal) relationships. They did not have the opportunities *or support* for getting to know one another and learning to work together in a meaningful way. Working together in a *meaningful* way depends on overcoming physical, attitudinal, and logistical barriers.

The hallmark of inclusive schools is togetherness and positive *interdependence,* which has both professional and personal benefits for teachers and therapists. There is consensus that no one person can effectively address the diverse education, social, and psychological needs of all children and focus on maximizing each person's contributions and performance through modeling, feedback, and mutual support. Everyone acknowledges and is comfortable with the fact that special education and related services personnel and regular education teachers bring unique but complementary skills to the special instruction process. Teachers learn about language instruction, and language interventionists learn about curriculum and classroom management skills.

No one person can effectively address the diverse needs of all children.

The team structure provides a supportive collegial atmosphere that enables professionals to practice creative thinking and problem solving. In addition to assuming new roles, adults learn new professional skills (as well as interpersonal skills). They learn to accept, trust, and help one another, to communicate accurately and unambiguously, and to resolve conflicts constructively. In the process of developing meaningful, reciprocal, and interdependent relationships they create a rich learning environment for all students.

SCHEDULING

Staffing arrangements in inclusive schools are different than traditional schools, where grouping of students with disabilities is based on what is judged to be the intensity of their needs. In traditional schools, staffing patterns are based on staff-to-student ratio and the percent of the day the student receives services. A special education teacher called a Resource Teacher may serve as many as 25 children with mild to moderate disabilities. Because they are considered to have minimal needs, these children receive special instruction weekly, for varying periods of time. Teachers with separate classes (usually called Self-Contained Classroom Teachers) serve children regarded as having more intensive needs. They may serve children with mild-moderate disabilities in classes with 12 to 15 children or children with severe and multiple disabilities in classes with 6 to 8 children. In traditional schools, language interventionists usually try to schedule at least a half hour of therapy every week or every other week for each child in their caseload. In inclusive schools, rather than serving children with the same "intensity of needs" in homogeneous groups, special education teachers are assigned to a grade level. The number of children for whom they are responsible depends on the students' instructional needs. Language interventionists in inclusive schools also function differently. In addition to providing direct support and team-teaching, they participate in team decision making focused on planning, coordinating, and monitoring language intervention efforts for the children on their caseload.

An example will illustrate how one inclusive elementary school has chosen to organize services. In the planning process, based on data indicating that the percentage of children eligible for special education services in the primary grades in the district is generally 15 to 16 percent, the Dalton School Primary Inclusion (DSPI) team predicted that there would be 10 to 15 children with disabilities at each primary grade level (K–3). (This is based on three classrooms at each level with average enrollment of 28 students.) When school started, the actual count of children eligible for special education services was 10, 12, 14, and 15 for kindergarten, first, second, and third grades, respectively. It was decided to distribute children with disabilities evenly among the classes and to assign a special education teacher and a teaching assistant to each grade level (the classroom-based special instruction arrangement described below). A language interventionist was assigned to serve all four levels and a physical therapist was assigned to serve children in grades K–6.

Staffing arrangements in inclusive schools generally fall into two broad categories: direct contact/service arrangements and consultation arrangements. Each arrangement, of course, requires different scheduling.

Direct contact/service arrangements include:

1. *Co-teaching.* The language interventionist and the special education teacher share responsibility for instruction for the entire class with the general education teacher. In addition to sharing teaching responsibilities, the classroom team equally shares instructional problem solving and decision making for all children (with and without disabilities). As this arrangement usually includes some children with severe disabilities, the team may also include an occupational and/or physical therapist and parents. The language interventionist might lead the class in brainstorming a list of guidelines (on a large piece of poster paper) before providing opportunities to practice some class presentations. The guidelines one class developed looked like this: (1) use a loud enough voice so that everyone can hear and look at the audience (most of the time); (2) begin by giving the name of whatever you are showing or naming the experience you are going to describe (e.g., "my first fishing trip"); (3) tell two or three things that you think are interesting about the object or the experience; and (4) ask if anyone in the class has questions or comments and wait long enough for people to think of a question or comment. Each child (including the children in the class with language disorders) copies the list of guidelines in her notebook and the large chart is posted in the classroom. The learning of the children with language disorders is further facilitated by several demonstrations (provided by students without disabilities) that highlight each of the guidelines.

In co-teaching, the general education teacher shares responsibility for instruction with either the language interventionist or the special education teacher.

2. *Classroom-based special instruction.* In the classroom-based direct services model, the language interventionist modifies and presents existing curriculum activities for individual children and/or groups of children with similar goals and objectives or expectations (ASHA, 1993). The special education teacher develops and provides modified activities and curricula in the regular classroom for individual children and/or a group of children with behavioral and/or academic difficulties in the regular classroom. Both the language interventionist and the special education teacher base their instruction on and draw from the classroom curriculum and routine activities. Decisions are also made as a team but since the language interventionist and the special education teacher are not in the classroom at all times, they may be less involved in problem solving and decision making for children without disabilities. This model differs from co-teaching in that most of the instruction provided by the support professionals (the language interventionist and the special education teacher) is for the children in the class who have special instructional needs. This special instruction and support may be provided individually or as part of a small group that includes both children with and without disabilities. In this model the support professionals serve a number of classrooms.

Consultation arrangements include:

1. *Collaborative support.* The language interventionist and the special education teacher participate as team members in decision making for children with special instructional needs. The support team, which includes the classroom instructional staff, family members, the special education teacher, the language interventionist, and other related services professionals, collaborate for continuous assessment, develop goals, plan programs, identify and arrange curriculum adaptations, and monitor program implementation and program effectiveness. The language interventionist and/or the special education teacher and the regular education teacher may provide some direct classroom-based services as a team. In this model, the support professionals consult and provide technical assistance and formal and informal training for many classrooms.

2. *Expert support.* After assessing the child, the support professional meets with the team (made up of the teaching staff, the special education teacher, and the parents) to provide intervention suggestions and recommendations. The expert consultant may also provide technical assistance and in-service training for those who will deliver the services.

All of these models have several things in common: They all call for collaboration and communication among administrative personnel, support personnel, teaching staff, and parents and they all present a major challenge where scheduling is concerned.

In co-teaching, particularly if there are a number of children with severe disabilities, the language interventionist and/or the special education teacher may be full time in the general education classroom. The success of co-teaching depends on total parity, recognition of each other's strengths, and commitment to common goals for the students. With classroom-based special instruction, the language interventionist and the special education teacher schedule regular blocks of time for their special instruction activities and also time for planning with the teaching staff how they can meet individual student language and communication objectives in the context of the classroom curriculum, daily routines, and interpersonal exchanges. When language interventionists and special education teachers serve as collaborative consultants to the classroom teacher they must allocate large time blocks for team meetings and blocks of time for classroom observations (to learn about the curriculum and the strengths

Functioning as collaborative consultants requires language interventionists and special education teachers to change the way they schedule their time.

and needs of the children as they relate to social and academic functioning and monitor the effectiveness of intervention strategies and children's progress). Collaborative consultation models may also include some direct classroom-based language intervention services, which are provided jointly by the language interventionists and/or the special education teacher and the classroom teacher.

MEASUREMENT AND EVALUATION STRATEGIES

Measurement and evaluation are different procedures with different purposes. Measurement is systematic data collection in order to evaluate the student's progress in developing targeted language and communication skills and to make decisions about progress. The basic steps in the measurement process are (1) determining what is to be measured, (2) defining the target behavior or event in observable terms, and (3) selecting an appropriate data-recording system for observing, quantifying, and summarizing the behavior (Tawney & Gast, 1984). Evaluation is analysis of the data collected in the measurement process for the purpose of decision making. Evaluation may be summative or formative.

Summative Evaluation and Formative Evaluation

Summative and formative evaluation differ in purpose, time, and level of generalization. **Summative evaluation** takes place after an intervention has been implemented (typically the annual review called for by the IDEA). The purpose is to document that the promised services have been provided and that goals and objectives have been achieved. **Formative evaluation** is undertaken before and during instruction to find out whether the planned intervention efforts are being provided and whether they are proving to be effective. Formative evaluation is primarily to assist identification of strengths and weaknesses in the intervention/teaching process.

Summative evaluation documents that services have been provided and goals have been achieved.

The results of formative evaluation show where there are strengths and weaknesses in the intervention process.

In most cases it is possible and desirable to use both qualitative and quantitative evaluation methods. Quantitative research and evaluation methods report results in numbers in an effort to describe, explain, and predict relationships. Qualitative methods are also concerned with description, but they are more concerned with describing with words, rather than with numbers. In collecting qualitative data, there is an effort to understand what is occurring. Qualitative methods are concerned with process rather than simply outcomes or products. The goal is to construct a picture of what is occurring. The focus is the *meaning* of behaviors. The assumption behind the use of qualitative data is that the meaning of behaviors cannot be separated from the context. Intervention is evaluated according to whether it results in socially valid (i.e., important and meaningful) changes in children's lives and whether it uses strategies that are socially valid (i.e., acceptable and sustainable) in the classroom and other natural settings.

Used in the broadest sense, qualitative methods include investigative methodologies and data collection procedures described as ethnographic, naturalistic, anthropological, or participant-observer. Qualitative methods are a way to examine the processes of teaching and learning, the intended and unintended consequences of the intervention procedures, the relationships among children and with adults, and the sociocultural contexts within which teaching and learning occur most effectively.

Authentic assessment is any measure that provides information about the child's school performance.

The term for assessment that provides both qualitative and quantitative information about the child's performance of skills in actual—rather than contrived—tasks in the child's natural environments is **authentic assessment** (Wiggins, 1989). At the most basic level, authentic assessment informs programming. It is not a single method but, rather, any measure that provides information about the child's behaviors in daily activities. Some methods for authentic assessment include observations, interviews, checklists, photographs, anecdotal records, and diaries. Checklists, anecdotal records, and observations are described below.

Checklists make it possible to obtain a great deal of information in a relatively short time. They can provide both specific and general information about children's understanding and use of different language forms, structures, and functions. An advantage of checklists is the potential to obtain information to address several different questions at once. Checklists can be used to document (typically with a checkmark) whether the student performed the targeted behavior when performance was appropriate and whether it was performed correctly or incorrectly.

Anecdotal records are a type of narrative recording. They may be written or recorded on audio- or videotapes. Notes about a student's use of language in specific contexts and activities and the appropriateness of an activity or certain materials in eliciting language are particularly useful. They may be recorded when the events occur or sometime thereafter.

Some professionals write notes with reminders and questions such as these:

1. "3/14 (10:30): Susannah said "Can I play?" twice (without being prompted) to Brandon and Kyle. They were playing the Fishing Game during free play. She seems to be developing a special friendship with Brandon."
2. "4/16: Need to remember to discuss with the team how to get Cory to respond to choice situations. Also, need to ask Donna for some ideas as to what to do to get Nicole to use words for feelings."

Anecdotal records provide an objective description of a specific behavior at a specific time in a specific situation. Every anecdotal recording should include the student's name, the date and time, a description of the behavior that occurred, where it occurred, and both the stimulus for and the response to the behavior. It should include everything that the student said and did in the situation (and to/with whom) as well as what is said and done to/with the student. Facts should be clearly separated from interpretations.

Interpreting written narrative data is simplified by providing an indication of the time and organizing the descriptions into three columns. Events that occur before the communicative utterance are recorded in the first column: the student's specific language or communication behaviors (verbal and nonverbal) are recorded in the second column; and the effect or response to the student's language/communication behavior is recorded in the third column.

Anecdotal records may be written or recorded on tape.

Observations are essentially a series of "snapshots" depicting different sequences of behaviors and events as they occur in their natural contexts. Selection of the most appropriate lens for the snapshots depends on the questions being asked, practical considerations (e.g., time available for data collection), and what dimension of the behavior is of concern (e.g., rate, duration). The methods for collecting observation data are (1) event or frequency recording; (2) duration and latency recording, and (3) interval recording.

Event or frequency recording involves counting the number of times the target behavior occurs during a specified time period. This method is appropriate for recording discrete behaviors of short duration with easily discernible beginnings and endings. Sentences, phrases, words, syllables, and phonemes are examples of discrete behavior units which, if not delivered at an extremely high rate, can be tallied. Frequency recording is realistic for classroom data collection because it can be incorporated easily into daily routines. The only data collection devices required are a pencil or pen and paper or a counter (hand-held or wrist-worn). When recording frequency of occurrences, it is critical also to record the number of trials (opportunities for the response) when performance is based on opportunity. For example, it is meaningless to record the number of "appropriate requests for assistance in the cafeteria" without a record of the number of times such requests were indicated.

Duration recording is used when the length of time a behavior occurs is of interest. The number of seconds or minutes from initiation to termination of the target behavior is recorded. Duration recording is most appropriate for (1) behaviors that occur at rates too high to make tallying a possibility; (2) behaviors that occur for extended time periods; and (3) behaviors that are variable in length

Duration recording provides information about how long the behavior persisted.

(e.g., conversation, dramatic play). One way of recording duration data is the time accumulation method. The stopwatch is started as the behavior begins, stopped when the target behavior ends, then restarted when the target behavior is begun again, and so on for the length of the observation period. Over time, **if** the stopwatch is not returned to zero, this produces a record of the accumulated time of instances of the behavior. **Latency** is the time between a stimulus, or prompt, and the student's response. Latency is a concern when it affects the functionality of a skill (for example, if the student takes so long to respond to a request for a toy that the peer starts playing with something else).

Interval recording permits fairly sensitive measurement of both duration and frequency simultaneously. The observation period is divided into equal time intervals (usually from 5 to 50 seconds) depending on the average frequency and duration of the behavior. Regardless of the number of times the target behavior occurs during an interval, the interval is checked only once. When more than one behavior is being observed or recorded, or when more than one child is to be observed and recorded, there may be separate rows of interval cells for each behavior or each child, *or* a single row of cells where a symbol is recorded (for the behavior or child). When using an interval recording system it is important to specify in advance the proportion of the interval in which the behavior must occur in order to be scored. For example, does the interaction have to occur for the entire interval to be scored? Or will it be scored if it occurs during part of the interval? If it needs to occur for only part of the interval, how long must it occur?

> Interval recording is especially useful when more than one behavior is being observed.

Summary

This chapter has considered six dimensions of programming in inclusive schools: (1) the focus of intervention; (2) methods and procedures for intervention; (3) the instructional environment; (4) professional relationships and responsibilities; (5) scheduling; and (6) measurement and evaluation. For teachers and language interventionists, as well as for families and administrators, inclusion is a new way of thinking *and* a new way of acting. This chapter has discussed ways that team members can collaborate to modify classrooms and other school environments to accommodate the needs of children with language and communication difficulties.

The approach to data collection and evaluation of behavior change described in this chapter encourages teachers and language interventionists to think broadly and to commit to documenting important, relevant, and functional language and communication outcomes.

REFERENCES

Alpert, C. L., & Kaiser, A. P. (1992). Training parents to do milieu language teaching with their language-impaired preschool children. *Journal of Early Intervention, 16,* 31–52.

American Speech-Language-Hearing Association. (1993). Guidelines for caseload size and speech-language service delivery in the schools. *Asha, 35* (Suppl. 10) 33–39.

Apolloni, T., & Cooke, T. P. (1978). Integrated programming at the infant, toddler, and preschool levels. In M. J. Guralnick (Ed.), *Early intervention and the integration of handicapped and nonhandicapped children* (pp. 147–166). Baltimore: University Park Press.

Au, K. H. (1980). Participation structures in a reading lesson with Hawaiian children: Analysis of culturally appropriate instructional events. *Anthropology and Education Quarterly, 11,* 91–115.

Bashir, A. S. (1989). Language intervention and the curriculum. *Seminars in Speech and Language, 10,* 181–191.

Blank, M., & White, S. (1986). Questions: A powerful but misused form of classroom exchange. *Topics in Language Disorders, 6*(2), 1–12.

Brinton, B., & Fukiki, M. (1989). *Conversational management with language-impaired children.* Rockville, MD: Aspen.

Brolin, D. E. (1991). *Life centered career education: A competency based approach* (3rd ed.). Reston, VA: The Council for Exceptional Children.

Brown, A. L., & Palincsar, A. S. (1987). Reciprocal teaching and comprehension strategies. In J. O. Day & J. G. Borkowski (Eds.), *Intelligence and exceptionality: New directions for theory, assessment, and instructional practice* (pp. 81–132). Norwood, NJ: Ablex.

Brown, W. H., Ragland, E. V., & Fox, J. J. (1988). Effects of group socialization procedures on the social interactions of preschool children. *Research in Developmental Disabilities, 9,* 359–376.

Bruner, J. S. (1975). The ontogenesis of speech acts. *Journal of Child Language, 2,* 1–19.

Bruner, J. S. (1978). How to do things with words. In J. Bruner & A. Garton (Eds.), *Human growth and development.* New York: Oxford University Press.

Bunce, R. H., & Watkins, R. V. (1995). Language intervention in a preschool classroom: Implementing a language-focused curriculum. In M. L. Rice & K. A. Wilcox (Eds.), *Building a language-focused curriculum for the preschool classroom* (pp. 39–72). Baltimore: Paul H. Brookes.

Burstein, N. D. (1986). The effects of classroom organization on mainstreamed preschool children. *Exceptional Children, 52,* 425–434.

Buttrill, J., Niizawa, J., Biemer, C., Takahashi, C., & Hearn, S. (1989). Serving the language-learning disabled adolescent: A strategies-based model. *Language, Speech, and Hearing Services in Schools, 20,* 185–204.

Byrne, B. M. (1984). The general/academic self-concept nomological network: A review of construct validation research. *Review of Educational Research, 54,* 427–456.

Carr, E., & Kologinsky, E. (1983). Acquisition of sign language by autistic children II: Spontaneity and generalization. *Journal of Applied Behavior Analysis, 16,* 297–314.

Cazden, C. B. (1988.) Classroom discourse: The language of teaching and learning. Portsmouth, NH: Heinemann.

Clark, G. M. (1994). Is a functional curriculum approach compatible with an inclusive education model? *Teaching Exceptional Children, 26*(2), 36–39.

Cole, K. N., & Dale, P. (1986). Direct language instruction and interactive language instruction with language-delayed preschool children: A comparison study. *Journal of Speech and Hearing Research, 29,* 206–217.

DeKlyen, J., & Odom, S. L. (1989). Activity structure and social interactions with peers in developmentally integrated play groups. *Journal of Early Intervention, 13,* 342–352.

Dittman, L. L. (1977). *Curriculum Is What Happens: Planning Is the Key.* Washington, DC: National Association for the Education of Young Children.

Donahue, M., & Bryan, T. (1984). Communicative skills and peer relations of learning disabled adolescents. *Topics in Language Disorders, 4,* 10–21.

Doyle, A., Connolly, J., & Rivest, L. (1980). The effect of playmate familiarity on the social interactions of young children. *Child Development, 51,* 217–223.

Duchan, J. F. (1995). *Supporting language learning in everyday life.* San Diego: Singular Publishing Co.

Englert, C. (1984). Measuring teacher effectiveness from the teacher's point of view. *Focus on Exceptional Children, 17*(2) 1–16.

Falvey, M. A., Grenot-Scheyer, Coots, J. J., & Bishop, K. D. (1995). Services for students with disabilities: Past and present. In M. A. Falvey (Ed.), *Inclusive and heterogeneous schooling* (pp. 23–40). Baltimore: Paul H. Brooks.

Fey, M., Cleave, P. L., Long, S. H., & Hughes, D. L. (1993). Two approaches to the facilitation of grammar in children with language impairment: An experimental evaluation. *Journal of Speech and Hearing Research, 36,* 141–157.

Friel-Patti, S. (1994). Auditory linguistic processing and language learning. In G. P. Wallach & K. G. Butler (Eds.), *Language learning disabilities in school-age children and adolescents* (pp. 373–392). New York: Merrill-Macmillan.

Fuchs, L. S., & Deno, S. L. (1991). Paradigmatic distinctions between instructionally relevant measurement models. *Exceptional Children, 57,* 488–500.

Gallagher, T. M. (1991). Language and social skills: Implications for clinical assessment and intervention with school-age children. In T. M. Gallagher (Ed.), *Pragmatics of language: Clinical practice issues* (pp. 11–14). San Diego: Singular Publishing Group.

Garcia, G. E. (1992). Ethnography and classroom communication: Taking an "emic" perspective. *Topics in Language Disorders, 12*(3), 45–66.

Goldman, J. A. (1981). Social participation of preschool children in same- versus mixed-age groups. *Child Development, 52,* 644–650.

Goldstein, H., Wickstrom, S., Hoyson, M., Janieson, B., & Odom, S. (1988). Effects of sociodramatic play training on social and communicative interaction. *Education and Treatment of Children, 11,* 97–117.

Hall, B. J. (1991). Attitudes of fourth and sixth graders toward peers with mile articulation disorders. *Language, Speech, and Hearing Services in Schools, 22,* 334–340.

Halle, J. W., Alpert, C., & Anderson, S. (1984). Natural environment language assessment and intervention with severely impaired preschoolers. *Journal of the Association for the Severely Handicapped, 4,* 1–14.

Halle, J. W., Marshall, A., & Spradlin, J. (1979). Time delay: A technique to increase language use and facilitate generalization in retarded children. *Journal of Applied Behavior Analysis, 12,* 431–439.

Hamre-Nietupski, S., McDonald, J., & Nietupski, J. (1992). Integrating elementary students with multiple disabilities into supported regular classes. *Teaching Exceptional Children. 24*(3), 6–9.

Hart, B., & Risley, T. (1968). Establishing the use of descriptive adjectives in the spontaneous speech of disadvantaged preschool children. *Journal of Applied Behavior Analysis, 1,* 109–120.

Hemmeter, M. L., & Kaiser, A. P. (1994). Enhanced milieu teaching: Effects of parent-implemented language intervention. *Journal of Early Intervention, 18,* 269–289.

Howell, K. W., & Morehead, M. K. (1987). *Curriculum-based evaluation for special and remedial education.* Columbus: OH: Merrill.

Johnson, D., & Johnson, R. (1986). Mainstreaming and cooperative learning strategies. *Exceptional Children, 52,* 553–561.

Johnson, D., & Johnson, R. (1991). *Teaching students to be peacemakers.* Edina, MN: Interaction.

Johnson-Martin, N. M., Attermeier, S. M., & Hacker, B. (1990). *The Carolina Curriculum for Preschoolers with Special Needs.* Baltimore: Brookes.

Kaiser, A. P., Hendrickson, J., & Alpert, C. L. (1991). Milieu language teaching: A second look. In R. G. Gable (Ed.), *Advances in mental retardation and developmental disabilities* (Vol. 4, pp. 63–92) London: Jessica Kingsley Publishing.

Kohl, F. L., & Beckman, P. (1984). A comparison of handicapped and nonhandicapped preschoolers' interactions across classroom activities. *Journal of the Division for Early Childhood, 8,* 49–56.

Langlois, J. H., Gottfried, N. A., Barnes, B. M., & Hendricks, D. E. (1978). The effect of peer age on the social behavior of preschool children. *Journal of Genetic Psychology, 132,* 11–19.

Leonard, L. B., Schwartz, R., Chapman, K., Rowan, L., Prelock, P., Terrell, B., Weiss, A., & Merrick, C. (1982). Early lexical acquisition in children with specific language impairments. *Journal of Speech and Hearing Research, 25,* 554–559.

Light, J. (1988). Interaction involving individuals using augmentative and alternative communication systems: State of the art and future directions. *Augmentative and Alternative Communication, 2,* 98–107.

Lougee, M. D., Grueneich, R., & Hartup, W. W. (1977). Social interaction in same and mixed-age dyads of preschool children. *Child Development, 48,* 1277–1287.

Menyuk, P. (1983). Language development and reading. In T. M. Gallagher & C. A. Prutting (Eds.), *Pragmatic assessment and intervention issues in language* (pp. 33–67). San Diego: College Hill Press.

Naremore, R. C., Densmore, A. E., & Harman, D. R. (1995). *Language intervention with school-age children: Conversation, narrative, and text.* San Diego: Singular Publishing Co.

Nelson, K., & Gruendel, J. (1981). Generalized event representations: Basic building blocks of cognitive development. In M. Lamb & A. Brown (Eds.), *Advances in developmental psychology* (pp. 131–158). Hillsdale, NJ: Lawrence Erlbaum.

Nelson, K., & Gruendel, J. (1986). Children's scripts. In K. Nelson (Ed.), *Event knowledge: Structure and function in development.* Hillsdale, NJ: Erlbaum.

Nelson, N. W. (1994). Curriculum-based language assessment and intervention across the grades. In G. P. Wallach & K. G. Butler (Eds.), *Language learning disabilities in school-age children and adolescents* (pp 104–113). New York: Merrill-Macmillan.

Noonan, M. J., & McCormick, L. (1993). *Early intervention in natural environments.* Pacific Grove, CA: Brooks/Cole Publishing.

Odom, S. L., Hoyson, M., Jamieson, G., & Strain, P. S. (1985). Increasing handicapped preschoolers' peer social interactions: A cross-setting and component analysis. *Journal of Applied Behavior Analysis, 18,* 2–16.

Odom, S. L., Peterson, C., McConnell, S. R., & Ostrosky, M. (1990). Ecolbehavioral analysis of early education/specialized classroom settings and peer social interaction. *Education and Treatment of Children, 13,* 316–330.

Odom, S. L., Stein, M. L., & Jenkins, J. R. (1983, May). Peer-initiation and individual contingency interventions for promoting social interactions: A cross-setting and component analysis. Paper presented at the annual meeting of the Association for Behavior Analysis, Milwaukee, WI.

Ostrosky, M. M., Kaiser, A. P., & Odom, A. L. (1993). Facilitating children's social-communicative interactions through the use of peer-mediated interventions. In A. P. Kaiser & D. B. Gray (Eds.) *Communication and language intervention services: Vol. 2. Enhancing children's communication: Research foundations for intervention* (pp. 159–185). Balitmore: Paul H. Brookes.

Owens, R. E. (1992). *Language development: An introduction* (3rd ed.), Columbus, OH: Merrill/Macmillan.

Owens, R. E. (1995). *Language disorders: A functional approach to assessment and intervention.* (2nd ed.) Boston: Allyn & Bacon.

Palincsar, A. S., & Brown, A. L. (1984). Reciprocal teaching of comprehension fostering and comprehension monitoring activities. *Cognition and Instruction, 1,* 117–175.

Paul, L., Rogers-Warren, A. K., & Spradlin, J. E. (1978). Teaching children to talk to one another. Paper presented at the fourth annual meeting of the Midwestern Association of Applied Behavior Analysis, Chicago.

Rees, N. (1980). Learning to talk and understand. In T. J. Hixon, L. D. Shriberg, & J. H. Saxon (Eds.), *Introduction to communication disorders.* Englewood Cliffs, NJ: Prentice Hall.

Rice, M. L. (1993). "Don't talk to him; he's weird": A social consequences account of language and social interaction. In A. P, Kaiser & D. B. Gray (Eds.), *Enhancing children's communication: Research foundations for intervention* (pp. 139–158). Baltimore: Paul H. Brookes.

Rice, M. L., Hadley, P. A., & Alexander, A. L. (1993). Social biases toward children with speech and language impairments: A correlative causal model of language limitations. *Applied Psycholinguistics, 14,* 445–471.

Risley, T., & Reynolds, N. J. (1970). Emphasis as a prompt for verbal imitation. *Journal of Applied Behavior Analysis, 9,* 501–508.

Rogers-Warren, A., Ruggles, T. R., Petterson, J., & Cooper, A. Y. (1981). Playing and learning together: Patterns of social interaction in handicapped and nonhandicapped children. *Journal of the Division for Early Childhood, 3,* 56–63.

Rogers-Warren, A. K., & Warren, S. F. (1980). Pragmatics and generalization. In R. L. Schiefelbusch & J. Pickar (Eds.), *Communicative competence* (pp. 432–467). Baltimore: University Park Press.

Rosenshine, B. (1983). Teaching functions in instructional programs. *Elementary School Journal, 85,* 335–339.

Ross, B. L., & Berg, C. A. (1990). Individual differences in script reports: Implications for language assessment. *Topics in Language Disorders, 10,* 30–44.

Sapon-Shevin, M. (1990). Student support through cooperative learning. In W. Stainback & S. Stainback (Eds.), *Support networks for inclusive schooling* (pp. 65–80). Baltimore: Paul H. Brookes.

Saville-Troike, M. (1982). *The ethnography of communication: An introduction* (1st ed.). Baltimore: University Park Press.

Sawyer, D. J. (1991). Whoe language in context: Insights into the current great debate. *Topics in Language Disorders, 11*(3), 1–13.

Silliman, E. R., & Wilkinson, L. C. (1994). Discourse scaffolds for classroom intervention. In G. P. Wallach & K. G. Butler (Eds.), *Language learning disabilities in school-age children and adolescents* (pp. 27–52). New York: Merrill/Macmillan.

Snow, C. E. (1984). Parent-child interaction and the development of communicative ability. In R. L. Schiefelbusch & J. Packar (Eds.), *The acquisition of communicative competence* (pp. 69–108). Baltimore: University Park Press.

Stainback, W., & Stainback, S. (1990). *Support networks for inclusive schooling.* Baltimore: Paul H. Brookes.

Stark, R. E., & Bernstein, L. E. (1984). Evaluating central auditory processing in children. *Topics in Language Disorders, 4,* 57–70.

Strain, P. S., & Odom, S. L. (1986). Peer social initiations: Effective intervention for social skills development of exceptional children. *Exceptional Children, 52,* 543–551.

Tawney, J., & Gast, D. (1984). *Single subject research in special education.* Columbus, OH: Merrill.

Tucker, J. (1987). Curriculum-based assessment is no fad. *The Collaborative Educator, 1*(4), 4–10.

Twardosz, S., Nordquist, V. M., Simon, R., & Botkins, D. (1983). The effect of group affection activities on the interaction of socially isolated children. *Analysis and Intervention in Developmental Disabilities, 13,* 311–338.

Vandell, D. L., & George, L. B. (1991). Social interaction in hearing and deaf preschoolers: Successes and failures in initiation. *Child Development, 52,* 627–635.

Vygotsky, L. (1962). *Thought and language.* Cambridge, MA: The MIT Press.

Vygotsky, L. (1978). *Mind in society: The development of higher psychological processes.* Cambridge, MA: Harvard University Press.

Wallach, G. P., & Miller, L. (1988). *Language intervention and academic success.* Boston: College-Hill Press.

Warren, S. G., McQuarter, R. J., & Rogers-Warren, A. K. (1984). The effects of teacher mands and models on the speech of unresponsive language-delayed children. *Journal of Speech and Hearing Research, 49,* 43–52.

Westby, C. E., & Costlow, L. (1991). Implementing a whole language program in a special education class. *Topics in Language Disorders, 11*(3), 69–84.

Wiggins, G. (1989). A true test: Toward more authentic assessment. *Phi Delta Kappan, 70*(9), 703–713.

Wiig, E. H. (1990). Language disabilities in school-age children and youth. In G. J. Shames & E. J. Wiig (Eds.), *Human communication disorders: An introduction.* (3rd ed., pp. 193–220). New York: Merrill/Macmillan.

Windsor, J. (1995) Language impairment and social competence. In M. E. Fey, J. Windsor, & S. F. Warren (Eds.), *Language intervention: Preschool through the elementary years* (pp. 213–240). Baltimore: Paul H. Brookes.

Yoder, P. J., Kaiser, A. P., & Alpert, C. L. (1991). An exploratory study of the interaction between language teaching methods and child characteristics. *Journal of Speech and Hearing Research, 34,* 155–167.

CHAPTER 9

Language Intervention with Infants and Toddlers

Ken M. Bleile

This chapter describes the major principles and procedures that underlie language intervention with infants and toddlers. Special attention is given to infants and young children with medical problems. Specifically, this chapter discusses the philosophical and research foundations of early language intervention, early intervention settings, safety precautions, assessment, and intervention. It extends the discussion of working with families that is provided in Chapter 4.

THE CHILDREN

The following descriptions are composites. They are provided to illustrate that language disorders in infants and toddlers often occur as part of larger developmental and medical problems. They underscore

The birth of an infant with disabilities affects families in many different ways.

the fact that, in most cases, the medical and developmental problems that give rise to language disabilities are unexpected—an eagerly awaited child is born with a genetic disorder causing mental retardation; a mother and father who are expecting one child, discover they are having twins, and the twins are born prematurely. Families differ enormously in how they cope with the unexpected difficulties associated with the birth of an infant with disabilities.

THOMAS. Thomas was born with Down syndrome, a genetic abnormality caused by an additional chromosome added to the 21st pair (Batshaw, 1991). Shortly after Thomas's birth, his mother learned that Down syndrome is the most common cause of mental retardation, affecting approximately 1 in 700 births, that most children with Down syndrome are moderately retarded, and that these children often suffer from heart conditions, weak muscle tone, and respiratory problems.

Although he was a difficult child to feed, Thomas developed slowly but steadily during the first months at home. At 6 months of age he underwent heart surgery to correct a faulty valve. During his time in the hospital for that surgery, Thomas appeared to regress, losing some of his earlier developmental gains. He was not yet babbling at one year. Language assessment at that time estimated his developmental level to be approximately that of a child 6 months of age. At 2 years of age Thomas was beginning to use single words to express his thoughts and needs. Language assessment at that time indicated that he was functioning at approximately the 12-month level.

JEAN AND JENNIFER. Mr. and Mrs. Smith were thrilled when they realized they were going to have a baby, and they were doubly thrilled—and shocked!—when a sonogram taken early in pregnancy revealed the presence of twin girls. The pregnancy proceeded normally until the 22nd week, when Mrs. Smith began to experience cramping. The babies, named Jean and Jennifer, were born in the 24th week, fully 3 months premature.

The tiny infants were placed in incubators in the hospital's neonatal intensive care unit (NICU), where they received around-the-clock medical attention. The Smiths were told that the infants were experiencing difficulty in breathing on their own: their lungs lacked surfactant, a secretion that is normally formed in the last month of pregnancy and that helps the lungs to breath (Metz, 1993). Both children were considered at risk for future developmental problems due to possible damage to their immature neurological systems (Bernbaum & Hoffman-Williamson, 1991).

Despite some medical problems, Jennifer grew steadily stronger. At 3 months (a few days after the expected full-term due date) she was discharged from the hospital, small but healthy. Jean's medical course was more complicated. Her neurological system was too immature to regulate her body, and her lungs were unable to supply the breaths needed to sustain life. At 2 months Jean was placed on mechanical ventilation, which kept her alive by breathing for her. Unfortunately, the lifesaving breaths administered by the machine damaged Jean's fragile, immature lungs, resulting in broncho pulmonary dysplasia (BPD). Jean survived these early medical crises, but she was not able to leave the hospital until near her first birthday. At home she continued to receive mechanical ventilation for 2 more months and she continued to breathe through a tracheostomy tube placed in her throat for another 3 months. At 24-months-old, developmental assessment indicated that Jean's language skills were approximately those of a child 14 to 16 months old; Jennifer's language development was near the 18-month level.

PHILOSOPHICAL AND RESEARCH FOUNDATIONS

The consequences of uncorrected language disorders are often severe. Adults with language disorders generally are less well educated and have lower incomes than their peers: Even persons with mild impairments in language are judged by their peers to be immature, tense, nervous, and afraid (Aram, Ekelman, & Nation, 1984; Crowe Hall, 1991; Hall & Tomblin, 1978; Silverman & Paulus, 1989). Early intervention seeks to act proactively, so that language disorders can be eliminated or reduced before they can adversely affect the child's social and educational development. For children such as Thomas who experience intellectual or cognitive impairments, the ability to use language effectively may mean the difference between living and working in a restricted or unrestricted environment.

> Early intervention seeks to eliminate or at least reduce language disorders.

Support for early intervention comes from research in neurology, language development, and psychology. The first two years of life is the most rapid period of neurological development. During this period the brain has more connections between cells than it will during any subsequent time, perhaps reflecting a greater potential for learning (Bach-y-Rita, 1990). The brain grows to approximately 70 percent of its adult size, myelinization occurs throughout the central nervous system, and most development of critical areas for language such as the cortex and hippocampus occurs (Damasio, 1990; Ojemann, 1991).

Because language development is intimately connected to the growth and development of the human brain, it is not too surprising that the first two years of life is the most rapid period of language development. As discussed in Chapter 1, this is the period when the young child begins to learn to control his speech mechanism, acquires and refines basic turn-taking skills, learns to understand literally hundreds of words, and begins to acquire the fundamental patterns of syntax. As discussed in Chapter 1, the foundations of social

development are also laid during the first two years (Yarrow, Rubenstein, & Pedersen, 1975). Family bonds establish a level of support
and security that helps the child to learn and grow socially.

Language disorders can interfere with bonding between the parents and the child, especially if the child also experiences concomitant
medical or cognitive deficits (Hock-Long, Trachtenberg, & Vorters,
1993). For example, as with many other parents of children with
Down syndrome, Thomas's parents needed a great deal of convincing
to believe that their son could benefit and learn from parent–child
interactions. Jean's parents also required assistance and support, as
they were unsure how to interact with their daughter during the
months when the tracheostomy precluded vocalization.

The efficacy of both early intervention in general and early language intervention in particular has been demonstrated in multiple
studies (Bricker, Bailey, & Bruder, 1984; Infant Health and Development Program, 1990; Mantovani & Powers, 1991; Ramey & Campbell,
1984; Warren & Bambara, 1989; Warren & Kaiser, 1988; White, Mastrapierl, & Casto, 1984; Wilcox, Kouri, & Caswell, 1991; Yoder, Warren, Kim, & Gazdag, 1994). To date, the largest study is one that was
conducted to investigate the effects of early intervention on intelligence in infants born prematurely at eight different clinical settings
(Infant Health and Development Program, 1990). Results of that
study indicate that children who received early intervention have
intelligence quotients from 6.6 to 13.2 points higher at 3 years of age
than children who received only routine follow-up. A striking finding
of the study was that children who did not receive early intervention
were 2.7 times more likely to have IQ scores in the mentally retarded
range at 3 years of age than those who did receive early intervention
(Bleile, 1995). Children with the lowest birthweights had the lowest
gains in intelligence.

INTERVENTION SETTINGS

The classroom is the intervention setting for most school-aged children with language disorders. The child care setting or the early
intervention program is only one of several important intervention
settings for infants and toddlers with language difficulties. Other natural environments for intervention include family day care settings
and the child's home. In all these settings the persons responsible for
language intervention are the child's early intervention team, which
includes the child's parents, an infant specialist, and at least one language interventionist with specialized training to work with children
under the age of 3 and their families.

While hospitals are excellent places to overcome medical problems, even the best medical facility is a poor setting in which to raise a
child (Fridy & Lemanek, 1993). In recognition of this, hospitals

attempt to discharge children as soon as possible. Thus the vast majority of infants and young children who need early language intervention are served by community-based language interventionists. This includes children with significant, life-threatening medical needs and children with in-place tracheostomies, seizure disorders, pervasive developmental delay, mental retardation, HIV, and fetal alcohol syndrome (FAS). Intervention is generally provided in the home for children with severe illnesses or those attached to relatively cumbersome medical equipment (as Jean was when she received mechanical ventilation). In the home, intervention is likely to be provided during quiet play and activities of daily living, possibly including those involving medical equipment, and it is provided anywhere the child frequents (e.g., the bedroom, kitchen, and living room). For example, Jean was taught simple names for parts of her tracheostomy.

Intervention for children who are not medically fragile may also be provided in the home because the home is a natural environment for children of this age. It is also provided in community child care settings, family day care homes, and early intervention programs. In these settings, it is provided in the context of interactions in activity centers, play areas, eating areas, and changing stations.

Safety Precautions for Infants and Toddlers Who Are Medically Fragile

The appendix of this chapter lists guidelines to follow for infection control with all children. Serving infants and toddlers who are medically fragile requires language interventionists to be able to use other basic safety procedures, including cardiopulmonary resuscitation (CPR) for children. Interventionists new to working with infants and toddlers with medical needs often feel that the medical issues are a barrier to establishing a relaxed, natural rapport with the child. After some time to adjust, however, most report that the child's medical needs cease to dominate their attention.

Where there are medical conditions such as those listed in Table 9.1, there may be sudden, even life-threatening changes in the medical status of the infant or toddler (Bernbaum & Hoffman-Williamson, 1991). It is important to be able to recognize and respond appropriately to emergency situations, if need arises. The most common physiological warning signs (or red flags) associated with mechanical ventilation, tracheostomy hazards, seizures, shunts, gastrointestinal conditions, and cardiac conditions are discussed in the following paragraphs. If physiologic warning signs are observed, the clinician should immediately contact a member of the medical or nursing staff.

Language interventionists must know CPR if they work with infants and toddlers who are medically fragile.

MECHANICAL VENTILATION. **Mechanical ventilation** is provided through a machine that breathes in and out for the patient. Jean, the child described at the beginning of this chapter, received ventilator assis-

TABLE 9.1   Medical concerns that can involve life-threatening changes in medical status

Concerns	Definition
Mechanical Ventilator	A machine that breathes in and out for patients with airway disorders whose lungs are unable to breathe without assistance
Tracheostomy	A surgical opening below the larynx on the anterior neck that acts as an artificial airway for breathing
Seizure	A relatively common type of abnormal electrical discharge in the brain that causes mild to severe changes in behavior and cognition
Shunt	A device that diverts excess cerebrospinal fluid from a ventricle to another part of the body, where the fluid is then safely absorbed
Gastrointestinal Conditions	Problems in one or more of three areas: controlled movement of food through the body, digestion of food, and absorption of nutrients
Cardiac Conditions	Medical problems affecting the heart that may occur either as isolated medical problems or in conjunction with other disabilities

tance through a tracheostomy tube for the first year of her life. The most commonly encountered physiological warning signs in children receiving mechanical ventilation include changes in skin color, exaggerated breathing, coughing, alteration in heart rate or respiratory rate, and either lethargy or irritability.

TRACHEOSTOMY.   **Tracheostomy** is a surgical opening below the larynx on the anterior neck (Handler, 1993). Persons receiving tracheostomy assistance breathe through a hole (stoma) placed in the anterior neck. Approximately 30 percent of children who receive tracheostomies also are ventilator assisted (Bleile, 1993). The most common daily hazards associated with tracheostomy care involve blockages that make breathing difficult or impossible. The physiological warning signs of blockage include a blue tint around the lips or nailbeds, flared nostrils, fast breathing, a rattling noise during breathing, mucus bubbles around tracheostomy site, coughing or gagging, clammy skin, restlessness, and either lethargy or irritability.

SEIZURES.   A **seizure** is a type of abnormal electrical discharge from the neurons in the cortex. Seizure disorders are prevalent among many populations of children with developmental disabilities, occurring in approximately 16 percent of children with mental retardation, and 25 percent of children with cerebral palsy, spina bifida, and hydrocephalus (Wallace, 1990). Thomas, the child described in the beginning of the chapter, is at risk for a seizure disorder because he is mentally retarded. The physiological warning signs associated with seizures include pallor, irritability, staring, nystagmus, changes in muscle tone, and vomiting.

A seizure is a sudden, involuntary disruption in the normal function of the CNS.

SHUNTS. A **shunt** is a device that diverts cerebrospinal fluid from a brain ventricle to another part of the body, where the fluid is then absorbed. Shunts are used with children with hydrocephalus, a condition in which the fluid-filled ventricles in the brain become enlarged. Approximately 60 percent to 95 percent of children with neural tube defects experience hydrocephalus (Charney, 1992). Physiological warning signs suggesting a shunt malfunction include headaches, vomiting, lethargy, and bulging fontanel (the soft spot on the head of the infant).

A shunt is a tube to drain excess cerebral spinal fluid from the brain ventricles to the abdominal cavity.

GASTROINTESTINAL CONDITIONS. **Gastrointestinal conditions** involve problems in one or more of three areas: controlled movement of food through the body, digestion of food, and/or absorption of nutrients. If a child cannot receive enough nourishment by mouth (per oral) to sustain life and continued growth, the youngster is fed via a gastrostomy placed into the stomach or a jejunal tube placed in the small intestine. Jean, the child described earlier, experienced feeding difficulties, but did not require tube feeding. Physiological warning signs of problems with a gastrostomy or jejunal tube include the presence of formula leaking from the tube at either the clamp or skin site, in and out movement of the tube, increased irritability, and emesis.

CARDIAC CONDITIONS. **Cardiac conditions** are medical problems affecting the heart. They may occur as isolated medical problems or in conjunction with other disabilities. Cardiac conditions are relatively common among children with Down syndrome. Thomas, the child with Down syndrome, had a cardiac condition requiring surgical intervention at 6 months of age. Physiological warning signs associated with cardiac conditions include changes in skin color, increased heart and/or respiratory rate, chest retractions, nasal flaring, and either lethargy or irritability.

ASSESSMENT

Assessment of children of all ages was discussed in Chapter 6 of this book. However, some assessment procedures are specific to infants and toddlers. The primary purpose of initial assessments is to determine if intervention is warranted (see Table 9.2). A parent interview or review of medical information is a source for this assessment. Either provides information about the child's background, the family's concerns, and the presence of any risk factors. The second source of information for the decision of whether intervention is warranted is assessment instruments (nonstandardized and standardized). As discussed in Chapter 6, nonstandardized assessments are particularly useful as they often provide insights about communication abilities that are not tapped by standardized test instruments. Standardized assessment instruments compare the child's performance to that of a standardized population.

In order for the language interventionist to get an accurate picture of how and when the child communicates in daily situations, assessment must involve as many of the persons and environments in the child's life as possible. For example, the assessment of Jean while in the hospital revealed that she was communicative with a favorite nurse during diaper changing, but grew increasingly withdrawn and quiet in situations where other children were present. If the child has a medical condition (as was the case with Jean), the language interventionist consults with a nurse or other qualified staff member knowledgeable about the child's medical status in order both to rule out the existence of medical complications that would interfere with the assessment and to be sure that assessment will not exacerbate the child's medical problems (Bleile & Miller, 1994).

Standardized assessments and phonological testings are performed in quiet, distraction-free locations when the child appears

> **Nonstandardized instruments provide insights that cannot be gained through administration of standardized tests.**

TABLE 9.2   Major purpose of three aspects of language assessments of infants and toddlers

Aspect of Assessment	General Purpose
Parent Interview	Better understand the family's perspective Identify areas in the child's history that might impact on the child's present and future language development
Nonstandard Assessment	Provide a first approximation of which language milestones the child has attained Sometimes serve as the sole means of assessment, especially with children who are otherwise untestable
Standardized Assessment	Allow the clinician to determine if a child is acquiring language at the same rate as other children

calm and alert. Either the parent or the language interventionist may attempt to elicit language from the child. Often parents are better at this because they are more familiar to the child. The child and the caregiver (or language interventionist) are positioned so that eye contact between the two is easily achieved and maintained. If a child has physical limitations or special motoric needs, positioning should be undertaken with guidance from occupational or physical therapy (Bleile & Miller, 1994).

Parent Interview

As noted above, assessment typically begins with a parent interview or, if the parents are unavailable, review of the child's medical chart or educational records. The language interventionist inquires about the family's concerns with such questions as "What brings you to the clinic?" "What are your major concerns?" or "Can you tell me why you brought your child for a language assessment today?" followed by more direct questions about the nature of the family's concerns, should such concerns exist. In addition to providing insights as to the family's perspective on the child's communication behavior, the parent interview helps to identify areas in the child's background that might impact on prognosis for future language development. Parent interviews last from 10 to 30 minutes, depending on the nature of the child's language difficulties, the ability of the parents to serve as reliable informants, and the language interventionist's style of interaction.

> The parent interview provides important insights as to how the family views the child's communication difficulties.

Because a child's physical well-being has an important influence on the rate of language development, a medical history is conducted. The language interventionist also tries to elicit information about the child's exposure to language both in and outside the home. Last, the family's perception of when the child obtained major language acquisition milestones is elicited. Examples of questions typically asked at this juncture are listed in Table 9.3. Other useful information at this point is whether there are medical, environmental, or genetic risk factors that could result in language disorders in the future.

Direct Assessment

After the parent interview is completed, assessment of the child's current language development typically requires from one-half to one hour. Most language interventionists use both nonstandard assessments and standardized assessments. As discussed in Chapter 6, *nonstandardized assessments* use observational techniques to determine which language milestones the child has attained. Sometimes nonstandardized assessment is used to get a general picture of the child's language; at other times nonstandardized assessment is the sole assessment of current language abilities. Nonstandardized assessment may consider language use, language content, and language form.

TABLE 9.3   Types of questions used to elicit background information

---

Questions

---

1. **Medical History**
   Did the mother or child experience pre- and perinatal medical complications?
   Does the child possess any diagnosed syndromes or conditions?
   Has the child ever been hospitalized?
   Does the child experience ear infections? If so, how frequently do or did they occur either presently or in the past?
   What is the child's current health status?

2. **Educational and Social Background**
   How many siblings and parents reside in the child's household?
   Does the child have contact with any children outside the home?
   Is the child presently or has the child in the past been involved in any educational programs?

3. **Language Milestones**
   At what age did the child begin to babble?
   At what age did the child say his or her first word?
   At what age did the child begin to put words together into sentences?
   How does the child typically express his or her wants and needs?

Language Use—Turn-taking skills and the use of sounds during interactions

Most children can be encouraged to play sound-gesture games such as "peekaboo" by 9 months of age (Capute, Palmer, Shapiro, Wachtel, Schmidt, & Ross, 1986), and by the end of the first year of life an infant can cover her own eyes in peekaboo and will initiate this and other sound-gesture games. As discussed in Chapter 1, infants first acquire the "my turn–your turn" aspect of language use in early interactions with caregivers, specifically daily routines such as mealtime, diaper changing, and dressing, and while playing such interaction games as peekaboo, and rolling a ball back and forth (Bruner, 1983; Snow & Goldfield, 1983). Additionally, turn-taking activities afford children excellent opportunities to acquire the meaning and phonological shape of words. Jean, described earlier, was taught the meaning of "ball" while rolling a bright red ball back and forth with the language interventionist. Jean was more attentive and motivated to learn the meaning of "ball" while playing this game than in other, more distracting situations.

Young children are most motivated to learn new words and meanings in social interaction contexts.

By 3 to 4 months of age an infant may coo, grunt, or squeal when spoken to, and by 7 months may vocalize on seeing a bottle. The language interventionist can expect an infant of 10 months to use a ritualized intentional gesture in conjunction with a short sound to obtain a desired object from a caregiver. Toddlers in the first months of their second year typically communicate using a combination of facial expression, gestures, single words, and vocalizations. By 16 to 18 months they can use words to express wants and needs, and by 20 months most can use words to relate experiences (Hedrick, Prather, & Tobin, 1984). The child's gradual ability to use sounds to interact with others is one of the most significant accomplishments of the first two years of life. At first, sounds are little more than an activity that accompanies interactions with caregivers, similar to eye gaze and arm waving. Gradually, however, sound replaces eye gaze and pointing as the child's primary means of communication, allowing the child to express the increasingly complex thoughts and needs permitted by the youngster's rapidly evolving neurological system. Thomas, the child with Down syndrome, experienced significant difficulties in learning to use vocal sounds rather than pointing and grunting to express his needs and wants.

Language Content—Receptive and expressive vocabulary

An infant 4 to 6 months old may respond to hearing her name. By 6 months she will respond to "no" with inflection, although she does not understand "no" if a different inflection is used (Hedrick, Prather, & Tobin, 1984). An infant 6 to 7 months old understands "bye-bye" and turns to look when a family member is named (example: "Where's daddy?"). Infants 8 to 9 months old respond to "no" if the language interventionist says it in a "flat" voice and they know the name of a few common objects. By 12 to 13 months they respond to a few simple commands without gestures, such as "sit down," "come here," "clap hands," and "stand up." Most toddlers can point to such body parts as the ears, eyes, hair, mouth, and nose by 16 months old and by 17 to 18 months they will lift a foot or point to a shoe when asked, "Where are your shoes?" Toddlers 20 months old are able to put a block "in the box" when given that command.

The notion that sound can signify meaning may be the most profound insight that infants have over the course of language learning. They learn that a certain group of sounds ("daddy") means one caregiver, that "mommy" means another caregiver, and that "kitty" means a strange little creature with soft fur. Typically, a child's receptive vocabulary (i.e., the words a child understands) is larger than the child's expressive vocabulary (i.e., the words the child speaks). All three children discussed in the beginning of this chapter experienced problems in word comprehension.

The awareness that sound can signify meaning is the most profound insight in early language learning.

Acquisition of expressive
vocabulary plays a central role
in language acquisition.

Many parents are able to report accurately the number of words a child regularly uses. Children typically acquire their first word by 11 months; they then produce two to three words by 12 to 13 months, four to six words by 14 to 15 months, and seven to 20 words by 16 to 17 months. By 20 to 21 months they have a single-word vocabulary of 50 words or more (Capute, Palmer, Shapiro, Wachtel, Schmidt, & Ross, 1986). To avoid the parent's listing only the words the child "says well," it should be explained that the parent is interested in the number of child words, not how well the child pronounces the words. Many times, parents begin by listing a few words, but remember more words as the assessment session continues. Acquisition of expressive vocabulary (words actually used for communication, rather than simply words the child understands) has a central role in language acquisition during the first two years of life. Researchers hypothesize that children first acquire words as isolated "items," somewhat analogously to how a person in a foreign country, for example, might learn a word for "dinner," another word for "taxi," and another word for "museum" (Ferguson & Farwell, 1975). In no sense is such a traveler "acquiring the country's language." Instead, the traveler is learning isolated words that are useful for meeting simple daily needs. The same may hold for the toddler in the early stages of word acquisition—the child learns a word for a favorite food, another to call a parent, and another to signal distress. Only later, after the child's vocabulary grows to approximately 50 words, do most children begin to show evidence that they realize that certain words can be classified as nouns, that others can be classified as verbs, or that certain classes of words begin with the same sound (and, therefore, can be pronounced similarly), while other words all begin with another sound (and so can be pronounced differently than other words) (Bleile & Fey, 1993).

Language Form—Phonology (pre-speech vocalizations, use of sounds and syllables in words and correct productions of consonants) and one area of syntax (combining words)

Pre-speech vocalizations may
be viewed as practicing for
speech.

Pre-speech vocalizations produced during the first year of life are thought to provide "practice" for later speech development (Locke, 1983; Locke & Pearson, 1992; Bleile, Stark, & Silverman McGowan, 1993; Vihman & Miller, 1988; Jusczyk, 1992). Through babbling, for example, the infant learns how to synchronize the velum, tongue, lips, and larynx for the purposes of producing sound. Around 3 to 4 months old many infants may be observed producing, or be encouraged to produce, cooing sounds, which are consonant-like noises made at the back of the mouth. Squeals, growls, raspberries, and trills are often heard when the infant nears 4 months old. Reduplicated babbling (repetitions of the identical syllable, such as ba-ba-ba) begins to appear near 6 months old and becomes well-established near 7 to 8 months old. Around 10 months old most infants produce nonreduplicated babbling (repetitions of different syllables, such as ba-di-du).

During the second year of life, phonological units (sounds and syllables) constitute the building blocks of words. Some investigators hypothesize that the phonological problems of a toddler may "grow into" an expressive language problem by the time the child is a preschooler, because the phonological problems place limitations on the child's ability to develop an expressive vocabulary (Paul, 1991). At 16 months children typically speak around 6 different consonants at the beginning of words and they may produce one (or no) consonants at the end of words. These consonants need not be "correct" relative to the adult language. Commonly produced word-initial consonants during this period are *b, d, m, n, h,* and *w,* and the most common word-final consonant is *t.* The most common syllable shapes of words are CV (consonant-vowel), CVCV, and, less frequently, VC and CVC. If the child is 24 months old, the child's speech should contain 9 to 10 consonants in the beginning of words, and 5 to 6 consonants in the end of words. The most common word-initial consonants are *b, d, g, t, k, m, n, f, s, w,* and *h,* and the most common word-final consonants are *p, t, k, n, s,* and *r.* Approximately 70 percent of the consonants produced by a child near 24 months old may be correct relative to the adult language. The following consonants should be produced correctly in two out of three word positions (initial, medial, final): *m, n, h, w, p, b, t, k, d,* and *g.*

Syntactic development represents an important expansion in the ability of the toddler to express ideas and needs. A child, for example, who speaks the single word "dog" must depend on the listener's understanding of the nonverbal context to know if the child is saying, "I want my dog," "The dog is panting," or "The dog is barking." A child who says, "Want dog," is more likely to have his needs met, because more of the request is included in the linguistic message. Sometime between 20 and 24 months a child can be observed to begin to combine words, and by 24 months many children speak regularly in two- and three-word sentences. When assessing a child's syntactic abilities, the language interventionist should remember that what seems like a sentence to an adult may be a single word for a child. Jennifer, for example, learned "got to go" as a single word, without having analyzed the phrase into separable units. Many times, children's "word phrases" are cliches used by adults in specific situations, such as "off we go" (while daddy picks up the child), or "bye-bye now" (while mother hangs up the telephone). Because the child always hears these words together, he makes the hypothesis that the

What seems like a sentence to an adult may be a single word for a child.

sounds are all one word. To avoid attributing to the child more knowledge of syntax than is possessed, a word should occur in combination with at least three other words before concluding the child is making a sentence rather than a word phrase. For example, "off we go" would not be considered a word phrase, unless one of the words occurred in at least two other utterances, such as "daddy go" and "go home."

Standardized assessment allows the language interventionist to determine if a child is acquiring language at the same rate as his peers and his relative communication strengths and weaknesses. The standardized assessment instruments listed below represent a range of options to use in assessing communication development with infants and toddlers. The list is divided into two parts: screening instruments and complete language evaluations.

Screening Tests

1. *Clinical Linguistic and Auditory Milestone Scale (CLAMS).* The *CLAMS* (Capute & Accardo, 1978) was developed by two well-respected developmental pediatricians to screen for language disorders in children from 0 to 2 years of age. Information on the *CLAMS* is obtained using parental report supplemented by direct observation. The test assesses 25 language milestones. The normative sample on which the *CLAMS* is based are 448 children, 69 percent of whom were Caucasian and 30 percent of whom were non-Caucasian (Capute, Palmer, Shapiro, Wachtel, Schmidt, & Ross, 1986). Approximately 20 minutes is required to complete the *CLAMS*.

2. *Rossetti Infant-Toddler Language Scale (Rossetti).* The *Rossetti* is a relatively new clinical instrument intended for use with children 0 to 3 years. Information on the *Rossetti* is elicited using incidental observation and parental report. Items were chosen for inclusion in the *Rossetti* based on "author observation, descriptions from developmental hierarchies, and behaviors recognized and used by leading authorities in the field of infant and toddler assessment" (p. 10). A normative sample was not obtained in the development of the *Rossetti*.

3. *Early Language Milestone Scale-2 (ELM-2).* The *ELM-2* (Coplan, 1993) is a screening instrument for use with children from 0 to 36 months old, and also assesses intelligibility in children 18 to 48 months old. Information on the *ELM-2* is obtained using parent report in conjunction with limited elicitation. The elicitation stimuli are real objects. The normative sample on which the *ELM-2* is based are 191 children aged from birth to 36 months. Approximately 1 to 10 minutes is required to complete the *ELM-2*.

4. *Receptive-Expressive Emergent Language Scale-2 (REEL-2).* The *REEL-2* (Bzoch & League, 1991) is a screening instrument for use with children 0 to 3 years old. The *REEL-2* is a new edition of an older instrument, and the theory on which it is based is now somewhat out of date. Information on the *REEL-2* is elicited using parental report. The normative sample on which the *REEL-2* is based are "language-advantaged Caucasian infants" (p. 7). The number of children composing the normative sample is not provided, nor is information available on how long the language interventionist should allow for test administration.

5. *Infant Scales of Communicative Intent (Infant Scales).* The *Infant Scales* (Saint Christopher's Hospital for Children, 1982) is a screening instrument for children from birth to 18 months old that relies on direct clinical observation of behaviors. The *Infant Scales* has been largely superseded by more recently developed screening instruments, although it is still used in some clinical settings in which obtaining parent reports is not feasible. No normative information on the *Infant Scales* is available, nor is there published information on how long the language interventionist should allow for test administration.

Language Evaluations

1. *Sequenced Inventory of Communicative Development (SICD).* The *SICD* (Hedrick, Prather, & Tobin, 1984) is a well-respected, in-depth language assessment instrument for use with children between 4 months and 4 years old. The *SICD* assesses both language reception and expression, using a combination of direct elicitation techniques and parental reports. The elicitation stimuli for infants and toddlers are real objects. The normative sample for the *SICD* were 252 children aged from 4 to 48 months. The *SICD* requires from between 30 minutes for infants to 75 minutes for children 24 months or older. Both English and Spanish versions of the test are available.

2. *MacArthur Communicative Development Inventories (CDI).* The *CDI* is a new, highly regarded language assessment instrument for use with children 8 months to 2 years, 6 months (Fenson, Dale, Reznick, Thal, Bates, Hartung, Pethick, & Reilly, 1993). The *CDI* uses one form for infants 8 to 16 months (Words and Gestures) and another for toddlers 16 months to 30 months (Words and Sentences). Information is elicited using parent questionnaires. The normative sample for the *CDI* were 1789 children aged 8 through 30 months. Parents are typically able to complete the *CDI* in 20 to 40 minutes, and speech-language language interventionists require approximately 10 minutes to score the results. Currently, only an English version of the *CDI* is available, although translations into several other languages (including Spanish) are underway.

3. *Preschool Language Scale-3 (PLS-3).* The *PLS-3* (Zimmerman, Steiner, & Pond, 1992) is an in-depth assessment instrument for use with children from birth through 6 years, 11 months. The *PLS-3* assesses both language reception and expression, using real objects and pictures. Earlier editions of the *PLS* tended to overestimate children's language development, perhaps because the normative sample on which the test was based was not completely representative of the United States population. The normative sample on which the *PLS-3* is based are approximately 1900 children balanced for geographical region and racial and ethnic origin. The PLS-3 requires less than 1 hour to administer and score.

INTERVENTION WITH INFANTS AND TODDLERS

Language acquisition requires two factors: an infant who is ready neurologically to learn *and* appropriate experiences.

Language acquisition depends crucially on the child's neurological readiness to learn, in conjunction with the availability of experiences afforded by the environment. The general educational strategy of early intervention is to manipulate the environment to maximize a child's opportunities to acquire language. In recognition that language acquisition depends on both the environment and the child's developmental readiness to learn, language intervention is said to "facilitate" or "stimulate" rather than "teach" language acquisition.

This section provides an overview of language intervention for infants and toddlers. The discussion focuses on underlying principles and procedures shared by most language interventionists and researchers rather than the tenets of a particular language intervention approach (Greenspan, 1985, 1992; MacDonald, 1989; MacDonald & Carroll, 1992; Wilcox, 1989). The topics considered include inclusion, the role of parents, intervention goals, and facilitative techniques. Issues are raised for consideration at the conclusion of each subsection.

As emphasized in Chapters 3 and 5, inclusion has brought language intervention out of the separate clinic room into the child's natural environments (Greenspan, 1985; MacDonald, 1989; Wilcox, 1989). Inclusion implicitly recognizes that language acquisition is different from other types of skill learning. Language differs from a specialized motor skill such as tennis, which involves acquiring certain specific motor skills best learned through direct instruction from a tennis instructor, in that it is acquired indirectly as a child performs activities and interacts with other persons. Restricting language intervention to a single person or even to a single discipline is unnatural. In effect, attempting to teach language a few hours each week is treating it as a type of motor skill. Inclusion assumes that children will more readily generalize when intervention occurs across a variety of settings and

Assuming that language can be learned with a few hours a week of instruction is treating it as a type of motor skill.

persons. This hypothesis is supported by Wilcox, Kouri, and Caswell (1991), who studied vocabulary acquisition in 20 children aged 20 to 47 months. Half the children were randomly assigned to receive individual therapy and the other half received treatment in a classroom-based early intervention program. Results of the investigation indicated that the two groups were equivalent in vocabulary acquisition, but that generalization of learning to the home setting was superior in those children who received treatment in a classroom setting.

The Role of Parents

Parents have a special role on the early intervention team because they are ultimately responsible for all treatment decisions affecting their child (Trout & Foley, 1989). Importantly, this special status is derived from parents' legal guardianship of their child rather than from such extraneous factors as the parents' sexual orientation, marital status, and whether the child is a biological offspring or adopted. The language interventionist's role is to serve as a resource to parents and to help them make the most informed decisions possible. This may involve providing written information about the nature of language development and a child's language disorder. Most language interventionists also hold frequent meetings with parents to answer questions as they arise. Demonstrations of intervention techniques often are excellent means to help parents understand language development and intervention issues.

Intervention Goals

It is important to realize that language is basically a tool. The clear lesson of research on language development is that a child acquires those aspects of language for which she has use (see the discussion in Chapter 1 and in the Assessment section of this chapter). Language intervention should provide the child with a tool to express feelings,

TABLE 9.4 Treatment goals for language intervention with infants and toddlers

Language Domains	Treatment Goals
Language Use	Turn-taking skills Vocalizations or speech during interactions
Language Content and Form	Receptive vocabulary Expressive vocabulary Pre-speech vocalizations Sounds and syllables in words Combining words

thoughts, and needs. To illustrate, Thomas loved to interact with people around him; early language goals for Thomas included facilitating babbling and participation in peekaboo games as ways to interact with his caregivers. Similarly, during one period in development, Jean appeared increasingly frustrated when adults could not understand what she wanted them to do; a language goal during this period focused on facilitating Jean's ability to name objects she wanted.

As with adults, children have different needs and thoughts, and what seems important and functional to one may be of little of no importance to another. For this reason, functionality is determined on an individual basis. For example, a language intervention goal for a particular child may include facilitating the use of words such as "hi" and "bye," while a vocabulary intervention goal for a child of the same age and developmental level might focus on facilitating the acquisition of words for various foods. Individual differences in functionality are particularly striking when comparing children with medical needs to their non–medically involved peers. Jean, for example, learned words for the mechanical ventilation and care of her tracheostomy far more quickly and with greater apparent interest than she did words for such things as trees, grass, and flowers. This is because Jean was surrounded by medical equipment, while she knew trees, grass, and flowers only through pictures in books. Stated differently, the names of parts of medical equipment were highly functional and interesting to Jean (as they are to many children with medical needs), while the names of objects outside the home represented abstract, vague concepts that she seldom directly experienced.

Language intervention goals for infants and toddlers should include facilitating the child's awareness of basic rules of conversation (language use), the knowledge of word meanings (language content), and the ability to vocalize and speak, and to combine words into sentences (language form). The following are examples of language intervention goals for children at different levels of language development.

Language Use Goals.   Intervention to facilitate language use can begin as early as the first months of life, when the child begins to be awake for more extended periods of time. An early language use goal for Thomas, for example, was increasing attention and mutual eye gaze. Early signs of the infant's involvement in interactions include eye widening, body movement, and smiling. For children between birth to 6 months, rattles and handheld toys are useful in facilitating interactions between the child and the speech-language language interventionist. Similarly, busy boxes excite the child and provide an activity that requires the joint attention of the child and caregivers. For children 6 months or older, noisemaking objects such as toy cars and drums are useful because they afford the child the opportunity to engage in reciprocal play. Jean and her care-

What seems important and functional to one child may be of little interest to another.

Language use (communication) begins at birth.

givers, for example, took turns patting a toy drum. Participation in sound–gesture games and daily activity routines such as diaper changing, bathing, and eating also provide excellent opportunities to facilitate the development of language use.

Toddlers benefit from such turn-taking routines as rolling a ball, putting together big-piece puzzles with an adult, and pointing and identifying pictures in books. Toddlers also can be encouraged to vocalize in interactions through simple manipulations that "violate social norms." Jennifer's caregivers, for example, "took Jennifer's turn" in peekaboo and tried to feed a shoe to a doll. Alternately, the adult might hide or withhold objects, forcing the child to vocalize in order to obtain a desired toy.

CONTENT AND FORM GOALS. Language content and form (both reception and expression) are often facilitated concurrently in naturally occurring contexts such as turn-taking routines or while playing. For example, changing the child's clothes provides opportunities to facilitate acquisition of the sounds, words, and syntax used with body parts, while mealtime offers chances to acquire aspects of language content and form associated with foods and actions such as opening, closing, chewing, and swallowing.

An important difference among language interventionists is whether they address language goals simultaneously or in sequence (Fey, 1986). The simultaneous targeting of language goals is sometimes called a horizontal approach and is depicted as a series of bidirectional arrows between language goals (a ↔ b ↔ c ↔ d ↔ e). The sequential targeting of language goals is sometimes called a vertical approach and is depicted as a series of unidirectional arrows between language goals (a → b → c → d → e). The horizontal approach

Language content and form are facilitated concurrently in naturally occurring contexts.

presents language "all at once" rather than focusing on only one or several language areas. To illustrate, within the horizontal approach the language goals for content, form, and use are presented simultaneously. Proponents of the horizontal approach observe that simultaneous learning is more typical than sequential learning in language acquisition. For example, the parent who says "please" is simultaneously modeling form (the sounds in "please"), content (the meaning of "please"), and use (the social functions of "please").

An argument against the horizontal approach is that it replicates an environment from which children with language disabilities have been unable to learn. Stated differently, a reason for language delay is that some children find it difficult to learn from an environment that presents content, form, and use simultaneously. The vertical approach provides more intensive, focused facilitation on selected language goals than does its horizontal counterpart.

An extreme version of a vertical approach would focus on a single language goal at a time. To continue the example of "please," a language interventionist using an extreme vertical approach might first facilitate use (the social purpose of "please"), then content (the meaning of "please"), and then form (the pronunciation of "please"). A difficulty with such an extreme version of a vertical approach is that content, form, and use are often closely bound together, making it difficult to facilitate them separately. For example, the content of "please" is difficult to facilitate without also facilitating its form.

Although either an extreme horizontal or vertical approach is possible, language interventionists often adopt a position midway between the two poles. Such language interventionists facilitate all aspects of language as they occur during an intervention activity (a horizontal approach), but also have additional language goals for specific aspects of language (a vertical approach). For example, while language interventionists for both Thomas and Jean attempted to stimulate all aspects of language in every intervention session, they also devoted time to facilitating specific areas of content, form, and use.

Facilitative Techniques

Early language intervention relies on naturalistic techniques that model aspects of language use, content, and form (Hart, 1985; Nelson, 1989). These techniques constitute in large measure the child's "language learning lesson." The techniques that follow can be adapted to facilitate many different aspects of language, depending on the child's developmental needs. The techniques described are presented separately for the sake of simplicity: In actual practice, they typically are used together.

TABLE 9.5   Summary of rationale for treatment goals

Language Domain	Rationale for Treatment Goal
Language Use	The fundamental rules of discourse and pragmatics are acquired in the course of interacting with caregivers in daily routines and simple games. An important development in discourse and pragmatics is the use of vocalizations and speech in interactions.
Language Content	The first steps in semantic development are undertaken as the child learns the names of familiar objects and persons in the environment.
Language Form	The principles of phonology are acquired as the child first babbles and then uses sound to say words. The ability to combine words into simple sentences represents a significant development in the acquisition of syntax.

VOCAL STIMULATION.   Vocal stimulation encourages the child's use of sound in play (Bleile, 1995). The following sequence was used to stimulate vocal development with Thomas.

1. The language interventionist spoke with Thomas's caregivers to determine times of the day when he was most likely to engage in vocal play. When Thomas was 6 months old, it was found that sometimes he could be induced to vocalize by setting a mobile in motion. This appeared to have a soothing effect and induced him to coo. When Thomas was 7 months, play with mirrors permitted him to look at his own facial expressions. He vocalized excitedly.

2. The language interventionist waited until Thomas began vocalizing, and then imitated the sounds produced by Thomas. For example, Thomas said a raspberry and then the language interventionist responded with a raspberry.

3. After a few "turns" imitating Thomas's babble, the language interventionist began introducing syllables that assessment indicated Thomas was able to produce. Thomas was "coaxed" into imitating the language interventionist.

4. Last, the language interventionist produced syllables slightly in advance of Thomas's developmental level. In many cases, Thomas attempted to imitate these new syllables. For example, the language interventionist babbled "da-da-da" when Thomas's babble was primarily composed of "b."

The purpose of vocal stimulation is to encourage the child's use of sound in play.

PARALLEL TALK.   **Parallel talk** provides linguistic labels that describe
the child's activities or those aspects of the environment to which the
youngster is attending. The rationale for engaging in parallel talk is
that the child is more likely to acquire those aspects of the language
that refer to things and actions that interest the child. The following
parallel talk sequence, for example, was used with Jean to facilitate
acquisition of "ball" and "book."

> *Jean picks up a ball.*
> Language interventionist: "Ball."
> *Jean rolls the ball.*
> Language interventionist: "Go, ball."
> *Jean picks up a book.*
> Language interventionist: "It's a book."

EXPANSIONS AND RECASTS.   Expansions and recasts "fill in the missing
parts" in the child's utterances while retaining the child's meaning.
Recasts are a specialized form of expansions, involving a change in
mood or voice. **Expansions** provide a more mature or more correct
version of the child's utterance while retaining word order. Expansions and recasts are often used to facilitate a toddler's syntactic development, but are also valuable techniques to facilitate aspects of
meaning and phonology. The following is an example of an expansion used with Jennifer to facilitate acquisition of two-word sentences.

> *Jennifer opens a book.*
> Jennifer: "Book."
> Language interventionist: "Book open." (expansion)
> *Jennifer points to a ball.*
> Jennifer: "Ball."
> Language interventionist: "It's a ball." (expansion)
> *Jennifer picks up the book and opens it.*
> Jennifer: "Book."
> Language interventionist: "Is the book open?" (recast)
> Jennifer: "Yes."

EXPATIATIONS.   **Expatiations** are similar to expansions, except that
new information is added. The following is an example of an expati-
ation used with Thomas to facilitate acquisition of [b] in the beginning of words.

> *Thomas points to a picture of a bee.*
> Thomas: "ee."
> Language interventionist: "Bee is buzzing."
> Thomas: "ee."
> Language interventionist: "Bees like honey."
> Thomas: "Bee."

BUILD-UPS AND BREAKDOWNS.   Build-ups and breakdowns expand and reduce sentences into their parts. The following is an example of a build-up and breakdown sequence that was used with Thomas to facilitate acquisition of the form and content for the word "ball."

Thomas rolls a ball.
Thomas: "Ball."
Language interventionist: "The ball is rolling." (expansion)
Thomas smiles.
Language interventionist: "Ball. Rolling." (breakdown)
Thomas laughs.
Language interventionist: "Ball is rolling." (expansion)

VERTICAL STRUCTURING.   **Vertical structuring** is designed to facilitate the acquisition of multi-word utterances. Within vertical structuring, the child says a word, which is followed by a contingent question by the language interventionist (Scollon, 1976). The result is that the child and adult create a multi-word sentence over several turns in conversation. The following is an example of vertical structuring that was used with Jennifer to facilitate the two-word sentence "Bike out."

> Vertical structuring is following single-word child utterance with contingent questions to eventually create a multi-word sentence.

Jennifer rides a tricycle to the door and then looks at the language interventionist.
Jennifer: "Bike."
Language interventionist: "Where?" (contingent question)
Jennifer: "Out."
Language interventionist: "Bike out." (expansion)
Jennifer: "Out."
Language interventionist: "Bike out."
Jennifer: "Bike out."

An important issue in early language intervention concerns who should be the agents of language change. Some language interventionists believe their major role on the early intervention team is to train parents and other team members to implement language intervention techniques. For example, a language interventionist might explain to a parent about recasts and then model this technique with the parent's child.

As discussed in Chapters 5 and 8, the philosophical underpinnings of a consultative approach to language intervention are similar to those for inclusion. Primarily, training a variety of persons to perform intervention techniques better reflects the nature of the language acquisition process, which typically occurs across a range of settings and persons. More practically, many persons on the early intervention team (especially parents) may have more opportunities than the language interventionist to interact with the child. Training

The use of parents and other early intervention team members is a way to increase interventionists without increasing the intervention budget.

them to perform simple intervention techniques greatly extends the number of treatment opportunities that the child receives.

Financial reasons may also motivate a language interventionist to assume a consultative role on an early intervention team. As the number of children requesting language services swells, early intervention teams are increasingly forced to become ever more efficient and cost sensitive. The use of parents and other early intervention team members (including aides) often represents an important way to "stretch" early intervention budgets.

The primary philosophical argument against consultative conception of the language interventionist's role is that other team members are not always well qualified to carry out the intervention techniques. This argument may not present itself within the horizontal approach, where the goal is to stimulate all areas of language acquisition simultaneously. However, vertical approaches require whoever is performing intervention techniques to identify those aspects of content, form, and use they are attempting to facilitate. Not all parents, aides, and other members of the early intervention team are sufficiently interested in or possess the abilities to carry out such treatments.

Most language interventionists take a middle ground between that of a consultative role and that of sole agent of language change. Language interventionists typically do not think of language as "their territory," and so view the training of parents and others as an important component of inclusion. For example, language intervention for Thomas, Jean, and Jennifer included training the parents and other team members. Training was achieved using a combination of written materials, in-services, and modeling. Additionally, the language interventionists provided some direct language intervention.

SUMMARY

When infants and toddlers experience language disorders that place them at risk for future educational and social failure, the goal of intervention is to act proactively before the child's language problem has negative consequences. Early language intervention is provided by a team that includes the child's parents and at least one professional whose educational training is in the study of language and its disorders. Locations where language intervention may occur include child care centers, family day care settings, early intervention programs, and the child's home. Language interventionists who work with infants and toddlers in any setting need to be knowledgeable about medical issues and safety precautions as well as having expertise in speech and language development, because many young children who need early intervention have concomitant medical and genetic disorders.

Language acquisition depends on neurological readiness in conjunction with experiences from the environment. The general purpose of language intervention is to maximize a child's opportunities to learn from his environment. This purpose is achieved by providing facilitation and support in natural environments, maintaining the parents' involvement in all decision making, developing language goals to guide intervention, and implementing facilitative techniques that maximize the effectiveness of the child's language learning environment.

REFERENCES

Administration on Developmental Disabilities. (1988). *Mapping the future for children with special needs: P. L. 99-457.* Iowa City, IA: University of Iowa Press.

Aram, D., Ekelman, B., & Nation, J. (1984). Preschoolers with language disorders: Ten years later. *Journal of Speech and Hearing Research, 27,* 232–244.

Bach-y-Rita, P. (1990). Brain plasticity as a basis for recovery of function in humans. *Neuropsychologica, 28,* 547–554.

Bailey, D., & Simonsson, R. (1985). *Family needs survey.* Chapel Hill: The University of North Carolina at Chapel Hill.

Batshaw, M. (1991). *Your child has a disability: A complete sourcebook of daily and medical care.* Boston: Little, Brown.

Bernbaum, J., & Hoffman-Williamson, M. (1991). *Primary care of the preterm infant.* Philadelphia: Mosby Year Book.

Bleile, K. (1993). Children with long-term tracheostomies. In K. Bleile (Ed.), *The care of children with long-term tracheostomies* (pp. 3–19). San Diego: Singular Publishing Group.

Bleile, K. (1995). *Manual of articulation and phonological disorders.* San Diego: Singular Press.

Bleile, K., & Fey, M. (1993). Issues and methods in the care of infants and toddlers. Annual convention of the American Speech-language-hearing Association, Anaheim, CA, November.

Bleile, K., & Miller, S. (1994). Toddlers with medical needs. In J. Bernthal & N. Bankson (Eds.), *Child phonology: Characteristics, assessment, and intervention with special populations* (pp. 81–109). New York: Thieme.

Bleile K., Stark R., & Silverman McGowan, J. (1993). Evidence for the relationship between babbling and later speech development. *Clinical Linguistics and Phonetics, 7,* 319–337.

Bricker, P., Bailey, E., & Bruder, M. (1984). The efficacy of early intervention and the handicapped infant: A wise or wasted resource? In M. Wolraich & D. Routh (Eds.), *Advances in developmental and behavioral pediatrics* (pp. 373–423). Greenwich, CT: JAI Press.

Bruner, J. (1983). *Child's Talk: Learning to use language.* New York: Norton.

Bzoch, K., & League, R. (1991). *Receptive-expressive emergent language test* (2nd ed.). Austin, TX: Pro-Ed.

Capute, A., & Accardo, P. (1978). Linguistic and auditory milestones during the first two years of life: A language inventory for the practitioner. *Clinical Pediatrics, 17,* 847–853.

Capute, A., Palmer, F., Shapiro, B., Wachtel, R., Schmidt, S., & Ross, A. (1986). Clinical Linguistic and Auditory Milestone Scale: Prediction of cognition in infancy. *Developmental Medicine and Child Neurology, 28,* 762–771.

Charney, E. (1992). Neural tube defects: Spina bifida and myelomeningocele. In M. Batshaw & Y. Perret (Eds.), *Children with disabilities: A medical primer* (pp. 471–488). Baltimore: Paul H. Brookes.

Coplan, J. (1993). *Early language milestone scale.* Austin, TX: Pro-Ed.

Crowe Hall, B. (1991). Attitudes of fourth and sixth graders toward peers with mild articulation disorders. *Language, Speech, and Hearing Services in Schools, 22,* 334–349.

Damasio, A. (1990). Category-related recognition defects as a clue to neural substrates of knowledge. *Trends in Neuroscience, 13,* 95–98.

Dunst, C., Trivette, C., & Deal, A. (1988). *Enabling and empowering families: Princi-*

ples and guidelines for practice. Cambridge, MA: Brookline Books.

Fenson, L., Dale, P., Reznick, J., Thal, D., Bates, E., Hartung, J., Pethick, S., Reilly, J. (1993). *MacArthur communicative development inventories.* San Diego: Singular Publishing Group.

Ferguson, C., & Farwell, C. (1975). Words and sounds in early language acquisition: English initial consonants in the first fifty words. *Language, 51,* 419–439.

Fey, M. (1986). *Language intervention with young children.* San Diego: College Hill.

Fridy, J., & Lemanek, K. (1993). Developmental and behavioral issues. In K. Bleile (Ed.), *The care of children with long-term tracheostomies* (pp. 141–166). San Diego: Singular Publishing Group,

Greenspan, S. (1985). *First feelings: Milestones in the emotional development of your child from birth to age 4.* New York: Viking Press.

Greenspan, S. (1992). *Infancy and early childhood: The practice of clinical assessment and intervention with emotional and developmental challenges.* Madison, CT: International Universities Press.

Hall, P., & Tomblin, B. (1978). A follow-up study of children with articulation and language disorders. *Journal of Speech and Hearing Disorders, 43,* 227–241.

Handler, S. (1993). Surgical intervention of the tracheostomy. In K. Bleile (Ed.), *The care of children with long-term tracheostomies* (pp. 23–40). San Diego: Singular Publishing Group.

Hart, B. (1985). Naturalistic language training techniques. In S. Warren & A. Rogers-Warren (Eds.), *Training functional language* (pp. 63–88). Baltimore: University Park Press.

Hedrick, D., Prather, E., & Tobin, A. (1984). *Sequenced inventory of communication development.* Seattle: University of Washington Press.

Hock-Long, L., Trachtenberg, S., & Vorters, D. (1993). The social worker's role with the family. In K. Bleile (Ed.), *The care of children with long-term tracheostomies* (pp. 203–222). San Diego, CA: Singular Publishing Group.

Infant Health and Development Program. (1990). A multisite, randomized trial. *Journal of the American Medical Association, 263,* 3035–3042.

Jusczyk, P. (1992). Developing phonological categories from the speech signal. In C. Ferguson, L. Menn, & C. Stoel-Gammon (Eds.), *Phonological development: Models, research, implications* (pp. 17–64). Timonium, MD: York Press.

Locke, J. (1983). *Phonological acquisition and change.* New York: Academic Press.

Locke, J. (1988). The sound shape of early lexical representations. In M. Smith and J. Locke (Eds.), *The emergent lexicon: The child's development of a linguistic vocabulary* (pp. 3–22). New York: Academic Press.

Locke, J., & Pearson, D. (1992). Vocal learning and the emergence of phonological capacity: A neurobiological approach. In C. Ferguson, L. Menn, & C. Stoel-Gammon (Eds.), *Phonological development: Models, research, implications* (pp. 91–130). Timonium, MD: York Press.

MacDonald, J. (1989). *Becoming partners with children: From play to conversation.* San Antonio: Special Press.

MacDonald, J., & Carroll, J. (1992). A social partnership model for assessing early communication development: An intervention model for preconversational children. *Language, Speech, and Hearing Services in the School, 23,* 113–124.

Mantovani, J., & Powers, J. (1991). Brain injury in premature infants: Patterns on cranial ultrasound, their relationship to outcome, and the role of developmental intervention in the NICU. *Infants and Young Children, 4,* 20–32.

McGongigel, M., Kaufmann, R., & Johnson, B. (Eds.) (1991). *National Early Childhood Technical Assistance System (NEC-TAS): Guidelines and recommended practices for the individualized family service plan (2nd ed.).* Chapel Hill, NC: National Early Childhood Technical Assistance System.

Metz, S. (1993). Medical management of the ventilator. In K. Bleile (Ed.), *The care of children with long-term tracheostomies* (pp. 41–55). San Diego: Singular Publishing Group.

Nelson, K. E. (1989). Strategies for first language teaching. In M. Rice & R. Schiefelbusch (Eds.), *The teachability of language* (pp. 263–310). Baltimore: Paul H. Brookes.

Ojemann, J. (1991). Cortical organization of language. *Journal of Neuroscience, 11,* 2281–2287.

Paul, R. (1991). Profiles of toddlers with slow expressive language. *Topics in Language Disorders, 11,* 1–13.

Paul, R. (1995). *Language disorders from infancy through adolescence: Assessment and intervention.* Philadelphia: Mosby Year Book.

Ramey, C., & Campbell, F. (1984). Preventive education for high-risk children: Cognitive consequences of the Caroline Abecedarian Project. *American Journal of Mental Deficiency, 88,* 515.

Saint Christopher's Hospital for Children. (1982). An assessment tool: The infant scales of communicative intent. *Update Pediatrics, 7,* 1–5.

Scollon, R. (1976). *Conversations with a one year old: A case study of the developmental foundation of syntax.* Honolulu: The University Press of Hawaii.

Silverman, F., & Paulus, P. (1989). Peer relations to teenagers who substitute /w/ for /r/. *Language, Speech, and Hearing Services in Schools, 20,* 219–221.

Snow, C., & Goldfield, B. (1983). Turn the page please: Situation-specific language acquisition. *Journal of Child Language, 10,* 551–569.

Trout, M., & Foley, G. (1989). Working with families of handicapped infants and toddlers. *Topics in Language Disorders, 10,* 57–67.

Vihman, M., & Miller, R. (1988). Words and babble at the threshold of language acquisition. In M. Smith and J. Locke (Eds.), *The emergent lexicon: The child's development of a linguistic vocabulary* (pp. 151–184). New York: Academic Press.

Wallace, S. (1990). Rise of seizures (Annotation). *Developmental Medicine and Child Neurology, 32,* 645–649.

Warren, S., & Bambara, L. (1989). An experimental analysis of milieu language intervention: Teaching the action-object form. *Journal of Speech and Hearing Disorders, 54,* 448–461.

Warren, S., & Kaiser, A. (1988). Research in early language intervention. In S. Odom & M. Karnes (Eds.), *Early intervention for infants and children with handicaps: An empirical base* (pp. 89–108). Baltimore: Paul H. Brookes.

White, K., Mastrapierl, M., & Casto, G. (1984). An analysis of special education early childhood projects approved by the joint dissemination review panel. *Journal of the Division of Early Childhood, 9,* 11.

Wilcox, M. (1989). Delivering communication-based services to infants, mothers, and their families: Approaches and models. *Topics in Language Disorders, 10,* 68–79.

Wilcox, M., Kouri, T., & Caswell, S. (1991). Early language intervention: A comparison of classroom and individual treatment. *American Journal of Speech-Language Pathology, 1,* 49–62.

Yarrow, L., Rubenstein, J., & Pedersen, F. (1975). *Infant and environment: Early cognitive and motivational development.* Washington, DC: Hemisphere.

Yoder, P., Warren, S., Kim, K., & Gazdag, G. (1994). Facilitating prelinguistic communication skills in young children with developmental delay II: Systematic replication and extension. *Journal of Speech and Hearing Research, 37,* 841–851.

Zimmerman, I., Steiner, V., & Pond, R. (1992). *Preschool Language Scale-3.* San Antonio, TX: The Psychological Corporation.

APPENDIX: INFECTION CONTROL GUIDELINES

Although the topic of colds and hand washing may seem mundane, young children have relatively weak immunological systems, and diseases carried by staff members are a primarily source of infection to children receiving early intervention services. The language interventionist should remain at home during illnesses such as colds and flu. Regardless of the number of sick days available, staff shortages, or other seemingly good reasons, the staff member who comes to work with an infection does children a great disservice. It is far better for a child with medical needs to miss a few treatment sessions because a language interventionist is ill than for the children to be exposed to infection.

Staff members who are well can still spread infection from a sick child to the other children with whom the language interventionist comes in contact. The following basic infection-control guidelines greatly reduce the chance that the language interventionist will carry disease from child to child.

Hand Washing

Most infections in early intervention centers and hospitals are carried from child to child by staff members. The most effective means to reduce spread of infection is through careful washing after intervening with each child. Other times when washing should be performed are when coming on or off duty, when the hands are dirty, after toilet use, after blowing or wiping one's nose, after handling soiled child secretions, and on completion of duty. To wash, the speech-language language interventionist wets the hands and forearms, applies soap, and washes all areas of the hands and forearms for 1 to 2 minutes, being careful to wash nailbeds and between fingers. Afterwards, the soap is rinsed from the hands and forearms thoroughly. A new paper towel is used to turn off the water faucet, and then the paper towel is discarded.

Toy Washing

Toys are another source of infection, because young children often place toys in their mouth or may place their finger in their mouth or nose after playing with an infected toy. Gloves are worn to clean possibly infected toys. Each toy is wiped down with warm, soapy water, and then rinsed. Next, the language interventionist sprays or wipes each toy with a disinfectant such as 1:10 solution of household bleach. The toy is then rinsed well and air dried for 10 minutes.

CHAPTER 10

Language Intervention in the Inclusive Preschool

Linda McCormick

The 1986 amendment to the Individuals with Disabilities Education Act (IDEA) (Public Law 99-457) brought about substantial changes in early childhood special education. Preschool children with disabilities are now eligible for the full range of protections and benefits that are available to school-age students, including the right to be educated in the general education environment (with whatever supports they need). The shift toward inclusive early education programs is apparent in two areas: (1) recognition of the importance of social competence, self-esteem, friendships, and communication skills as priority outcomes at the preschool level, and (2) new roles for early childhood special educators as co-teachers, support personnel, and consultants.

The implicit assumptions underlying separate services for young children with disabilities were that their disabilities are such that (1) they need very different, intensive, and specialized services that can only be provided in separate settings, and (2) they are unlikely to benefit from the experiences provided to their peers in general early education settings. There is now a substantial research base countering these assumptions (e.g., Peck, Odom, & Bricker, 1993; Salisbury & Smith, 1993; Strain, 1990). When young children with disabilities are provided with the supports they need (i.e., integrated special services, environmental and curricular adaptations, individualized methods and materials), they thrive in inclusive settings.

> Young children with disabilities thrive in inclusive settings when they have needed supports.

Montgomery's (1995) observations (presented on p. 337) highlight some of the benefits that inclusive classrooms provide to children with disabilities. Daily interactions with peer models and exposure to a greater variety of experiences provide children with disabilities with continuous opportunities to observe, learn, and practice age-appropriate social, communication, and cognitive skills. Language, cognitive, and motor-skill development outcomes for children with disabilities in inclusive programs are equal to and, in many cases, surpass those of peers in separate special education classes (Strain, 1990). They also demonstrate higher levels of social play and more appropriate social interactions than peers with disabilities in separate settings (Demchak & Drinkwater, 1992; Fewell & Oelwein, 1990; Lamorey & Bricker, 1993). Also, they are more likely to initiate interactions with peers, and their play skills are decidedly more advanced than peers in separate settings.

> Developmental outcomes for children in inclusive programs are equal to or better than those of peers in separate education programs.

Finally, another important benefit of the decision to place a child in an inclusive program is the increased probability for inclusion as the child gets older (Miller, Strain, McKinley, Heckathorn, & Miller, 1993). Children of matched demographics and developmental levels who were placed in inclusive preschool programs were significantly more likely to be in inclusive elementary classes several years later than were their peers who started off in segregated preschool programs.

> Whether inclusion is successful depends on the available supports, not the severity or pervasiveness of the child's disability.

Whether inclusion is successful depends on the available resources, not the severity or persuasiveness of the child's disability: There is no evidence that children with certain conditions or levels of disability are better candidates for inclusion than others. The one qualifier attached to the assertion that inclusion seems to benefit *all* young children is that there must be planning, staff training, and, most importantly, adequate supports.

Inclusive programs also have benefits for children *without* disabilities. They continue to achieve positive developmental outcomes comparable to those achieved in programs that do not include children with disabilities, *and* they demonstrate greater understanding of and sensitivity to individual differences (Odom & McEvoy, 1988; Strain, 1990). Children in inclusive classrooms demonstrate patience,

---

INCLUSION, OBSERVATION, OUTCOME

Judith Montgomery

The interaction among children is so powerful that I often feel we adults intrude when we try to treat communication disorders. How presumptuous to assume that children would want to imitate *us* when it is clear that they are imitating other children around them all the time! I like the idea of all children learning together to the extent to which each is capable, and with the support that each one needs. I have long been interested in the concept of inclusion—and in educating children, and in the need to collect treatment outcome data. Recently, I discovered a way to combine all three interests.

Inclusion uses that strong natural support in the environment. Inclusion says that not everyone learns the same way. But children do indeed learn. And when we can measure that learning, we will have another form of treatment outcome.

Over a period of time, I observed a class that uses an inclusion model. The class consisted of 14 2- to 4-year-old children. Seven of them had diagnoses of autism, pervasive developmental delay, cerebral palsy, unknown neurological dysfunction, developmental disability, and moderate-to-severe mental retardation. The descriptive terms used in the children's evaluations were staggering; 5 years ago all of these children would have been placed in self-contained classrooms.

Instead, these seven children were placed in a typical preschool with seven children without disabilities. The former group received the support services they needed in the classroom, including speech and language treatment and physical and occupational therapy several times per week.

After the children had experienced 4 months of a daily, typical preschool curriculum, I observed the following actions of the seven students with disabilities:

- They all learned where to hang their coats.
- They all could identify their own "bucket" for storing materials to take home each day.
- Four of the children learned to climb the fence in the backyard.
- Two learned to "pump" on the swings.
- All of them learned to fingerpaint; five preferred the painting easel.
- All of them knew where the painting shirts were kept and three of them told on their peers if they forgot to put them on before beginning to paint.
- All of the children played in the playhouse—sometimes with peers, but just as often by themselves, frequently redoing an action they saw someone doing earlier.
- Six learned to sit on the rug square with their own name on it. (One waited until everyone else sat down and then crawled over to hers.)
- All seven children loved singing and watching their peers sing in the big circle.
- All learned to play at the water table, the bean table, and the flour table.
- Every child, with or without disabilities, was reminded at least once a week not to drink the water on the water table.
- Three of the children with disabilities liked to wear dress-up clothes and walk around laughing.
- All of the children "wrote" messages to each other and two of them learned to "deliver" them to the intended child's "mailbox."
- Three of the children with disabilities learned to play "gas up the cars" in the play yard.
- Four of them imitated unusual and fun words heard in the stories that were read in class.
- One child with disabilities learned to clean up the inside toy area.
- No one learned how to clean up the outside toy area!
- Everyone loved art projects (and had to carry one home every time).
- Everyone held hands to go outside to play or line up for the bus.

There were other observations that space precludes listing, but, clearly, these are fine examples of functionally based outcomes or skills that have made a significant difference in the lives of these children and their families. No formal tests were used. Children were not pulled out to check if they were learning new skills.

The children were simply observed. So, next time you wonder if our intervention techniques are effective and if you can measure their outcome reliably, consider just watching and recording what is going on in a typical situation for that person. It works.

From Asha, April 1995

compassion, and acceptance of others—the attitudes and values that will enable them to be helpful and effective friends, neighbors, and coworkers with one another when they become adults.

This chapter will describe intervention and instructional strategies for young children with language and communication impairments in inclusive early education settings. These strategies are compatible with best practices in both early childhood special education (ECSE) *and* general early childhood education (ECE). Language and communication difficulties may be the child's only disability or they may be secondary to another disability; for example, learning disabilities, attention disorders, orthopedic impairments, multiple disabilities, hearing impairments, visual impairments, serious emotional disturbance, autism, mental retardation, or traumatic brain injury.

Strategies To Encourage Language and Communication

Young children with disabilities are similar to their peers in that they learn from repeated and sustained interactions with objects, events, and persons in their environment. However, they are also different from their peers in that they often (1) fail to generalize, (2) are less goal oriented, (3) have a shorter attention span, (4) show less persistence, (5) experience difficulties expressing themselves, and (6) lack social competence. Learning certainly occurs, but for children with disabilities it does not occur incidentally: It requires planning and use of special instructional strategies. They are likely to need more prompts, more direct instruction, and more opportunities for practice than their typical peers. Although very few experiences in inclusive early childhood programs are *specifically* designed for the purpose of teaching language, the majority of activities in these settings function that way in that they stimulate and encourage language naturally.

Arranging learning experiences along a continuum according to degree of intrusiveness is useful when deciding which instructional approaches to try first. The less intrusive instructional strategies are, the higher preference they should be given. The ultimate goal is for planned intervention strategies to "blend in" so well in the classroom that they are virtually indistinguishable from ongoing activities. Thus, planned intervention strategies that are very similar to naturally occurring learning experiences are likely to be the least intrusive. Least intrusive procedures have other advantages. Their similarity to naturally occurring experiences generally translates to providing as few prompts as possible and using natural prompts (e.g., a gestures, pictures). Thus, fading prompts is much easier once the child demonstrates the desired response. A second advantage is that least intrusive procedures are easier to implement across different settings.

For children with disabilities, learning does not occur incidentally.

Arrange the Environment

Intervention strategies that rely on environmental structuring are preferred strategies because they are near the "least intrusive" end of the intrusive-unintrusive continuum. Environmental structuring to facilitate engagement and interaction is an important procedure in the best practices of both ECE and ECSE (Bredekamp & Rosegrant, 1992; DEC recommended practices, 1993). Specifically, both fields advocate

- selecting materials that are conducive to social play and cooperation in order to increase peer interactions;
- selecting and using materials and activities that are preferred by the children to increase the likelihood that children will engage with the materials and tasks;
- assisting children in the development of interactive play themes based on their interests;
- limiting and clearly defining choices of activities and materials to help children select and engage in appropriate classroom activities;
- staying in close proximity to children in order to take advantage of opportunities to assist engagement and peer interactions; and
- designing activities and play areas that accommodate a small group of children so that there is the peer proximity conducive to social and play interactions.

There are two reasons for using classroom routines and activities to teach language and communication skills (Bricker & Cripe, 1992; Fey, 1986; Roberts, Bailey, & Nychka, 1991). One reason is the substantial data suggesting that language and communication skills learned in individual therapy sessions often fail to generalize to everyday environments (e.g., Leonard, 1981; Rogers-Warren & Warren, 1984; Warren & Kaiser, 1986). A few hours of speech and language therapy per week and/or teaching only during specific classroom language activities generally are not sufficient to achieve most communication objectives for preschoolers experiencing language and communication difficulties. The second reason is that it is intuitively logical (and there are now substantial data to support this logic) to use the many naturally occurring communication opportunities as a context for teaching language and communication skills (Kaiser, Ostrosky, & Alpert, 1993).

Many environments are arranged so that children have little need to use language. Materials, toys, activities, drinking water, and foods (whatever they want or need) are *too* available. They have no reason to use language because the can easily "help themselves" to whatever they want or have it routinely provided by the adults in the environment. Attention to arranging the environment to increase opportunities for language and communication may be the single most essential

ECSE and ECE both advocate environmental structuring to facilitate engagement and interaction.

Unfortunately, many environments are arranged so that children have no need to use language to be successful.

element of language intervention in inclusive preschool programs. Assuming that children attend to, learn, and talk about what interests *them,* not what interests the adults in the environment, or necessarily what interests their peers, the goal is to arrange the environment so that there are more reasons to initiate communicative behavior. Planning focuses on identifying circumstances that give rise to use of language and positive social interactions and arranging to have these circumstances occur more frequently (Haring, Neetz, Lovinger, Peck, & Semmel, 1987; Hemmeter & Kaiser, 1990; Ostrosky & Kaiser, 1991).

Ostrosky and Kaiser (1991) have outlined seven environmental arrangement strategies to increase the number of opportunities to elicit communication. Initially the adult must notice what the child is interested in, establish joint attention to the focus of attention, and encourage the child to attempt communication. Thus, *in addition to the environmental arrangement strategies,* the teacher or another adult provides nonverbal cues and prompts (e.g., the teacher may shrug her shoulders, raise her eyebrows, and tilt her head expectantly). Over time these are faded so that children are responding to the naturally occurring communication opportunities that are provided by the environmental arrangement strategies.

As suggested by Ostrosky and Kaiser (1991), the seven strategies are (1) making interesting objects, materials, and activities available; (2) placing desired objects out of reach or blocking access to objects and activities; (3) providing materials that require assistance to operate; (4) offering materials out of context; (5) providing inadequate portions; (6) failing to provide sufficient materials; and (7) doing something to elicit protest.

1. Make interesting objects, materials, and activities available. Because young children are more likely to initiate communication about things that interest them, increasing the number of interesting objects, materials, and activities in the environment has a high probability of increasing language use *and* increasing the number of teaching opportunities for adults. The first task is to generate a list of attractive and appealing objects, materials, and activities. The teacher and/or the language interventionist determines the children's object and activity preferences by noting their attention focus and interviewing family members and other adults. This analysis of children's attention focus often points up definite sensory preferences—for example, auditory feedback, visual stimulation, tactile stimulations. Many children, particularly those with severe disabilities, are most interested in response-contingent materials (e.g., a battery-operated bear that marches and plays music when a switch is activated). As an aside, because the subset of materials and activities that are of interest to children with disabilities may be very small, it is a good idea to rotate toys on a regular basis to help maintain children's interest.

Analysis of children's attention focus often points up definite sensory preferences.

Although not interesting themselves, some items are important because they give the child access to interesting activities. For example, a communication board may not be particularly interesting, but it makes it possible for the child to (1) request art materials and preferred centers, and (2) answer calendar and weather questions during morning circle—these interest him very much. A tape recorder with a loop tape that plays the repeatable refrain ("ee-i'-ee-'i-o) lets the child join singing of "Old MacDonald" at circle time.

2. Place desired objects out of reach or block access to objects and activities. The number and variety of circumstances in which requesting is necessary in order to receive desired objects and activities can be multiplied by simply placing objects (toys, materials, games, foods) that the child finds desirable, attractive, and interesting on a shelf out of reach (but within view), or in clear plastic bins, and restricting access to high-interest activities. For example, if riding is a child's favorite outdoor activity, there is a high probability that placing a gate at the entry to the outside area where wheel toys are parked will increase the rate of requests.

3. Provide materials that are difficult to operate. Providing toys that the child cannot activate without assistance also encourages requesting. A jack-in-the-box with a wind-up, an unopened bottle of bubbles, a mechanical toy with a hard-to-turn switch, and a swing are examples of toys and play equipment for which the child may need some assistance. The idea, of course, is for the child to recognize the need for help and ask for it. If the child does not request assistance, a verbal or nonverbal prompt (e.g., "What do you want?" or "Say 'help'.") is provided.

> Toys which the child cannot access without assistance prompt requests for help.

4. Offer objects or materials out of context. Creating silly situations by offering objects or materials out of context has a high probability of eliciting a vocalization, comment, or protest. Examples include attempting to put another child's (or an adult's) sweater on the child, or hanging a picture upside down. The idea is to create an absurd situation that violates the child's expectations.

5. Provide inadequate portions of needed or desired objects or materials. Giving the child only a small portion of what is needed or desired is another way to elicit a protest and/or a request. The adult controls the amount provided so that the child has some, but not all, that he wants or needs. For example, during snack time, small servings of juice, fruit, and crackers are provided with the understanding that more is available upon request. Peer modeling often comes about as a bonus with this strategy and the next—for example, a peer may say "Tell Miss Joy you need more" or even "Say 'more juice'."

6. Fail to provide needed objects or materials. Intentionally "forgetting" to give the child the materials necessary or desired for a favorite activity is similar to the above. However, with this strategy, no portion of the needed materials—or none of the needed objects— is provided. For example, the adult may "forget" to put out any crayons, paste, or scissors for an art activity or "mistakenly" provide a nonfunctional or inappropriate item (e.g., an empty paste container). This strategy requires children to problem-solve and indicate what is wrong or missing. The missing materials are cues for communicating that something is wrong or missing.

    7. *Do something that the child does not like.* Doing something that the child does not want or providing an item that she does not like creates an opportunity to prompt the child to say "No thank you" or "Don't do it that way." For example, when the child points to the top shelf she is offered the container of Tinkertoys rather than the container with magnets and is prompted to say "No, I want magnets." Like the other strategies, this should be carried out in a warm, engaging manner so as not to be frustrating to the child. The adult must be extremely sensitive to prevent this strategy from becoming intrusive to the point that the activity is no longer creative and spontaneous. The slightest indication that this strategy is detracting from the activity or in any way frustrating the child should be a signal to immediately terminate it.

    A study by Kaiser, Ostrosky, and Alpert (1993) offers encouraging evidence that training teachers to use the seven environmental arrangement strategies (together with milieu teaching techniques, which are described below) also enhances the use of augmented communication systems (manual signing or a communication board) by preschool children with disabilities. After instruction on the strategies, the teachers increased the frequency and variety of strategies they used, generalized their use of the procedures to other children and other settings, and maintained their use over time. There were associated increases in total child-communicative responses and in spontaneous use of targeted signs.

    There are two caveats concerning all of these environmental arrangement strategies that need to be understood before they are used. One caveat has to do with the possibility of frustrating the child; the other has to do with fostering dependence. Adults must know and be sensitive to the child's tolerance for frustration. If there is any indication that the child is feeling frustrated, the request for communication should be immediately withdrawn (and the child should be given the desired item or provided access to the desired activity). The point is to encourage language and communication, *not* to upset and frustrate the child with too many communication demands. The concern expressed by many adults—that arranging the environment so that the child must request desired objects and activities will foster dependency—is a valid concern. (Adults are often especially concerned about not fostering dependency where children with disabilities are concerned.) The issue reduces to a matter of balancing language/communication objectives with dependency goals. This environmental arrangement strategy should not be used unless

Stop the procedure if denying the child access seems to frustrate the child.

language/communication objectives take precedence over independence objectives.

Arrange Activities and Routines

Routines help children learn sequences of appropriate behaviors because they learn to anticipate what will happen next and "fill in the slots." A routine is a sequence of interactive events that is repeated frequently and always in exactly the same way. Examples of routines include games (e.g., peekaboo); rhymes, jokes, and songs (e.g., "When you're happy and you know it . . . "); social amenities and courtesies (e.g., "please," "excuse me"); daily caregiving activities (e.g., toileting, dressing, bathing); storytelling; and activity formats (e.g., morning circle, show and tell, snack preparation, clean up). Over the past decade there has been a great deal of support for using routines to help children learn sequences of appropriate behaviors, including language and communication skills (e.g., Hunt, Goetz, Alwell, & Sailor, 1986; Hunt & Goetz, 1988; McCormick, 1990).

As discussed in Chapter 8, instruction in the context of routines relies on a prompting procedure that is also used in milieu teaching (described in a following section)—time delay. The adult begins the routine and then prevents continuation at a point of maximum motivation in the sequence. When a well-established routine is interrupted (particularly when the interruption is at a point where there is maximum anticipation of a positive next substep) there is a high probability that the child will either produce the behavior that is expected at the point of interruption or indicate a desire for the routine to continue. Relying on the child's need and desire to move on to the next step and to finish the routine, the adult simply waits at the point of interruption.

Use of routines as a context for facilitating and supporting language and communication was also discussed in Chapter 8.

In most environments there is no need to establish new routines to teach language. There are already numerous routines in place throughout the day. All that is necessary is to take advantage of the opportunities for language teaching that existing routines present. Following are the steps to follow in planning for using routines to promote development and use of language and communication skills:

1. Select a routine that the child enjoys. Almost any routine can be used, but some are better than others. The best routines are those that involve a variety of objects and materials that the child finds attractive, interesting, and desirable and that require many repeated actions. Once instruction within the context of one routine is under way, other routines can be selected and used.

2. List the specific steps in the routine and the language skills and/or concepts that can be elicited at each step. It is possible to teach new language forms and functions *and* provide opportunities to practice and thus generalize forms and functions learned in other contexts. For example, a simple toothbrushing routine provides an excellent opportunity for teaching new vocabulary (e.g., *toothbrush, toothpaste, water, spit, drink, up, down,* etc.) and requesting. When planning, it can be helpful to have a script of the routine. Figure 10.1 shows a sample script for snack preparation.

   3. Decide when and how the routine will be interrupted. The possibilities for interrupting a routine are numerous (Halle, Alpert,

FIGURE 10.1   Sample script for snack preparation

		Time __10:30__
		Location __Snack Area__
Routine __Snack Preparation__		Materials __Napkins, Cups, Food__
Sequence of Events	**What You Might Say**	**What Child(ren) Might Say**
Announce snack time.	"It's time to eat! What do we need to do?"	"Wash hands."
Send children two or three at a time to wash hands.	" _____ and _____ go first to wash hands. Who is sitting next to _____ ?" "Who is sitting next to _____ ?" "Who will go when they return?"	" _____ ." " _____ ." " _____ and _____ ."
Remind children of designated leaders for snack time. Rehearse leader duties.	"Who are our hosts and hostesses today?" "What do they do first?" "Then what?" "Then what?"	" _____ , _____ and _____ ." "Get out napkins and cups and food." "Put napkins and cups on the table." "Put apples on the plate."
By the end of leader duty rehearsal, all have returned from washing hands and all go to chairs at the snack table. Host/hostess prepares and distributes napkins and places crackers on a plate. When child asks, the apples are passed and/or the juice is poured when asked for.	"We're ready now. Why aren't you eating?"	"Want apple." "No food." "Pour juice." "No juice." "Thank you."

Developed by L. McCormick, 1990.

& Anderson, 1984). These procedures, described in the environmental arrangements section, include:

- withholding or delaying provision of expected objects or actions;
- providing an incomplete set of materials; and
- making "silly" mistakes.

4. *Decide how the desired responses will be prompted if time delay alone does not elicit the targeted behaviors.* Possibilities include modeling the desired response (e.g., "Say *I need a napkin*") and providing a verbal direction (e.g., "Can you tell me what's wrong?").

A variation of the interrupted routine, the interrupted chain strategy, is particularly effective with students with severe disabilities (e.g., Hunt & Goetz, 1988). A behavior or response chain is a sequence of behaviors that requires at least three steps for completion. The interrupted behavior chain strategy is slightly different from the use of routines. In contrast to the routines strategy, where the routine is interrupted or the expectations of the routine are violated in order to elicit child communication efforts, in the interrupted chain strategy a specific instructional trial is inserted into the middle of the sequence.

An example from a study by Hunt, Goetz, Alwell, and Sailor (1986) demonstrates application of the interrupted chain strategy. It was used with Nate, a 6-year-old nonverbal student with severe mental retardation. Prior to the intervention, when Nate wanted a hug, he walked up to the teacher or other familiar adult and reached out, putting his arms around the adult's neck or pushing his head against the adult's body. When he wanted help with dressing or to go outside, Nate pulled at the nearest adult. He communicated opposition by crying, pushing objects away, opening or closing his eyes, or physically leaving the situation.

The purpose of the intervention was to teach Nate to use a picture communication book that is attached by a key clip to the waistband of his pants. The first objective for Nate is to point to the "want" card in his communication book. The initial step toward this objective is for Nate to pull the open communication book up to above waist level. The four response chains selected for Nate were (1) playing catch in the classroom or at recess; (2) preparing to go out to recess; (3) approaching and hugging an adult; and (4) playing with a See'n Say during leisure time. The first three sequences were behavior chains that were performed independently and spontaneously; the fourth was to be taught through systematic instruction. In the first chain, an instructional trial was inserted after Nate threw the ball to his partner in the six-step ball-playing chain. In the second chain, a four-step chain for recess preparation, an instructional trial was inserted just after Nate's classmates were dismissed to go to recess. In the third chain, an instructional trial was inserted while Nate's arms were

> The purpose of the intervention with Nate was to teach him to use a communication book.

around an adult in a three-step hugging behavior chain. In the fourth chain, an instructional trial was inserted while Nate was pulling on the cord of the See'n Say in a toy-play chain with five steps.

The first instructional target for Nate—pulling his open communication book with the word "want" displayed to above waist level—was inserted into the "playing catch in the classroom or at recess behavior" chain at the predetermined point in the sequence. When Nate attained criterion on that target, a second target was taught within the second behavior chain, and so on until all of the target communication responses were acquired.

Activity-based intervention is a naturalistic teaching strategy that adapts principles and procedures from more traditional early childhood special education practice into inclusive and developmentally appropriate contexts. Intervention on children's individual goals and objectives is embedded in planned curriculum activities, routines, and child-initiated interactions (Bricker & Cripe, 1992). The goal of activity-based intervention is to develop targeted skills while the child participates in the activities that he finds interesting and appealing.

Activity-based intervention applies behavioral learning principles, but they are applied very differently than in traditional behavioral programs. There is no attempt to teach children to respond to specific cues under specific conditions; rather, activity-based intervention focuses on teaching functional skills and generalizable skills. Functional skills are skills that children need to be independent in self-care and social activities and routines in their environments. Generalizable skills are skills, such as requesting, that can be practiced and used in many different settings throughout the day.

> Activity-based intervention teaches functional and generalizable skills in the context of interesting and appealing activities.

Determining how skill objectives for each child can be taught and/or practiced in the context of daily classroom activities as well as preparing a classroom environment that is stimulating and interesting for all children are teacher responsibilities. For example, eating independently (a self-help objective), picking up a cracker (a fine motor objective), and requesting more (a language objective) would be facilitated and practiced at snack time. Each child's individual goals and objectives would be incorporated into curriculum activities such as playing in the block center or participating in an art activity.

Losardo and Bricker (1994) describe a "trip-to-the-store" activity to illustrate program design of activity-based intervention. This activity, in which several object names are introduced, is designed to have a logical beginning and outcome. The interventionist arranges the environment to resemble an actual grocery store. Shelves are stocked with plastic food items and empty containers with the labels intact. The interventionist begins the activity by asking children to complete shopping lists that include the target words to be taught. After the children arrive at the store, they are encouraged to get shopping carts and make their food selections. Object names appropriate to a grocery store setting are introduced.

Play-based intervention is described as an "inclusive curriculum" that integrates intervention strategies to strengthen developmental processes and increase functional skills across cognitive, social-emotional, communication and language, and sensorimotor domains (Linder, 1993). It is an outgrowth of the transdisciplinary play-based assessment process developed by Linder (1990). Transdisciplinary play-based intervention (TPBI) uses the objectives in the child's individualized program to generate specific intervention strategies that are integrated into the child's daily routine. The procedures are designed to be used with children from infancy to age 6. They can be implemented in almost any play environment using whatever play materials and opportunities are available in that environment. Most frequently used play environments are the home, infant and toddler programs, and preschool and kindergarten classes. Linder (1993) provides instructions for developing a play-based storybook curriculum but, generally speaking, the TPBI can be incorporated into almost any curriculum model.

Play-based intervention can be implemented in any play environment.

The use of play as an intervention context with young children with disabilities is relatively recent. It is only in the past 15 years that interventionists have begun to capitalize on the natural proclivity of children to play by using it as a setting for assessment (Linder, 1990), intervention and instruction (e.g., Linder, 1993; McGee, Krantz, & McClannahan, 1985), peer tutoring (Strain & Odom, 1986), and specifically, language intervention (Warren & Gazdag, 1990). However, recognition of the important role of play in development and learning is not new. Play is a spontaneous activity through which children experiment with life experiences. It is also the context for constructing an understanding of objects and events and learning how to talk about them. Cooperative play is the occasion for a variety of social and communicative interactions. It is a natural medium through which children learn acceptable modes of social interaction—sharing, taking turns, accepting responsibility—that are typically areas of difficulty for children with disabilities (Johnson, Christie, & Yawkey, 1987). They learn that, to enjoy interactions with others, aggression must be controlled and various rules must be followed.

Play takes many forms with young children. There is *sensorimotor play,* where children learn to use their senses to explore and manipulate objects. There is *functional play,* where children explore and learn about relationships among objects and between objects and events, and *constructive play,* where they learn to create. In *dramatic play,* they learn to make-believe, and in *game play,* they learn about prescribed rules. Play can be child-initiated and child-directed or adult-initiated and adult-directed. Children may play alone, in proximity to other, or in interaction with others. However they play, the content and style of their play will reflect their development and their culture.

As noted, Linder's TPBI process integrates intervention in four domains: cognitive, social-emotional, communication and language, and sensorimotor. The recommendations, with respect to language and communication goals, are to incorporate instruction into play and routine activities such as mealtime and snacktime, bathing, hand washing, brushing teeth, dressing, and toileting. TPBI incorporates some aspects of activity-based instruction, already described, and milieu teaching and interactive modeling, described in the next section. At the preschool level, the role of the adult (ECE teacher, ECSE teacher, language interventionist, or other support staff) is to provide an enriched environment and then to treat the child as a conversational partner, facilitating learning through warm and positive natural conversational interactions. Times when the child is interested in and manipulating objects are seized upon as opportunities to name and label the objects and model conversational discourse and semantic and grammatical constructions. The initial focus is on increasing cognitive and pragmatic skills, with the idea that increased mean length of utterance and more advanced grammatical structures will follow.

Facilitate and Support

The curriculum in most early childhood programs is based on the belief that the natural curiosity and exuberance of children should be nurtured in a meaningful and intellectually stimulating manner. Most curricula combine child-chosen play in a carefully arranged environment with planned developmentally appropriate activities (Feeney, Christensen, & Moravcik, 1995). Learning experiences are organized into thematic or topical units. The unit theme or topic is essentially the core around which appropriate activities are planned and organized so as to integrate learning in different developmental areas. It is selected or developed to reflect the interests, abilities, and specific concerns of the children in the program. The teacher engages the children in in-depth exploration of the theme by introducing a range and variety of theme-related materials, people, and experiences over a period of time, which can range from one or two weeks to several months. Learning experiences help children relate information, knowledge, objects, and actions to the theme. They are provided in the contexts of child-initiated play activities, one-to-one instruction, small-group activities, and large-group activities. Activity descriptions are sent home on a regular basis, with suggestions for parents to provide experiences at home and talk about aspects of the theme. All themes include a variety of both familiar and new vocabulary.

Basic facilitation strategies are procedures to facilitate development and use of language forms and communication skills that early childhood educators use with *all* children (Roberts, Bailey, & Nychka, 1991). These strategies are used in the context of routine activities (e.g., snacks, washing hands before lunch, bathroom breaks, recess) and curriculum activities. The six most common basic facilitation strategies are (1) engaging the child; (2) commenting about the child's interests and activities; (3) responding to communicative attempts; (4) allowing time for the child to respond; (5) using rational modeling; and (6) expanding and extending child utterances. These strategies are listed and briefly described on Table 10.1.

Special facilitation strategies are procedures that are used with young children who are not acquiring language at the same rate as their peers. Special facilitation strategies include (1) prompting a

> Basic facilitation strategies are early childhood education procedures that are generally used with all children.

> Special facilitation strategies are special education procedures that are generally used with children with special needs.

TABLE 10.1   Basic facilitation strategies

- ***Engage the child.*** Follow the child's attentional focus, show a sincere interest, and draw the child into interactions through actions or words related to the attentional focus. Initially accept any child behavior that is an indication of interest as a communicative effort.
- ***Comment and ask questions about the child's interests and activities.*** Use questions and comments to encourage children to talk about what they are doing and to express their feelings. Comment in order to provide a model of language describing what the child is doing or focused on. Use *wh-* questions and open-ended questions (e.g., "Tell me about _____") to encourage children to formulate their thoughts and express them in a meaningful way.
- ***Respond to all communicative efforts.*** To teach the child how powerful communication can be, try to provide what is requested and/or continue the topic of the child's communication.
- ***Allow time for the child to respond.*** Wait at least five seconds after speaking, look expectantly at the child, and use verbal or gestural cues to encourage the child to take a turn and thus keep the conversation going. If the child does not respond, repeat or rephrase the previous utterance.
- ***Use rational modeling.*** Describe the relationships between objects, actions, people, and events over time and through space. For example, when the child says "Brendyn cry," say "Yes, Brendyn is crying because he hurt his knee when he fell."
- ***Expand and extend child utterances.*** Restate or rephrase the child's utterances, adding omitted words. Expansions are a means of modeling a structurally more complex utterance for the child while at the same time confirming for the child that his or her message and its intent was understood. Extensions add new information.

higher level of response; (2) promoting peer interactions; (3) encouraging use of particular materials; and (4) teaching communication to replace challenging behaviors. Table 10.2 describes and provides some examples of how these special facilitation strategies are used with preschoolers.

TABLE 10.2   Special Facilitation Strategies

- ***Prompt word retrieval and higher level of responses.*** Prompt word retrieval with gestures, describing attributes, providing information about the function or category of the word, or by using a familiar phrase or sentence with the word omitted. Always try to elicit the most mature form of communication the child is capable of producing. Systematically fade prompts as the child demonstrates the target response.
- ***Promote peer interactions.*** Promote peer interactions through: (1) peer-mediated models where socially competent peers are taught to initiate interactions with less skilled classmates; (2) adult-mediated models where the adult encourages and prompts communicative responses toward less skilled peers; (3) direct instruction where children are taught to initiate communicative interactions; and (4) group models using cooperative learning or affection activities. (Affection activities are typical group games and songs such as "Simon Says" and "The Farmer in the Dell," which are modified to incorporate physical affection; e.g., a hug, pat on the back, high five, or handshake.)
- ***Encourage use of particular materials.*** Providing materials designed for two or more children sends a message about the importance of playing together. Similarly, providing duplicates of materials and toys sends a "play together and communicate" message. (Blocks foster cooperative building projects; housekeeping toys and clothing prompt children to act out familiar and meaningful routines.) How toys and other play materials are placed is a factor in communication. Placing materials so that children are face to face typically encourages communication. For example, there is considerably more communication across a dishpan full of sand or water when children are facing one another than with a large sand/water table (where children stand side by side). Easels are an exception. When placed so that children stand side by side there is more communication (than when they are arranged back to back).
- ***Teach communication skills to replace challenging behaviors.*** Sometimes young children who lack language skills use undesirable/disturbing behaviors (e.g., tantrums, hitting, screaming, crying, whining) to achieve their communication goals (Donnellan, Mirenda, Mesaros, & Fassbender, 1984). What this tells us is that the child does not have appropriate ways to get his or her needs met. The teacher must identify the communicative intentions of the undesirable behavior (e.g., "I want attention," "I want help," "I don't want to do this") and teach more acceptable ways of expressing the intended messages.

Two language intervention procedures that systematically apply the special facilitation strategies presented in Table 10.2 are milieu teaching and interactive modeling. These teaching approaches share the following basic characteristics (Kaiser, Ostrosky, & Alpert, 1993):

- Teaching occurs in the child's natural environments (e.g., home, school).
- The environment is arranged to encourage and support child communication.
- Teaching occurs in response to the child's interests.
- Communicative efforts are acknowledged and rewarded by providing natural consequences.

Milieu teaching, originally developed to facilitate acquisition of language and communication skills in preschool programs, has been expanded to include teaching of cognitive, social, motor, and adaptive skills (Brown, McEvoy, & Bishop, 1991; Nordquist, Twardosz, & McEvoy, 1985). Also, it is now also used with school-age children.

Milieu Teaching

Recall from Chapter 8 that milieu teaching is an umbrella term for a number of strategies that take advantage of a child's interest in material, activities, or other children to elicit particular behaviors. The basic difference between milieu teaching strategies and other language intervention procedures is not so much the nature of the strategies as when they are applied (Hart & Risley, 1975). It is their *incidental* use in unplanned interactions that is important and the fact that they are initiated by the child. Table 10.3 lists the basic assumptions of milieu language intervention (Alpert & Kaiser, 1992).

Milieu teaching is based on observations of caregivers interacting with normally developing children (Hart & Risley, 1975), which found that the categories tend to (1) talk about objects, events, and/or relations that have attracted the child's attention; (2) model, imitate, and expand desired and actual child-communication efforts; (3) repeat

> The defining characteristic of milieu teaching procedures is their *incidental* use in unplanned adult–child interactions.

TABLE 10.3   Basic assumptions of milieu language intervention

- The child's natural environment(s) is the best setting for language intervention.
- The most effective language teachers are the significant others in the child's life.
- The child's focus of interest should set the occasion for language training episodes.
- The focus of training should be functional language.
- Language training should focus simultaneously on linguistic forms and their functions, and strategies for language learning.
- Training episodes should be brief and positive.

and clarify words, statements, and requests that the child does not seem to understand; and (4) use such techniques as higher speech frequencies and stress to call the child's attention to important sentence elements. Over the past 15 years, researchers and practitioners have used this approach to teach young children request functions (Warren & Kaiser, 1986), basic semantic relations (e.g., action-object relationships) (Scherer & Olswang, 1989; Warren & Bambara, 1989; Warren & Gazdag, 1990), and specific vocabulary words (Yoder, Kaiser, & Alpert, 1991; Warren, 1992) and early language skills using spoken (Yoder, Kaiser, & Alpert, 1991) or signed modes of communication (Carr & Kologinsky, 1983; Oliver & Halle, 1982).

The environment is arranged to increase the opportunities for language and communication.

Implementation of milieu language teaching requires planning, preparation, and practice. The basic elements are arranging the environment to create reasons for communication (as previously discussed), identifying communication or language targets, and applying the teaching procedures. There is no limit to the number of language targets that can be taught with milieu language teaching procedures. Typical intervention targets include increasing the frequency of communicative behaviors, production of longer and more complex utterances, and expression of familiar functions with more advance forms. For example, the specific language targets for 5-year-old Lori are: (1) using labels to request desired foods at snack time; (2) saying *more song, more drum,* and *more play* when appropriate during music time; and (3) expression of familiar functions after snacks and at other clean-up times (e.g., *wash, spill, wipe, dry, all done,* and *pick up*).

Some questions to assist selection of specific targets for milieu teaching are:

- What objects does the child come into contact with most frequently in routine activities in the classroom and other school environments?
- Who are the child's favorite people? (Adults and peers the child seems to want to interact with the most are high-probability communication partners.)
- What forms is the child expected to use (or respond to) most often in the greatest number of contexts? (Examples might include "yes" and "no," the child's name, food labels, names for family members, teachers, and favorite peers, a word for bathroom, labels of preferred activities, etc.)
- What functions would enable the child to be more effective in the greatest number of contexts? (Consider requesting, protesting, greeting, and questioning.)

As noted, the basic assumption of the milieu teaching model is that language learning can be enhanced by increasing the child's rate of appropriate engagement with people and objects. It differs from most other naturalistic intervention models in that it uses explicit prompts for specific communicative behaviors. The explicit prompts for communication follow the child's attentional focus. The child is *repeatedly* prompted to use more advanced language forms and structures.

The four basic milieu teaching procedures are: (1) modeling; (2) mand-modeling; (3) time delay; and (4) incidental teaching. All four procedures require the immediate presence of an adult to mediate between the child and the desired or needed object or activity.

The **modeling procedure** is straightforward. The adult follows the child's attentional focus: When the child demonstrates an interest is an object or activity, a word or function is modeled (e.g., "Say *paint*" or "Say *I want the puzzle*"). A correct imitation of the model is followed by praise, verbal expansion, and immediate access to the desired object and/or activity. If the imitation is not correct or the child does not respond, the model is repeated (and the child is given access to the desired object and/or activity).

The **mand-model procedure** adds one element to the modeling procedure—a mand. (*Mand* is Skinner's (1957) term for a request.) Skinner identified use of mands as one of two functions of verbal behavior; the other is describing or labeling. The mand-model procedure teaches these important communication skills:

- establishing joint attention as a cue for verbalization;
- turn-taking; and
- responding to verbal requests or instructions.

After a request or direction, the child is presented with a request and, if necessary, a model of the desired communicative behavior. This is the sequence of steps in the mand-model procedure:

1. When the child focuses attention on or approaches an object or activity, the adult says "Tell me what this is," or "Tell me what you want," or "Tell me what you want to do."
2. If the child's response is less than he is capable of (or if he does not respond), a model of the desired response is presented (as in the modeling procedure). Another possibility, when the child provides a partial response, is for the adult to elaborate the mand (e.g., "Give me the whole sentence") and then provide a model.
3. If the child responds appropriately, the adult confirms the child's communicative attempt (e.g., "That's good"), provides a verbal expansion (e.g., "You want to work on *Beauty and the Beast* puzzle today"), and gives the child the desired object and/or activity.
4. An incorrect response is followed by a corrective model (e.g., "Say *want puzzle*") and the child is then given access to the desired object and/or activity.

The four milieu teaching procedures are modeling, mand-modeling, time delay, and incidental teaching.

The **time delay procedure** uses a systematic wait procedure. When the child shows an interest in an object or activity, the adult delays responding until the child requests or comments. This is the sequence of steps in the time delay procedure:

1. The adult faces the child with an expectant look while displaying something that the child wants (e.g., a pitcher of orange juice, a favorite toy) or something that provides access to a desired activity (e.g., the gate to the sandbox area).
2. The adult establishes and maintains eye contact with the child and waits a specified time (e.g., 4 to 15 seconds) for the child to attempt communication.
3. If the child does not attempt to communicate, the adult models the desired language behavior.
4. If the child responds, the adult confirms the child's effort (e.g., "That's good"), provides a verbal expansion (e.g., "You want some orange juice"), and immediately provides the desired object and/or access to the desired activity.
5. As with the other procedures, an incorrect response is followed by a corrective model (e.g., "Say *want juice*") and access to the desired object and/or activity.

The **incidental teaching procedure** is used to elicit more elaborate language and improve conversational skills. This is the sequence of steps in the incidental teaching procedure:

1. The adult focuses full attention on the child who has just initiated a communicative interaction (a verbal or nonverbal request or command).
2. The adult asks the child to elaborate on the communication (e.g., "Please say which of the wagons you want").
3. If the child does not produce as good an elaboration as she is capable of, the adult prompts again or provides a model of the elaborated response (e.g., "Say *I want the big red wagon today.*")
4. The adult confirms the child's communicative effort (e.g., "That's right"), repeats what the child said, and provides the requested object and/or activity.

The language requirements placed on a child depend on the child's ability level and prespecified language/communication targets. Three activities in the typical preschool setting that afford particularly good opportunities for milieu language teaching are (1) eating times, (2) creative activities (e.g., free play, art, music, outside play, games, field trips, circle time), and (3) transition times. At eating times, food and drink are provided contingent upon requesting behavior (depending upon the child's capabilities). In addition to request forms, the names of foods and food-related items (napkins, dishes, silverware) and polite forms such as "please" and "thank you" can be taught at eating times. Keep in mind that objects and activities are *never* withheld: they are simply delayed as a tactic to teach language. If the child does not produce the desired language behavior after two or three prompts, the food or drink (or other object or activity) is always provided anyway. Creative activities provide numerous opportunities for adults to elicit requests and comments and encourage use of longer and more complex utterances. There are opportunities for children to communicate what they want to *do,* what they want to *hear,* what they want to play or work with, and where they want to *go.* Transitions between activities also provide numerous opportunities to prompt language use. Before transition to a new activity, children can be prompted to request assistance putting away materials, taking off outdoor clothing, or finishing a particular task. They can be asked and prompted to name the next activity and prompted to greet the adult and peers upon entering the new activity.

Interactive Modeling

Interactive modeling was first described and validated by Wilcox (1984). As noted in Chapter 8, this procedure has been referred to by a variety of names, including *recasting* (Nelson & Gruendel, 1986); *interactive language instruction* (Cole & Dale, 1986), and *focused stimulation* (Leonard, Schwartz, Chapman, Rowan, Prelock, Terrell, Weiss, & Merrick, 1982). Basically it provides children with a high density of lexical models, in a conversational format that is embedded in ongoing activities. Responses are neither required nor elicited. The steps in interactive modeling are outlined below (Wilcox, Kouri, & Caswell, 1991). Note that it begins very much like milieu teaching.

Interactive modeling is also discussed in Chapter 8.

1. ***Establish joint attention.*** The adult establishes joint attention with the child by (1) responding to the child's interaction initiative, (2) following the child's lead (e.g., engaging in parallel or cooperative play), or (3) attending to whatever interests the child in an activity. Joint attention is established when the adult and the child are visually attending to the same environmental event or jointly manipulating an item.
2. ***Label the focus of attention.*** Once joint attention is established, the adult describes the child's nonverbal behavior by naming the item the child is focusing on or playing with. For example, if the child is dressing a doll, the adult gets a doll, begins dressing it, and says "doll."
3. ***Respond and expand.*** If the child produces the target word following the model, the adult responds to the intent of the communication and then expands it with a semantically related two-word combination. For example, if the child says "doll" after the adult model, the adult might say, "Yes, dressing the

dolly." Thus the adult response acknowledges comprehension of the child's utterance and produces a semantically related expansion.

4. ***Correct and model again.*** If the child imitates an item incorrectly, the adult says "no" and again provides the correct model. For example, if the child says "kitty" while picking up another toy animal, the adult would say, "No, that's a _____ ." At no time is a corrected production required, and the adult's tone is always conversational rather than corrective.

5. If the child produces a target word in the absence of an adult model, the adult provides the same type of feedback as in Step 3 above.

Focused stimulation exposes the child to repeated examples of specific words in contexts where the meaning and the function of the word are obvious.

Wilcox and colleagues (1991) compared the effectiveness of interactive modeling used in a classroom with more structured individual intervention procedures provided in a separate setting. They found that use of target words as measured by treatment data was equal for the children in the two intervention conditions. However, the young children in the classroom intervention condition demonstrated greater generalization of target words to the home environment.

There are several conceptual and procedural differences and similarities between milieu language teaching and focused stimulation. Where the stated purpose of milieu language teaching is to increase the child's production of language and communication behaviors by mediating engagement with people and objects, focused stimulation concentrates on exposing the child to repeated examples of specific target linguistic forms in contexts that make both the meaning and the function of the form obvious. Whereas milieu teaching procedures take advantage of unplanned opportunities as occasions for facilitating communication, focused stimulation plans opportunities for presentations of targeted forms and structures. Neither approach *requires* the child to respond. However, milieu teaching procedures strongly encourage child responses by providing explicit prompts for and specifically praising communicative efforts. Focused stimulation may use a storytelling format, asking the child questions to elicit specific linguistic features presented in the story. Similar to milieu language teaching, focused stimulation procedures can be used effectively by parents as well as professionals.

PEER SUPPORT STRATEGIES

Research has shown that children with disabilities interact with other children more frequently in inclusive settings than in segregated settings (e.g., Guralnick & Groom, 1988; Paul, 1985). However, in the absence of adult intervention, peers without disabilities are more likely to select classmates without disabilities as playmates than those with disabilities (Beckman, 1983; Peterson & Haralick, 1977). Increasing interactions between children with and without disabilities results in more opportunities for classmates with disabilities to learn appropriate social and communicative responses.

Peers are natural partners in social and communication interactions with classmates with disabilities; they are also natural facilitators. There is now a substantial body of research demonstrating the effectiveness of peer support intervention strategies (also called peer-mediated interventions) in facilitating development of social, language, and communication skills and increasing social interactions between children with and without disabilities in inclusive settings (Goldstein, Kaczmarek, Pennington, & Shafer, 1992; Goldstein & Wickstrom, 1986; Odom & Strain, 1984; Strain & Odom, 1986). Peer support interventions may take the form of (1) teaching peers to initiate interactions with their classmates with disabilities, (2) teaching peers to respond to their classmates with disabilities, (3) peer modeling, and/or (4) cooperative learning practices.

Most research has focused on teaching peers to direct social initiations to classmates with disabilities (Odom & Strain, 1984; Strain & Odom, 1986). Social initiations include play organizers (i.e., "Let's play with these blocks."), shares (i.e., "Here, you can play with this now."), physical assistance, and affection (e.g., hugging, patting, holding hands). The first step in all peer support intervention is to select socially competent children to serve as support peers. Then these support peers are taught how to initiate behaviors that elicit or support the interactions of their classmates with disabilities. Preparation of peers for peer-initiation intervention begins with selection of socially competent peers who have age-appropriate play skills, either no history with the child with disabilities or a positive history, and expressed willingness to participate. Daily lessons of 20 to 30 minutes are scheduled to teach the specific social initiations (Strain & Odom, 1986). The lessons typically follow the standard format shown in Table 10.4.

> Peers are natural facilitators of social and communication interactions.

TABLE 10.4 Format for teaching peer-initiation strategies

1. **Discuss** the importance of making new friends, sharing, playing cooperatively with others, and helping one another.
2. **Describe** the target initiations for that day's lesson: play organizing, sharing, physical assistance, or affection.
3. **Model** the target social initiation with another adult playing the other child role. (On about half the occasions, the adult playing the child with disabilities should be nonresponsive in order to provide an opportunity to demonstrate persistence.)
4. **Prompt** rehearsal of the initiation strategies (with adult verbal support and feedback).

Equally important as teaching peers without disabilities to initiate communication is teaching them how to respond to the initiations of their classmates with disabilities so that the classmates have an opportunity to experience the reinforcing nature of interactions. The peer-response strategy described by Goldstein, Kaczmarek, Pennington, and Shafer (1992) may be used with, or as an alternative to, teaching peers to *initiate* interactions. Drawing from research considering social and communicative interactions among preschool children with and without disabilities, Goldstein and colleagues determined that one particular setting event—mutual attention to an object or activity—was more likely than any other event to be followed by a communicative response. Of the four communicative functions that were effective in obtaining responses from communication partners (comments, requests for information, requests for action, and simple acknowledgment), commenting seems to occur most frequently and have the greatest probability of eliciting a response.

Preschoolers can be taught to attend to, comment on, and acknowledge the behavior of their classmates.

When preschoolers without disabilities were taught to attend to, comment on, and acknowledge the behavior of their classmates with disabilities, they were successful in improving rates of interaction for four of their five classmates with disabilities (Goldstein et al., 1992). (The five preschoolers with disabilities who participated in this study exhibited significant language, social, and cognitive deficits: four were diagnosed as autistic and the fifth was diagnosed as pervasive developmental delay.) Peer training involved six direct instruction lessons that focused on three facilitation strategies: (1) mutual attention to a play activity, (2) commenting about ongoing activities, and (3) general acknowledgment of the partner's communicative behaviors. Each training session began with an overview of the step to be trained and a review of the previously leaned steps. This was followed by descriptions of the requirements of the step, adult modeling of the step in isolation and within the complete sequence of steps, adult–child demonstrations with practice, and child–child practice. Posters were used to illustrate the strategies during the training and the demonstrations. The 10 peers who participated in this study required between 11 and 16 sessions to attain an 80 percent mastery criterion with the steps during triadic interactions (two peers without disabilities and a classmate with disabilities) in a free-play situation. Table 10.5 shows Goldstein and colleagues' format for teaching peer response strategies.

Group instruction provides many opportunities for peer modeling and observational learning.

The possibilities for peer modeling and observational learning are an important advantage of group instruction. In inclusive programs, learning of a wide range of behaviors, including social, language, and communicate skills, occurs naturally as a result of children with disabilities watching the performance of peers without disabilities. Teachers can increase modeling by ensuring that "models" use

TABLE 10.5   Format for teaching peer-response strategies

Teach peers to

1. establish mutual attention by moving in front of the classmate with disabilities and looking at him, the toys he is playing with, *or* what he is doing;
2. say the name of the classmate;
3. say the classmate's name a second time and, if he does not respond, tap him on the shoulder and say his name again;
4. talk about what the classmate is doing and wait for him to respond (to take a turn in the exchange); and
5. talk about the activity again after the classmate responds.

naturally occurring opportunities. For example, the teacher might say "Jordan, could you show Soo Jin what to say when she is the store-keeper?" or "Mark, when we go outside, will you remind Taylor how to ask when it is his turn to pull the big wagon?" According to the classic research of Bandura (1969), the effectiveness of modeling is increased when the sex, age, and other characteristics of the model closely resemble those of the imitator and when the modeled behavior is reinforced. For example, noting that Jordan received more juice when she said "More please," Sarah makes an effort to produce the same request.

Based in the work of Johnson and Johnson (1991, 1994), the cooperative learning model structures activities to teach children to encourage one another, elaborate on each other's successes, and work toward common goals. As a teaching strategy, cooperative learning has four basic elements: (1) positive interdependence, (2) face-to-face communication, (3) individual accountability, and (4) group process. Positive interdependence is working together and depending upon one another to accomplish a common goal. Participants are expected to use some form of communication and appropriate interpersonal and small-group skills (e.g., turn-taking) and to feel individually responsible for the group's efforts.

Cooperative learning differs from the other peer support strategies in that the emphasis is on fostering cooperative interactions. The dynamics of the groups and the cooperative interactions are viewed as the context for learning and practicing social, language, and communicative skills. The focus on social skills, along with the structure that is inherent in cooperative learning lessons, provides an ideal context for language learning and practice of communication skills. The teacher and the language interventionist should work together in developing and implementing cooperative learning lessons. Table 10.6 shows the steps in developing a cooperative learning lesson (Johnson & Johnson, 1991).

TABLE 10.6   Steps in planning and implementing a cooperative learning lesson

Steps	Procedures
1. Select a lesson.	Select a lesson/activity that is simple, straightforward, motivating, and developmentally appropriate. Some examples for preschoolers include making jello; painting a mural; making a farm, fire station, zoo.
2. Specify two objectives for the lesson.	Specify a cognitive objective and a social/language skill objective for the lesson. Ideally, one of these will be a new objective and the other will be a practice objective.
3. Assign children to groups.	Use small groups initially. *Gradually* move from pairs, to triads, and then to groups of four or five (in that order). Mix children of different ability levels, sexes, ethnic and cultural backgrounds, and language skills.
4. Introduce the objectives and what it means to be cooperative.	Discuss the objectives and how they will be used. Define cooperation and talk about cooperative behaviors that are appropriate and desirable (e.g., taking turns, asking for materials, sharing, looking at and listening to a speaker, saying nice things, helping others).
5. Model the steps and provide directions.	Explain the lesson with clear, step-by-step directions and demonstrations. If possible, show the steps in a sequence of pictures. Ask children to describe what they will be doing before beginning the lesson.
6. Observe and provide feedback.	Observe and provide positive feedback for cooperation. Provide assistance only if absolutely necessary. Clarify directions and/or answer questions related to the objectives.
7. Evaluate and debrief.	At the end of the lesson, take time to reflect on what they learned and what they said and did during the lesson. Especially talk about the cooperation and comment about how well they worked together.

PLANNING

The early childhood educator should have a support team comprised of the child's parents and all, or some combination, of these professionals (depending on the child's needs): early childhood special education specialist, language interventionist, occupational therapist, and physical therapist. There should be a teaching plan for children with disabilities which addresses their needs in the areas of (1) social interactions and social skill development, (2) cognitive development, (3) emotional development, and (4) physical competence (NAEYC & NAECS/SDE, 1991). There should also be provisions for regular monitoring.

Team planning on at least a weekly basis is essential. Weekly meetings provide an opportunity for the team to discuss children's progress toward identified goals and objectives, whether—and how— present instructional strategies and/or materials should be modified, and activities and expectations for the coming week. Planning for the whole class generally involves identification of a theme, as well as specific curriculum lessons and activities, materials, and targeted skills in line with the theme. Additionally, there should be intensive and individualized planning for the children in the class with disabilities. Noting the anticipated activities for the week, the team identifies specific skill targets, environmental arrangements, instructional strategies, and peer support strategies for children with disabilities. Figure 10.2 shows planning for Josie, a 4-year-old with Down syndrome whose language is at approximately the 30-month level.

The matrix format lends itself well to planning how to embed particular instructional targets into daily routines.

CHILDREN FROM CULTURALLY AND LINGUISTICALLY DIVERSE POPULATIONS

It is especially challenging to respond to the needs of young children with disabilities who come to the preschool or early intervention setting with limited English and limited knowledge of the content, roles, and rules common to such settings (Barrera, 1993). The issue is not so much English-only instruction versus instruction that uses both English and non-English languages—as it is with older populations. Rather, in early childhood education the issue is how to meet the child's developmental needs. Barrera (1993) states these concerns as: (1) how to make young children from culturally and linguistically diverse populations feel emotionally secure, and (2) how to establish and maintain meaningful communication. It is difficult for children to feel emotionally secure in an environment where they cannot express themselves as they have learned to do or understand the language being used around them. Similarly it is difficult for them to learn through a communication medium that is insufficiently developed.

Guidelines for working with young children from culturally and linguistically diverse populations are similar to those for the development of any multicultural curriculum. Most important is to draw material directly from the children's homes and communities and capitalize on the language skills that the children bring to school, regardless of whether these skills are in English or in another language (Williams & De Gaetano, 1985). According to cross-cultural research, early mother-child interactions (e.g., peekaboo) and the prelinguistic skills developed from these interactions can be quite different across cultures (Richman, Miller, & LeVine, 1992). It is not difficult to imagine the confusion young children must experience

Capitalize on whatever language and communication skills the child has at the present time.

FIGURE 10.2   Example of matrix planning format

Weekly Planning Matrix

Child's name: _Josie_   Date:

Team Members Present: _Judy, Denise, Ferrell, and Christy_

Schedule	Behavior Target(s) in Routine/Activity	Environmental Arrangement	Instructional Strategies	Peer Support Strategies
Arrival/Free Play	Indicate (point + vocal) desired toy or center	Preferred toys placed out of reach	Time delay Modeling	Peers model toy and center requests
Morning Circle	Raise hand ("here"); gestures for songs	Place Josie between Ashley and Alice	Interrupt the routine Visual prompts Modeling	Peer modeling— Ashley and Jason
Art/Small Groups	Take turns and request (point + vocal) materials	Cut/paste activity Provide inadequate portions	Time delay Modeling Mand-Model	Cooperative learning structure
Transition	Participate in cleanup		Verbal prompt Physical assistance	Peer assistance Peer modeling
Bathroom	Follow the toileting and washing routines	Pull-up pants	Describe actions as performed + Partial physical assistance	
Outdoor Play	Request shoes Make play choices Take turns with buggy	Swing seat Wheel toys	Time delay Modeling Mand-mode	Peer (Ashley) to initiate play requests
Storytime	Respond to action requests in the story	Big books Other props	Verbal prompts Partial physical prompts	Peer (Alice) modeling
Bathroom	Follow the toileting and washing routines	Pull-up pants	Describe actions as performed + Partial physical assistance	
Lunch	Request choice of drink and food	Inadequate portions Food in plastic containers	Modeling Time delay	Peer (Ashley) modeling
Clean-up	Place containers in can		Verbal prompts Modeling	Peer modeling
Preparation for Home	Request help with sweater/coat Wave good-bye		Time delay Physical prompts	Peer modeling

when their prelinguistic and nonverbal skills are not recognized as culturally imbedded. They may be viewed (and treated) as if they "do not have language" only because they are not responding as expected in the intervention setting.

Children must have well-developed communication skills before they can be expected to benefit from instruction that uses language to provide information and teach abstract concepts (Barrera, 1993). There should be a clear distinction between the *development* of language and the *use* of language as a medium for instruction. When children are learning language (either a first language or a second language), the emphasis should be on learning and practicing basic communication skills. When the language system has developed sufficiently, *then* children are ready to deal with the more complex demands of communication for learning (e.g., to explain a concept or define a word).

> Reasonably well-developed communication skills are necessary if a young child is to benefit from instruction that uses language.

Structure the program in such a way that all of the children in the class understand ongoing routines and have the opportunity to express themselves to the best of their abilities, whether they are fluent in English or not. Failure to do this can affect children's self-esteem and confidence. If they are not able to keep up with their peers, their egocentric perspective may lead them to blame themselves and conclude that they are not as competent as their peers.

There is no reason to assume that children with disabilities cannot learn a second language to the level to which they can learn a first language. Barrera (1993) makes the point that the misperception that children with disabilities cannot handle two languages is most often used to support the exclusive use of English, which is already a second language for many children. Based on her own experience, Barrera contends that 3- and 4-year-olds with disabilities (even those with communication disorders and mental retardation) can develop second-language proficiency at a rate and to a level commensurate with their first-language development.

To capitalize on existing skills, introduce new concepts and skills in the child's strongest language system. When the child's strongest language is not English and it is not possible to introduce concept and skills in the strongest language, then carefully incorporate strategies suitable for non-native speakers of English into the teaching situation. These strategies are similar to those previously described—strategies used with monolingual children with language delay or disorder.

> Introduce new concepts in the child's strongest language system.

SUMMARY

Crucial to the success of an inclusive preschool is flexibility on the part of the teachers and the related services personnel as well as commitment to team collaboration and joint decision making. The importance of embedding instruction on important objectives into the context of ongoing classroom activities and routines, adapting and rearranging materials, controlling access to materials, adapting the structure of activities, providing opportunities for peer interactions, and interspersing instructional trials within activities must all be taken into consideration in program planning.

Ultimately, meeting the needs of young children with disabilities rests on the collaboration and cooperation of educators in the fields of early childhood education and early childhood special education. One response to the call for educators with these transdisciplinary skills has been the development, in many universities, of preservice teacher education programs that integrate early childhood special education and early childhood education knowledge and skills (Bredekamp & Willer, 1992; Johnson & Johnson, 1992; Lowenthal, 1992; Miller, 1992).

REFERENCES

Alpert, C. L., & Kaiser, A. P. (1992). Training parents as milieu language teachers. *Journal of Early Intervention, 16,* 31–52.

Bailey, D. B., McWilliam, P. J., & Winton, P. J. (1992). Building family-centered practices in early intervention: A team-based model for change. *Infants and Young Children, 5,* 73–80.

Bandura, A. (1969). *Principles of behavior modification.* New York: Holt, Rinehart & Winston.

Barrera, I. (1993). Effective and appropriate instruction for all children: The challenge of cultural/linguistic diversity and young children with special needs. *Topics in Early Childhood Special Education, 13,* 461–487.

Beckman, P. (1983). The relationship between behavior characteristics of children and social interaction in an integrated setting. *Journal of the Division of Early Childhood, 7,* 69–77.

Bredekamp, S. (1987). *Developmentally appropriate practice in early childhood programs serving children from birth through age eight.* Washington, DC: National Association for the Education of Young Children.

Bredekamp, S., & Rosegrant, T. (1992). *Reaching potentials: Appropriate curriculum and assessment for young children* (Vol. 1).

Washington, DC: National Association for the Education of Young Children.

Bredekamp, S., & Willer, B. (1992). Of ladders and lattices, cores, and cones: Conceptualizing an early childhood professional development system. *Young Children, 47*(3), 47–50.

Bricker, D., & Cripe, J. (1992). *An activity-based approach to early intervention.* Baltimore: Paul H. Brookes.

Brown, W. H., McEvoy, M. A., & Bishop, N. (1991). Incidental teaching of social behavior *Teaching Exceptional Children, 24*(1) 35–38.

Carr, E. G., & Kologinsky, E. (1983). Acquisition of sign language by autistic children: Spontaneity and generalization effects. *Journal of Applied Behavior Analysis, 16,* 297–314.

Carta, J., Schwartz, I., Atwater, J., & McConnell, S. (1991). Developmentally appropriate practice: Appraising its usefulness for young children with disabilities, *Topics in Early Childhood Special Education, 11,* 1–19.

Cavallaro, C. C., Haney, M., & Cabello, B. (1993). Developmentally appropriate strategies for promoting full participation in early childhood settings. *Topics in Early Childhood Special Education 13,* 293–307.

Cole, K., & Dale, P. (1986). Direct language instruction and interactive language instruction with language-delayed preschool children: A comparison study. *Journal of Speech and Hearing Research, 29,* 206–217.

DEC recommended practices: Indicators of quality in programs for infants and young children with special needs and their families. (1993). Reston, VA: Division for Early Childhood of the Council for Exceptional Children.

Demchak, M. A., & Drinkwater, L. (1992). Preschoolers with severe disabilities: The case against segregation. *Topics in Early Childhood Special Education, 11*(4), 70–83.

Donnellan, A. M., Mirenda, P. L., Mesaros, R. A., & Fassbender, L. L. (1984). Analyzing the communicative functions of aberrant behavior. *Journal of the Association for the Severely Handicapped, 9,* 201–212.

Feeney, S., Christensen, D., & Moravcik, E. (1995). *Who am I in the lives of children?* Columbus, OH: Merrill/Prentice Hall.

Fewell, R. R., & Oelwein, P. L. (1990). The relationship between time in integrated environments and developmental gains in young children with special needs. *Topics in Early Childhood Special Education, 10*(2), 104–116.

Fey, M. E. (1986). *Language intervention with young children.* Newton, MA: Allyn and Bacon.

Goldstein, J., & Wickstrom, S. (1986). Peer intervention effects on communicative interactions among handicapped and nonhandicapped preschoolers. *Journal of Applied Behavior Analysis, 19,* 209–214.

Goldstein, J., Kaczmarek, L., Pennington, R., & Shafer, K. (1992). Peer-mediated intervention: Attending to, commenting on, and acknowledging the behavior of preschoolers with autism. *Journal of Applied Behavior Analysis, 25,* 289–305.

Guralnick, M. J., & Groom, J. M. (1988). Peer interactions in mainstreamed and specialized classrooms: A comparative analysis. *Exceptional Children, 5,* 415–425.

Halle, J. W., Alpert, C., & Anderson, S. (1984). Natural environment language assessment and intervention with severely impaired preschoolers. *Topics in Early Childhood Special Education, 4,* 1–14.

Haring, T. G., Neetz, J. A., Lovinger, L., Peck, C., & Semmel, M. I. (1987). Effects of four modified incidental teaching procedures to create opportunities for communication. *Journal of Applied Behavior Analysis, 14,* 387–400.

Hart, G., & Risley, T. R. (1975). Incidental teaching of language in the preschool. *Journal of Applied Behavior Analysis, 8,* 411–420.

Hemmeter, M. L., & Kaiser, A. P. (1990). Environmental influences on children's language: A model and case study. *Education and Treatment of Children, 13*(4), 331–346.

Hunt, P., & Goetz, L. (1988). Teaching spontaneous communication in natural settings through interrupted behavior chains. *Topics in Language Disorders, 9,* 58–71.

Hunt, P., Goetz, L., Alwell, M., & Sailor, W. (1986). Using an interrupted chain strategy to teach generalized communication responses. *Journal of the Association for persons with Severe Handicaps, 11,* 196–207.

Johnson, E., & Johnson, K. M. (1992). Clarifying the developmental perspective in response to Carta, Schwartz, Atwater, and McConnell. *Topics in Early Childhood Special Education, 12,* 439–457.

Johnson, D. W., & Johnson, R. T. (1991). *Learning together and alone: Cooperation, competition, and individualization* (3rd ed.). Englewood Cliffs, NJ: Prentice-Hall.

Johnson, J. E., Christie, J. F., & Yawkey, T. D. (1987). *Play and early childhood development.* Glenview, IL: Scott, Foresman and Company.

Johnson, R. T., & Johnson, D. W. (1994). An overview of cooperative learning. In J. S. Thousand, R. A. Villa, & A. I. Nevin (Eds.), *Creativity and collaborative learning: A practical guide to empowering students and teachers* (pp. 31–44). Baltimore: Paul H. Brookes.

Kaiser, A. P., Ostrosky, M. M., & Alpert, C. L. (1993). Training teachers to use environmental arrangement and milieu teaching with nonvocal preschool children. *Journal of the Association for Persons with Severe Handicaps, 18*(3), 188–199.

Kaiser, A. P., Yoder, P. J., & Keetz, A. (1992). Evaluating milieu teaching. In S. F. Warren & J. Reichle (Eds.), *Causes and effects in commu-*

nication and language intervention (Vol. 1, pp. 9–47). Baltimore: Paul H. Brookes.

Lamorey, S., & Bricker, D. D. (1993). Integrated programs: Effects on young children and their parents. In C. A. Peck, S. L. Odom, & D. D. Bricker (Eds.), *Integrating young children with disabilities into community programs* (pp. 249–270). Baltimore: Paul H. Brookes.

Leonard, L. (1981). Facilitating linguistic skills in children with specific language impairment. *Applied Psycholinguistics, 2,* 89–119.

Leonard, L., Schwartz, R., Chapman, K., Rowan, L., Prelock, P., Terrell, B., Weiss, A., & Merrick, C. (1982). Early lexical acquisition in children with specific language impairment. *Journal of Speech and Hearing Research, 25,* 554–564.

Linder, T. W. (1990). *Transdisciplinary play-based assessment.* Baltimore: Paul H. Brookes.

Linder, T. W. (1993). *Transdisciplinary play-based intervention.* Balitmore: Paul H. Brookes.

Losardo, A., & Bricker, D. (1994). Activity-based intervention and direction instruction: A comparison study. *American Journal of Mental Retardation, 98,* 744–765.

Lowenthal, B. (1992). Collaborative training in the education of early childhood educators. *Teaching Exceptional Children, 24*(4), 25–29.

Mahoney, G., & Robinson, C. (1992). Focusing on parent-child interaction: The bridge to developmentally appropriate practice. *Topics in Early Childhood Special Education, 12,* 105–120.

McCormick, L. (1990). Intervention processes and procedures. In L. McCormick & R. Schiefelbusch (Eds.), *Early language intervention* (2nd ed.). Columbus, OH: Merrill/Macmillan.

McGee, G. G., Krantz., P. J., & McClannahan, L. E. (1985). The facilitative effects of incidental teaching on preposition use by autistic children. *Journal of Applied Behavior Analysis, 18,* 17–31.

McLean, M. E., & Odom, S. L. (1993). Practices for young children with and without disabilities: A comparison of DEC and NAEYC

practices. *Topics in Early Childhood Special Education, 13,* 274–292.

Miller, P. S. (1992). Segregated programs of teacher education in early childhood: Immoral and inefficient practice. *Topics in Early Childhood Special Education, 11,* 39–52.

Miller, L., Strain, P., McKinley, J., Heckathorn, K., & Miller, S. (1993). *Preschool placement decisions: Are they predictors of future placements?* ERIC Reproduction Number 360–771. Pittsburgh, PA: Research Institute on Preschool Mainstreaming.

Montgomery, J. (1995). Inclusion, observation, outcome. *Asha, 37,* 7.

National Association for the Education of Young Children & National Association for Early Childhood Specialists in State Departments of Education. (1991). *Guidelines for appropriate curriculum content and assessment in programs serving children ages 3 through 8.* Washington, DC: National Association for the Education of Young Children.

Nelson, K. (1989). Strategies for first language learning. In M. Rice & R. Schiefelbusch (Eds.), *The teachability of language* (pp. 263–310). Baltimore: Paul H. Brookes.

Nelson, K., & Gurendel, J. (1986). Children's scripts. In K. Nelson (Ed.), *Event knowledge: Structure and function in development.* Hillsdale, NJ: Erlbaum.

Novick, R. (1993). Activity-based intervention and developmentally appropriate practice: Points of convergence. *Topics in Early Childhood Special Education, 13,* 403–417.

Nordquist, V. M., Twardosz, S., & McEvoy, M. A. (1991). Effects of environmental reorganization in classrooms for children with autism. *Journal of Early Intervention, 15,* 135–152.

Odom, S. L., & Brown, W. (1993). Social interaction skills interventions for young children with disabilities in integrated settings. In C. A. Peck, S. L. Odom, & D. D. Bricker (Eds.), *Integrating young children with disabilities into community programs* (pp. 30–64). Balitmore: Paul H. Brookes.

Odom, S. L., & McEvoy, M. (1988). Integration of young children with handicaps and normally developing children. In S. Odom & M. Karnes (Eds.), *Early intervention for infants and children with handicaps: An empirical base* (pp. 241–268). Baltimore: Paul H. Brookes.

Odom, S. L., & McEvoy, M. (1990). Mainstreaming at the preschool level: Potential barriers and tasks for the field. *Topics in Early Childhood Special Education, 10*(2), 48–61.

Odom, S. L., & Strain, P. S. (1984). Classroom-based social skills instruction for severely handicapped preschool children. *Topics in Early Childhood Special Education, 4*(3), 97–116.

Oliver, C. B., & Halle, J. W. (1982). Language training in the everyday environment: Teaching functional sign use to a retarded child. *Journal of the Association for the Severely Handicapped, 8*, 50–62.

Ostrosky, M. M., & Kaiser, A. P. (1991). Preschool classroom environments to promote communication. *Teaching exceptional children, 23*(4), 6–10.

Paul, L. (1985). Programming peer support for functional language. In S. Warren & A. K. Rogers-Warren (Eds.), *Teaching functional language* (pp. 289–307). Austin, TX: Pro-Ed.

Peck, C., Odom, S., & Bricker, D. (Eds.) (1993). *Integrating young children with disabilities into community programs: Ecological perspectives on research and implementation.* Baltimore: Paul H. Brookes.

Peterson, N. L., & Haralick, J. G. (1977). Integration of handicapped and nonhandicapped preschoolers: An analysis of play behavior and social interaction. *Education and Training of the Mentally Retarded, 12*, 234–236.

Richman, A. L., Miller, P. M., & LeVine, R. A. (1992). Cultural and educational variables in maternal responsiveness. *Developmental Psychology, 28*, 614–621.

Roberts, J. E., Bailey, D. B., & Nychka, H. B. (1991). Teachers' use of strategies to facilitate the communication of preschool children with disabilities. *Journal of Early Intervention. 15*, 358–376.

Rogers-Warren, A., & Warren, S. (1984). The social basis of language and communication in severely handicapped preschoolers. *Topics in Early Childhood Special Education, 4*(2), 57–72.

Salisbury, C. & Smith, B. (1993). *Effective practices for preparing young children with disabilities for school,* ERIC Digest EDO-EC-93-2. Reston, VA: Council for Exceptional Children.

Scherer, N. J., & Olswang, L. B. (1989). Using structured discourse as a language intervention technique with autistic children. *Journal of Speech and Hearing Disorders, 54,* 383–394.

Skinner, B. F. (1957). *Verbal behavior.* New York: Appleton-Century-Crofts.

Strain, P. (1990). Least restrictive environment for preschool children with handicaps: What we know, what we should be doing. *Journal of Early Intervention, 14,* 291–296.

Strain, P., & Odom, S. L. (1986). Peer social initiations: Effective interventions for social skills development of exceptional children. *Exceptional Children, 52,* 543–551.

Warren, S. F. (1992). Facilitating basic vocabulary acquisition with milieu teaching procedures. *Journal of Early Intervention, 16,* 235–251.

Warren, S. F., & Bambara, L. M. (1989). An experimental analysis of milieu language intervention: Teaching the action-objective form. *Journal of Speech and Hearing Disorders, 54,* 448–461.

Warren, S. F., & Gazdag, G. (1990). Facilitating early language development with milieu procedures. *Journal of Early Intervention, 14,* 62–86.

Warren, S. F., & Kaiser, A. P. (1986). Incidental language teaching: A critical review. *Journal of Speech and Hearing Disorders, 51,* 291–299.

Wilcox, M. J. (1984). Developmental language disorders: Preschoolers. In A. Holland (Ed.), *Language disorders in children* (pp. 101–128). San Diego, CA: College Hill.

Wilcox, M. J., Kouri, T. A., & Caswell, S. B. (1991). Early language intervention: A comparison of classroom and individual treatment. *American Journal of Speech-Language Pathology,* September, 49–62.

Williams, L. R., & De Gaetano Y. (1985). *ALERTA: A multicultural, bilingual approach to teaching young children.* Reading MA: Addison-Wesley.

Winton, P. J., McWilliam, P. J., Harrison, T., Owens, A. M., and Bailey, D. B. (1992). Lessons learned from implementing a team-based model for change. *Infants and Young Children, 5,* 49–57.

Yoder, P. J., Kaiser, A. P., & Alpert, C. L. (1991). An exploratory study of the interaction between language teaching methods and child characteristics. *Journal of Speech and Hearing Research, 34,* 155–167.

CHAPTER 11

Facilitating Literacy in Young Children

Mary Ross Moran

Language purposes change when children undertake schooling. At home and in nonacademic preschools or day care settings, children emphasize immediate interpersonal language functions—listening and speaking—to meet needs, bond with others, and learn acceptable behaviors within family and community. Home and nonacademic preschool environments feature face-to-face conversations with caregivers, built upon shared knowledge and common experiences. Communications are context-dependent; persons and objects talked about are likely to be present or known to both speaker and listener. Communicative uses of language—referential, persuasive, and social functions—become means to move into larger groups and to share the cultural values of the broader society. This chapter explores these changes as it reviews the language demands of beginning literacy instruction, optional literacy approaches, combined approaches, and programs for learners with special needs during early childhood.

SCHOOL DEMANDS

This chapter explores changes in the demands of communication when the child starts school.

Schooling requires a shift in focus through primary grades between the ages of 5 and 8 years. In contrast to natural conversations, schools typically feature ritualized question-and-answer formats based on vicarious experiences from oral reports or reading, rather than on direct shared experiences. Information is presented in a context-independent manner; teachers talk about people and objects beyond students' and teachers' first-hand knowledge. Noncommunicative uses of language, concept formation, rehearsal, and management functions gain importance as instruments for structured rather than spontaneous lessons.

Tizard and Hughes (1984) confirmed this contrast. Home talk that they recorded was characterized by "real attempts to communicate being made on both sides," but when primary students talked at school, "conversations with adults were mainly restricted to answering questions rather than asking them, or taking part in minimum exchanges" (p. 9).

For beginning readers and writers, the need to span time and space makes demands different from those of listening and speaking. Beginning readers must fill in information that writers have left out as assumed common knowledge. Novice writers must anticipate what an absent reader should be told and what can be taken for granted as shared information.

"Learning to disembed language from the concrete, social context in which children first learn to speak is a crucial task for being able to gradually make the transition into the instructional uses of language that prevail in classrooms . . . it might be more accurate to say that a child is learning to embed print into contexts that are increasingly complex and removed from the here and now" (van Kleeck, 1990, p. 39).

The extent to which children are prepared to read and write depends on childrearing practices.

Although the wish to join adult society motivates children to try to read and write, they come to school variously prepared to do so. As Heath (1982) demonstrated in her studies of three communities, the extent to which children are prepared to shift to school literacy is a function of language patterns within childrearing practices. In one community Heath studied, home language prepared children to label, explain, and engage in question–answer displays of knowledge beyond the immediate environment. In another community, labels and explanations were common, but information from books was not valued equally with direct experience. In a third community, both labels and explanations were uncommon; instead, personal reactions to events were talked about and valued.

Differing preschool language patterns thus produce variations between teachers' expectations and children's language styles. Children using language patterns of communities two and three are at a disadvantage in traditional literacy lessons, not because they are unready to learn, but because they have not practiced teacher-accepted ways to display their learning.

Even when parents foster school-like exchanges, contrasts occur. Juliebo (1985) reported four. At home, (1) children initiate learning by asking questions, (2) parents and children construct activities together, (3) literacy events are part of everyday life, and (4) feedback tends to focus on what children can do well. At school, teachers initiate learning activities, which they construct without children's help, literacy is set apart from life in separate contrived lessons, and feedback tends to correct errors. Juliebo concluded that school literacy lessons may not become meaningful and relevant for those entering schools from language-rich and print-rich home environments that have encouraged a more independent learning style.

When children with disabilities enter school, they can be expected to differ in the childrearing practices and language patterns to which they have been exposed and in the extent to which disabilities interfere with reading and writing. Those with oral language disorders who meet early academic failure are reclassified as having learning disabilities (Snyder, 1984).

As recently reviewed by Wallach and Butler (1995), research has offered some answers to practitioners' questions about the connections between language and literacy. It is now clear that students who read and write gain more than those competencies—they obtain access to learning in a broad sense, including opportunities to participate in their cultures as well as to develop more sophisticated oral language. Furthermore, the consensus is that spoken and written language interact so that each influences the other, although one is more prominent than the other at varied stages of child development.

Being able to read and write is critical for children to gain access to learning.

Typically developing 3-year-old children do write and read (Durkin, 1982; Goodman, 1986; van Kleeck, 1990) at a period when oral language is not yet considered established (Karmiloff-Smith, 1979; Johnston, 1988). This evidence supports a prediction that children with oral language disorders can nevertheless engage in reading and writing and profit from literacy instruction. The question is how a given individual learner's opportunities to do so might be enhanced. As Wallach and Butler (1995) point out, program planners must exercise "a healthy skepticism about 'the best' and 'only' way to teach reading and writing" (p. 3).

The issue in debate for beginning literacy instruction is which methods or combinations offer optimal conditions for students with disabilities that include limited language. According to Chiang and Ford (1990) and Weaver (1991), studies of United States beginning literacy instruction for students with language disorders are limited.

However, some insights emerge from related information about (1) what typically developing prereaders discover through emergent literacy events prior to schooling, (2) natural learning preferences of those who write and read at their own initiative prior to schooling, and (3) contrasts between two prevalent approaches to reading instruction including attempts to combine approaches, as illustrated by three studies of early literacy experiences by at-risk students.

Emergent Literacy

Adams (1990) used the term *prereaders* as preferable to describe those who have not been exposed to formal reading instruction because ". . . **emergent literacy** . . . is defined differently by different authorities" (p. 55). Nevertheless, the latter term is often used to describe the ability of early learners in print-oriented societies to construct meanings about, and make sense of, print before being introduced to literacy instruction (van Kleeck, 1990).

Repeatedly, observers have reported that children in literate families come to school knowing a great deal. Goodman (1986) argued that wanting to be literate and therefore imitating literate behaviors is natural for children in societies that value print. According to Harste, Woodward, & Burke (1984b), children learn critical distinctions between drawings and writings, as well as finer distinctions between individual alphabetic letters, words, lists, and connected text. They know that words are composed of a variety of letters, and that many have a specific sound-symbol correspondence. Prereaders predict, confirm, and self-correct to create meaning as they pretend to read. They use their life experiences to interpret a text, and they come to integrate varied cues into strategies for improved meaning making.

Miller (1990) reported that in high-print homes, learners manipulate, transform, make up, and write down language. They become **metalinguistic;** that is, they can step back from literacy experiences and think or talk about them as process. They use language to ask questions and thus learn more about language. In studies reported by van Kleeck (1990), children displayed metalinguistic competence as they made reasonable predictions when they did not understand what was said to them or what they saw in print. They also distinguished between everyday talk and school instructional discourse. They knew that teachers tell information, ask students to report current events or facts from readings, and ask questions for specific answers determined in advance.

As prereaders develop literacy prerequisites, they come to consider more and more what it is that they know. Among the important preliterate metalinguistic competencies, van Kleeck later (1995) identified form components as "(1) knowledge of print and book conventions; (2) conscious knowledge of the sound component of language,

Marginal notes:

Wanting to be literate and imitating literate behaviors are natural for children in societies that value print.

Children from high-print homes have important preliterate metalinguistic competencies.

or phonological awareness; and (3) letter knowledge, including their names, shapes and sounds" (p. 35). According to van Kleeck, these form competencies are teachable, but because "many will have acquired the majority of the skills discussed herein in their homes . . . not all children will need such training. This is true even of phonological awareness" (p. 46).

Schickedanz (1986) described how homelike emergent literacy activities can be incorporated into preschool settings to replace early direct teaching of decoding or printing. Typical preschool events of making lists of supplies needed, writing recipes, posting student names for chores and leadership, writing procedures for book checkouts, labeling spaces where classroom materials are to be put away, and other routine daily actions support literacy by providing a print-rich environment that makes none of the artificial demands of direct lessons.

These suggestions recall Nelson's (1989) principles for first-language teaching. He recommended that learners (1) engage in active exchanges with fluent partners; (2) see adults as models instead of direct teachers; (3) have chances to compare their productions with adult models to discover discrepancies; (4) be allowed to ignore multiple examples of one system and not move forward in it while simultaneously showing rapid learning in another system; (5) benefit from incorporating language into scripted events of meal preparation, pet care, chores, and other predictable events; (6) be exposed to wholes before parts; and (7) be permitted to demonstrate individual rates for acquiring proficiency. Teachers who agree that adults support early oral language by reacting to intent rather than form and by encouraging risks instead of compliance to rigid structures see that literacy lessons can do the same.

As noted by Rhodes and Dudley-Marling (1988), both oral-language-learning and early-literacy environments allow children to see language used in meaningful contexts that are interactive and social. "It's our view that reading and writing development are guided by the same language-learning principles that govern oral language development. Children learn language, oral or written, to fulfill personal, communicative intentions" (p. 25).

Learner-Initiated Literacy

Evidence drawn from studies of children who have begun to write and read on their own initiative prior to formal instruction suggest some natural learning preferences. One of them is that writing precedes reading, contrary to the way schools introduce instruction. Jensen (1993, p. 291) quoted one writing expert as saying in an interview ". . . young children can learn to write before they can read. They can write anything they can say, whereas they can read only a

Researchers have learned a great deal from observing children who begin to write and read without instruction.

fraction of the words they can say. And so writing is easier, quicker, and in a sense, more 'natural' than reading—certainly more easily and naturally learned." Goodman (1986) estimated that 50 percent of 3-year-olds practice writing incorporating at least some letterlike forms. Moxley (1982) found that early readers typically emerge from self-taught writers. "This approach to reading by preschoolers resembles what might be called a language arts approach, a holistic involvement with several related language activities" (p. 211).

Durkin's (1982) longitudinal research revealed further that students who learned to write and read before school did so with the aid of "(a) a literate environment; (b) adult models who read; (c) interesting experiences that were discussed; (d) availability of someone who answered questions and responded to requests related to reading, writing and spelling; (e) availability of materials for writing; and (f) positive contacts with books and reading" (p. 2).

Mothers of early readers tell us that their children prefer to get meaning cues from pictures or the context rather than sounding out words.

According to Torrey (1979), preschool readers use learning processes different from those of school-taught readers. Mothers of early readers have documented that their children did not spontaneously sound out words, but preferred meaning cues from pictures or known words surrounding unfamiliar ones. Torrey summarized the reported learning experience of early readers helped by adults: (1) discovery was guided; (2) meaning was emphasized over form; (3) coercion was avoided in favor of free choice; and (4) active engagement took precedence over passive instruction (p. 137).

In contrast to Torrey's reports of direct print-to-meaning methods used spontaneously by preschool readers, van Kleeck (1995) interpreted Adams's (1990) conclusions about fluent readers as "supporting training that emphasizes form" (p. 29). Adams's finding that "Fluent readers" not only "process every letter they read" but also "translate print to speech by subvocalizing when they read" was said by van Kleeck to "implicate a thorough knowledge of sound-letter correspondences" (p. 29). Perhaps this contrast can also be interpreted to mean that if children have been taught to decode print through sound they will do as they have been taught, but that, left to their own devices without formal instruction, they can also construct meaning from print without going through the sound system. What the contrast clearly underlines is that there is more than one way to learn to read, and that teachers might enhance early formal instruction by considering the methods of those who learned at home.

Rhodes and Dudley-Marling (1988), for example, recommended that school literacy environments duplicate the conditions under which children have learned to read before they come to school. Homelike conditions to support learner-initiated growth include ensuring that students are (1) exposed to a wide range of reading materials, (2) hear books read and discussed, (3) see others reading and writing for life purposes, (4) have easy access to books and writing materials, (5) have adults around who pretend that children's intentions about writing are realized and who act as if they understand the text because they can figure out the intent, and (6) have adults who answer questions, immerse them in print, and respond to the functions and not the forms of early attempts.

Examples of Early At-Risk Learners

Contrasting reports of studies of at-risk children as they approached literacy tasks offer further insights. Thomas, Rinehart, and Wampler (1992) reported kindergarten-year findings from a three-year study of four children to compare their talk with their literacy tasks as they moved from a Headstart program through first grade. During the Headstart year, the investigators had concluded that (1) those with the most developed oral language had the best understanding of the functions of reading and writing; (2) those who actively engaged in talking with adults and those whose families frequently read to them had better oral language; (3) those who scribbled at home had better performance in writing; and (4) time devoted to oral language promoted interest in writing.

Three subjects entered traditional skills-based, basal-driven kindergarten classrooms; the fourth entered a more flexible classroom. As participant-observers over three months, the investigators recorded data over circle time, reading, activities, recess, and lunch. In contrast to Headstart procedures and the fourth classroom, three kindergarten routines limited class talk to directions, regulations, and information from teachers to students. Neither student talk nor writing was included in the program. The researchers concluded that, after one year of formal instruction, three of the four had learned (1) that there is only one correct way to write and that the invented spellings and scribblings of Headstart were wrong; (2) that reading is defined as pronouncing words correctly and quickly; and (3) that writing is form rather than a function of expressing meaning. "In revealing literacy to these young learners piecemeal, not at all in the natural way they learned oral language through meaningful social settings with accompanying context, these teachers appear to be limiting how these children define literacy" (p. 161).

In contrast, Franklin (1992) reported a case of a 3-year-old diagnosed with "a severe expressive language delay" (p. 46) whose preschool years were spent in an environment where literacy events were tied together. Teachers read to children every day, then wrote down students' dictated responses to each reading. Later, children read books with predictable refrains and told their own stories spun from them, which teachers wrote down and read aloud. At no time

Revealing literacy to young learners piecemeal appears to be limiting.

were children expected to copy conventional alphabetic symbols, complete worksheets, or pronounce aloud letters or words presented in print, but they were permitted time and encouragement for scribbling and looking at books with adults who engaged in dialogues about readings. By the second preschool year, the boy with a language disability was printing his name, although only four lessons had directly taught this skill. By age six, he wrote his name fluently, recognized and printed all upper- and lower-case letters, and read several predictable books reliably. Franklin concluded that many youngsters with language problems "who are immersed in a print-rich setting and are allowed to participate actively in reading and writing activities teach themselves about the forms, functions, and conventions of print" (p. 48).

These contrasts point up the impact of early experiences on children's concepts of literacy as well as their response to instruction. Early experiences with print may result in many different levels of knowledge and performance. For some learners, the chances to continue to develop these understandings become limited once they enter schools that offer instruction in conflict with their expectations. Schools should open doors to literacy; instead, some close them.

Cases in Literacy (1989) reported the experience of another child with a disability who ended first grade displaying abilities to write her name and pronounce at sight about 20 words. The school's approach to providing remedial instruction for this learner included the general curriculum teacher's substituting a set of books with highly regular spelling but nonsense sentences such as "Jan ran for the fan," because the student was unsuccessful in matching letters and sounds or recognizing whole words as taught within the adopted basal-reader program. However, the child was also pulled out of the class 30 minutes a day to work with a remedial reading teacher who employed student-chosen library books, predictable books, the child's and other children's dictated experience stories written down, and other natural materials to combine reading and writing instruction. Despite intent to help her, teachers confused this learner by offering strategies useful in one setting that would not transfer to another, and by patching together an incoherent combination of piecemeal instruction.

OPTIONAL LITERACY APPROACHES

The two opposing views of beginning literacy are called *code emphasis* and *whole language.*

The following discussion contrasts two opposing views of beginning literacy—**code emphasis** and **whole language.** Code emphasis implies that code breaking occurs by translating print to sound. Phonological awareness is a prerequisite, and the ability to pronounce words at sight or sound them out is the route to comprehending text from letters to words to sentences. In contrast, whole language emphasizes contextual meaning as it combines listening, speaking, reading, and writing activities. To whole-language advocates, any language experience is valued, and phonological skills are no more important than others, although they interact with meaning cues and word-order cues to help learners construct new meaning as they decode the text both top to bottom (whole to part) and bottom to top (part-to-whole), thus making use of their explicit language knowledge along with prior knowledge of how the world operates.

The next section first presents principles, prerequisites, assessment, instructional organization, examples of typical lessons, and considerations of what constitutes disability under code-emphasis approaches, followed by implications of methods for students entering school with language disabilities. Then, there are contrasting descriptions of whole-language principles, prerequisites, assessment, intervention organization, sample literacy lessons, and concepts of disability, followed by implications of whole-language instruction for students with disabilities.

Instead of recommending an either–or choice, the discussion closes with examples of how some code-emphasis strategies can work within a whole-language framework. An eclectic program offers students with oral language disorders multiple strategies for beginning literacy.

> This chapter suggests using code-emphasis strategies within a whole-language framework.

CONTRASTS BETWEEN TWO APPROACHES

Over the past decade, traditional code-emphasis approaches that begin with individual letters or words matched to speech have been challenged by whole-language approaches that emphasize the integration of entire texts for related listening, speaking, reading, and writing. According to Shuy (1986), the shifts began with research in oral language. The field of psycholinguistics debated the usefulness of larger units of connected text. Entire essays or book chapters became the subject of study instead of minute parts of individual sentence structure. At the same time, the field of sociolinguistics replaced concepts of objective, universal, static competencies with subjective, variable, dynamic functions. These shifts led to options for early literacy instruction.

> Code-emphasis approaches begin by teaching individual letters or words matched to speech: Whole-language approaches emphasize the integration of listening, speaking, reading, and writing.

Principles

Both code-emphasis and whole-language advocates describe comprehension as the goal of reading. However, the two approaches differ in convictions about how comprehension occurs.

Recoding is translating printed symbols to phonemic counterparts and vice versa.

To describe how code-emphasis approaches work, the term **recoding** was assigned by Goodman (1973) to the process of translating printed symbols to phonemic counterparts and vice versa. Recoding exchanges one code for another. A sound symbol is substituted for a visual symbol in reading, and a visual for a sound symbol in writing. In contrast, the term **decoding** means translating a code to a noncode; the process of code breaking. Reading always requires decoding, because meaning must be constructed around the text that appears on printed pages (Orasanu & Penney, 1986). However, reading need not include recoding printed letters to sounds. Decoding can proceed directly from print to meaning without going through the sound system. Similarly, writers can encode words without first pronouncing them (Moxley, 1982).

According to code-emphasis advocates, recoding is the essential route to decoding, which unlocks the meaning that resides in the text page, after which comprehension occurs when readers match print information with words and concepts stored in memory through oral-language competence. However, whole-language advocates consider recoding unnecessary—though an option as a last-resort strategy—whereas decoding is a necessary but not sufficient step toward comprehension. In whole-language approaches, readers construct meaning by combining prior vocabulary, word order, and topic knowledge with decoding of text pages.

Prerequisites

The two approaches assign varying roles to cues that use (1) prior competence in a first language, and (2) prior schemas or concepts about how the world operates. Code-emphasis views hold speech as primary, with reading and writing as secondary language codes. Whole-language advocates view listening, speaking, reading, and writing as an interactive network that is mutually supportive throughout the primary years, rather than hierarchical (Goodman, 1986). Both views consider competence in oral language important, but with different emphases.

Language skills considered prerequisite to code-emphasis tasks emphasize sounds (phonological awareness, phonic analysis and synthesis), whereas whole-language lessons focus on meaning (semantic) and word-order (syntactic) cues. Both approaches make varied use of word-building (morphological, structural analysis) cues. Although many code-emphasis advocates talk about segmentation and other phonologicial abilities as clearly prerequisite to literacy instruction, others point out that these subskills can just as likely be considered results of literacy or reciprocal with reading–writing processes. The issue is not settled (Brady & Shankweiler, 1991; van

Kleeck, 1990). In her examples of how workbook pages used in early reading instruction prepare learners to pass readiness tests, Durkin (1982) reported that when explicit measures of code-emphasis readiness activities were administered to children who had already learned to read through whole-language procedures, "certain children who could read did less well on the test than others who had not participated in the program and could not read" (p. 3).

Whole-language advocates are not concerned with specific language prerequisites. Instead, they see any language experience as reinforcing all others. Because listening, speaking, reading, and writing form an interactive network, there is no predetermined order in which they should be experienced in instruction.

Schemas, or recurring and therefore predictable events in human experience, occur in code-emphasis approaches only in final stages, when subskills are said to come together so readers can grasp an entire text. In contrast, whole-language approaches center on prior schemas and topic knowledge at the outset, before attention is given to new information in text.

> Both approaches make varied use of word-building cues.

Assessment

Code-emphasis approaches to assessment center on hierarchical skills presumed to underlie more complex tasks. Thus, the focus is on either alphabetic codes or isolated words. For example, Bryant (1986) called for alphabetic-code measures of ". . . not only single letter-sound correspondences, but syllables and complex orthographic sequences as well" (pp. 67–68). Majsterek and Ellenwood (1990) concluded from reviewing literature on code-emphasis approaches that "One aspect of a child's oral language, phonological awareness, has been consistently linked to later reading development and eventual reading performance" (p. 11). They went on to recommend examples of screening measures they described as promising and developmentally appropriate for prekindergarten children considered at risk for delayed literacy. They suggested three procedures: sound blending, sound categorization, and word segmentation.

More comprehensive examples of measures of phonological processes were described by van Kleeck (1990), who suggested that both letter detection and phonological awareness are component skills in children's ability to realize the formal relationship between speech and print. She stressed that research has validated that "phoneme segmentation ability on entry to school was the best predictor of 39 measures of reading achievement 2 years later" (p. 33).

> Code-emphasis approaches recommend assessment of sound blending, sound categorization, and word segmentation.

A collection of reports edited by Brady and Shankweiler (1991) described numerous phonological assessment procedures. Measures featured combinations of word, syllable and phoneme segmentation, alliteration, letter-sound matching, syllable rhyming, and other tasks at multiple levels of phonological awareness and varied dependence on memory.

At the whole-word level, Perfetti (1986) identified standards based on rapid word naming. Code-emphasis advocates tend to value word-recoding fluency over other competencies. For example, arguing that less fluent readers have poor comprehension, Carnine, Silbert, and Kameenui (1990) offered guidelines for reading rates only, not for rates plus accuracy, and they based their standards on readability levels of materials, not on empirical data about how fast real students pronounced the materials. Housbrouck and Tindal (1992) described their procedure for measuring rate plus accuracy in one-minute timed oral recodings. The measure was a middle score of words correctly pronounced immediately on presentation.

Among researchers who have conducted programmatic studies of relationships between oral language and literacy, Catts (1993) reported that "phonological awareness has been shown to be related to early reading achievement, especially word recognition" (p. 950). He also found that "semantic-syntactic language abilities accounted for individual differences in reading comprehension over and above that accounted for by phonological awareness and rapid naming." Catts addressed a controversy between early psycholinguistic reading experts who "argued that these higher level language abilities are of primary importance in learning to understand printed materials" and others who "have proposed that although semantic-syntactic language abilities are very important for reading comprehension, word recognition skills play an independent role in explaining variability in comprehension, especially in the early school grades" (p. 956).

Although the purpose of recoding is to provide a route to meaning, researchers have identified learners who can pronounce words but do not assign meaning to those words (Perfetti, 1986). Teachers refer to such readers as *word-callers* rather than *readers*. Assessment of pronouncing words aloud without an accompanying measure of comprehension does not tell examiners whether students are decoding, as opposed to merely recoding.

Adams (1990) drew the connection between rapid word recoding and meaning when she summarized as follows: "Laboratory research indicates that the most critical factor beneath fluent word reading is the ability to recognize letters, spelling patterns, and whole-words effortlessly, automatically and visually. The central goal of all reading instruction—comprehension—depends critically on this ability" (p. 54). Her emphasis on visual methods supports an inference that phonic methods are merely preliminary to whole-word fluency.

Students who know how to accomplish a recoding task—say, pronouncing a set of high-frequency words–are expected to recognize those words whether they are presented in isolation or in meaningful context. Because skills are said to emerge separately, code-emphasis advocates measure them in isolation and separated from meaning. For example, readers may be asked to apply phonics generalizations to pronounce nonsense words, or writers may be instructed to spell words dictated outside a clause frame, or to spell to dictation words that they cannot recode at sight, because an adopted spelling text bears no relation to an adopted basal reading text.

Writing skills are measured apart from reading in code-emphasis procedures, typically by using indirect measures that require students to judge appropriateness of grammatical usage or spelling rather than direct measures that ask students to create original text. Indirect measures on standardized norm-referenced tests ask testees to read the materials before making judgments; therefore, the extent to which reading influences low results cannot be established (Moran, 1987). Direct measures of writing under code-emphasis have tended to count how many whole words are written in a timed writing, calculate a percentage of words spelled correctly, or examine how many letters are joined together (Deno, 1985). Even though students are actually writing the words, as distinct from just selecting them under indirect procedures, code-emphasis methods do not combine direct quantitative methods with quality examinations of original text judged for appropriateness of form for audience and purpose.

Reading and writing assessment that would express whole-language theory and practices have yet to become widespread; only about 10 states use whole-language methods on statewide competency tests (Henk & Rickelman, 1992). In contrast to code-emphasis value on tests, whole-language advocates emphasize continuous during-instruction monitoring by recording how learners participate in daily reading and writing. Finding strengths on which to build is viewed as the assessment goal of choice to learn whether students are ready to engage in specific literacy events and how they might be helped to profit more from them (Weaver, 1991).

For example, Watson (1985) suggested classroom observation along with interviews as natural ways to gather information. She recommended watching how students attend to print even when someone else is reading to them. Among 10 questions she asks readers is to recount what they try when they encounter a passage that does not make sense, and how they use context of known words or topic knowledge to make educated guesses about unfamiliar text. Cases in Literacy (1989) recommended, ". . . we must add assessments of actual performances—ongoing analyses of students completing a variety of literacy tasks initiated by either the student or the teacher. Literacy events are described by observing and interviewing, not by testing" (p. 24).

The critical factor underlying fluent reading is the ability to recognize letters, spelling patterns, and whole words effortlessly, automatically, and visually.

Ten states use whole-language methods on statewide competency tests.

Rhodes and Dudley-Marling (1988) presented a set of guidelines for observing readers and writers within a whole-language framework. They recommended watching both teacher- and student-initiated silent reading over varied materials and purposes in natural settings without interference or prompts by observers. They suggested that observations be recorded daily, summarized regularly, and supported by audio or videotapes. They listed several types of interview questions useful as follow-up for observations, which they argued should always be used to confirm or disconfirm the results of any norm-referenced tests that schools may require.

Rhodes and Dudley-Marling (1988) also suggested that within a whole-language context, miscue analysis following oral reading can help teachers discover the extent to which students use semantic and syntactic cues in making oral substitutions for unfamiliar words. Asking students to insert appropriate words in passages from which, say, every seventh word has been deleted can measure the ability to use semantic and syntactic cues in adopted subject-matter textbooks. Multiple readings can reveal fluency. During oral sharing times or when writing about reactions to readings, ability to retell main plot points in sequence, to predict, draw inferences, determine conclusions are all strengths to be discovered by interactions between teachers and readers or writers.

Instructional Organization

Code-emphasis and whole-language approaches differ in the extent to which they focus on language competencies.

The two initial-literacy approaches differ in inclusion of, focus on, and sequence of language competencies. Listening and speaking apart from oral recoding play limited roles in code-emphasis instruction, which also typically separates reading from writing exercises that center on subskill instruction. Reading instruction awaits readiness as demonstrated by phonological awareness tasks of letter-sound matching, rhyming, alliteration, or sound blending, or until a vocabulary of rapidly pronounced words in isolation reaches a reliable preset figure. Writing instruction is delayed until recoding of printed text has reached a predetermined competency level.

In code-emphasis instruction, recognition of meaning begins with grapheme-phoneme relationships. Pronouncing words is the route to linking them with meanings stored in oral-language memory. Access to oral vocabulary automatically permits recognized words and their combinations perceived in accurate sequential order to lead to comprehension of the larger text. Similarly, writing is a process of building letter forms into words, clauses, sentences, and paragraphs. Reading lengthy connected passages is delayed until underlying subskills of letter and word identification are demonstrated. Writing instruction may be limited to handwriting and spelling drill and practice, or fill-in-the-blank grammar exercises offered on the assumption that discrete skills come together later to permit creation of original text.

Code-emphasis strategies follow a procedure that Weaver (1988) described as bottom-up and part-to-whole. That is, strategies emphasize alphabetic letter-to-word or word-to-sentence progressions. Readers examine parts of texts minutely to pronounce individual words so they can recognize them as part of their stored oral vocabulary. Bottom-up strategies look at details first, then arrive at the meaning of the entire text by putting those details together.

Simmons and Kameenui (1989) reported that code emphasis reserves the introduction of structural (morphological) and contextual (semantic and syntactic) analyses "until students have developed proficiency in basic applications of the phonics code" (p. 35). In other words, meaning making occurs following recoding of print to sound. As the final stage of the instructional sequence they described, Simmons and Kameenui said that passage reading required the reader "to orchestrate all the previously reviewed component skills" (p. 36).

Perfetti (1986) described a three-stage code-emphasis procedure beginning with words stored in memory. First, lexical access—recognizing a word—allows conceptual features associated with the name code to be recovered from storage. Second, retrieval of concepts from storage permits a comparison of the recovered information to the sentence encoded through lexical access; that is, the text is compared against what is already in the reader's meaning repertoire. Third, the larger unit—the entire text—is comprehended by constantly updating the overall meaning in relation to the understanding of each sequential sentence in a longer passage.

In contrast, whole-language instruction begins with entire texts instead of parts of texts. Using top-down reading instruction, teachers guide learners through strategies that examine titles, bold headings, captions, charts, graphs, or pictures to predict what the text is about. After activating prior knowledge about the topic by asking oral questions for oral answers, whole-language teachers help students use their grasp of their first language by making educated guesses about unknown words based on known words in the context.

Whole-language instruction begins with entire texts instead of parts of texts.

As Orasanu and Penney (1986) have pointed out, words have varied meanings depending upon the larger context. Only after the whole text has been considered do whole-language advocates turn to examining any component parts, and they may not do so at all if readers are successful at constructing new meanings with initial top-down strategies.

Whole-language instruction from the first lesson combines listening, speaking, reading, and writing into related activities with authentic communicative purposes. Students use the same vocabulary and concepts across four integrated language competencies as they engage in related everyday activities. No hierarchical order of language competencies is implied. Thus writing need not await reading proficiency ". . . writing is not always used to serve reading and follow reading . . . just as often writing can come first, and reading can serve writing" (Jensen, 1993, p. 291). As Chiang and Ford (1990) pointed out, "the importance of process-oriented writing programs becomes even greater as educators realize that writing also assists readers in appreciating and understanding text" (p. 32).

Whole-language instruction combines listening, speaking, reading, and writing into related activities.

Whole-language instruction assumes that oral language, still undergoing development from ages 3 through 8 (Karmiloff-Smith, 1979), is refined by early reading and writing whether undertaken spontaneously by children before entering school or introduced in school. Literate activities contribute linguistic concepts not available through oral utterances. For example, the unit called a *word* is more readily identified in print than in the speech stream.

In whole-language instruction, because speech is not considered the route to meaning, readers need not use a part-to-whole progression beginning with recoding alphabetic letters or isolated words. Instead, learners may employ a whole-to-part-to-whole strategy, based on the entire discourse unit being considered, along with semantic and syntactic cues at sentence level, before any identification of smaller units like single words. The ability to grasp the overall purpose and point of a piece of written language enables readers to predict with greater accuracy the details later provided by decoding

Lack of skill in decoding single words does not prevent text comprehension.

single words and their arrangements in sentences. For example, a heading that includes the word *health* increases the likelihood that words such as *doctor* or *nurse* will be decoded quickly and accurately and that a word not now stored in a sight vocabulary, such as *hospital*, might be decoded by an educated guess based on the preceding known words being used as semantic cues. Lack of skill in decoding single words in isolation—whether by recoding methods or direct print-to-meaning methods—does not prevent readers from obtaining the gist of the text (Moxley, 1982).

According to whole-language advocates, assignment of meaning depends on the broad social context in which the text is read as much as on the graphemic material encoded in the text. Readers pull out relevant features of the text and combine them to produce the most probable interpretation of what is on the page, which is then tested against knowledge of the real world.

Contrasting Examples of Literacy Lessons

In a summary of code-emphasis approaches to literacy instruction, Sawyer (1991) characterized such lessons as a routine based on basal reading texts, workbooks, and tests. The teacher is a manager who distributes and collects prepared worksheets, conducts subskills lessons according to a scripted manual, and presents hierarchical skill explanation-demonstrations over phonics and spelling rules.

Simmons and Kameenui (1989) offered an example of a pure part-to-whole sequence of code-emphasis lessons that begin with phonemic awareness activities of segmenting individual sounds and blending them into words, and progress through sound-symbol association lessons, pronunciation of regular and irregular words in isolation to automatic recoding levels, and ultimately to reading an entire connected passage which, they suggested, should contain primarily words that can be successfully pronounced by segmenting, sound-blending, and sound-symbol associations. They added that any words that do not conform to these requirements should be pre-taught individually as sight words. No mention was made of combining semantic (meaning) or syntactic (word-order) cues with phonic and graphic (word-shape) cues.

In a series of lessons to help readers with specific language disabilities to identify words efficiently, Dana (1991) offered an approach to code-emphasis instruction. Using a task-analytic approach, Dana employed a sounding chart to teach 10 phonics generalizations that apply often—though not entirely reliably. Effectiveness was demonstrated in two studies conducted by the originator with students with special learning needs and by three colleagues who used the approach with readers with severe disabilities.

Sawyer (1991) pointed out that, in contrast to code emphasis, a sample whole-language lesson employs neither teachers' manuals nor explicit directions for delivery. Harste (1989) emphasized that no two whole-language classrooms will look alike because "whole language isn't an orthodoxy—there's no one right way to do it—but rather . . . it's an invitation to inquiry, an invitation for teachers to take charge of their classroom once again" (p. 6).

One typical example of a long-standing whole-language approach is a language experience lesson, in which students' dictated or student-written oral narratives, explanations, or arguments are typed by a teacher or aide, presented as reading instructional materials, then revised on paper by students as a composition activity, culminating in a final communicative product. Thus, students respond repeatedly to text they have generated themselves, with oral reading aloud and listening to one another's stories, oral discussion, and writing integrated to reinforce one another.

Contrasting Views of Disabilities

Code-emphasis advocates' notions of disabilities focus on identifying specific subskills lacking in unsuccessful readers and writers, characterizing those missing skills as deficits, and attempting to instill them

Code-emphasis advocates target the specific skill deficits of children with disabilities.

through remedial intervention. The emphasis is on changing the behavior of the individual rather than attempting to modify the demands on readers or writers (Weaver, 1991).

Furthermore, code advocates draw inferences about students' deficits by measuring their responses to test items that may vary in difficulty or familiarity. Skills are viewed as either mastered or not mastered; readers and writers are not expected to vary in performance as a function of task type or purpose (Lipson & Wixson, 1986).

Whole-language advocates talk instead about mismatches between learner competencies and task demands. Shuy (1986) said that, instead of asking whether students can recognize or write individual words, investigators want to know about prior language and concepts, and how students conceptualize an entire passage and relate it to their lives. Rather than trying to identify static skills, researchers acknowledge that variations in competencies occur at all levels of ability, depending upon the dynamic interactions among text passages and students' prior knowledge of a first language and schemas about how the world works. Because so many dynamic competencies intertwine, it is impossible to separate the contribution of any specific variable to reading or writing success, and no single variable can be held constant to study others as a possible single cause of a literacy problem (Harste, Woodward, & Burke, 1984a).

When whole-language advocates Lipson and Wixson (1986) and Weaver (1991) described alternative ways of looking at disabilities, they pointed out that language competencies work in concert with task demands, purposes, and social expectations to cause variations in the effectiveness of reading and writing processes. A disability may show up under certain demands and circumstances, but not under others. This approach acknowledges sociocultural context, the type of discourse being attempted, and the task demands imposed by text difficulty and other conditions such as teacher questions or purposes—all of which interact with language, motivation, and interests displayed by learners. Studies have shown that readers classified as disabled according to specific criteria can perform as well as average readers on many tasks. The problem is to specify which conditions give rise to success for students with specific reading characteristics. Furthermore, performance on many measures varies for able readers as well. Variation is normal. Studies have also shown variations in performance by good readers on word-recognition tasks, depending on (1) whether words are represented in adopted basal readers, (2) the frequency of word occurrence, (3) whether materials are expository or narrative, (4) how syntactically difficult the text is, (5) length of the passage, and (6) whether a stated purpose for reading was established in advance. Thus Lipson and Wixson and Weaver

> Whole-language advocates consider the sociocultural context, the type of discourse attempted, and the task demands imposed by the difficulty of the text.

concluded that a useful view characterizes a reading or writing disability as a relative, rather than absolute, phenomenon that resides not in the learner but in a mismatch between the student's strengths and the environmental conditions under which the learner is asked to perform.

Rhodes and Dudley-Marling (1988) agreed: "We believe that reading and writing failures cannot be adequately explained simply by pointing to disabilities or problems intrinsic to the child. Learning to read and write is a matter of an interaction between students and their learning environments . . . certain classroom environments are much more likely to foster literacy development than others, especially for learning disabled and remedial readers" (p.78).

A reading or writing disability may be relative, rather than an absolute, phenomenon.

Implications of Interventions for Students with Disabilities

Simmons and Kameenui (1989) reviewed research on beginning reading instruction for low-achieving readers. They concluded that "although research findings support phonics-based programs, results do not endorse all phonics programs unequivocally," with more positive results coming from programs that are systematic and intensive (p. 35). Dana (1991) questioned the feasibility of teaching multiple phonics generalizations to students who had already demonstrated an inability to memorize rules.

For beginning readers with language disabilities, code-emphasis or recoding approaches may present problems in requiring phonological awareness, stored oral vocabulary, rule induction, and memory for linguistic material. Recoding print to sound could be expected to be difficult for students with language disabilities who demonstrate during primary school years (1) chronic conductive hearing loss associated with recurring middle-ear pathology; (2) high-frequency sensorineural hearing loss associated with failure to discriminate consonant sounds, identify alliteration, or rhyme syllables; (3) insufficient memory to hold subcomponents in mind to build toward a grasp of an entire passage; or (4) inadequate stored oral vocabulary to permit automatic assignment of meaning after whole words are recoded. Furthermore, for students with disabilities who lack a conceptual base because they could not explore their world and label incoming perceptual motor stimuli, limited word meanings are stored to be activated by recoding. "In such cases, phonics does not serve much purpose. This is an especially crucial issue with hearing- and language-disordered children" (Hasenstab & Laughton, 1982, p. 12).

Code-emphasis approaches may present problems for beginning readers with language disabilities.

As many experts have pointed out, phonics generalizations constitute an inexact science even for students with normal hearing and speech. According to van Kleeck (1990), students must first learn that each letter represents a sound, then "one of the child's subsequent tasks will be to realize how truly rough this correspondence is" (p. 36). Some learners demonstrate only limited pattern recognition and inductive reasoning from pattern examples, but code emphasis requires a number of rules governing probable pronunciation of graphemes according to surrounding graphemes, then decisions about whether rules apply or if the stimuli are exceptions in the English system. Recoders must judge readily when a pattern does and does not apply—a considerable cognitive load on readers with disabilities. Karmiloff-Smith (1979) said that even typically developing children over 5 years old are still organizing generalizations about language, but do not yet have procedures for exceptions—a feature of later development.

Code-emphasis approaches place many demands on metacognitive skills.

In addition, code-emphasis approaches make considerable demands on metacognitive functioning. Unfortunately, speech and language problems interfere with stepping back from language to think about and become aware at a conscious level of how language works. Metalinguistic ability has been identified as central to beginning reading and writing (Weaver, 1988, 1994), but lacking in students with language disorders (Catts, 1993; Kamhi, 1987). Disadvantages of code-emphasis approaches for students with language problems do not, however, mean that children with oral language disabilities cannot learn to read. Torrey (1979) has pointed out that self-taught readers demonstrate "that it is possible to become a skillful reader without ever showing much reliance on phonics" (p. 134).

Whole-language approaches appear to offer some advantages for students with language disabilities. Among strategies employed by beginners who initiate reading by asking adults to help them, "reliance on a links-of-a-chain approach for decoding sounds is conspicuously missing" (Moxley, 1982, p. 212). The first advantage of whole-language approaches is that they recognize the emphases applied by self-initiated readers and writers.

If reading material need not be recoded into speech, students have access to meaning directly from print. A step is bypassed. Silent reading (without subvocalizing) is faster than oral reading because students are not slowed down by having to pronounce words. Because meanings can be understood when pronunciation is unknown, the size of the reading vocabulary can move ahead of oral vocabulary, and students can read words they never have an opportunity to use orally. Children with oral language disorders might also find, as have many with hearing impairments, that seeing words in print can be meaningful even if speech counterparts are not within their repertoires.

Readers draw meaning from a combination of semantic (meaning), syntactic (word order), and, as a last resort, graphic and phonic (word shape and letter sounds) cues found in the text. New information in the reading is then combined with prior knowledge of the world, which has no counterpart in the text. Thus the decoding of words in sentences is important but not enough for comprehension (Orasanu & Penney, 1986). Emerging data on the role of prior knowledge in comprehension of texts make attempts to increase word knowledge inadequate as means to improve assignment of meaning to decode the recoded text.

Perhaps the major advantage of whole-language approaches is that there is no need to delay reading or writing until so-called prerequisites have been established. That is, oral vocabulary or word order need not reach specific levels of competence before reading is introduced, nor must reading be well under way before writing is undertaken. Students with language disorders who do not readily master reading are not deprived of writing instruction. In traditional recoding programs, it is not unusual to find youngsters of grade six or seven still being drilled on phonics and still recognizing words at a level classified as about grade one, while being deprived of subject content and writing instruction because they lack those recoding skills. If only a speech route to literacy is assumed, then students who become stalled along that route do not move from word recognition into higher level comprehension skills or into composing meaningful writing. This deprivation is avoided under whole-language approaches.

Encouraging writing along with or prior to reading promotes active involvement because writers initiate rather than receive messages. Some have suggested that writing may from this point of view be considered a developmentally easier task than reading, because writers need only construct and not reconstruct meanings initiated by others (Jensen, 1993).

The whole-language approach offers advantages for beginners with language disorders because it provides redundancy. The same vocabulary and topics are introduced for listening, concept building, oral discussion of word meanings, sight reading, spelling, and formulating original text, both orally and in writing. Along with orally discussing what words can mean in various contexts, students practice putting those same stored words to work within meaningful statements that they compose themselves and either dictate to an adult or write in their own fashion. Connected materials generated by students then become the basis for reading instruction—as beginners learn to recognize stored words in meaningful contexts they have composed themselves—and for writing instruction, as learners revise their own products according to feedback from peers and teachers. Because all newly learned words can be read and written as well as discussed, students can choose the emphasis they want to place on these competencies on any given day.

> Whole-language approaches appear to have some advantage for children with language disabilities.

> A major advantage of whole-language approaches is that there is no need to delay instruction until certain prerequisites are achieved.

Chiang and Ford (1990) deplored "a disturbing paucity of research on whole-language approaches with students with LD. This is in part due to the incompatibility of the whole language philosophy with research designs that primarily focus on the artificial manipulation of small parts of language instruction. This often makes comparisons between whole language programs and more traditional programs difficult" (p. 32). Agreeing with the finding that "Formal research on the effects of whole language upon remedial or learning disabled students . . . seems sparse," Weaver (1991, p. 41) added that anecdotal reports support the use of these procedures to the same degree as with students who are not labeled as having a disability.

COMBINED APPROACHES TO LITERACY INSTRUCTION

As she contrasted models of literacy, Weaver (1988, 1994) described two views as constituting (1) part-to-whole, bottom-up, and outside-in—from text to reader, or (2) whole-to-part along with part-to-whole, top-down prior to bottom-up, and inside-out—reader to text—as well as outside-in. Weaver thus depicted a code-emphasis approach as moving in only one direction, but a whole-language emphasis as offering opportunities to include part-to-whole, bottom-up, and text-to-reader organization within the broader framework.

Aspects of a code-emphasis approach can be merged into a whole-language framework.

The following section offers additional expert support for an eclectic approach to beginning literacy instruction, then illustrates how aspects of a code-emphasis approach can be incorporated into the whole-language framework. O'Shea and O'Shea (1990) advocated a combined approach for students with disabilities: "At the risk of being accused of 'fence-sitting' over the issue of which theoretical model and instructional practices are most appropriate for explaining and treating reading problems . . . all are considered as having contributed in some way . . ." (p.89).

Chiang and Ford (1990) advocate taking the best from both the reductionist view, that learning is enhanced when complex tasks are broken down into smaller parts, and the holistic view, that tasks are best learned if left intact. "It is not our intent to suggest that assessment and instruction methodology for students with learning disabilities be restricted to just one of these viewpoints. Instead, we advocate moving toward a balance in using approaches represented by both viewpoints when working with children with reading problems" (p. 31). They go on to argue that acceptance of the principles of whole language need not imply rejection of other approaches as ". . . other effective methods can bring about a more balanced perspective" (p. 34). Chiang and Ford also pointed out that a variety of remediation procedures must be available to meet the varied needs of those with specific learning problems.

Adams (1990) similarly supports the combination of two approaches. Her conclusion, after reviewing the literature on beginning reading instruction, is that balanced systematic skill instruction combined with meaningful materials produced the best results.

How is the recommended combination to be organized for instruction? Whole language should be emphasized as the general framework for instruction, with code emphasis embedded in brief applications in early decoding strategy lessons. Materials, activities and literacy events, topical organization, emphasis on problem solving for meaning, direct teaching of strategies, focus on learner-directed growth, and adjustments to meet individual needs should be drawn from the whole-language philosophy.

EMBEDDED CODE EMPHASIS

For beginning readers, in the view of members of the Commission on Reading (Anderson, Heibert, Scott, & Wilkinson, 1985), phonics instruction has a limited place. Generalizations and strategies should be taught simply and over a short period of time to help learners identify words in their oral vocabularies quickly and accurately so that decoding supports the meaning-construction process.

Grossen and Carnine (1993) were more specific about recommended brevity of phonics instruction. They supported the selection of code-based materials for an initial instructional period which they defined as "only the first few months of reading instruction," after which "students must learn quickly to move beyond sounding out to sight-word reading" (p. 25). However, they cautioned that whole-language approaches are mistaken in "completely deemphasizing the language code. There is no research to support such a move" (p. 25).

In agreement with teaching both meaning-centered and code-emphasis approaches, van Kleeck (1995) nevertheless differs from other experts in that she argues for emphasizing form and meaning separately. Contending that a meaning-centered approach leaves form "to chance" but code emphasis teaches it "systematically" (p. 30), she also points out that "phonics . . . focuses too narrowly on sound-letter correspondences and often ignores crucial skills underlying them" (p.32). She goes on to describe a two-stage preliteracy development program that would first teach a meaning foundation centered on showing how print is both meaningful and enjoyable. She proposes that this stage be delivered over preschool or kindergarten, adding, "it seems critically important that the lessons of this meaning foundation stage be learned before any systematic form emphasis begins" (p. 36). She proposes to follow a meaning foundation stage with an intensive form foundation stage emphasizing

The role assigned to phonics in beginning literacy is limited but critical.

phonological awareness and alphabetic knowledge—the teachable skills underlying sound-letter correspondences. For children who need these foundations ("Not all children . . ." p. 46) "the separate focus on form and meaning would continue into the first and perhaps even the second grade" (p. 47). Again, van Kleeck recommends that the two approaches be emphasized separately during a period that she calls preliteracy. In other words, her sequence is not literacy instruction but is prerequisite to it in that these foundations provide the metalinguistic base for literacy lessons.

Most other experts have discussed formal school literacy instruction over the primary grades. In placing phonic analysis and synthesis into the broader structure of whole-language approaches, Weaver (1988) suggested that teachers "Directly teach only the most basic letter-sound correspondence," and "Give additional help in internalizing letter-sound patterns only to children who seem especially able to benefit from such instruction" (p. 401).

Because it is only through association of letters with speech sounds that "the code is finally 'cracked' with the realization that each sound in speech is represented, more or less, by one phoneme" (van Kleeck, 1990, p. 36), some code-emphasis instruction could be expected to benefit learners. The role assigned to phonics in beginning literacy is limited but critical.

One reason phonics lessons should be incorporated is that explicit associations of letters with speech sounds gives rise to invented spelling, one of the features of emergent literacy that experts say should be encouraged. Weaver (1988) even suggested that phonics generalizations could be taught mainly through children's own writing by encouraging functional spelling in early writings and first drafts, supplemented by repeated readings of enjoyable materials. Although van Kleeck (1990) claimed that many children make these associations without explicit instruction, Brady and Shankweiler (1991) concluded that most children have to be taught the grapheme (letter)–phoneme (sound) connection by direct instruction.

Worksheets have very limited, if any, usefulness in beginning reading.

In comparing code-emphasis approaches to beginning reading with whole-language instruction, Grossen and Carnine (1993) applaud the whole-language move away from worksheets, which have "no research base whatsoever where learning to read is concerned" (p. 25). Weaver (1988, 1994) agrees that phonics instruction embedded in a holistic framework should make no use of fragmented worksheets or isolated tasks but should instead incorporate phonics instruction within meaningful text when other language cues have not led to comprehension.

Only after students have employed multiple contextual strategies should teachers introduce the phonological strategy, which should continue to be deemphasized in favor of meaning, word-order, and word-shape cues, according to O'Shea and O'Shea (1990). Following initial instruction, teachers should recommend declining use of phonic cues. The process of sounding letters to recode to speech is much slower and less efficient than the immediate visual recognition of entire words, as advocated by Perfetti (1986) and Adams (1990), or the use of semantic or syntactic language cues (Weaver, 1988, 1994). Therefore, use of phonic cues may be effective for recoding single words in isolation but it becomes—for readers of connected text late in the primary years—a strategy of last resort to be applied after more efficient schema and language context strategies have been applied to the whole text. "When all systems are permitted to operate, as they do in natural language settings, the amount of graphemic information needed is significantly less than that necessary if presented in isolation" (Harste et al., 1984a, p. 103).

Emphasis on semantic and syntactic language cues first, followed by phonics strategies, would appear to be consistent with a recommendation by Catts (1993) that intervention programs should target semantic and syntactic processes as well as phonological awareness.

However, language experts tend not to recommend along with language interventions the schema development that reading experts have emphasized as critical to accompany text comprehension. Weaver (1988, 1994) followed early psycholinguistic reading experts such as Smith (1971) and Goodman (1973) in presenting numbers of ways to design initial literacy lessons to help learners apply semantic, syntactic, and phonological language cues to aid text comprehension, but she went on to point out that decoded text must be joined with prior knowledge of how the world operates to construct new meanings. This entire process is what experts in the field currently define as reading.

SOURCES FOR READING AND WRITING

Available individual reading texts should feature trade books as found in libraries, both literary and popular, both fiction and nonfiction, and some in paperbacks that can be taken home or carried around in pockets. Big books with oversize type and pictures should be on hand for group modeling and sharing, with teachers delivering top-down models for exploring them. Predictable books with refrains that are readily memorized, wordless picture books for spontaneous invention, student-produced writings ranging from hand-printed cards to laser-printed classroom publishing, and environmental labels placed around classrooms to designate common objects and order classroom routines constitute some of the materials to be read by classroom groups.

Among the best books for beginners are trade books as found in libraries, books with predictable refrains, wordless picture books, and student-produced writings.

Writing materials should include a variety of implements for handwriting, from crayons to felt pens to pencils and pens of all sizes, along with slates, chalkboards or dry-pen boards, individual tablets, all manner of readily available paper for scribbling and drawing at will, and typewriters and computer word processors when available. Oversized tablets and overhead transparencies to record group compositions allow teachers to model writing. Opaque projectors can show student writing products to groups for discussion.

ACTIVITIES AND LITERACY EVENTS

Because "whole language researchers have shown there's no inherent order in the way language is learned," Harste (1989) argued that whole-language lessons can start anywhere, so long as they begin with whole texts instead of parts. Summarizing whole-language emphases, Harste identified continuous language models, flexible and open-ended activities, collaborative group assignments, and using language daily for real purposes that meet genuine student needs.

Chiang and Ford (1990) offered lists of activities for whole-language lessons. Students typically share reading of big or predictable books aloud with discussion or telling of stories similar to those read, and they may dictate or write reactions to the books, followed by journal writing, then more group activities in which discussion, reading, and writing take equal turns.

Repeated readings of familiar books are recommended.

Over time, facilitators gradually increase the complexity of shared book sessions. Also, repeated readings of familiar books can occur in groups or be included in individual reading times. Repeated readings can be combined with teacher-led predictions about what could be expected next, followed by teacher open-ended questions for which divergent responses are accepted. Time is always set aside for sustained silent reading of up to 30 minutes. During short periods of teacher-guided reading by individuals, teachers make observations and conduct interviews over strategies in use and make suggestions for strategies to be tried. Sawyer (1991) recommended that facilitators also read aloud from more complex material than students are capable of reading themselves.

Large-group collaborative writing may follow teacher modeling of writing process. Composing sessions begin with prewriting brainstorming and move through several drafts, revisions, and final editing, followed by individual conferences over writing, with decisions about which products are to be included in individual portfolios.

Graham and Johnson (1989) offered some cautions for introducing literacy events to students with disabilities. Prereading activities are needed to activate prior knowledge, set goals, introduce key concepts and vocabulary, and provide advance organizers. During-reading activities should include three readings over most texts, mapping procedures to identify text structure, inserting questions into text rather than waiting until all text has been read, asking students to look back at text to locate answers, and simple summaries of text as brief as one sentence. All these teacher-initiated text supports were shown by Graham and Johnson to be based on investigations with students with disabilities.

Topical Organization

An eclectic program excludes typical code-emphasis basal reading materials featuring unconnected narratives followed by discrete skills applications. Instead, Beck (1985) suggested that reading and writing stimuli be organized into topical units. That is, multiple reading passages over related information would be made available for reading and writing instruction for a lengthy period. Although Beck did not address this factor, student-generated language experience materials could be organized by themes just like published materials. That is, teachers and students could negotiate and originate materials on specific related topics over weeks of instruction.

Reading and writing stimuli may be organized into topical units.

Grouping reading and writing topics according to thematic content promotes building of schemas as recurring events in human experience and activating of prior knowledge about specific topics. For instance, a topical choice might be family celebrations that could help children from several cultures develop schemas for experiences

that would include, for example, a typical American birthday party. Schemas would include the expectation that guests would attend, present gifts, play games, sing "Happy Birthday" as candles are blown out, and then eat cake. Minor variations in details do not detract from basic schemas. An analogy can be drawn between plot and story. The same plot—child finds pet, loses pet, regains pet—can be realized in multiple stories differing in details. Proximity in time of associated materials would enhance recall and discussion of similarities and differences. Facilitators could establish prior knowledge for weeks of work by building on immediately preceding reading and writing texts.

Problem Solving for Meaning

"Readers need functional responses to their reading to learn that how they read makes a difference in their lives" (Moxley, 1982, p. 23). To this end, Moxley recommended changing instructional emphasis from form to consequences. Meaning-based activities can permit readers and writers to check their own perceptions with those of others reacting to the same or similar texts, and the emphasis can be placed on the functional consequences in their lives of having read or written a particular material. Was there an idea in a text that they had never thought of before? What did they learn that they could apply to a hypothetical situation? How can writing down an idea permit reflective thinking about what it means? Concern with meaningful consequences is a shift away from too much arrangement of prior constraints that have been typical of code-emphasis approaches. Examples of prior constraints include requiring accurate formation of letters before words can be written, or correct spelling before composition instruction is undertaken. Focus on consequences means that such matters are ignored if the end result of the attempt is a genuine communication: The test is the effect on the reader of a student paper, not the form of the written product. Similarly, an emphasis on consequences in reading would imply that a reader is considered successful if the gist of the material is grasped, even if many words cannot be recoded on demand. The goal of reading and writing is thus shifted from demonstrating mechanical prowess to exhibiting an ability to receive and initiate meaningful communications.

> Meaning-based activities permit beginning readers and writers to check their perceptions with those of others reacting to the same or similar texts.

Direct Teaching of Strategies

During part of each day's work, facilitators work with individuals to help them develop specific strategies for reading and writing. For students with disabilities, O'Shea and O'Shea (1990) recommended emphasis on semantic relationships within entire texts as the primary system for identifying unfamiliar words, meanings of which should be checked against readers' real-life experiences. Teachers should present syntactic (word order) and morphological (roots, prefixes, suffixes) cues as supporting semantic (meaning) cues.

Construction of new meaning during reading is based on selective use of semantic, syntactic, morphological, graphic, and perhaps phonic cues in the text as well as knowledge of how language works and previous life experiences. Studies cited by Orasanu and Penney (1986) found that readers gained in comprehension performance without improvement in recoding fluency. Though rate and accuracy on oral reading tests throughout strategy training remained essentially stable, the comprehension-monitoring strategies they engaged in were successful in improving their grasp of the text. That is, readers who did not recode additional text were nevertheless able to improve their ability to understand that text by applying cognitive strategies to discover organizational principles that made the text more accessible.

According to Lipson and Wixson (1986), strategy training can help overcome weaknesses in academic texts, which are typically not well organized. Although teachers might change text to make connections more explicit, such modifications may be too time-consuming. Instead, direct teaching of strategies is suggested by Weaver (1988) to enable readers to ask for just as much help as they need to move forward, but not to become overdependent on teacher questioning.

In oral reading, teachers should correct only those substitutions that disrupt meaning.

When oral reading is conducted one-to-one so teachers can offer strategy help, Graham and Johnson (1989) suggested that teachers should correct only those oral substitutions that disrupt meaning. Rather than providing ongoing correction as is featured in some code-emphasis approaches, teachers should limit their comments and interruptions during oral reading, according to O'Shea & O'Shea (1990). The reasoning is that students will continue to take risks and make predictions only if they perceive that it is safe to do so.

Learner-Directed Growth

Among differences between traditional classes and whole-language frameworks, one of the most growth-enhancing is the shift from external control of events by teachers in the former and the opportunities for student control of their own learning activities in the latter. Learners should be encouraged to undertake self-directed activities.

The shift from teacher control to learner control is among the most appealing aspects of whole-language frameworks.

Negotiating topical themes between teachers and students, then using student-chosen books from among selections provided to fit the theme, then permitting students to decide in what order and for what periods of time most tasks will take place, then asking learners to form their own flexible groups for sharing, for group writings, or for feedback about writings—all these opportunities for choice support responsible student decision making.

As described by O'Shea & O'Shea (1990), a developmental shift of control from the adult to the child is conceptualized by teaching that anticipates competence before it is demonstrated. Thus, beginners read a great deal of text before they have all the skills to do so, but teachers support them by modeling self-guided verbalizations and strategies that are being taught along with the contextual reading. Harste (1989) would place major responsibility for discovery on learners. After facilitators offer diverse strategies to readers and writers, it is up to students to "search for patterns that connect" (p. 7).

Adjustment of Demands

Because "language variation, including variation in comprehension, is the norm rather than the exception" (Harste et al., 1984a, p.104), children who enter school with language disabilities share with other learners the fact that variation in competencies depends on the demands placed on them and the contexts in which they are asked to perform. Therefore, one of the major instructional needs of an eclectic approach is to adjust relative emphases of integrated language instruction to meet individual needs.

For example, if whole-language environmental observation and interview assessment procedures reveal that one primary student lacks schemas or prior specific topic knowledge, that student needs more emphasis on concept building through direct experiences to be talked about both while they are occurring and afterward. On the other hand, a second student whose entering schemas are well developed but whose decoding strategies reveal that graphic shape and size of words are typically ignored may need to write more so the print code becomes more visually familiar as she creates word configurations that are meaningful to her. As another example of meeting individual needs, Franklin (1992) described a natural literacy approach that asks young children to develop at their own pace. Intended for students of all ethnic and racial backgrounds, the program emphasized reading and writing words important to learners' own cultures.

In many situations, teachers can modify task demands rather than trying to modify student behavior.

Teachers modify demands rather than asking students to do all the changing. "If one accepts language variation, and with it variation in what was learned, one can appreciate a language learner's current achievements and language experiences for what they are" (Harste et al., 1984a, p. 104). The relevant question is not the level of a student's language skills, but the conditions under which a primary reader and writer can and will apply whatever competencies have been achieved (Weaver, 1991). Facilitators discover those conditions and modify experiences accordingly.

In Goodman's (1982) opinion, the key to helping students is to lead them to value themselves as language learners and users, and to value the language process as interactive and constructive. He insisted that learners who have been told that they have reading or writing deficits "must set aside the pathological view of self," rid themselves of labels, and focus on the strengths they used to develop oral language (p. 89).

The requirements teachers place on learners when conducting a code-emphasis classroom can gradually adjust to the modified demands of a transitional classroom that combines the two approaches, with approximately equal time devoted to each, followed by a shift to a total whole-language framework with limited code emphasis embedded in early instruction. Anderson (1991) addressed a process to be followed to effect the change. He outlined and charted a four-stage, gradual transition to show how personnel assignments, space, time, grouping, materials, activities, and evaluation programs would all change over a period of time so that adjustments need not be abrupt.

EFFECTIVE PROGRAMS FOR LEARNERS WITH SPECIAL NEEDS

Perhaps the program with the longest history of combining whole-language philosophy with some embedded code-emphasis tasks is Reading Recovery. Developed in New Zealand by Clay (1985) and imported to this country primarily by faculty at Ohio State University, the program has been studied over a decade. Clay (1985) described the program in detail, and Weaver (1988,1991) summarized features of the program and results of effectiveness studies.

Students selected for Reading Recovery are those who have completed one year of literacy instruction, after which they score at the lowest levels of their peer groups. About ten percent of groups by age 6 develop inappropriate strategies or cannot coordinate strategies into a useful system to decode text. For 3 to 6 months of tutorial instruction delivered 30 minutes per day, students engage in the following tasks (Clay, 1985, p. 56): (1) oral rereading of one or more books read in prior tutoring sessions; (2) oral rereading of a book read for the first time the previous day, while the teacher records substitutions or mispronunciations with notations; (3) intensive individual instruction in specific strategy needs discovered through earlier observation and analysis; (4) writing a story; (5) examining a new book using prereading, top-down strategies to predict what it is about; and (6) oral reading of the new book.

> Students selected to participate in Reading Recovery have scored at the lowest levels of their peer groups.

Weaver expressed some reservations about the extent to which this intensive tutorial program could be called a whole-language approach. However, participants clearly read entire texts repeatedly, then discuss them with the teacher, who offers multiple strategies including top-down cue systems based on contextual cues. When students write, they select topics and generate original texts for direct evaluation. Reading and writing are combined.

However, there is no attempt to use topical organization, students do not choose initial books but only those to reread, oral reading is emphasized over silent, and teachers note and comment on code-emphasis gaps that intensive instruction is then designed to fill. Assessment employs standardized norm-referenced measures to supplement ongoing observation records. Students work in genuine communicative interactions with a tutor but not with one another.

Most students demonstrated average performance in reading and writing after only 14 weeks in the program.

Clay reported that most participants left the program after up to 14 weeks of instruction with average performance in reading and writing, then maintained those levels as long as three years later. Weaver (1991) reported that Clay later cited, in an unpublished paper, government figures to show that only 1 percent of children who participated in the New Zealand program were subsequently referred for additional remedial assistance. Weaver's (1991) report of the Ohio studies stated that two-thirds of those participants left the program with average levels of achievement compared to their peers. They maintained gains over two years following their dismissal from the program.

As another example of the type of collaborative assessment and intervention planning that could support an eclectic approach to beginning literacy instruction for students with language disabilities, Silliman, Wilkinson, and Hoffman (1993) described how a transdisciplinary team composed of an ASHA-certified speech-language pathologist who also is a classroom teacher, a deaf educator, a school social worker, and a teaching assistant joined forces to design goals for students with language disabilities. The perspective of listening, speaking, reading, and writing as interrelated communicative processes emerging from social contacts informed the team's efforts to (1) facilitate strategies to help students learn how to learn, and (2) ease the shift from oral to literate communication. Authentic assessment procedures included closed and open types of observational tools. What they called closed systems included rating scales and checklists for both student self-evaluation and teacher judgment, records of how much help students requested in which types of literacy tasks, analysis of both works in progress and completed products, and previously determined observations of oral interactions. Open systems included teacher anecdotal daily notes, running records of observations and interviews about strategy use, maps of classroom interactions, and transcripts of teacher–student and student–student oral discourse (p. 61).

Authentic assessment is also discussed in Chapter 8.

Results of studies of these procedures showed that one of the most effective techniques was the immediate jotting of Post-it notes to catch readers/writers using effective strategies. Videotaping was also helpful. Following a one-year pilot program, the procedure was adopted as a means to "think of assessment as an integrated, continuous, and natural part of the everyday activities of the classroom, because any teaching-learning interaction contains potential assessment information" (p. 71).

Another example of an attempt to apply whole-language philosophy to a program for students with language disabilities was reported in detail by Westby and Costlow (1991). The setting was a self-contained classroom for 8 to 10 children per year, ages 5 to 9 years, all with delayed and disordered oral language and listening skills. Facilitators included a teacher and aide who were always present plus a speech-language pathologist for half a day, and part-time volunteers.

Instruction for the entire morning was based on language activities surrounding cooking, art, science and building projects organized according to topical themes. Children talked about, listened to others talk about, read about, and wrote about the activities in which they engaged. For half the morning, some worked on pretend play and creative dramatics while others engaged in group story reading, storytelling, and oral reporting about books previously read. Afternoon sessions were individualized, and included mathematics instruction or therapies outside the classroom.

Although none of the children who left this special communication classroom at age 9 prior to the implementation of the experimental whole-language activities had demonstrated reading and writing skills, ". . . after 3 years of the whole language program, it was extremely rare for a child to leave the program without some functional reading and writing skills, and many children were able to be mainstreamed into regular classes" (p. 73).

SUMMARY

If they want to facilitate literacy, teachers and others working with children during the early childhood period of the primary grades must evaluate assumptions about the nature and purposes of reading and writing instruction. Code emphases or recoding approaches, delivered in isolation from meaningful social language interactions with adults and peers, conflict with widespread acceptance of a philosophy that connections must be made among listening, speaking, reading, and writing. Whole-language principles can govern an instructional organization that includes limited phonics generalizations for those students who can use them. Phonic as well as graphic cues can supplement semantic, syntactic, morphological, and pragmatic cues within a cultural context. Materials, literacy events, topical structure, emphasis on meaning, learner-directed growth, and adjustment of individualized demands foster authentic communicative interactions.

An eclectic approach to beginning reading and writing fosters literacy by incorporating some features of two opposing views. Learners with language disorders deserve to gain control over literacy facilitated by professional personnel who lose no time over debates about instructional methodology, but instead help learners to apply multiple strategies.

REFERENCES

Adams, M. J. (1990). *Beginning to read: Thinking and learning about print*. Cambridge, MA: MIT Press.

Anderson, G. (1991). Teacher transition from a skills to a whole language classroom. In J. Hydrick (Ed.), *Whole language: Empowerment at the chalk face* (pp. 179–184). New York: Scholastic.

Anderson, R. C., Heibert, E. H., Scott, J. S., & Wilkinson, I. A. (1985). *Becoming a nation of readers: The report of the Commission on Reading*. Champaign, IL: Center for the Study of Reading.

Beck, I. (1985). Comprehension instruction in the primary grades. In J. Osborn, P. Wilson, & R. Anderson (Eds.), *Reading education*. Lexington, MA: Lexington Books.

Brady, S. A., & Shankweiler, D. P. (Eds.). (1991). *Phonological processes in literacy*. Hillsdale, NJ: Lawrence Erlbaum Associates.

Bryant, P. (1986). Phonological skills and learning to read and write. In B. Foorman & A. Siegel (Eds.), *Acquisition of reading skills* (pp. 51–69). Hillsdale, NJ: Lawrence Erlbaum Associates.

Carnine, D., Silbert, J., & Kameenui, E. (1990). *Direct instruction reading* (2nd ed.). Columbus, OH: Merrill.

Cases in literacy (1989). Newark, DE: International Reading Association.

Catts, H. W. (1993). The relationship between speech-language impairments and reading disabilities. *Journal of Speech and Hearing Research, 36,* 948–958.

Chiang, B., & Ford, M. (1990). Whole language alternatives for students with learning disabilities. *LD Forum, 16,* 31–34.

Clay, M. (1985). *The early detection of reading difficulties*. (3rd ed.). Portsmouth, NH: Heinemann.

Dana, C. (1991). An alternative approach to phonics instruction. *Teaching Exceptional Children, 23,* 32–37.

Deno, S. (1985). Curriculum-based measurement: The emerging alternative. *Exceptional Children, 52,* 219–232.

Durkin, D. (1982). *Getting reading started*. Boston: Allyn & Bacon

Franklin, E. A. (1992). Learning to read and write the natural way. *Teaching Exceptional Children, 24,* 45–51.

Goodman, K. (1973). Psycholinguistic universals in the reading process. In F. Smith (Ed.), *Psycholinguistics and reading*. New York: Holt, Rinehart & Winston.

Goodman, K. (1982). Revaluing readers and reading. *Topics in Learning and Learning Disabilities,* 87–93.

Goodman, K. (1986). *What's whole about whole language*. Portsmouth, NH: Heinemann.

Graham, S., & Johnson, L. (1989). Research-supported teacher activities that influence the text reading of students with learning disabilities. *LD Forum, 15,* 27–30.

Grossen, B., & Carnine, D. (1993). Phonics instruction: Comparing research and practice. *Teaching Exceptional Children, 25,* 22–25.

Harste, J. (1989). Preface. In D. Watson, C. Burke, and J. Harste, *Whole language: Inquiring voices* (pp. 5–7). New York: Scholastic.

Harste, J., Woodward, V., & Burke, C. (1984a). Examining our assumptions: A transactional view of literacy and learning. *Research in the Teaching of English, 18*(1), 84–108.

Harste, J., Woodward, V., & Burke, C. (1984b). *Language stories and literacy lessons*. Portsmouth, NH: Heinemann.

Hasbrouck, J. E., & Tindal, G. (1992). Curriculum-based oral reading fluency norms for students in grades 2 through 5. *Teaching Exceptional Children, 24,* 41–44.

Hasenstab, M. S., & Laughton, J. (1982). *Reading, writing and the exceptional child.* Rockville, MD: Aspen.

Heath, S. (1982). Narrative skills at home and school. *Language in Society, 11,* 49–76.

Henk, W. A., & Rickelman, R. J. (1992). Trends in statewide reading assessment: A closer look. *Reading Horizons, 33,* 73–82.

Jensen, J. M. (1993). What do we know about the writing of elementary school children? *Language Arts, 70,* 290–292.

Johnston, J. (1988). Specific language disorders in the child. In N. Lass, L. McReynolds, J. Northern, & D. Yoder (Eds.), *Handbook of speech-language pathology and audiology* (pp. 685–715). Toronto: B. C. Decker.

Juliebo, M. (1985). The literacy world of five young children. *Reading-Canada-Lecture, 3,* 126–136.

Kamhi, A. (1987). Metalinguistic abilities in language-impaired children. *Topics in Language Disorders, 7,* 1–12.

Karmiloff-Smith, A. (1979). Language development after five. In P. Fletcher & M. Garman (Eds.), *Language acquisition.* Cambridge, England: Cambridge University Press.

Lipson, M. Y., & Wixson, K. K. (1986). Reading disability research: An interactionist perspective. *Review of Educational Research, 56*(1), I I 1–136.

Majsterek, D., & Ellenwood, A. (1990). Screening preschoolers for reading learning disabilities: Promising procedures. *LD Forum, 16,* 6–14.

Miller, L. (1990). The roles of language and learning in the development of literacy. *Topics in Language Disorders, 10,* 1–24.

Moran, M. (1987). Options for written language assessment. *Focus on Exceptional Children, 19*(5), 1–10.

Moxley, R. (1982). *Writing and reading in early childhood: A functional approach.* Englewood Cliffs, NJ: Educational Technology Publications.

Nelson, K. E. (1989). Strategies for first language teaching. In M. L. Rice & R. L. Schiefelbusch, *The teachability of language* (pp. 263–310). Baltimore: Paul H. Brookes

Orasanu, J., & Penney, M. (1986). Comprehension theory and how it grew. In J. Orasanu (Ed.), *Reading comprehension: From research to practice.* Hillsdale, NJ: Lawrence Erlbaum Associates.

O'Shea, D., & O'Shea, L. (1990). Theory-driven teachers: Reflecting on developments in reading instruction. *LD Forum, 16,* 80–91.

Perfetti, C. (1986). Cognitive and linguistic components of reading ability. In B. Foorman & A. Siegel (Eds.), *Acquisition of reading skills* (pp. 11–40). Hillsdale, NJ: Lawrence Erlbaum Associates.

Rhodes, L. K., & Dudley-Marling, C. (1988). Readers and writers with a difference. Portsmouth, NH: Heinemann.

Sawyer, D. (1991). Whole language in context: Insights into the current great debate. *Topics in Language Disorders, 11,* 1–13.

Schickedanz, J. (1986). *More than ABC's: The early stages of reading and writing.* Washington, DC: National Association for the Education of Young Children.

Shuy, R. (1986). Changing linguistic perspectives on literacy. In J. Orasanu (Ed.), *Reading comprehension: From research to practice* (pp. 77–88). Hillsdale, NJ: Lawrence Erlbaum Associates.

Silliman, E., Wilkinson, L., & Hoffman, L. (1993). Documenting authentic progress in language and literacy learning: Collaborative assessment in classrooms. *Topics in Language Disorders, 14,* 58–71.

Simmons, D. C., & Kameenui, E. J. (1989). Direct instruction of decoding skills and strategies. *LD Forum, 15,* 35–38.

Smith, F. (1971). *Understanding reading.* New York: Holt, Rinehart, and Winston.

Snyder, L. (1984). Communicative competence in children with delayed language development. In R. Schiefelbusch and C. Pickar (Eds.), *Communicative competence: Acquisition and intervention.* Baltimore: University Park Press.

Thomas, K. F., Rinehart, S. D., Wampler, S. K. (1992). Oral language, literacy, and schooling: Kindergarten years. *Reading Horizons, 33,* 149–166.

Tizard, B., & Hughes, M. (1984). *Young children learning: Talking and thinking at home and school.* London: Fontana.

Torrey, J. (1979). Reading that comes naturally. In T. Waller & G. MacKinnon (Eds.), *Read-*

ing research (pp. 117–144). New York: Academic Press

van Kleeck, A. (1990). Emergent literacy: Learning about print before learning to read. *Topics in Language Disorders, 7,* 25–45.

van Kleeck, A. (1995). Emphasizing form and meaning separately in prereading and early reading instruction. *Topics in Language Disorders, 16,* 27–49.

Wallach, G. P., & Butler, K. G. (1995). Language learning disabilities: Moving in from the edge. *Topics in Language Disorders, 16,* 1–26.

Watson, D. (1985). Watching and listening to children read. In A. Jaggar & M. Smith-Burke, (Eds.), *Observing the language learner* (pp. 115–128). Newark, DE: International Reading Association.

Weaver, C. (1988, 1994). *Reading process and practice.* Portsmouth, NH: Heinemann.

Weaver, C. (1991). Whole language and its potential for developing readers. *Topics in Language Disorders, 11,* 28–44.

Westby, C., & Costlow, L. (1991). Implementing a whole language program in a special education class. *Topics in Language Disorders, 11,* 69–84.

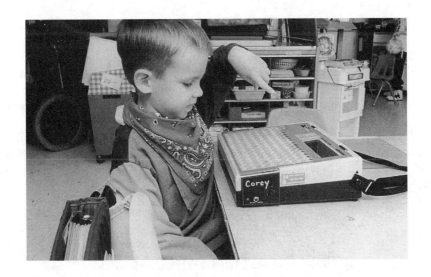

CHAPTER 12

Special Needs of Young Children with Severe Disabilities

Mary Jo Noonan and Ellin Siegel-Causey

As discussed throughout this text, the current trend in service delivery for young children with disabilities is intervention in natural environments, or "full inclusion" (Noonan & McCormick, 1993). Until very recently, full inclusion was available only for some special education students who had mild disabilities and received most of their education in the mainstream of general education classes. Special education professionals believed that students with more significant disabilities would be better served in smaller, more controlled school settings that allowed intensive, one-to-one instruction. We have now learned, however, that it is possible to fully include students with severe disabilities. With proper supports, all children can participate in the general education setting, and all students benefit.

For very young children, **full inclusion** means that infants and toddlers are served in natural environments, such as their home or a day care center, and preschool and elementary school students attend regular classrooms in their neighborhoods (Sailor, Gee, & Karasoff, 1993). For elementary-age students with severe disabilities, special education may include **community-based instruction,** that is, instruction in home and other community locations to address daily living and functional life skill needs. Together, full inclusion and community-based instruction are considered "best practice" for children with severe disabilities. This chapter will discuss strategies for assessing communication needs and designing appropriate interventions for students with severe disabilities in natural school and community settings.

Full inclusion and community-based instruction are "best practice" for children with severe disabilities.

YOUNG CHILDREN WITH SEVERE DISABILITIES

The primary purpose of communication intervention for young children with severe disabilities is to provide them with an effective means to participate in family and community life. Communication is a means of social participation when it enables children to influence the people and events around them (Goldstein & Kaczmarek, 1992). Children control their environments when they communicate their choice of playmates for recess, ask their parents for a kiss, or tell their teacher that they have had enough to eat. Effective communication (i.e., effective social participation) provides freedom and independence to children who are otherwise very dependent because of the severity of their disabilities.

Children with severe disabilities need extensive and ongoing supports in order to participate in natural environments.

Children with severe disabilities have diverse characteristics, but they share the need for extensive and ongoing supports (e.g., personal assistance, special equipment) in order to participate in school, home, and community activities. They also exhibit a wide array of disabilities. For most, significant mental retardation is their primary disability. Others have physical and neurological disabilities that interfere with their intellectual capacity to such a degree that performance is similar to the performance of others who have mental retardation; this is referred to as "functional retardation" (Guess & Mulligan, 1982). Still others have mental retardation in addition to physical, neurological, visual, and/or hearing impairments, which compound the debilitating effects of mental retardation. Behaviorally, children with severe disabilities have obvious delays in basic skills associated with everyday living. For example, these children may be delayed in learning to dress themselves, feed themselves, walk, take care of their toileting and personal hygiene needs, or express their feelings and desires.

Communication characteristics of young children with severe disabilities are as diverse as their general characteristics (Guess, 1980).

Some children with severe disabilities learn to talk in simple phrases and understand most of what is said to them, but their development of speech is delayed. Some understand speech and communicate through pointing, gesturing, or using an augmentative communication system, but do not speak. Others communicate primarily through emotional responses, such as crying or smiling, and do not seem to understand speech, nor do they attempt to use language verbally or nonverbally.

Children with severe disabilities have a range of speech, language, and communication problems. For example, their speech may be unintelligible due to oral-motor coordination difficulties associated with cerebral palsy or due to behavioral problems (e.g., speaking too rapidly) and they may demonstrate echolalia (imitative speech), repetition or perseveration, irrelevant speech, or distortions in pitch or intonation. Although children with severe disabilities have diverse characteristics, a number of common educational needs have been identified:

Children with severe disabilities have a range of communication problems.

Communication is an important educational goal for the vast majority of young children with severe disabilities. Given the presence of severe mental retardation (actual or functional) and a likelihood that there are multiple disabilities, it is difficult to imagine a child with severe disabilities who does not have significant communication needs.

Systematic and consistent intervention is needed to provide sufficient opportunities to learn the relationship between natural cues, the communication skill being taught, and natural consequences (Snell & Brown, 1993). Children with severe disabilities learn slowly, and they often fail to notice the relevant features of what is being taught (Ford & Mirenda, 1984). Therefore, it is important that teaching techniques focus the child's attention on the relevant features of the skill. Errorless or near-errorless instructional procedures should be used to minimize confusion when learning new skills.

Teaching techniques must emphasize independence. This means that intervention procedures should eliminate *all* prompts and independence should be taught directly (Noonan & McCormick, 1993). Eliminating prompts and teaching initiation will ensure that children do not become "prompt dependent" and unable to use their communication skills independently (Reichle & Sigafoos, 1991). Furthermore, children should be provided with an augmentative communication system as a means to independent communication if they are unable to use speech effectively.

Teaching children to initiate interactions helps avoid prompt dependency.

Intervention should occur in actual settings where the communication skills are required to reduce the need for generalization (Kaiser, 1993). Typically, children with severe disabilities do not generalize learned skills to new situations. Teaching techniques that facilitate generalization should be included in all intervention programs.

ASSUMPTIONS

All children communicate in some way.

An important assumption of this chapter is that *all children communicate in some way,* even if they are not intentionally trying to control their environment (McCormick & Noonan, 1984). For example, an infant winces when she is uncomfortable, or a child says "ah" when an activity stops. Recognizing that all young children communicate means that there will always be a starting point for intervention.

A second assumption of this chapter is that *communication intervention should enhance participation in natural environments* (Goldstein & Kaczmarek, 1992). This second assumption influences the nature of communication objectives, the selection of priorities, and intervention methods. For example, new vocabulary words may include a variety of foods to enhance a child's participation during family mealtimes; or printed words may be included on a communication board of photographs so that a wide range of people can understand the augmented communication system.

Communication assessment and intervention techniques described in this chapter are relevant to young children who use speech, augmentative communication systems, and/or other nonverbal/gestural means of communication. Specific considerations for selecting and teaching augmentative communication systems are described in detail in Chapter 13.

FORMULATING COMMUNICATION OBJECTIVES

Procedures for ecological assessment and planning are described in Chapter 7.

Communication objectives for young children with severe disabilities are established following the ecological assessment and planning process described in Chapter 7. The purpose of this process is twofold: first, to determine present and future communication needs associated with home, school, and community activities selected by the child's family and intervention team; and second, to determine present abilities associated with communication needs. The procedures described in Chapter 7 for determining present and future communication needs (i.e., creating a vision and conducting discrepancy analyses) are recommended for identifying broad communication goals for children with severe disabilities. Additional assessment procedures, however, may be required to identify present communication abilities and obtain information needed to formulate specific short-term communication objectives associated with each goal. For example, if a young child is using one-word utterances, and most of the utterances seem to be requests, a more detailed assessment of pragmatic functions may be desired. This additional assessment will provide information on the variety of pragmatic functions in the child's repertoire, and how frequently the functions are demonstrated. A complete assessment of these functions would not have been obtained through the discrepancy analysis. Five assessment strategies are described below to provide information about a child's present levels of communication associated with goals identified through the ecological assessment and planning process. These strategies are particularly relevant to young children with severe/multiple disabilities.

Identifying Present Communication Abilities

As noted above, information concerning a child's present communication abilities is often necessary to formulate specific, short-term instructional objectives. The assessment strategies for assessing present communication abilities are: standardized assessments, communication /language sample, behavioral assessment/functional analysis, ABC analysis, and oral-motor assessment. A thorough assessment will probably require two or more strategies.

STANDARDIZED ASSESSMENTS. There are many standardized assessments that are commercially available for use with children who have severe disabilities and/or children with mild to severe language disabilities. Some of these are components of communication training programs, while others are assessment instruments only. Figure 12.1 lists examples of standardized assessments (covering verbal and nonverbal skills) and indicates the dimensions of communication addressed by each.

Decisions on selecting and administering standardized assessments should be based on the dimensions of communication/language that are of concern. For example, a test appraising the use of symbolic forms would not be relevant for a child who is nonverbal or who does not have an augmentative communication system; without words or symbols there would be no linguistic forms to assess. Instead, an assessment of nonlinguistic communicative forms (e.g., head, limb, or body movements, facial expressions, alternating gaze, shrugging, extending hand/arm, touching object/person, moving toward/away, etc.) would be applicable (Kaiser, Alpert, & Warren, 1987; Rowland & Stremel-Campbell, 1987; Siegel-Causey & Downing, 1987).

An important concern involving standardized communication assessments is that most were normed on *young* children (often toddlers and preschoolers) with normal language development or mild language delays. Because the reliability and validity reported for a standardized test are only applicable for populations comparable to the norm group (Salvia & Ysseldyke, 1985), tests normed on children who are very young or who have mild language delays cannot be scored and interpreted for older children or those with severe disabilities. The tests might be useful, however, as an item-by-item assessment

Most standardized assessment instruments do not include children with severe disabilities in the norm population.

FIGURE 12.1   Standardized assessments appropriate for young children with severe disabilities

Assessment/Program	Communication Dimension			
	Vocabulary	Syntax	Semantics	Pragmatics
Communication Training Program (Waryas & Stremel-Campbell, 1982)		✓	✓	✓
Environmental Prelanguage Battery (Horstmeier & MacDonald, 1978)		✓	✓	
Environmental Language Inventory (MacDonald, 1978		✓	✓	
ICP: Initial Communication Processes (Schery & Wilcoxen, 1982)			✓	✓
PALS: Program for the Acquisition of Language with the Severely Impaired (Owens, 1982)	✓	✓	✓	✓
Communication and Symbolic Behavior Scales (Wetherby & Prizant, 1993)	✓	✓	✓	✓

of skills (without calculating a summary score), or as a guide to the content for assessment.

It is also important to note whether the tests can be modified for children using augmentative communication systems. If children with augmentative communication systems were not included in the standardization sample, the test should be interpreted only on an item-by-item basis, or used as a guide for assessment content.

COMMUNICATION/LANGUAGE SAMPLE.   The language sample (Miller, 1978) was described in detail in Chapter 6. For young children with severe disabilities, it is particularly useful for assessing the adequacy of their

Language sampling procedures are also discussed in Chapter 6.

communication repertoires. For example, a communication/language sample analysis of the functions associated with language *use* may reveal that a child communicates to make simple requests (e.g., asking for a toy) or to protest and express dissatisfaction (e.g., saying, "no more"), but rarely answers questions, and does not contribute to conversation.

The language sample can also be used with children who are nonverbal to evaluate the functions and effectiveness of gestural communication. One such communication/language sample indicated that a nonverbal child communicated a wide range of requests, but had frequent difficulties in communicating the exact nature of his request. When the interventionist tried to guess what he wanted, the child often changed his request if something equally appealing was named. For example, he wanted help retrieving something he had dropped, but indicated he wanted a drink when the interventionist guessed what he wanted and asked if he was thirsty.

BEHAVIORAL ASSESSMENT/FUNCTIONAL ANALYSIS. Behavioral assessment is a direct observation assessment technique. Its main purposes are to quantify (i.e., measure) a behavior of interest and to identify what seems to be controlling or maintaining it (Bijou, Peterson, & Ault, 1968; Nelson & Hayes, 1979). The first step is to operationalize the behavior by writing a behavioral definition (e.g., "A *nonverbal request* occurs when Tommy points to something, with or without vocalizing, or when he alternates glance between an object and an adult, with or without vocalizing"). Next, the behavior is quantified by observing and recording a relevant and measurable characteristic of it, such as frequency of nonverbal requests. Other types of measurement used in behavioral assessment include percent, duration, latency, rate, interval recording, and time sampling. (For a more extensive discussion of measurement techniques in behavioral assessment, the reader is referred to Brown & Snell, 1993.)

In addition to quantifying the behavior, events that occur before (antecedent) or after (consequent) may be altered to determine what may be controlling the behavior (Baer, Wolf, & Risley, 1968). For example, a child's favorite games can be placed out of reach to determine whether the arrangement will result in the child's making requests. Antecedent and consequent alterations not only illustrate what *may* be maintaining or reinforcing a behavior, but also allow the interventionist to evaluate potential intervention strategies.

Similarly, behavioral assessment techniques may be used to conduct a functional analysis. In a functional analysis, behavioral assessment data are carefully examined to determine what use or purpose a behavior serves for a child (Iwata, Dorsey, Slifer, Bauman, & Richman, 1982). This is an important part of communication assessment because some young children use inappropriate behaviors, such as

The effect of varying antecedent and consequent events is useful information when planning intervention.

A functional analysis yields
hypotheses about the purpose
that the inappropriate behavior
is serving for the child.

tantrums or self-injurious behavior, to communicate when they lack socially acceptable communication skills (Donnellan, Mirenda, Mesaros, & Fassbender, 1984).

A functional analysis yields hypotheses about what purpose an inappropriate behavior is serving. For example, several days of data collection might indicate that a preschooler begins biting her hand at about 10:30 each morning. The functional analysis also indicates that the child gets increasingly active as lunchtime approaches. One hypothesis is that the child bites her hand when she is hungry. Teaching an appropriate communication skill that serves the same purpose as the behavior of concern will test this hypothesis. The preschooler who bites her hand may be taught to ask for a snack. If the hypothesis is correct, and both behaviors do indeed serve the same purpose, then reinforcing only the appropriate communication behavior will result in a decrease in the inappropriate behavior.

ABC ANALYSIS.   This assessment strategy is a behavioral assessment technique utilizing continuous recording (Bijou et al., 1968; Brown & Snell, 1993). The evaluator lists each child behavior ("B"), the events that precede or are antecedent to the behavior ("A"), and those that follow or are consequent to the behavior ("C"). Typically, the evaluator records the observations in a three-column A-B-C format (see Table 12.1). The duration of the ABC analysis may include several short segments (e.g., six 10-minute intervals throughout the day), or one or more long segments (e.g., two 1-hour intervals).

Following the observation(s), the data are reviewed to identify patterns of behavior: antecedent-behavior relationships, behavior-consequent relationships, and/or antecedent-behavior-consequent relationships. This information allows the evaluator to assess communication/language behavior *in context*. Contextual information (noted in the antecedent and consequent columns) is helpful in identifying the content and use functions of the child's communicative responses (e.g., the child said "me," and pointed to a juice box in response to a peer getting a soda; "me" is serving the function of a request).

The communication/language sample, behavioral assessment, and ABC analysis are informal observational assessments. They should focus on the individual's typical and spontaneous behavior, be conducted by familiar persons, and employ real-life materials and situations. This will result in information regarding meaningful activities at home, at school, and in the community.

MOTOR ASSESSMENT.   Baseline information on areas of motor development related to the development and production of speech must also be considered in a thorough communication assessment of children with severe disabilities, particularly those who have multiple

TABLE 12.1   Sample portion of an ABC analysis

Antecedent	Behavior	Consequence
T. lifts child and carries child to tilt table	Licks upper lip	
Places child supine on tilt table	Head right, right arm extended, left arm flexed, increased tone	
	Head hyperextended to right, moans, appears to be biting lip (?)	T. says "relax, relax, what's the matter?" & fastens knee strap (T. leaves)
	Tone decreases	
Another child calls out	Mouth opens, head extends back and to the right	
The other child whines and whines	Head moves slowly back and forth	
T. returns, unstraps child, puts her arms behind child's shoulders	Lifts head and chest up (anticipates being picked up?)	T. pauses to talk to aide, lifts child and places child prone in the block area
	Moves head slowly side to side	
etc.		

disabilities. Three areas of motor development are important to communication assessment (Morris, 1971; Morris & Klein, 1987):

Head control, including neck and shoulder stability, provides support enabling effective operation of the muscles involved in articulation and respiration.

Respiration and phonation are assessed to determine the extent to which the child is able to coordinate respiration and phonation. A coordinated pattern enables the child to produce a steady vocalization that may eventually be modified to articulate speech sounds.

Normal development of oral-motor patterns for eating coincides with acquisition of oral-motor skills necessary for articulation. Oral-motor patterns, such as chewing, sucking, swallowing, and biting, are reduced to specific components and/or refined to produce speech sounds. For example, the articulation of "m," "p," and "b" is based on the oral-motor patterns of lip smacking and lip rounding for sucking. While *babbling,* infants practice vowel and consonants sounds of

> The three areas of motor development to be concerned with are head control, respiration and phonation, and oral-motor patterns.

speech. Eventually, intonation patterns are added, and adults assign meaning to the speech sounds (e.g., "ma-ma," "hi").

In addition to assessing the normal motor behaviors—head control, respiration and phonation, feeding patterns, and babbling—abnormal motor responses, particularly those associated with neuromotor disabilities (e.g., cerebral palsy), must also be evaluated because they often interfere with speech development (Morris & Klein, 1987).

Postural tone describes muscle tensions.

ABNORMAL POSTURAL TONE.   Postural tone refers to muscle tenseness throughout the body. If a child's muscle tone is abnormally low (hypotonic), chest stability required for deep, regular breathing may be lacking; head control is likely to be poor; and there will be limited phonation. If the child's muscle tone is abnormally high (hypertonic), normal breathing patterns will be inhibited by stiffness in the chest. Abnormal tone is also likely to affect the lips, tongue, and palate, thus making oral-motor movements for articulation difficult.

ABNORMAL PATTERNS OF MOVEMENT.   Abnormal motor patterns, such as uncontrolled movements caused by fluctuating muscle tone or primitive reflex patterns, interfere with normal movement patterns in the speech musculature. One such pattern is the assymetrical tonic neck reflex (ATNR). When the head is turned to one side, there is a significant increase in muscle tone and the arm and leg extend on the face side. The child's jaw may deviate to the face side, and the increase in muscle tone may be accompanied by tongue thrust and jaw thrust.

LACK OF SELECTIVE MOVEMENT.   Selective movements refer to movements that are isolated or differentiated from larger patterns of movement (e.g., pointing with the index finger rather than reaching out with the arm and hand). Selective movements are more mature and sophisticated as compared to gross, undifferentiated movements. Such differentiation in oral-motor patterns allows for independent tongue, lip, and jaw movement. Children with neuromotor disabilities often lack selective oral-motor movement, and thus have great difficulties with the refined oral-motor patterns required for articulation.

Children with neuromotor disabilities typically have difficulties with the refined oral-motor patterns required for articulation.

SECONDARY OR COMPENSATORY MOVEMENT PATTERNS.   Children with abnormal reflexes and motor patterns frequently develop secondary or compensatory patterns that affect or interfere with speech. For example, a child with a strong flexion pattern may sit with a rounded back that eventually results in a sunken chest structural deformity. This structural deformity, in turn, results in shallow, abnormal breathing patterns.

The assessment of normal and abnormal oral-motor patterns should be conducted by a transdisciplinary team, including a physical therapist, occupational therapist, and/or speech-language therapist. Specific guidelines for assessing oral-motor functioning are beyond the scope of this chapter. An excellent oral-motor assessment, *Pre-speech Assessment Scale* (Morris, 1984), provides thorough directions for assessing each area of oral-motor behavior described above (see also Morris & Klein, 1987).

Communication Profile Assessment

Baseline assessment information for young children who are communicating nonsymbolically may be organized across cognitive, social, communicative, and motor domains. The Communication Profile Assessment (Siegel-Causey & Wetherby, 1993) is a strategy for organizing this baseline information in six areas:

COMMUNICATIVE FORMS. Assessment data on communicative forms includes a comparison of vocal and gestural forms. Consideration should be given to both conventional forms recognized by most people, as well as those that are idiosyncratic. Initial communicative forms might include generalized movements, vocalizations (undifferentiated vowels, laughs, cries), facial expressions (smiles, grimaces), head and eye orientation to object/actions of interest, reaching toward desired object, movement of the body to request action, and withdrawal to avoid activity.

Initial communication forms may include generalized movements, vocalizations, facial expressions, and head and eye orientation.

COMMUNICATIVE FUNCTIONS.   Communicative functions are the reasons a child communicates. There are three broad categories of communicative functions: using communication (1) to regulate the behavior of others, (2) to engage in social interaction, and (3) to reference joint attention. Table 12.2 lists communication functions and provides examples. It should be determined whether the child uses any of these three communication functions and how these messages are conveyed.

DEGREE OF INTENTIONALITY.   The degree of intentionality in a child's communication responses must be inferred from observable behavior displayed during interactions. One approach to inferring intentionality at the preverbal level is to define intentional communication using behavioral criteria, such as (1) alternating eye gaze between goal and listener; (2) persistent signaling until the goal is accomplished or failure indicated; or (3) changing the signal quality until the goal has been met (Bates, 1979; Bruner, 1978; Harding & Golinkoff, 1979). The more such behaviors are displayed, the more confident the interventionist can be that the behavior was intentional communication.

TABLE 12.2   Communication functions and examples

Communicative Function	Examples of Forms
Behavior Regulation: To get others to do something or to stop doing it	
Request Object/Action	Child looks at or reaches toward object
	Child gives object when assistance is needed to open or activate it
	Child holds up empty cup for refill
Protest Object/Action	Child pushes other's hand away to stop getting tickled
	Child cries when toy is pushed away
	Child throws unwanted toy
Social Interaction: To draw attention to self	
Request Social Routine	Child taps other's hand to request continuation of game
	Child looks at other and laughs to keep game going
Request Comfort	Child reaches toward mother when upset
	Child raises arms to get picked up
	Child wiggles in chair to get other to adjust his position
Greet	Child waves "hi" or "bye"
	Child extends arm in anticipation of other shaking hand to say goodbye
Call	Child tugs on other's pant leg to get notice from other
	Child vocalizes to get other to come
Show Off	Child vocalizes, looks at other, laughs to get reaction
	Child hides under jacket and laughs until other notices
Request Permission	Child holds up cookie to ask permission to eat it
Joint Attention: To draw attention to object or event	
Comment on Object/Action	Child shows book to get other to look at it
	Child points to photograph to get other to look at it
Request Information	Child holds up box and shakes it with questioning expression to ask what's inside
	Child points to picture and vocalizes to ask what it is

Adapted from Siegel-Causey & Wetherby (1993).

READABILITY OF SIGNALS OR FORMS.   Readability refers to the clarity of a communicative signal and ease with which a signal can be interpreted. For nonsymbolic children, readability is influenced by the degree of familiarity of persons interacting with the children as well as the conventionality of the communicative signals.

> Familiar persons will be more competent at interpreting the child's signal.

REPAIR STRATEGIES.   Children who do not use symbolic communication may be faced with frequent communication breakdowns because of the more limited readability of the signals. Repair strategies describe the child's ability to modify his communication when the desired effects are not obtained. An absence of repair strategies would be reflected in abandoning a communicative goal if it is not immediately achieved. The ability to modify a signal to repair communicative breakdowns promotes successful social exchanges.

CAPACITY FOR SYMBOLS. Although some children do not use symbols expressively, they may understand words or nonverbal symbols (e.g., pictures, sign language). Therefore, receptive language and comprehension response strategies should be evaluated. It is also important to evaluate cognitive skills that are correlates of language (i.e., tool use, causality, imitation, and functional object use). In other words, the child's communicative strategies should be considered in reference to other problem-solving and learning strategies.

As one completes the child's profile, it is important to consider the influence of the activities, and the patterns of interactions currently used by staff within these activities. From the child's perspective, what is there to communicate about in each familiar activity? These questions may help the interventionist not to discern what the child does (already accomplished in assessment process), but rather to discover the potential communication content that the child could communicate about.

Baseline assessment techniques (standardized assessments of vocabulary, syntax, semantics, and/or pragmatics; communication/language sample; behavioral assessment; and oral-motor assessment) and the Communication Profile Assessment are used to provide detailed information on children's present levels of performance. The next step is to gather these assessment data, along with information on parent priorities and discrepancy analysis results (refer to the planning and assessment process described in Chapter 7). All of this information will be reviewed and discussed when formulating communication objectives.

Formulating Communication Objectives

The list of goals identified through person-centered planning and the parent interview should be reviewed by the parents and professionals. The most important of these goals should be identified as intervention goals. Determining which are the most important can be facilitated by judging each against a set of functional criteria. Several checklists, rank-ordering formats, and rating scales for prioritizing goals have been suggested (cf., Falvey, 1989; Rainforth, York, & Macdonald, 1992; Snell & Brown, 1993). They are all quite similar and include considerations such as the following:

There are certain considerations that can help interventionists to prioritize goals and objectives.

- is preference of parent;
- is preference of child;

- is age-appropriate;
- is immediately useful and functional;
- increases ability to control environment/make decisions;
- is needed throughout the day and across multiple settings;
- allows greater access to age-appropriate activities and natural environments;
- enhances social interaction with peers; and
- facilitates the performance of many other skills ("tool skill").

Once communication goals have been established, baseline assessment information pertinent to the selected goals is reviewed. This information includes performance levels on prioritized goals, adaptations that may be needed (alternative or augmentative approaches), and/or possible intervention techniques that may aid in designing interventions. For example, if a prioritized goal is for the child to request assistance when needed, ABC analysis results indicate when and where the child might need assistance, as well as the percentage of time when the child effectively requests assistance. Such detailed baseline information will help the intervention team develop three to five short-term objectives for each communication goal.

Given that young children with severe disabilities learn slowly and frequently fail to generalize, *an ideal communication objective is one that targets a generalized skill*. According to Horner and McDonald (1982), a generalized skill is one that is performed in natural situations when appropriate, and is not performed when inappropriate. Generalization is demonstrated when a child performs a skill correctly in settings where intervention did not occur. It is not necessary to wait for a child to acquire a skill in one teaching situation before addressing the concern of generalization: Generalization may be promoted when a child is *first learning* a skill, rather than afterwards.

Objectives may be developed to address one of three types of generalization: (1) stimulus generalization, (2) response generalization, and (3) stimulus and response generalization. A communication objective that addresses stimulus generalization can be generalized across persons, settings, or situations (e.g., "Tommy will say "hi" when he encounters familiar people in the classroom, in the cafeteria, and on the playground"). In objectives that address response generalization, the communication behavior itself is generalized: a group of skills that serve the same purpose (a "response class"), rather than a discrete skill, are taught (e.g., Deana will point to 'fine' on her communication board, smile and nod her head, or say "o.k." when someone asks how she is). In objectives that address both stimulus and response generalization, a response class is demonstrated across stimuli (e.g., Lily will point to "want" or a photo on her communication board, or to the item itself, to initiate a request to the teacher, the physical therapist, or a playmate at recess).

A generalized skill is one that is performed spontaneously in natural situations.

There are three types of generalization.

TEACHING FUNCTIONAL COMMUNICATION SKILLS

Communication intervention in natural settings *ensures* that communication skills are functional and demonstrated when and where they are needed. When the natural setting is a home or a regular classroom, instruction does not occur during a "communication training" period. Instead, it occurs throughout the day when the communication skills are required or meaningful (Kaiser, 1993). For example, rather than teaching a new communication board picture (a cup to indicate "drink") in isolation, the child is taught to point to the picture to request a drink during breakfast or when arriving at school. Teaching in the natural situation eliminates the need to generalize from the teaching setting to a natural one. Teaching across several natural situations throughout the school day promotes generalization to other untrained settings.

Teaching across natural settings promotes generalization.

A matrix format (adapted from Mulligan & Guess, 1984; and Savage, 1983) for integrating basic skills objectives (such as communication skills) into a child's daily schedule is depicted in Figure 12.2. In the first column, the child's daily schedule of activities is listed. Basic skill objectives are noted across the top of the matrix and are infused into the schedule with checkmarks indicating the activities that provide a meaningful context for instruction. Because these communication objectives/activities were identified through the discrepancy analysis (see Chapter 7), at least one activity is appropriate for each communication objective. Embedding communication skills into other instructional activities teaches functional relationships among skills, with each skill serving as a natural stimulus for the next, and as a natural consequence to the preceding skill (Guess et al., 1978).

Chapter 7 discusses how to do a discrepancy analysis.

Establishing a Symbolic Communication Repertoire

For children without symbolic skills (i.e., words, sign, communication board symbols) or with very limited symbol usage, the general goal is to teach one or more signals or symbols for controlling the environment. (Potential communicative signals include behaviors such as vocalizations, changes in muscle tone, eye gazing, or body movements.) Because communication is a reciprocal process, intervention may address the behavior of the interventionist or the child. A dual focus on child and interventionist recognizes that interactions are influenced by what both the initiator and responder do rather than assuming that one partner has deficits to remediate (Siegel-Causey & Wetherby, 1993).

Communication/language intervention should match the child's skills regardless of the nature or the mode of expression. There are four intervention strategies that are tailored to the child's skill levels and allow the child to experience control of interactions as she

Student Carrie Y.

Semester Fall

Year 1995

Daily Schedule and Activity Objectives	Basic Skill Objectives															
	Communication							Fine motor					Gross motor			Etc.
	greet familiar persons	request needed items	request assistance	indicate task completed	answer single questions	comment to continue conversation	identify sight words	maintains grasp	points with index finger	grasps small items	moves wheelchair forward	pulls self to stand	full elbow extension	transfers to chair		
7:45–8:00 Arrival/Put away personal items	✓	✓	✓		✓		✓			✓	✓		✓			
8:00–8:30 Grooming																
Toothbrushing	✓	✓								✓		✓				
Face washing	✓	✓					✓		✓							
Hair brushing	✓		✓													
8:30–8:50 Circle time																
Socialization	✓			✓		✓										
Songs				✓		✓		✓	✓	✓			✓			
Daily Schedule		✓		✓		✓		✓	✓							
8:50–9:30 Centers		✓		✓												
Select items	✓						✓	✓	✓	✓						
Etc.																

initiates, maintains, and/or terminates communication exchanges: enhancing sensitivity, increasing opportunities, sequencing experiences, and utilizing movement (Siegel-Causey & Wetherby, 1993). This section reviews each of these strategies and concludes with a description of facilitated communication, a controversial approach to teaching symbolic communication to children with autism who do not use speech.

ENHANCING SENSITIVITY.   Studies of early communication interactions between the caregiver and infant show that caregiver sensitivity is vital to the infant's acquisition of communication skills (Bakeman & Adamson, 1984; Odom, 1983; Snow, 1984). Caregivers of nondisabled infants typically are sensitive to signals of readiness to communicate (e.g., the child's direct gaze or leaning forward). Furthermore, they allow the child to take turns during interactions, and they wait until the child has finished responding before taking their turn (Clark & Seifer, 1983). The caregiver's ability to discern the child's signals and to assign meaning to the child's expressions promotes communication exchanges.

Interventionists can enhance their sensitivity to children's signals and capitalize on opportunities for communication in two ways. First, the interventionist should be familiar with the child's nonsymbolic behavior. Some children with severe disabilities communicate at a nonsymbolic level in a manner similar to young children without disabilities. These children may move unintentionally in ways that can be communicative, such as opening their mouth, turning their head, or touching an object. The interventionist can observe and use an ABC analysis to help identify the child's nonsymbolic behaviors that may be communicative in nature.

Second, the interventionlist should assign meaning or intentionality to the child's nonsymbolic behaviors. Although it is not always clear if a child's communicative behaviors are intentional, it is important that the interventionist respond to nonsymbolic behaviors as though they are intentional. For example, the child may smack her lips when she has finished a bite of food. If the interventionist gives the child a bit of food each time she smacks her lips, the child learns to smack her lips to request more food.

INCREASING OPPORTUNITIES.   In order to learn to communicate, children must have opportunities to interact with others. For many children with severe disabilities, however, their need to communicate seems to have been eliminated. In home and at school, these children are usually dressed, fed, and cared for with minimal participation expected or required from them (MacDonald, 1985). Furthermore, interventionists may view the children as responders, not initiators. Changing the views and expectations of adults toward individuals

Interventionists learn about the child's signals from watching and talking with the caregiver(s).

with severe disabilities may greatly improve interactions (Affleck, McGrade, McQueeney, & Allen, 1982). Three intervention techniques are recommended for increasing opportunities for communication:

Three techniques for increasing opportunities for communication are (1) utilize motivating situations, (2) create communication opportunities, and (3) interrupt behavior chains.

1. Utilize motivating situations. In designing instructional programs, interventionists should take note of situations that are highly motivating and/or likely to promote communication. Highly motivating situations, such as activities with favorite peers or games, can provide natural reinforcers for targeted communication behaviors. Group activities in which adult attention is given contingent on each child's communicative responses promotes communication through modeling and reinforcement.

2. Create communication opportunities. Interventionists can create opportunities for communication by delaying their anticipation of the child's needs and desires. Halle (1984) focused on arranging the environment to increase the need and motivation to communicate. For example, a child may expect a teacher to provide a snack, a gesture within a fingerplay game, or a certain object at a certain moment. If the teacher hesitates (time delay), the child may become impatient and demand that the teacher follow through. The child is thus motivated to communicate a need/desire.

The technique of interrupting behavior chains is also discussed in Chapter 8.

3. Interrupt behavior chains. Stopping a child in the midst of a task and requiring a communicative response (e.g., requesting to continue the activity) is very effective in teaching children an initial communication response (Goetz, Gee, & Sailor, 1985; Hunt, Goetz, Alwell, & Sailor, 1986). For example, after a child looks at a book and starts to put it away, the interventionist physically blocks the child from placing it on the book rack. The child must point to a communication card that says "want" to be permitted to complete the task.

Scripting is also discussed in Chapters 8 and 10.

SEQUENCING EXPERIENCES.   Organizing daily activities into a regular, sequential format allows children to become familiar with recurrent patterns and to assume a definite role in the activity (Yoder & Reichle, 1977). This is sometimes referred to as "scripting." For example, a mother's utterances repeated several times in a game with her infant establishes a predictable, familiar pattern. Games, familiar routines, and community activities such as ordering food in restaurants or grocery shopping with a friend often can have a component of "your turn–my turn" that helps the child learn to express himself.

Two suggestions for providing sequencing experiences are:

1. Provide natural, recurring events. There are numerous daily activities where successive routines are possible, such as self-help activities (bathing, dressing, mealtime), leisure activities, and transition times (between activities, between environments). The redundancy of routines and recurring events appears to encourage the child to anticipate what may occur next (Writer, 1987).

2. *Respond contingently to child behaviors.* The intervention-ist can respond to reflexive, unintentional, or intentional behaviors of the child in an immediate and reliable manner. For example, an inter-ventionist can establish give-and-take play with an electronic game, stop the game, and then begin the game again contingent on any type of "impatient" behavior (e.g., whining). Later, restarting the game can be made contingent on a more specific communication behavior, such as the child's making eye contact with the interventionist.

UTILIZING MOVEMENT. Jan van Dijk developed a communication ap-proach for children who are deaf-blind that uses movement to stimu-late awareness and cognitive growth (van Dijk, 1986). Some aspects apply to children with severe disabilities. van Dijk believed that movement develops children's awareness of themselves and of their bodies as vehicles to explore the world, and encourages their under-standing of the separation of self from the environment. Because some of the activities in this approach require the instructor to lift, hold, or bear some of the child's weight; these activities, therefore, are appropriate only for young children who weigh less than 45 to 50 pounds.

van Dijk's movement-based approach is complex and contains many levels of intervention. This section describes only the initial levels. The reader is advised to consult other articles that more thor-oughly explore the entire theory (Stillman & Battle, 1984; Writer, 1987).

Resonance activities, the first level of movement activities, are designed to shift the child's focus of attention from self to the exter-nal world of people and objects. The adult establishes and maintains direct physical contact with the child, moves with the child, pauses, and waits for the child to signal for the movement to start again. The pauses allow the child to initiate a signal (e.g., smile, vocalization, physical contact) that indicates a desire to continue. During the movement dialogues the adult or child may modify the movement. For example, rocking side to side instead of forward or back, or adding a new noise during the movement, which the other partner copies. The purpose is to demonstrate to the child how her behavior produces a change in the environment or activity. Within resonance activities, an elementary form of dialogue is established, with both the child and adult having the opportunity to respond to each other's movements as if they were engaged in conversation.

Coactive movement, the second level of movement activities, in-creases the physical distance between the communication partners. The gradual physical separation requires children to pay greater attention and to associate their own actions with what they observe. The same start-stop format is maintained, and the adult continues to respond contingently to any of the child's signals as valid communications

The first levels of Van Dijk's movement-based approach include resonance activities and coactive movement.

(Writer, 1987). Coactive movements can become more complex by introducing movement sequences (e.g., roll, rock, jump) that are within the child's repertoire. Given consistent structure and repetition, the child may learn to anticipate the order and sequence of movements and to signal if the sequence is stopped or altered. Coactive movement encourages the child to move from the world of the concrete and physical to a more abstract level, where the adult and child maintain a dialogue without direct physical contact.

A primary goal of the movement approach is to promote the child's awareness of other people. Gradually the child becomes aware of the effect of her own behavior to initiate or change a movement cycle. At the later coactive level, the child begins to function without as much support, first spatially, then temporally. The child gradually begins to recognize the social aspect of her communication skills: Communication with another person yields the changes in the movement cycle.

FACILITATED COMMUNICATION.   Facilitated communication is a relatively new and very controversial approach for children with autism who do not use speech (Biklen, 1990; Crossley & Remington-Gurney, 1992). Children communicate with the assistance of a "facilitator," a person who physically guides their hand to spell out messages on a communication board. The facilitator must adopt supportive attitudes (e.g., nonpatronizing, self-effacing), assume that the child is a competent communicator, and believe that communication is extremely important.

The assistance provided through facilitation looks very much like the direct instruction approach of graduated guidance (an approach in which an interventionist provides only as much physical assistance as needed for a child to make a response, and reduces assistance as the child demonstrates increasingly more independence). Although such physical guidance is often an effective technique for teaching children to point and use a communication board (Sigafoos, Mustonen, DePaepe, Reichle, & York, 1991), facilitated communication has become very controversial. Critics describe these concerns. First, the literature includes only a few examples in which facilitation was successfully faded and children communicated independently (Wheeler, Jacobson, Paglieri, & Schwartz, 1993). When facilitation is not faded, it raises the question, "Who is generating the message, the child or the facilitator?" A number of carefully designed experimental studies have indicated that in many instances the facilitator is controlling the communication, not the child (Cummins & Prior, 1992; Hudson, Melita, & Arnold, 1993; Prior & Cummins, 1992; Shane, 1993; Smith & Belcher, 1993; Wheeler et al., 1993). Many professionals are concerned about this issue because there have been serious incidences in which parents have been accused of child abuse through facilitated messages supposedly communicated by their child. Court-ordered studies of these specific incidences demonstrated empirically that the facilitator was the author of the accusations, not the child (Shane, 1993). Even in the absence of such serious accusations, there is concern for subjecting families to great psychological pain by giving them false hopes and leading them to believe that children have intellectual and communication skills beyond what was previously believed.

Facilitated communication is the center of considerable controversy.

Other points of controversy concerning facilitated communication include the lack of adequate answers to such questions as (1) how can a child spell out messages without looking at the communication board while pointing or typing?; (2) how can a child who has never learned to read or write suddenly demonstrate the ability to spell out messages?; and (3) why are the proponents of facilitated communication reluctant to conduct controlled studies of their procedure? (Calculator, 1992; Shane, 1993). Because of these unresolved issues, many professionals do not recommend the use of facilitated communication as described by Biklen and his colleagues (Biklen, 1990; Biklen, Morton, Gold, Berrigan, & Swaminathan, 1992; Crossley & Remington-Gurney, 1992). It is important, however, that concerted efforts be made to teach children with autism who are nonverbal to communicate with augmentative systems (such as a communication board) using empirically supported procedures, such as direct teaching methods (prompts, reinforcement, graduated guidance, etc.).

Expanding the Communication Repertoire

When children demonstrate one or more symbolic communicative responses reliably (i.e., repeatedly and across several situations) they have met the goal of *establishing a symbolic communication repertoire*. The next major goal is *to expand the child's communication repertoire* across the dimensions of form, content, and use. As noted in Chapter 7, generalized communication goals and objectives are determined through person-centered planning and are modified with consideration of the baseline assessment information. This approach to developing instructional objectives results in form, content, and use goals referenced to home, school, and community activities.

The first goal is to establish a symbolic communication repertoire.

The second goal is to expand the child's repertoire in the dimensions of form, content, and use.

Communication *forms* are expanded by building grammatical structures, such as two-word combinations (e.g., noun-verb, verb-noun, adjective-noun) and three-word combinations (e.g., noun-verb-noun, adjective-noun-verb). Expansion of communication *content* focuses on developing the child's vocabulary, semantic functions (e.g., agent, action, object, possession), and combinations of semantic functions. And, expanding communication use involves increasing pragmatic functions in frequency (i.e., a function is used more often), type (i.e., new functions are added), and across situations (e.g., school, home, one-to-one, in groups). Objectives for expanding communication repertoires will frequently focus on form, content, and use *concurrently*. A child's grammar is built in the context of an expanding vocabulary and an increasing number of semantic functions; and interventions to build grammar, vocabulary, and semantic functions occur as the child uses communication more often, for increasingly more purposes, and in a growing number of situations.

TEACHING GENERALIZED SKILLS.   As noted in the description of generalized objectives, teaching generalized skills means that generalization is taught in the initial stages of skill acquisition rather than after the skill has been acquired. Teaching generalized skills incorporates the generalization strategy of "train sufficient exemplars" (discussed in Chapter 8) in the instructional program because more than one stimulus or response variation is taught concurrently for each objective (Horner, Sprague, & Wilcox, 1982). Additionally, Chapter 8 described two other generalization techniques ("train loosely" and "use intermittent reinforcement schedules") that may be included in an instructional program to facilitate generalization. Once the skill has been acquired and demonstrated across the training exemplars, it is important to assess for generalization with one or two untrained stimuli that are a part of the stimulus or response class targeted for generalization. For instance, if a child learns to sign "more" to request more drink, play, and hugs, the child may be assessed under situations requiring a request for more toothpaste and more cereal.

> Techniques to increase generalization are also discussed in Chapter 8.

DIRECT TEACHING STRATEGIES.   As noted in Chapter 8, direct teaching refers to instructional techniques that present the child with a consistent stimulus-response-consequence (S-R-C) arrangement (Snell & Brown, 1993). Children with severe disabilities must learn to recognize the S-R-C relationships that naturally occur. The intent of direct teaching is to *highlight* these relationships by assisting the child with prompts, cues, and motivational techniques. As learning occurs, the instructional assistance is gradually eliminated and the child demonstrates the skill in the presence of the natural stimuli and consequences.

> It is critical for children with severe disabilities to recognize stimulus-response-consequence relationships.

Although direct teaching requires consistency, it is most effective when implemented in the course of naturally occuring activities. *Incidental teaching,* described in detail in Chapter 8, is one approach for doing this. The hallmark of incidental teaching is that communication skills are taught at times throughout the day when the skills are needed (Kaiser, 1993). These natural times for instruction are usually determined by a child action (e.g., "when the child needs assistance," or "when the child looks at mom or dad"), rather than at times predetermined by the teacher. When incidental teaching occasions occur, instruction is implemented exactly as planned. In this way, incidental teaching promotes learning through consistent instruction, as well as generalization through instruction across multiple situations in the presence of natural stimuli. Furthermore, incidental teaching helps children learn to initiate communication because the occasions for instruction are natural events rather than verbal prompts from an adult.

DESIGNING INTERVENTION PROGRAMS. A written intervention program specifying the generalized communication objective and teaching procedures should be developed for each communication objective. Incidental teaching is usually the preferred teaching strategy because it promotes generalization. Child performance data from previous intervention programs may help identify types of prompts, prompting arrangements, and motivational strategies most likely to promote rapid learning. Assessment data, particularly baseline information, may indicate which prompts are likely to help a child make a correct response.

Figure 12.3 is an example of an incidental teaching program for the generalized communication skill of making a request. There are seven major components of an intervention program:

Incidental teaching is also discussed at length in Chapters 8 and 10.

1. The desired *child response* is described in behavioral terms. If response generalization is the objective, the response variations are described behaviorally.
2. Environments, activities, and times of day that will serve as the *instructional contexts* are identified. If incidental teaching techniques are used, the "occasion for instruction" is also described.
3. If a complex communication skill, such as a conversational skill, is the objective, a *task analysis* is included (see Chapter 8).
4. *Prompting techniques,* including specific prompts, stimulus variations (if stimulus generalization is the objective), or prompt sequences that are delivered prior to the child's response, are delineated. If prompts change from one step of a task analysis to the next, each prompt is noted. Prompts that are provided if the child fails to respond or makes an incorrect response (sometimes called "correction procedures") are also described.
5. *Motivational consequences,* including reinforcers that are natural consequences to the child's communication response (see Chapter 8), and an indication of when the consequences are provided (e.g., "each time the correct response occurs," "every third correct response," "on the average of every three correct responses") are described. Consequences for no response or incorrect responses (e.g., "interventionist attends to another child if no response is given within 5 seconds," "incorrect response is ignored") are also indicated.

FIGURE 12.3   Sample incidental teaching program

Student: Tommy K.		Date Program Initiated: 01/08
Objective:	Tommy will say "hi" when he encounters familiar people in the classroom, in the cafeteria, and on the playground. (Criteria: 4 consecutive correct responses & 2 consecutive correct generalization probes.)	

ANTECEDENTS	STUDENT RESPONSE	CONSEQUENCES
Occasions/Settings for Instruction: Whenever Tommy encounters familiar peers or adults in the classroom, in the cafeteria, or on the playground	Tommy says "hi."	For Correct Response: Smile at Tommy and peer or adult; facilitate peer or adult responding/ conversing with Tommy if necessary (e.g., say, "Tommy remembers you. Maybe you'd like to ask Tommy what game he'd like to play").
Instruction: 1. Approach Tommy, alternate glance beteen peer or adult & Tommy, wait 4 seconds (time delay). After 2 consecutive correct: 2. Approach Tommy & wait 4 seconds. After 2 consecutive correct: 3. Observe Tommy from a distance; approach only to implement correction procedure.		For Incorrect or No Response: Whisper "hi" in Tommy's ear. If Tommy says "hi," consequate as correct response. If no response, model correct response.
Generalization Probe: Observe Tommy at assembly and in school office when submitting attendance card (no instruction).		

6. *Generalization strategies,* such as training across settings or using natural maintaining contingencies, that are in addition to the stimulus or response variations specified in the generalized skill objective or the occasions for incidental teaching, should be indicated.

7. And finally, *data collection procedures,* detailing when and how data will be collected (see Chapter 8), are indicated.

Written instructional programs are essential to effective intervention because prompting, motivational, and generalization strategies should be implemented precisely as written each time the skill is taught.

SUMMARY

Young children with severe disabilities have diverse characteristics but share a need for interventions directed at establishing or expanding their communication repertoires. Working from the assumption that all children communicate in some way, goals aimed at establishing a communication repertoire focus on teaching symbolic communication skills. And for children who already communicate symbolically, goals are to build the communication repertoire by increasing communication forms and functions. For all children with severe disabilities, the goal of communication intervention is to enable them to communicate more effectively and across a greater range of situations.

REFERENCES

Affleck, G., McGrade, B. J., McQueeney, M., & Allen, D. (1982). Promise of relationship-focused early intervention in developmental disabilities. *The Journal of Special Education, 16*(4), 413–430.

Baer, D. M., Wolf, M. M., & Risley, T. R. (1968). Some current dimensions of applied behavior analysis. *Journal of Applied Behavior Analysis, 1,* 91–97.

Bakeman, R., & Adamson, L. B. (1984). Coordinating attention to people and objects in mother–infant and peer–infant interactions. *Child Development, 55,* 1278–1289.

Bates, E. (1979). *The emergence of symbols: Cognition and communication in infancy.* New York: Academic Press.

Bijou, S. W., Peterson, R. F., & Ault, M. H. (1968). A method to integrate descriptive and experimental field studies at the level of data and empirical concepts. *Journal of Applied Behavior Analysis, 1,* 175–191.

Biklen, D. (1990). Communication unbound: Autism and praxis. *Harvard Education Review, 60,* 291–314.

Biklen, D., Morton, M. W., Gold, D., Berrigan, C., & Swaminathan, S. (1992). Facilitated communication: Implications for individuals with autism. *Topics in Language Disorders, 12*(4), 1–28.

Brown, F., & Snell, M. E. (1993). Measurement, analysis, and evaluation. In M. E. Snell (Ed.), *Instruction of students with severe disabilities* (pp. 152–183). Columbus, OH: Merrill.

Bruner, J. (1978). From communication to language: A psychological perspective. In I. Markova (Ed.), *The social context of language* (pp. 17–48). New York: John Wiley and Sons.

Calculator, S. (1992). Perhaps the emperor has clothes after all: A response to Biklen. *American Journal of Speech-Language Pathology, 1,* 18–20.

Clark, G. N., & Seifer, R. (1983). Facilitation of mother–infant communication: A treatment model for high-risk and developmentally delayed infants. *Infant Mental Health Journal, 4*(2), 67–81.

Crossley, R., & Remington-Gurney, J. (1992). Getting the words out: Facilitated communication training. *Topics in Language Disorders, 12*(4), 29–45.

Cummins, R. A., & Prior, M. P. (1992). Autism and assisted communication: A reply to Biklin. *Harvard Education Review, 62,* 228–241.

Donnellan, A. M., Mirenda, P. L., Mesaros, R. A., & Fassbender, L. L. (1984). Analyzing the communicative functions of aberrant behavior. *Journal of the Association for Persons with Severe Handicaps, 9,* 201–212.

Falvey, M. A. (1989). *Community-based curriculum.* Baltimore: Paul H. Brookes.

Ford, A., & Mirenda, P. (1984). Community instruction: A natural cues and corrections decision model. *Journal of the Association for Persons with Severe Handicaps, 9,* 79–88.

Goetz, L., Gee, K., & Sailor, W. (1985). Using a behavior chain interruption strategy to teach communication skills to students with severe disabilities. *The Journal of the Association for Persons with Severe Handicaps, 10,* 21–30.

Goldstein, H., & Kaczmarek, L. (1992). Promoting communicative interaction among children in integrated intervention settings. In S. F. Warren & J. Reichle (Eds.), *Causes and effects in communication and language intervention* (pp. 81–111). Baltimore: Paul H. Brookes.

Guess, D. (1980). Methods in communication instruction for severely handicapped persons. In W. Sailor, B. Wilcox, & L. Brown (Eds.), *Methods of instruction for severely handicapped students* (pp. 195–225). Baltimore: Paul H. Brookes.

Guess, D., Horner, D., Utley, B., Holvoet, J., Maxon, D., Tucker, D., & Warren, S. (1978). A functional curriculum sequencing model for teaching the severely handicapped. *AAESPH Review, 3,* 202–215.

Guess, D., & Mulligan, M. (1982). The severely and profoundly handicapped. In E. L. Meyen (Ed.), *Exceptional children and youth: An introduction* (2nd ed., pp. 263–303). Denver: Love.

Halle, J. (1984). Arranging the natural environment to occasion language: Giving severely language-delayed children reason to communicate. *Seminars in Speech and Language, 5*(3), 185–197.

Harding, C., & Golinkoff, R. (1979). The origins of intentional vocalizations in prelinguistic infants. *Child Development, 50,* 33–40.

Horner, R. H., & McDonald, R. S. (1982). Comparison of single instance and general case instruction in teaching a generalized vocational skill. *Journal of the Association for the Severely Handicapped, 7*(3), 7–20.

Horner, R. H., Sprague, J., & Wilcox, B. (1982). General case programming for community activities. In B. Wilcox & G. T. Bellamy (Eds.), *Design of high school programs for severely handicapped students* (pp. 61–98). Baltimore: Paul H. Brookes.

Horstmeier, D. S., & MacDonald, J. D. (1978). *Environmental prelanguage battery.* Columbus, OH: Merrill.

Hudson, A., Melita, B., & Arnold, N. (1993). Assessing the validity of facilitated communication: A case study. *Journal of Autism and Developmental Disorders, 23*(1), 165–173.

Hunt, P., Goetz, L., Alwell, M., & Sailor, W. (1986). Using an interrupted chain strategy to teach generalized communication responses to students with severe disabilities. *Journal of the Association for Persons with Severe Handicaps, 11*(3), 196–204.

Iwata, B., Dorsey, M., Slifer, K., Bauman, K., & Richman, G. (1982). Toward a functional analysis of self-injury. *Analysis and Intervention in Developmental Disabilities, 2,* 3–20.

Kaiser, A. P. (1993). Functional language. In M. E. Snell (Ed.), *Instruction of students with severe disabilities* (pp. 347–379). Columbus, OH: Merrill.

Kaiser, A., Alpert, C., & Warren, S. (1987). Teaching functional language: Strategies for language intervention. In M. Snell (Ed.), *Systematic instruction for persons with severe handicaps* (3rd ed., pp. 247–272). Columbus, OH: Merrill.

MacDonald, J. D. (1978). *Environmental language inventory.* Columbus, OH: Merrill.

MacDonald, J. D. (1985). Language through conversation. In S. Warren & A. Rogers-Warren (Eds.), *Teaching functional language* (pp. 89–122). Baltimore: University Park Press.

McCormick, L., & Noonan, M. J. (1984). A responsive curriculum for severely handicapped preschoolers. *Topics in Early Childhood Special Education, 4*(3), 79–96.

Miller, J. F. (1978). Assessing children's language behavior: A developmental process approach. In R. L. Schiefelbusch (Ed.), *Bases of language intervention* (pp. 269–318). Baltimore: University Park Press.

Morris, S. C., & Klein, M. D. (1987). *Pre-feeding skills.* Tucson, AZ: Therapy Skill Builders.

Morris, S. E. (1971, November). *Pre-speech and language therapy for the cerebral palsied infant: Its role in the prevention of communication disorder.* Paper presented at the

Annual Convention of the American Speech and Hearing Association, Chicago.

Morris, S. E. (1984). Pre-speech assessment scale. Clifton, NJ: Preston.

Mulligan, M., & Guess, D. (1984). Using an individualized curriculum sequencing model. In L. McCormick & R. L. Schiefelbusch (Eds.), *Early language intervention* (1st ed., pp. 299–323). Columbus, OH: Merrill.

Nelson, R. O., & Hayes, S. C. (1979). Some current dimensions of behavioral assessment. *Behavioral Assessment, 1,* 1–16.

Noonan, M. J., & McCormick, L. (1993). *Early intervention in natural environments: Methods and procedures*. Pacific Grove, CA: Brooks/Cole.

Odom, S. (1983). The development of social interchanges in infancy. In S. G. Garwood & R. R. Fewell (Eds.), *Educating handicapped infants: Issues in development and intervention* (pp. 215–254). Rockville, MD: Aspen.

Owens, R. E. (1982). *PALS: Program for the acquisition of language with the severely impaired*. Columbus, OH: Merrill.

Prior, M. P., & Cummins, R. A. (1992). Questions about facilitated communication and autism. *Journal of Autism and Developmental Disorders, 22,* 331–338.

Rainforth, B., York, J., & Macdonald, C. (1992). *Collaborative teams for students with severe disabilities*. Baltimore: Paul H. Brookes.

Reichle, J., & Sigafoos, J. (1991). Establishing spontaneity and generalization. In J. Reichle, J. York, & J. Sigafoos (Eds.), *Implementing augmentative and alternative communication* (pp. 157–171). Baltimore: Paul H. Brookes.

Rowland, C., & Stremel-Campbell, K. (1987). Share and share alike: Conventional gestures to emergent language for learners with sensory impairments. In L. Goetz, D. Guess, & K. Stremel-Campbell (Eds.), *Innovative program design for individuals with dual sensory impairments* (pp. 49–75). Baltimore: Paul H. Brookes.

Sailor, W., Gee, K., & Karasoff, P. (1993). Full inclusion and school restructuring. In M. E. Snell (Ed.), *Instruction of students with severe disabilities* (pp. 1–30). Columbus, OH: Merrill.

Salvia, J., & Ysseldyke, J. E. (1985). *Assessment in special and remedial education* (3rd ed.). Boston: Houghton Mifflin.

Savage, S. (1983). Individualized critical skills model (ICSM). Alameda, CA: Training and Resources Group, California Department of Education, Personnel Development Unit.

Schery, T. K., & Wilcoxen, A. G. (1982). Initial communication processes. Monterey, CA: Publishers Test Service, CTB/McGraw-Hill.

Shane, H. C. (1993). The dark side of facilitated communication. Topics in language disorders, 13(4), ix-xv.

Siegel-Causey, E., & Downing, J. (1987). Non-symbolic communication development: Theoretical concepts and education strategies. In L. Goetz, D. Guess, & K. Stremel-Campbell (Eds.), *Innovative program design for individuals with dual sensory impairments* (pp. 15–48). Baltimore: Paul H. Brookes.

Siegel-Causey, E., & Wetherby, A. (1993). Non-symbolic communication. In M. E. Snell (Ed.), *Instruction of students with severe disabilities* (pp. 290–318). Columbus, OH: Merrill.

Sigafoos, J., Mustonen, T., DePaepe, P., Reichle, J., & York, J. (1991). Defining the array of instructional prompts for teaching communication skills. In J. Reichle, J. York, & J. Sigafoos (Eds.), *Implementing augmentative and alternative communication* (pp. 173–192). Baltimore: Paul H. Brookes.

Smith, M. D., & Belcher, R. G. (1993). Brief report: Facilitated communication with adults with autism. *Journal of Autism and Developmental Disorders, 23*(1), 175–183.

Snell, M., & Brown, F. (1993). Instructional planning and implementation. In M. E. Snell (Ed.), *Instruction of students with severe disabilities* (pp. 99–151). Columbus, OH: Merrill.

Snow, C. E. (1984). Parent-child interaction and the development of communicative ability. In R. L. Schiefelbusch & J. Pickar (Eds.), *The acquisition of communicative competence* (pp. 69–107). Baltimore: University Park Press.

Stillman, R., & Battle, C. (1984). *Callier-Azusa Scale (H), Scales for the assessment of com-*

municative abilities. Dallas: Callier Center for Communication Disorders.

van Dijk, J. (1986). An educational curriculum for deaf-blind multihandicapped persons. In D. Ellis (Ed.), *Sensory impairments in mentally handicapped people* (pp. 375–382). London: Croom-Helm.

Waryas, C. L., & Stremel-Campbell, K. (1982). *Communication training program*. Hingham, MA: Teaching Resources.

Wetherby, A. M., & Prizant, B. (1993). *Communication and symbolic behavior scales—(1st ed.)*. Chicago: Riverside Publishing.

Wheeler, D. L., Jacobson, J. W., Paglieri, R. A., & Schwartz, A. A. (1993). An experimental assessment of facilitated communication. *Mental Retardation, 31,* 45–59.

Writer, J. (1987). A movement-based approach to the education of students who are sensory impaired/multihandicapped. In L. Goetz, D. Guess, & K. Stremel-Campbell (Eds.), *Innovative program design for individuals with dual sensory impairments* (pp. 191–223). Baltimore: Paul H. Brookes.

Yoder, D., & Reichle, J. (1977). Some current perspectives on teaching communication functions to mentally retarded children. In P. Mittler (Ed.), *Research to practice in mental retardation, education, and training, Volume II* (pp. 199–205). Baltimore: University Park Press.

CHAPTER 13

Supporting Augmentative and Alternative Communication

Linda McCormick

The student who has little or no functional speech needs an array of supports in order to take full advantage of opportunities for cognitive and social interactions in inclusive school settings. The field of augmentative and alternative communication (AAC) focuses on providing communication options for persons of all ages who are not able to use natural modes such as speech, gestures, or handwriting to meet their daily communication needs. AAC interventions involve electronic and nonelectronic applications

While the history of AAC as a field spans only a little more than three decades, the sum of its accomplishments is impressive (Zangari, Lloyd, & Vicker, 1994). In the early 1970s, there were fewer than a dozen published reports of hearing individuals with severe expressive communication disability using manual signs, communication boards, or modified typewriters to augment or replace speech. Today there are hundreds of books, chapters, periodicals, and newsletters devoted exclusively to AAC information and research reports. Most university personnel preparation programs now have at least one AAC course, and there is a professional organization for persons interested in the AAC field that publishes a quarterly journal.

> There has been a shift from narrow conceptualizations of language to the broader phenomena of communication.

Two trends in the 1980s contributed to the dramatic growth in AAC research and applications. One of these trends was a direct consequence of passage of PL 94-142: The public schools began serving increasing numbers of students with severe disabilities, many of whom had little or no functional speech. The other trend was theoretical—a shift in the field of speech and language disorders from narrow conceptualizations of language to a focus on the broader phenomena of communication. Moving away from preoccupation with trying to determine the cause of speech difficulties and teaching sound and word production to considering the *effect of communication difficulties* and working to develop the ability to communicate at a level adequate to meet the individual's communication needs in home, educational, vocational, and community environments was a major paradigm shift.

Initially there was some concern that introduction of an AAC system would interfere with acquisition of speech. The many reports describing increased speech following implementation of an AAC system have finally put these concerns to rest (e.g., Daniloff, Noll, Fristoe, & Lloyd, 1982; Kohl, Karlan, & Heal, 1979; Prinz & Shaw, 1981; Romski, Sevcik, & Ellis-Joyner, 1984; Silverman, 1980). There is now a substantial literature (reviewed by Abrahamsen, Romski, & Sevcik, 1989) indicating that, in addition to acquiring communicative use of an AAC system, AAC users demonstrate positive gains in (1) speech production and comprehension (if they are exposed to speech in conjunction with corresponding nonspeech symbols), (2) attention span, (3) task orientation, and (4) social skills.

> Legislative provisions for assistive technology have been included in both IDEA and ADA.

In recognition of the importance of assistive technology for individuals with disabilities, congress included legislative provisions supporting assistive technology in both the Individuals with Disabilities Education Act (IDEA) and the Americans with Disabilities Act (ADA-PL 101-336). The regulations for the IDEA describe an **assistive technology device** as

> "... any item, piece of equipment, or product system, whether acquired commercially off the shelf, modified, or customized, that is used to increase, maintain, or improve the functional capabilities of children with disabilities." (Federal Register, 1992)

This definition is broad. It includes a range of devices from low technology to high technology items as well as computer software.

The IDEA regulations describe an **assistive technology service** as

". . . any service that directly assists a child with a disability in the selection, acquisition, or use of an assistive technology device." (Federal Register, *1992*)

Both laws have a requirement stating that individuals with disabilities are to have whatever assistive devices they need. Assistive technology includes battery-powered toys, hearing aids, wheelchairs, computers, eating systems, augmentative communication devices, special switches, and a wide range of other devices that have the potential to improve an individual's ability to learn, compete, work, and interact with others. School districts are required to provide assistive technology devices and services to eligible children (if necessary to ensure the provision of a free appropriate public education). School districts must (1) evaluate the student's technology needs, (2) secure needed devices (through purchasing or leasing), and (3) provide intervention, training, and support to use the technology. After assistive technology needs have been determined, technological devices and services are provided as special education, related services, or supplementary aids and services. AAC systems are one type of assistive technology.

The field of AAC as it is today reflects three major paradigm shifts. As set forth by Mirenda, Iacona, and Williams (1990) these current perspectives also have broad implications for the future of this rapidly expanding field.

- ***Inclusionary assessment procedures.*** Past assessment procedures offered limited candidacy for AAC to persons able to demonstrate certain cognitive prerequisites. Today's inclusionary assessment procedures make AAC available for *all* persons with disabilities (including those with the most severe intellectual disabilities) (Kangas & Lloyd, 1988).

  > Inclusionary assessment makes AAC available for all persons with disabilities.

- ***Focus on functionally relevant communication.*** Past intervention practices targeted specific, isolated speech and language skills. Current procedures target integrated, functionally relevant communication abilities (Romski & Sevcik, 1988).

  > Intervention targets integrated, functionally relevant communication abilities.

- ***Recognition that communication is multimodal.*** Past intervention efforts often provided or taught only a single device or technique. Now most AAC systems involve a collection of devices, techniques, symbols, and strategies that can be used interchangeably (Reichle & Karlan, 1985; Vanderheiden & Lloyd, 1986).

  > There is recognition that communication is multimodal.

Discussion of these three trends is integrated throughout the chapter. The first section presents an introduction to basic terms and concepts and an overview of the various AAC options. This is followed by a discussion of gestural and graphic communication method. Finally, the remainder of the chapter deals with assessment and intervention consideration. Throughout, there is some discussion of the broader area of assistive technology but, for the most part, the focus of the chapter is on AAC.

BASIC TERMS AND CONCEPTS

Recognizing the need for standardization of terms and definitions, the field of AAC has worked to achieve agreement on a core set of terms (ASHA, 1991; Lloyd & Kangas, 1990; Lloyd & Blischak, 1992). This section provides definitions and some discussion of these terms.

AUGMENTATIVE AND ALTERNATIVE COMMUNICATION (AAC).   The term **augmentative and alternative communication** refers to the total arrangement for supplementing and enhancing an individual's communication—the communication device, the communication technique, the symbol system, and the communication skills that are necessary for access to or use of the system. The narrower term "alternative communication" should be used only when it is clear that the approach is a *substitute* for natural speech and/or handwriting. The term "augmentative communication" is used only when it is clear that the approach is an *addition* to natural speech and/or handwriting. In most cases the most appropriate term is the broader augmentative and alternative communication or AAC. AAC is now conceptualized as necessarily *multimodal,* meaning that it involves more than one modality, or mixed modalities. Because AAC is multimodal, an AAC system typically requires multiple devices, techniques, symbols, and strategies that are used interchangeably: It does not consist of a single device or technique (Vanderheiden & Lloyd, 1986).

ASSISTIVE COMMUNICATION DEVICE.   An **assistive communication device** is the means of displaying and/or transmitting intended messages. AAC communication devices are available in many shapes, forms, and sizes, ranging from simple paper and pencil devices to sophisticated electronic and computer-based devices (Kraat & Sitver-Kogut, 1991). Because there is external assistance involved, communication with an assistive device is said to be **aided communication.** The most common nonelectronic assistive communication devices are communication boards, communication books, and communication cards. These devices and high-tech electronic devices will be described later in the chapter.

COMMUNICATION TECHNIQUE. The **communication technique** is the method for indicating or forming symbols to transmit messages to a communication partner (ASHA, 1991). Techniques are sometimes differentiated as aided or unaided. As noted above, techniques that require an external device such as a communication board, book, or display are said to be **aided techniques. Unaided communication** utilizes techniques such as gesturing, signing, or speech that do not require external support. In this chapter we will adopt another common approach for labeling and differentiating the two types of techniques as (1) **gestural mode techniques,** and (2) **graphic mode techniques** (Mustonen et al., 1991). Gestural mode techniques are the body movements and facial expressions used to achieve gestural mode communication (signs and gestures). Techniques for graphic mode communication include direct selection, scanning, and encoding. Most graphic mode techniques have fewer motor requirements than gestural mode techniques.

The two types of unaided techniques are gestural mode techniques and graphic mode techniques.

Direct selection means selecting, typically through pointing, the desired symbol from a set of available symbols. The student may use any body part or an assistive device (i.e., a switch) to select a symbol. When motor control does not permit pointing with either a finger or a pointing device (e.g., a dowel rod or a light beam pointer attached to a head band), direct selection can also be accomplished with a fist, elbow, toe, or heel. Another option is "eye pointing" (looking at the desired symbol for an extended time) if the individual is not able to point using a gesture or a pointing device. Because each pointing response indicates a single message element, direct selection requires fewer movements to transmit a message then scanning or encoding.

Scanning is the second choice when direct selection is not a viable option. All that is necessary for an individual to use a communication board with a scanning response strategy is the ability to signal yes or no when a desired symbol or symbol set appears or is highlighted in some way. There are several scanning possibilities. With linear scanning, the symbols that the user selects from are presented one at a time. With row-column scanning, entire horizontal rows are presented. The AAC user selects first a row and then a symbol in one of the columns in the row. In block scanning, a block or set of items is selected first and then either row-column or linear scanning is used to select a symbol within the set. With direct scanning, selection begins at some point on the display and the AAC user somehow indicates which direction the highlighter should move. All of these scanning methods are accomplished either through manual scanning (a partner points to or highlights the scanning sets and specific symbols) or electronic scanning. Electronic scanning devices typically have a grid of small lights controlled by switch activation.

Encoding, the third graphic mode communication technique, requires higher cognitive skills because the AAC user must select from a code to indicate a message from a message array. The code must either be memorized or be available on a chart. The simplest type of encoding scheme includes a large chart on which is printed a series of messages that the individual might want to use, such as "I'm ready to go" or "I need more." The messages are numbered consecutively. This chart is used with a communication board that has the same number of cells as there are messages. Each cell contains one of the numbers that appear on the chart. Encoding may be combined with either direct selection or scanning. A one-step or two-step scanning strategy could be used with the communication board to signal the number of messages that the user wants to communicate. With this strategy, only a single response is required to transmit one or more multi-element messages. It is possible to overcome the major limitation of this arrangement—the relatively small number of available messages—by always ensuring that this message is on the chart: "The message I want is not on the board. Please use another board."

SYMBOLS.   **Symbols** are auditory, visual, or tactile images or signs that suggest or stand for a concept or idea. The term "symbol" has a broad meaning in AAC terminology. It includes exact representations, such as photographs and drawings, as well as abstract representations (e.g., written and spoken words, Braille) and everything between these two extremes. Use of the term also extends to representations for gestural communication such as facial expressions, body positions, and eye gaze.

The greater the iconicity, the easier it is to identify the meaning of the symbol.

Iconicity refers to the ease with which the meaning of a symbol can be recognized, an important consideration when selecting symbols for an AAC system. The greater the iconicity, the easier it is to recognize the symbol's meaning. At one end of the iconicity continuum are symbols that, because they allow for total iconicity (they resemble their referents), are said to be transparent symbols. The meaning of a transparent symbol is easily recognized or can be easily guessed. A line drawing or a photograph of a tree or flower is an example of a transparent symbol. At the other end of the iconicity continuum there are *opaque* or arbitrary symbols. When there is only an arbitrary relationship between the symbol and its referent, the symbol's meaning is not immediately apparent or easily guessed; it must be learned. The written or spoken word "tree" is an example of an opaque symbol. At some point near the middle of the iconicity continuum there are symbols that can be recognized *if* additional information is available or with minimal training (Reichle, York, & Sigafoos, 1991).

STRATEGY. A strategy is a specific plan and the skills needed in order to use the AAC system (the device, the symbol system, and the techniques) for communication (ASHA, 1991). Each AAC user needs to develop his or her own unique strategies to accomplish basic communication goals. Gaining someone's attention, changing and maintaining a topic, and making repairs when a message is not understood are examples of strategies. Most strategies are taught in an instructional context, however, AAC users also discover some strategies on their own.

COMMUNICATION OPTIONS

Recall that this chapter uses the terms gestural mode and graphic mode techniques rather than the terminology unaided and aided techniques to refer to the method for indicating symbols to transmit messages. Gestural communication techniques are like speech in that they are easily available and portable. They have an advantage over speech in that they require less sophisticated motor skills. Their advantage over graphic mode techniques is that there is no need to worry about constructing (or securing funds to purchase) or carrying around a communication device. Where symbolic gesturing (specifically, manual signing) is concerned, the major disadvantage is the relatively limited audience. Despite the fact that sign language is the third most used non-English language in the United States and the major communication system for more than half a million individuals, most environments do not include potential communication partners. In many settings such as fast-food restaurants, or delis, an AAC user can communicate more effectively by pointing to pictures of desired food choices (either on the wall, a menu, or a communication board) than with manual signing.

Gestural Communication

Similar to their speaking partners who use natural speech, most AAC users employ gestural communication. Basically, the two gestural communication options are demonstrative gesturing and symbolic gesturing (Mustonen et al., 1991).

> The two gestural communication options are demonstrative gesturing and symbolic gesturing.

DEMONSTRATIVE GESTURING. **Demonstrative gesturing** involves behaviors such as pointing, reaching, showing, offering, and giving objects; touching others; and head movements that are used intentionally to convey meaning. Some gestures (e.g., pointing, reaching, showing, offering, and giving) are used to convey a desire for an object, attention, or interaction *or* to direct attention. Others (e.g., touching others) communicate affection and/or encouragement. Finally, head movements (specifically, nodding) are a means of conveying yes and no responses. All potential AAC users should be taught the gestures for yes and no if they do not already have them.

Symbolic Gesturing.   **Symbolic gesturing** is not as easy to understand as demonstrative gesturing because the forms are not always closely related to their meanings. There is a wide variety of symbolic gestures, ranging from generally understood signs such as a wave for "good-bye" to symbols that are part of formal manual sign languages. Hamre-Nietupski and colleagues (Hamre-Nietupski, Stoll, Holtz, Fullerton, Flottum-Ryan, & Brown, 1977) compiled a list of over 160 generally understood gestures. The advantages of using natural gestures for communication are (1) they are easily understood without the listener's needing special training, and (2) they typically involve gross motor movements that are manageable for persons with physical disabilities.

Amer-Ind is a gestural system based on American Indian hand talk. It falls somewhere in the middle between natural, generally understood signs and manual language symbols. Dr. Madge Skelly developed Amer-Ind in the 1970s from the hand talk she learned as a child from her Iroquois relatives. The Amer-Ind system has 250 concept labels, each with multiple meanings. The basic features of Amer-Ind that make it very appropriate for some AAC users are (1) concreteness, (2) flexibility, and (3) lack of grammatical structure.

Manual sign systems are at the other end of the symbolic gesturing continuum. The three types of manual sign systems are (1) systems that are alternatives to (rather than paralleling) spoken language; (2) systems that parallel spoken English, and (3) systems that supplement other means of transmitting language (Beukelman & Mirenda, 1992).

American Sign Language (ASL) is the language of most deaf persons in North America. It is an example of an alternative system. ASL is not a manual version of English. It does not use English word order, there is no form of the verb *to be,* no passive voice, no articles, and there are no signs for pronouns. With ASL, it is possible to convey an entire statement with a single sign.

Manually Coded English (MCE) is the term for systems that parallel English. They directly code English word order, syntax, and grammar. One such system is Sign English (Woodward, 1990), which is also known as Pidgin Sign English. Sign English uses ASL signs with English word order. Signs are typically accompanied by gestures and vocalizations. Another MCE system, Signed English, also borrows liberally from the vocabulary of ASL. Signed English was originally developed for use by preschoolers with hearing impairments, but it has been expanded considerably and is now used by many older students.

Fingerspelling is an example of the third type of manual sign system: It supplements other means of transmitting language. Fingerspelling is spelling words with manual alphabet, which consists of 26 letters that have one-to-one correspondence with traditional orthography. In fingerspelling, one hand is held in front of the chest and words are spelled letter by letter.

Even for those students whose severe physical limitations may preclude the use of many signs expressively, there is value in using gestural communication as receptive input. Exposing students to simultaneous speech and gestural communication (called total communication) may assist auditory processing and enhance receptive vocabulary. The two major disadvantages of gestural communication are (1) the motor requirements, and (2) potential communication partners. Because of the motor coordination required to form and produce manual signing many of the same students who have difficulty with speech also have difficulty forming manual signs. The pool of potential communication partners is limited to those persons who understand and can converse with signs.

It is logical to assume that exposing students to simultaneous speech and gestural communication has some advantages for understanding and learning language.

Graphic Communication

Graphic communication resembles gestural communication in that it is also visually based. However, unlike gestural communication symbols, which are temporal and dynamic, graphic communication symbols are spatial and static. Because graphic symbols remain visible they do not place the same memory requirements on the AAC user and communication partners. Graphic communication options may be two-dimensional or three-dimensional. They range from abstract representations that are opaque to exact representations that are clearly transparent. Some collections of symbols are properly termed symbol **sets** while others, because they are rule-governed, can be called symbol *systems*.

ABSTRACT REPRESENTATIONAL SYMBOLS. Students who cannot use speech but are functionally literate typically use traditional orthographic symbols to communicate messages. Use of *traditional orthography* has obvious advantages: (1) the ability to communicate unlimited messages, and (2) the ability to be readily understood by all potential communication partners who are literate (unless the AAC user has a computer-based device that has voice output in addition to a visual display). When provided with a display (electronic or nonelectronic) of printed letters, words, syllables, phrases, or sentences, the AAC user can create an unlimited number of messages. Training focuses on teaching a technique (e.g., writing, pointing, typing) that will produce the desired output. Traditional orthography may be used alone or in combination with other symbols.

The most common alphabet-based symbol systems are traditional orthography, Morse code, and braille.

Other alphabet-based symbol systems are Morse code and braille. When used in AAC applications, the *Morse code* dots and dashes are transmitted via microswitches to an emulator that translates them into letters and numbers (Beukelman & Mirenda, 1992). Morse code emulators are available for most computer-based devices. *Braille* is an option for AAC users who are visually impaired. Braille characters may be produced with a slate and stylus (a small device that permits the user to press braille dots from the back of a paper), a braillewriter (a device similar to a typewriter), or by using a computer and one or another of the available software programs.

Blissymbols, a symbol system developed by Charles Bliss, was originally intended as an international second language. The system consists of approximately 100 symbols that can be used singly or combined in different ways. Blissymbols are black line drawings on white background of discrete, meaning-based units that represent concepts. The structure of Blissymbolics is similar to that of printed ideographic Chinese characters. Some are pictographic in that they depict the outline of the concept represented, others are ideographic in that they show a shape related to an idea associated with the referent, and still others are arbitrary (totally opaque). Blissymbols can be used to convey messages about the here and now as well as the past and the future. They are appropriate for students who are capable of more sophisticated symbolization than pictures, but not yet ready to use traditional orthography. Materials for teaching the Blissymbol system are distributed by Blissymbols Communication International. Figure 13.1 provides examples of Blissymbols.

Blissymbols are most appropriate for students who are capable of using relatively sophisticated symbolization.

Exact Representational Symbols.   Real objects, parts of objects, miniature objects, photographs, and line drawings all come under the heading of "exact representational symbols." Real objects that are closely associated with a referent, miniature objects, and parts of objects may be attached to a communication board and used as symbols. Particularly useful for students who have dual sensory impairments, *tangible symbols* have the advantage of being tactilely discriminable and highly iconic (Rowland & Schweigert, 1989). For example, a spoon might be used as a symbol for "hunger"; a cassette tape might be used as a symbol for "music"; the lid of a toothpaste tube might be used as a symbol

Figure 13.1   Examples of Blissymbols

music   emotion   ear   time

for "brushing teeth"; and a piece of terrycloth or a piece of a sponge might be a symbol for "washing" or "bathing." Using miniature objects rather than real objects (if the student is able to recognize that the miniature object represents the referent) has a definite advantage because of limited space on a communication board.

Clear color or black and white *photographs* showing actual objects, actions, people, places, and activities are often used on the communication boards of very young children and students with intellectual disabilities. Several investigators have considered characteristics of photographs that have implications for their use as communication board symbols. One study found an advantage for color photographs over black and white photographs (Mirenda & Locke, 1989). Another (Dixon, 1981) found some advantages for using objects cut out from color photographs rather than the entire photograph. Reichle and colleagues (1991) note that the context in which an item appears in a photograph may affect recognizability. For example, a photograph of a lightswitch may be recognized more readily if it is photographed with a lamp next to it.

Line drawings may be very detailed and realistic representations of concepts, or sketchy outlines. Rebuses are pictures that represent words or syllables. There are many types of rebuses, but the most readily available collection is obtainable from the American Guidance Service. Developed originally to assist reading instruction, the system has been adapted and expanded for use as communication symbols. Another popular pictographic symbol set, Picture Communication Symbols (PCS), includes more than 1800 simple line drawings, and is available in a number of formats (sticker, colored stamps, symbol books that can be photocopied, software programs) from Mayer-Johnson Company. Pictographs may be used alone or with printed letters or words (for AAC users who have some reading skills).

There are at least a half dozen other sets of line drawings or graphic symbols that have been produced specifically for communication boards that are available commercially. Some of these symbol sets such as Picsyms (Carlson, 1984) and Pictogram Ideogram Communication (PIC) symbols (Johnson, 1985) contain ideograms as well as pictographic symbols. **Ideograms** present a character or graphic symbol representing an idea rather than a picture of a particular concept. For example, a heart shape might represent "feeling."

> Ideograms present concepts with character or graphic symbol rather than a picture.

SYSTEM ACCESS AND DESIGN

As noted in the introduction, there is strong evidence suggesting that providing an AAC system does not in any way interfere with or jeopardize acquisition of oral language skills. In fact, in some cases it seems to facilitate comprehension and development of speech. Thus there is no risk involved in providing an AAC system to every child with a severe expressive communication disorder. The challenge is designing and implementing an optimal system for each student. Fortunately, considering the extensive knowledge and competency requirements, this is not the classroom teacher's responsibility. Actually, it is not the responsibility of any one professional (or even a team of professionals from a single discipline). At the very least, design and development of an optimal AAC system requires a team made up of the student, the family and other caregivers, teachers, therapists, paraprofessionals, and an assistive technology specialist. Most classroom teachers need to learn only how best to communicate with students who are using ACC systems, and how to facilitate their communication with peers. The first step for the AAC team is to assess the child's capabilities and needs. The data from this assessment aid design and/or selection of the communication device, symbol selection, and selection and arrangement of vocabulary.

Assessment

Assessment is an on-going process that begins with compilation of information about the student's capabilities, his communication needs, and personal preferences (and those of the family). Because AAC systems are multimodal, whether to use gestural techniques or graphic techniques need not be an issue. The initial focus is on the student, not the technology. Consider the following:

> The initial focus of assessment is on the student, not the technology.

- What are the student's communication needs and goals?
- Where and with whom does the student want and need to communicate?
- What are the student's language, cognitive, sensory, and motor skills and capabilities that will facilitate communication?
- What are potential barriers to the student communicating in his natural environments?

Thus, the first step is assessment of the student's mobility, manipulation abilities, communication, cognitive/linguistic skills, and sensory/perceptual abilities (Mirenda et al., 1990).

MOBILITY ASSESSMENT. Mobility assessment considers appropriate seated positioning and ambulation variables. A physical and/or an occupational therapist generally conduct this assessment. If the student cannot assume and maintain a stable, well-aligned seated position independently, the therapists determine how much assistance will be required. Because most students with severe physical disabilities spend

portions of their day in positions other than sitting (e.g., supported standing), the team must also consider these positions and decide how the AAC system will be used during transitions.

MANIPULATION ASSESSMENT. Manipulation assessment is concerned with evaluating the student's fine motor skills relative to the motoric requirements of both gestural mode techniques (signing and gesturing) and graphic mode techniques (direct selection, microswitch activation, or scanning). The occupational therapist typically takes the lead in assessing hand use to determine whether the student will be able to form signs and/or point with the index finger. Assessment then considers the efficiency of head movement, eye gaze, or other body parts for direct selection (pointing). There are a number of easy-to-use formal protocols for fine motor assessment related to the use of signs (Dunn, 1982), microswitches (York, Hamre-Nietupski, & Nietupski, 1985) and other adaptive communication devices (Goossens' & Crain, 1986).

COMMUNICATION ASSESSMENT. Generally, two assumptions can be made about the student's communication: (1) that she is already communicating at some level (at least with family members and other familiar persons); and (2) that communicative competence is minimal. It is rarely the case that a child does not participate in communicative interactions at some level even though she does not use what we think of as standard forms of communication. It is also rare to find that a child with severe physical disabilities has acquired communicative competence. This is because, as discussed in Chapter 1,

All students participate in communicative interactions at some level.

communicative competence is acquired in the context of reciprocal interaction between an infant and caregivers. Severe physical disabilities disrupt the bonding and the reciprocity that is normally established in the context of feeding, sucking, and early vocalization. Thus, most children born with physical disabilities severe enough to interfere with the development of speech have not experienced the normal reciprocal interactions through which communicative competence is acquired.

The language interventionist and the teachers on the team may use the ecological inventory procedure (described in Chapters 7 and 12), or some modification of that procedure, and direct observations to collect the information they need about how the student presently responds to communicative opportunities and obligations. The goal of observations in the student's natural environments and/or interviews with family members and other caregivers and friends is to determine how the student currently exerts control over her environments. Specifically, the communication assessment generates information about

- how the student currently communicates in different contexts;
- how effective and functional present communication modes are in her different contexts;
- what the student currently communicates about; and
- motivational factors that have the potential to affect the student's communication (Mirenda & Smith-Lewis, 1989).

Data collected through these observations and the ecological inventory process also suggest naturally occurring opportunities when communication partners can replace the yes/no questions they are asking with more appropriate language forms.

Decisions regarding the specific communication modes the student will need to learn for different environments require information about the demands of the environments and the nature of the communicative intents in those environments. Some communicative intents lend themselves best to graphic mode techniques (e.g., ordering by pointing to a picture at the counter of a fast-food restaurant). In other cases, gestural mode techniques provide a more natural and appropriate means of communicating intent (e.g., greeting a friend or rejecting a second helping of food).

COGNITIVE/LINGUISTIC ASSESSMENT. Cognitive/linguistic assessment considers receptive language skills and major cognitive attainments related to communication. The focus is on determining (1) how the student presently understands the world; (2) how communication can best be facilitated within this understanding; and (3) the extent to

> Some communicative intents lend themselves to graphic mode techniques; others are better expressed through gestures.

which the student can meet the cognitive demands of the various symbol sets or systems. There are a number of standardized nonverbal tests, such as the Bracken Basic Concept Scale (Bracken, 1984) and the Leiter International Performance Scale (Arthur, 1950), that, when properly used, may yield useful information about the student's cognitive level. These tests are *not* administered to establish a mental age score *or* to determine "readiness" for an AAC system. Rather, they are used to get a picture of the student's present level of ability relative to such cognitive processes as causality, object permanence, and categorization, and to contribute information for decisions about appropriate symbol systems and vocabulary.

SENSORY/PERCEPTUAL ASSESSMENT. Sensory/perceptual assessment considers the student's ability to process incoming information (functional vision skills, functional hearing, and tactile abilities). Information about sensory loss and functional use of sensory modalities is critical in the selection of AAC system options. Assessment of tactile perception is most challenging, as there are very few reliable assessment procedures in that area.

Environmental Assessment

The goal of environmental assessment is to develop a comprehensive list of activities with potential communicative opportunities and obligations so that instructional objectives can be directed to prepare the student for participation in these contexts (Reichle et al., 1991). The classroom schedule is a starting place for this assessment, which should generate a list of priority communication opportunities and their symbol vocabulary requirements.

Environmental assessment should generate a list of priority communication opportunities and their symbol vocabulary requirements.

Other concerns in the environmental assessment include the preferences and skills of potential communication partners. Anyone who has serious reservations about any aspect of the system is not likely to use it. Variables that seem to influence the preferences of the AAC candidate, family, and peers are the appearance of the system, portability, and/or durability. The ages and the literacy skills of potential communication partners are taken into account, because if the output of an AAC system cannot be readily understood by untrained listeners (which is often the case with manual signs or low-quality synthetic speech), there will be frequent communication breakdowns. The time and skills required to learn the system are another consideration, particularly where manual signs and sophisticated computer devices are concerned. If there are no professionals available with the expertise to design and develop a particular "high-tech" AAC system and teach the student how to use it, then that system is not a viable option.

The potential impact of the AAC system on the student's "appearance of normality" or *perceived* communicative competence is also a concern. Among the variables thought to influence perceptions of communicative competence are the intelligibility of the message, the rate and accuracy of message delivery, the pragmatic skills of the user, the grammatical completeness of the message, and the ability of the communication partner to develop effective response strategies (Hoag & Bedrosian, 1992; Kaiser & Goetz, 1993).

AAC System Requirements

When the team has a clear picture of the student's current capabilities and needs, the focus shifts to selection of (1) communication device(s), (2) communication techniques, (3) the symbol systems or symbol sets that will be provided and taught, and (4) the communication strategies that need to be developed. Figure 13.2 provides a format for planning the student's AAC system requirements.

Demonstrative gesturing is easiest.

GESTURAL MODE COMMUNICATION REQUIREMENTS.   Recall that gestural communication options include demonstrative gesturing and symbolic gesturing. With both gestures and signs, as with graphic symbols—discussed in the following section—iconicity is a major factor in how easily learned and how easily understood the symbols are. Demonstrative gesturing (e.g., pointing, showing, offering and/or giving objects, touching, head nodding, etc.) places the fewest requirements on the student because most gestures are, by definition, highly transparent and because teaching of gestures typically begins with behaviors already in the student's repertoire.

The ease with which signs can be learned is also influenced by their configurations; specifically, the shape or shapes assumed by the hands, the orientation of the hand/arm to the body, and the part of the body from which the sign or gesture is produced. Doherty's (1985) review of the literature found that the easiest signs to learn are (1) two-handed signs that require contact between the hands; (2) symmetrical signs; (3) signs produced within the user's visual field; (4) signs that require the same simple handshape and hand movement to be used repeatedly; (5) highly transparent signs; (6) signs that are conceptually dissimilar to other signs that the user is trying to learn; and (7) signs that are motivating and functional for the user.

GRAPHIC MODE COMMUNICATION REQUIREMENTS.   Graphic mode communication requirements are more extensive in that they include not only requirements associated with the symbol system but also requirements associated with the technique and the device. As discussed earlier, graphic symbols are similar to gestures and signs in

FIGURE 13.2   Suggestions form for team planning meetings

What Are Possible Communication Techniques for This Student?

Graphic   *Gestural*

Direct Selection _____   Demonstrative Gesturing _____

Scanning _____   Symbolic Gesturing _____

Encoding _____

What Are Graphic Symbols/Sets This Student Can/Will Use?

Nonelectronic

Board _____   Book _____   Cards _____   Vest _____   Other _____

Electronic (specify)

1.

2.

What Type of Graphic Symbol Characteristics Does This Student Need?

Size? _____   Placement? _____   Number? _____

List an Initial Graphic Symbol Vocabulary for This Student.

```



```

List Gestural Symbols or Symbol Sets This Student Can/Will Use.

```



```

Describe an Initial Gestural Symbol Vocabulary.

```



```

Time and date for the next meeting? _____

Place for the next meeting? _____

that they vary along a continuum of iconicity, with transparent symbols at one end and opaque symbols at the other extreme. Mirenda and Locke (1989) have identified a hierarchy of difficulty for nouns across 10 different symbol sets. This is the hierarchy (from most transparent to most opaque): real objects, color photographs, black and white photographs, miniature objects, black and white pictographs, Blissymbols, and written words. Most students with severe intellectual and severe expressive communication difficulties are not able to use the last two systems (Blissymbols and written words) well enough to permit functional communication.

At least one investigation has looked at the specific motor and cognitive requirements of graphic communication techniques. In a comparison of the response latencies and number of errors of elementary school-age children using two different techniques (direct selection and row-column scanning), Ratcliff (1987) found significantly more errors and somewhat longer response latencies using scanning. Because the subjects in this study demonstrated normal cognitive and motor development, these findings confirm what has been the "conventional wisdom" of the field—that scanning places greater cognitive demands on users than does direct selection.

Scanning places greater demands on the student than does direct selection.

FUNDING. Funding must be considered when selecting an AAC system. Despite the increased legislative support for assistive technology, funding continues to be an issue where electronic communication devices are concerned. Both families and professionals frequently report lack of information about sources of funding (Morris, 1990). Fortunately, many of the devices that are effective for children are relatively low cost. (Some of these devices are described in the next section.)

System Development

Design and development of the AAC system has a dual focus: (1) meeting the student's immediate communication needs in his present natural environments, and (2) projecting what expansions are likely to be needed. Beukelman, Yorkston, and Dowden (1985) call these "today needs" and "tomorrow needs." Data collected through the ecological inventory process are valuable when the team makes decisions about specific techniques, symbol systems, and vocabularies. A major goal of the planning process is to identify the communication techniques and strategies that will give children increased control of their environment.

SELECTING A DEVICE. There are a number of low-cost communication devices and strategies that, because they can use different types of symbols (pictures, words, letters), are appropriate for nonreaders as well as readers. These devices basically divide themselves into two selection methods: direct selection and scanning. Recall that direct selection requires the user to directly indicate his vocabulary choice using a finger, hand, eye gaze, pointer, or other indicating method. The most common low-tech direct selection devices are communication boards or charts, communication books, communication cards, communication vests, communication aprons, and E-trans.

A *communication board* or chart typically has a flat surface with an array of two-dimensional symbols displayed in a matrix format. The size of communication boards depends on the AAC user's needs, abilities, and physical limitations, and they range from lapboard-size single-sheet displays to smaller miniboards. Single-sheet displays may be fitted beneath plexiglass or some other protective covering on a lap tray, or folded in half and equipped with carrying handles (similar to a briefcase). Another design that is appropriate for children with limited head and neck control is a board that stands as a trifold. AAC users with a large vocabulary and the ability to turn pages or flip cards may use multipage boards. Photo albums and three-ring notebooks are often modified to be used as *communication books,* with the number of pages and the number and arrangement of two-dimensional symbols on the pages determined by the AAC user's needs and abilities. There are a variety of commercially produced notebooks available in different sizes, construction materials, and colors. *Communication cards* with two-dimensional symbols are carried in wallets with plastic windows such as those designed for credit cards or business cards, or they may be attached to a keychain. A *communication vest* with attached objects or symbols may be worn by the child's communication partner. The partner and the child communicate by indicating desired vocabulary symbols on the vest. A *communication apron* with attached objects or symbols may be worn by the communication partner or the child. Symbols or words may be attached upside down on the apron so that the wearer can read them right side up.

E-trans, or eye-transfer system, is a clear Plexiglas rectangle with a square or circle cut out in the center. Objects, pictures, symbols, alphabet, numbers, or words and phrases are attached to the frame by Velcro, clear contact paper, or plastic pockets. The child uses eye gaze to indicate a desired selection, or possibly a series of eye gazes to encode and expand message selections. An E-trans can be purchased commercially or homemade. (The plastic may be cut by a local plastics company.)

Recall that scanning is a technique in which vocabulary items are offered to the child, either visually or auditorily. The child typically selects from the array by activating some type of switch. The most

There are almost unlimited possibilities when it comes to designing communication boards.

common low-tech scanning devices are loop tapes, communication clocks, or the sequential scanner. An *endless loop tape,* a switch, and a tape recorder can be used to construct a simple auditory-scanning voice-output device. The endless loop tape or telephone answering-machine tape (available in 15-, 30-, and 60-second lengths) allows messages to be recorded. The child pushes a switch plugged into the remote jack of the tape recorder to produce the prerecorded message. The *communication clock* (also called a rotary scanner or dial scanner) has a hand that rotates when an attached switch is activated. The switch can stop the hand at any point on the clock face. Objects or symbols are mounted on the clock face. The child stops the hand at one of the symbols or objects to communicate. Communication clocks come in a variety of sizes and are available with lights, adjustable speeds, musical cues, and counterclockwise hand movement. The *sequential scanner* is a switch-activated device with two to four compartments. Objects or symbols are placed in the compartments, which are illuminated in sequence with the switch.

Electronic communication devices may produce speech and/or written output. They are expensive but, in recent years, both the size and the cost of electronic communication devices have been reduced, making them more easily available (Mustonen, Locke, Reichle, Solbrack, & Lindgren, 1991). Most electronic devices, such as Pegasus (Words+, Inc.) shown in Figure 13.3, are boxlike objects that the student can carry or place on a wheelchair tray. They are pro-

> Electronic communication devices may produce either speech or printed output.

FIGURE 13.3   Pegasus

grammed with words or phrases that are spoken when certain areas of the keyboard are pressed. There may be only one or two available words or many phrases and sentences represented by printed text, pictures, or photographs. Among the advantages of electronic systems is the ease with which messages can be produced. Even young children and students with limited cognitive skills can use them, producing messages that are far more sophisticated than their actual language skills. For example, when Julie touches the door symbol on her display, her electronic aid produces the phrase, "I'm ready to go now."

Another advantage of electronic devices for both the AAC user and communication partners is the potential to communicate without first taking whatever steps are necessary to get a listener's attention. It is not necessary for the listener to move close to the user and look at the display in order to receive the communication. A third advantage is the ability to store messages to be used at a later time (in conversation or written text). More capable AAC users can even use their electronic devices as portable lap-top computers, thus integrating the functions of communication and word processing. Finally, electronic communication devices can clarify a qualitatively poor selection response. Consider, for example, students who do not have precise aim with a head pointer. Some electronic communiation devices can add increments of time to allow a user time to establish contact with a particular symbol. A symbol is not electronically selected until the cumulative contact time reaches a predetermined criterion.

> The potential to communicate without first taking steps to get a listener's attention is an important advantage of electronic communication devices.

SELECTING COMMUNICATIVE FUNCTIONS AND VOCABULARY. Decisions regarding initial vocabulary are particularly important because, as Mirenda and colleagues (1990) remind us, "the vocabulary provided through a system will directly determine its functionality for the user as well as the motivation of the user to communicate with the system" (p. 14). Reichle and colleagues (1991) emphasize the importance of analyzing the communicative obligations and opportunities in the candidates' environments as the basis for selecting an initial repertoire of communicative functions to teach. To maximize the possibility of generalization across stimulus conditions, give first priority to *communicative intents that can be used across several situations*. Reichle and colleagues (1992) give as an example the rejecting response "I don't want to do this," which can be used when the AAC user is offered an item that he does not want; when an item that is normally desired is rejected because the AAC does not want more; and when the AAC user (for whatever reason) wants to discontinue an activity.

Another consideration when selecting initial instructional targets is *idiosyncratic gestures that are already in the AAC candidate's communication repertoire* (Reichle et al., 1992). Examples might include headshakes to indicate "yes" and "no," a side-to-side hand motion to indicate "no more," and crotch holding to indicate a need to use the bathroom. The first two behaviors are usually considered socially acceptable; there may be a decision not to retain the third. Some factors to consider, in addition to social acceptability, when deciding whether to retain an idiosyncratic gesture that is already in the candidate's repertoire are (1) how clearly the gesture conveys the intended message; (2) whether the gesture involves the production of undesirable reflex patterns; and (3) whether the gesture constitutes a challenging (inappropriate) behavior.

The ecological inventory process is also discussed in Chapters 7 and 12.

In addition to providing information about the communicative obligations and opportunities in the candidate's environments, data collected through the ecological inventory process and direct observations assist the selection of vocabulary. Factors to consider when selecting specific vocabulary items are (1) the iconicity of the sign or symbol; (2) how many opportunities there will be to use the sign or symbol; (3) whether the sign or symbol is generic; (4) how many characteristics the sign or symbol shares with other vocabulary targets; and (5) the motoric characteristics (if a manual sign is being considered) (Reichle et al., 1992). Iconicity is important (for both gestural mode communication and graphic mode communication) because signs and symbols that are more guessable are easier to learn and easier for listeners to decipher. The more opportunities there are for the AAC learner to use the vocabulary item, the quicker it will be acquired and the greater the likelihood it will be maintained.

Generic symbols are preferable because they have broader application than specific vocabulary items. For example, teaching the generic sign or symbol for "drink" has advantages over teaching the specific vocabulary item "orange juice." With the former, the AAC user can request any number of different types of beverages. When selecting initial vocabulary in both the graphic and gestural modes, the similarity of signs and symbols will affect how quickly they are learned. The more characteristics that new vocabulary items share with previous items, the more difficult they are to discriminate and thus, to learn. The motor complexity of signs also affects ease of learning. Signs and gestures that require contact between both hands or between hand and body seem to be the easiest to acquire. Figure 13.4 shows a planning form that synthesizes Reichle's (1991) suggestions concerning the types of information that should be assembled and discussed at team planning meetings.

INSTRUCTION AND PRACTICE

Technology may be viewed as an equalizer that permits many students with severe and multiple disabilities to participate in activities

FIGURE 13.4   AAC planning form

AAC SYSTEM PLANNING

AAC Candidate: _____   Today's Date _____

Team Members

WHEN/WHERE Does the Student Need/Want to Communicate?

WHAT Are the Student's Current Strategies for Meeting His/Her Communication Obligations/Opportunities?

What Functions Does the Student Need to Learn to Meet His/Her Communication Obligations/Opportunities?

What Forms Does the Student Need to Learn to Meet His/Her Communication Obligations/Opportunities?

Technology permits many students with severe and multiple disabilities to participate in activities with their nondisabled peers.

in the general education classroom. Computers are an example. They make it possible for students with severe physical disabilities who, despite the ability to generate ideas and form sentences, cannot hold a pencil to express themselves through written communication. Some students are able to use a standard computer keyboard with a few minor modifications. For example, the Apple IIGS computer allows the keyboard to be modified so that a student, who can touch a key but has trouble releasing it in a timely fashion, can avoid accidentally typing long strings of repeated letters (because of difficulty releasing). On Apple II computers, a simple hard plastic keyguard with latches allows the student to press two keys simultaneously or, for students who use the Macintosh, there is a system resource called "Sticky Keys" which converts simultaneous keyboard commands into simple sequential steps. A similar software resource is available for IBM and compatible computers.

Students who cannot use the standard keyboard with adaptations can use an alternative computer access device. Various keyboard emulators are available that allow a student to point with a mouse to letters on a picture of a keyboard on the screen. One of several pointing alternatives for a student who cannot use a handheld mouse is a device called the Headmaster (available from the Prentke Romick Company). The Headmaster allows pointing with head motions, using a headset transmitting an ultrasound signal. Alternatives to the standard keyboard include the Unicorn Expanded Keyboard (Unicorn Engineering, Inc.) that looks like a 14-inch by 21-inch piece of hard plastic with a paper overlay, the Power Pad (Dunamis, Inc.), and the Muppet Learning Keys (Sunburst Communications), which is a colorful board with letters (in alphabetical order), numbers from zero to nine, a paint box of colors, and various other "buttons."

If even one muscle of the body can be consciously controlled, the student can write with a computer (and control environmental devices using a switch). Any part of the body can be used: a finger, hand, arm, leg, foot, chin, forehead, or tongue. The movement can be large or small; it can be powerful or have very little force. All that matters is that the movement is reliable (can be repeated) and that it is under voluntary control.

Computerized speech synthesis is a technological advance that has been especially beneficial for AAC users. When computerized speech is synthesized, rules have been coded into the software that allow the computer to "translate" anything the person types into speech output: The computer produces sounds that simulate the sounds of a person speaking the typed-in letters, word, or sentences. This is called text-to-speech. When computerized speech is digitized, an actual human voice has been translated into data that can be stored on a disk in words or phrases. This speech is usually of superior quality to the robotic-sounding synthesized speech, but it has the disadvantage that the user may only use those particular words or phrases that have been digitized.

Most critical in planning for AAC instruction is to avoid these assumptions: (1) that children with severe expressive communication difficulties have had an opportunity or the conditions essential to acquisition of communicative competence, and (2) that provision of an AAC system will somehow "automatically" result in the acquisition of communication skills. Plan for *direct* training of specific techniques. Also plan for expanding system use and conversational participation in present and future environments once the student masters initial communication skills.

The very fact that a student has an AAC system and knows how to generate messages will not increase appropriate communication or promote meaningful changes in her daily life unless she has appropriate instruction and support to use it effectively to initiate and participate in conversations (Basil, 1992; Newell, 1992). Research suggests that AAC users tend to be responders, seldom initiating conversations with others (Angelo & Goldstein, 1990). When initiations do occur, they are often limited to object or action requests rather than requests for information that have the potential to initiate conversations. Some possible reasons why students may not use their AAC system include (1) an inadequate symbol system (the student may not have the necessary symbols to encode the types of messages needed to initiate a conversation); (2) lack of conversational/discourse skills; (3) embarrassment because of having to rely on a nonspeech mode of communication; (4) potential communication partners who do not understand the AAC user's symbols; and (5) decreased motivation because of the failure of past efforts to use communication to affect the environment.

For a student to gain proficiency in using aided and/or unaided AAC systems in the classroom, teachers and peers must begin to use the system(s) (paired with verbal communication) in communication directed to the student. For example, in the case of a voice-output device, the teacher and peers should simultaneously point out and/or activitate cells on the device when they speak to the student. In the case of gestural communication, the teacher and peers should learn and use the manual signs that the AAC user will be expected to learn. "Total immersion," where the teaching staff signs and speaks simultaneously (using a sign for each word [Signed English]), is the ideal when teaching gestural communication, but it is not a realistic expectation in most classrooms. However, generally the teaching staff and peers can learn a signing vocabulary with the student(s). One way to begin integrating gestural communication into the daily routine is to look up and learn a small set of key signs for each activity, as well as

It is important not to assume that children with severe communication difficulties have had the opportunities to acquire communicative competence.

Begin by learning a small set of signs for each activity in the daily routine.

a set of relationship words such as "when," "after," and "before" that can be used throughout the day.

Ideally, instruction is designed to promote initiating (as well as responding) behaviors, and it is provided in the context of daily routines and curriculum activities. When selecting routines and activities as training contexts, consider: (1) whether motivation to communicate is inherent in the activity; (2) whether there is ample opportunity for the student to see symbols being used repeatedly, interactively, and meaningfully; and (3) the potential to enhance, clarify, and add to whatever communication (speech and/or gestures) the student is presently using in the activity.

Although most naturalistic instructional procedures described in Chapters 8, 10, and 12, such as milieu language teaching, were not originally developed to teach AAC users, they are appropriate instructional approaches. Milieu teaching is used most frequently with children with severe expressive communication difficulties. As discussed in Chapters 8 and 10, the fundamental assumption underlying the use of milieu teaching is that the potential for communication can be increased by creating situations where children need communication in order to secure desired objects and activities. Adults can then provide natural consequences for communication attempts and build upon these communication efforts to create shared meaning. Milieu teaching has been particularly effective in teaching early language skills using gestural communication (Carr & Kologinsky, 1983; Oliver & Halle, 1982; Rogers-Warren & Warren, 1980; Schepis et al., 1982). Romski and Sevcik (1988) used it to teach a computer-based AAC system to adults with severe disabilities.

Environmental Arrangement Strategies

Students must have opportunities to use their AAC system in naturally occuring interactions.

Similar to learning any other skills, the key to learning to use an AAC system is practice. Students should have as many natural opportunities as possible to use their AAC system to communicate. One of the most serious problems for AAC users is that potential communication partners often fail to see and, therefore, to take advantage of naturally occurring communication opportunities. Potential communication partners must often be cued to notice and respond to initiations and to prompt the student to use the AAC system. Training peers in the use of the AAC system may be crucial if the system is to be used on a generalized basis. For example, Hunt, Alwell, and Goetz (1991) trained a student with severe disabilities and a peer to have conversational exchanges using a communication book, but use of the device did not generalize to other peers until these other peers received brief instruction in how to use the book during conversational exchanges. Similarly, use of the book at school did not generalize to the student's home (despite the parents' involvement in determining and selecting the system) until the parents received brief training in how to use the book to converse with the student. The objectives for the training session were to teach student peers the following: (1) to make comments by referring to pictures in the communication book, (2) to cue the AAC user to take another "turn" by asking him a question related to a picture in the book, and (3) to wait after the student answered the question to give him an opportunity to make additional comments or introduce a new topic. Oral instructions were accompanied by demonstration and followed by a brief role-playing activity with the teacher. Training was generally conducted individually or with pairs of students.

Recall from Chapter 10 these suggestions and examples of environmental arrangement strategies to encourage and support the use of language:

Chapter 10 also discusses environmental arrangement to encourage and support language learning and use.

- Provide interesting objects and materials.
- Encourage choice making by offering two or more objects or activities.
- Provide materials that cannot be operated without assistance.
- Provide only a subset of the materials needed for an activity.
- Provide small portions of each type of needed materials.
- Place desired objects within view but out of reach.
- Create situations that violate expectations.
- Provide an unwanted object or materials.
- Block access to materials or activities.

Used alone or in combination with milieu teaching procedures, these strategies can be as effective in encouraging communication with an AAC system as with oral language.

Milieu Teaching Procedures

Refer back to the discussion of milieu language teaching interactions in Chapters 8 and 10. Recall that these procedures are brief and positive, carried out in natural environments, and child-initiated (Rogers-Warren & Warren, 1980; Warren' & Kaiser, 1986). The four general principles of milieu teaching are:

Milieu teaching is discussed at length in Chapters 8 and 10.

1. ***Follow and attend.*** Take advantage of the focus of the child's attention to comment, model a response, or ask a question.
2. ***Make it profitable to use language***. Show the child that using language is the best way to get desired materials and participate in desirable activities.
3. ***Create situations to elicit language.*** Arrange the environment to increase the probabilities for language and communication.
4. ***Respond and expand***. Determine the child's level and require an expanded form or structure before providing the desired event, materials, or services.

Functional Communication Training

Although all behavior has communicative value, it is not necessarily the case that all behavior that is used for communication is appropriate and socially acceptable. Behaviors such as hitting, pushing, biting, screaming, and pulling someone's arm—which are potentially harmful to the student and/or others—fall into the category of problem behaviors (also called challenging behaviors). As discussed in Chapter 8, functional communication training is teaching students with severely limited communication skills alternative communicative responses that serve the same function as their problem behaviors.

> Functional communication training teaches students communicative responses to replace their problem behaviors.

Functional communication training has been successful in reducing disruptive behavior (Hunt, Alwell, Goetz, & Sailor, 1990), severe aggression and self-injurious behavior (Durand & Kishi, 1987), stereotyped behaviors (Wacker et al., 1990), and a variety of communication problems (Carr & Kemp, 1989). Several studies have taught students to use unaided AAC systems (manual signs) as a means of requesting and thus reducing challenging behaviors (Bird, Dores, Moniz, & Robinson, 1989; Durand & Kishi, 1987). Others have taught the use of communication devices to request desired objects and activities as an alternative to their problem behaviors.

Durand (1993) evaluated the effectiveness of teaching aided AAC systems to three students who exhibited aggression, self-injury, and tantrums. These students with severely limited communication skills (a 3-year-old, a 5½-year-old, and a 15-year-old) participated in the study. Following assessment of the function of their challenging behaviors, the students were taught to use their voice output communication devices to request desired objects and activities (e.g., social attention, breaks from work). Multiple baseline data collected across the three students indicated that not only did the students use their devices successfully, but also the intervention reduced their challenging behaviors. Durand attributes the success of the functional communication to three factors: the electronic communication devices were easy to operate, they provided immediate feedback (vocal output), and the consequences were highly reinforcing.

Conclusion

These guidelines serve as a summary of the major points of the discussion of instruction and practice:

- An AAC system is best learned in a supportive environment with appropriate instruction provided in the context of ongoing activities.

- All components of the student's multimodal AAC system should be taught concurrently in the context of ongoing meaningful, reinforcing, and interactive activities.
- Ensure maximum opportunities for children to experience receptive use of their AAC system.
- Plan for continuous reassessment and evaluation of the system (including vocabulary, devices, techniques, and symbols).

ROLES AND RESPONSIBILITIES

As emphasized at the beginning of this chapter, a team approach is imperative for working with augmentative and alternative communication (ACC) users. In addition to the AAC candidate, her family or caregivers and close friends, and present and potential employers, the team includes representatives from general and special education, speech-language pathology, and physical and occupational therapy. Other disciplines that may be involved are psychology, social services, vocational counseling, computer technology, medicine, and rehabilitation engineering.

Guidelines for collaborative teaming for students who are AAC users are basically the same as those for teams concerned with students who use speech as their primary communication mode. The roles and responsibilities of the different disciplines on the team depend on the needs and preferences of the AAC candidate and the family (Beukelman & Mirenda, 1992). However, it is possible to identify a core of basic competency requirements for the primary team members. The roles and responsibilities typically assumed by the language interventionist as suggested by the American Speech-Language-Hearing Association (ASHA) (1989) are shown in Table 13.1.

Chapter 5 discusses collaborative teaming.

TABLE 13.1 Roles and responsibilities suggested for the language interventionist on the AAC team

- Identification of appropriate AAC candidates;
- determination of appropriate AAC systems;
- development of intervention plans to promote "maximal functional communication";
- implementation of the intervention plans;
- evaluation of intervention outcomes;
- evaluation and awareness of new AAC technology and strategies;
- advocacy in the AAC area;
- provision of in-services for professionals and consumers; and
- coordination of AAC services.

Table 13.2   Roles and responsibilities suggested for the teacher on the AAC team

- Adapting the curriculum for the AAC user;
- preparing and maintaining documentation;
- writing goals and objectives for AAC users;
- assessing cognitive abilities;
- acting as liaison between the team and family members;
- assessing social capabilities;
- providing for ongoing skill development;
- identifying vocabulary to be provided in the AAC users system;
- providing information about students' motivation and attitudes toward AAC techniques; and
- determining students' communication needs.

Similarly, there has been some research considering the competency needs of teachers on AAC teams. Based on a survey of over 200 special education teachers nationwide who serve on school district teams responsible for providing AAC services, Locke and Mirenda (1992) have identified the roles and responsibilities assumed by special education teachers on AAC teams. The roles and responsibilities shown in Table 13.2 were indicated by a majority (at least 70 percent) of the special education teachers who responded to the survey.

The roles of physical and occupational therapists on AAC teams have also been discussed (Stowers, Altheide, & Shea, 1987). Physical therapists are typically responsible for carrying out gross motor assessments related to the use of AAC techniques, ensuring appropriate positioning and seating, constructing adaptive equipment as needed for positioning and seating, and providing in-service to other team members about positioning and seating. Occupational therapists usually assess the fine motor abilities and visual perceptual skills needed for AAC. Additionally, they evaluate motivation and potential occupational roles in different environmental settings. Occupational therapists also assume primary responsibility for remediating functional deficits that impair performance of fine motor skills, constructing adaptive devices for the arms, hands, and head, and providing in-service to other team members concerning use of fine motor abilities (Stowers et al., 1987).

Summary

The three trends noted in the introduction to this chapter—inclusionary assessment procedures, focus on functionally relevant communication, and recognition of the multimodal nature of communication—

have contributed to the growth of the number of communication options available to children with severe disorders. Most important has been the recognition that communication is a right, not something that children must somehow "be ready for." Children are no longer denied communication devices and instruction because they do not demonstrate certain cognitive and/or social behaviors judged to be prerequisite to communication. Once it is determine that a child is not developing intelligible speech at the expected rate, there is now a framework to assist professionals and parents to make the decisions necessary to provide an AAC system that will afford the child maximum participation in a variety of environments with a wide range of communication partners.

REFERENCES

Abrahamsen, A. A., Romski, M. A., & Sevcik, R. A. (1989). Concomitants of success in acquiring an augmentative communication system: Changes in attention, communication, and sociability. *American Journal on Mental Retardation, 93*(5), 475–496.

American Speech-Language-Hearing Association. (1989) Competencies for speech-language pathologists providing services in augmentation communication. *Asha, 31,* 107–110.

American Speech-Language-Hearing Association. (1991). Report: Augmentative and alternative communication. *Asha, 33* (Suppl. 5), 9–12.

Angelo, D. H., & Goldstein, H. (1990). Effects of a pragmatic teaching strategy for requesting information by communication board users. *Journal of Speech and Hearing Disorders, 55,* 231–243.

Arthur, G. (1950). *The Arthur Adaptation of the Leiter International Performance Scale.* Chicago: C. H. Stoelting.

Basil, C. (1992). Social interaction and learned helplessness in nonvocal severely handicapped children. *Augmentative and Alternative Communication, 2,* 71–72.

Beukelman, D. R., & Mirenda, P. (1992). *Augmentative and alternative communication: Management of severe communication disorders in children and adults.* Baltimore: Paul H. Brookes.

Beukelman, D. R., Yorkston, K. M., & Dowden, P. A. (1985). *Communication augmenta-*tion: *A casebook of clinical management.* San Diego: College-Hill.

Bird, F., Dores, P. A., Moniz, D., & Robinson, J. (1989). Reducing severe aggressive and self-injurious behaviors with functional communication training: Direct, collateral and generalized results. *American Journal of Mental Retardation, 94,* 37–48.

Bracken, B. (1984). *Bracken Basic Concept Scale (BBCS).* San Antonio, TX: The Psychological Corporation.

Burkhart, L. J. (1993). *Total augmentative communication in the early childhood classroom.* Eldersburg, MD: Linda J. Burkhart.

Carlson, F. (1984). *Picsyms categorical dictionary.* Lawrence, KS: Baggeboda Press.

Carr, E. G., & Kemp, D. C. (1989). Reducing behavior problems through functional communication training. *Journal of Applied Behavior Analysis, 18,* 111–126.

Carr, E. G., & Kologinsky, E. (1983). Acquisition of sign language by autistic children: Spontaneity and generalization effects. *Journal of Applied Behavior Analysis, 16,* 297–413.

Daniloff, J., Noll, J., Fristoe, M., & Lloyd, L. (1982). Gesture recognition in patients with aphasia. *Journal of Speech and Hearing Disorders, 47,* 43–49.

Dixon, L. S. (1981). A functional analysis of photo-object matching skills of severely retarded adolescents. *Journal of Applied Behavior Analysis, 14,* 465–478.

Doherty, J. E. (1985). The effects of sign characteristics on sign acquisition and retention: An integrative review of the literature. *Augmentative and Alternative Communication, 1,* 108–120.

Dunn, M. (1982). *Pre-sign language motor skills.* Tucson, AZ: Communication Skill Builders.

Durand, V. M., (1993). Functional communication training using assistive devices: Effects on challenging behavior and affect. *Augmentative and Alternative Communication, 19,* 168–176.

Durand, V. M., & Kishi, G. (1987). Reducing severe behavior problems among persons with dual sensory impairments: An evaluation of a technical assistance model. *Journal of the Association for Persons with Severe Handicaps, 12,* 2–10.

Goossens', C., & Crain, S. (1986). *Augmentative communication assessment resource.* Wauconda, IL: Don Johnston Developmental Equipment, Inc.

Hamre-Nietupski, S., Stoll, A., Holtz, K., Fullerton, P., Flottum-Ryan, M., & Brown, L. (1977). Curriculum strategies for teaching nonverbal communication skills to verbal and nonverbal severely handicapped students. In L. Brown, J. Nietupski, S. Lyon, S. Hamre-Nietupski, T. Crowner, & L. Gruenewald (Eds.), *Curricular strategies for teaching functional object use, nonverbal communication, problem solving and mealtime skills to severely handicapped students* (Vol. 7, Part 1, pp 94–250). Madison, WI: Madison Metropolitan School District.

Hoag, L. A., & Bedrosian, J. L. (1992). Effects of speech output type, message length, and reauditorization on perceptions of the communicative competence of an adult AAC user. *Journal of Speech and Hearing Research, 35,* 1363–1366.

Hunt, P., Alwell, M., & Goetz, L. (1991). Interacting with peers through conversational turntaking with a communication book adaptation. *Augmentative and Alternative Communication, 7*(2), 117–126.

Hunt, P., Alwell, M., Goetz, L., & Sailor, W. (1990). Generalized effects of conversational skill training. *Journal of the Association for Persons with Severe Handicaps, 15,* 250–260.

Johnson, R. (1985). *The picture communication symbols—Book II.* Solana Beach, CA: Mayer-Johnson.

Kaiser, A. P., & Goetz, L. (1993). Enhancing communication with persons labeled severely disabled. *Journal of the Association for Persons with Severe Handicaps, 18,* 137–142.

Kangas, K., & Lloyd, L. (1988). Early cognitive skills as prerequisites to augmentative and alternative communication use: What are we waiting for? *Augmentative and Alternative Communication, 4,* 211–221.

Kraat, A. W., & Sitver-Kogut, M. (1991). *Features of portable communication devices.* Wilmington, DE: Applied Science and Engineering Laboratories.

Light, J. (1988). Interaction involving individuals using augmentative and alternative communication systems: State of the art and future directions. *Augmentative and Alternative Communication, 4,* 66–82.

Locke, P., & Miranda, P. (1992). Roles and responsibilities of special education teachers serving on teams delivering AAC services. *Augmentation and Alternative Communication, 8,* 200–214.

Lloyd, L. L., & Blischak, D. M. (1992). AAC terminology policy and issues update. *Augmentative and Alternative Communication, 8,* 104–109.

Lloyd, L. L., & Kangas, K. A. (1990). AAC terminology policy and issues update. *Augmentative and Alternative Communication, 6,* 167–170.

Morris, M. W. (1990). Assistive technology funding: A user-friendly workbook. Washington, DC: RESNA Technical Assistance Project.

Mirenda, P., Iacona, R., & Willams, R. (1990). Communication options for persons with severe and profound disabilities: State of the art and future directions. *Journal of the Association for Persons with Severe Handicaps, 15*(1), 3–21.

Mirenda, P., & Locke, P. (1989). A comparison of symbol transparency in nonspeaking persons with intellectual disabilities. *Journal of Speech and Hearing Disorders, 54,* 131–140.

Mustonen, T., Locke, P., Reichle, J., Solbrack, M., & Lindgren, A. (1991). An overview of augmentative and alternative communication systems. In J. Reichle, J. York, & J. Sigafoos (Eds.), *Implementing augmentative and alternative communication* (pp. 1–38). Baltimore: Paul H. Brookes.

Newell, A. F. (1992). Today's dream—Tomorrow's reality. *Augmentative and Alternative Communication, 8,* 81–88.

Oliver, C., & Halle, J. (1982). Language training in the everyday environment: Teaching functional sign use to a retarded child. *Journal of the Association for Persons with Severe Handicaps, 8,* 50–61.

Ratcliff, A. (1987). *A comparison of two message selection techniques used in augmentative communication systems by normal children with differing cognitive styles.* Unpublished doctoral dissertation, University of Wisconsin-Madison.

Reichle, J. (1991). Defining the decisions involved in designing and implementing augmentative and alternative communication systems. In Reichle, J. York, & J. Sigafoos (Eds.), *Implementing augmentative and alternative communication: Strategies for learners with severe disabilities* (pp. 39–60). Baltimore: Paul H. Brookes Publishing Co.

Reichle, J., Mirenda, P., Locke, P., Piche, L., & Johnson, S. (1992). Beginning augmentative communication systems. In S. F. Warren & J. Reichle (Eds.), *Causes and effects in communication and language intervention* (pp. 131–156). Baltimore: Paul H. Brookes.

Reichle, J., & Karlan, G. (1985). The selection of an augmentative system of communication intervention: A critique of decision rules. *Journal of the Association for Persons with Severe Handicaps, 19,* 146–156.

Reichle, J., York, J., & Sigafoos, J. (Eds.). (1991). *Implementing augmentative and alternative communication: Strategies for learners with severe disabilities.* (pp. 39–60). Baltimore: Paul H. Brookes.

Rogers-Warren, A., & Warren, S. (1980). Mands for verbalization: Facilitating the display of newly trained language in children. *Behavior Modification, 4,* 361–382.

Romski, M. A., & Sevcik, R. A. (1988). Augmentative and alternative communication systems: Considerations for individuals with severe intellectual disabilities. *Augmentative and Alternative Communication, 4,* 83–93.

Romski, M. A., Sevcik, R. A., & Ellis-Joyner, S. E. (1984). Nonspeech communication systems: Implications for language intervention with mentally retarded children. *Topics in Language Disorders, 5,* 66–81.

Rowland, C., & Schweigert, P. (1989). Tangible symbols: Symbolic communication for individuals with multisensory impairments. *Augmentative and Alternative Communication, 6,* 226–234.

Schepis, M., Reid, D., Fitzgerald, J., Faw, G., van den Pol, R., & Welty, P. (1982). A program for increasing manual signing by autistic and profoundly retarded youth within the daily environment. *Journal of Applied Behavior Analysis, 5,* 363–379.

Silverman, F. (1980). *Communication for the speechless.* Englewood Cliffs, NJ: Prentice Hall.

Skelly, M. (1979). *Amer-Ind gestural code based on universal American Indian hand talk.* New York: Elsevier.

Stowers, S., Altheide, M. R., & Shea, V. (1987). Motor assessment for aided and unaided communication. *Physical and Occupational Therapy in Pediatrics, 7*(2), 61–78

Vanderheiden, G. C., & Lloyd, L. L. (1986). Communication systems and their components. In S. W. Blackstone (Ed.), *Augmentative communication: An introduction* (pp. 49–161). Rockville, MD: ASHA.

Wacker, D. P., Steege, M. W., Northup, J., Sasso, G., Berg, W., Reimers, T., Cooper, L., Cigrand, K., & Donn, L. (1990). A component analysis of functional communication training across three topographies of severe behavior problems. *Journal of Applied Behavior Analysis, 23,* 417–429.

Warren, S. F., & Kaiser, A. P. (1986). Incidental language teaching: A critical review. *Journal of Speech and Hearing Disorders, 51,* 291–299.

Woodward, J. (1990). Sign English in the education of deaf students. In H. Bornstein (Ed.), *Manual communication: Implications for education* (pp. 67–80). Washington, DC: Gallaudet University.

York, J., Hamre-Nietupski, S., & Nietupski, J. (1985). A decision-making model for using microswitches. *Journal of the Association for Persons with Severe Handicaps, 10,* 214–223,

Zangari, C., Lloyd, L. L., & Vicker, B. (1994). Augmentative and alternative communication: An historical perspective. *Augmentative and Alternative Communication, 10,* 27–59.

CHAPTER 14
Children with Culturally
Diverse Backgrounds

Betty H. Bunce

Maria is informed that she will have a new child, José, in her first-grade classroom. José and his family have newly immigrated from Mexico and speak Spanish in the home. José has only limited proficiency in English. His vocabulary consists of a few words such as Coke, hamburger, car, hi, bye, and please. José will be the only child with a native language that differs from English in Maria's classroom. Marie is monolingual in English and has never taught a child who speaks a language other than English. Her immediate dilemmas are how best to incorporate José into the classroom and how to meet his language and academic needs while continuing to meet the needs of her 24 other students.

José is six years old and a competent speaker of Spanish. He has had one semester of schooling in Mexico. He is eager to learn about his new country, but, at the same time, apprehensive about his new school. José's dilemmas are how to gain acceptance in his new school, how to learn English, and how to do the academic work required of monolingual speakers of English.

With an estimated 2.5 million school-age immigrants (Jennings, 1988; see report of the Stanford Working Group, 1993, for other estimates of children with limited English proficiency), this kind of scenario occurs with a variety of themes throughout the United States. In some cases, the class may have several language minority children from a variety of language and socioeconomic backgrounds. In other cases, there will be bilingual teachers and bilingual programming for several students of one language background. Another variation involves older children who may or may not have achieved facility in English and/or academic work. Still a different scenario is the child who is language-disordered in his first and/or second language. In any case, some of the concerns are the same. The teacher needs to be able to facilitate the language and academic achievement of the child, and the child needs to be accepted in the classroom and achieve both linguistic and academic competence.

This chapter addresses two specific concerns: how to facilitate the linguistic and academic achievement of the bilingual/bicultural child, and how to identify and provide the needed special programming for the bilingual child with a language impairment. There are several issues affecting both of these concerns. These issues are discussed at length in the following sections: (1) philosophies regarding second-language learning; (2) sociocultural factors; (3) language proficiency and academic achievement; (4) types of programs and instructional tactics; and (5) assessment and intervention.

> This chapter addresses procedures to facilitate achievement of the bilingual/bicultural child and special programming for the bilingual child with a language impairment.

PHILOSOPHIES REGARDING SECOND-LANGUAGE LEARNING

Lindfors (1987) has delineated two viewpoints regarding the learning of a second language that have important educational implications. One approach, the audiolingual method, focuses on automatic mastery of utterance form. The second approach focuses on communication or on achieving communicative competence. Although people favoring the audiolingual method consider communication to be an eventual goal, an underlying assumption is that the second-language learner needs to develop some language structure and then learn to communicate. On the other hand, people favoring the communication viewpoint assume that such separation between form and use is not possible. They believe that the first language is learned in interactive contexts and that the second language is best acquired in the same manner. In both cases, beliefs about language learning affect teaching strategies and expectations.

> One view focuses on mastery of form; the second view focuses on communicative competence.

For the audiolingual approach, oral pattern practice is an important instructional procedure. This is accomplished through structured drill with immediate correction of errors. The learner must memorize and recite sentences or passages as part of the drill. Procedures to facilitate the shift to a communicative situation are provided after practice on correct production of form. Correct phonological production is often emphasized. Therefore, much time is spent on discrimination activities between phonological systems of the first and second language. Sometimes the emphasis may be on sounds used in the second language, but not in the first. A major assumption involved in the audiolingual approach is that language learning is broken down into parts and practiced, and then the pieces are put together again. A second assumption of the audiolingual method is that the first language can interfere with the learning of the second language. Therefore, prohibitions against using the first language may be made. Finally, the audiolingual method emphasizes speech production.

Proponents of communicative competence place emphasis on communication from the beginning. This viewpoint assumes that language form and use cannot be separated; therefore, it is more global and context-oriented. Wholes are not broken down into parts (at least initially). Instructional procedures would emphasize interactive meaningful experiences rather than controlled pattern practice on correct form. Errors in form are tolerated, and corrections are made only if communication breaks down. Comprehension of language is emphasized and usually precedes production (see Krashen & Terrill, 1983, for further elaboration of the natural approach to second-language learning, particularly in classroom settings).

> The communicative competence view assumes that language form and use cannot be separated.

The communicative competence point of view is similar to prevailing views of how children acquire their first language (e.g., Bates, 1976; Berko-Gleason, 1993) and to the interactionist perspective as presented in this text. It is assumed that the children will acquire the rules of the second language much as they acquired rules in the first language. That is, through being immersed in the context, the child will construct novel sentences to communicate intent. A second assumption is that the child will adopt some of the same strategies used in acquiring the first language, so that overgeneralizations of rules and overextentions of vocabulary may occur. However, the first language is not expected to interfere with the learning of the second.

> The communicative competence view assumes that children acquire the rules of a second language much as they acquire the rules of their first language.

The two viewpoints represent the end points on a learning style scale. The audiolingual method utilizes a bottom-up approach, whereas communicative competence uses a top-down approach. The two viewpoints can also be divided on how language proficiency is perceived. The audiolingual (or interference) view appears to suggest that there are two distinct proficiencies that can interfere with each other (cf. Lado, 1957). The communicative competence position suggests one general language proficiency that can be represented by two different surface forms (Cummins, 1979, 1984).

In summary, these two positions or philosophies of second-language learning lead to different kinds of policies regarding instructional methods. The audiolingual favors pattern practice of correct oral productions, practice on parts before insertion into whole, sequential linear learning, and little facilitation of first-language usage. The communicative competence method favors using the second language within meaningful communicative situations, allows errors of form, starts with the global and then proceeds to parts, and supports further development of the first language. The focus in this chapter is on *facilitating communicative competence* of bilingual/bicultural children.

SOCIOCULTURAL FACTORS

A child learning English as a second language brings to the task knowledge of her first language and myriad other cultural and personal factors. These cultural and personal factors can affect the academic achievement of the child. Many of the factors contribute to academic achievement (e.g., broader understanding of concepts underlying word meanings, ability to analyze linguistic structure, broader understanding of different ways of interacting). However, other factors may be less positive due to what Iglesias (1985b) calls communication mismatch between teacher and child. This mismatch is due to linguistic differences and misunderstandings in ways of interacting. Teachers need to be aware of possible causes of communication failure in the school environment in order to circumvent misunderstandings and to facilitate academic achievement and acceptance of the bilingual/bicultural child in the school system. Teachers must be aware of their own cultural ways of interacting and how these may affect children who do not share their culture or language. In addition, teachers need to respect these differences as differences and not deficiencies.

> As discussed in Chapter 8, classroom interactions tend to be interactions that are familiar to middle-class children.

Saville-Troike (1979) described the culture of the American school as one that "serves primarily to prepare middle-class children to participate in their own culture" (p. 141). This means that the classroom interactions extend to interactions already familiar to middle-class children. For example, these children are familiar with "test questions," where the adult asks a question, the child responds, and the adult then evaluates the appropriateness of the response ("What color is the box?" "Brown," "That's right"). To some children learning English as a second language, this is a peculiar interaction because adults in their culture do not ask questions about something they already know.

To the monolingual, monocultural teacher, this classroom conversation is a natural, obvious way to facilitate the learning of students. However, awareness that this interaction may not be a natural way of interacting for all students will help the teacher locate possible areas of confusion. The child's failure to respond may be due not to lack of knowledge, but to differences in styles of interaction. The child may be more familiar with learning by observation and indicating knowledge through demonstration. The child may also not be accustomed to responding individually or to the group at large.

How turn-taking is achieved in a classroom may also be an area of cultural difference. Raising a hand before responding may be strange to some children. It also may limit who responds to the teacher's questions or participates in the activities. Differential demands placed on students due to teacher expectations may also be a factor. For example, classroom interaction literature has indicated that teachers allow less time for responses to students they perceive as being low achievers (Rowe, 1969) and provide more explicit elicitations for high achievers (Cherry, 1978). Reasonable response time and explicit elicitations need to be provided to all children. By providing more explicit cues or by modeling a problem-solving procedure the teacher can teach more than just content. The students learn what are the important features of a problem and how to analyze a situation. They also learn what kind of response is expected.

Iglesias (1985a) also notes that children must learn to use language differently in different situations with different tasks and teachers. Heath (1986) suggests that success depends less on the specific language the children know and more on how they use the language they know. She lists some common teacher expectations of children's language use, which include the ability to: (1) use language to label and describe events; (2) participate in a test question format, in which the teacher asks a question, the child responds, and the teacher evaluates the response; (3) use language to recount past events or information in a predictable format and order; (4) use language to request and clarify information; and (5) follow oral and written directions with little sustained adult supervision. These expectations may not be realistic for all children, particularly children whose culture and language may be different from the teacher's. Therefore, the teacher needs to consider some of the assumptions behind classroom routine and recognize areas of possible conflict. The teacher may also need to provide more explicit examples or cues, to vary the way information is elicited, and to provide alternative ways to respond. Other aspects of school culture may also be unfamiliar. For example time, space, and materials are highly organized. A sequence of time blocks structures each day. Desks and other classroom furniture are usually organized in a linear fashion, either in rows or with several desks forming blocklike units. Areas of

Teachers need to consider the assumptions behind their classroom routines and to recognize the problems they pose for children whose culture and language are different from the teachers'.

the room are designated for certain activities. Children are also organized into lines for moving outside of classrooms or into homogeneous (top, middle, bottom) groups for reading and other academic instruction.

The linearity of organization of time, space, and materials may not be difficult for a child from the mainstream culture who is accustomed to schedules and to using materials in prescribed ways. However, there are cultures within as well as outside the United States in which such order is not natural (cf. Garcia, 1992; Heath, 1983; Iglesias, 1985b). Thus, the organization and use of materials in a step-wise fashion may be inexplicable to a child who is accustomed to a more holistic, active, or associative learning style. The materials themselves may be unfamiliar and threatening. Children unfamiliar with boundaries around time, space, and materials may have difficulty adjusting to the school environment.

Individual differences in social interaction style may also be a factor in the acquisition of a second language. Children who are outgoing and who are allowed to interact with peers can increase the amount of meaningful input they receive. This in turn increases their second-language learning by providing additional practice in both comprehending and producing the new language. Some children make good use of a few routine phrases in order to initiate and maintain the interaction. Although many of the good second-language learners described by Wong-Fillmore (1983) were socially outgoing, another group also achieved good oral language skill: active observers. These children were participants, but their participation did not necessarily include being talkative. Other scholars have also noted that some children learning a second language have a silent period before they begin talking in the second language (Bunce, 1995; Tabors & Snow, 1994). Bunce estimated that the length of the silent period for some of the children in their program was three to five months. Teachers need to be aware of these individual differences in language-learning style and to provide opportunities for interaction and for observation of meaningful, comprehensible input within the classroom.

In summary, not all communication mismatches are due to linguistic differences and not every child knows the instruction conversational style. In addition, not all students learn best through individual instruction and responses or from a part-to-whole sequence. School linear organizational style may be unfamiliar and threatening to children. When there are sociocultural differences between teachers and children, there are many opportunities for miscommunication and for erroneous assessments of children's skills to occur (Garcia, 1992). Being aware of these possible areas of difficulty will help the teacher make adjustments and/or provide the necessary support to help the bilingual/bicultural child succeed. Teachers will

> The organization and use of materials in a step-wise fashion is extremely difficult and threatening for some children.

need to find instructional methods that encourage children to learn both English and academic skills.

LANGUAGE PROFICIENCY AND ACADEMIC ACHIEVEMENT

Proficiency in language is difficult to determine. It is not an all-or-nothing situation, but rather a gradual process. One concern is the level of proficiency in the second language that is needed for the child to succeed academically. Studies of the French immersion programs indicate that students not only achieved proficiency in French and English but also reached high levels of academic achievement (Lambert & Tucker, 1972). Baetens-Beardsmore and Swain (1985) also document academic achievement by bilingual children attending various types of schools in Europe. Other scholars have documented the cognitive advantages to being bilingual (e.g., Ben Zeev, 1977; Ianco-Worral, 1972).

However, while positive effects of bilingualism are being documented, many bilingual children are not experiencing academic success (Cortes, 1986; Cummins, 1984; Iglesias, 1985a). Cummins suggests that a level of proficiency is needed before the cognitive advantages of being bilingual are realized. In addition, there are different kinds of language proficiencies. For example, some second-language learners have good oral language skills and yet do not succeed academically.

Cummins (1984) describes two language proficiencies that help explain the differences in achievement: *basic interpersonal communicative skills (BICS)* and *cognitive/academic language proficiency (CALP)*. To help explain the differences, Cummins conceptualizes language proficiency along two continuums. The first continuum concerns the amount of environmental or contextual support. At one end is context-embedded language where the language is supported by paralinguistic and situational cues. The other end is context-reduced language where the linguistic cues themselves must carry the message. Much of everyday conversation involves context-embedded language, whereas the language of the classroom is closer to the context-reduced end of the continuum.

> Much of everyday conversation involves context-embedded language.

The second continuum concerns levels of cognitive involvement in performing communicative tasks. At the top (this continuum is placed vertically) are relatively undemanding and largely automatic tasks requiring little cognitive involvement, while at the bottom are cognitively demanding communicative tasks. It is possible for a communicative task to be cognitively undemanding and context-embedded (e.g., routine greeting), or cognitively undemanding and context-reduced (e.g., writing a letter to a friend), or context-embedded and cognitively demanding (e.g., persuading another to your point of view), or both context-reduced and cognitively demanding (e.g., writing a research paper).

Chamot (1981, cited in Cummins, 1984) differentiates between BICS and CALP using Bloom's taxonomy (Bloom & Krathwohl, 1977). BICS involves *knowledge, comprehension* (basic understanding), and *application* (use in a particular concrete situation). CALP involves higher level cognitive skills of *analysis* (breaking down wholes into parts), *synthesis* (putting elements into a whole), and *evaluation* (judging adequacy of ideas).

Cummins's conceptualizations regarding BICS and CALP are important. Because children can converse in context-embedded situations does not mean they have the language skills needed to succeed in a decontextualized academic setting. It should be noted, however, that a person may have good academic language skills in the second language but not good oral interpersonal skills (as well as vice versa). This usually occurs when the CALP skills are already developed in the first language, as in the adult's learning a second language. It may be that BICS and CALP have somewhat independent development. This would mean that academic training does not depend on first developing oral language skills. Wong-Fillmore (1985) notes that immersion programs have shown that it is possible to develop academic and second-language skills simultaneously.

> The ability to converse in context-embedded situations should not be taken as evidence that a child has the language skills to succeed in decontextualized settings.

Cummins (1979, 1984) suggests that first- and second-language academic skills are interdependent. He conceptualizes a "dual iceberg" representation of bilingual proficiency. A common underlying proficiency can be represented by surface features of either language. Therefore, it should be relatively easy to transfer academic knowledge from one language to the other. He provides some evidence for this from studies of bilingual immersion programs.

In summary, because a child can use language in oral conversations does not mean the child can use language proficiently in an academic situation. If a general proficiency is represented by two surface forms, then developing academic skills in the child's first language should transfer to the child's second language. Pflaum (1986) describes just such an occurrence. In any case, educators must plan for acquisition of both kinds of language skills.

TYPES OF PROGRAMS AND INSTRUCTIONAL TACTICS

A variety of educational programs and settings have been devised to meet the needs of children who are learning English as a second language. In *immersion programs,* students are placed in classes where the instruction is in their second language. The classes consist of students at a similar level of proficiency in the language of instruction. The teacher is usually bilingual and knowledgeable about the culture of the students (cf. Lambert & Tucker, 1972, for description of French/English Immersion programs). Bilingualism is an educational goal in the immersion programs.

In the United States there are a variety of bilingual programs where the students use some combination of their first and second languages. Richard-Amato (1988) lists three types of bilingual programs: transitional, maintenance, and enrichment. In transitional programs, students learn most of the subject matter in their first language until they are ready to be placed into an all-English class. In the maintenance programs, students continue to have part of their education in their first language throughout their school years. In the enrichment programs, students are taught a second language to broaden cultural horizons or for some future visit to a foreign country (typical foreign language classes taught in junior or senior high school and usually not designed for language-minority groups).

In transitional programs, children learn most of the subject matter in their first language.

Other types of programming for language-minority students involve submersion into the mainstream classroom with or without some support from English as a second language (ESL) classes. The educational goal is to enhance English and academic skills. There is no emphasis on the first language, though it may be used to teach some of the content. The ESL classes are similar to the transitional bilingual classes where the emphasis is on learning English for eventual placement in all English classes. Placement in special ESL classes may range from a few weeks to two or three years, depending on the school system involved and the student's proficiency in English.

Richard-Amato (1988) suggests that optimal programming for ESL students might be to combine ESL classes with various levels of mainstreaming. Students at beginning levels would be mainstreamed into courses in music, art, and physical education. High school courses might include home economics and industrial arts. During intermediate levels, more mainstream classes would be added but the remainder of the core courses would be taught in the first language. The advanced student would be mainstreamed into most subjects, though some classes might utilize what Richard-Amato calls *"sheltered" English* (p. 224). Sheltered English is an instructional approach that is used to make academic instruction in English understandable to students who speak a language other than English (Freeman, Freeman, & Gonzales, 1987). The students are "sheltered" in that they do not compete academically with native English speakers because the class includes only second-language learners. Teaching strategies would include using many extralingusitic cues such as props, visual aids, and body language. Additional strategies would employ linguistic cues such as the use of repetition and pauses, short sentences, and frequent comprehension checks. Some of the "sheltered" English strategies are similar to "motherese" strategies (e.g., repetition, short sentences, emphasis on joint attention, focus on comprehension, etc.) used to facilitate the acquisition of a first language.

A major problem for school districts is that only one or two students may speak any given language, and it is not feasible to hire bilingual teachers for only a few students. Also, qualified bilingual teachers may be difficult to find. Therefore, the teachers of ESL classes may be monolingual, but have special training in working with bilingual students. In this case the special programming would not include core content taught in the students' first language. Richard-Amato (1988) suggests that the mainstream classroom can be an appropriate environment for second-language acquisition if comprehensible, meaningful input is provided.

> **It is a major problem for school districts when only one or two students speak any given language.**

Programming for the individual student might take a variety of forms. For example, if José (returning to the case example in the introduction) was in a bilingual program, the instruction would be in Spanish for at least part of the day. Reading instruction might be in both languages. The more successful bilingual programs usually provide half-day or alternate day programs in which one language is used at a time. This is in contrast to programs that provide ongoing translations or an alternating back and forth between the two languages (Richard-Amato, 1988). Good communication between the bilingual teacher and the mainstream classroom teacher is needed. For example, Diaz, Moll and Mehan (1986) describe children who were at different reading levels in Spanish, but were put in the lowest reading groups in their English reading class. Much of what was demanded in English groups was letter-sound connections with little context support (CALP skills involving analysis, synthesis, and evaluation). With this type of instruction, all of the students appeared to be at the same low reading level. However, when tested on comprehension, many of the students demonstrated that they understood what they read in English in spite of their halting oral reading. The type of instruction did not reveal what some of the students were able to read and understand. Diaz and colleagues (1986) advocate using a bilingual reading approach that includes a focus on writing. For example, the child may dictate a story that is written down by the teacher and subsequently read her dictated story. Later on, the children can write their own stories using invented spellings, if necessary. The focus on writing allows active interaction within a specific context. All of these activities allow a pairing of BICS and CALP skills so that the child's knowledge is extended within a meaningful framework.

> **Most critical is to extend the child's knowledge within a meaningful framework.**

If José were in an ESL program with some mainstreaming into the regular classroom, then all instruction would be in English. ESL instruction would probably involve training vocabulary and syntactic structure in both comprehension and production. In addition, some tutoring of academic subjects may be included in the ESL instruction. In the first-grade classroom, the teacher, Maria, would focus on ways to integrate José into the classroom, to communicate with him, and to effectively teach him the academic content. Specific objectives might be: (1) to provide José with opportunities to interact with peers and teachers within a communication situation; (2) to increase his oral language skills; (3) to increase his literacy skills; and (4) to extend his knowledge of math, social studies, science, and other content area subjects.

A variety of activities and procedures could be used to achieve these objectives. An underlying concept would be that *meaningful input is most effective*. Some of the following procedures, summarized in Table 14.1 and then further described, involve classroom management techniques that foster communication in the classroom. Other suggested techniques focus on how the academic content could be taught. Also, most of the activities are appropriate for the non-ESL student and can be done within the classroom to facilitate the learning of all students. A few of the techniques may be more easily achieved within a preschool or kindergarten class; however, it is important to find ways to increase communicative opportunities for bilingual students in any classroom.

These procedures are for classroom facilitation of communication and learning.

1. **Set up a buddy system.** The buddy is someone, usually a peer, who can be available to help the ESL student find materials and places, and in general be a resource person who is available to explain instructions and answer questions. At first, this may be achieved through nonverbal means such as gesturing, pointing, or demonstrating. Having a buddy or buddies will increase the amount of language interaction the ESL child receives. Some teachers use a buddy system routinely so that all students have a resource peer/partner with whom to check work, to brainstorm ideas for projects, to help edit writing, and the like.
2. **Focus on communication.** The teacher may need to use more gestures and demonstrations and avoid using overly complex sentence structure when talking. However, use of single words without contextual support is not suggested. The child needs to be able to use her nonlinguistic knowledge to help in understanding the new language.
3. **Use role-playing as a way to provide contextual support.** Dramatic play activities are especially rich environments to stimulate language. Also, acting out stories (or historical events) can help make what has been read comprehensible to the ESL student.
4. **Use peer teaching and modeling of responses.** During or after explanations be sure to include a peer demonstration of what is to be done. Provide several practices so that understanding of the concept will more likely occur. In some cases, explanations given by peers will be more effective.

TABLE 14.1 Increasing communication opportunities for bilingual students

What To Do	What It Is	How It Helps
1. Set up a buddy system.	Designate a classroom peer.	Someone is available to help ESL students find materials and other resources.
2. Focus on communication.	Use gestures and short sentences.	Use of nonlinguistic as well as linguistic knowledge helps comprehension.
3. Use role-playing to provide contextual support.	Act out situation or dramatic play scenarios.	Stimulates language use and increases knowledge.
4. Use peer teaching and modeling of responses.	Have a peer demonstrate activities and provide explanations.	ESL student may comprehend better and be more likely to imitate a peer.
5. Use group work and cooperative learning.	Children working on assignments or projects in groups (usually 2–5 children in each group).	Group work may be the norm for a particular culture and more comfortable for a particular child; also it provides opportunities for ESL students to contribute to a project.
6. Record instructions on audiotapes.	Make recordings of important information.	Tape allows for repetition of instructions; repetition can aid in understanding word boundaries.
7. Allow observations.	Let the ESL student observe without pressure to respond.	ESL students often need an "input" phase or silent period before producing a new language.
8. Provide descriptions.	Describe what the student is observing.	Helps the student learn both language content and form within a specific context.
9. Provide opportunities for speaking.	Provide small-group or one-to-one activities where it is easy for the ESL students to talk but where they are not pressured to do so.	Students may feel more comfortable talking in a small group where they can choose when to speak.
10. Accept simplified syntactic forms.	Allow short sentences that may or may not be grammatically correct. Use expansions or recasts to provide information on form.	The focus is on communicating not on grammar; however, the use of expansions and recasts can aid in the learning of correct grammatical forms.

TABLE 14.1   Increasing communication opportunities for bilingual students (continued)

What To Do	What It Is	How It Helps
11. Use global holistic activities.	Holistic activities begin with a top-down focus, starting with the whole and proceeding to the parts.	Nonlinguistic knowledge as well as linguistic knowledge can more easily be used in holistic activities. If a structure is learned within a context, it is more likely to be used appropriately than if learned in isolation.
12. Teach literacy skills through a whole-language focus.	Whole-language activities involve listening, speaking, reading, and writing in an interactive rather than sequential manner.	Literacy activities such as reading and writing may be taught simultaneously with oral language.
13. Use tutors who speak the child's first language.	Designate a volunteer adult or classroom peer who knows the child's first language.	Tutors may translate information between teacher and child or between children so that the ESL student can communicate with others and continue to develop academically while learning English.
14. Make content area books available in the child's first language.	Use literature, math, social science, and science books written in the child's first language.	Helps advance the academic skills of the child who is literate in her first language and is in the process of learning English.
15. Provide reading materials in the ESL student's linguistic or cultural group.	Use stories written in English, where the protagonist is from the ESL student's linguistic or cultural group, and available to all children.	Helps provide all of the children in the classroom some knowledge about and appreciation for different cultures.

5. **Use some group work and cooperative learning.** Group work can be a way to employ peer demonstration and teaching. For some children, group work is more appropriate to their home culture. It also provides an opportunity for ESL students to contribute to a project.

6. **Record instructions on audiotapes.** Sometimes repetition will allow the student time to figure out what the instruction means. In oral language, it is not always clear where word boundaries are, and sometimes repeated listening will aid this process. Also, for some center activities, it is helpful to have audio instructions paired with written instructions and/or illustrations.

7. **Allow the ESL student time to observe without pressure to respond.** Remember that many children learning a second language have a silent period before they begin speaking.

8. **Describe what the student is observing.** This may help the student learn both language content and form within a specific context. Observation of real situations is more effective than rote memorizing of surface forms.

9. **Provide opportunities for the ESL student to speak, but do not pressure her to do so.** This can probably best be achieved through small-group activities where the student may be more comfortable in responding. However, one-on-one conversations with the teacher may also be effective.

10. **Accept simplified syntactic forms.** Focus on what is being communicated. Make corrections only indirectly by expanding or recasting. Expansions are restatements that expand the utterance by using correct grammar (e.g., child says, "Boy walk house," teacher says, "Yes, the boy walk*s to the* house"). Recasts retain the basic information while syntactic structure is altered (e.g., child says, "Boy walk house," teacher says, "You're right, the boy *is walking* to the house. Where will he walk next?"). In both cases the conversational topic is maintained. The purpose of the expansions and recasts is incidentally to provide a model but to keep the focus on the communication.

11. **Use global, holistic activities that focus on meaning before using part-to-whole activities.** Holistic activities begin with a top-down focus. That is, they present the whole and then proceed to the part. A sociodrama, or choral reading, or a summary of a story all provide an overview or more holistic presentation so that the child can use nonlinguistic knowledge to understand (cf. Anim-Addo, 1992, for a description of the use of sociodrama in a classroom). The lack of contextual support in many oral drills or worksheets makes it difficult to use nonlinguistic knowledge. Also, transfer of rotely learned forms to conversation is difficult.

12. **Teach literacy skills through whole-language activities.** Whole-language activities involve listening, speaking, reading, and writing in an interactive rather than sequential manner (cf. Goodman & Goodman, 1986; or Norris & Hoffman, 1993, for description of whole-language activities; or Huddleson, 1985, on using a six-level ESL series that provides oral and written communication activities). That is, the child does not have to first engage in listening, then speaking, then reading, then writing. Therefore, the teacher does not have to wait for good oral control of the English language before teaching reading and writing. Some examples of whole-language activities include:

    a. *Language-experience stories*. These are stories dictated by the student(s) and written down by the teacher, often on a chart for later reference. The story is based on a shared experience. Often these stories are written following field trips. However, any shared experience can be used (e.g, film, film strip, guest speaker, favorite recess activity, class science project, etc.). After the stories have been written, the group (or individual) reads them. Often the children copy the story and read it again to themselves. Children are able to decode the story because it is written in their own words.

b. *Choral reading and/or poetry activities.* The class can partici-pate in choral reading activities by reading in unison or by having different groups read different lines. Often ESL chil-dren can join in even if they do not know all of the words. Reading and writing activities involving poetry also can improve literacy skills. Songs and fingerplays are appropriate activities within preschool and kindergarten classes. ESL chil-dren may first participate during songs and fingerplay activi-ties. The repetitiveness of these activities helps provide support for the interaction.

c. *Predictable books or stories.* These books have recurring lines that can be predicted from earlier presentations. Allow the children to join in with the reading. (See the Appendix at the end of the chapter for a list of various titles.)

d. *A story that is read and retold by puppets.* First, the teacher could manipulate the puppets, later the children could do this. The story could be audiotaped and the tape, book, and puppets made available so that the children could listen, read, and retell the story later. Writing materials could be made available for the children to write their own stories involving the puppets. Invented spellings would be acceptable. (See Seawall as cited in Lindfors, 1987, for description of this type of activity used in a bilingual kindergarten.)

e. *Other writing activities.* The students can keep a journal, write a story from a story starter (e.g., "I like to play with . . . "), write a caption to a picture, or write a story on a topic of their choice. In all cases invented spellings would be acceptable.

13. **Use tutors who speak the child's first language.** This is not always possible, but if there are personnel available, make use of their knowledge to extend the teacher's knowledge of the child's language and culture as well as helping the child in content areas and other subjects.

14. **Make content area books available in the child's first lan-guage.** This is particularly helpful for the older ESL students who have literacy skills in their first language.

15. **Provide reading materials where the protagonist is from the ESL student's linguistic or culture group.** (See the Ap-pendix for a list of various titles; see also Pisant, 1992, for addi-tional resources.)

These are just a few of the instructional tactics that may help the teacher provide appropriate language and academic activities for the ESL child (or children) in the classroom. Many of these activities are also appropriate for use with special ESL classes. Of course there are many other activities that can facilitate acquisition of literacy and language skills. Many of the activities in the basal readers are appropriate or can be easily adapted. Again, the more context support, the more likely the ESL student will understand. Hands-on math and science activities are also important in facilitating learning for the ESL student.

ASSESSMENT AND INTERVENTION

Assessing children who are learning English as a second language presents many challenges.

There are many assessment issues involving children who are learning English as a second language. Some of these issues revolve around the testing instruments themselves. Other issues concern the use of tests for placement in special programs. For example, appropriate placement in ESL programs, bilingual classes, and mainstream classes may be facilitated by some assessment of skill levels. Also, assessment of communication skills is important in identifying handicapped bilingual, bicultural children who are in need of more specialized programming. Assessment is also important is determining appropriate intervention and in documenting progress. Finally, assessment can provide information regarding the student's progress in English and academic skills.

Bias may not be completely eliminated, but it can be limited.

The development of nonbiased procedures for assessing bilingual, bicultural children is difficult. A book edited by Hamayan and Damico (1991) is devoted to ways bias can be limited in the assessment of bilingual students. As described by these and other scholars, some standardized test measures are available, particularly for the Spanish-English bilingual (see Cheng, 1987; Cole & Snope, 1981; Deal & Yan, 1985; Hamayan and Damico, 1991; Mattes & Omark, 1984, for listings of testing instruments). However, not all of these instruments are appropriate for all dialects of a particular language. Also, some tests are direct translations from English, which may alter the way certain concepts are expressed in the first language. Furthermore, there may not be appropriate norms provided. Finally, cultural factors may influence the assessment process.

In evaluating assessment instruments, Mattes and Omark (1984) suggest that the examiner note such features as:

1. *The purposes and construction of the tests.* Are the tests appropriate for the population to be tested? Is the test based on a theoretical model?
2. *Linguistic and cultural appropriateness.* Is the dialect of the tests appropriate? Are the types of required tasks and stimuli appropriate for the population?

3. *Adequacy of the norms.* How was the test standardized and on what population? Is the normed population an appropriate comparison group?
4. *Reliability and validity of the test instruments.*

Cheng (1987) underscores that care must be taken to ensure that test items are familiar to the children. She suggests that household objects such as items for baking; some kinds of furniture; sports such as football, hockey, skiing; buildings and signs such as hospitals, traffic signs; and historical events and people such as Thanksgiving, Halloween, George Washington, and Abraham Lincoln would not be appropriate test items for Asian-language minority children. These items may also be inappropriate test items for other ESL children.

A variety of scholars (e.g., Bernstein, 1989; Chamberlain & Medeiros-Landurand 1991; Lewis, Vang, & Cheng, 1989) caution that there can be cultural influences on assessment. For example, Chamberlain and Medeiros-Landurand list such factors as problems due to cultural misconceptions of the roles and expectations of a particular task. Although some children consider the assessment process as one linked to evaluation and promotion and work hard to demonstrate what they have learned, other children may not consider the assessment process a part of the learning process and may be less motivated to demonstrate their knowledge. Also, there may be stereotyping due to differences in cultural behavior. Some children may appear inattentive and be labeled as having comprehension difficulties; yet, they may be attending to the task but in a manner different than that expected by the evaluator. For example, children may be paying attention to the evaluator but have their eyes lowered as a sign of respect. The evaluator may expect the student to pay attention by maintaining eye contact and, therefore, may think the child is not attending and perhaps does not understand the task. Other cultural factors that could impinge on the assessment process include differences in viewpoints on competition and cooperation (individual versus group success); time (some children may not understand "speed" testing); proximity (some children may find the formal relationship of the testing situation to be stressful); gender of the participants (some children may respond differently to female versus male evaluators); and cognitive style (some children may use a global, intuitive style rather than the reflective, analytical style valued in many educational testing situations).

> Children in some cultures are taught that lowering their eyes shows respect for adults.

Another issue concerns the type of assessment instruments. Many of the language tests available are discrete point tests, which focus on knowledge of specific elements of phonology, grammar, and vocabulary, rather than integrative tests, which examine the ability of the student to utilize several skills at the same time (Oller, 1979; Damico, 1991). Also, some tests require integrative skills and yet evaluate only discrete items (e.g., having students write an essay in which only certain grammatical forms are judged). As yet, no comprehensive standardized instruments exist for testing children who speak English as a second language.

A variety of remedies for the assessment dilemmas have been suggested. Some of these include development of local norms for standardized tests, development of teacher-made checklists, and the use of criterion-referenced tests. It may be that qualitative assessment of the children's language skills within naturalistic settings provides the most relevant information. In particular, Richard-Amato (1988) suggests that test tasks should relate to the classroom communication situations.

The placement of students in bilingual or ESL classes depends on many factors. One is the availability of such classes. Another factor is English-language proficiency of the students. A third factor is how this proficiency is assessed and what criteria are used for placement. Cummins (1984), in discussing the differences between basic interpersonal communicative skills (BICS) and cognitive/academic language proficiency (CALP), estimated that it may take only two years for a child learning to speak English as a second language to reach peer-appropriate conversational skills, but may take five to seven years for the same child to reach grade norms on the language skills needed for academic work. If the children are judged to have reached English proficiency based on their conversational skills alone, then they may be dismissed prematurely from ESL classes.

> Two years may be sufficient for a child to learn peer-appropriate conversational skills, but 5 to 7 years is required to become competent enough for academics.

The decision on placement may be made by reviewing students' scores on such tests as the Bilingual Syntax Measure (Burt, Dulay, & Hernandez-Chavez, 1976), by students' performance on criterion-referenced tests such as Assessment of Basic Skills, Spanish Edition (Brigance, 1984), or by teacher checklists. Teacher-made tests may be the most effective because they may include items particularly relevant to a specific situation.

Richard-Amato (1988) describes a checklist that may be helpful in grouping students within a classroom setting or in determining types of placement. She provides a description of typical language behaviors of students at beginning, intermediate, and advanced levels of second-language proficiency in a classroom setting. Within each grouping she has three levels ranging from low to high. For example, typical behaviors exhibited by the low beginner would include dependence upon gestures, facial expression, pictures, and even a translator. The middle beginner would demonstrate some comprehension, but only when the speaker provides gestural clues, speaks slowly, and uses concrete referents. He may show some recognition of written segments, and may speak haltingly and be able to write short sentences. The high beginner may comprehend more in social conversation and may be able to make wants known, though with frequent errors in grammar, vocabulary, and pronunciation. The high beginner may be able to read a simple test and write short sentences. Richard-Amato continues the checklist format describing behavior for the intermediate and advanced students. Behavioral descriptions included for the intermediate levels are: (1) has difficulty with idioms but has greatly increased vocabulary knowledge; (2) makes frequent errors in grammar and pronunciation; (3) comprehends substantial parts of conversations but may need frequent repetitions; (4) understands and uses more complex structures in reading and writing but still has difficulty with abstract language. For the advanced student, items included were: (1) comprehends conversational and academic discourse most of the time; (2) speaks fluently but makes occasional errors; (3) reads and writes with less difficulty; and (4) is able to comprehend and use both concrete and abstract language. In addition to language proficiency, Richard-Amato suggests that teachers should also test for competency in content areas. At first, the testing may be given in the student's first language by aides or tutors with appropriate language backgrounds. This information would be important in making placement decisions regarding sheltered or mainstreamed classes. Students are much more likely to succeed if they have appropriate background knowledge.

> In addition to assessing language, teachers should also test for competency in content areas.

Assessment of Bilingual/Bicultural Children with Impairments

Kathy was a 3½-year-old girl who was the oldest of two children of a German-speaking mother and English-speaking father. Although both German and English were spoken by both parents in the home, German was the dominant language. Kathy was referred to a University speech and language clinic by her father, who was a doctoral student at the university. He was concerned about her German and English language acquisition. The family wanted her to be bilingual in German and English. At the time of the referral, Kathy spoke in two- to three-word sentences in German, but often omitted the sounds at the end of words. She spoke only a few English words. The dilemma for the speech and language clinic staff members was how to assess this child's speech and language development.

In developing an assessment plan, it is important to be careful not to misdiagnose the child's difficulty with language. For example, several scholars (Cummins, 1984; DeBlassie & Franco, 1983; Erickson & Walker, 1983; Mercer, 1983) have found inordinate numbers of language minority students placed in special education programs based on test scores normed on English-speaking students. As a result, many of the children were misdiagnosed as having mental retardation, learning disabilities, or language disorders. At the same time, some children with impairments may not have been identified because their difficulties were attributed to being speakers of English as a second language. In any case, Erickson and Walker suggest that if 8 percent to 12 percent of the school-age population have impairments then there must be a sizable number of bilingual children who also have impairments. Therefore, procedures for identifying and treating these children need to be developed. All of the issues raised earlier regarding the use of different types of assessment measures need to be addressed.

DeBlassie & Franco (1983) suggest that it is not necessary to throw out the standardized tests, but teachers should remember that many of these tests have been standardized on middle-class monolingual speakers of English. Tests should be used in conjunction with other measures (e.g., observations, teacher checklists, adaptive behavior data, personality assessment, medical and developmental data). DeBlassie and Franco's model for nondiscriminatory assessment involves the collection of history, current characteristics, and specific treatments or interventions. It is important to compare behavior in both languages. For Kathy, the child referred to earlier in this section, there was information from her parents that she deleted important grammatical endings from words in both languages.

Tests should always be supplemented with information from other sources.

Roussel (1991) has provided an annotated bibliography of communicative ability tests that have been used with children learning English as their second language. Some of the tests screen for language dominance (particularly between Spanish and English); whereas other tests assess English language proficiency. Roussel cautions that many of the tests do not provide reliability or validity measures. Also, for some tests, normative information is not available.

This lack of reliable and valid testing instruments makes it especially difficult to identify a bilingual child with speech and language impairments. The surface deviations may be due to a disorder or to a stage in development of the second language. Damico, Oller, and Storey (1983) believe that the assessment of the student's ability to use language for communication is more helpful in identifying the bilingual child with language impairments than are assessments of morphological and syntactical structures. Specifically, they examined language samples for non-normative patterns using surface-oriented syntactic criteria and the following pragmatic criteria: (1) linguistic nonfluencies; (2) revisions; (3) delayed responses; (4) nonspecific vocabulary; (5) inappropriate vocabulary; and (6) poor topic maintenance. The different criteria identified different subgroups as language-disordered. The results indicated that the pragmatic criteria were better predictors of achievement and teacher ratings seven months later than were the syntactic assessments. Earlier, Damico and Oller (1980) demonstrated that teachers trained to look for pragmatic difficulties made significantly more appropriate referrals than did teachers trained to use traditional morphological and syntactic deviancies as the basis for referrals.

Mattes and Omark (1984) developed an inventory for rating bilingual childrens' communication skills in both the first and second languages. The inventory, Bilingual Oral Language Development (BOLD), uses a + or – to rate 20 different behaviors (e.g., comments on own actions and other's actions, describes experiences, attends to speakers, follows directions, initiates interactions). It is recommended that these behaviors be evaluated on direct observations and on information from teachers and parents. This type of inventory can help determine the language in which the child functions best. The inventory can be modified if some behaviors are not typical of the child's culture. Cheng (1987), in her book on assessing Asian children's language, also provides a variety of checklists that rate functional communication, nonverbal behavior, and overall behavioral patterns. Adler (1991) provides an Assessment Instrument for Multicultural Clients for use by a speech-language pathologist. This instrument involves different rating scales of the client's language proficiency including structure, intelligibility, and comprehension.

Another instrument that can be effective for evaluating young children's skill in both languages is the Speech/Language Assessment Instrument (SLASS, Hadley & Rice, 1993). This observational tool evaluates the child's use and understanding of language and is completed by an adult familiar with the child (e.g., a parent or teacher). The adult rates the child on a variety of skills using a one- to seven-point rating scale with one being very low ability, four being the normal ability for age, and seven being very high ability. Although this instrument was developed primarily as a way to rate the skills of children with speech and language impairments in English, it can be used to rate these abilities in two languages by having the parent or an adult familiar with the child and both languages rate the child in both languages. For Kathy, this would be accomplished by having her parents rate her language skills in English and in German. Such a rating scale may reveal that the child is communicating appropriately in the home language but is not in English, or, as was the case for this child, not communicating effectively in either language.

As part of a comprehensive evaluation, Mattes and Omark (1984) suggest that standardized tests may be used; however, in many cases there are no tests available. Therefore, an inventory of communication skills may be an appropriate first step. In addition, adaptive behavior inventories may be used. One such measure that has normative data on nonwhite children is the Adaptive Behavior Inventory for Children (Mercer, 1979). Other informal measurements include language samples and criterion-referenced tests (e.g., Brigance Comprehensive Inventory of Basic Skills, 1983; Spanish Language Assessment Procedure, Mattes, 1984). Story retelling tasks may also be helpful in judging children's comprehension of content and effectiveness in describing events. The most appropriate measures are often assessment instruments developed at a local level (cf. Mattes & Omark, 1984, for suggestions for developing local assessment instruments).

The most appropriate instruments are assessment instruments developed at a local level.

These instruments are developed for a target population with a specific content and focus and are normed using the local population. Bilingual children are thus compared to local peers rather than to a national sample.

Shipley and McAfee (1992), in their handbook on assessment, provide information on phonemic, grammatical, and pragmatic contrasts between Hispanic English and standard English and between Asian English and standard English. These contrasts can help the clinician become aware of possible confusions that children learning English as a second language may have between the structures of the two languages. The knowledge is helpful is determining what pattern or structure might be typical of some speakers and what pattern might signal an impairment. Other sources (e.g, Cheng, 1989, 1995; Screen & Anderson, 1994) provide information on speech and language services in multicultural settings.

Assessment of Kathy at the clinic involved observation of the child playing with her parents. During that time, a language sample was taped, and an informal communication inventory was completed noting how Kathy communicated her needs and thoughts. This inventory was similar to the SLASS (Hadley & Rice, 1993). Because of the parents' concern about their daughter's deletion of final sounds from words, a phonological inventory was completed. In addition, the parents completed the MacArthur Communicative Development Inventory: Words and Gestures (Fenson, Dale, Reznick, Thal, Bates, Reilly, & Hartung, 1993) to document words and phrases Kathy understood and produced in English and in German. Although, Kathy had a history of ear infections, hearing testing completed at the time of the evaluation indicated hearing was within normal limits.

Results of the evaluation of Kathy's language skills indicated that she primarily used one- and two-word utterances to communicate. Words usually consisted of consonant–vowel syllables. Longer utterances were in German (2 to 3 words). Sometimes the sentences appeared to be a mixture of English and German. Much of her communication depended on gestures. The phonological inventory indicated she used the following English consonant sounds: *m, p, b, n, t, w, h, sh,* and *f.*

Recommendations for general intervention goals for Kathy were

1. to increase her understanding and production of English vocabulary (her parents were to continue speaking German in the home to allow for improvement in German language skills);
2. to increase the length of her utterances;
3. to increase intelligibility by decreasing the number of open syllables produced (consonant–vowel syllables) and increasing the number of closed syllables (consonant–vowel–consonant syllables); and
4. to increase correct production of /k/.

Other recommendations included that she be enrolled in a language preschool classroom with intervention provided in the classroom, if possible. Alternatives included receiving therapy at the clinic setting three times per week and attending a preschool or play group where she would be interacting with other children her age.

In summary, the bilingual exceptional child needs to be identified and to have an appropriate intervention program provided. To attain needed services, information concerning language abilities in the first language is necessary. Also necessary is information on adaptive functioning, educational achievement, and language abilities in the second language based on integrative and communicative functions. Discrete point assessments of surface morphological and syntactic functions are not enough.

Language Intervention with Bilingual Children Who Have Language Impairments

Intervention programs for bilingual children who have language impairments will depend on several variables including age and severity of the disability, attitude and goals of the family, resources and available social interactions, and vocational expectations (Erickson & Walker, 1983). The availability of programs is also a factor. Evans (1983) describes several programs for bilingual children under the age of six with language impairments. Some programs involve parents extensively, whereas others encourage parental involvement but do not require it. Some programs also serve nonhandicapped children. The content of the intervention and the extent to which the first language is incorporated into the programming also vary. Most infant and preschool programs focus on basic self-help and language skills rather than academic instruction.

Some programs require parent involvement; others just encourage it.

For some of the programs, the language of instruction was the child's first language. However, according to Erickson and Walker (1983), most programs do not provide intervention in the child's first language because further schooling in the United States will require knowledge of English and it may be better to have the child focus on one language rather than two. Also, a continuing problem is the lack of personnel proficient in languages other than English. Bilingual paraprofessionals may be a solution. Paraprofessionals can be used as interpreters, referral sources and, to some extent, providers of intervention.

LAP: A Model Program

Rice and Wilcox (1995) describe a model preschool at the University of Kansas that provides programming for children who have language impairments, who are developing language in a typical manner, and who are learning English as their second language. The language skills of all children are facilitated within an inclusive classroom setting. The children are 3 to 5 years old. All children attending the Language Acquisition Preschool (LAP) receive an initial screening to document their language development. Assessment instruments include the Peabody Picture Vocabulary Test, Revised (Dunn & Dunn, 1981), the Reynell Test of Language Development (Reynell, 1985), an articulation test, and a language sample. For the ESL children, interpreters are available to provide translations for the children. Periodic retesting of the children is done to document progress.

The LAP, as described by Rice and Wilcox (1995), is designed to develop language skills in a naturalistic preschool group setting. The curriculum is language-focused, whereby language skills are facilitated throughout all curriculum activities. This language-focused curriculum model views children as active learners who learn best when they plan and carry out activities. The overall purpose of the classroom is to provide a language-rich environment conducive to language learning. The schedule of activities includes those that are routine (e.g., calendar time), and those that change daily (e.g, dramatic play). There is also a balance between activities that are child-centered (e.g., center activities where the children can choose between activities and the level of their participation in the chosen activity) and activities that are more teacher-directed (e.g., large-group activities). The schedule is organized in the following manner:

The purpose of the LAP is to provide a language-rich environment conducive to language learning.

Entry and Free Play	with children arriving and playing until all have arrived
Circle Time	with greetings, calendar, roll call and special announcements
Center Time	where the child chooses to participate in one of four available centers (art table, dramatic play, blocks area, and quiet area)
Story Time	
Sharing Time	where children respond to questions from other children about "show and tell" items
Outdoor Play	
Snack Time	
Large-/Small-Group Time	a teacher-directed time where problem solving, classification, and pre-academic activities are presented
Music and Fingerplay Time	

The longest scheduled period is the play center time where the children are free to choose and plan their activities. Adults are present to respond to and interact with the children. In the quiet area, the adult is available to read stories or play with puzzles with the child. There is plenty of adult input, and less talking is expected from the child. At the art table the adult may use modeling and narration to provide ongoing descriptions of what the child is doing. For example, at the art table the adult might say, "This play dough feels soft and squishy, . . . or . . . I need some glue to paste the hat on the man . . . or . . . You need some glue, too." The block area is where a moderate amount of verbal activity from the children takes place. Again, the adult may model or provide narration of what the child or the adult is doing. Verbal output from the children is usually highest in the dramatic play center. It is the area where the child can act out a situation such as making dinner, being a doctor, going to the store, and playing dress-up (for further elaboration see Bunce & Watkins, 1995; Bunce, 1995; Rice, 1995).

For the new ESL children, interpreters are initially available to help each child adjust and to provide explanations to the child concerning LAP classroom activities and routines. They also provide the teachers with needed information regarding cultural differences. For the language-delayed children, speech-language graduate students plan therapy programs under the supervision of the classroom teacher, who is a certified speech-language pathologist. Therapy is conducted within the classroom setting while the child is interacting with the materials and other children. Intervention is achieved through a concentrated normative model (CNM). As described by Rice (1995), the normative aspects emphasize the commonalities of development across children and conform to normative models of language development. They also recognize that language is a specific domain of development. The concentrated aspect of the model: (1) recognizes the need to emphasize or highlight specific language skills; (2) focuses on language in the classroom; and (3) allows for special techniques to direct children's attention to specific language forms. It also allows for much redundancy (e.g., the child is surrounded by language focusing on the child's interests and activities). Operational guidelines as described by Rice (1995) for the CNM model include:

> Interpreters are available to help new ESL children adjust and help the teachers understand cultural differences.

1. Language intervention is best provided in a meaningful social context.
2. Language facilitation occurs throughout the entire curriculum.
3. Language curriculum is rooted in content themes.
4. Language intervention begins with the child.
5. Verbal interaction is encouraged.
6. Passive language learning and overt responses are encouraged.
7. Children's utterances are accorded functional value.
8. Valuable teaching occasions can arise in child-to-child interactions.
9. Parents are valuable partners in language intervention programming.
10. Routine parent evaluations are an integral part of the program. (pp. 32–37)

Specific intervention techniques used within the concentrated normative model, described by Bunce and Watkins (1995), include (1) providing many opportunities for language use; (2) using focused contrasts; (3) modeling appropriate sounds, structures, and functions; (4) providing event casts; (5) using open questions, expanding and recasting children's utterances; (6) providing redirects and prompted initiations; and (7) using scripted play.

For example, to facilitate the acquisition of vocabulary, Kathy would be surrounded by language describing what she is doing. Comments, not questions, would be used by the adult. If she were at the block area and playing with a dollhouse, an adult could describe her actions, pausing for comments from Kathy. Kathy would not be required to make a response. If /k/ was to be facilitated, words such as wal*k*, li*k*e, tal*k*, could be inserted into the conversation (e.g., the doll is wal*k*ing, she li*k*es to tal*k* to her mother). To facilitate production of longer sentences and to highlight the importance of grammatical forms, sentences involving focus contrasts could be used. For example, the adult could say, "The mommy *is* walk*ing* to the house. Look, she walk*ed* in," as the child plays with the dolls. The close proximity of the two grammatical forms allows the child, over time, to begin to understand the differences in meaning. If the child comments, the adult can expand on the child's utterances. For example, if the child said, "Baby cry," the adult can respond, "Yes, the baby is crying." Different techniques can be used within one interaction. The resulting conversation may look like the adult is just "playing" with the child. However, the conversation is tailored to meet the child's communication needs.

The LAP procedures can be used in any setting and at any time where there are opportunities for adult–child interactions.

These intervention techniques can be used anytime there is opportunity for interaction between a child and adult or between children. There may be more opportunity for such interaction during the dramatic play activity. Here, the play theme supports the child's knowledge, but also elaborates on it. For example, a grocery store scenario is often familiar to the child but it also allows for expansion of the child's knowledge, particularly of the words associated with it (e.g., food items, phrases such as "How much does this cost?" or "That is five dollars," etc.). Again, an emphasis can be placed on highlighting appropriate grammatical forms. A further advantage of providing intervention in the classroom is that interactions between children can be facilitated. For example, an adult can prompt a child to initiate to another child by saying, "Ask Jay how much the banana is," or "Ask Lisa if you can have a turn," or "Say, 'Lisa, my turn now.' " Therefore, a major advantage of providing language intervention within the classroom is that appropriate form, function, and use can be taught at the same time. There is no need to teach a form in isolation and then provide for generalization to an appropriate context. The context is learned with the form (see Bunce, 1995; or Bunce &

Watkins (1995) for further elaboration of how the intervention techniques are embedded into the different preschool activities).

Most of the ESL children attending the LAP preschool have not been delayed in their first language development. Typically these children have approached monolingual norms after 14 months in LAP (Bunce & Shirk, 1993). However, several children, such as Kathy described above, have been both language impaired and learning English as a second language. These children receive intervention following the techniques described above. Research on the development of language skills of these children is just beginning. So far, the children have all made progress in their English language skills, and parents report much improvement in their first language skills as well.

School-Based Intervention

Intervention in the public school setting has been provided by a variety of specialists including speech-language pathologists and special education teachers. However, a bilingual child with language impairments may receive only ESL services because the language problem is assumed to be due to a language difference. Not much has been written regarding specific instructional or intervention techniques for bilingual children with language impairments. However, techniques already discussed as being helpful for second-language learners are appropriate, especially those that include: (1) focusing on meaning; (2) teaching vocabulary and syntax within a context; (3) allowing time for comprehension to develop before insisting on production; (4) using a peer buddy; (5) using predictable books; and (6) incorporating parents and significant others in the teaching.

A variety of techniques used with monolingual children with language impairments may also be helpful. These interventions involve various aspects of language including pragmatics (use in context), semantics (meaning), morphology and syntax (grammatical forms and word order), and phonology (sound system). The specific focus of the intervention depends on the child's needs. However, the most effective programming involves all aspects. When possible, the intervention should not focus only on basic interpersonal communicative skills (BICS), but should also include skills that foster cognitive/academic language proficiency (CALP) as discussed by Cummins (1979, 1984).

Many of the techniques used with monolingual children with language impairment are also appropriate for bilingual children.

PRAGMATICS. The appropriate use of language within a context is the goal of any language intervention program. It does not matter that a child can understand and produce language forms in a clinical setting if the child does not use language to get needs met, to make routine greetings, to follow turn-taking rules, and to make repairs when communication breaks down. Routine activities are a starting point. Allowing the child to observe and take part in appropriate interactions is important. A peer buddy may provide a model. (Remember that active, though silent, observation may play an important role in language development for many children.)

Within a kindergarten or preschool setting, activities such as show and tell can teach question-and-answer routines (e.g., "What do you have?" "A truck," "Where did you get it?" etc.). Snack time can also be used to teach and practice appropriate language to get needs met ("Please pass the juice," "I need more crackers," "More cookie," etc.).

Within an elementary classroom, routines such as lunch count, roll call, and procedures for passing out and handing in materials can be used to teach specific responses to a specific situation. For example, during roll call, the child who is learning English as a second language may first respond nonverbally by raising his hand; later the appropriate classroom verbal response may be required. If this child is the helper and responsible for passing out papers, the teacher can demonstrate what is needed and at the same time provide a verbal description. The child can, at first, perform the task without speaking but later may use language while doing the task. Other classroom activities can provide opportunities for children to observe and take part in classroom discourse. It is very important for children learning English as a second language to know the classroom procedure for asking questions on assignments, for requesting help, and for requesting additional information. How to ask clarifying questions may be a particularly important skill for all the children to learn. Teachers also need to be aware of each child's culture and ways of interacting within the culture. The test question format in which the teacher asks a question, the child answers, and then the teacher evaluates the response may be new to the child. Cultural mismatches need to be avoided when possible.

> A first priority for children learning English as a second language is to learn how to ask questions and request information and assistance.

SEMANTICS.   As children learn to use language to get their needs met, they learn meanings of words and concepts. Some activities may be specifically focused to enhance vocabulary. Various activities can be used to teach vocabulary, ranging from object and picture labeling to reading stories. When possible, new vocabulary should be used in context so the child can understand the use as well as the meaning of the word or concept. This may be particularly important if the concept is not marked in the child's first language. Various kinds of classification activities are also helpful in improving conceptual knowledge. Activities such as matching, categorizing, and choosing the different item in a set can help extend the child's academic language proficiency.

SYNTAX AND MORPHOLOGY.   Many procedures facilitate syntactic and morphological development. Sentence rearrangement games help focus the student on the various ways in which content could be said. Question games provide practice in asking and answering questions. Role playing and story retelling provide practice with syntactic structures within a certain context. Various sequencing activities, including sequence patterns and sequential story games or puzzles, can be used. Having the child generate a story that is written down for later rereading improves oral language and literacy skills. For the primary (and older) students, writing activities may be helpful, particularly if the emphasis is on the process, not a perfect product. Invented spellings would be allowed so the child can focus on the content (cf. Edelsky, 1982; Lloyd, 1992, for description of writing in a bilingual program).

The child who, after an initial period of adjustment, does little or no combining of words to form sentences may need help learning word-order rules in English. One way to provide a focus on the demarcation of word boundaries and word order rules is to use a miniature linguistic system (MLS) procedure (e.g., Bunce, Ruder, & Ruder, 1985; Goldstein, 1983). The MLS focuses on syntax, but also on teaching a system so that generalization to nontrained items is facilitated. The MLS can be used to train any structure that can be broken into two components. Examples include:

> A miniature linguistic system can be used to teach word-order rules.

verb | object
preposition | object
adjective | object
adjective | subject
subject | verb-object
adjective-subject | verb-object

A matrix of 16 or 25 squares (depending on whether it is a 4 by 4 or 5 by 5 matrix) outlines the training steps. For example, if the verb + object construction is to be taught, then all of the nouns are placed across the top of the matrix (see Figure 14.1) and all of the verbs are listed on the side of the matrix. In the case of a 4 by 4 matrix there are four different nouns and four different verbs. The first verb is paired with each noun to form four different combinations. Each combination is taught separately. For example, if the verbs chosen were *touch, push, drop,* and *wash* and the nouns were *car, ball, chair,* and *truck* then the first training item would be "touch car." After the child can indicate the correct item, the next structure consisting of the first verb and the second noun is trained (i.e., "touch ball"). In a similar manner "touch chair" and finally "touch truck" are trained. After the first verb has been paired with the four nouns, the first noun is paired with the rest of the verbs. In this case, the fifth, sixth, and seventh training steps would be "push car," "drop car," and "wash car." A check of the comprehension of other possible structures within the matrix (e.g., *push, drop, wash,* paired with each of the nouns) usually indicates generalization to untrained structures. This means that after training seven

FIGURE 14.1   MLS training matrix for verb-object combinations

	Noun 1 (car)	Noun 2 (ball)	Noun 3 (chair)	Noun 4 (truck)
Verb 1 (touch)	Training 1	Training 2	Training 3	Training 4
Verb 2 (push)	Training 5			
Verb 3 (drop)	Training 6			
Verb 4 (wash)	Training 7			

combinations, the child learns 16 combinations. In addition, children often understand verb-noun combinations utilizing different lexical items so they usually have learned many more than 16. The miniature linguistic system provides a systematic way for children to distinguish between word boundaries.

Once the child has learned some verb-object combinations, subjects may be added and a new matrix formed. For example, four nouns can be listed along the side of the matrix (e.g., boy, girl, man, woman) and four verb-object combinations across the top (e.g., touch car, push ball, drop chair, wash truck). Again, the margins of the matrix are trained. That is, the first subject is paired with all the verb-object combinations, and then the first verb-object combination is paired with all of the subjects. The training items are "boy touch car," followed by "boy push ball," "boy drop chair," "boy wash truck," "girl touch car," "man touch car," and "woman touch car." Again, each training item is trained to criterion before the next item is taught. Generalization to untrained combinations is expected. Theoretically, the child should be able to understand any combination of subject-verb-object, which is now a total of 64 different combinations. This is not including any other vocabulary words the child may know and could insert into the subject-verb-object construction. The use of articles can be added relatively easily once the basic subject-verb-object pattern is established. Adjective-noun constructions, prepositional phrases, and other constructions can be trained and the basic subject-verb-object pattern expanded (e.g., becoming adjective-subject-verb-preposition-object).

In using the MLS, Bunce and colleagues (1985) suggest three important training procedures: (1) initial training should focus on comprehension because generalization to production without further training sometimes occurs; (2) a variety of exemplars should be used to represent the components (e.g., several different cars are used so the child understands that the term refers to a class of objects not just one particular referent); and (3) training should involve the use of contrasts (e.g., if the target item is "touch car," then foils include a different verb paired with car and a different object paired with touch). The use of contrasts ensures that the child focuses on both aspects of the construction, learning the concept of "touch" as well as of "car." Just pointing to a picture of someone "touching" is not enough because there are two pictures of someone "touching" something. Likewise, just pointing to a picture with a car is not correct because there are two pictures with cars. The training can be done using pictures representing the constructions or by using objects with the teacher or clinician performing the actions.

> The use of contrasts helps the child learn both aspects of the construction.

Using a miniature linguistic system is an example of working with a particular component of language. It provides a means for the child to analyze syntactic rules and note word boundaries, and it also teaches some vocabulary. The effectiveness of the miniature linguistic system is that generalization to untrained structures is planned and expected. However, the child then needs to use the structures within a naturalistic setting, such as a classroom. Training the structures is only the beginning. Generalization to settings outside the training situation is the main goal. The teacher who is aware of the child's abilities can do much to foster this transfer through conversations, stories, songs, role playing, and other activities.

PHONOLOGY. In the case of the bilingual child who is language impaired, the primary focus should be on developing communication. As the child's ability to use language improves, often pronunciation also improves. However, some children may need specifically tailored intervention in order to learn the sound system of a language. Providing children with good speech models may help. Articulation therapy provided by a speech-language pathologist may be necessary to help some children discriminate between the sound systems of the two languages. This discrimination may be aided by teaching the alphabet or phonic skills (or the articulation therapy may aid the learning of the alphabet and phonic skills).

> Some children need special help to learn the sound system of English.

If José were a 5-year-old kindergarten child with a language impairment, what kind of programming might he receive? Several options may be available. For example, José might be placed in a language classroom where he would receive intensive language therapy as well as academic work, he might be placed in a preschool setting to enhance his language skills before focusing on academic skills, or he might be placed full or part time in an ESL class. It is also possible that José's language problems would be assumed to be due to his lack of exposure to English and he would be placed in a kindergarten class with or without ESL programming.

In any case, the classroom teacher would need to seek ways to help José achieve in the classroom. Again, utilization of a buddy system and use of peer models would be helpful. Teacher observation of José's communication skills (as well as language skills) would be important. The use of the Bilingual Oral Language Development (Mattes & Omark, 1984) could be a starting point in assessing José's language skills, as well as procedures described earlier by Damico and colleagues (1983) that focus on pragmatic criteria (poor topic maintenance, delayed responses, nonspecific vocabulary, etc.). Language samples also can provide information on José's use of both English and Spanish. Information from the parents concerning José's development would be important to consider, as well. More formal assessment involving standardized and criterion-referenced testing might then be done. Formal testing in Spanish may depend on availability of Spanish-speaking professionals.

While observations and testing are being completed, the classroom teacher will be providing programming through routine activities in the classroom. Singing, show and tell, story time, snack time, and center time with a variety pre-academic activities are rich environments for language learning. In addition, the speech-language pathologist, special education teacher, and/or ESL teacher may be involved in setting up programming. The kind of programming will vary depending on the setting and the needs of the child.

Many of the language intervention activities described earlier may be appropriate for José. However, these are just a few of the many activities possible in a classroom or clinical setting. In any case, the emphasis needs to be on improving both basic interpersonal communication skills and cognitive and academic language skills. In addition, when developing appropriate intervention activities, the following intervention principles, summarized in Table 14.2, should be considered:

1. Begin intervention where the child can be successful. Train through strengths, not weaknesses; that is, make sure the child can respond correctly at least 30 percent to 50 percent of the time with support. If the child can respond correctly 60 percent of the time with no support, then monitoring of the skill may be important but the target is not necessarily an intervention target. The child is already well on the way to mastery. If the target is not produced correctly with support at the 30 percent level, then be careful in choosing that target because what will be practiced is error responses. Some simplification of the response may first need to be taught.

2. Base intervention on testing (both formal and informal) and observations.

3. Choose to remediate those items that will have the greatest effect on the child's life (e.g., help most in making the child a competent communicator, help in academic achievement, etc.)

4. Plan for generalization from the very beginning:
   a. Have a variety of contrasts available in order to highlight the discrimination to components you want the child to make. For example, if you want the child to focus on the preposition "in," have the one object pictured *in* another object, then *on* the same object (and maybe *beside* it, too). This presentation forces the child to attend to the location of the object rather than focusing on either of the two objects as the component being trained.
   b. Train in a variety of contexts (including the classroom— you may have to set up situations to provide the extension activities).
   c. When the child can perform for you, set up the task so it can be done for others.
   d. Train strategies that make sense and work in more than one situation.
   e. Train concepts, rather than rote memory.

5. If training on isolated features is done (sometimes this is both needed and effective), be sure to end training at a more global level. For example, if work is on syntax involving question reversals (e.g., "Did you go?" versus "You did go?"), be sure to eventually have the question used in a real conversation. Sometimes this can be achieved through role playing. Just being able to respond appropriately when asked to do so is only one step. The next step is to produce the response when needed in "real life."

6. Break things down into smaller components only as far as needed to get the response, particularly if the tasks need to become automatic. For example, if you can get a child to produce the correct

TABLE 14.2 Intervention principles

Principles	Guidelines
1. Begin intervention where the child can be successful.	a. Train through strengths. b. Begin training where the child can respond correctly 30–50% of the time with support. c. Don't practice error responses. d. Some simplification of the response may first need to be taught.
2. Base intervention on testing (formal and informal) and observations.	a. Assess child's skills using formal and informal testing. b. Develop intervention plan based on child's needs and strengths. c. Continue to assess needs and progress through observations and additional testing.
3. Choose to remediate those items that will have the greatest effect on the child's life.	a. Focus on communication first. b. Teach vocabulary and structure that is important for academic achievement.
4. Plan for generalization.	a. Use a variety of contrasts in order to highlight the discrimination between components. b. Train in a variety of contexts. c. Vary the interactants (when the child can do the task for you, set up the task to be done with others). d. Train strategies that work in more than one situation.
5. If training on isolated features is done, end training at a more global level.	a. First train the isolated form, (e.g., question reversals), then use in "real" conversations. b. Use role play as a intermediary step to "real" conversations, if necessary.
6. Simplify target structures only as far as needed to get the appropriate response.	a. If you can get correct production of a sound at the syllable level, don't train at the sound level. b. If child can produce the target form (with cuing) in a sentence, don't practice at the word level.
7. Assess as you remediate.	a. Attend to gains and losses within each session. b. Use probes periodically to assess progress. c. Use formal testing as needed.
8. Train first in comprehension, then in production.	a. Model appropriate responses within a context. b. When possible, have children make nonverbal responses (e.g., pointing, responding to directions, etc.) to target items. c. Probe for production; may not need to train.
9. Follow the child's lead.	a. Attend to child's focus. b. Let child's interests provide the content to be trained.
10. Let the child be the teacher.	a. Child can demonstrate new knowledge when playing teacher. b. Teacher can assess child's competencies. c. Child is motivated to do the task.

sound at the syllable level, don't work at the sound level. Later, as part of training analysis skills, it may be appropriate to focus on part-to-whole activities.

7. Continue to assess as you remediate. This does not mean a multitude of formal testing, it means you attend to gains (and losses) within each session. Procedures need to be changed if progress is not being made. What is appropriate for one child is not always appropriate for another.

8. If possible, train first in comprehension, you may get transfer to production without training.

9. Take advantage of "teachable" moments. This means following the child's lead. Let the child's interest provide the content to trained. For example, if the child is involved in building with the blocks, describe what she is doing. Also, join in and build with the child or provide additional props and describe the action. For an older child, reading or discussing the book the child has selected, or getting the child to tell about the story she has written or what has happened in ballgames at recess, are all opportunities to teach language.

10. Let the child be the "teacher." Sometimes you can better assess what a child understands about a task if you switch roles.

SUMMARY

Bilingual/bicultural children have special educational needs. These needs can best be met by teachers and special educators who are aware of both linguistic and cultural factors influencing educational achievement. Appropriate programming depends on flexibility in designing ways to facilitate their learning of both linguistic and academic skills. Achieving this flexibility is not easy, but must become a goal if the educational needs of bilingual children are to be met.

REFERENCES

Adler, S. (1991). Assessment of language proficiency of limited English proficient speakers: Implications for the speech-language specialist. *Language Speech & Hearing Services in Schools, 22,* 12–18.

Anim-Addo, J. (1992). Drama with young learners in school. In P. Pisant (Ed.), *Language, culture and young children: Developing English in the multi-ethnic nursery and infant school* (pp. 110–122). London: David Fulton Publishers.

Baetens-Beardsmore, H., & Swain, M. (1985). Designing bilingual education: Aspects of immersion and "European School" models. *Journal of Multilingual and Multicultural Development, 6,* 1–15.

Bates, E. (1976). *Language and context: The acquisition of pragmatics.* New York: Academic Press.

Ben Zeev, S. (1977). The influence of bilingualism on cognitive strategy and cognitive development. *Child Development, 48,* 1009–1018.

Berko-Gleason, J. (1993). *The development of language* (3rd ed.) New York: Macmillan.

Bernstein, D. K. (1989). Assessing children with limited English proficiency: Current perspectives. *Topics in Language Disorders, 9*(3), 15–20.

Bloom, B. S., & Krathwohl, D. R. (1977). *Taxonomy of educational objectives: Handbook I: Cognitive domain*. New York: Longman.

Brigance, A. H. (1983). *Comprehensive inventory of basic skills*. North Billerica, MA: Curriculum Associates.

Brigance, A. H. (1984). *Assessment of basic skills: Spanish edition*. North Billerica, MA: Curriculum Associates.

Bunce, B. H. (1995). A language-focused curriculum for children learning English as a second language. In M. L. Rice & K. A. Wilcox (Eds.), *Building a language-focused curriculum for the preschool classroom (Vol. I): A foundation for lifelong communication* (pp. 91–103). Baltimore: Paul H. Brookes Publishing Co.

Bunce, B. H. (1995). *Building a language-focused curriculum for the preschool classroom (Vol. II): A planning guide*. Baltimore: Paul H. Brookes Publishing Co.

Bunce, B. H., Ruder, K., & Ruder, C. (1985). Using a miniature linguistic system in teaching syntax: Two case studies. *Journal of Speech and Hearing Disorders, 50,* 247–253.

Bunce, B. H., & Shirk, A. (1993, November). *Children learning English as a second language: Classroom language facilitation*. Poster session presented at the American Speech-Language-Hearing Association Convention, Anaheim, CA.

Bunce, B. H., & Watkins, R. V. (1995). Language intervention in a preschool classroom. In M. L. Rice & K. A. Wilcox (Eds.), *Building a language-focused curriculum for the preschool classroom (Vol. I): A foundation for lifelong communication* (pp. 39–71). Baltimore: Paul H. Brookes Publishing Co.

Burt, M., Dulay, H., & Hernandez-Chavez, E. (1976). *Bilingual syntax measure*. New York: Harcourt Brace Jovanovich.

Chamberlain, P., & Medeiros-Landurand, P. (1991). Practical considerations for the assessment of LEP students with special needs. In E. B. Hamayan & J. S. Damico (Eds.), *Limiting Bias in the assessment of bilingual students* (pp. 111–156). Austin: Proed.

Cheng, L. (1995). Integrating language and culture for inclusion. San Diego: Singular Publishing.

Cheng, L. (1987). *Assessing Asian language performance*. Rockville, MD: Aspen Publications.

Cheng, L. (1989). Service delivery to Asian/Pacific LEP children: A cross-cultural framework. *Topics in Language Disorders, 9*(3), 1–14.

Cherry, L. (1978). A sociolinguistic approach to the study of teacher expectations. *Discourse Processes, 1,* 373–394.

Cole, L., & Snope, T. (1981). Resource guide to multicultural tests and materials. *ASHA, 23,* 639–649.

Cortes, C. E. (1986). The education of language minority students: A contextual interaction model. In *Beyond language: Social and cultural factors in schooling language minority students* (pp. 3–34). Los Angeles: Evaluation, Dissemination and Assessment Center, California State University.

Cummins, J. (1979). Linguistic interdependence and the educational development of bilingual children. *Review of Educational Research, 49,* 222–251.

Cummins, J. (1984). *Bilingualism and special education: Issues in assessment and pedagogy*. Clevedon Avon, England: Multilingual Matters.

Damico, J. S. (1991). Descriptive assessment of communicative ability in limited English proficient students. In E. B. Hamayan & J. S. Damico (Eds.), *Limiting bias in the assessment of bilingual students* (pp. 157–217). Austin: Proed.

Damico, J. S., & Oller, J. W. (1980). Pragmatic versus morphological/syntactic criteria for language referrals. *Language, Speech and Hearing Services in Schools, 11,* 85–94.

Damico, J. S., Oller, J. W., & Storey, M. E. (1983). The diagnosis of language disorders in bilingual children: Surface-oriented and pragmatic criteria. *Journal of Speech and Hearing Disorders, 48,* 385–394.

Deal, V., & Yan, M. (1985). Resource guide to multicultural test and materials, Supplement II. *ASHA, 26,* 6, 43–49.

DeBlassie, R. R., & Franco, J. N. (1983). Psychological and educational assessment of bilingual children. In D. R. Omark & J. G. Erickson (Eds.), *The bilingual exceptional child* (pp. 55–68). San Diego: College Hill Press.

Diaz, S., Moll, L. C., & Mehan, H. (1986). Socio-cultural resources in instruction: A context-specific approach. In *Beyond language: Social and cultural factors in schooling language minority students* (pp. 187–230). Los Angeles: Evaluation, Dissemination and Assessment Center, California State University.

Dunn, L. M., & Dunn, L. M. (1981). Peabody Picture *Vocabulary Test—Revised*. Circle Pines, MN: American Guidance Service.

Edelsky, C. (1982). Writing in a bilingual program: The relation of L1 and L2 texts. *TESOL Quarterly, 16,* 211–228.

Erickson, J. C., & Walker, C. L. (1983). Bilingual exceptional children: What are the issues? In D. R. Omark & J. G. Erickson (Eds.), *The bilingual exceptional child* (pp. 3–22). San Diego: College-Hill Press.

Evans, J. (1983). Model preschool program for handicapped bilingual children. In D. R. Omark & J. G. Erickson (Eds.), *The bilingual exceptional child*. San Diego: College-Hill Press.

Fenson, L., Dale, P. S., Reznick, J. S., Thal, D., Bates, E., Reilly, J. S., & Hartung, J. P. (1993). *MacArthur Communicative Development Inventory: Words and Gestures*. San Diego: Singular Publishing Group.

Freeman, D., Freeman, Y., & Gonzales, G. (1987). Success for LEP students: The Sunnyside sheltered English program. *TESOL Quarterly, 21,* 361–367.

Garcia, G. E. (1992). Ethnography and classroom communication: Taking an "emic" perspective. *Topics in Language Disorders, 12,* (3), 54–66.

Goldstein, H. (1983). Training generative repertoires with agent-action-object miniature linguistic systems with children. *Journal of Speech and Hearing Research, 26,* 76–89.

Goodman, K., & Goodman, Y. (1986). *What is whole about whole language?* Portsmouth, NH: Heinemann.

Hadley, P. A., & Rice, M. L. (1993). Parental judgments of preschoolers' speech and language development: A resource for assessment and IEP planning. *Seminars in Speech and Language, 14,*(4), 278–288.

Hamayan, E. V., & Damico, J. S. (1991). *Limiting bias in the assessment of bilingual students*. Austin: Proed.

Heath, S. B. (1986). Sociocultural contexts of language development. In *Beyond language: Social and cultural factors in schooling language minority students* (pp. 143–186). Los Angeles: Evaluation, Dissemination and Assessment Center, California State University.

Heath, S. B. (1983). *Ways with words*. Cambridge: Cambridge University Press.

Hudelson, S. (1985). *Hopscotch*. New York: Regents Publishing Co.

Ianco-Worrall, A. (1972). Bilingualism and cognitive development. *Child Development, 43,* 1390–1400.

Iglesias, A. (1985a). Communication in the home and classroom: Match or mismatch. *Topics in Language Disorders, 5,* 29–41.

Iglesias, A. (1985b). Cultural conflict in the classroom. In D. N. Ripich & F. M Spinelli (Eds.), *School discourse problems* (pp. 79–96). San Diego: College-Hill Press.

Jennings, L. (April, 27, 1988). Panel: School must aid immigrants in "struggle to succeed". *Education Week, 7* (31), 1–2.

Krashen, S., & Terrill, T. (1983). *The natural approach: Language acquisition in the classroom*. Oxford: Pergamon.

Lado, R. (1957). *Linguistics across cultures*. Ann Arbor: University of Michigan Press.

Lambert, W. E., & Tucker, G. R. (1972). *Bilingual education of children: The St. Lambert experiment*. Rowley, MA: Newberry House.

Lewis, J., Vang, L., & Cheng, L. (1989). Indentifying the language learning difficulties of the Hmong: Implications of context and culture. *Topics of Language Dissorders, 9*(3), 21–37.

Lindfors, J. W. (1987). *Children's language and learning* (2nd ed.). Englewood Cliffs, NJ: Prentice-Hall, Inc.

Lloyd, P. (1992). Children's developmental writing. In P. Pisant (Ed.), *Language, culture and young children: Developing English in the multi-ethnic nursery and infant school* (pp. 98–109). London: David Fulton Publishers.

Mattes, L. J. (1984). *Spanish Language Assessment Procedures: A Communication Skills Inventory*. Oceanside, CA: Academic Communication Associates.

Mattes, L. J., & Omark, D. R. (1984). *Speech and language assessment for the bilingual handicapped*. San Diego: College-Hill Press.

Mercer, J. R. (1979). *SOMPA: System of Multicultural Pluralistic Assessments*. New York: Psychological Corporation.

Mercer, J. R. (1983). Issues in the diagnosis of language disorders in students whose primary language is not English. *Topics in Language Disorders, 3* (3), 46–56.

Norris, J. A., & Hoffman, P. R. (1993). *Whole language intervention for school-aged children*. San Diego: Singular Publishing Group.

Oller, J. W. (1979). *Language tests at school*. London: Longman.

Pflaum, S. W. (1986). *The development of language and literacy in young children*. Columbus, OH: Charles E. Merrill.

Pisant, P. (1992). *Language, culture and young children: Developing English in the multi-ethnic nursery and infant school* (pp. 110–122). London: David Fulton Publishers.

Reynell, J. K. (1985). *Reynell Development Language Scales*. Los Angeles: Western Psychological Services.

Rice, M. L. (1995). The rationale and operating principles for a language-focused curriculum for preschool children. In M. L. Rice & K. A. Wilcox (Eds.), *Building a language-focused curriculum for the preschool classroom (Vol. I): A foundation for lifelong communication* (pp. 27–38). Baltimore: Paul H. Brookes Publishing Co.

Rice, M. L., & Wilcox, K. (1995). *Building a language-focused curriculum for the preschool classroom (Vol. I): A foundation for lifelong communication*. Baltimore: Paul H. Brookes Publishing Co.

Richard-Amato, P. A. (1988). *Making it happen: Interaction in the second language classroom*. New York: Longman.

Roussel, N. (1991). Annotated bibliography of communicative ability tests. In E. B. Hamayan & J. S. Damico (Eds.), *Limiting bias in the assessment of bilingual students* (pp. 320–343). Austin: Proed.

Rowe, M. (1969). Science, silence, and sanctions. *Science, 6,* 11–13.

Saville-Troike, M. (1979). Culture, language, and education. In H. T. Trueba & C. Barnett-Mizrahi (Eds.), *Bilingual multicultural education and the professional: From theory to practice* (pp. 139–148). Rowley, MA: Newberry House.

Screen, R. M., & Anderson, N. B. (1994). *Multicultural perspectives in communication disorders*. San Diego: Singular Publishing Group, Inc.

Shipley, K. G., & McAfee, J. G. (1992). *Assessment in speech-language pathology: A resource manual*. San Diego: Singular Publishing Group, Inc.

Stanford Working Group. (1993). *A blueprint for the second generation*. Stanford, CA: Stanford University.

Tabors, P. O., & Snow, C. E. (1994). English as a second language in preschool programs. In F. Genesse (Ed.), *Reading, writing, and schooling* (pp. 103–125). New York: Cambridge University Press.

Wong-Fillmore, L. (1983). The language learner as an individual. In M. Clake and J. Handscombe (Eds.), *On TESOL'82: Pacific perspectives on language learning & teaching*. Washington, DC: Teachers of English to Speakers of Other Languages.

Wong-Fillmore, L. (1985). Teacher talk as input. In S. Gass and C. Madden (Eds.), *Input in second language acquisition* (pp. 17–50). Rowley, MA: Newberry House.

Appendix

Selection of Predictable Books

(Predictable books have limited text per page, repeated patterns, strong rhythms, and supportive illustrations.)

Bayer, A. (1984). *My name is Alice*. New York: Dutton.

Brett, J. (1985). *Annie and the wild animals*. Boston: Houghton Mifflin.

Brown, R. (1984). *If at first you do not see*. London: Anderson Press.

Carle, Eric. (1982). *What's for lunch?* New York: Putnam.

Gibbons, G. (1981). *Trucks*. New York: Crowell.

Ginsburg, M. (1980). *Kittens from one to ten*. New York: Crown.

Goss, J. L., & Hardste, J. (1985). *It didn't frighten me*. Worthington, OH: Willowisp.

Lobel, A. (1981). *On Market Street*. Toronto: Scholastic.

Lobel, A. (1984). *A rose in my garden*. New York: Greenwillow.

Mayer, Mercer. (1983). *Just Grandma and me*. Racine, WI: Golden Books.

Parish, P. (1980). *I can, can you?* New York: Greenwillow.

Wildsmith, B. (1982). *Cat on the mat*. Toronto: Oxford Press.

Zolotow, C. (1983). *Some things go together*. New York: Crowell.

Children's Literature and Different Cultures

Asian Americans

Bunting, A. E. (1982). *The happy funeral*. New York: Harper & Row. (K–4th grade.) Chinese customs are presented simply and reverently by a little Chinese American girl giving a first-person account of her grandfather's funeral.

Chandler, D. (1978.) *Favorite stories from Cambodia*. Portsmouth, NH: Heinemann. (3rd–6th grade.) This title includes 12 stories and is presented as a supplementary reader. Comprehension exercises are included and may be helpful to Cambodian children learning English.

Clark, A. N. (1979). *In the land of small dragon*. New York: Viking. (K–3rd grade.) A picture book with a retelling of the Vietnamese version of the Cinderella story.

Coutant, H. (1974). *First Snow*. New York: Alfred Knopf. (Preschool–K.) Lien spends her first winter in New England with her sick grandmother, who provides an acceptance of death through her explanation of the first snowfall. Also communicates the values of Vietnamese culture and customs.

Friedman, I. R. (1984). *How my parents learned to eat*. Boston: Houghton Mifflin. (K–3rd grade.) In a simple, but appealing story a small Japanese American girl describes the courtship of her parents and their adjustment to two styles of eating.

McHugh, E. (1983). *Raising a mother isn't easy*. New York: Greenwillow. (4th–6th grade.) A story of adoption and of cultural (Korean American) assimilation.

Nha-Trang. (1978). *Favorite stories from Vietnam*. Portsmouth, NH: Heinemann. (3rd–6th grade.) Sixteen stories from Vietnam written in simplified vocabulary. Comprehension exercises are included.

Paek, M. (1978). *Aekyung's dream*. Chicago: Children's Press. (1st–6th grade.) Aekyung, a Korean immigrant, adjusts to confusing customs and a new language in the United States.

Pinkwater, M. (1975). *Wingman*. New York: Dodd, Mead. (3rd–6th grade.) Chen Chi-Wing, or Donald Chen, as he is known at school, is the only Chinese American at P. S. 132 in New York.

Sadler, C. (1982). *Treasure mountain: Folktales from Southern China*. New York: Atheneum. (4th–6th grade.) Six tales of Chuang, Han, T'ung, and Yao tribes. Nice to read aloud and a good source for storytelling.

Sadler, C. (1981). *Two Chinese Families*. New York: Atheneum. (3rd–6th grade.) Contemporary life styles in China through the eyes of two different families are portrayed.

Uchida, Y. (1983). *The best bad thing*. New York: Atheneum. Rinko, the only girl in a Japanese American family, is worried when Mama decides to help a family friend.

Vuong, L. D. (1982) *The brocaded slipper and other Vietnamese tales*. Philadelphia: Lippincott. (3rd–6th grade.) Five tales that are useful in contrasting the similarities between Vietnamese and American folk literature.

Wolkstein, D. (1983). *The magic wings: A tale from China*. New York: Dutton. (2nd–4th grade.) A Chinese folktale that is excellent for reading aloud or for storytelling. Excellent illustrations.

Yashima, T. (1955). *Crow Boy*. New York: Viking. (K–2nd grade.) A moving story, with excellent illustrations, portraying Japanese school life.

European Americans

Cole, J. (1983). *Bony-legs*. New York: Macmillan. (Preschool–3rd grade.) A simple retelling of one of the Baba Yaga stories.

DePaola, T. (1986). *Watch out for the chicken feet in your soup*. Englewood Cliffs, NJ: Prentice-Hall. (K–3rd grade.) A charming story that can help children adjust to the ideas that differences are interesting and that there is nothing wrong with people who have a foreign accent.

Levoy, M. (1972). *The witch of 4th street and other stories*. New York: Harper & Row. (1st–4th grade.) Eight stories describe the lives of immigrant families from different countries living in New York in the early 1900s.

Norris, G. (1976). *A feast of light*. New York: Alfred Knopf. (3rd–6th grade.) Ulla, a 9-year-old Swedish immigrant, at first refuses to make friends and has trouble learning English.

Sandlin, J. (1981). *The long way to a new land*. New York: Harper & Row. (K–3rd grade.) A story about the emigration of a Swedish family to America.

Snyder, S. K. (1979). *The famous Stanley kidnaping case*. New York: Atheneum. (3rd–6th grade.) The family is in Italy, where Amanda's mother has inherited property that she can have only if they live there a year. The kidnapers don't bargain for holding five children captive.

Hispanic Americans

Blue, R. (1971). *I am here: Yo estoy aqui*. New York: Watts. (K–3rd grade.) A 5-year-old Puerto Rican girl who just emigrated to the United States is frightened when she cannot understand the language of her kindergarten class.

Brown, T. (1986). *Hello, amigos*. New York: Holt. (Preschool–3rd grade.) A photo essay of a day in the life of Frankie Valdez.

Ets, M. (1959). *Nine days to Christmas*. New York: Viking. (K–2nd grade.) A story about a little girl in Mexico City and her preparations for a Posada. Describes a typical day for a middle-class family in Mexico City.

Galarza, E. (1971). *Barrio boy*. South Bend, IN: University of Notre Dame Press. (1st–4th grade.) An autobiography of a Mexican child who comes to the United States.

Galbrith, C. (1971). *Victor*. Boston: Little, Brown. (2nd–4th grade.) Victor, from a Spanish-speaking family, finds school difficult. Then school begins to change—children may now speak Spanish as well as English, and invitations to Parents' Night are sent in both English and Spanish.

Madison, W. (1971). *Maria Luisa*. Philadelphia: Lippincott. (3rd–6th grade.) Maria Luisa and her brother move to San Francisco, where she enrolls in an ESL class. She learns to adjust to a new school and to a big city.

Molnar, J. (Ed.). (1972). *Graciela: A Mexican-American tells her story*. New York: Watts. (3rd–6th grade.) Graciela describes her migrant Chicano family's annual trip to pick produce in Michigan.

Sandoval, R. (1977). *Games, Games, Games*. Garden City, NY: Doubleday. (K–6th grade.) Illustrated descriptions of traditional Mexican children's games.

Wolf, B. (1978). *In this proud land: The story of a Mexican American family*. Philadelphia: Lippincott. (4th–6th grade.) This is the story of a family as they live and work together.

Native Americans

Baylor, B. (1981). *God on every mountaintop*. New York: Scribner's. (4th–6th grade.) Myths of the Southwest native Americans are told.

Baylor, B. (1976). *Hawk, I'm your brother*. New York: Scribner. (K–3rd grade.) This is the story about a boy who learns to live harmoniously with nature.

DePaola, T. (1983). *The legend of bluebonnet*. New York: Putnam. (K–4th grade.) A story of a Commanche Indian girl who sacrifices what she loved best to save her tribe.

George, J. C. (1972). *Julie of the Wolves*. New York: Harper & Row. (4th–6th grade.) A Newbery Medal winner about an Eskimo girl who runs away and becomes lost on the tundra.

Gobel. P. (1983). *Star Boy*. New York: Bradbury Press. (2nd–5th grade.) An adaptation of a Blackfoot tale explaining why the Sun Dance lodge is round.

Hirschfelder, A. G. (1986). *Happily may I walk: American Indians and Alaska natives today*. New York: Scribner's. (4th–6th grade.) Describes contemporary Native American cultures.

Hofsinde, R. (1964). *Indians at home*. New York: William Morrow. (4th–7th grade.) Describes the building of Indian homes and the life and customs of each home. Also describes changes that modern times have made.

Leech, J., & Spencer, Z. (1979). *Bright Fawn and me*. New York: Crowell. (K–4th grade.) A young Cheyenne girl looks after her younger sister at an Indian trading fair.

Syme, R. (1975). *Geronimo, the fighting Apache*. New York: William Morrow. (3rd–5th grade.) A biography of Geronimo.

abstract modeling Various situations and the verbalizations that accompany the situations from which the child extracts regularities; a term associated with social learning theory.

accommodation Modification of existing cognitive structures in accordance with new information.

adaptation The process of adjusting to the demands of the environment.

aided communication Communication techniques that require an external device such as a communication board, book, or other display.

apraxia A neurological disorder affecting the ability to plan speech movements.

assimilation The process by which new information and new experiences are incorporated into an organism's existing cognitive schemata.

augmentative and alternative communication (AAC) The total arrangement for supplementing and enhancing communication—the device, the technique, the symbol system, and communication skills.

authentic assessment Assessment that provides qualitative and quantitative information about the performance of skills in actual—rather than contrived—tasks in the child's natural environments.

autism A disorder originating in the first few years of life that is characterized by self-absorption, inability to interact socially, repetitive behavior, and language dysfunction (e.g., echolalia).

causality The ability to anticipate what consequences will follow from a certain cause or what cause is likely to produce a particular consequence.

cerebral palsy An umbrella term for any disorder of movement or posture that results from a nonprogressive abnormality (either damage or disease) to the immature brain.

clinical judgment Statements about an individual's abilities based on the professional's clinical experience, intuition, and knowledge of development and impairment.

code emphasis An approach to learning to read that focuses on translating print to sound; it emphasizes parts, rather than the whole.

cognitive hypothesis Belief that language is an expression of developing conceptual knowledge.

cognitive referencing A method of determining language disability that compares language abilities with level of cognitive functioning (as measured by a nonverbal intelligence test).

communication The exchange of ideas, information, thoughts, and feelings.

community-based instruction For elementary-age students with severe disabilities, instruction in home and other community locations to address daily living and functional life-skill needs.

concept analysis A procedure through which the critical or relevant attributes of a concept are identified.

conductive hearing loss Hearing loss due to abnormalities or problems associated with the outer or middle ear; usually a malfunction or blockage that prevents clear transmission of sound waves to the inner ear.

contingent query In discourse and conversation, statement of a comment, a request for clarification, and a clarifying response.

critical-period hypothesis Theory, originating with Lenneberg (1967), that there is a critical period for language learning; it is based on the belief that the brain's left hemisphere is no longer able to acquire language after lateralization for language has occurred.

cue validity Term from the competition model that accounts for the order of acquisition of some elements of a language; a measure of how available and reliable a cue is in a given language.

decoding The process of translating a code to a noncode, or the process of code breaking.

demonstrative gesturing Behaviors in gestural communication such as pointing, reaching, showing, offering, giving objects, touching others; and head movements that are used to convey intentional meaning.

direct instruction Teacher-guided instruction focused on mastery of specific skills and concepts.

directive function The use of vocal and gestural signals of language to intentionally influence the attention and actions of others.

direct selection Selecting, typically through pointing, desired symbols from a set of those available for aided communication.

duration recording A behavioral assessment procedure that is used when the length of time a behavior occurs is of interest; time may be reported in seconds, minutes, or percentages.

dynamic assessment Evaluation procedure associated with Vygotskian: the a child's functioning with supportive cues from others is compared to static assessment with no assistance.

dysarthria   A group of related speech disorders that result from disturbed voluntary control over the speech mechanism.

echolalia   Repetition of what is said by other people; the repetition may be immediate, an exact repetition produced within seconds, or delayed.

ecological communication model (ECO)   An assessment and intervention approach where the focus is to enhance interactive and conversational behaviors of young children within the context of natural social and learning contexts with parents, teachers, interventionists, and peers.

ecological model   A theory, originating in biology, which states that an organism cannot be studied apart from its environment; that behavior cannot be understood without considering its context.

emergent literacy   The ability of early learners in print-oriented societies to construct meanings about, and make sense of, print even before being introduced to literacy instruction.

empowerment   A process that supports family members in gaining control over life circumstances and in providing nurturing and care for others.

encoding   Method of selecting from a code to indicate a symbol or message from an array.

enhanced milieu teaching (EMT)   Specific procedures to enhance language learning, including environmental arrangement of toys, responsiveness, and incidental language teaching techniques.

equilibrium   The end result of accommodation and assimilation; coming into balance of the child's cognitive structures and information provided by the environment.

expansion   Responding to a child's utterance with a more sophisticated version of the utterance, usually retaining the child's word order.

expatiations   An adult's presentation of a more mature version of the child's utterance, with new information added.

extension   Responding to a child's utterance with a comment that adds information to the established topic.

fading   The gradual removal of an instructional prompt so that the desired behavior is performed independently or with only naturally occurring supports.

fetal alcohol syndrome (FAS)   A condition resulting from the mother's use of alcohol during pregnancy; children tend to be small for their gestational age and to remain small after birth; children may have mild to moderate retardation, congenital heart defects, joint abnormalities, and facial deformities (droopy eyelids, wide nose, flattened midface).

formative evaluation   Monitoring of behaviors before and during instruction to find out their effects.

full inclusion   Providing educational and therapeutic services in natural environments such as the home, day care center, or regular classroom.

gestural mode techniques   The body movements and facial expressions used to achieve gestural mode communication (signs and gestures).

grammatical morphemes   Morphological inflections that do not carry independent meaning when they stand alone but subtly affect the meaning of sentences.

graphic mode techniques   Direct selection, scanning, and encoding techniques used for augmentative and alternative communication.

holophrastic   The use of a single word by a child to communicate a meaning that an adult would say with a sentence.

iconicity   The ease with which the meaning of a symbol can be recognized; the greater the iconicity, the easier it is to recognize the symbol's meaning.

ideograms   Line drawings that present a character or graphic symbol to represent an idea (i.e., a heart to represent "feeling").

illocutionary stage   The second communication stage described by Bates (1976), in which the child begins to use conventional gestures and vocalizations to intentionally affect the behavior of others.

imitation   Performance of a response that matches, or approximates, the behavior of a model.

incidental teaching   A procedure used to elicit more elaborate language and communication skills; one of the four basic milieu teaching procedures.

interactive modeling   Increasing the frequency of exposure to targeted language features to increase, the probability that they will be learned; also called recasting.

interval recording   A recording procedure in which the observation period is divided into equal time intervals; permits fairly sensitive measurement of both duration and frequency simultaneously.

language   An abstract system with rules governing the sequencing of basic units (sounds, morphemes, words, sentences) and rules governing meaning and use.

language-learning disabled   Label for children in the learning disabilities category whose problems are exclusively in the areas of speech and language.

language sampling   A procedure for recording productive language during play, while telling stories, or in conversational exchanges.

latency Time between a stimulus, or prompt, and the subsequent response.

lateralization The localization of function or activity (as of verbal processes in the brain) on one side in preference to the other.

linguistic mapping Verbal labeling or modeling by adults to increase the child's use of requesting, vocal commenting, and vocal imitation.

locutionary stage The third communication stage described by Bates (1976), in which the child uses words to convey intentions.

mand Behavioral term for a request or direction.

mand-modeling Providing a model *plus* a mand, or request; one of the four basic milieu teaching procedures.

marital subsystem In family systems theory, the interactions between the partners who head the family; one of four major subsystems within the family system.

means-end understanding The ability to separate problem-solving process from problem-solving goals.

metalinguistic The ability to talk about language, from a phonological, semantic, or syntactic perspective.

milieu approaches Methods for increasing communication skills, such as contingent imitation, responsivity, following the child's lead, linguistic mapping, and social routines; providing language models; and embedding teaching within routines.

mixed hearing loss Hearing loss that is a combination of conductive and sensorineural.

modeling Demonstration of a desired motor or verbal behavior; "showing how"; one of the four basic milieu teaching procedures.

morphology The rules governing how the words of a language are formed.

motherese The term used to refer to a style of speaking that adults characteristically use to simplify their language when speaking with infants and young children.

object permanence The understanding that objects continue to exist even when not immediately perceptible; that people, places, and things exist independent of one's own perceptions.

opaqueness The degree of difficulty in recognizing the meaning of a symbol; at the negative end of the iconicity continuum, the meaning of a symbol is not immediately apparent or easy to guess.

organization The process by which existing schemata are combined into new and more complex intellectual structures.

parallel talking A particular feature of motherese where adults describe the actions of young children who are not able to describe the same actions themselves.

parent-child subsystem As applied in family systems theory, the interactions between parent(s) and child within the family system; one of four major subsystems within the family system.

performatives Specific speech acts in which the intent or goal is actually accomplished by the act of speaking.

perlocutionary stage The first of the communication stages described by Bates (1976), in which the infant's behaviors are undifferentiated and not intentionally communicative; adults infer meaning.

pervasive developmental disorder (PDD) A diagnostic category used by psychiatrists and psychologists for children who meet some but not all of the criteria for autism.

phonological disorders Disorders of the speech-sound system common in children.

phonology The science of the speech sounds of a language, the rules governing their distribution and sequencing, and the stress and intonation patterns that accompany them.

pragmatics Linguistics concerned with the effectiveness of language in achieving desired functions in social situations; factors include attitudes, personal history, the setting, the topic of conversation, and the details of the preceding discourse.

preconcepts Early schemata in the course of development; the concepts that infants begin constructing at birth.

prompting The use of assists or supports that increase the likelihood that the learner will give a correct response; can be thought of as "priming."

recasts Responses that are similar in meaning to what the child has said, yet differ in linguistic structure of mood or voice.

recoding The process of translating printed symbols to phonemic counterparts, and vice versa.

regular education initiative (REI) An educational philosophy with the basic premise that general education should have primary responsibility for the education of all students, with support from special education.

reinforcement Any event that immediately follows a response *and* has the effect of increasing the probability that the response will be repeated.

relational words Utterances that make reference across entities.

reliability The extent to which a test consistently measures the same attribute or behavior; or observers providing a consistent record.

responsivity The degree of sensitivity in responses to children, particularly in the context of communication; the behavioral "match" of the adult's responses to the child's communication.

scaffolding Providing a child with sufficient support to use and/or understand language (verbal or written) at a level more complex than could be grasped or produced independently.

scanning Selecting a symbol or symbols from an array that is displayed by a communication partner or by an electronic or computerized device in a predetermined configuration.

schemata (sing. schema) The models, or mental structures, created by humans to represent, organize, and interpret their observations and experiences.

schemes for relating to objects The infant's ability to perform specific actions or action sequences consistently and habitually on a variety of objects.

semantic map An outline that helps in brainstorming or generating ideas related to a central topic; consists of a key question or topic, strands, strand supports, and relationship lines.

semantic relations Earliest relational meanings; combinations of two or more words to convey more and different meaning than any one of the words alone could convey.

semantics The rules used to create and understand the meanings associated with words and word combinations.

sensorineural hearing loss Hearing loss that is the result of damage or disease in some portion of the inner ear, auditory nerve, and/or the neural pathways; may be genetic in origin or caused by disease or injury before, during, or after birth.

shaping A procedure for systematically teaching the sequential steps in a task analysis.

sheltered English An instructional approach that is used to make academic instruction in English understandable to students who speak a language other than English. Students in sheltered English classrooms compete only with other second-language learners.

situated pragmatics Instruction that provides contextual support to help children with language and communication disorders understand and be more included in the social and cultural mainstream.

spatial relationships Recognition of an object's position in space and of the relationship of one object to another.

specific language impairment (SLI) A label for children with language impairment that "cannot be attributed to deficits in hearing, oral structure and function, or general intelligence."

speech acts A speaker's goal or intent in using language.

speech The oral modality for language; the expression of language with sounds.

substantive words Specific entities or classes of entities that have certain shared perceptual or functional features.

summative evaluation Assessment after intervention that has been implemented for the purpose of documenting goals and objectives achieved.

symbolic gesturing The use of symbolic behaviors such as waving (i.e., to convey "good-bye") to communicate meaning in gestural communication.

symbols In the field of augmentative and alternative communication, the auditory, visual, or tactile images or signs that suggest or stand for a concept or idea.

syntax The rules for the way in which linguistic elements (words) are put together to form phrases and sentences, what sentences are acceptable, and how to transform sentences into other sentences.

task analysis Breaking down a skill into small steps to make it easier to assess and/or teach.

theory An orderly set of statements that explains and predicts behavior and is subject to scientific verification.

time delay A systematic wait procedure whereby, when the child shows an interest in an object or activity, the adult delays responding until the child requests or comments; one of the four basic milieu teaching procedures.

unaided communication Communication that utilizes techniques such as gesturing, signing, or speech, which do not require external support.

universal grammar A concept associated with linguistic theory that is the innate formal system of principles that constrain representation, as well as parameters that may be reset according to a given language's characteristics.

validity The extent to which a test measures what it says it measures.

vertical structuring An adult's responding to single-word utterances with contingent questions in order to facilitate production of longer utterances.

whole language One approach to learning to read that focuses on contextual meaning as it combines listening, speaking, reading, and writing activities.

zone of proximal development From Vygotskian theory, the distance between actual and potential development; the difference between the developmental level of the child when independently engaged in problem solving; and the child's competence when guided by caregivers or in collaboration with more capable peers.